Elements of Structured Finance

Elements of Structured Finance

ANN RUTLEDGE AND SYLVAIN RAYNES

WITH SPECIAL CONTRIBUTION BY NENAD ILINCIC, CFA

OXFORD
UNIVERSITY PRESS

2010

OXFORD
UNIVERSITY PRESS

Oxford University Press, Inc., publishes works that further
Oxford University's objective of excellence
in research, scholarship, and education.

Oxford   New York
Auckland   Cape Town   Dar es Salaam   Hong Kong   Karachi
Kuala Lumpur   Madrid   Melbourne   Mexico City   Nairobi
New Delhi   Shanghai   Taipei   Toronto

With offices in
Argentina   Austria   Brazil   Chile   Czech Republic   France   Greece
Guatemala   Hungary   Italy   Japan   Poland   Portugal   Singapore
South Korea   Switzerland   Thailand   Turkey   Ukraine   Vietnam

Copyright © 2010 by Oxford University Press, Inc.

Published by Oxford University Press, Inc.
198 Madison Avenue, New York, New York 10016
www.oup.com

Oxford is a registered trademark of Oxford University Press

Library of Congress Cataloging-in-Publication Data
Rutledge, Ann.
Elements of structured finance / Ann Rutledge, Sylvain Raynes.
        p. cm.
Includes index.
ISBN 978-0-19-517998-9   1. Finance.   I. Raynes, Sylvain. II. Title.
HG101.R88 2009
332—dc22   2009003123

9 8 7 6 5 4 3 2

Printed in the United States of America
on acid-free paper

Contents

Elements of Structured Finance

The Brave New World of Structured Finance

Shakespeare originally coined the phrase. Aldous Huxley made it the title of his satirical novel about a political system that re-engineered people to fit society. In the 1990s, when structured finance was becoming institutionalized in the American capital markets, anxious bankers of the traditional-art-not-science school of credit demonized it as a dehumanized form of banking: the brave new world of structured finance.

Nevertheless, structured finance caught on. By the early 2000s, a structured finance mania had gripped the global debt capital markets. When the market imploded in 2007, some observers saw a reprise of the U.S. savings and loan crisis, others a replay of the 1929 financial system collapse, with credulous, greedy investors willingly sucked in by leveraged financing schemes wrapped in academic mumbo-jumbo. However, with hindsight, the collapse of the financial system of 2007–2008 is likely to be viewed as a referendum on the modern fiduciary conscience. Structured finance is capable of marshaling unimaginable quantities of money—but to what end? It is difficult to base a persuasive economic case for structured finance on what has been achieved thus far.

To see the good in structured finance we must look instead to its essence, i.e., to its theory. Although structured finance is a way for corporations to raise capital, it is not itself corporate finance but rather, an information-based financial decision process that unifies the core financing, operating, and investing activities inside the corporation from a cash flow perspective. Structured finance links financial intention to performance, then outcome, and closes the loop when it relates the outcome back to the original intention. *Ceteris paribus*, negative feedback indicates that the system is in equilibrium, that it does not need more cushion or control, and this translates into a more favorable cost of capital when next financing; positive feedback indicates that the ratings and the reality of the transaction are not in equilibrium, which translates into a higher risk premium or higher capital costs after adding more structural protection the next time around. Theoretical structured finance places a much greater emphasis on economic planning and governance, thereby promoting capital efficiency. By contrast with corporate finance, where resource decisions are made by a handful of senior decision-makers, the governance routines of structured finance are carried out within a control structure (the bond indenture) that is supposed to leave very little to chance or discretion. In principle, if the terms of the contract are violated, investors can sue for damages in a court of law. Within structured finance, therefore, the philosophy of ownership and governance is closest to that of a republic with a constitution, just as the ownership structures and forms of governance within corporate finance are closest to a monarchy with a king and a cabinet.

To carry the political theme further, structured finance does away with the corporation's crown of immortality, the going-concern assumption, by breaking the corporation down into the economic units of which it is composed, which are finite and terminal. The economic consequence of deconstructed financing is that structured securities are not backed by a presumed infinite reserve of once-and-future wealth. When obligors of assets backing the securities stop paying their bills, the securities stop paying investors. Further borrowing by direct recourse to the corporation to prop up performance is strictly forbidden. Therefore, the analysis of credit quality in structured securities must take place entirely within the transaction.

Since structured finance is financial democracy in action, it is vulnerable in the same ways that political democracy is. No matter how well-designed the structuring process may be, financial literacy is the key to good governance. For a structured transaction to be carried out in accordance with the true economic intent in the bond indenture, the market, broadly defined, must be literate in the elements of structuring, otherwise the entire exercise risks turning into the beggar-thy-neighbor free-for-all witnessed in the subprime meltdown. Once this point is understood, the usual excuses for structured finance illiteracy no longer seem quite so self-evident. Structured finance is not an esoteric form of babble. Learning to speak it does not dehumanize the speaker, nor does it diminish the role of judgment: only a financial culture that rewards effortless gain can do that. Since structured finance is not a dialect of corporate finance but an altogether different way of speaking about value that is simultaneously intuitive, logically self-determined, mathematical, and transparent, newcomers to this type of finance are not necessarily disadvantaged. In the final analysis, structured finance is not just for the experts. It belongs to everyone whose wealth is touched by it, which is to say, everyone.

The purpose of this book is to demonstrate by stages how the practice of structured finance can be carried out in accordance with its theory. When this is done, substantial gains in capital efficiency can be achieved through the more targeted use of data and information, learning through feedback, and the realignment of financial incentives with bona fide value-creation. Any capital that can be conserved through this process can be redeployed to the frontier of innovation, and to improvements in the delivery of social services, and support for the arts and other things that enable us to adapt to our changing world, without reducing our current wealth. Such claims do not rest on empirical observation but are axiomatic. Hence, when we consider how well we are providing, not only for ourselves but for our children and their children, as far into the future as our imagination can stretch, structured finance paradoxically may be the most optimistic, human-centered form of finance.

Part I

▷

Intermediate Structured Analysis

1

Elements of Securitization Law

The ability to finance a corporation off-balance-sheet through issuing structured securities starts, not with finance, but with the law. For this reason alone, a chapter on legal analysis should occupy first position in a book on the elements of structured finance. But a second reason for putting the legal chapter first is that, unlike the economics analysis underlying off-balance-sheet finance, which is internally consistent because it is mathematical, the legal theory of off-balance-sheet finance has yet to be formalized. The law is piecemeal, relatively unexamined and disconnected from the economics. Moreover, within U.S. securitization law at least, glaring lacunae have been present from the beginning. Their persistence has enabled certain powerful market institutions to circumvent the self-imposed rules and principles of risk transfer, at first selectively and invisibly, and later on a scale that has put the market itself in jeopardy. That is not to say that all the recent problems in the structured finance market are due only to legal breaches, but certainly they have been due to a breakdown in market ethics, of which legal breaches have been part and parcel from the beginning. Some, but not all of the problems with securitization law are unintended. Since the practice norms of securitization law evolved by and large as a synthesis of existing laws, without the benefit of economic insight, most legal practitioners failed to grasp the economic meaning of structures they were allowing to go to market. However, some leading legal practitioners, collectively and individually, have also exploited the general ignorance, by watering down or perverting customary structuring rules for the benefit of clients and constituents. If securitization law is to become fair, the invisible game-playing going on must come to light, the gap in perspectives between the law and economics must be narrowed and awareness about the violations of practice norms must develop. This is why we, as nonlawyers, wound up writing a chapter on legal analysis, albeit from an economic standpoint, and placed it at the start of this book.

1.1 THE ECONOMIC IMPACT OF DOUBLE-COUNTING

As noted above, securitization law is riddled with inconsistencies, at least in the U.S., the world's largest structured finance market. Paradoxically, the two inconsistencies that matter most today were once important developments in U.S. law, and not only supported the growth and development of supported commercial enterprise but also supported financial innovation. However, one could argue that the law has not kept up with financial innovation; that the value of these ideas is thoroughly depreciated; and that, unreformed, they stand in the way of the return of system stability and market rationality.

One such depreciated idea comes from the nineteenth century American concept of bankruptcy as reorganization, an opportunity to restore a troubled company to commercial health, and not simply an orderly liquidation. In its day, the decision to design a solution benefiting the entire capital structure, and not just the creditors, was a material departure from the precedingt English law, which American law had mirrored up until the time of the railroad crisis. Just how revolutionary this departure was is a matter of historical debate, but at the very least, one can say this new philosophy of bankruptcy helped to get the U.S. railroads up and running. Its significance in the history of financial ideas was the acknowledgment in law that capital is not just physical but also metaphysical, and that the measure of its value is not just the liquidation proceeds of the physical good, but the cash flows from future business generated by those capital assets. Quite plausibly this is an innovation that spurred the growth and development of capital markets in the U.S. for many decades to follow, by conserving the intangible value of enterprise and shortening the recovery time for corporations at the brink of insolvency.

Nevertheless, today one could rightly reason that securitization now does what our bankruptcy code was originally designed to do, i.e., recapitalize and restructure, and does it better. By enabling corporations to raise large amounts of capital flexibly, securitization allows them to grow, reposition, and steer clear of bankruptcy long before it is imminent, with no strings attached other than the consensual terms of the indenture. With securitization, the strictly metaphysical concept of capital as *the firm's ability to generate future cash flows* comes full circle. In a world with equal access to securitization, bankruptcy becomes unnecessary, and furthermore, inexcusable: a consequence of using flexible debt finance irresponsibly. In its day a hallmark of legal innovation and commercial efficiency, in a world with securitization U.S. - style bankruptcy is something of an economic albatross. Even after changes to the Bankruptcy Code in 2005 (BAPCPA) to reduce the power of insolvent corporations in workout mode (the "limited exclusivity" reform), the philosophy of bankruptcy as reorganization, with the imposition of the automatic stay, positively undermines the discipline of securitization because it favors the management of nonproductive companies over shareholders and long-term stakeholders.

The other inconsistency comes from U.S. commercial law, which was revamped in the 1950s (30 years before the advent of securitization) to facilitate transparency in commercial transactions involving transfers of ownership of real and intangible goods. The beauty of good commercial law is precisely that it averts the problem of multiple sales of the same good—the commercial equivalent of double pledges. However, in U.S. commercial law, the distinction between a pledge and a sale is fuzzy. This makes perfect sense, because the health of the productive economy does not hinge on that distinction: In exchange for a $10,000 working capital advance from my creditor, I pledge an asset of a commensurate value. If I fail to repay the sum, my creditor can liquidate my asset and keep the proceeds. Have I not, effectively, sold my asset for $10,000? But with the advent of securitization, it has become impossible for third parties to distinguish between a financing where the lender has recourse to the borrower plus some assets held in trust for it (a *pledge*), and one where the lender has no recourse to the borrower but agrees to be repaid strictly from cash flows appending to some assets held in trust on its behalf (a *sale*). In the first case, the lender expects to be exposed to the borrower's bankruptcy risk until repayment. In the second case, if the borrower effectively has irrevocably transferred ownership of the assets to the lender as the basis of repaying the loan, these assets logically should not be entangled in a future bankruptcy. The latter case illustrates the meaning of the phrase *isolate the assets from the risk of the borrower's bankruptcy.*

The phrase *true sale* was coined to signify an intention that is invisible under present-day U.S. commercial law: to conduct a financing where the transfer of ownership really is a sale, not a pledge. Yet, 30 years and trillions of dollars later, the legal debates surrounding the interpretation of *true sale* continue. Since the law both dictates market conduct and reflects market practice, there are lawyers who argue that off-balance-sheet finance does not really exist since there is no difference between a pledge and a sale under the law—an opinion that flies in the face of practical reality. There are also debates in which semantic games about the word *recourse* feature prominently. An example would be an assertion that non-recourse finance cannot exist because all investors have recourse to something, whether that something is the borrower or its assets. This interpretation turns the meaning of the word *recourse* on its head and obfuscates its materiality. At the heart of the debate is an economic question: *to whose balance sheet does the asset append?* It cannot simultaneously be on both the buyer's (lender's) and the seller's (borrower's) balance sheet. A framework of law, or accounting for that matter, that permits an asset to be characterized as being simultaneously owned by multiple parties is devoid of ethical conscience.

To return to the theoretical paradigm, securitization economics hinges on the ability to isolate certain financial assets from the bankruptcy risk of a corporation and value them on a balance sheet that has next to no operational risk. Whatever the assets appeared to be worth when they belonged to the seller (it was impossible to know except through financial statement disclosures and by observing the health of the company) they now are worth the present value of future asset cash flows adjusted by the propensity of the underlying obligors (who are different from the borrowing corporation itself) to default or prepay their obligations. The *new* financing of old assets therefore attracts a *new* economics whereby new investors are promised a rate of return that fairly reflects, not the corporation's repayment risk, but the payment risk of the asset cash flows filtered through a structure engineered for a target maturity and risk profile. Investors at the top of the capital structure accept a lower rate of return than the market premium for the company's default risk because they expect that their rights in the asset cash flows are legally secure; otherwise, they will never accept a lower rate of return than the cost of company debt since, for an arm's-length transaction, it would not make sense to accept a lower rate of return than the benchmark. Moreover, the near risk-free rate that they are accepting in return for a senior position in the cash flow proceeds does not address the legal risk described above, namely of being reclassified as creditors to the corporation in an insolvency and forced to share proceeds with on-balance-sheet lenders of assets they have already bought. Effectively, the unresolved ambiguity of the bankruptcy code allows the company creditors to double-count the security package provided by their assets: first with the cash proceeds from the securitization, and once again via the claw back. The greater the legal uncertainty about bankruptcy remoteness, the greater the incentive for corporations to borrow large sums, spend them unaccountably, then declare bankruptcy and claw back assets they have already monetized. Today this can all be done legally.

Failure to characterize *sale* definitively under commercial law may put the *on-balance-sheet* lenders at greater risk, right up to the moment default is declared. If the assets that are alleged to have been taken off-balance-sheet (sold) continue to be counted as if they still belong to the company, both creditor groups are expecting to be repaid from the same resource; both are underestimating the true amount of borrower leverage; and neither side is being properly compensated for the true borrower default risk. The *off-balance-sheet* lenders at the top of the capital structure (representing most of the value of the transaction) have not agreed to bear the risk of the borrower defaulting, but the company is likely to prop them up with company resources as long as possible because they are the cheapest to repay. Invisibly, they are being preferred to the on-balance-sheet lenders with on-balance-sheet assets, at least until such time as the corporation uses up these resources and declares bankruptcy. Again, a rational strategy for a mature corporation facing intense market competition and impossible shareholder expectations may be to securitize, to cash out the value of the firm, then put itself into bankruptcy through this preference repayment scheme.

In sum, the failure to bring securitization law and related laws in line with the economic meaning of securitization has created compelling but perverse incentives that expose not just structured investors but more traditional creditors to corporate bankruptcy. For banks, which are not subject to the bankruptcy code in the U.S., the game also involves double-counting of assets held on-balance-sheet and assets warehoused in off-balance-sheet structures, where the game is one of regulatory or accounting arbitrage. For certain such off-balance-sheet vehicles (those that trade or reinvest principal receipts in new securities, which are substantially investment holding companies if not in name) the law may compound the problem by failing to require the type of disclosures that are typical for investment-holding companies.

In sum, in an era when the U.S. derives much of its domestic growth and income at the intersection of information technology and finance, the failure of securitization lawyers to codify customary market norms and rules in the law—whether from inertia, ignorance or the seduction of easy money-has put the most well-developed segments of the U.S. economy at enormous risk. To reform the accounting and regulatory frameworks and the law so as to prevent double-counting, the starting point is to make the legal term *true sale* an unambiguous embodiment of the trinity of its economic meanings.

1.2 THE TRINITY OF TRUE SALE

A litmus test of whether or not a structured transaction entails a *true sale* and hence deserves better capital treatment than on-balance-sheet financing, involves three elements, each discussed in greater length below:

1. The credit structure is truly non-recourse
2. Assets under the credit structure are identifiable and countable
3. The exchange of assets for value takes place at fair value.

A "yes" to all three elements signals that the sale is "true" for this transaction.

Reflecting on the types of transactions that have gone to market in the name of structured finance, it should be immediately apparent that not every transaction is in fact a "true sale" securitization, because not every transaction is non-recourse in its security structure. For example, fully- or even partially-supported Asset Backed Commercial Paper (ABCP) where the assets being financed are not the property of the financing vehicle, generally stands in violation of the first element above. Future flow transactions by definition violate the second element because they presume the existence of receivables that have not yet been created. Transactions with market value "credit structures" are premised upon a trading strategy where price and fair value are disconnected. They violate the third element. To be clear, a "no" to any of the three tests is not necessarily a disaster in the making. However, "no" to any one of them points to potential weaknesses in the integrity of the transaction structure and provides useful feedback to the analyst on issues that may merit closer analysis and inspection.

True Sale Element: Non-recourse

As explained above, the non-recourse standard ensures that the same asset will not be in two places at the same time. Double-counting means that either the structured investor or the lender to the corporation is being preferred. It is impossible to know which without identifying and counting the assets belonging to each. However, the assets of a corporation are not identifiable or countable under the public financial reporting rules. Assets are only countable when they belong to an off-balance-sheet issuer. However, asset-liability parity is a condition precedent to structured finance involving the transfer of ownership of assets from the borrowing corporation to the lenders. Thus, by definition, recourse cannot be permitted in the credit structure.

As discussed above, the word *recourse* in the credit sense is sometimes confused with its meaning in ordinary English, which is broader and less specific. In structured finance, recourse is defined to mean that the lender continues to rely on the borrower for repayment. Non-recourse means that the lender takes ownership of certain assets in exchange for the cash value of the assets rather than relying on the borrower for repayment. It is therefore meaningless to speak of the lender having *recourse to asset cash flows* related to receivables it has already purchased.

Another source of confusion about *recourse* arises from commercial transactions, where buyers typically have rights to return goods to the seller and demand their money back in full, for example, if the goods are defective or if they are returned within a limited period of time. Since the buyer's put option is so basic to certain types of commercial transaction, and it is a kind of recourse albeit not credit recourse, non-recourse *in an absolute and total sense* is clearly an impossible standard for structured finance, which is only related to the funding of financial assets.

Non-credit recourse situations in the context of off-balance-sheet finance, typically ABCP and credit card securitizations, can nevertheless lead to payment shortfalls due to *dilution*. Dilution means that the buyer has exercised its right to return the good and the transaction will now be under-collateralized unless the seller takes action.[1] In such cases, the seller has an obligation to buy back the good at full price, and to maintain asset-liability parity, the seller must also simultaneously and symmetrically repurchase the receivable at par or substitute it with a fresh receivable that is a financial equivalent. Dilution is said not to violate the principle of true sale because it is unrelated to credit risk, and any interim exposure to the seller can be mitigated by establishing up-front dilution reserves.

The litmus test of recourse in the credit sense turns on the owner of the option. A borrower in a secured transaction who initiates the buy back of a receivable at par or who substitutes an equivalent credit is engaging in economic recourse, because the lender ultimately is depending not on the value of the receivables but the ability of the seller to go on repurchasing or replacing nonperforming receivables. A useful way to understand this distinction is with reference to the value of the option that the borrower is giving up. In commercial transactions, where counterparty and market risk are inseparable, the buyer of goods self-insures by accepting and occasionally exercising the right of return of defective receivables or defective promises made at the time of sale. The point of structured finance, however, is to insulate the investor from the counterparty risk of the borrower. The senior noteholder accepts a new rate of return that is different-less than-the seller's cost of capital. By accepting a lower rate of return for less risk, the buyer of the credit (the investor) consents to giving up its general right of recourse to the assets on the seller's balance sheet but retains specific rights to return defective receivables under situations where the assets failed to meet the *a priori* conditions of sale. This right of return always belongs to the investor, not the borrower.

True Sale Element: Asset Identification

It is not impossible to pledge assets that have not been preselected or that remain uncounted (*blanket liens*) but it is impossible to sell something that has not first been identified. The imperative of asset identification therefore follows from the definition of true sale. It is a necessary but not a sufficient condition to achieving true sale treatment, since identification does not prevent the asset from being returned, which raises a potential red flag about the first true-sale element, or from being sold at a price away from fair value, the third true sale element.

True Sale Element: Fair Value

What is a "true" sale? Part of the answer has already been provided in the context of U.S. commercial law. It signifies the intention to transfer ownership: a real sale, not a pledge. However, the economic meaning of a true sale is *an exchange of value at an equilibrium price*. The truth of a true sale lies in the convergence of price and apparent value at the time of sale. This convergence is also the basis of market value theories that equate the two. An untrue sale is one that takes place at a price known to be away from value. The effect of an untrue sale is always to give advantage to one party at the expense of another. The sale of an asset to an off-balance-sheet investor at a price above value is an unjust transfer of wealth from the buyer to the seller. The transfer of a good below value (fraudulent conveyance) is an unjust transfer of wealth from the seller to the buyer. Sales by insolvent companies suspected of taking place away from value can be voided by the receiver or the bankruptcy court. This right applies retroactively over a time frame that varies according to the jurisdiction, but up to one year is common. In this way, financings that involve transfers where price and value diverge may come back to haunt the participants and even cause the transaction to unwind.

1.3 THE PROCESS OF LEGAL STRUCTURING

Bankruptcy-remoteness is the key to off-balance-sheet financing, but bankruptcy law is not the only material legal concern. The process of securitization intersects with several other legal domains: securities law, securities regulation, bank regulation, and commercial, consumer, contract, fiduciary, and tax laws. The next two sections provide a factual discussion of the legal process that culminates in the issuance of structured securities, with an emphasis on U.S. law. While each of these dimensions is essentially technical, securitization law is embedded in a mosaic of practice and culture. That is where our discussion begins.

Securitization and the Culture of Law

The law determines what kind of transactions may come to market, by controlling structuring activity at each step in the process. Since the law works differently in each jurisdiction, the legitimate paths to risk transfer via a sale mechanism differ by country.

In a Civil Code legal system, the law regulates conduct with explicit rules that make certain behaviors permissible and everything else illegal. As a prelude to securitization readiness, Civil Code countries typically undertake the following steps:

1. Research the elements of law pertaining to the securitization process and its operations
2. Ascertain whether it is feasible under the framework of existing laws
3. Revise that framework if needed to make way for the new piece of legal infrastructure
4. Draft and promulgate the law

Once enacted, the new securitization law becomes the central reference for all legal and operational processes related to the structuring of deals.

The Anglo-Saxon (English) legal tradition, championing custom and principle over rule and order, works by the reverse logic. Virtually anything is permitted unless the law expressly forbids it. Hence, new financial processes do not need special laws to be legal or enforceable. They need elements of the process to exist a priori in the law as concepts, laws, rulings, or practices. The next section presents the elements of U.S. securitization law, which is among the most complex of securitization law frameworks.

Legal Jurisdiction over Securitization

Securitization lawyers fulfill a crucial role prior to the origination of a deal, assembling the bond documentation, providing bankruptcy opinions, registering ("perfecting") the security interest, shepherding the securities through registration, and, in the event of bankruptcy litigation, defending the independence of the trust. This section deals with the steps to launching a transaction:

- Selling or transferring a financial asset
- Perfecting the security interest and assigning the underlying collateral
- Achieving bankruptcy-remoteness
- Registering, disclosing, distributing, and trading structured securities
- Determination of the eligibility of structured securities for investment

Table 1.1 provides a flowchart of the legal issues arising at each step.

Sale or Transfer of Financial Assets

In what sense do receivables exist under the law? Can they be pooled, subdivided, transferred, or sold? What about intangibles? Or future receivables: contracts that do not exist but whose future existence is highly probable? What mechanisms exist to reflect a change of ownership? How does conflicting evidence of ownership get resolved? Modern capitalist societies can take for granted that the law has addressed these questions, but in many emerging markets, it is where the legal analysis of securitization begins. Even in established markets, the law may be far ahead of accounting practice, particularly with respect to pooling, subdividing, transferring, and sale of assets, where the accounting framework has been unable to delve below the threshold of the company so as to treat substructures meaningfully and consistently.

In the U.S., the authority on commercial law is the Uniform Commercial Code (UCC), a national model that each of the states (except Louisiana) adopts, sometimes with modifications. First drafted in 1953 by a national body to rationalize interstate commerce, the UCC's goal is one of "continued expansion of commercial practices through custom, usage, and agreement of the parties." It has been revised several times since then, to keep pace with changing commercial practice.

Securitization, a non-traditional way of raising capital, is an example of change in commercial practice to which the UCC has responded. In 1994, the UCC modified Article 8 by introducing the *financial asset* as a generic term to describe the various

TABLE 1.1

Legal steps to creating a bankruptcy-remote transaction

	ITEM	AGENT	GOVERNING LAW(S)	ISSUE
1	Sale or transfer of a financial asset	Debtor	UCC Articles 8–9	The mechanics of sale or transfer of financial assets. Legal relationships between seller and buyer.
2	Bankruptcy-remoteness: true sale	Debtor	Bankruptcy Act; case law is sketchy	Interpretation as to the "true sale" nature of the transaction.
3	Setting up the SPE	SPE	State; case law is less sketchy	The SPE must conform to the requirements of independence from the originator and seller.
4	Nonconsolidation	SPE	Bankruptcy Act 105(a); UCC; FDIC Act; NAIC Regulations	Interpretation as to why the SPE should not be consolidated onto the balance sheets of the bankrupt corporation, as a point of equity.
5	Setting up the SPE	SPE	State laws of incorporation	Minimize voluntary/involuntary bankruptcy.
6	Tax Issues	SPE	State and National tax laws	Minimize entity-level taxes.
7	Security Registration Requirements	SPE	Securities Act of 1933; Securities Exchange Act of 1934; Trust Indenture Act of 1939; Investment Company Act of 1940	U.S. securities laws have a raft of requirements surrounding registration that pertain to the timing and content of information to be disclosed.
8	Investor Eligibility	SPE	Securities Act of 1933, ERISA	Securities Act of 1933 sets eligibility criteria for nonregistration. ERISA lays out guidelines for pension funds.
9	Perfecting the security interest and assigning the underlying collateral	Debtor	UCC Articles 8–9;	The mechanics of creating a valid security interest.
10	Assignment of underlying collateral	Debtor	Depends on the collateral: ships, aircraft are national; deeds of title on real property can be national or state, depending on the regulator.	The physical collateral, when material

forms of collateral treated in Article 9, governing sales or transfers of personal property and intangibles. The 1994 version of Article 8 also added language to describe the handling of securities in a digital world.

UCC Article 9 details how to create valid security interests in five classes of nonreal property[2] arising out of commercial financing transactions:

- Accounts
- Chattel paper
- Instruments and promissory notes
- General intangibles and payment intangibles
- Securities and investment property

In 2001, Article 9 underwent substantial rationalization in ways that favored securitization. In the latest version, a sale or transfer of any of these classes qualifies for true sale treatment and automatically creates a security interest. However, the mere existence of a security interest is not enough. To be valid, it must also be perfected. This is achieved when the steps under the UCC have been correctly followed and the security interest "attaches" to the new owner. What follows is a high-level review of processes that, in practice, are intensively mechanical and detailed.[3]

For a security interest to attach, three things are needed:

1. A debtor empowered to make the transfer
2. Consideration for the transfer
3. An authenticated security agreement itemizing the collateral

Different collateral types are perfected differently. For accounts and chattel paper, the most common method is by *filing* a financing statement, usually with the official registrar where the debtor resides. This system helps the transferee to determine whether the collateral has already been pledged by searching the public records for prior liens. Taking *possession* of the collateral, directly or in the care of a third party, is an alternative mechanism. It is the strongest way of perfecting an interest but not feasible for all collateral types. Securities holdings, for example, cannot be possessed physically, although they can be placed under the *control* of the transferee. Lottery winnings perfect *automatically* upon attachment.

These comments apply to creating a valid security interest in the financial asset. Most beneficial interest holders of securitizations will also want to perfect proceeds from the collateral, which the law treats separately. Article 9 provides guidance on perfecting the proceeds of collateral.

Assignment of the Physical Collateral under U.S. Law

Depending upon the type of asset, the physical collateral can be an important component of value in case of default and liquidation. This is clearly the case for commercial buildings, homes, or even automobiles. It is most certainly not the typical case for credit card or trade receivables. Wherever the collateral is considered to have an important cash liquidation value, a security interest in it must be taken and perfected. For the most part, the guidelines on perfecting a security interest are asset- and also state-specific. In general, states take the lead in providing a titling system for real estate, while Article 9 of the UCC gives guidance on sales of accounts and contracts secured by personal property.

Achieving Bankruptcy-Remoteness under U.S. Law

The bankruptcy analysis involves an ex ante determination that the assets transferred to the issuer would not wind up in the bankruptcy estate of the ultimate borrower and cause precisely the same cash flow uncertainty that securitization was designed to avert. Note that the issuer is not the borrower, who is also referred to as a seller or transferor. The issuer is an off-balance-sheet vehicle currently referred to as a Special Purpose Entity (SPE) and previously referred to as a Special Purpose Vehicle (SPV). In both cases, it is called "special" mainly because its only purpose is to hold the assets, but also because it has been specially constituted to exist under the radar or beyond the reach of parties that might destroy its fragile economics by putting it into bankruptcy. Bankruptcy-remoteness is ultimately what allows the SPE to issue securities at the intrinsic value of the assets it acquires—in other words, at fair value.

If the seller is a debtor under the U.S. Bankruptcy Code, bankruptcy analysis should identify suitable defenses against potential attacks on the trinity of true sale from the seller's trustee. Such attacks could be launched along the following lines:

1. True Sale: The transfer of assets from the seller to the SPE is a bona fide sale and not a loan. If a judge views the sale by the (now) bankrupt seller as a loan, the assets transferred to the SPE will be classified as property of the bankruptcy estate. Under the automatic stay provision of the U.S. Bankruptcy Code, the SPE will be unable to collect on those assets to pay investors until the reorganization plan is in place and it is unclear what resources will be available to the SPE thereafter. In addition, the court has the ability to void and recover prior distributions from the SPE.

2. Perfection of the Security Interest: The trustee must have a valid security interest that attaches to the collateral. In the U.S., perfection is achieved in accordance with the previous subsection, *Assignment of the Physical Collateral under U.S. Law*.

3. Non-consolidation: The SPE is viewed as being inextricably linked to the seller, whether from an opinion of the court that both are in fact the same company or that their affairs are "hopelessly intertwined." If the SPE is deemed to be substantively the same entity as the seller, the Bankruptcy Code gives the court broad equitable powers to handle the creditors of the seller and the SPE as equals. The bankruptcy judge may then claw back the assets of the SPE and use them to satisfy the seller's outstanding liabilities in respect of all the creditors' claims.

4. Sale at Fair Value: In securitization, the assets are re-underwritten and sometimes revalued. However, the purchase of assets at a price materially different from book value, may attract a charge of fraudulent conveyance (sale at a "fake" price) if the seller winds up in bankruptcy.

5. No Preference: Asset transfers to an SPE need to be reviewed for possible re-characterization as preference. This charge applies generally to debt payments not made in the ordinary course of business or pledges of additional collateral by the seller to certain creditors.

6. No Executory Contracts: Contracts involving the delay of performance by both parties until a future date may be voidable under the Bankruptcy Code and thus present a degree of uncertainty that is not appropriate for securitization.

From the early days of the rated structured market, bankruptcy-remoteness of the SPE was established via a *true sale opinion* from a law firm of good standing and repute. The opinion was intended to provide the legal comfort that the transfer of assets was a sale and not a loan. Key determinants in the true sale opinion were the intention of the parties as to a sale or borrowing, the level of recourse the SPE had to the seller, the benefits to the SPE of owning assets (can the SPE, for example, freely transfer them?), the degree of control retained by the seller over the assets and the price at which sale occurred. A bankruptcy judge would review these factors and also take into consideration the accounting and tax treatments of the transaction. It was also generally necessary for the SPE to receive a *non-consolidation opinion* from a law firm of good standing and repute. This was done by overcoming hurdles in terms of both corporate formalities and financial separateness. The former to defeat potential charges that the SPE and the seller are "one and the same", and the latter to refute possible claims that its financial affairs are "hopelessly intertwined" with those of the seller.

However, the ambiguity surrounding pledge and sale discussed above created a vacuum that the accounting framework finally stepped into with the concept known as the Financial Accounting Standards Bureau (FASB) 140. For an SPE to achieve true-sale treatment, FASB 140 mandated a double-SPE structure and a two-step process, effectively allocating the burden of proof that a sale had taken place to the first SPE and the burden of proof of nonconsolidation to the second SPE. The first transfer had to take place place sufficiently close (>90%) to the nominal value of the assets to avoid a charge of fraudulent conveyance. The second transfer did not need to take the form of a true sale. However, the second SPE was responsible for conducting lien searches on the assigned collateral and obtaining a first perfected security interest, both in the collateral and its proceeds. For Collateralized Debt Obligations (CDOs), revolving transactions whose popularity skyrocketed after 2000, a true sale opinion was generally not required even though the transferor purchased assets in arm's-length non-recourse transactions for full consideration from a variety of sellers. This was also the case for ABCP where, as noted earlier, true sale was the exception rather than the rule. FASB 140 also might require several substantive consolidation opinions from the intermediate (first) SPE to address various consolidation risks. If established as a corporation, the main concern would be vis-à-vis majority shareholders. As a limited partnership, the concern would be that its assets would be consolidated on the books of an insolvent limited partner with a majority interest or a general partner. As an LLC (Limited Liability Company), substantive consolidation opinions might be required in relation to all its members. In addition, as was true prior to FASB 140, a sole issuing SPE would bear the burden of proof in respect of all the points related to bankruptcy remoteness. Please note that this paragraph is written mainly in the past tense because the accounting framework recently repudiated the off-balance-sheet treatment provided under FASB 140.

For sellers that are not debtors under the U.S. Bankruptcy Code (mainly banks and insurance companies) the consequences of insolvency depend upon the insolvency regime established by the regulator. For most insurance companies, although the National Association of Insurance Commissioners (NAIC) provides model guidelines for handling insolvency, implementation is primarily a matter of state law with significant interstate variation.

Financial institutions under the jurisdiction of the Financial Institutions Reform, Recovery and Enforcement Act of 1989 (FIRREA) are not subject to an automatic stay. Their securitizations are often structured as a loan, not a sale. Where the Federal Deposit Insurance Corporation (FDIC) is authorized or required to act as a receiver or conservator (to insured state depository institutions and banks) the risk has always been there that the FDIC would exercise its broad powers to override transaction arrangements and consolidate the assets of the SPE with the receivership estate of the bank or depository. In 1999, FDIC issued a ruling (12 CFR Part 360; RIN 3064-AC28, also known as the "Securitization Participation Rule") to clarify its intentions neither to undo transactions with minimum conditions for a bona fide transaction in place (the existence of a written security agreement and grant of the security interest for full consideration) nor to undo true sale transactions that looked to the outside world like a securitization or participation by meeting FDIC criteria and conforming to generally accepted accounting rules. Since the motive of the FDIC's 1999 ruling was to conform to the accounting framework ultimately adopted for securitization, FAS 140, the question remains open whether changes to the securitization accounting paradigm might motivate the FDIC to rethink its position on consolidation in light of more recent experience. For non-FDIC-insured banks, the analysis rests on state banking law.

Setting up the SPE: Corporation and Tax Requirements

This sub-section concerns the bankruptcy-remoteness of the SPE from the standpoint of investors, who might attempt to force it into bankruptcy. It is the reverse-image of the discussion of bankruptcy-remoteness from the seller's standpoint. The crux of the analysis lies in the extent to which all possible risks of voluntary bankruptcy or involuntary bankruptcy are contained. At the heart of SPE bankruptcy protection are (i) insertion of nonpetition language, both voluntary and involuntary, into the documents of incorporation; (ii) limiting the business scope and powers of the SPE to the bare minimum required for it to service the debts it has issued; (iii) imposing restrictions on changes to the capital structure, for example, by the assumption of additional debt or, more radically, merger, consolidation, or sale of the SPE's assets, any of which could materially affect the repayment certainty of the SPE's obligations; (iv) subordinating or capping fees, expenses, indemnities, and other uses of SPE cash, to protect the SPE against technical default; and (v) appointing independent directors and requiring their consent, as fiduciaries, on decisions that could affect the well-being of beneficial interest holders in the SPE.

Implementation will vary somewhat in accordance with the entity form of the SPE, which may be established as either a trust, a corporation, a limited partnership, or an LLC. It may also vary with the laws of the state in which the entity is established. For instance, in 2002, the State of Delaware enacted the Asset-Backed Securities Facilitation Act, which seeks to eliminate the potential for conflicting interpretations in the laws as they relate to securitization and SPEs. That law legislates for a safe harbor for the true sale of assets from the transferor, which may add muscle to the true sale analysis. It also permits fiduciary duties to be defined within the governing agreement of an SPE and protects fiduciaries that rely in good faith on the provisions of the governing agreement from liability for breaches of fiduciary duty. This supports the independent director's ability to fulfill its duties to the SPE while avoiding possible conflicting requirements under the common law of the State.

Tax Structuring

In many cases, structured securities are created to achieve a financing economy, but the tax consequences of the structuring must also be examined to insure that the goal is also achievable under US tax law.[4] The framework for tax analysis is a combination of case law and statutes.

The primary question in the tax analysis is whether the securitization qualifies as equity or "debt for tax." If the former, an income tax liability will be incurred. Here, the most recent communication from the Internal Revenue Service (IRS), the U.S. tax authority, is that of Notice 94-47, 1994-1 C.B. 357, issued in May 1994. The tax analysis looks at the timing, character, and source of taxable income or loss to determine the tax impact on transaction participants. The answer depends on the conclusions of a "facts and circumstances" investigation that asks questions related to the benefits and burdens of ownership of beneficial interests, details of the servicing arrangement, and the formal relationships between the transferor and the transferee, to determine the substance of the transaction. The type of asset being securitized is important, as mortgage loan securitizations allow the transferor more flexibility under REMIC tax legislation and obviate the need for the same benefits-and-burdens analysis.

A second hurdle in tax-mitigation in the initial structuring is the selection of an issuing vehicle that is not subject to entity-level taxation. This is not an issue for Real Estate Mortgage Investment Conduits (REMICs), which are not subject to entity-level taxes, but for non-REMIC types of transactions, a "check-the-box" regulation issued by the Treasury (Regulation 301.7701–3) simplified the rules to permit SPEs to be structured as partnerships or "disregarded entities," i.e., a situation whereby distinct legal taxpayers have elected to treat all income tax operations as if they were consummated by the owner, and thus avoid entity-level taxation.

On an ongoing basis, tax liability is determined based upon the sale or financing characterization and details about the debt instruments acquired. For example, is the interest stated? Was the instrument issued at an original issue discount? Was it acquired at a discount or premium? All these factors influence U.S. income tax accounting rules.

Registration, Disclosure, Distribution, and Trading

Once the legal structuring work is dealt with, the next raft of legal issues are the securities laws governing the registration, marketing, and trading of structured securities. Key laws in this framework include:

- The Securities Act of 1933
- The Securities Exchange Act of 1934
- The Sarbanes–Oxley Act of 2002
- The Trust Indenture Act of 1939
- The Investment Company Act of 1940
- Regulation AB

The Securities Act of 1933 is a disclosure statute designed to provide "full and fair disclosure of the character of securities sold in interstate and foreign commerce through the mails." It governs the who, what, where, when, and how much, of securities registration.

The Securities Exchange Act of 1934 governs all facets of securities trading in public markets, including registration and reporting responsibilities for securities in the secondary market. The main reporting requirement falls under Section 15, to which issuers registered under the 1933 Act with 300 or more registered securities holders are liable. Section 12(g) of the 1934 Act may require issuers of structured securities with equity-like payment characteristics that are held by more than 500 recorded investors in aggregate to file a registration statement identifying each owner of the securities. Issuers required to register under either of these sections must file annual (Form 10-K), quarterly (Form 10-Q), and interim (Form 8-K) reports. For structured securities, the content requirements have been modified to permit the type of format presented in servicer reports. All issuers of structured securities are subject to fraud liability under 10b-5. They are also required to fulfill CEO and CFO certification requirements under Section 302 of the Sarbanes–Oxley Act of 2002, using a Revised ABS Certification Statement.

The Trust Indenture Act of 1939 requires that a trustee of debt securities registered under the 1933 Act should file a trust indenture disclosing the names of each obligor and attesting to its independence from conflicts of interest. It also sets forth the rights and duties of qualified indentures.

The Investment Company Act of 1940 regulates publicly owned investment companies that engage in investing, reinvesting, and trading in securities, not merely by disclosure (in the case of the 1933 and 1934 Acts) but also substantively. Its provisions are in many ways inimical to structured securities. For example, multiple classes of securities and investments in other investment companies are prohibited. The key question for issuers of structured securities is avoiding registration.[5] Rule 3a-7 was designed by the SEC as an exemption for the securitization. However, it is not a blanket exemption: each transaction must be analyzed to determine that it is 3a-7-eligible. The original permission granted by the SEC to exempt structured finance from the registration requirements was based upon a confidence in the market's ability to police itself that since has been undermined:

Nevertheless, the fundamental issue is whether structured financings in fact present opportunities for abuse similar to those presented by registered investment companies. We conclude that all structured financings, regardless of the nature of their underlying assets, theoretically present the opportunities for abuses similar to those that led to the enactment of the Investment Company Act. The industry, however, has been remarkably free of abusive practices, due primarily to the requirements thus far imposed by the market itself.

Based on this record, we recommend that the (Securities & Exchange) Commission adopt an exemptive rule to permit all structured financings to offer their securities publicly in the United States without registering under the Investment Company Act, provided that the financings meet certain conditions that would codify present industry practice. The conditions would limit the scope of the rule to issuers that invest in assets that have scheduled cash flows; primarily hold the assets to maturity (i.e., have limited portfolio management); issue nonredeemable securities; issue publicly only debt or debt-like securities rated in the top two investment grades, the payment of which depends on the cash flows of the underlying assets; and whose assets are held by a qualified trustee. In addition, we recommend that the Commission seek public comment on whether section 3(c)(5) should be amended so that all structured financings are subject to the same requirements for exemption.[6]

Regulation AB ("Reg AB") was promulgated by the SEC in 2004 as a comprehensive set of rules and forms governing the registration, disclosure, and reporting requirements for asset-backed securities under the Securities Act of 1933 and the Securities Exchange Act of 1934. It was designed to both replace and enhance the prior SEC registration framework. Note that Reg AB remains valid in part or in full at the time of writing and is also valid for structured securities that do not fit the Reg AB definition of "asset-backed".The 1933 Act changes took effect as of December 31, 2005 while the 1934 changes took effect in full in March of 2007.

Item 1101 of Reg AB defines an asset-backed security as:

... a security that is primarily serviced by the cash flows of a discrete pool of receivables or other financial assets, either fixed or revolving, that by their terms convert to cash within a finite time period, plus any rights or other assets designed to assure the servicing or timely distributions of proceeds to the security holders; provided that in the case of financial assets that are leases, those assets may convert to cash partially by the cash proceeds from the disposition of the physical property underlying such leases.

Reg AB includes master trusts, which are aggregations of multiple "discrete pools." It includes securities with prefunded amounts not to exceed 50% of the offering proceeds in a maximum one-year prefunding period. Revolving periods in structures backed by amortizing assets are permitted, up to a maximum of three years and subject to eligibility criteria that keep the pool homogeneous. It excludes securities backed by nonperforming assets, most credit default swaps, and disallows pools where over 50% of the receivables are delinquent.[7]

Securities registered under Reg AB require a raft of new data disclosure requirements that were added as a result of canvassing the securitization industry or that mirror the disclosure items in paragraph 19 of FASB 140. *Sponsors* must disclose significant amounts of backup on their securitization experience and program, and the relatedness of that experience to the current transaction. They must also disclose their material roles and responsibilities in the transaction, as well as data on the size, composition, and growth of the servicer portfolio and adverse history, if any. The *Depositor* must disclose its ownership structure, activities, and continuing duties in the current transaction. *Issuers* must disclose the nature and amount of the equity contribution (if any); the market price and price basis of the securities if they are securities within the meaning of the 1933 Act, and the expenses incurred in selecting and acquiring pool assets that are payable out of proceeds, as well as the amounts paid. *Servicers* must disclose the length of time they have been involved in servicing assets; the size, composition, and growth of their portfolio of serviced assets; material changes to their servicing policies or procedures in the past three years; their financial condition; statistical information on advances, if material; default or early amortization experiences under servicer-related triggers; and previous, material noncompliance with their servicing criteria. They must also discuss the factors that are material to the servicing of the assets of the current transaction and their procedures to handle them. *Trustees* must disclose their prior experience in handling similar ABS transactions, whether or not they independently verify distribution calculations, and their access to transaction accounts, compliance with covenants, credit enhancement applications, pool substitutions, and underlying data. *Originators* who originate 20% or more of the assets in the transaction must provide information on their origination program and activities. Unaffiliated originators who originated between 10 and 20% of the securitized assets must be identified.

In many cases, the disclosure requirements under Reg AB mirror and reinforce the reporting requirements under GAAP.

Investor Protection

The U.S. securities law framework regulates through a registration and disclosure framework that sets criteria of eligibility for institutional and private buyers. The Employee Retirement Income Security Act of 1974 (ERISA) is a federal law supervised by the Department of Labor that regulates behavior. It sets minimum standards for most voluntarily established pension and health plans in private industry; imposes *fiduciary responsibilities* on plan investment managers who manage and control plan assets; institutionalizes grievance and appeals processes for plan participants; and empowers participants to sue for benefits and breaches of fiduciary duty. ERISA has stringent conflict of interest and prohibited transaction rules that made it difficult, historically, for ERISA plans to invest in asset- and mortgage-backed securities, but many prohibitions have since been eliminated, albeit piecemeal.

Market Regulation of the Structured Finance Sectors

A network of supra-national, national, and local financial system regulators and standards bodies have overlapping jurisdiction over the securitization/structured finance markets, with tax regulation separately administered. At the supra-national level, the Basel Committee provides a framework for capital regulation; the U.S. has its own version, with different definitions and calculations. In the U.S., the regulatory system consists of federal and state governments, securities, banking, and insurance industry regulators, and the standards bodies for the accounting and derivative industries.

A shortlist of key regulatory institutions with oversight of activities touching on the securitization or structured finance market is provided below:

- Basel Committee on Banking Supervision
- Securities and Exchange Commission
- Federal Reserve System and its seven-member Board
- Office of the Comptroller of the Currency (OCC) under the Treasury Department
- Federal Deposit Insurance Corporation (FDIC)
- Office of Thrift Supervision (OTS), which superseded the FHLBB as the regulator of mortgage institutions
- National Association of Insurance Commissioners (NAIC)
- Commodity Futures Trading Commission (CFTC)
- International Swaps and Derivatives Association (ISDA)
- American Institute of Certified Public Accountants (AICPA)
- Financial Accounting Standards Board (FASB)
- SEC-designated credit rating agencies, called Nationally Recognized Statistical Rating Organizations (NRSROs)

Quasi-Regulatory Role of NRSROs

The role of NRSROs as de facto regulators runs through the parts of the Securities Act of 1933, the Securities Exchange Act of 1934, the Investment Company Act of 1940, the Secondary Mortgage Market Enhancement Act of 1984, and of course Basel II, in relation to registration and disclosure of primary market securities, eligible investments, and capital charges.[8] Its origin has been identified as an undated mimeographed ruling by John W. Pole, Commissioner of the OCC from 1928 to 1933, whereby national banks could carry bonds with investment-grade ratings by established rating agencies of BBB, or higher, at cost, while noninvestment grade and defaulted bonds required "haircuts".[9]

Eventually, this practice became codified in U.S. securities law in 1975, under the net capital rule 15c3-1 of the Securities Exchange Act of 1934, whereby ratings from designated agencies (NRSROs) would form the computational basis for broker-dealers to determine their required net capital.

Since 2000, the question of whether NRSRO ratings are suitable proxies for direct examination and regulation has come under increasing scrutiny from a number of standpoints, particularly as they relate to structured ratings. A list of the more trenchant objections from a structural perspective is given below:

- There are too few NRSROs to handle the demand for their business due to ambiguous licensing requirements and innovation is being stifled (Lawrence J. White)
- Separation of market pricing and regulatory assessment activities is impossible when the main input in the price of a structured security is also the main input in assessing its risk.
- Separation of regulatory assessment and structuring activities is impossible when the NRSRO effectively does the structuring work for the investment bank.

To solve the problem, we must begin with the observation that structured finance is not corporate finance. Corporate finance is a committee process. Structured finance is a production process. Today's NRSROs are simply not organized to produce structured ratings of sufficient quality for capital to change hands. They lack the requisite processes, data architecture, technical expertise, and legal incentives to fill this role. If structured finance is to live up to its promise, consistent rules and standards must be promulgated on production and conduct in this sector, and they must be enforced.

1.4 LAW AND THE THEORY OF MEASURE

Structured finance implies that it is possible to create investment products with predictable risk–return profiles through precise risk measurement and management.

In order to measure the risk–return properties of certain investments, their raw materials must be amenable to measurement. Mathematically, the following properties must obtain for the set of assets backing the investments in order for them to be measurable quantities:

- the empty set will have a measure of $\emptyset$; and
- the measure of the sum of the elements will be equal to the sum of the measures of each element (*countable additivity*).

The law, through the mechanism of the trinity of true sale, appears to play an important role of preparing the ground of structured finance for mathematical measurement so that the fair value of structured securities can be calculated. A legal interpretation of the first mathematical property is that something of *no* value (*nothing*) cannot be represented as having *some* value (being *something*). To represent nothing as something is to commit fraud. Moreover, under the second property of measurability, the trinity of true sale imposes a meaning on the conditions placed on the set of loan collateral in the SPE that is both legal and mathematical by giving them properties of a Darboux sum, which insures their measurability. The first true sale condition, non-recourse, defines the set of loan collateral sold to the SPE as an upper Darboux sum: the expectation that some loans may default means that the sold assets must have a value greater than or at least equal to the amount of liabilities if the SPE is going to be able to pay its debts without recourse to the seller. The second true sale condition, asset identification, makes the set of loan collateral in the SPE a lower Darboux sum as well. That is because asset identification and valuation is carried out from zero via a process that assigns a certainty-equivalent (minimum) value to each granular asset, an amount generally insufficient to cover SPE liabilities. For the sale to be true, the seller must be seen to have conveyed assets in an amount sufficient, but no greater than required, to satisfy SPE liabilities. Mathematically, this is equivalent to saying that the minimum of the upper Darboux sum must equal the maximum of the lower Darboux sum. Therefore, their intersection defines the third true sale requirement: fair value.

Structured finance taking place outside the trinity of true sale is not amenable to measurement. In practical terms, this means that it is impossible to say definitively which assets belong to the corporation, which belong to the SPE, and whether, therefore, the same assets are being counted multiple times in a given transaction. The accounting term for the ambiguous transfer of interest is the Variable Interest Entity (VIE) concept discussed in the next chapter.

END-OF-CHAPTER QUESTIONS

1. What is the fundamental jurisprudential difference between legal systems based on a Civil Code framework of law and the Anglo-Saxon system? Name national markets that engage in securitization and characterize their legal underpinnings from a systems standpoint.

2. What is the impact of such differences on the practice of securitization from a legal standpoint? What are the disadvantages and advantages of each system, from a multiplicity of policy and economic perspectives?

3. Do credit rating agencies have a regulatory role in securitization? Which ratings agencies—what role?

4. Name the international accountancy standards organizations and describe the role they play in securitization. Do the same for the international derivatives standards organization.

5. Define the term recourse. Discuss the differences in meaning from the legal and economic standpoints, giving examples of both and highlighting where the legal and economic meanings do not overlap. What does the presence of recourse do to a securitization transaction?

6. How does the Securities & Exchange Commission regulate securitization? How does the Federal Reserve System regulate securitization? Characterize the philosophies of regulation for each institution. What is the significance of recent changes to the framework of regulation following the subprime mortgage crisis?

7. What is the role of the Federal Deposit Insurance Corporation in the U.S. financial system? Does the FDIC have a right to undo securitizations assembled by banks in FDIC receivership?

8. What is the meaning of the term "safe harbor" and how does it relate to securitization law?

9. In which type of law do we find the definition of a sale? What is the name of this law in the U.S. legal system? How does this law facilitate or impede securitization activities? What is the meaning of "true sale" in the context of securitization law?

10. Describe the feature of the U.S. bankruptcy code that makes it necessary, not only to pledge but also to sell the assets slated for securitization.

11. Describe how the structure of the law has influenced the development of the securitization markets in the United States.

12. What is fraud? Give examples of fraudulent activity in securitization.

APPENDIX: THE TRINITY OF TRUE SALE AND THE DARBOUX-INTEGRAL

As indicated above, we can properly formalize the true sale in mathematical terms by having recourse to the concept of a Darboux sum.[10] The latter is closely related to the Riemann sum, so that in the limit they are identical. In essence, the Darboux sum is a generalization and extension of the Riemann sum.

Consider the real interval $[a, b]$ partitioned into n subintervals as follows:

$$a \equiv x_0 < x_1 < x_2 \ldots .. < x_n \equiv b$$

Next, let $f : [a, b] \to$ be a bounded, nonnegative function and let $P \equiv (x_0, x_1, \ldots x_n)$ be a partition of a interval $[a, b]$. Now define the following $2n$ subinterval values:

$$M_i \equiv \max f(x) \, x \in [x_{i-1}, x_i)$$

$$m_i \equiv \min f(x) \, x \in [x_{i-1}, x_i)$$

The upper Darboux sum is defined as: $U_{f,P} \equiv \sum_{i=1}^{n} M_i(x_i - x_{i-1})$

The lower Darboux sum is defined as: $L_{f,P} \equiv \sum_{i=1}^{n} m_i(x_i - x_{i-1})$

Now, we can easily define the upper Darboux-integral U_f as $U_f \equiv \min[U_{f,P}]$ over all possible partitions P of the interval $[a, b]$. Similarly, we can define the lower Darboux-integral L_f as $L_f \equiv \max[L_{f,P}]$ over all possible partitions P of the interval $[a, b]$. Finally, when the condition $U_f = L_f$ holds, we say that the function $f(x)$ is Darboux-integrable and we express this circumstance as follows:

$$V \equiv \int_a^b f(x) \, dx = U_f = L_f$$

In structured finance, the analogy is clear. The x-interval $[a, b]$ represents the assets as they are found on the seller's, or the corporation's balance sheet. Once the assets are transferred to the SPE, they are represented by the values $f(x) = y$. Thus, the function $f(x)$ represents the legal transfer-function corresponding to the subject-securitization.

It follows from Darboux-theory that a true sale can only take place if the function $f(x)$ is Darboux-integrable and that the fair market value of the subject-assets is none other than the Darboux-integral V of $f(x)$. Therefore, if D is the total amount of structured debt issued in connection with the subject-securitization, the trinity of true sale implies that we have a true sale if *and* only if the condition $D = V$ holds at closing, for in that case, the fair market value V of the assets is numerically equal to the aggregate debt D issued by the SPE. In passing, the n subinterval discrepancies $[m_i, M_i]$ stand for the "uncertainty" in the cash flow properties underlying the assets, i.e., their respective prepayment and default propensities.

In plain English, this means that non-recourse can only be credible if the aggregate asset value transferred to the SPE either equals or exceeds the nominal value of the aggregate SPE debt D issued, i.e., $U_f \geq D$ holds. Similarly, identification of the assets requires us to transfer something that is identifiable as such, but not necessarily in an amount sufficient to compensate the seller for the assets transferred to the SPE, i.e., $0 \leq L_f \leq D$. When these two conditions have the same meaning, which means they become "identical," the sale is true.

2

Elements of Securitization Accounting

2.1 PREFATORY REMARKS FROM A NON-CPA

In the 1990s, the accounting standards-setter in the United States, the Financial Accounting Standards Board (FASB), began to standardize corporate accounting under Generally Accepted Accounting Principles (GAAP). The process gave rise to many debates internally and vis-à-vis non-U.S. standards-setters on the best model for securitization accounting. In the main, through their rulings, the European standards-setters have endeavored to keep structured finance within the traditional boundaries of corporate finance, whereas the Americans have sought to promote off-balance-sheet securitization by imposing a minimum of reporting norms reflecting existing U.S. market custom and practice. In a sense, the global debates over how to absorb securitization into accounting have been playing out a dilemma that has existed since the birth of modern accounting in the 1950s, over whether to make it a normative or a descriptive discipline.

The securitization accounting debates remain unresolved and, in the authors' view, are irresolvable in their present form. Accounting is a language of corporate finance developed by accountants, mostly for accountants, with special evolved language objects for describing events deemed (by accountants) to have a material impact on the financial position of corporations. At the other end of the granularity spectrum is structured finance, an ensemble of micro-processes that enable the corporation to be described as the sum of discrete packets of quantifiable value that can be bundled or partitioned and sold off, with cash proceeds used to purchase new discrete packets of quantifiable value. This style of financing enables the corporation to be conceptualized dynamically as it moves continuously through the cycles of birth, seasoning, maturation, burn-off, death, and regeneration. Conventional structured finance risk measures are able to reflect and report material changes in value far below the accounting framework's threshold of materiality, such as changes in the composition of delinquencies, the rate of cumulative loss formation etc. It would be inaccurate to say that such conditions go unreported in GAAP. Rather, they are unmeasurable and therefore unreportable under GAAP due to the materiality constraint.

Even the most primitive structured risk measurement environment, like the Back of the Envelope (BOTE) discussed at length in Chapter 4, is a better choice for reporting on structured finance transactions than the accounting framework. It simplifies without oversimplifying to the point of making irreparable changes to practice norms. Here it may also be appropriate to note that the incidence of fraud in securitization was *de minimus* prior to FAS 125, the first GAAP pronouncement on securitization, and its replacement FAS 140, but has risen exponentially since 2000. While the accounting profession cannot be blamed for the deterioration of market standards, we must nevertheless point out that GAAP accounting fails to curtail data abuses that can lead to exaggerated value claims and delayed recognition of risk. In conclusion, the more structured finance is mainstreamed to suit the accounting model for corporate finance, the greater the opportunity for misrepresentation.

Accounting Authorities

FASB is the U.S. professional standards-setting body for financial reporting, whose mission is to establish and improve standards of financial accounting and reporting to provide information that is useful to users of financial statements (present and potential investors, creditors, and other capital market participants) in making rational investment, credit and similar resource allocation decisions.[1]

Established in 1973 as a successor to the Accounting Principles Board (APB), FASB is accountable to three institutions: the SEC (Securities and Exchange Commission), the AICPA (American Institute of Certified Professional Accountants), from whom it derives its authority, and the Financial Accounting Foundation (FAF), the self-regulatory, nonprofit 501(c)(3) corporation that bears responsibility for FASB appointments and operational oversight. The FAF has 11 board members who represent key professional bodies within the U.S. financial reporting network.[2] The AICPA is the professional designation body for the U.S. accounting profession. It contributes to the accounting framework dialogue through the Accounting Standards Executive Committee (AcSEC) as well as Emerging Issues Task Force (EITF), the designated organization for interpreting and contextualizing new financial developments within GAAP.[3] The SEC retains the final power to issue accounting pronouncements and to overrule those of FASB.

FASB pronouncements are the result of consultations within the community of institutions responsible for corporate risk measurement and financial reporting. GAAP has the finality of law in the accounting world. Considerable documentary detail on the discussions and debates on elements of the GAAP framework can be found on the FASB website: www.fasb.org. Its hierarchy of principles was revised and published in May 2008 as FAS 162, with a goal of informing and instructing the reporting entities about the rules of financial disclosure. Earlier versions had been written for an auditor readership.

Outside the U.S., the supranational accounting authority is the International Accounting Standards Board (IASB), which issues International Financial Reporting Standards (IFRSs), formerly known as International Accounting Standards, or IAS.

The IASB is recognized by the SEC as an accounting authority. National accounting authorities also have multichannel roles in the development of accounting standards.

2.2 ACCOUNTING UNDER GAAP: STRUCTURE AND CONTENT

Visualize the GAAP approach to accounting for cash securitizations as a decision tree with two trunks and five main branches (Figure 2.1), corresponding to different reporting treatments for the same transaction—or six, if one includes the exemption for investors who hold their investment to maturity. GAAP reporting rules are not symmetrical for borrowers and investors, hence the two trunks. Branching arises from a decision to preserve certain traditional accounting distinctions as the system has continued to evolve.

Consistency with the tradition has come at the expense of analytical consistency, as the following examples illustrate:

- The rules for investor reporting depend on whether or not the investor plans to hold the security to maturity. A financial purist would say the value of a security does not change when it changes hands, even if the new owner has a different cost of capital.

- Investor reporting rules also depend on whether the collateral is mortgage-related (governed under FAS 65) or not (governed under FAS 115). Mortgage-backed securities originally were structured with less credit risk and more recourse than ABS (Asset-Backed Securities). They were bought and traded mainly in dealer markets with the government sponsored enterprises serving central market making and guarantee functions. However, the market-customary differences between ABS and RMBS (Residential Mortgage-Backed Securities) have been steadily eroding under market-wide pressures for standardization.

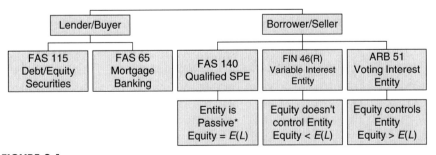

FIGURE 2.1
GAAP decision tree for cash securitization: two trunks, five branches.

- Sell-side institutions are treated under GAAP in accordance with (effectively) their degree of exposure to operational risk:

  – Traditional entities fund their financial assets and their operations on-balance-sheet: their operational risk exposure is high. The litmus test under Fin 46 (R) for belonging to this category is that the equity holder has ultimate control over the entity's decision processes, absorbs its asset and earnings risk, and provides excess cushion to debt holders. This type of entity follows ARB 51.

  – The classic off-balance-sheet issuer, a QSPE (Qualified Special Purpose Entity) is created specifically and solely to hold the cash flows resulting from a true sale of receivables and pass them through to the beneficial interest holders. It has low operational risk exposure, related primarily to the funds collection and payment routines provided by the servicer, which should have de minimus discretion over the use of funds. The equity of the QSPE is typically sized to match the expected loss. This type of entity follows FASB 140, which defines its nature and scope.

  – The VIE (Variable Interest Entity) is a hybrid, a state in between that of an operating entity and a passive vehicle: a non-QSPE. VIEs may have explicit or implicit recourse to the borrower but they do not have voting rights. They absorb the lion's share of the financial and operational risks of the assets, but not their totality. They use fair value metrics to estimate this risk on a run-rate basis. Whoever bears the majority of the financial risk must consolidate the investment on its balance sheet if it does not sell 51% or more of such expected loss to a third party. This type of entity follows Fin 46(R), which sets the criteria for determining who must consolidate and for calculating the accounting expected loss, a concept different from Expected Loss as used in structured finance and in this text.

The astute reader of this chapter will recognize instantly that the VIE category was created for off-balance-sheet transactions structured in violation of the trinity of true sale. Their liabilities are not Darboux sums. That gives a certain logic to the rule of sizing the risk on the asset side and ignoring the rates of return on the liability side, since the liability holders are not pricing the naked asset risk in their cost of capital but are counting on recourse, implicitly or explicitly, to some other institution for the unknown risks hidden in the structure. The question on which Fin 46(R) provides guidance is *who*. But note that permission to delay the calculation of risk creates the opportunity for the risk to grow in the funding structure without restriction. Future losses may balloon way beyond initial expectation. Also, the mechanics of calculating expected losses under Fin 46 (R), described in two subsequent sections, is easily manipulated.

What all this means is that, *ceteris paribus*, securities issued out of VIEs (ABCP, CDOs, or paper issued by SIVs, synthetic lease-backed conduits, complex structured vehicles and covered bond structures) are intrinsically much riskier than ABS or RMBS. This is not to assert that all VIEs are badly structured. Unfortunately, it is virtually impossible to test this assertion because the securities issued from VIEs also tend to be exempt under the Investment Holding Company Act of 1940. The lack of a mandatory disclosure regime creates a wall of opacity that makes apples-to-apples comparison impossible, particularly in ABCP, where program administrators are permitted to withhold all credit information below the portfolio level. In sum, the intrinsic instability and black-box nature of the VIE, coupled with the non-analytic expected loss measurement method under Fin 46 (R)-2, make it both a flexible financing platform for banks and a convenient launch pad for half-baked structures and pyramid schemes. Wherever it is economically feasible to restructure a VIE as a true sale SPE with bona fide structured finance risk measures, it is possible to continue to have flexibility without loss of market order or discipline. Any transaction that fails when it is thus converted is a sham.

2.3 FAS 125/140: TRUE SALE SECURITIZATION

Prior to FAS 125 (1996) financial assets on the balance sheet were accounted for as indivisible units, not because of any genuine impediment to identifying or valuing asset pools but because the reporting focus was the company. Data mining of the assets was believed not to yield material[4] information that was not already in the company's financial statement analysis.[5] In reality, however, details about the assets are material to the valuation of structured securities. A reporting language that cannot reflect these basic elements of value is not only useless to investors in structured securities, but may also distort company value.

For accounting information to be useful in the brave new world of structured finance, it would need to *follow the money* off-balance-sheet and back on again. FAS 125 was the first pronouncement to attempt to do this. It replaced the more traditional risk-and-reward approach and posited a *financial-components approach*. This was conceived as a compromise between reckoning in categorical terms and reckoning in cash flow terms. It allowed the slicing and dicing of cash flows between multiple owners to be minimally described without going wholly for cash flow accounting,[6] a step in the right direction. FAS 125 did not distinguish clearly between true sale and Enron-style transactions that should not have been deconsolidated.[7] FAS 140, *Accounting for Transfers and Servicing of Financial Assets and Extinguishments of Liabilities*, replaced FAS 125 in September 2000 as the master document for GAAP accounting of public and private companies that raise funds via private or public market securitizations.

The gist of FAS 140 was to correct the oversights of FAS 125 and to lay out more stringent criteria for deconsolidation.[8] Because it defines true sale securitization from an accounting standpoint, FAS 140 has a legal as well as an accounting dimension. Its guidance on isolating assets from bankruptcy risk[9] was crafted to mirror market practice and to reinforce legal true sale conventions from the accounting perspective, filling a vacuum in U.S. securitization law itself.[10] Its accounting significance was the creation of a new accounting object, a special category of issuer that qualifies for deconsolidation called a Qualifying Special Purpose Entity or QSPE, qualifying because it conforms in all respects to FAS 140 criteria.[11] QSPEs purchase financial assets[12] and associated ownership rights obtained under the sale,[13] and simultaneously issue nonrecourse debt.[14] The scope of operations of a QSPE is restricted under its limited-purpose charter, with its rights and responsibilities expressly spelled out in the operating agreement known as the Pooling and Servicing Agreement or PSA. True sale criteria are satisfied by a facts-and-circumstances determination of whether the seller's stated motivation is aligned with how the structure works and the seller's scope of duties. The true sale and nonconsolidation opinions required by rating agencies and the two-step (double-SPV) transfer process required by the accountants are positive requirements in achieving deconsolidation.[15]

To prohibit recourse in QSPEs on the grounds of incompatibility with deconsolidation, it must first be identifiable in the context of a transaction.

Unfortunately, recourse takes many forms, and the financial motivation to disguise it is powerful. FAS 140 deals with the complexities of recourse with a simple principle. Since sale means the surrender of effective control, the seller may not exert control over assets belonging to the QSPE. This logic extends to the discussion of implicit recourse via options. Investor puts are allowed, but not seller calls.[16] Paradoxically, the legal analysis of recourse rests on the opposite principle. It is all right for the seller to be able to control the assets on the balance sheet of the QSPE, but it is not all right for the investors to be able to put default risk back to the seller, otherwise on-balance-sheet senior creditors are provided with a window through which they can attack the true sale from a legal perspective. The legal and the accounting conceptions of recourse are thus both necessary for the economic analysis of recourse to be comprehensive.

Revolving QSPEs

FAS 140 also provides guidance on off-balance-sheet warehousing of assets through the ramp-up phase to be deconsolidated. Beneficial interest is evidenced by a variable funding note (VFN), whose principal balance increases with the transfer of new asset originations, up to the authorized amount. Then, whenever market conditions are suitable, the bank merely sells (puts) the VFN back to its own warehouse vehicle, which immediately sells its assets to a QSPE in an amortizing term transaction. If the VFN *put* complies with FAS 140 sale criteria, and the Transferor holding a residual is excluded from bidding on the assets in the second step, the vehicle is a QSPE.

2.4 FAS 156: ACCOUNTING FOR SERVICING (FAS 140 BRANCH)

FAS 140 addresses the transfer and servicing of assets and the extinguishment of liabilities for a company financing itself off-balance-sheet, but does not address the seller's ongoing servicing liability qua servicer. That is the role of FAS 156, *Accounting for Servicing of Financial Assets, an amendment of FASB Statement No. 140*, promulgated in March 2006. The need for a FAS 156 is a tacit but self-evident admission that the static accounting framework is inadequate for the dynamic reporting requirements of structured finance. FAS 156 succeeded in moving the accounting framework closer to continuous measurement in time. However, nothing in the FAS 140 branch of rulings moved the analysis closer to measurement on a continuous scale.

2.5 FIN 46 (R): VARIABLE INTEREST ENTITY ACCOUNTING

FASB Interpretation Number 46 (Fin 46), first promulgated in April 2003 and subsequently revised, is an interpretation of ARB 51 that establishes rules for identifying the controlling entity of the VIE and consolidating the risk onto that party's balance sheets. Since Fin 46 (R) strikes the authors (who are structured finance purists) as misguided if not downright dangerous. Since we are not accountants, we will not linger on its significance within the accounting framework. The main point of this section is to show that Fin 46 (R) Expected Loss is both anomalous and easily manipulated from the standpoint of proper structured finance. The Fin 46 (R) Expected Loss concept is a measure of the variability of residual income from the assets. Its calculation, illustrated in Table 2.1, is as follows:

1. Provide estimates of the cash flows over a one-year time horizon and their associated probabilities. Their sum-product is the mean one-year cash flow.
2. Calculate the negative differences between the mean and weight each difference by the probability of occurrence (the same probabilities as in 1). Take their present value: the sum of these present values is the Expected Loss.[17]

For example, say the hurdle rate is 5% and two cash-flow scenarios are contemplated $100 in an up market (50% probability) and $80 (50% probability) in a down market. From this calculation, we conclude that the VIE must consolidate a Fin 46 (R) Expected Loss of $4.76 on its balance sheet, or else sell 51% of it to a third party.

Note that the determination of key variables in the first two columns is completely at the seller's discretion. The variance is unbounded, and there is really no way for an independent third party to replicate or judge the appropriateness of these estimates. That makes it easy for the seller to slant them to suit a particular outcome. In short, the Fin 46 (R) expected loss is meaningful in an accounting sense, but it has no economic meaning in the structured finance context.

By contrast with the accounting "Expected Loss", the Expected Loss calculation used in the analysis of structured securities backed by loan assets is not a measure of operating cash flow risk but the projected cumulative net loss on a static pool, i.e.

TABLE 2.1

Calculating an accounting E(L) for a VIE

ESTIMATED CASH FLOWS	PROBABILITY	E[CASH FLOWS]	FAIR VALUE	VARIANCES	E[LOSS]	FV E[LOSS]
$100	0.5	$50	$47.62	$10	$5	$4.76
$80	0.5	$40	$38.10	($10)	($5)	($4.76)
Portfolio	1.0	$90	$91.43	$0	$0	$0

defaults less recoveries. A static pool expected loss typically has much less variability than do operating cash flows. It is amenable to third-party estimation and critique. It has both an accounting and an economic meaning. By contrast, the capital structure of a QSPE bases the size of the equity on the static pool Expected Loss so that its expected earnings and losses are zero.

2.6 FAS 115: DEBT/EQUITY INVESTOR ACCOUNTING

The principal pronouncement in GAAP on securitization for investors is FAS 115 (1993), *Accounting for Certain Investments in Debt and Equity Securities.* The approach applies to all classes of investor in the capital structure. The analysis begins by classifying the strategy of the investor in one of three ways:

- Trades principally for near-term sale are carried on the balance sheet at fair value. Changes in current earnings are reflected in the income statement.

- Securities that are Available for Sale (AFS) are also carried on the investor's balance sheet at fair value, with changes reflected in Other Comprehensive Income in the equity accounts but not in current earnings. This changes if fair value drops below its amortized historical cost basis for more than a temporary period.[18] The security is then treated as impaired; the unrealized loss is recognized as a current loss on the income statement.

- Hold to Maturity (HTM) has the least onerous requirements. These securities are carried at an amortized historical cost basis subject to write-downs. However, the HTM decision means the investor intends to hold it to maturity. Changes on the basis of changing interest rates, prepayment rates or the need for liquidity are not permitted, and certain types of securities do not permit HTM as a choice, IOs (Interest Only) being an example. Investors may decide to reclassify an original HTM as AFS but risk jeopardizing management credibility. The reverse, i.e. reclassifying an AFS security as HTM, is permitted only under stringent conditions.

2.7 FAS 65: ACCOUNTING FOR MORTGAGE SECURITIZATIONS

Basically, mortgage loan securitizations follow FAS 65 (1982), with additional guidance that is complicated and depends upon the strategy, the term of the investment and the risk grade. As mentioned earlier in this chapter, these accounting distinctions are becoming further removed from reality as the distinction between mortgage and non-mortgage instruments for the purpose of repackaging has been eroded. Further changes are likely as the accounting viewpoint moves toward convergence.

2.8 FAS 159: THE FAIR VALUE OPTION

In addition to mandating different treatments for different strategies, investor accounting also lacks clear guidance on how to make the (mandatory) determination that a reduction in security value is no longer temporary. The authors note the artificiality of this requirement, since structured securities have a payment promise of timely interest and ultimate principal. A reduction in value that seems permanent can reverse itself (for example, from recoveries) and the determination that the first determination was wrong is just as judgmental. In the meantime, recognizing a false value reduction can have regrettable knock-on effects on the economics of the transaction as well as its holder. FAS 159 (February 2007), *The Fair Value Option for Financial Assets and Financial Liabilities*, is an alternative that permits fair value measurement on qualifying investments (debt and equity securities from VIEs are a notable exception) in accordance with FAS 157.

2.9 FAS 157: FAIR VALUE MEASUREMENT

FAS 140 defined *fair value* as "the amount [for which something] could be bought or sold in a current transaction between willing parties, other than in a forced or liquidation sale." If price was not readily available as a fair value proxy, other information acceptable to the market (e.g. present values, option prices, matrix prices, risk-neutral spread models, or fundamental analyses) is allowed. AICPA 92 dictated that the fair value analysis should be audited as to its reasonability and appropriateness, and sets guidelines on the auditing process. Sarbanes–Oxley also emphasized the significance of internal controls on the fair value analysis, and the auditor's role in opining on the risk management system for performing fair value calculations. FASB revisited these questions with FAS 157, *Fair Value Measurements*, issued in September 2006, which went into effect for financial statements issued after November 15, 2007. The purpose of FAS 157 was to create a convergent definition of fair value within GAAP and provide additional guidance to prevent too much model risk or manipulation in the measures being reported.

An overall critique of FAS 157 is beyond the scope of this chapter. However, some general observations are in order. First, FAS 157 displays more financial sophistication than earlier pronouncements. This is apparent even in small ways, for example, the new definition of fair value addresses the question of "when" and not just "how much," as indeed it must:

… the price that would be received to sell an asset or paid to transfer a liability in an orderly transaction between market participants at the measurement date.

FAS 157 also stipulates a framework for allowable valuation techniques. The framework permits three philosophies of valuation based on market prices (market), estimated income (income), and replacement cost (cost), respectively. FASB expressed a strong preference for the market approach. However, the emphasis on market value that has become de rigueur over the past 30 years betrays a limited understanding on the part of its strongest advocates, many of whom have never set foot inside a market, about the intrinsic instability of price as a proxy of value.

40 • ELEMENTS OF STRUCTURED FINANCE

The emphasis on empirical data also releases FASB from the necessity of opining about fair value from a theoretical perspective. In this way, the accounting profession is continuing to edge toward adopting the elements of the shrink-wrapped structured finance measurement and reporting approach, all the while sidestepping the need to dictate norms, which a robust fair value theory would require.

END-OF-CHAPTER QUESTIONS

1. Identify the key components of the structure of the U.S. accounting authority, the FASB, and the accounting framework, GAAP. Do its rulings and disclosure requirements have the effect of law? What are the consequences of violating GAAP?
2. Identify the most important securitization accounting standards under GAAP and explain how they function.
3. Debate the authors' assertion that "even the most primitive risk measurement environment" within the framework of structured finance is superior to that of securitization accounting today.
4. Characterize the taxonomy of reporting requirements for suppliers and seekers of capital under GAAP. Contrast this with the customary reporting requirements in structured finance and securitization.
5. What feature of the GAAP framework is incompatible with the principles of risk measurement in securitization?
6. What does GAAP say about fair value and fair value measurement?

3

Deconstructing the Corporation

This chapter offers a perspective on operations and operational risk in three linked but distinct spheres, the structured finance micro-market, macro-market, and meta-market, in that order. The micro-market of operations relates to the timely incremental movements of cash through accounts in the payment system, and corresponding title and custody arrangements governed under the indenture. The macro-market, depicted in those ubiquitous "Securitization 101" box-and-arrow diagrams, deals with the deconstruction of roles originally carried out by the bank in on-balance-sheet lending that have been redistributed across different institutions to facilitate the off-balance-sheet transaction. Meta-market refers to the mesh of credit, operating, and governance systems through which structured transactions flow, changing the velocity of money, and transforming the structures of capital and risk, as they move. From a comprehensive risk governance perspective, each sphere needs to be understood interactively as well as on its own terms. But this is a market that still lacks crossover expertise between those who design transactions, those who carry out instructions, and those who safeguard financial system integrity. Were it otherwise, structured finance would never have come to be called, not inappropriately, *the shadow financial system.*

3.1 MARKET MICRO-STRUCTURE

Operations of a Brain-Dead Company

Businesses cannot be run by rules, like machines. They need managers of skill and experience who, in turn, need flexibility to make good decisions in dynamic, unpredictable environments. However, flexibility also allows managers to put their own interests before those of the firm, which is why no operational platform is free of agency problems.

Compared to the operational challenges of capital-intensive firms, the requirements for servicing an amortizing loan pool are simple indeed, which makes the true sale Special Purpose Entity (SPE) (under FASB 140, the QSPE) more amenable to rule-based governance and automation. That is fortunate, since, for the borrower to capture the desired cost of funds arbitrage, the SPE must be structured to satisfy a paramount concern for bankruptcy-remoteness and accept rigorous constraints on its scope of operations (see chapters 1 and 2). In short, the ideal SPE is a sleek funding "machine" that brings together near-uniform principles of structuring and underwriting to put securities into the market with assembly line operations to service them. Servicers, trustees, custodians, and swap counterparties are the proverbial cogs in the machine. Their importance to its operations is evidenced by their seniority in the payment waterfall. In the same way, the inextricable relationship between certain service providers and the availability of the management of the asset cash flows is evidenced in the structure of compensation—usually (and problematically[1]) a percentage of the outstanding principal balance of the assets.

Never forget, however, that the machine is only a metaphor. Service personnel are human. Their clients are human. To err is human. And human "machines" can also deceive. For structured finance to have integrity as a source of corporate finance and not be a mere casino, the human factors must be thoroughly understood and tightly managed. In some cases, more automation is the answer. In other cases, retaining a crack team of professionals to deal flexibly with the unexpected may be the answer. In sum, structured finance has a standardized micro-market aspect that reduces discretion, as befits a "brain-dead" company. But the optimal degree is not zero for structured finance, any more than it is for corporate finance. Operational excellence requires a balance between automation and skilled human intelligence. Between operating companies and SPEs, the optimal balance point will not be identical, but each will have one. To remain optimal, operating results will need to be continuously monitored, and the fulcrum may need to be reset periodically. The task of finding the optimal balance point is greatly facilitated by the use of feedback loops, about which more will be said throughout this book.

The Paramount Role of the Servicer

Since the true sale SPE must be *brain dead* to avert jeopardizing its bankruptcy-remote status, the internal operations of an SPE must be pared to the bare minimum required for servicing the deal. Many subroutines under the minimum set can be competitively outsourced, but in most markets this is not true of servicing, which tends not to be viewed as a commodity but a special service whose quality may suffer if it is separated from the original lending relationship, not to mention the nontrivial risk of disclosing confidential information to a competitor. Because servicing generally stays with the originator/seller, the servicer's role remains a hybrid of principal and agent in structured finance: a difficult, intrinsically conflicted balance that may lead the seller/servicer to act in ways not reflected in the instructions found in the Pooling and Servicing Agreement (PSA) and ultimately not in the interest of the investor. Servicer abuse usually takes the form of economic recourse that may be invisible to the outside world, but that is contrary to the intention if not the mechanics of the bond indenture. The problem of agency conflicts is compounded by transaction complexity and information asymmetries that make it hard to detect, report, or react within the time frame of a transaction.

Constitution: The Pooling and Servicing Agreement

The seller/servicer, investors, and all agents are bound under the bond indenture, which encompasses all the contracts in the transaction. The most important operational document is the PSA. Among other things, it spells out precisely how to segregate cash inflows from the general accounts of the seller; how to set up the trust accounts; how and to whom the funds of the trust are to be reinvested or distributed.[2] The inflexibility of the blueprint enhances well-structured securitizations and exacerbates the litigation risk in poorly structured or infeasible[3] transactions. The PSA becomes all-important to the analysis of structured securities when modeling the deal because it is the definitive, contractually binding transaction structure. Analysts may use other sources of information to form judgments about a target transaction. The disclosure process follows a well-known hierarchy of information quality where "1" is the least, and "3" the most authoritative:

1. "the Deal Deck" (PowerPoint presentation)
2. the Prospectus or Offering Memorandum or Offering Circular (marketing disclosure document)
3. the PSA

3.2 PAYMENT MECHANICS

The Structure of Accounts

Cash flows in a true sale securitization must pass from the borrower to the SPE that owns the receivables. In the U.S., they typically flow directly into the *trust account* or *accounts* owned by the SPE, bypassing the overnight risk of seller default (*commingling risk*); but this is not the only pattern. Non-U.S. markets see a wider variety of borrower payment mechanisms and account structures, including:

- *Direct debit*, whereby the payment is debited electronically from the ultimate borrower's account and credited to the account of the bank, then swept into the trust account at $t + 1$.
- *Bank check*, whereby the ultimate borrower writes a check from its own banking account in favor of the lender (Originator). In some instances, the Originator moves the funds into the trust accounts as a next step, for example when the Originator remains the lender of record for reasons of banking law or practice. In other cases, the Originator does not use separate accounts; allegedly this has been a common practice among investment grade originating banks and corporations in Europe.
- *Direct collection* is commonly the first collection step in markets with poorly developed cash management infrastructure and plentiful labor. It is found particularly commonly in securitizations where the ultimate borrowers live away from urban areas. When there is direct collection, multiple levels of transmission between the ultimate borrower and the ultimate investor are also very common.

Payment Risk

Tables 3.1 and 3.2 categorize the ongoing roles and duties of key agents handling the asset- (table 3.1) and liability-side cash flows (table 3.2) of the SPE.

Note that although the trustee is in charge of protecting the investors' interest, overall responsibility for process integrity itself belongs to no one. A sound accounts structure must defeat several layers of potential risk to a cash flow en route from an ultimate borrower to an ultimate lender. Each of the aforementioned payment mechanisms is exposed to these risks in varying degrees, as detailed in table 3.3.

The Time Line

Figure 3.1 and box 3.1 show a generic timeline of the monthly cash cycle in ABS transactions. Time is counted in discrete time intervals labeled *collection periods*. A *record date* separates each collection period. Its length typically but not necessarily follows the pattern of payment dates in the underlying receivable. When this is not the case, the rationale for the basis difference should be probed, and the risks of cash flow diversion or yield erosion, quantified and properly addressed.

During the collection period, cash is swept daily into the *collection account*. While sitting idle, it may be invested in *eligible investments*, which are usually short-maturity, highly rated liquid paper. They must be liquid because cash must be available by the next *distribution date* for remittance to investors. Every month, the trustee goes through a series of steps in order to fulfill its obligations vis-à-vis the trust. These steps are usually staggered in time to allow the trustee to pursue errors and inconsistencies in the calculations. All transactions carry out these steps, whether or not they are recognized as such. Revolving asset classes, like Collateralised Bond Obligations (CBOs) and Asset-Backed Commercial Paper (ABCP), may have additional special provisions.

3.3 TRANSACTION DIAGRAMMING

The best way to begin to visualize the transaction is to reconstruct the "deconstructed" financial operations in a flow chart using deal information in the prospectus. Best, because as a description of cash flows and institutions, the transaction diagram describes the interface between the micro- and the macro-market structure. All parties involved in the transaction, e.g. originator, seller, issuer, servicer, trustee, investor,

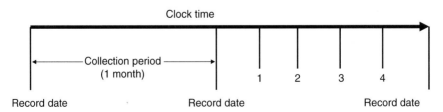

FIGURE 3.1
The operating cycle of ABS transactions.

▶ **Box 3.1**

▶ **1. Determination Date**

This step focuses on the asset side of the SPE balance sheet. Prior to the Determination Date, the Servicer prepares reports outlining all relevant asset attribution and performance parameters for the most recent Collection Period, and forwards them to the Trustee for review. In these reports, all cash flow quantities must be tallied (interest, penalty interest, principal collections, defaults, prepayments, recoveries, surety bond payments, delinquencies, etc.) and, since certain portions of the loan payment may not belong to the deal, ownership of the cash flows correctly partitioned.

▶ **2. Calculation Date**

This step focuses on the liability side of the SPE balance sheet. On the Calculation Date, the Servicer computes the amounts due to bondholders and all third parties based on the legal documents. The rules may be complicated and include features like triggers and spread capture provisions. These amounts are then turned into transfer instructions from the Collection Account to the various sub-accounts set-up on the Closing Date for the benefits of each party. Although there may be an unlimited number of sub-accounts, there is only one Collection Account. At the conclusion of this step, the entire contents of the Collection Account have been allocated to one party or another.

Under normal circumstances, if the structure benefits from a surety bond, any interest shortfall is transformed into a demand note to the Surety Provider. Principal shortfalls may be accumulated and need not be paid until the Legal Final Maturity Date, since the promise to ABS investors is normally for timely interest but ultimate principal only. Surety providers have significant discretion as to the manner in which they will make good on their guarantee and outright immediate refunding of a troubled transaction is usually a last resort measure. An impending call on a surety bond will usually trigger pre-emptive action before the actual demand note is written out.

▶ **3. Distribution Date**

On this date, the servicer passes the amounts calculated in step 2 to the paying agent with payment instructions to pay the ultimate recipients. With a central clearing institution, the cash changes hands one extra loop. The paying agent passes the instructions to the shareholder of record, the CSD(Central Securities Depository), which disburses funds to broker-dealers, who distribute them to the ultimate claimholders.

If a surety bond exists and has been called, the associated cash is remitted prior to the Distribution date and is thus available for distribution to the sub-accounts. At this time, the Collection Account is empty.

▶ **4. Payment Date**

On this date, the amounts now sitting in the sub-accounts are wired to their intended recipients (Servicer, Noteholders via DTCC, Trustee, etc.) and the sub-accounts are now empty. ◀

financial guarantor, need to be linked together along the lines of cash and title. Institutions whose direct involvement terminates at closing do not belong on the transaction diagram. Conventionally two diagrams are drawn, one for the closing and one for the ongoing cash flows. Figures 3.2 and 3.3 illustrate the primary and secondary market situations for a hypothetical deal.

Activities Underlying the Closing Flows

In this diagram (figure 3.2), individual obligors have previously entered into financial agreements involving the purchase of physical collateral under a loan or lease entailing fixed monthly payments. The lender of record (the transferor) retains the title until the loan is repaid, but it is transferred to the issuer at closing. In the U.S., the transferor previously will have filed UCC-1 statements (liens) on the collateral to secure the rights to it, and these statements will now be in its possession. At closing, the UCC-1 statements are to be transferred to the issuer. At the same time, investors will deliver cash to the issuer in exchange for asset-backed notes. The issuer will use this cash to effectively purchase the collateral and step into the shoes of the transferor. From this point on, the issuer has legal ownership of the equipment via the trustee and the investors have equitable ownership through the notes. Simultaneously, if there is a monoline insurer involved, it has delivered a surety bond to enhance the security of the notes for the benefits of the investors.

Third Parties (Not in the Diagram)

The essential services prior to the close are the advisory, underwriting, and distribution services, for which the investment bankers receive an underwriting commission; the documentary and legal opinion (true sale/nonconsolidation) services from lawyers, who are compensated with legal fees; and accounting support work that may include structuring advisory, asset-level due diligence, or shadow modeling. Rating agencies assess the creditworthiness of the transaction tranches and receive a fee, usually as a fraction of a percentage of total issue size. In some cases, external consultants such as appraisers and other professionals may be involved to further value the cash potential of the assets dedicated to the structure.

Activities Underlying Ongoing Flows

Every month, the ultimate obligors remit cash to the issuer. As discussed in the preceding section, this is ideally done through a lockbox account, usually located at the servicer's place of business. This cash is then swept daily or weekly into the collection account under the control of the trustee that applies it in accordance with the priority of payments. Just as indicated in the illustration, payment shortfalls typically will fall to the subordinated tranches first. If there is no lockbox account, the investor has an overnight risk that the funds, commingled with the funds of the seller, could be caught up in a seller bankruptcy. Periodically, the servicer passes the proceeds to paying agents and instructs them about the funds to be disbursed to liability holders in the capital structure. As mentioned earlier, the servicer and trustee (as well as the swap counterparties in many cases) are part of the capital structure. They tend to

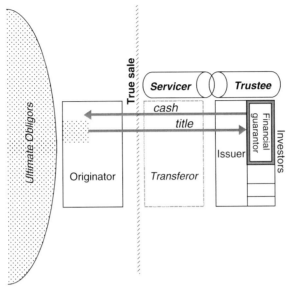

FIGURE 3.2
Diagram of closing cash flows (primary market).

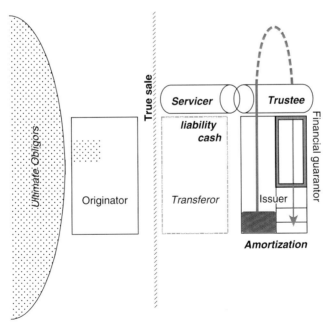

FIGURE 3.3
Diagram of ongoing cash flows (secondary market).

collect their fees ahead of note holders, to insure the soundness of the transaction's fundamental operations.

Third Parties (Not in the Diagram)

After the transaction goes to market, third parties involved in its original structuring maintain a low-level of involvement with it. Rating agencies charge a small monitoring fee each year to maintain the status and relevance of the rating. However, this does not necessarily imply that the ratings on structured deals are systematically reviewed; the quality, frequency, and intensity of ratings review is case-by-case. Other forms of third-party post-market support may include mark-to-market advisories on behalf of non-buy-and-hold investors, and audit work. Data vendors are among the most active parties in the secondary market phase. Their business model is to obtain their data from trustees, and clean and publish it in raw form or added-value formats, also known as modeling software.

3.4 MARKET MACROSTRUCTURE

A market consists of a buyer and a seller, who exchange goods for other goods or capital. A distributed market has agents, who enable buyers and sellers to find each other and deal across distances. Regulators, professional support providers, and data vendors outside the market (but looking in) contribute to market stability and permanence. The ensemble of these six institutional roles

- Buyers
- Sellers
- Agents
- Professional support providers
- Regulators
- Data vendors

forms the boilerplate operational infrastructure of modern distributed markets. Virtually every category of institution that defines a tertiary market is found in the structured finance market:

- Buyers

  - Investors in the SPE
  - Financial guarantors (monolines)
  - Intermediaries

- Sellers

  - Originators
  - Transferors
  - Issuers (the SPE)

- Agents

  - Intermediaries, (bringing together the buyer and seller)
  - Collateral managers/servicers/program administrators
  - Custodial agents/trustees
  - Clearing and settlement agents
  - Issuing and paying agents

- Professional Support Services

  - Rating agencies (at origination)
  - Lawyers
  - Accountants

- Regulators

  - Accounting standards boards
  - Supra-governmental agencies
  - Governmental agencies
  - Rating agencies

- Data Vendors

  - Specialty financial media
  - Rating agencies

Once primarily a target for safety-seeking investors, ABS' universe of *buyers* has widened, but most of the paper that goes into the market is still highly rated (that is the point, after all, because it reduces the overall funding cost to the borrower) and good data are lacking on what percentage of the paper is cannibalized by the banks in conduits or left unsold on the banks' balance sheets.

In addition to the ultimate investor, the *financial guarantor* (also known as a surety bond provider, monoline insurance company, or "wrapper") has had an important role in developing the structured market as a buyer of contingent credit risk. The financial guarantor model is presently broken for structured finance, but historically surety bonds were purchased for the senior tranche of securitizations by unknown sellers, which were at best low investment grade without the wrap. By agreeing to honor the original payment promise on the security it wrapped, the financial guarantor interposed its own balance sheet to raise the rating and create liquidity. As pointed out in the micro-market section, the surety bond indenture promised to pay timely interest and ultimate principal to investors per the original indenture, to insulate them from cash flow interruption up to the AAA level; it did not promise not to prepay the contract amount.[4] At an early point in the structured market's history, financial guarantors played a key role in building investor confidence in transactions from unknown sellers. In the 2000s, they once again played a key role in developing the synthetic market—the same sector that ultimately broke their business model.

The *seller* is frequently the *originator* of the underlying collateral. The third-party nature of the structured market means that the originator and the seller need not be the same institution, and a few deals have transpired where by the originator and seller were unrelated. The more typical pattern is the multi-step asset sale process carried out under the 2000–2009 version of FASB 140 in U.S. GAAP, which required transactions claiming off-balance-sheet treatment (QSPEs) to use a double-SPE structure. In the double-SPE model, the borrowing company (the *depositor*) sells the assets to an intermediate SPE, known as the *transferor*, who then "transfers" them to the *issuer*, the second SPE. Regardless of whether the sale takes place in one step or two, the *issuer* is always an SPE, and, as the reader will recall from chapter 1, is always independent of the seller.

Agents are facilitators, not principals. Since their role is to limit risk, constraints must be applied to how they handle the property of others. This is particularly true if, as in the case of sellers-turned-servicers, the property used to belong to them. Agents typically operate within a tiered structure of discretionary power. Their degree of allowable discretion may not be apparent except in the details of their duties: a custodian acts like a trustee but a collateral manager acts at times like a hedge fund. An informed analysis of operating risk must therefore not only keep track of which agents are handling which duties, but also assess whether their degree of discretion matches their job description.

Prior to origination, the agent with the most discretion over the structured transaction is the *arranger*, a commercial or investment banking intermediary that supplies financial advisory services on the transaction and arranges for it to be placed with investors through one or more *placement agents.* Usually the arranger is the lead agent. The team undertaking to structure the transaction and place the securities with investors is known as the *underwriting syndicate. Structuring the transaction* means creating a design for redistributing the risks of the pool across different classes of securities. Credit risks will be apportioned to the classes at a contract rate of return that, ideally, matches the risk of their investment, and noncredit (basis or price) risks will be contracted out to one or more *swap counterparties* whose credit is consistent with their ability to support the investors appropriately.[5]

The banking intermediary's control over the deal at the design stage is related to its dual role as agent and principal. Since the "agent" in charge of structuring the securities may become an inadvertent "principal" (investor) in the unsold part of the undertaking, dealing strategy must address both possibilities. In practical terms this means, in addition to satisfying investors and the rating agency, the bank may need the backing of its credit committee from the beginning. In banks where credit committees are powerful, the deal will have to be structured conservatively to meet internal investment guidelines. Banks whose business model relies mainly on fees tend to be less sensitive to credit risk, but may still require certain minimal ratings on the retained tranches to avoid having to de-lever, which could hurt the market perception of its financial strength, and reduce the scale of underwriting activities producing the fee income that drives its business.

In many ways, the arranger has considerable freedom to design a transaction but the arranger does not have the freedom to make structural choices that affect credit quality. Such credit-determining choices are regulated by the SEC-licensed *credit rating agencies*, which assign credit ratings and also publish reports on the transactions they rate.[6] At the same time, the placement agent in the arranging bank will be constrained by *investor* appetite for risk attributes: rating, maturity, collateral type, and geographic origin. The role of the arranging bank throughout the origination process is to bring these supply- and demand-side constraints into alignment iteratively, so as to produce a transaction for the market, and a market for the transaction.[7]

After bringing the two sides together, the rating agency and (if all has gone well) the bank intermediary exit the transaction, leaving the parties listed in table 3.1 to execute the transaction. Note that while the roles of financial arranger and independent arbiter of value are intrinsic to the viability of the structured finance market, nothing is intrinsic about banks doing the arranging or rating agencies acting as the independent arbiters of value. Separation of the advisory and placement functions, and perhaps also movement of the origination and trading of structured securities into an exchange environment are viable ways of further deconstructing the macro-market and making it more efficient, particularly if market discipline is improved by investors having to rely less on ratings and more on their own capital and intelligence.[8]

Once the transaction closes and is performing in the secondary market, the agents under contract perform critical roles, ranging from moving money to providing checks and balances that reduce the likelihood of payment errors that could hurt either the seller or the buyer.[9]

The agents that will need, and are given, the most discretionary authority are those that will be involved in managing the collateral and moving money, and must play the roles of in situ manager and in extremis cop. Given that the buyer and seller's relationship is essentially adversarial, these duties are spread out between two institutions: a *servicer* (with a sell-side allegiance) to carry out the duties and responsibilities stipulated in the indenture, and a *trustee* (with a buy-side allegiance) to ensure that the duties and responsibilities are being properly carried out. Generally speaking, a *trustee* is an individual or organization that holds or manages and invests assets for the benefit of another. In a structured transaction, the trustee is legally obligated to make all trust-related decisions with the beneficiary's interests in mind, and may be liable for damages if it fails to do so.[10] The shortcoming of this arrangement is the underlying assumption that the trustee can avert extraordinary risk for investors simply by performing ordinary supervisory duties. This might be the case if the trustee has a high degree of domain expertise and has invested in systems with added-value data capture, and the servicer maintains high standards of operational integrity. But as a practical matter, the trustee is paid only to supervise mechanical tasks under the PSA, like the clearing and settlement of trust funds, the safeguarding of trust assets, and the required reporting to transaction stakeholders. The trustee is not paid to assume the risk of servicer malfeasance. Indeed, that risk is hard to measure ex ante and probably impossible to compensate adequately from ordinary transaction cash flows.

Not all trust and custody work is equally specialized or compensated. The degree of specialization depends on the specifics of the deal, and compensation follows.

Transactions involving specialty assets like SME loans or large commercial leasing assets involve more judgment and so are better compensated. So is trustee work involving more complex, coordinative, judgmental asset administration services, for example, for deals with a revolving period during which the principal balance does not decline and the return of principal is applied to the purchase of new collateral. The party that performs the portfolio selection role is a *collateral manager*, who agrees to be bound by the terms of a collateral management and other transaction documents. This role entails considerable discretion over the purchase and sale of collateral.

In transactions where market pricing forms an important component of the security structure, the fine line between collateral management and hedge fund investing becomes invisible. This twist can introduce an adversarial element to the relationship between the active collateral manager and the investor, especially when the collateral manager's fee is senior to investors' claims. Not every collateral manager has this degree of discretion, but all collateral managers must be prepared to do more than just follow rules. Assets must sometimes be substituted, even in passive transactions. At times, the manager must decide between competing rules in the PSA because market conditions make operating completely within the transaction constraints infeasible. For example, the security- and portfolio-level eligibility criteria sometimes combine in an intricate fashion so that no permissible security can be found, and yet the security must be purchased to produce sufficient yield to pay investors. Investing the principal proceeds in riskless securities or amortizing the deal before the start of the amortization period are not options. Clearly, the role of collateral manager can have a very material impact on security performance and value. Where this is true, the collateral manager is generally well compensated.

Agents with the least discretionary authority perform generic roles. They may be *clearing agents*, who collect funds and verify transaction information; *settlement agents*, who finalize the sale and oversee the transfer of title from seller to buyer; and *issuing and paying agents*, who provide basic payment and administrative services on behalf of investors, especially in multi-seller ABCP conduits.

Sitting across the table from the trustee is the *servicer* whose duties and rights are defined in the PSA, described in the micro-market section above. Some transactions have *backup* (or *successor*) *servicers* under contract to step in and manage the cash flow operations if the seller/servicer becomes insolvent. Contingent servicing may be further subclassified into *hot*, *warm*, *cool* or *cold* backup. It is well to bear in mind that backup servicing is motivated by the legal goal of *bankruptcy remoteness* of the SPE from the seller, which can never be fully achieved operationally so long as the servicer and the seller are one and the same. On paper the idea looks fine, but there is always a certain irresolvable tension between servicing and backup servicing arrangements, since institutions that are suitable backups are probably also competitors. They might well be selling their service in order to poach the seller's clients. In sum, the contingent operational risk of the seller/servicer going under remains an unresolved flaw in the design of the structured finance market.

Other agents stand outside the transaction. They may be involved at the origination or secondary market phase. Some of the more important agents are described below.

TABLE 3.1

Roles and duties carried out in respect of the assets of an SPE

ORIGINATOR	SELLER	TRANSFEROR	SERVICER	ISSUER
Originates loans or accounts receivable.	Sells vintages of loans/accounts receivable.	May on-lend loans or accounts receivable to issuer.	Collects/processes receivable cash flows under indenture.	**Issues securities. Owns receivables. Owes repayment.**
Receives spread income, "points."	Receives proceeds at "Fair Value."	Double-SPE structure, may realize gain.	Receives a fee as an agent.	**Collects cash in trust accounts.**

TABLE 3.2

Roles and duties carried out in respect of the liabilities of an SPE

SERVICER	ISSUER	TRUSTEE	INVESTOR	RATING AGENCY
Collects/processes data about receivable cash flows as per the indenture.	**Issues securities. Owns receivables. Owes repayment.**	Checks cash flow modeling work, publishes/distributes servicer data in reports.	Receives trustee reports.	Receives trustee reports. Keeps the rating "fresh."
Receives fee as an agent.	**Collects cash in trust accounts.**	Receives nominal fee income.	Receives proceeds at "Fair Value."	Receives fee as a rating agent.

DTC

Wholesale clearing function: receives funds from servicer via I&P (Issuing/Paying Agent) and distributes them to ultimate investors. Receives a clearing fee.

TABLE 3.3

Non-credit risks to payment certainty

RISK	EXPLANATION	PAYMENT SOLUTION/MITIGANT
Counterparty	For borrowing/lending activity not documented expressly as a loan, the likelihood that the seller will become insolvent.	All cash flow interactions involving agents or principals carry at least transitory counterparty risk so long as the cash flow is in their possession. Avoid exposure to entities whose credit quality is much lower than the credit of the securities they are handling.
Commingling	An insolvent seller has cash flow liabilities but will fail to discharge its obligations, including disbursing asset cash flows due to the trust.	All non-lock box solutions, although *direct debit*'s superior information trail is compensatory to some degree. Potential loss must be estimated and reserved for if cannot be structured away.
Netting/offset	An insolvent seller will attempt to offset its liabilities with assets of the same counterparty, for example, offsetting an ultimate borrower's mortgage payment by the balance on deposit.	All non-lock box mechanisms. When the right of offset is enabled in banking law (commonly the case) the bond indenture must repudiate it expressly.
Payment system	Cash flowing through the financial system is arrested due to operational breakdown or credit emergencies of the government.	All structured finance transactions carry at least transitory payment system risk so long as the cash is flowing through that jurisdiction. Avoid exposure to financial systems whose systemic soundness is much lower than the credit of the securities they are handling.

Professional Support Services are the providers of legal, accounting, tax, rating agency, and other ancillary services performed prior to closing, who are only marginally and peripherally involved in the operations of the SPE once it is in the secondary market. The role of lawyers and accountants in relation to structured deals was briefly discussed in chapters 1 and 2, respectively. The activities of rating agencies, while not systematically addressed, is covered by the technical content in the chapters that follow.

All these agents come to the transaction because they are licensed to carry out the will of the regulators. *Regulators* are responsible for making and enforcing the state of play in the market. Most markets are subject to a hierarchy of regulators ranging from grass-roots, self-regulatory associations to national governmental and multi-lateral institutions at the highest level. Because structured finance intersects many markets and political jurisdictions, it is potentially subject to several forms of regulation.[11]

Data Vendors are the institutions that aggregate and publish market performance statistics. Trustees were the first to play the role of data vendors, in so far as they supervised the aggregation and transmission of performance data by the servicers ("servicer reports"). Over the past decade, a handful of private companies have made a business of repackaging and selling trustee reports online to the market. In recent years, rating agencies have joined the fray to supply not only raw data but also added-value metrics on a subscriber basis.

3.5 MARKET META-STRUCTURE: TO BUILD A BETTER MODEL

The jury is really still out on why the systemic issues in the structured finance market that preceded market collapse were ignored for so long. One factor is surely the market-wide resistance to standardization and blind adherence to the fallacy that structured finance is about custom-tailoring when quite the opposite is true: Structured finance is the industrial process for risk standardization. Another likely factor is inertia. The market had been running on autopilot for 20 years since the late 1970s, when, in the wake of the collapse in 1998 of Long Term Capital Management (LTCM), a multi-strategy hedge fund directed by market wizards with impeccable academic and Wall Street credentials, hedge funds began entering structured finance in droves. The complex, dynamic, leveraged trade flow through channels like market-value Collateralized Debt Obligations (CDOs) and basket-index trading completely transformed the market from its original buy-and-hold character. A third factor is undoubtedly fear, i.e., the fear of experts confronted by a big hole in a subject they thought they knew well. The mutability and the complexity of the structured finance market inspires this fear in just about everyone who has carved out a living in one quadrant or another of the market.

Structured finance is an OTC market. Although most bond markets started out as OTC platforms, this is a matter of convention rather than necessity. Today some of the biggest financial derivative markets are housed in exchanges that did not start out there. And, as suggested elsewhere, there is nothing essential about banks being in the role of arranger, or rating agencies being the market's independent arbiter. An organized, exchange-model structured finance market would work just as well. The exchange could facilitate both roles, as the designer of the contract market and a force for reporting and disclosure, compliance, and enforcement.

At this juncture, the closest thing structured finance has to an exchange is the SEC-licensed credit rating agency, technically referred to as a Nationally Recognized Statistical Rating Organization (NRSRO). In some sense, it can be said to design *contract markets* for structured product trading,[12] although the rating agency emphasis is overwhelmingly oriented toward the primary market and is not accountable to the shortcomings in product durability, design quality, or safety that only show up in the secondary market. Rating agencies lack the statistical sophistication to conceptualize structured securities as being subject to continuous shifts in volatility, to measure credit volatility continuously or to build mechanisms that anticipatorily adjust the level of credit enhancement to promote continuous, liquid trading the way exchange clearinghouses do for contract markets. Rating agencies do not set minimum standards of risk sophistication and capital adequacy for their clients, nor do they expel those who fail to measure up. They do not provide comprehensive oversight, central coordination, or a clearinghouse safety net to backstop failed trades. Although the interface to the Central Securities Depository (CSD), i.e., Depository Trust & Clearing Corporation, and wholesale clearing & settlement services through International Central Securities Depositories is evolving,[13] the need to answer to many masters simultaneously has held back achievement of the goal of straight-through processing.[14] In truth, central administration via a competent, independent administrator could perhaps take the efficiency of the structured market model to a much higher level, while putting its regulation on a more objective, comprehensive footing.

END-OF-CHAPTER QUESTIONS

1. Why do the authors characterize securitization as a "deconstruction" of the corporate operating platform? What are the potential benefits or gains for companies, of separating the operating and financing functions: (a) in the statement of cash flows (SFAS 95, 1987); and (b) operationally via securitization? What are the potential risks or losses that arise from the separation of activities: (a) informationally; and (b) operationally?

2. Explain the role of each of the six types of market player (buyers, sellers, etc.) and fit them to the main functions carried out in securitization markets.

3. Review the role of each agent in securitization, classifying them by the degree of discretion they have over the resources they manage. How does your analysis change for revolving deals? Identify the critical weaknesses in the design of the agents' functions and propose mitigants to those weaknesses.

4. Who is the issuer of a structured security?

5. Choose a deal prospectus and analyze it using the transaction diagram format. Array "asset-side" functions to the left of the divide between the issuer's assets and liabilities, and "liability-side" functions to the right of the divide.

6. Describe the main financial events in the calendar of a structured security and describe the underlying activities. What would be the impact of disruptions to the calendar at these event-times, and what parties mainly would be affected?

7. Identify the defining macro-level features of the structured finance marketplace. Compare and contrast these to the macro-level features of other capital market sectors in advanced economies.

8. Referencing the discussion of the operational platform to that of the regulatory platform (chapter 2), characterize the suitability of the regulatory infrastructure to regulate the operations under its jurisdiction. In what functions do the biggest gaps arise? Contrast this analysis with your knowledge of problems that have arisen in the structured finance market. Were these problems foreseeable from a systems design standpoint?

4

BOTE: The Static Valuation Model

4.1 BOTE: A STATIC, SELF-CONSISTENT VALUATION TOOL

The premise of securitization is for a company to deploy its capital more efficiently by using its financial assets rather than its entire balance sheet to raise working capital. This idea represents a paradigm shift in financial thinking that allows the company to grow and prosper financially at the speed of its own success when the following economic conditions are true:

1. The firm is financially solvent, i.e., the steady-state yield of its financial assets is greater than or equal to its arm's-length cost of debt capital
2. The firm's financial asset base is diversified, i.e., the pooled payment risk of its financial assets is less than its own payment risk
3. To grow, the firm needs the working capital locked up in its assets
4. The market can understand the value proposition of the off-balance-sheet financing, which is not the same as that of general, unsecured corporate debt.

Securitizations are a special type of structured finance transaction whereby the funding arbitrage alluded to in conditions 1. and 2. above is achieved by transferring financial assets off-balance-sheet, and thus more clearly into the light of day, through a well-designed capital structure.

The back-of-the-envelope (BOTE) method refers to the original, semi-self-consistent valuation approach used for structured securities. *Self-consistent* really means drawing information about the transaction directly from performance data coming out of the transaction.

Since capital efficiency is maximized through self-consistent risk measurement, this attribute deserves an explanation.

Corporate finance is built on a foundation of proxy data: financial statement ratios concerning liquidity, leverage, return on assets, asset turnover and the like that are indirect measures of payment *quality*. They facilitate quality *comparisons*, for example, between different issuers or different instruments but do not produce information that can be directly used to value securities.

For valuation, a mapping must be established between the proxy variables and default or loss statistics that indicate the real value of the assets. A credible mapping is one that the users agree makes sense, that is independent, and that shows stable long-run empirical associations between proxy data and performance returns.[1] The Black–Scholes equation is one such a model for the options market. It is not a self-consistent approach, however. One of its factors, time, is inside the deal, but the other, volatility, comes from exogenous market prices, e.g. a proxy of risk.

By contrast, the BOTE is semi-self-consistent. Its inputs, cumulative principal losses, and total capital cushion, are cardinal measures of value, not proxies. Capital cushion is measured directly from the transaction structure. The cumulative loss estimate is derived from peer transactions. However, to the extent it can be replaced by data coming directly from the deal, BOTE analysis is capable of becoming fully self-consistent. Self-consistency shifts the belief structure of the market away from proxies and toward greater reliance on science and statistics. That is an evolutionary development, one that permits the belief system about value to correct itself in time using objective data feedback.

The BOTE came into existence in the 1980s when the market needed something simple and intuitive to understand security value from brain-dead SPEs. In the past two decades, it has been replaced by more sophisticated models that promise greater capital precision because they consider the impact of time and variability on transaction value and risk. Although its static approach is a fatal flaw from the standpoint of structuring and pricing, the BOTE is nonetheless a highly useful paradigm for thinking about the value proposition of structured transactions. No different from any other model, it is a starting point for thinking systematically about deals. By agreeing to submit to the rules, we discover transaction truths that cannot be seen with the naked eye. Also, the simplicity and pervasiveness of the market's institutional memory for BOTE analysis make it uniquely convenient as a starting point for discussing security value in structured finance.

The essence of the BOTE is its ability to capture the "four quarters for a dollar" analysis, which forces you to answer this question:

If I securitize $1 of assets, how does every last cent get allocated to liabilities?

The process of working through to the answer is relatively simple, but it is not trivial. By forcing the analyst to explain how capital is utilized in the structure, the BOTE analysis gets to the heart of value.

It also gets to the heart of risk, by testing the *asset–liability parity* assumption. Asset–liability parity means, that when the securities go to market, every dollar of liabilities is backed by a dollar or more of current assets. After origination, the ratio of assets to liabilities may turn out not be enough to repay the investors in full, but that is the risk they are getting paid to take. It is irrational for the transaction to be insufficiently collateralized at closing because no investor willingly buys a security with a known, uncompensated financial loss. When asset–liability parity conditions are violated, the transaction structure is said to be infeasible. If a transaction is infeasibly structured at closing, it is not a transaction at all but rather a deceptive form of on-balance-sheet corporate borrowing.

4.2 RISK MEASURE AND RATING SCALE

In the BOTE approach, the measure of security credit quality is expressed as the ratio of the amount of total capital, or credit enhancement (CE), available to cushion the impact of expected cumulative losses, $E(L)$, on the collateral pool, for one or more classes of security (j):

$$\frac{CE_j}{EL} = n_j \rightarrow r_j \tag{1}$$

where the following scale for mapping the ratio n to its associated credit grader is typical:

Rating	CE/E(L)
Aaa	5
Aa	4
A	3
Baa	1.5–2
Ba and below	< 1.5

Both quantities, CE and $E(L)$, are conventionally expressed as percentages of the initial asset pool balance.

The Meaning of CE and $E(L)$

The estimated cumulative loss statistic, commonly referred to as the expected loss or $E(L)$, is established at closing based on the historical pool performance of homogeneous pools of receivables in a liquidation scenario. The forecast cumulative loss is the most important variable in credit structuring. More details are provided on where and how to derive the $E(L)$ in chapter 5.

CE is also sometimes referred to as *credit support*. At the highest level of generalization, credit support can come in the form of third party guarantees, or it can be capital in the transaction that is contingently allocated to a certain tranche (or tranches) in a certain priority. The first type is referred to as "external CE" and the second type is referred to as "internal CE." When external CE is provided to a particular tranche, for example, through bond insurance, a credit default swap, a Letter of Credit (LOC), or some other counterparty risk transfer mechanism, the focus of the risk analysis switches to the counterparty. The BOTE method references internal CE only.

Internal CE can be classified in one of five basic forms: excess spread (XS), reserves, subordination, overcollateralization or triggers. All CE is a redistribution of asset cash flows, but each form has a different utility function and cost to the structure.

XS, defined as the difference between the asset earning and funding rate, arises when assets are refinanced under a new capital structure that reduces the overall funding cost.

The reduction in senior expenses frees up capital for reallocation to other liabilities, to improve (enhance) their credit profile. Note that the generation of *XS* is the primary motivation for doing a structured deal. If this cannot be achieved, the justification for the deal is not obvious and should be probed.

Reserving involves the holding of cash in the structure for the benefit of designated claimholders and can take different forms. Reserve funds can be established at closing from proceeds, and held for the benefit of certain classes of investors until the store of funds is fully drawn down. They can be designed to be dynamic, with step-up or step-down features fed from (or feeding) *XS* in the cash flows available for distribution. Reserve mechanisms that are unfunded at closing and fed dynamically from *XS* are often referred to as Spread Accounts. For purposes of calculating the portion of *CE* from reserve funds, only reserves funded at closing are considered. Reserves funded from *XS* are accounted for in the *XS* calculation to avoid double-counting. Note that reserving is expensive because it takes the form of cash, and that the most efficient reserve mechanisms are those that hold negative carry and asset–liability mismatch in balance.

Subordination is the result of designing credit tranches that place certain investors in a senior position to others in the capital structure. The word "subordination" describes any hierarchical payment relationship in general parlance, but in the context of *CE* it usually signifies priority in the allocation of principal.[2] *Overcollateralization*, or O/C, is essentially the same concept as subordination except that there is no junior investor, or rather that the seller is the junior investor. O/C occurs when the market is unwilling to buy a subordinated bond at any price and coupon. The percentage of overcollateralization may be said to reflect the arm's-length market consensus of the $E(L)$ on the pool.

Triggers are a form of contingent credit enhancement. If certain specified conditions that are false at closing become true within the lifetime of the deal, the payment instructions under the trigger will shift, creating a different priority of payments that offers additional protection to certain classes of investor at the expense of others. At closing, the expected value of a trigger is supposed to be zero. In practice, risk-neutrality in trigger-setting is hard to demonstrate, much less to achieve, given the informational asymmetry about asset performance between sellers and everyone else. The analysis of triggers is beyond the capacity of the BOTE model, which does not capture the effects of time or probability on which triggers depend.

4.3 TRANSACTION ANALYSIS (FIRST ATTEMPT)

The following example illustrates a simple application of the BOTE. The first attempt highlights a common mistake made in analyzing structured securities. Begin by assuming these a priori data for a hypothetical transaction:

WAC (Weighted Average Coupon)	14%	
WAM (Weighted Average Maturity)	60	
Servicing Fee	1%	
Reserve Fund	1%	
Class A tranche size	90%	
Class B tranche size	10%	
Class A Interest Rate	7%	
Class B Interest Rate	10%	

WAI (Weighted Average Interest cost)

$$0.9 \times 0.07 + 0.1 \times 0.10 = \quad 7.3\%$$
$$E(L) \quad 5\%$$

We can rate the two classes, A and B, by carrying out four steps:

1. Determine the maximum amount of credit enhancement (*CE*) available to each class
2. Reduce the maximum to a certainty-equivalent *CE* amount
3. Compute the ratio of *CE* to $E(L)$
4. Read the rating off the rating table

The analysis below shows the amount of credit enhancement available to each class, in the worked example, in order of liquidity:

Class A	**Class B**
Excess Spread (*XS*)	Excess Spread (*XS*)
Reserve Account	Reserve Account
Subordination	–

Amounts of credit enhancement are computed in reverse-order for each category, as follows:

Subordination, the size of the Class B, is available only to the Class A, in the amount of 10%. Since the sum of the classes is 100%, the transaction does not have any overcollateralization. The reserve account, available to both the Class A and the Class B, is given as 1%. Since, as noted above, the BOTE does not recognize time, it is impossible to pro-rate it meaningfully between the classes. The correct procedure is to double-count the reserve amount. Here, double-counting is not such a bad practice because we are also double-counting the amount of credit cushion required by our rating scale, which is quite capital-intensive. The virtue of double-counting is that it results in consistency of treatment from deal to deal.

The reserve fund and subordination percentages are easily determined. Both are known at closing. They can simply be read off a term sheet. By contrast with the static quantities, *XS* does not materialize as an object in the term sheet. The amount of total available *XS* is uncertain. It depends on default and prepayment rates that are unknown when the deal closes. The *XS* spread amount must first be estimated as a maximum number and then reduced to an informed certainty-equivalent estimate, as illustrated below in the third transaction attempt.

The first step in computing XS is to compute the gross spread (GS) on an annual basis: $WAC - SF - WAI$, thus

$$GS = 14 - 1 - 7.3 = 5.7\%$$

Considering the approximately five-year term of the transaction, total XS would then be

$$XS = 5 \times 5.7 = 28.5\%$$

We would now have:

Class A CE:	XS + reserve account + subordination
Class A CE:	28.5% + 1% + 10% =39.5%
Ratio $CE/E(L)$:	39.5%/5% ≈ 8
Rating:	**Aaa (or better)**

Class B CE:	XS + reserve account
Class B CE:	28.5% + 1% = 29.5%
Ratio $CE/E(L)$:	29.5%/5% ≈ 6
Rating:	**Aaa (or better)**

We are done, aren't we? *Unfortunately, we are not! What has gone wrong?*

4.4 TRANSACTION ANALYSIS (SECOND ATTEMPT)

This first attempt was erroneous because we forgot that the percentage amounts of CE should all be expressed in terms of the initial outstanding principal balance of the pool. But multiplying the annual XS by WAM is also wrong: It is tantamount to assuming that our $100 of initial principal will remain outstanding for the entire five-year term, dramatically overstating the amount of XS. In reality, XS is a function of a changing pool balance because consumer loans amortize. As a collateral pool matures and the principal balance of the loans in the trust pays down, the income earned on a gross spread of 5.7% will also decline. The XS analysis above totally neglected this financial reality.

To correct the overstatement, an *average life (AL) concept* is needed. AL is used to synchronize and standardize the repayment horizon of all structured finance deals for ease of rating and pricing. Mathematically, it represents the maturity date for a hypothetical bullet-maturity equivalent of the pool that would yield an identical dollar amount of interest as the actual pool. The AL formula simplifies the calculation of periodic interest, by reducing the problem of finding the area under the curve at each time step to one of finding the area of a rectangle. The AL compensates for the overstated amount of principal balance outstanding on the y-axis by exactly understating its maturity on the x-axis. This concept is shown graphically

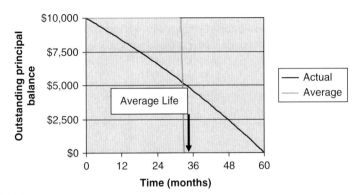

FIGURE 4.1
The average life.

in figure 4.1 for a simple $10,000 amortizing loan with a 60-month maturity and constant interest rate.

Without going into mathematical detail here[3] it can be shown that the average life t^a of a loan with initial principal balance P_0, periodic interest rate r and maturity T can be defined as:

$$t^a = \frac{1}{P_0} \int_0^T t \, dp \tag{2}$$

In equation (2), dp is the principal amortization schedule of the loan. After some simple algebra, if one inserts the usual equation for dp (see chapter 6) into equation (2), the result is:

$$t^a = \frac{T}{1 - (1+r)^{-T}} - \frac{1}{\ln(1+r)} \tag{3}$$

For a 14% APR loan with a 60-month maturity, equation (3) yields:

$$t^a = 33.45 \text{ months} \approx 2.8 \text{ years}$$

This yields:

$$XS = 2.8 \times 5.7 = 16.0\% \text{ (not 28.5\%)}$$

4.5 TRANSACTION ANALYSIS (THIRD ATTEMPT)

CE calculations are supposed to represent certain quantities of additional capital delineated in section 4.2. Initial reserves, subordination, and overcollateralization, are all disclosed directly in the prospectus, but *XS* must be approximated. After multiplying the annual *XS* rate by the *AL*, the portion of the *XS* that is unlikely to materialize should also be eliminated. By convention, three adverse events are said to reduce quantity of XS to be relied on as CE: elevated prepayments, adverse prepayments, and the timing of XS in relation to the timing of losses. In the BOTE, these effects are manually estimated and adjusted for. Note that these manual calculations are redundant in a cash flow modeling environment, where they are handled automatically via the cash flow model.

Elevated prepayments are associated with unexpectedly early amortization of the principal balance of loans compared to historical prepayment rates and can reduce interest income below expected levels, so that the absolute amount of available XS on pools with elevated prepayments is less than anticipated. The method of manually reducing XS for elevated prepayments is beyond the scope of this chapter but deserves mention here. It proceeds by running a cash flow model at elevated prepayment speeds (1.5 or 2 × expected case) and reducing total XS by the amount of reduction in the stressed case. An example of the first six months of a cash flow run showing the impact of a PSA of 200 (where the normal speed is 100) is provided in Table 4.1.

Even if historical prepayment rates materialize, the composition of prepayments and defaults is such that loans with above average coupon rates are more likely to refinance or default, and hence income from them cannot be counted on. A stress test sometimes carried out is to assume the top 20% of the loans by APR drop out of the pool at time 0. Measure the reduction in WAC, multiply this number by the AL and subtract it from total XS. Table 4.2 shows this analysis.

If credit losses take months to manifest, as is typically the case except with subprime collateral, and if XS is most abundant at the beginning of the transaction, a material portion of XS may leave the structure before it can be utilized as CE. It is known in the trade as use-it-or-lose-it (UIOLI). XS released back to the issuer is a net reduction of spread availability. One way to estimate the amount of UIOLI is to calculate the amount of XS generated between time step 0 and the required write-off time (30, 60, 90, or 120 days), and subtract this from total XS. This concept is illustrated in figure 4.2, where the square-shaped markers represent the cumulative loss curve and the diamond-shaped markers show the decreasing trend in monthly XS.

From figure 4.2, it is evident that less than the 16% of XS estimated above can be credited to this structure. Applying this analysis to the case at hand, given the 5% $E(L)$, we would reduce XS by 2% for elevated prepayments, 0.67% for adverse prepayments and (say) 4.33% for UIOLI, leaving us with an estimated XS of 9%. The credit ratings for the classes must be recomputed, and the following results are obtained:

Class A CE: 9% + 1% + 10% = 20%
Ratio $CE/E(L)$:   20%/5% = 4

Rating: **Aa**

Class B CE: 9% + 1% = 10%
Ratio $CE/E(L)$:   10%/5% = 2

Rating: **Baa**

TABLE 4.1
XS reduction due to elevated prepayments

PSA	200	AL	4.51	Δ XS	(2%)	PREPAID	LIFETIME XS	13.59%	11.59%
	LOANS	CPR	SMM	INTEREST COLLECTED	SCHEDULED PRINCIPAL	PREPAID PRINCIPAL	SENIOR EXPENSES	XS/ANNUALIZED PSA=1	XS/ANNUALIZED PSA=2
0	2,000.00	0.2%	0%						
1	1,999.34	0.4%	0.033%	$300,000	$130,413	$9,975	$232,500	0.23%	0.23%
2	1,998.01	0.8%	0.067%	$298,596	$131,673	$19,892	$231,412	0.22%	0.22%
3	1,996.03	1.2%	0.101%	$297,080	$132,901	$29,739	$230,237	0.22%	0.22%
4	1,993.39	1.6%	0.134%	$295,454	$134,095	$39,506	$228,977	0.22%	0.22%
5	1,990.11	2.0%	0.168%	$293,718	$135,254	$49,180	$227,632	0.22%	0.22%
6	1,986.20	2.4%	0.202%	$291,874	$136,377	$58,751	$226,202	0.22%	0.22%
7	1,981.65	2.8%	0.236%	$289,922	$137,462	$68,208	$224,690	0.22%	0.22%
8	1,976.48	3.2%	0.271%	$287,866	$138,508	$77,539	$223,096	0.22%	0.22%
9	1,970.70	3.6%	0.305%	$285,705	$139,515	$86,734	$221,422	0.22%	0.21%
10	1,964.31	4.0%	0.340%	$283,443	$140,480	$95,782	$219,668	0.21%	0.21%
11	1,957.33	4.4%	0.374%	$281,080	$141,403	$104,672	$217,837	0.21%	0.21%
12	1,949.78	4.8%	0.409%	$278,619	$142,282	$113,396	$215,930	0.21%	0.20%

TABLE 4.2

XS reduction due to adverse prepayments

APR (%)		ORIGINAL POOL			ADJUSTED POOL		
		BALANCE ($)	%	*WAC (%)*	BALANCE ($)	%	*WAC (%)*
≥	<		ORIGINAL			HAIRCUT=20%	
19.5		0	0.00	0.00	0	0.00	0.00
18.5	19.5	0	0.00	0.00	0	0.00	0.00
17.5	18.5	0	0.00	0.00	0	0.00	0.00
16.5	17.5	0	0.00	0.00	0	0.00	0.00
15.5	16.5	9,279,051	3.03	0.48	0	0.00	0.00
14.5	15.5	15,387,995	5.02	0.75	0	0.00	0.00
13.5	14.5	38,656,474	12.62	1.77	1,900,601	0.62	0.09
12.5	13.5	65,896,474	21.51	2.80	65,896,474	26.91	3.50
11.5	12.5	99,898,689	32.61	3.91	99,898,689	40.80	4.90
10.5	11.5	42,028,122	13.72	1.51	42,028,122	17.16	1.89
9.5	10.5	23,000,087	7.51	0.75	23,000,087	9.39	0.94
8.5	9.5	12,152,049	3.97	0.36	12,152,049	4.96	0.45
7.5	8.5	0	0.00	0.00	0	0.00	0.00
6.5	7.5	0	0.00	0.00	0	0.00	0.00
5.5	6.5	0	0.00	0.00	0	0.00	0.00
4.5	5.5	0	0.00	0.00	0	0.00	0.00
TOTALS		$306,298,941	100.0	**12.33**	$244,876,022	80	**11.67**

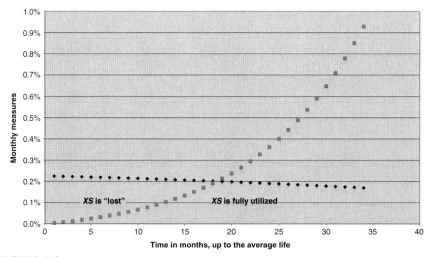

FIGURE 4.2

Use it or lose it (UIOLI) illustrated.

Note the significant difference between this result and what we obtained in the naïve case. The role of *AL* and dynamic *XS* adjustment are just two of structured finance's many nonintuitive facets that can cause credit analysts to fall into traps.

4.6 SHORTCOMINGS OF THE BOTE ANALYSIS

As a tool for structuring and pricing, the BOTE method has three shortcomings, two related to the credit scale and one to the input measures. First, it stops at the investment-grade boundary (BBB/Baa). Therefore, it cannot be used to rate securities whose credit quality is below investment grade. Second, it is an integer scale, which implies that credit quality is assumed discontinuous. This is evidently false, since the definition of credit quality in this environment is a ratio, not an integer. That means the user must interpolate to find the rating between the points, but there is no specific guidance on this other than that credit scales are exponential, so the midpoint between (for example) A and AA will be somewhere between 3 and 3.5; it will not be exactly 3.5. Third, as alluded to above, the BOTE method recognizes neither time nor probability. The point about time is obvious from the metric itself, where *CE* is measured at closing ($t = 0$) and $E(L)$ is measured at maturity ($t = T$). A model that recognized time would show the changing values of the cumulative loss curve and its incremental impact on the amount of *CE* as functions of time. Furthermore, a model that recognized probability would have some measures indicating the pattern of deviation from the expected case ratio. BOTE does not recognize probability except in the trivial sense of assuming but not showing that the $E(L)$ is the mean. All three of these shortcomings reflect the improper carryover of corporate finance thinking into structured finance.

End-of-chapter questions

1. You are an investor in the Class A or Class B tranche. All you know about the underlying risk/return characteristics of the pool is that the WAC is *the risk free rate* + *4%*. What is your optimal class size and class interest rate, given what you know.

2. Describe the essential features and delineate the steps of the BOTE approach. What problems does it solve?

3. What measures of risk and return are incorporated in the BOTE value concept? What are the pluses and minuses of this conception of risk and return?

4. Define $E(L)$ (expected loss) and identify which part of the capital structure the $E(L)$ in the BOTE formula refers to?

5. Define asset-liability parity, first in economic, then in legal and finally in mathematical terms.

6. Choose a deal prospectus and use the BOTE to solve for the expected loss given the structure and the ratings.

7. Explain the following statement: Given that the BOTE model was used to rate the transaction, it should be possible using the capital structure and ratings on each tranche to back out the expected loss, which should be the same expected loss for each tranche.

8. Even after the third attempt to rate the sample transaction using the BOTE we are not entirely finished, since the results tell us we can "optimize" the design by restructuring ad hoc. Why and how would you propose to do this? What is the result when you carry out your proposal? What is the significance of these results?

9. A banker shows you the vintage data on three static pools (table 4.3). Please construct the base curve for Pool C (express it as a percentage of absolute loss rather than as a percentage of aggregate cumulative loss) and explain your method. Normalize the curve from 0 to 100% when you are finished.

10. Pool C provides the collateral backing a transaction with this capital structure:

   - $100 transaction with a senior sub-structure
   - $WAC = 12\%$
   - $80 of Class A Notes issued at par, coupon $= 6\%$
   - $20 of Class B Notes issued at par, coupon $= 11\%$
   - AL of Class A Notes $= 1.5$ years
   - AL of Class B Notes $= 3.5$ years
   - $5 reserve account funded at closing
   - Servicing fees (the only senior expense) $= 1\%$

TABLE 4.3

XS reduction due to elevated prepayments

POOL A	POOL B	POOL C	BASE CURVE (A)	BASE CURVE (A+B)/2
0.15%	0.32%	0.26%		
0.23%	0.52%	0.36%		
0.52%	1.02%	0.96%		
1.05%	1.82%	1.33%		
1.81%	2.92%	–		
2.67%	4.32%	–		
4.03%	6.02%	–		
6.00%	7.42%	–		
7.55%	8.52%	–		
8.50%	9.32%	–		
9.03%	9.82%	–	=9.03/9.51	=?
9.35%	10.02%	–	=9.35/9.51	=?
9.46%	9.82%	–	=9.46/9.51	=?
9.51%	9.82%	–	100%	100%
9.51%	9.82%	–	100%	100%

What will be the enhancement on the Class A Notes? What will be the approximate rating of the Class A Notes using the BOTE method?

APPENDIX: BASIC LEXICON OF STRUCTURED FINANCE

The table of acronyms and definitions below highlights the financial terms most commonly used in everyday structured finance analysis. The universe of variables that matter in structured finance analysis is, in the end, rather limited. The skill of analysis resides in understanding the deep structure of their interrelatedness, a theme that leads into the next chapter and continues through to the end of this book.

Common Term of Art	Definition
WAC	Weighted average coupon of the assets in the pool (%).
WAM	Weighted average maturity of the assets in the pool (months).
WAI	Weighted average interest rate of the liabilities backed by the pool (%).
Class or Tranche	The position of the bondholder within the capital structure. The terms of each class usually differ in substance from every other class. Classes may also be subdivided into sub-classes, which often have staggered maturities. Structured transactions have any number of classes. In the priority of payments, the last class is usually referred to as "equity." Classes may also be referred to as "tranches."
Credit Support	Capital protection for a structured security, and which can take various forms.
Credit Enhancement (*CE*)	The aggregate amount of credit support to a class of structured securities issued by a SPE. Credit enhancement is usually expressed as a percentage of the initial principal balance of the assets in the pool. Three of the many types of credit support will be considered below. In many instances, credit support and credit enhancement are used interchangeably.
Servicing Fee	The fee charged for executing the financial operations of the SPE. In these notes, we will assume that the trustee fee is subsumed within the servicing fee, although they are formally separate.
Subordination	The amount of the pool represented by the issued classes junior to the senior-most class; in some cases, the main subordination is equity.

Over Collateralization (O/C)	The amount of the pool that has not been certificated nor sold to an investor. Overcollateralization is equal to the aggregate asset balance less the aggregate liability balance.
Expected Loss $E(L)$	Strictly speaking, $E(L)$ is an ex ante statistical estimate of the cumulative percentage of credit losses in the pool expressed as a percentage of the initial balance. It has also come to be used as the "most certain guesstimate" in models that use point estimates (not distributions) as inputs.
Standard Deviation of Losses	Statistical estimate of the dispersion with respect to the mean of the loss distribution. This term cannot be used in conjunction with the second definition of $E(L)$ above.
Excess Spread	Interest collected on assets within a structured pool in excess of what is required to make coupon payments on the liabilities backed by that pool and the servicing fee, or else the difference between the asset earning and funding rates. Excess spread is a significant form of credit enhancement in structured finance.
Reserve Account	A collateral account, usually in the form of cash, funded from proceeds at closing and another form of credit enhancement. Reserve accounts may be referred to as reserve funds. Other terms for related concepts: spread account, a reserve account funded from XS; sinking fund, an account in which reserves are allowed to build from incoming cash flows to offset future liabilities.
Yield Spread Account	A liquidity account created for transactions closing with a negative XS position in order to artificially make the XS positive. The yield spread account can only be drawn down to supplement interest payments of eligible classes. It is not a form of credit enhancement.

5

Piecing the Credit Together

This chapter focuses on cultivating credit judgment and learning about the source materials available for that purpose. Credit judgment is guided by *credit intuition*, an executive ability that enables the analyst to identify the salient drivers of a transaction and synthesize them into a view on its investment quality: *credit understanding* or *credit insight*. The process of developing credit judgment can be positively influenced by gaining familiarity with structured finance-specific source materials. In fact, knowing where these source materials are and how to use them properly may be the biggest obstacles to becoming a competent structured credit practitioner.

The cardinal uncertainty in structured credit analysis is whether the value of the collateral backing the securities is *"just enough"* for investors to realize a return of capital at an appropriate return on capital. The imperative of *just enough* also holds true in corporate finance, where the lender's art is finding the fine line between financing terms so onerous that they could bankrupt the client and financing terms so lax that they allow the client to divert borrowed funds to other, inappropriate uses.[1] However, unlike corporate finance where by the analysis of value is not built from the ground up, but instead projected forward on an invisible time line with an infinite horizon (the going-concern assumption),[2] in structured finance capital structure uniquely determines financial value, and financial value also uniquely determines the capital structure. For structured finance, credit intuition and understanding have to be grounded in the transaction itself, which is to say, the fine details of payment risk and cushion.

Unfortunately, a structured transaction is less accessible to intuition than the anthropomorphic corporation. How do we come to know it? Where do we look? A full treatment of the topic requires an investigation into the following categories of reference materials:

1. Source material on the structure of individual transactions
2. Source material from the annals of transaction structure history
3. Source material on the assets being securitized

4. Source material on the methods used to assess the securities' payment certainty

Market practitioners need to develop strong technical, quantitative competencies to implement or evaluate structured credits. This which was the rationale for our writing *"Elements of Structured Finance"*. Along the way, structured finance practitioners also need to develop judgmental competencies for selecting and using source materials to guide them in structuring or valuation, which is, in turn, our rationale for writing this somewhat inward-looking chapter.

5.1 SOURCE MATERIAL ON THE TRANSACTION STRUCTURE

What is the authoritative version of the transaction in the market? As simple as it sounds, this not an easy question to answer. A formally correct response would be the final transaction documents that bind the parties together and compel them to execute the funding design. This is the blueprint for the market microstructure, described at length in chapter 3. However, structured deals are a work in process. It is typical for them to continue to be refined right up to the closing day, and not atypical for them to be misinterpreted and misjudged, not only at purchase but also in the secondary market.

As a matter of practice, the closing docs are rarely consulted before or after the transaction closes unless the transaction becomes the subject of litigation. Only then do they become the central reference for the intent of the transaction. Nor can it be said that dealmakers or structurers have detailed, deep, or technical knowledge of the transaction as it is documented. This role belongs to the lawyers and archivists, who are experts in the documentation but often unskilled at reading the economic intent from the literal text.[3] In short, while deal documents are authoritative, they are not a reliable guide to the live transaction. Live deals take shape in the minds of transactors who are working impressionistically from a combination of anecdote and knowledge of past deals.[4]

Good *script knowledge* is essential to developing structured credit judgment. Script knowledge means the ability to conceptualize the transaction documents and the modeling environment, and move seamlessly between the two. Script knowledge is evidenced by an ability to render liability subroutines faithfully from the PSA into a scripting or programming language. It is a first milestone on the path to structural knowledge, although by no means the last. Script knowledge used to be the exclusive preserve of quants and IT professionals. That has changed. However, while the market has become more receptive to the role of a *structuring banker*, in some environments analysts still must downplay good script knowledge to avoid being sidelined as mere technical support help. Leaving stereotypes aside, however, the structured market as a whole relies on practitioners with good script knowledge to ensure that the structure mirrors the transaction intent. Script knowledge therefore precedes the development of structured credit intuition on the road to mastery. Until the transaction has been conceptualized, there can be no intuition of its credit character.

The next learning stage actually consists of a series of milestones culminating in a capacity to hold in mind the array of elements that constitute the unique value of the transaction. Call it *visualization*. Analysts who can visualize the transaction can reproduce any one of a number of its different, essential facets at will. For example, by graphing the flow of cash and the transfer of title (the market macrostructure, chapter 3), inferring the expected loss and its variance from historical data, valuing the assets, executing the waterfall, assessing the payment certainty of the liabilities and evaluating the quality of transaction design. Each visualization is an aspect of credit intuition, a tool for the analyst to be able to interrogate the transaction ever more incisively:

What are you (the transaction) saying?
What are you not saying?
What are you worth?
How much am I willing to pay for you?

The last stage in the development of structured credit judgment is deep credit understanding, manifested by the ability to reduce the complexity of the transaction to simple truths about strategy and motivation, value and price, that are invisible to the untrained eye. Deep credit understanding reveals instantaneously what otherwise becomes perceptible much more slowly during and after the time when the deal is taking shape.

The sheer volume of specialized learning required in order to feel confident in structured credit judgment can be daunting. However, the attainment of credit insight can be itself a powerful motivator, on a par with professional recognition, and perhaps more powerful than monetary compensation alone. The pleasure derived from the development of credit judgment is self-reinforcing, as new insights stoke the desire to learn how, do more, and see further out in time, as new learning feeds new thresholds of understanding. An analyst's professional development advances like this, recursively, on the same iterative path where the design of a transaction itself takes shape, albeit over a much longer time frame, and perhaps imperceptibly.

Learning to Read the Prospectus

Reading comprehension is critical to developing credit intuition. Unfortunately, there is no way of getting around the need to read and comprehend the structure of the deal. Fortunately, reading comprehension can be sharpened and improved through the repetition of doing deals: reading the prospectus; learning to focus selectively on the material passages; developing a vocabulary of common terms and structures; learning to spot and question uncommon usages; and observing how the terms and structures play themselves out in real time so as to mold structured credit insight to nonlinear yield space where raw intuition often fails.

Like reading a detective novel, piecing the credit together is a process of reconstruction through a combination of fact-finding and intuition which begins with a set of hypotheses about how the transaction structure transforms asset cash flows into securities and their value, then zigzags toward confirmation or rejection and replacement with new, better hypotheses, until the process concludes with an investment decision. Inputs are added to the analysis until either (i) a hypothesis emerges that seems to fit the relevant data comfortably enough, or (ii) the analyst's time simply runs out. This is where the analogy with detective fiction breaks down. The novel concludes with precise certainty about causality that can never be replicated in the primary structured market given the asymmetries of information between buyers and sellers, and the pressure for quick decision-making because analyst time is itself capital.

Transaction reconstruction begins with the transaction description, but which one? The final PSA contains the definitive waterfall but, as alluded to earlier, it is not the most common or most convenient reference document. Prior to origination it is incomplete, and after origination it is bundled together with many other documents. Early drafts of the PSA are a reasonable substitute, though the structure may have changed in the interim. The same is true of summary deal marketing documents like the *prospectus*, *offering memorandum* or *offering circular*.[5] These are the most accessible and readable sources on transaction mechanics and structure, but with two caveats. First, prospectuses are time-sensitive. They may reflect a version of the transaction no longer contemplated. Second, unlike the indenture, the deal description in marketing materials is not legally binding. Therefore, the analyst should be on the lookout for misinformation that may unduly flatter the credit without overtly misstating facts. Nevertheless, prospectus disclosures are much more reliable than more informal materials like Power Point presentations that constitute part of the marketing package. In the hierarchy of representative materials, the prospectus is a good compromise between expediency and reliability.

What matters in the prospectus? The vital prospectus sections are the *cover page* and a set of pages that commonly begins on page 2. These are often framed by a visible border and referred to collectively as the *term sheet*.[6]

The term sheet and the glossary of defined terms, if it exists, are the essence of the transaction. Other prospectus sections contain data ranging from mildly useful to utterly useless.

Cover Page

The cover page presents the summary of the transaction liabilities:

- Size of the offering (how much money is being raised)
- Date the securities are to be offered (the *closing*)
- Names, sizes, coupon amounts, prices, maturity dates, average lives, and expected ratings of tranches offered under the prospectus
- Financial advisors, underwriters, external credit enhancement providers, and, potentially, other financial service providers necessary to take the deal to market

The cover page publishes the key data on the capital structure from which the deterministic amounts of credit enhancement can be calculated on each tranche: subordination, initial overcollateralization, reserve funds, yield supplement, and spread accounts. Note that *XS* spread is not typically disclosed in the term sheet but must be inferred from a combination of the structure and static pool data. Moreover, it is often the case that some tranches present in the capital structure are not offered in the prospectus. At times, the lower part of the structure is held back on the seller's balance sheet, and sometimes the mezzanine is sold via a different, private transaction. Conventionally, the prospectus will have certain disclosures on the name, size, and maturity date of the tranches not offered, to give the prospective investor a snapshot of the deal, but sensitive information like rating, price, and coupon on the non-offered tranches is not always disclosed.

Term Sheet

The prospectus *term sheet* discloses how the transaction is intended to work.[7] Typically it contains enough information to allow the analyst to visualize and model the transaction, but not enough to interpret cash flows, *XS* or other dynamic components of credit enhancement that must be worked out from the asset-side data. The ordering of topics in the term sheet begins by describing the parties to the transaction moving on to a discussion of assets followed by a description of the capital structure, including sections on the securities and available credit enhancement.

The main focus will usually be the liabilities, with disclosures on capital structure, credit enhancement and pay down mechanics. However, the parties and asset discussions are integral to credit understanding. The parties are important as a guide to transaction operations. That section should have enough disclosure to graph the entire flow diagram (see chapter 3). Note that insufficient data to render the transaction flows is a credit red flag: *What is being hidden, and why?* The usefulness of the assets discussion is limited, more often than not, by the omission of static pool data used to rate the securities. Regulation AB, where it applies, requires the disclosure of issuer static pool history in connection with securities registration. Eventually, this requirement should bring $E(L)$ information into the prospectus. Until that happens, the prospectus can be relied upon for nuance on the asset type and risk grade, but not for measure. Some prospectuses do provide stratified sample data on credit-sensitive variables such as loan balance, coupon, maturity, loan-to-value, portfolio loss, etc. Any of these may be useful in developing credit intuition, sometimes more via what is omitted than by what is provided.[8] No credit data that are disclosed should be ignored, but neither should they be uncritically applied. Remember that in credit, as in life, data can be disclosed to conceal as well as to reveal.[9]

Transaction Analysis

As previously noted, whereas the BOTE method outlined in the last chapter is inadequate for structuring, its simplicity makes it a fine roadmap for putting the pieces of a credit already outstanding back together again, and taking it on a test drive. Its simplicity also makes it appropriate for illustrating this piecework process.

The choice of BOTE as a roadmap will guide which data to select and how to use them. In the BOTE, the risk of the deal is defined as the cumulative $E(L)$ and the capital cushioning as the initial CE amount, pared down dynamically according to the terms of the transaction. The security-level risk measure is defined as CE divided by $E(L)$. Once the transaction enters the secondary market, the relationships between risk, capital and rating can be inverted to extract proprietary information about the $E(L)$ once the rating is given.[10] Instead of asking, "What is the rating of the deal?," we ask, "What is the $E(L)$ that drove this structure and this rating?" and rearrange the terms to extract transaction-implied $E(L)$ for each rated tranche, j, given its associated CE_j:

$$\frac{CE_j}{n(r_j)} = E(L)$$

Since the $E(L)$ should be the same for each tranche, whenever more or less the same $E(L)$ is obtained from different tranches, the result is more or less believable.

Note that in a real transaction, the $E(L)$ does not change tranche-wise as it relates to the pool, not the liabilities. In addition, the BOTE-implied $E(L)$ will always vary to some degree unless the BOTE was used originally to structure the deal and the CE analysis is precise. The goal is not to seek precision but merely a well-rounded answer, i.e. one that includes all material information. To obtain a well-rounded answer, a few pieces of the credit puzzle need to be prepared including, at a minimum

- The four-quarters-for-a-dollar analysis: the initial principal balance of the collateral must precisely equal the sum of the class sizes on the liability side
- The calculation and allocation of CE to each tranche, based on the prospectus description
- A rationale for extrapolating and interpolating the integer scale by resourceful application of existing ratings source material (any official, public material is fair game)
- The test drive: a dynamic interpretation of the static analysis

The details of each point are expanded in the text below:

(1) **How is the aggregate principal balance of the assets allocated to the liabilities?**

If the entire capital structure is being offered in the prospectus, the answer is straightforward: it is identical to the dollar amount of offered securities. If most of the capital structure is being offered in the prospectus and the asset amount is given, the structure of subordination for the offered securities can be worked out. If details on the unoffered portions are not forthcoming and the asset base is not given, the analyst must extract it using data disclosed in the prospectus. The prospectus should contain the minimum data set enabling the derivation of the initial pool balance from asset–liability parity conditions. If this cannot be demonstrated from the prospectus, it is reasonable to infer under-collateralization.

(2) **Obtain subordination and over-collateralization levels via (1) above.**

The disclosure on reserve funds is typically straightforward. To avoid double-counting care should be exercised to include only the initial reserve fund amount. Target reserve amounts are funded from XS, which is separately calculated. XS calculations require both WAC and WAI information. WAI should be calculated directly from the cover page. *WAC* can be calculated using a stratified sample of the asset pool, if it is disclosed in the prospectus. If there is no disclosure, *XS* should not be imputed from target reserve fund amounts but should be assigned a value of zero. This may seem punitive, but target amounts disclosed in a marketing document cannot be reliably credited, and it is impossible to back out the $E(L)$ while solving for the *XS* simultaneously. The *XS* analysis can be revisited after a hypothetical $E(L)$ has been obtained.

(3) **Levels on the integer scale must be interpolated for notches ($+/1$ and $-/3$) and extrapolated to take it below BBB.**

The interpolation should not be linear since the credit scale is exponential. Ratings below BBB can scaled with reference to historical default percentages. To illustrate the last point, suppose an idealized bond default study published by an NRSRO provides indicative default rates on BBB, BB and B securities five years from issuance, as shown in table 5.1.

In this study, BB securities with an average life of five years or less evidence less than 10% probability of default. This makes 10% the ceiling for $E(L)$ (with zero recoveries) for corporate bonds of this rating level and maturity. Is 10% material? Yes. Is it probable? No. Our second observation is that, $CE/E(L) = 1$ is an important threshold. What would $CE/E(L) < 1$ mean? Simply that, in the expected case, there would be insufficient *CE* to cover losses. Putting these two arguments together, we would not be inclined to make the rating factor of BB $<= 1$ on an expected case, because although the default probability is material (and could entail losses of up to 100% of the defaulted amount), it is far less than 50%. Therefore, if we want to construct a rating factor for BB consistent with market information on BB default risk, the ceiling must be less than 1.5 and the floor higher than 1.0, which would imply a security default should expected losses actually materialize.

(4) **Test drive of the structure using the BOTE as a roadmap.**

Suppose the deal information in table 5.2 is found on the cover page of a hypothetical structured transaction' prospectus. Once the work of items (1)–(3) is performed $E(L)$ can easily be calculated. If the original ratings were assigned using the BOTE, $E(L)$ should be identical for all tranches in the structure, as illustrated in this hypothetical example. Assuming no reserve fund and zero *XS*, the equilibrium $E(L)$ implied on the pool by this structure is 3%. If *XS* is positive, then the securities are better than the

TABLE 5.1

Hypothetical bond default study results

TERM /*AL*	1	2	3	4	5
Baa2	0.1700%	0.4700%	0.8300%	1.2000%	1.5800%
Ba2	1.5600%	3.4700%	5.1800%	6.8000%	8.4100%
B2	7.1600%	11.6700%	15.5500%	18.1300%	20.7100%

ratings indicate. The amount of equity, 3.5%, is larger than the $E(L)$, which implies the expected-case value of the residual cash flow is 0.5%, not 0%. To be clear, this exercise does not signify that the empirical $E(L)$ is indeed 3%; it only produces the ratings-implied $E(L)$, which may be quite different from the truth. The simultaneous derivation of $E(L)$ at 3% is presented in table 5.3.

We can take the analysis one step further and look for relative value across the capital structure by comparing the ratings-implied $E(L)$ with our ex ante $E(L)$ from an independent collateral analysis. If our independently determined $E(L)$ is approximately 2.5%, our ex ante ratings on the securities would be higher than the official ratings, because total CE has risen by 50 bps while the risk has gone down by 50 bps, i.e. sufficiently to change the economics at the margin. That analysis is displayed in table 5.4, with the addition of hypothetical average life calculations.[11]

TABLE 5.2

Liability-side data on cover page (1)

SECURITIES	CLASS PERCENTAGE	RATING	RISK PREMIUM	MATURITY
Class A	85.0%	AAA	0.35%	5 yrs
Class B	6.5%	A−	1.10%	8 yrs
Class C	5.0%	BB	4.00%	8 yrs
Equity	3.5%	N/R	−	−

TABLE 5.3

Backing out an implied $E(L)$

SECURITIES	CLASS PERCENTAGE	RATING FACTOR	IMPLIED RATING
Class A	85.0%	5.00	AAA
Class B	6.5%	2.83	A−
Class C	5.0%	1.17	BB
Equity	3.5%	0.00	N/R

TABLE 5.4

Liability-side data on cover page (2)

SECURITIES	RATING	RATING FACTOR	RISK PREMIUM	AVERAGE LIFE
Class A	AAA	6.00	0.25%	2.5 yrs
Class B	AA−	3.40	0.50%	3.5 yrs
Class C	BBB−	1.40	2.50%	3.5 yrs
Equity	N/R	0.00	−	−

TABLE 5.5
Finding an economic arbitrage

SECURITIES	ARBITRAGE PER ANNUM	LIFETIME ARBITRAGE
Class A	0.10%	25 bps
Class B	0.60%	210 bps
Class C	1.50%	525 bps
Equity	–	–

Annual and lifetime credit arbitrage opportunities would be assessed as in table 5.5. Suppose, on the other hand, that our ex ante $E(L)$ is 5%. This would mean that, in the expected case, Class C would suffer a 1.5% loss. Suffering a loss in the expected case is contrary to rational expectations, not to mention common sense.

Having demonstrated the method, two caveats on the all-purpose usefulness of the BOTE roadmap are in order. First, the method does not work on tranches where the main source of credit enhancement is provided externally, i.e., highly rated *wrapped* tranches of transactions by a subprime or non-rated seller who needs a financial guaranty to issue securities. The optical rating stems from the counterparty providing the protection. The real (*standalone*) rating is lower. This must be true otherwise the guarantor could charge a profitable premium. Ratings on insured tranches must be *looked through*. This means that the counterparty's undisclosed attachment point the *shadow* rating, representing the rating agency's credit assessment on the tranche, must be used in its place. Since the shadow rating is not a matter of public record nor disclosed to the guarantor, it must be inferred. Knowing something about the guarantor's strategy may be useful, to limit the feasible range of values to a likely answer. Was the guarantee offered to capture a rating arbitrage or a regulatory capital arbitrage? Is the guarantor simply buying the business? Each answer would imply a different strategy and associated rating level.

The second caveat is, if the BOTE is not used to rate the transaction, it will be impossible to compute a unique $E(L)$. Rating methods that consider time or probability, or both, usually require less enhancement than the BOTE. Moreover, the BOTE will not work on complex deals, i.e., those with waterfalls allowing cash to move up as well as down. Since few deals today are rated using the BOTE, and most are complex, this is a fairly serious shortcoming.[12] In short, the BOTE should be abandoned where it frustrates intuition rather than assist it. Eventually, every analyst will outgrow the BOTE roadmap and will replace it with a structuring tool, not to structure but to reverse-engineer the deal so as to interrogate it.

However, since human intuition is no match for computational power, the analyst must be trained in the use of more powerful valuation approaches, involving more modeling intensity, or else credit insight will be lost and errors of judgment will be committed. Many valuable insights can be gained by learning to model. Cash flow modeling is the language of transaction value, and learning deal-speak means having to go live in that environment. It is not sufficient just to sightsee or read books. But, the model must ultimately reside in the mind. Modelers who attempt to apply formulas without understanding the deal as a value proposition deliver a worthless product, just as analysts trying to price a deal without the discipline of a mathematical model and a fixed set of measures inevitably deceive themselves, and the people they counsel, with the shallowness of their analysis.

5.2 THE HISTORY OF STRUCTURAL CONVERGENCE

History is a rich archive of structural experiments. Until the mid-1990s most deals consisted of sequential-pay credit tranches and static reserve funds. These structures locked up more spread in the securities than was required for their credit designations. In the mid-1990s, the problem of excessive over-collateralization began to be redressed through embedded or outright triggers intended to sculpt the waterfall more finely while still defending the structure against extremes of payment uncertainty. In early 2000, market pressures leading to spread compression, rising prepayment risk and aggressive use of prefunding gave rise to a raft of new structural features, such as sub-classes of money market and term notes of staggered-maturities. Traditional CMO tranches, like Planned Amortization Classes, Targeted Amortization Classes, interest-only and principal-only securities, Z- and NAS-bonds were used more aggressively than ever in agency transactions while private-label RMBS structures featured multiple-pool transactions with distinct sets of liabilities eventually cross-collateralized in the form of a common block. The history of the experiments and the convergences between different structured market sectors is a macro-level source of structural ideas. The history of successes and failures along the path to convergence is full of expensive lessons that provide a rich and fruitful learning environment for serious structured credit analysis.

Source Material on the Assets Being Securitized

Recall that the credit risk in the SPE collateral is the main structural driver.[13] Although it is just estimate, it must still approximate the truth, otherwise the securities will perform outside the boundaries of expectation. Source material used to determine the credit risk in the SPE collateral is private, informally provided and virtually unregulated. This situation seems to flout the ideal of regulation by disclosure, but it came about because rating agencies, who have the final say about SPE collateral risk, sought to maintain quality control and independence from market pressure by disclosing as little as possible to the outside about the specifics of their collateral measurement processes and measurement outcomes. Overall the process worked well as long as the structured market was in its infancy, although even then it lacked the redundancy of checks and balances. When it malfunctioned, no single institution outside the rating agency sphere knew enough about the technical specifications of the process to regulate or replace their risk assessment function. That is why disclosures on source material and its uses are such an important and overlooked aspect of institutionalizing the market.

The first thing to know about source material for the structured transaction is that the seller's balance sheet information is unusable. Both items on its balance sheet related to the assets, *Accounts or Loans Receivable* and a related *Provision for*

Doubtful Accounts, are too unrefined for vintage- and cash-flow centric structured analysis. They even go by a different term of art: the *servicer's portfolio*. Instead, the focus is on *vintages*: loans made by the same originator with homogenous seasoning. Within vintages, underwriting characteristics are merged into the basic unit of analysis known as the *static pool*.

To avoid selection biases, pooling should proceed by a random selection of loans underwritten under a uniformly applied loan policy. Prior to pooling, the original credit and investment guidelines should be reviewed to determine the target risk–return features of the collateral, the consistency with which the guidelines were applied and the performance results.

Once a pool-cut is available, the most important risk measure by far is the cumulative loss on the pool, or $E(L)$. As risk measures go within financial theory, the $E(L)$ is both powerful and unique. With regard to its power, $E(L)$ is a cardinal measure of risk that translates directly into a fair value metric. This makes it a better information source than financial statement ratios, which are *ordinal measures* of value, and arguably also better than market-determined prices or rates of return, which are only value *proxies*. With regard to its uniqueness, only the $E(L)$ measures total (life-time) risk, whereas every other conventional measure reflects average (periodic) risk. An $E(L)$ that is properly determined can be placed within an envelope of capital protection (CE) that mitigates and modulates its impact on security value over the life of the risk exposure. A proper determination starts with a static pool's measurement method. This will not work with a revolving portfolio because its statistics are too easily manipulated in ways that the sidebar below on *Altruism 125* illustrates.

The Lifecycle of Risk: Delinquency, Default, Loss

Although the expected loss is the focus of the asset-side analysis in structured finance, it is important to answer the more fundamental question: What is a loss?

The definition of loss follows the convention in the structured market. Unlike the accounting loss, measured as the principal balance outstanding and accrued interest at the time of default, the structured finance loss signifies the ultimate shortfall on the initial principal balance net of recoveries at maturity. In general, the accrual convention does not apply to structured finance, which relies on pure cash flow accounting. In addition, accrued interest, which is meaningful at the level of the individual loan, loses its significance in the context of pooling.[14]

> #### ▶ Portfolio and Static Pool Measures Compared
>
> A deadly strain of a new virus, *Altruism 125*, has gripped New York City. Two training hospitals, H1 and H2, are attempting to measure the associated mortality rate. H1's measurement method proceeds as follows:
>
> - Every Friday for 24 successive weeks, count the total number of people diagnosed with, and the number confirmed to have died of, *Altruism 125*.
> - The ratio reaches a steady-state after 10 weeks, at 4%.

H2's measurement method proceeds as follows:

- Every Friday for 8 successive weeks, count the total number of people diagnosed with *Altruism 125*.
- After the eightth week, do not add anyone new to this cohort, but continue to follow it through time, tallying the number of people confirmed to have died or recovered from *Altruism 125*, until the outcomes of the entire cohort are accounted for.
- After 24 weeks, the ratio reaches 10% cumulatively.

H1's approach leads to a portfolio average measure. H2's produces a static pool measure. Note that although both hospitals are measuring the same phenomenon and population, different methods are off by a staggering 250%—or, put another way, the difference between a non-prime (4%) and a sub-prime (10%) pool.

The first method by H1 is technically incorrect for measuring the breakout rate of a disease, and also incorrect for measuring the expected loss on a pool. It introduces a suppressed data problem by partitioning the states of being as dead/not dead. In fact, *not dead* really means *not dead yet*, a category that will continue to overstate the number of *survivors*, as the subset that continues to die off is replenished with the newly sick.

If the incidence of *Altruism 125* accelerates, the mortality rate will improve but for the wrong reason, namely that the death rate is not keeping up with the infection rate. This is known as the *denominator* or *pipeline effect*. But, since the epidemic of *Altruism 125* is self-limiting, as soon as the number of newly sick begins to taper off, the death statistic will start to balloon in proportion to the number of *survivors*. In common parlance, this is referred to variously as *tail risk* or *the suppressed data problem*.

The second method by H2 correctly poses the states of being as *death/survival* because it is based on cumulative measurements, not averages. As a result, the estimate gets closer and closer to the true mortality rate (of that population) with the passage of time. If the etiology of *Altruism 125* changes for some reason (immunological response or the introduction of new drugs) the characteristic mortality of the population will actually change. Then, the old statistic will not have the same predictive power, any more than the $E(L)$ measure would apply to loans originated by the same lender but based on a different underwriting policy.

Losses are the last stage of a process that begins when the borrower is current, then progresses to a state of non-currency or delinquency. Delinquency is the nonpayment event. Default is the tipping point in the delinquency state, when the underwriter judges that the loan will not be repaid and decides to initiate foreclosure. The loss is determined after the foreclosure process is completed and the liquidated proceeds have been received. Each of these credit events (delinquency, default, loss, recovery) should be recognized in strict accordance with chronological time to prevent misrepresentation of loan quality, because the value of a loan is established based on the contractually agreed terms within a temporal context. However, as noted in other chapters of this book, there is no regulatory guidance to enforce truthful disclosures about loan status.

A snapshot of a hypothetical delinquency state, with a typical grace period for U.S. consumer debt, is given in table 5.6.

TABLE 5.6

Typical loan delinquency states

0–4 DAYS	5–30 DAYS	31–60 DAYS	61–90 DAYS	91–120 DAYS	>120 DAYS
Most prime borrowers are almost always here.	This bucket can be liquidity or credit impairment. A high incidence can be purely cultural.	This bucket is about credit. The challenge to borrowers to make two payments (to become current) is significantly higher than to make one.	Write-offs begin here, often, when the pool is distressed.	Write-offs typically begin here.	Check for lax collection practices when write-offs take place here.

TABLE 5.7

An example of loan delinquency transitions

	0–4	5–30	31–60	61–90	91–120	>120	CHECK
0–4	0.98	0.02	0	0	0	0	1
5–30	0.01	0.95	0.04	0	0	0	1
31–60	0.005	0.126	0.86	0.009	0	0	1
61–90	0	0.001	0.2	0.79	0.009	0	1
91–120	0	0	0.0005	0.19	0.7095	0.1	1
>120	0	0	0	0	0	1	1

This snapshot only shows the one-way transition, from current to defaulted. Transition happens in the opposite direction, too, as delinquent accounts repair to a lesser delinquent state or *cure* and are returned to *current* status. Note that the transition from *current* to 5-30 days delinquent (*bucket one*) dominates other transitions as a determinant of ultimate defaults.

A hypothetical delinquency transition matrix in table 5.7 describes the transition of accounts between states. The rows represent the percentage of accounts in each state at time $(t − 1)$ that transition in to other states (columns) at time (t). In this picture, 98% of all accounts remain current from one period to the next while 1% of accounts curently one-period delinquent will cure in the next period, versus a cure rate of 0.5% for accounts now two periods delinquent. Two percent of all current accounts will slip into delinquency the following month. This number doubles (4%) for accounts already in bucket 1, but declines going from bucket two to bucket three (0.9%), etc. It is logically impossible for delinquencies to change faster than one bucket per month.

Recency versus Contractual Delinquency

A delinquency should only be able to *cure* (return to *current* status) when the obligor has made all payments currently due. Under some policies, the collection platform is allowed to cure the account even when payments, or portions thereof, are still outstanding. This practice, referred to as *recency* accounting in contrast to the proper *contractual* reckoning, is illegal in some jurisdictions, frowned upon in many more and universally misleading. Recency makes it next-to-impossible to calculate the actual loss of yield, and therefore, the ultimate loss on the loan. Although this should be disclosed somewhere in the prospectus of term securitizations, there need not be any disclosure on recency methods for loans financed with in ABCP conduits, where market practice has long and successfully resisted many forms of disclosure considered the norm in term securitizations.

▷ Identifying Recency Accounting

... for fiscal years ended 1999 and 1998, the period of delinquency was based on the number of days more than 50% of the scheduled payment was contractually past due.

   Translation: The borrower only needed to pay 50% of the due amount to be counted as *current*. Note that nowhere does the bad word *recency* appear—on the contrary, only the good word *contractual*! The reader must be prepared to have a working definition of recency to identify it in documents. ◁

The Empirical Loss Curve: Basis of the Expected Loss Analysis

Losses in a static do not move linearly across time. Early on, they accelerate, reach a maximum, decelerate and finally taper off. The S-shaped unfolding of losses from origination to amortization is referred to as a *static pool loss curve*, or more simply, *the loss curve*.

   Vintage loss curves are associated with assets of different risk grades from different lenders where, after a while they become iconic. *Issuer loss curves* are the basis for predicting future performance on new structured transactions. The practice of using issuer loss curves in forecasting started with rating agencies, who made the express assumption that lenders' underwriting guidelines and collection practices give rise to characteristic loss and recovery patterns that are somewhat stable over time. Loss curves used in transactions are generally constructed from prior loss curves or raw-vintage loss data from the lender. When no prior static pool history is available, they are constructed using *peer* static pool history from lenders believed to have similar underwriting and collection characteristics.

   Loss curves are constructed on a spreadsheet by arraying cumulative loss data in columns, with each row representing a new temporal data point. In this way, apples are always compared to apples and the problem of averaging across time is avoided. The analyst selects all or a subset of the issuer's vintages and computes an average or *base* curve for forecasting losses on the new transaction, then normalizes it from 0 to 1. Each point on the normalized curve becomes the *percentage-of-completion* of the loss curve. Three points have a special significance. The first is the point in time when defaults begin, i.e. where the curve formally takes shape. If write-offs occur on the 91st day, this will be the fourth time step. The second is when the *loss-to-liquidation ratio*, expressed as the monthly amortization due to defaults divided by total monthly amortization, reaches its inflection point. This roughly corresponds to the time when the rate of acceleration reaches a maximum. This corresponds roughly to the parameter t_0 on the theoretical loss curve in chapter 6. The third point occurs at termination, where the number on the y-axis is the historically realized cumulative loss, or the expected cumulative loss if data points are missing given the pool's average maturity.

Loss Curve Projection

When all loss data are disclosed empirically,[5] from closing to maturity, the last data point is the cumulative realized loss for a given pool. The loans behind it were originated months or years prior to the current pool in question. Newer vintages may be more representative of the lending environment. However, by definition they are incomplete and must be extrapolated if the base curve is to be constructed properly.

Table 5.8 illustrates base curve extrapolation in a tabular format. In general, there are two methods for extrapolation: the additive method and the multiplicative method.

Additive Method

This method is a simple shifting algorithm that resets each new data point based on the difference between the previous and the target point for the base curve. If the base curve is defined by y_i, $i = 1, 2, 3, \ldots N$, the target curve by g_i, $i = 1, 2, 3$, and the

TABLE 5.8
Base curve construction for projecting loss curves

POOL 1	POOL 2	AVERAGE	BASE CURVE 1	BASE CURVE AVG.
0.13%	0.33%	0.23%	1.19%	2.30%
0.33%	0.66%	0.50%	3.03%	4.96%
0.67%	1.13%	0.90%	6.18%	9.02%
1.00%	1.52%	1.26%	9.18%	12.60%
2.50%	3.03%	2.77%	22.96%	27.61%
3.90%	4.23%	4.07%	35.81%	40.59%
6.73%	6.37%	6.55%	61.80%	65.40%
7.35%	6.80%	7.08%	67.49%	70.67%
8.12%	7.33%	7.73%	74.56%	77.15%
9.08%	7.97%	8.53%	83.38%	85.15%
9.97%	8.55%	9.26%	91.55%	92.48%
10.05%	8.60%	9.33%	92.29%	93.14%
10.22%	8.71%	9.47%	93.85%	94.53%
10.35%	8.80%	9.57%	95.04%	95.60%
10.75%	9.05%	9.90%	98.71%	98.86%
10.89%	9.14%	10.01%	100.00%	100.00%

target-curve data stop at $i = n$, then for the point $g_i, i = n + 1, n + 2, n + 3, ...N$, the rule is:

$$g_i = g_{i-1} + (y_i - y_{i-1}) \tag{1}$$

In this case, the new cumulative expected loss estimate for the pool is

$$E(L) \equiv g_N = g_n + (y_N - y_n) \tag{2}$$

Multiplicative Method

This is a ratio method whereby each new data point is set equal to the previous data point multiplied by the ratio of the target and previous data points for the base curve. Using the identical nomenclature, this rule is:

$$g_i = g_{i-1} \frac{y_i}{y_{i-1}} \tag{3}$$

In that case, the new cumulative expected loss estimate for the pool is

$$E(L) \equiv g_N = g_n \prod_{i=n+1}^{N} \frac{y_i}{y_{i-1}} \tag{4}$$

The main difference between the two lies in their assumptions about credit loss behavior. The first says losses are additive in time, and that we can just step off from where we are to compute remaining loss. The second assumes that the credit loss process feeds on itself and so must be viewed logarithmically. However, when the data trail is too new to establish a trend line, the multiplicative method may lead to unrealistic answers. More intricate methods of loss curve construction making increasingly realistic assumptions about the default process are introduced in the Advanced Part (chapters 14–24).

Analysts should be cognizant of the main shortcomings of loss curve extrapolation. Aside from the problem of projecting the future from the past, which is intrinsic to forecasting itself, the sheer mindlessness of loss curve projection is a major shortcoming. For example, what if the historical curves have a different maturity than the pool being securitized? It would be too easy to copy, cut, and paste, glossing over the fact that the actual loss curve is 25% to 33% longer. Such transactions would be under-collateralized vis-à-vis their credit benchmarks.

Accounting for Recoveries

Many games played in structured finance happen at the level of counting and reporting losses. The regulatory vacuum of reporting standards for delinquencies, defaults, losses and recoveries creates opportunities to game the system by delayed recognition of loss, use of recency accounting and the accelerated recognition of recoveries. Recovery data are particularly open to question. Like loss data, they too are private and informally provided by the arranger on behalf of the seller. But unlike cumulative loss data, ex-post facto reconciliation is not possible because the final numbers are never checked by anyone involved in the securitization process. The serious analyst needs to devise a roundabout way of determining the accuracy of the recovery numbers he uses. One such method is to investigate the method of record keeping that produced those numbers.

Of the three ways to account for recoveries,

- *Cash basis*, recognizing the loss and recovery amounts *when* they occur
- *"Accrual" basis*, attempting to match the cash inflow with the cash outflow by attributing them to the same time period
- *Estimated basis*, netting a constant percentage of recoveries from gross losses with an episodic true-up

the first two are factual, the third is not. Sellers who provide estimated rather than historical recoveries may be more tempted to exaggerate or manipulate results in their favor.

Figures 5.1a and 5.1b illustrate this point graphically. At the top in both figures we show the cumulative default curve. The above three treatments of losses based on it can be found near the center: cash-based, smoothed ("accrual") and managed. Recovery curves are also provided for reference: marginal curves for the cash-based and smooth treatments at the bottom, and a cumulative recovery curve associated with the managed loss curve to highlight the potential deception.

A cash-based loss curve associates recovery amounts with the actual period of the cash inflow. It is the choppiest and the riskiest looking, but appearances are deceptive. In fact, it is more accurate and provides the greatest transparency because it is purely

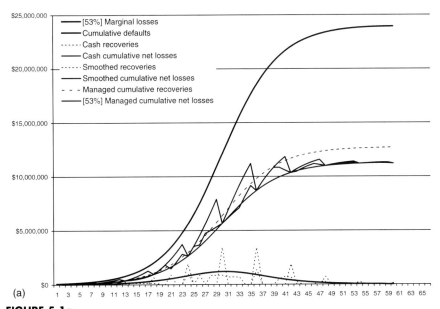

FIGURE 5.1a

Loss curve under three treatments.

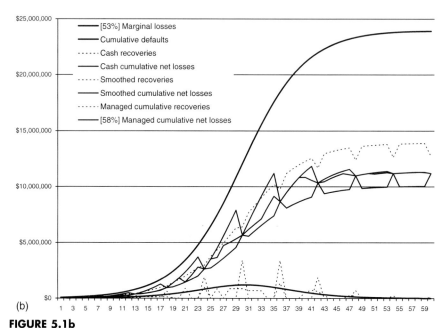

FIGURE 5.1b

Loss curves: managed treatment twists the truth.

cash-based. The smoothed or accrual loss curve associates the recovery amount with the loan at the time of default. It is less precise in a cash flow sense (which matters most in securitization) but it preserves the original relationship between the loan and its recovery, which may offer important information on the original loan.

The managed loss curve assumes a constant 47% loss severity and adjusts the differences when recoveries are received. To highlight what is wrong with this approach, the cumulative managed recovery curve is presented. Figure 5.1a shows the case where the estimated 53% recovery amount is realized. In figure 5.1b, the point is stretched and a 58% recovery amount is claimed, with true-ups only at the points in time where the actual cash comes in. It is difficult to prove ex ante that the number is wrong since recovery amounts are not legally disclosed in any reporting system. However, the rewards for stretching the truth are significant, because the convention of estimating cumulative losses is backward-looking, and loss curves with 18 to 30 months' of seasoning look substantially lower under the managed than the cash treatment, enabling the seller to go to market with an unjustifiably low credit enhancement based purely on optical differences.

Loss Curves and Loss Distributions

Economic processes usually operate at two distinct levels: macro and micro. The macrostructure is described in the loss distribution or distributions, which imply a much richer data set for analysis. Reference to the loss distribution makes it possible for the analyst to replace the $E(L)$ with the standard deviation of losses as the risk measure. Loss variance is the true risk of the pool, not the expected loss. Keeping the micro and macro levels separate and distinct also makes it easier to isolate the local risk from global, systemic risk. Consistent underwriting should produce a characteristic distribution with a microstructure of risk that relates to the intrinsic vagaries of outcome in the lending decision. Changes in the underwriting rules and disturbances in the macro-economy may cause shifts in the risk distribution itself. When these modalities can be drawn out of the data, the structure of credit enhancement can be fine-tuned so that the originator or sellers are properly compensated for the quality of their originations, and not unduly penalized for risks in their environment over which they have no control.

Figure 5.2a shows a set of 21 hypothetical loss curves (including the average, in bold) sampled from a normal distribution with a mean of 5% and a standard deviation of 8% and where the inflection point is randomized around a mean of 25 months. Figure 5.2b shows the histogram and the cumulative distribution function computed from these curves.

5.3 A REVIEW OF PAYMENT CERTAINTY VERSUS VALUE

Every transaction feature represents an economic tradeoff that may favor the buyer or the seller. Some features serve to conceal, some to highlight. Yet the transaction structure is empty until it is fed by assets, which will have a particular payment profile. The security outcomes are ambiguous unless and until they can be compared to each other on the same credit scale. Although the premise, and the promise, of structured

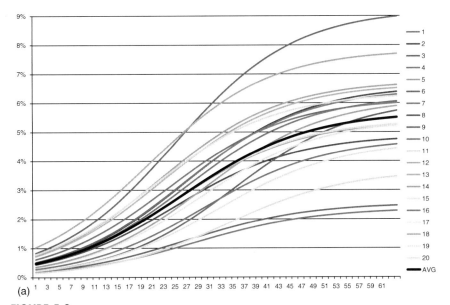

(a)

FIGURE 5.2a
Hypothetical sample of cumulative loss curves from a pool.

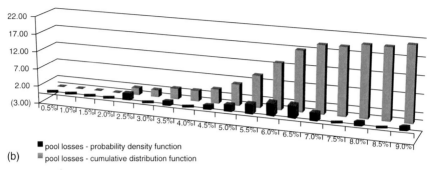

(b)
- ■ pool losses - probability density function
- ▨ pool losses - cumulative distribution function

FIGURE 5.2b
Loss curve cumulative distribution function and probability density function.

finance is precise credit risk measurement, this goal is hindered by the lack of uniform standards of risk measurement and the lack of uniformity of the credit scale. Instead of playing by a set of common rules in the marketplace, market players have relied on rating agencies for product standardization. In reality, however, structured rating systems are rife with biases and inconsistencies. In some cases, these have been massively exploited; in other cases, they have passed entirely under the radar.

The current lack of standards notwithstanding, certain simplifying generalizations can be made about contemporary valuation methods, and about the results they produce. These are represented in figure 5.3. As discussed at length in chapter 4, corporate finance analysis employs proxies of value (financial statement ratios, other rule-of-thumb relationships) where the link to value is established via a mapping process. A similar approach exists for structured finance: the benchmark pool method,

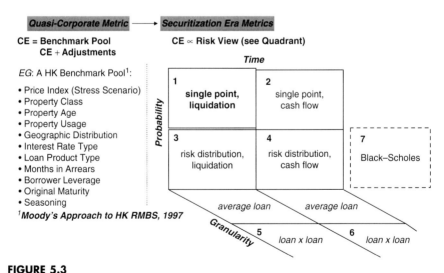

FIGURE 5.3
Atlas of structured valuation approaches.

located to the left of the corporate/structured divide in figure 5.3. This method tends to develop in new markets that lack the kind of static pool performance data depth that makes a self-consistent approach feasible, and they tend to be superseded when static pool data become available. In this approach, one or more rating agencies dictate, usually without validation:

1. Criteria of the asset to be sold to the SPE ("benchmark pool")
2. Formulas to transform real asset pools into benchmark pool equivalents
3. Required credit enhancement for a target rating given the benchmark pool

Benchmark pool methods are like recipes, providing guidance on selecting the right ingredients in the right proportions to get the desired rating result. Their main disadvantage is inconsistency caused by the absence of empirical validation, resulting in too much or too little enhancement in relation to the true risk. Some valuation approaches that appear more sophisticated than they really are behave much like benchmark pools, for example, rating agency methodologies in respect of collateralized debt obligations (CDOs), both cash and synthetic, whereby ratings rather than empirical data are the main collateral risk measure. CDOs as a market sector have never performed well, and an important reason for this empirical fact is their cookbook-like simplicity, which belies the real complexity of valuing securities backed by dynamic credit portfolios.[15]

Bona fide structured-finance valuation models, located to the right of the corporate/structured divide, use direct value inputs: interest, loss, default, recovery, delinquency, principal balance, time-to-maturity, yield, etc. The main variations in valuation methods are given along three dimensions: time/timeless (1–2), probabilistic/certain (3–4) and aggregated/granular (5–6). A seventh variation, really a different paradigm altogether, is the treatment of structured securities as derivatives based on the application of some variant of the Black–Scholes formula. The security risk-measures characteristic of each approach appears in the main quadrant.

Valuation approaches represented in the left column (squares 1 and 3) do not have time as a variable. Such models are focused on the liquidation value of the collateral, and are somewhat removed from the funding question since they leave out the main variable in finance.

Methods depicted in the right column (squares 2 and 4) are centrally concerned with the time value of all financial processes inside the transaction assessed within a cash flow model.

The choice "in time, or not in time" can be further refined by choosing to use highly certain point estimates as inputs (top row, squares 1–2) or impounding the risk microstructure in the value analysis (bottom row, squares 3–4). Models that avoid probability are said to be "stress-based" where the stress scenario has a user-defined significance. S&P has historically had an express preference for basing its rating criteria on stress scenarios, where the ability to withstand certain defined stresses defines the rating. Models that use probability can better satisfy the requirements for financial engineering because they permit continuous analysis across the sample space and allow the allocation of capital to be fine-tuned. However, statistical approaches are only as scientific as the input data permit. Unfortunately, the availability of large statistical default data sets on credit performance is still limited, though this is changing with the subprime crisis. The last choice relates to granularity: should the assets be treated as homogeneous (5) or should they be decomposed into subpools of different risk profiles, so that the vagaries of pool composition can be simulated with respect to transaction outcome (6). In general, granularity becomes important when working with pools of heterogeneous collateral, where pool averages may not accurately depict the risk.

Generally speaking, as the choice of method moves down and to the right, the value analysis can become more precise whereas moving up and to the left makes the analysis simpler and less data-driven. Precision is indeed a desideratum of any valuation method, but the choice of method should also reflect practical considerations like the quality and volume of collateral data, the structural intensity of the transaction, and the time pressure on the analyst. In the end, the choice of method will also be a matter of one's own preferred style of credit analysis.

Each square in the schematic has its own characteristic measure of payment certainty and value. These measures are delineated in table 5.9.

Metrics displayed in the left column produce "man on the street" or "rule-of-thumb" ratings that are essentially ordinal rankings. Note that the BOTE metric, $CE/E(L)$ in the upper left quadrant, is quintessentially an ordinal ranking. Although the collateral measures are cardinal, the ratio does not directly measure security value. It is a classic *distance from the credit event* measure. The same is true for the BOTE measure adjusted to reflect the impact of the distribution in the lower right quadrant.

Metrics displayed in the right column are *default* or *loss probabilities*, or *reductions of yield*. These measures can be used directly for valuation. Since the mid-1980s, rating agencies have based their rating definitions on one or more of these measures. Practically speaking, the upper-right-hand corner measures defaults in a single-scenario, stress-based framework. Whereas loss and yield reduction results can also be compiled from single cash flow scenarios, and can be meaningful within a certain context, they do not add up to a rating. On the other hand, all three risk measures can be reproduced via simulation. This is the meaning of the measures in the lower-right column. Defaults are an indirect measure of performance because they do not provide vital information on the severity of losses, whereas losses or reductions of yield (both of which Moody's has claimed their ratings represent) can be used to derive a fair price if information is available from the market about the clearing price of different credit grades at key-rate maturities (*yield spread curves*).

Finally, table 5.10 presents the main "sectors" of the structured market as variations in the production process of structured securities as well as profiling their key elements. Only the first is a legitimate process revolution; collateralized debt and VIE sectors are not.

This chapter on piecing the credit together must end, although it has barely scratched the surface. Armed with the knowledge of basic conventions presented thus far, and with your intelligence as a compass, you are now ready to embark on your own adventures in structured credit analysis.

TABLE 5.9
Models and metrics: a matrix presentation

#	T	P	G	METRIC(S)	EXPLANATION
1	0	0	0	$\dfrac{CE}{EL} = n \to r$	CE is really $E(CE(0))$ and EL is really $EL(T)$. n is a rating multiple.
2	1	0	0	$\dfrac{CE - u_L}{\sigma_L} = n \to r$	Same comments apply.
3	0	1	0	$R\left(P(0) - \sum\limits_{t=1}^{t} \dfrac{p(t)+i(t)}{(1+r)^t}\right) > 0 \to ri - 1$	$R()$ refers to a stress scenario that *defines* the rating, r. A positive residual equates to a failed test and defines the rating.
4	1	1	0	$\dfrac{1}{MC}\sum\limits_{i=1}^{MC}\left(P(0) - \sum\limits_{t=1}^{t}\dfrac{p(t)+i(t)}{(1+r)^t}\right) = p, \mu_{loss}, \mu_{\Delta IRR} \to r$	This method uses a MC simulation, in which the average outcome (default, average security loss or average reduction in yield) defines the rating.
5	0	1	1	no practical example	–
6	1	1	1	same as (4)	This method requires MC simulation of a matrix of exposures.
7	1	1	0	Black–Scholes equation or equivalent	Merton default model.

TABLE 5.10

Structured market sectors: key focal points and omissions

SECTOR	KEY FOCUS	KEY OMISSION
"Actuarial" – ABS, RMBS, CMBS	Total risk analysis, implemented through the use of a cumulative loss curve function in the assets. Security-level measure is the average reduction of yield.	Most complete analytical paradigm of the three, though implementations may have shortcomings. Salient omission is a failure to use the same framework of analysis for repackaged securities.
"Default" – CDO, CBO, CLO	Risk analysis is based on the default probability as expressed in the rating and an assumed binomial process generating losses.	Most generic framework for analyzing structured securities. Use of the rating introduces a series of errors that have come to be exploited by users.
"Eclectic" – ABCP, SIV	Marginal risk analysis that benchmarks the original capital model (each ABCP conduit has its own template; SIVs follow their Capital Model).	Most like a benchmark pool method: the cash flow significance of each factor is not expressly modeled out.

END-OF-CHAPTER QUESTIONS

1. What is credit judgment in structured finance? Why and how does it matter?

2. Describe the learning stages of structured credit judgment. What are your natural strengths and weaknesses? Knowing your own strengths and weaknesses, how do you propose to develop yourself as a structured analyst or structured transactor?

3. Identify the key source material used in structuring and valuing structured transactions. Classify each type of material as to: (a) its informational importance, and (b) its degree and type of regulatory supervision.

4. Someone once referred to the difference between corporate and structured finance as "sampling with and without replacement." In what sense might this be an apt description? What impact does it have on the measurement of risk and return in structured securities?

5. Identify the states of credit impairment, from incipience to resolution. Discuss how miscategorization of loan status can alter its financial value. Identify various tactics for masking loan quality that have been discussed in this chapter, and name the laws or regulations put in place to prevent such misdemeanors.

6. Name the key inputs into a rating or valuation model and explain how to obtain them.

7. What is a static pool? Why is it the analytical basis for securitization? What is a loss curve? How is the empirical loss curve constructed? What is the difference between a loss curve and a loss distribution?

8. Discuss the differences in valuation approaches for different structured finance vehicles, as described in chapter 8.

9. Find the $E(L)$ on the collateral backing transaction XYZ by referencing the following classes of securities issued from the SPE and their assigned ratings:

Class A	85.0%	AAA
Class B	6.5%	A
Class C	5.0%	BB
Equity	3.5%	N/R

6

Analysis of Asset-Side Cash Flows

Recall from chapter 1 that the motivation to finance assets off–balance sheet is the ability to improve the funding economics in a non-recourse financing by fostering competition among investors or separating the default risk of the assets from the default risk of the borrower. The latter case characterizes *securitization*, a refinancing based on a more abstract *economics* analysis justified via static pool analysis. Because asset cash flow properties of the target pool are independent of the liabilities, they can also be analyzed without knowledge of the liabilities, and, conversely, liability mechanics can be analyzed without knowledge of the target pool of assets. On the other hand, what cannot be ascertained easily is whether the liability structure is feasible for a target pool until its asset cash flow properties are also known. Nevertheless, since each side can be modeled as a separate problem, we divide the topic of cash flow modeling into two chapters, one on assets and the next one on liabilities.

6.1 MODELING RISKLESS CASH FLOWS

The modeling and valuation of risky and "riskless" cash flows takes place in two very different environments. The primary emphasis of this chapter is on the temporal impact of aggregate pool losses (defaults minus recoveries) on structured security value. Prepayment modeling is only of secondary interest since bona fide prepayments clearly reduce the uncertainty of principal repayment. For this reason, this chapter presents a perfunctory prepayment model that serves only to track the negative impact of prepayments on XS. A more serious treatment is found in chapter 10. Nevertheless, some preliminary observations about the inadequacy of traditional prepayment conventions for credit-oriented cash flow modeling are in order.

The original structured securities spawned from mortgages were CMOs (Collateralized Mortgage Obligations). The raison d'être of mortgage repackaging was to create "value" by separating principal and interest cash flow receipts to create securities with a new risk profile and maturity. None of the original CMOs were deemed to have material credit risk. In the case of "agency" paper, credit risk was transferred to Government Sponsored Entities (GSEs). While a small percentage of the market had outright backing by the U.S. government via GNMA (Government National Mortage Association) guarantees, a much larger percentage was backed by companies estabished by the U.S. government, FNMA (Federal National Mortgage Association) and FHLMC (Federal Home Loan Mortgage Corporation). They were not, in fact, government-supported institutions, but they did carry AAA ratings by the major U.S. rating agencies and had other special benefits under their charters. In the case of the early non-agency CMO market, credit risk was deemed commensurate with historical experience on conforming 30-year fixed rate mortgages which, until the mid-1980s, had been very low.

In 1985, the Public Securities Association (or PSA, the predecessor U. S. broker-dealer association) developed a standard model of prepayment risk for the CMO market. Up until that time, the most sensitive model in use was the CPR: Conditional Prepayment Rate. CPR is usually defined as the annualized ratio of the difference between actual amortization $T(t)$ and scheduled amortization $S(t)$ during the period, over the aggregate pool balance at the beginning of the period $P(t-1)$ less scheduled amortization.[1]

$$CPR(t) = 12 \frac{T(t) - S(t)}{P(t-1) - S(t)}.$$

The PSA model used the CPR as a building block. It described a typical path of prepayments as an linearly rising CPR index during the ramp-up period (PSA ramp) and constant thereafter.

Elements of the PSA model:

- Prepayments increase at a constant rate over $0 < t < t_0$ (the inflection point) at 30 months, whereupon they remain constant as a percentage of the remaining principal balance outstanding.
- The rate of increase defines the index. A PSA 100 curve means that the conditional prepayment rate (CPR) is cumulatively 6%, or an annualized rate of increase of 0.2%, over 30 time periods, whereas a PSA 200 curve would rise twice as fast, reaching 12% at month 30.
- The unit of change is the single month mortality (SMM), equal to $1 - (1 - CPR)\hat{}(1/12)$, which is convex, matching the convexity of principal amortization.
- In using the PSA model to stress prepayments, the inflection point never varies, only the prepayment velocity.

Figure 6.1 is a graphic representation of the PSA model.

Although the inadequacies of the PSA curve for prepayment forecasting have been in evidence for decades, it is still used as a standard measure for modelers to speak to each other about prepayments on low-default pools in equivalent terms, and to reverse-engineer each others' modeling outcomes.

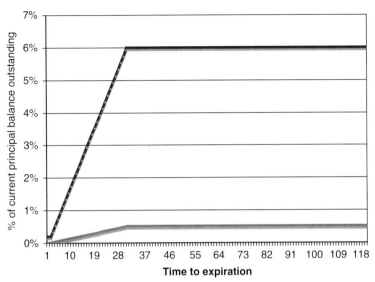

FIGURE 6.1
Conditional payment rate and single month mortality.

The PSA model is absolutely incompatible with the standard credit modeling approach for RMBS, however, because credit modeling uses $P(0)$—initial principal— as the denominator of all measures. It is an absolute, not a relative risk measure. For this reason, it cannot be used in the model we will build using the relationships in this chapter and the next.

6.2 MODELING RISKY CASH FLOWS

In structured finance, transaction failure is first and foremost a failure of asset valuation. It is far more difficult to estimate the cash flow generating capacity of the assets in the pool than to model the liabilities, because the structure of liabilities follows the condition of the assets. Everything else about liability coding is strictly a matter of logic. This is true even when the assets are strictly amortizing, as in this chapter. Revolving asset environments (chapter 8) raise the valuation challenge to an even higher level.

In order to model asset-side cash flows, the basic performance characteristics (parameters) of the asset pool must first be ascertained. All cash flow estimates are based on the pool's summary financial characteristics. Normally, pool-level data is given to the analyst by the issuer in a format similar to that found in the source materials discussed in chapter 5, and the analyst will have to synthesize the pool's performance characteristics from the raw data. In this chapter however, asset-side parameters are presented as such for ease of exposition.

In this and all further treatments, time t will be divided into discrete collection periods, and will thus take on integer values only; in other words $t \in [0, 1, 2, \ldots, T]$.

This nomenclature also implies the condition $\Delta t = 1, \forall t \in [0, T]$.[2] Since time intervals are numerically always equal to one month, we omit them wherever redundant.

Basic collateral data are presented as follows:

Number of loans in the pool: $N(t)$, $N(0) \equiv N_0$
Weighted Average Coupon (periodic): $\frac{WAC}{12} = r$
Weighted Average Maturity (months): $WAM = T$
Current pool balance: $V(t)$, $V(0) \equiv V_0$
Expected loss as a % of V_0: $E(L)$

6.3 ORGANIZATION OF THE CASH FLOW MODEL

The building of the cash flow model should be implemented on a single spreadsheet. Conceptually, the cash flow model has different regions with different functions:

1. the Assumptions section is where parameters representing the transaction to be modeled are stored, including basic collateral data and details of the target capital structure.
2. the Asset side is where cash flow estimates are conducted.
3. the Liability side is where the payment instructions on the target capital structure are carried out.
4. the Evaluation section immediately following the liability analysis is where ratings or valuations on this scenario are carried out.
5. the Yield Spread curves representing current capital market equilbrium rates of return for different credit ratings are also integral to the valuation process, although their inclusion in the cash flow modeling process is not discussed until chapter 13.

Our style of cash flow modeling starts in loan space and proceeds to dollar space. It analyzes the states of the various loans in the pool as a function of time and derives cash flow quantities from their loan status. This is a good modeling approach, both theoretically and practically, because strictly speaking, dollars depend upon the borrower's payment activity. The unit of borrower activity is the loan account. Therefore, it makes sense to model the dollars of the target loans based upon a hypothesis about the states of the loans over the time horizon of the deal, i.e., $t \leq T$.

Loans can be classified in terms of one of five states:

- performing as per the contractual schedule
- prepaying in full
- defaulting, in accordance with definition in the Credit & Investment Manual
- prepaying in part, having paid the most recent scheduled payment due in full
- defaulted, but still paying in full or part in a "bankrupt borrower" status

In this treatment, we simplify the task by assuming the loans belong only to one of the first three states. After establishing our hypothesis of borrower loan states, we can work out the corresponding cash flows algebraically.

The cash flow engine should be organized as follows on the spreadsheet:

1. Each row represents a collection period (month, quarter, etc.).
2. *Time*: the left-most column (of the asset section) is set aside for time t,
3. *Loan States*: immediately to the right of "time" are three columns corresponding to loans of different payment states: Current, Defaulted, fully Prepaying. Current loans remain in the pool until maturity; Defaulted and fully Prepaying loans are amortized at the time step when they default or prepay, respectively.
4. *Cash Flows*: immediately to the right of loan states are related cash flow activity levels, shown as the five italicized items below:

    (a) Current loans make *Scheduled Interest* and *Scheduled Principal* payments;
    (b) The balance outstanding of Defaulted loans is recorded as a *Defaulted Principal* amount. Associated *Recoveries* are recorded when they are recognized, usually with a time lag;
    (c) Prepaying loans pay off their entire remaining balance (*Prepaid Principal*) after first making the required payment for the current time step, via (a) above.

5. *Principal Amortization*: the aggregate, initial pool balance, V_0, must pay down to zero via the principal amounts recorded in 4 above: Scheduled Principal, Defaulted Principal and Prepaid Principal. Note that, as Recoveries and Scheduled Interest are not principal quantities, they are not part of the amortization.
6. *Collateral Evaluation*: the analysis conducted in steps 1–5 is summarized in three columns: *Available Funds*, the quantity of periodic cash collected that can be used for claims payment; *Total Principal Due*, the amount of amortization from the current period, which becomes the principal pass-through amount on the liabilities, and *Cumulative Principal Due*, the rolling sum of Total Principal Due amounts.

The algebra of these defined terms is supplied below. A more exhaustive treatment on cash flow modeling desiderata is provided in chapter 12.

6.4 FORECASTING THE EXPECTED LOSS

By definition, the expected loss is the first moment of the credit loss density function. Although we will develop this concept further in chapter 9 please remember that the loss density function is of primordial significance in assigning ratings to structured securities. Normally, the choice of distribution would be the subject of intense discussion because it has a direct impact on credit enhancement requirements, which, in turn, have an impact on the cost of the transaction. In most cases however, the normal or lognormal distribution is selected by default.

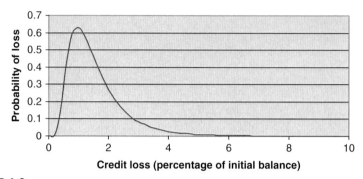

FIGURE 6.2
A lognormal credit loss distribution.

Remember that any loss density function $f(L)$ must in general satisfy the basic boundary condition $f(L) = 0$, $\forall L > 1$, where the loss L is expressed as a fraction of the pool's initial principal balance. This means that losses in excess of 100% of the pool cannot occur. In addition, negative credit losses are usually assumed infeasible whereas in reality they are possible in structured and corporate finance. Negative credit loss could occur as the outcome of a foreclosure process whereby the liquidated proceeds would exceed the amount unpaid loan balance. An example of a lognormal credit loss distribution is given in figure 6.2 below. In this example, $E(L)$ would be about 1.5%.

Modeling the Credit Loss Curve

Two important observations about credit loss modeling need to be made at the outset:

- The main challenge of modeling cash flows *is* the estimation of credit losses from the loss distribution;
- Credit loss is loss of principal, not interest, although loss of principal necessarily entails foregone interest.

The loss *curve* should never be confused with the loss *distribution*. The loss curve is the path of cumulative losses within a single pool, which at closing is as forecast. Eventually, with the passage of time the forecast is replaced by the actual path of realized losses, which may or may not follow the original forecast. The loss distribution is the ensemble of possible paths of the cumulative loss curve on an arbitrarily large number of sample pools of loans originated under identical underwriting guidelines to that of the target pool. It represents the risk of loss.

In this chapter, you are given the parameters for constructing a cumulative loss curve. In chapter 9, we will simulate the cumulative loss curve by specifying the cumulative distribution function of losses and applying a sampling routine to it.

A *logistic curve* is by far the most appropriate formalism to use in describing the path of cumulative losses over time. It is also an apt formalism for describing the life cycle of of a phenomenon (in this case, static pool losses) from inception to maturity, burnout, and death. Algebraically, the credit loss curve's Cumulative Distribution Function $(CDF)^3$ is thus expressed as

$$F(t) = \frac{a}{1+be^{-c(t-t_0)}} \equiv CDF \tag{1}$$

The analytical behavior of equation (1) can be surmised intuitively by inspection of its form. The mathematical intuition is that, when the exponential term in the denominator is close to zero, the quantity $F(t)$ becomes equal to the constant a, hence equation (1) is asymptotic to a as $t \to \infty$ since the denominator tends to 1 at $t \to \infty$. Also, since the value of the exponent is negative for $t < t_0$ and positive for $t > t_0$, we can readily see that the marginal loss curve, depicted with the lower-case $f(t)$, must rise monotonically from zero, reaching a maximum at $t = t_0$ and then decrease monotonically after $t > t_0$. In practice, the position of the inflection point $\ln(b)+t_0$ is often selected as the time step where the *loss-to-liquidation* ratio, defined as the ratio of current defaults divided by the monthly amortization, achieves zero slope. The parameter c determines the steepness of the curve around the inflection point (which may be considered the correlatedness of the assets in the pool) with larger values producing a steeper curve. Finally, parameter b rescales the length of the lifecycle. With appropriate choices of its four parameters, equation (1) replicates well the credit-loss behavior of most asset pools through time.

By definition, the following continuous time relationship holds between the CDF and the probability density function (PDF) for monthly defaults: $dF(t) = f(t)\,dt$. Thus, in our spreadsheet approximation, we may define *marginal* or monthly losses in pool percentage terms as

$$f(t) = F(t) - F(t-1)$$

With time measured in months, examples of credit loss CDF and PDF are given in figures 6.3 and 6.4 respectively for the following typical values of the parameters a, b, c, and t_0:

$$a = 0.1$$
$$b = 1$$
$$c = 0.1$$
$$t_0 = 55$$
$$T = 120$$

In practice, values for parameters b and c in the range above can cover a wide range of loss curve scenarios.

Account-Space Adjustment

The percentage of accounts in default will not always be equivalent to the percentage of defaulted dollars. If defaults turn out to be concentrated in the accounts with

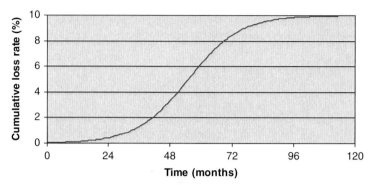

FIGURE 6.3
A CDF of credit losses.

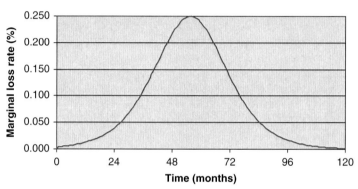

FIGURE 6.4
A PDF of credit losses.

higher balances, assuming equivalency could result in a material underestimation of principal loss.

To adjust the loss curve for discrepancies, multiply the cumulative percentage of defaulted loan-accounts (*account-space*) by the ratio of cumulative defaulted dollars (*dollar-space*) over account-space defaults. To illustrate, if dollar-space defaults are 10% but the cumulative number of defaulted loans is 12.5%, apply the ratio to each $F(t)$.

A technical note: the ease of switching from loan- to dollar-space values stems from the linear parameter in equation (1). This method only works on defaults, not losses, i.e. the product of default and recovery. Recoveries on defaults may operate according to a different process, discussed later in the chapter.

Account–Space Calculations

We begin by forecasting defaults as a percentage of total initial pool balance, $F(t)$, and then map our results back to account-space, $L(t)$, by multiplying $F(t)$ by $N(0)$.

For instance, with an assumed initial pool count of 2000 loans, $N(0)$, assume we wish to simulate an expected loss value of 10% of the account base or 200 accounts $L'(T)$. In effect, we are saying that over the life of the pool (120 months), precisely 200 accounts will default over time following the pattern shown in equation (1).

Normalization of Loss Curves

Note that the curve L(t) does not exactly reach the target $E(L)$ of 10% when the logistic curve is used. That is because 10% is only reached when t becomes arbitrarily close to $+\infty$. However, infinite time will never be reached over the lifetime of any loan with finite maturity. Thus, loss curves like equation (1) normally require normalization in order to properly reflect the expected loss known to be applicable to the pool under study. To correct the error on both the marginal and cumulative loss curves, it is necessary to normalize each monthly entry.

Define $L(t)$ as the cumulative non-normalized account-space loss curve, $l(t)$ as the marginal non-normalized account-space loss at time t, $n_D(t)$ as the marginal, normalized account-space loss at time t, N_0 as the initial number of accounts and D_r as the cumulative account-space default rate. We have by definition: $E(L) = N_0\, D_r$. Now, normalize defaults so that cumulative defaults at $t = T$ are indeed equal to the chosen value $E(L)$ adjusted for account-space utilization as shown above:

1. Convert $F(t)$ to $L(t)$: $L(t) = F(t) \cdot N(0)$.
2. Convert $L(t)$ to $l(t)$: $l(t) = L(t) - L(t-1)$.
3. Normalize $l(t)$ as follows:

$$n_D(t) = \frac{l(t)\, N_0\, D_r}{\sum_{t=1}^{T} l(t)} = \frac{l(t)\, N_0\, D_r}{[L(T) - L(0)]}$$

Table 6.1 shows the values of $F(t)$, $L(t)$, and $L'(t)$ for the last two time steps using the parameters assumed in the example.

6.5 PREPAYMENTS IN A SIMPLE CASH FLOW MODEL

Serious prepayment modeling is difficult and has yet to achieve its final form. Although many variables affect the level of prepayment in structured pools, the most important one by far is the prevailing interest rate environment. Prepayment

TABLE 6.1
CDF $t = 119, 120$

N	F(T)	L(T)	L'(T)
119	9.983%	199.668	199.968
120	9.985%	199.700	200.000

modeling thus amounts to interest rate prediction, a notoriously inaccurate science. A fuller treatment of this topic is presented in chapter 10.

Even if many reliable prepayment models exist, all are *conditional* prepayment models. If interest rates are assumed to be known, corresponding pool prepayment rates can be determined fairly precisely. Of course, to assume that interest rates are known is to assume the problem away. However, except for RMBS, prepayment is a secondary credit issue since very few borrowers have the necessary incentive to prepay solely based on interest rate variations. The variability of prepayment behavior within the relatively short-maturity asset pools of most ABS asset classes is largely driven by factors other than interest rates, none of which are any more predictable. The prepayment formula provided below has the functional form of a PSA curve but as a function of the initial principal balance (as per the discussion in section 6.1). This particular implementation assumes that, over the life of the 10-year transaction, 20% of the pool's initial account inventory will prepay at one point or another (figure 6.6).

The marginal prepayment curve indicates that the monthly account-space prepayment rate $g(t)$ begins at 0 and rises linearly until it reaches a steady-state at the inflection point t_{0p}. We will compute monthly account-space prepayments using the cumulative prepayment curve $G(t)$:

$$n_P(t) = G(t) - G(t-1).$$

Resist the temptation to calculate prepayments directly from the marginal curve $g(t)$, as it will result in too high an estimate—the equivalent of Riemann integration using the right-hand point instead of the midpoint.

From figure 6.6, we can easily define $G(t)$ as:

$$G(t) = \begin{cases} \frac{at^2}{2}, & 0 \le t \le t_{0p} \\ \\ \frac{at_{0p}^2}{2} + (t - t_{0p})\, a\, t_{0p}, & t_0 \le t \le T \end{cases} \tag{2}$$

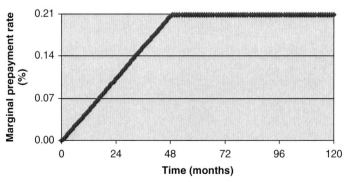

FIGURE 6.5
Marginal prepayment curve.

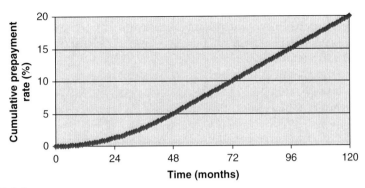

FIGURE 6.6
Cumulative prepayment curve.

Here, parameter a is the slope of the straight line from 0 to t_{0p} in figure 6.5, and we have assumed $t_{0p} = 48$. To normalize this loan-space cumulative function, we use the fact that at $t = T$, the following account-space boundary condition holds by assumption:

$$\int_0^{t_{0p}} [at]\,dt + (T - t_{0p})\,a\,t_{0p} = N_P$$

Solving for the slope a, defined via equation (2), we find:

$$a = \frac{N_P}{\frac{t_{0p}^2}{2} + (T - t_{0p})\,t_{0p}}$$

Here again, note the linearity of $G(t)$ with respect to parameter a.

We are now ready to compute cash flows from an asset pool with the above default and prepayment characteristics.

6.6 ASSET CASH FLOWS

Assume pool assets consist of N_0 level-pay loans, each with a periodic coupon r, a maturity of T months and a time-dependent principal balance $B(t)$ with $B(0) \equiv B_0$.

A level-pay loan is defined via the following first-order, linear differential equation:

$$M\,dt = r\,B\,dt - dB \tag{3}$$

In equation (3), M is the periodic payment, a constant number by definition. Equations like (3) are all solvable, and the solution can be looked up in any calculus textbook. The minus sign in equation (3) stems from the fact that the loan's principal balance is decreasing as time increases. Equation (3) reflects the principal balance of the level-pay loan as the solution of an ordinary differential equation. Equations (4a) and (4b) describe the same phenomenon as a periodic process, a better formalism for describing cash flows in our model. Skipping the details of derivation, we have:

$$B(t) = \frac{M}{r} \left\{ 1 - (1+r)^{t-T} \right\}$$ (4a)

for the balance in advance and, of course,

$$B(t-1) = \frac{M}{r} \left\{ 1 - (1+r)^{t-1-T} \right\}$$ (4b)

for the balance in arrears.

The two boundary conditions $B(0) = B_0$ and $B(T) = 0$ can be satisfied by setting:

$$M = \frac{B_0 r}{1 - (1+r)^{-T}}$$ (5)

In the remaining subsections, we use the relationships expressed in equations (4a) and (5) to partition the monthly payment into interest and principal cash flows, and use these elements to describe such activities through time with respect to the "average" loan in a target static pool.

Ending Loan Count

At the end of each monthly period, the number of remaining loans is:

$$N(t) = N(t-1) - n_D(t) - n_P(t)$$ (6)

Interest Collections

To calculate the interest collected during the month, we can use equation (4) and the definition $I(t) = [N(t-1) - n_D(t)] \, r \, B(t-1)$, to yield:

$$I(t) = [N(t-1) - n_D(t)] \, M \left\{ 1 - (1+r)^{t-1-T} \right\}$$ (7)

The right-hand side of this equation is the product of the number of live accounts and the interest rate. The left-most term is the performing loan count, $N(t-1)$ being the number of loans outstanding in arrears and $n_D(t)$ being the number of loans written off in the current period.

Principal Collections

Monthly principal received consists of (a) regular or scheduled principal $P_R(t)$ and (b) prepayments $PP(t)$.

(a) Regular principal is computed via the scheduled monthly amortization given by equation (4), where the part in the curly brackets represents the change in the discount factor by which the balance amortizes:

$$P_R(t) = [N(t-1) - n_D(t)] \frac{M}{r} \left\{ (1+r)^{t-T} - (1+r)^{t-1-T} \right\}$$ (8)

(b) Prepayments are equal to the number of prepaid loans multiplied by the ending balance at time step t. We use the balance in advance to calculate the prepayment since the scheduled monthly amortization has already been made via the equation in (a) above:

$$PP(t) = n_P(t) \frac{M}{r} \left\{ 1 - (1+r)^{t-T} \right\} \tag{9}$$

The algebra of total principal $P(t)$ receipts for the period would be computed as:

$$P(t) = PP(t) + P_R(t),$$

Note that while the quantity $P(t)$ is not a defined term in this cash flow model, it is a variable in other types of structure, for example, in market value CDOs.

Defaults

Defaulted balances $D(t)$ are equal to the number of defaulted loans multiplied by the outstanding principal balance at time $t - 1$:

$$D(t) = n_D(t) \frac{M}{r} \left\{ 1 - (1+r)^{t-1-T} \right\} \tag{10}$$

Recoveries (or Loss Given Default)

Defaulted balances are usually subject to recoveries $R_C(t)$, for instance if the collateral is sold or auctioned off after a time delay t_r and the proceeds are fed back through the trust. We would then have:

$$R_C(t) = D(t - t_r) \left[1 - LGD(t - t_r) \right] \tag{11}$$

In equation (11), $LGD(t - t_r)$ is the *loss given default* as a percentage of the loan's outstanding principal balance at the time of default, $t - t_r$, where t_r represents a delay in recoveries. The value of LGD is time-dependent since the value of the recoveries will depend on the coincident values of the collateral in the secondary market and the loan's outstanding principal balance. The time-dependent phenomenon is displayed in figure 6.7 where we show a typical loan amortization curve next to an asset depreciation curve, normally a durable good, like a car.

LGD at $t = 0$ is a relatively small number corresponding to the difference between the retail and wholesale value of the asset, then rising monotonically until approximately $t = 40$ and declining monotonically from 40 to 120, including the region $96 \leq t \leq 120$ for which $LGD < 0$.

In the middle of the range, the recovery amount as a percentage of the loan's outstanding principal balance would tend to be the smallest, since the gap between the loan's principal balance and the asset's depreciated value is relatively larger than either before or after that. Conversely, when both curves intersect (around $t = 96$), recoveries would theoretically be 100% since the value of the asset is now equal to the outstanding loan balance. Beyond that point, there would be a credit "profit" instead of a credit loss, although most jurisdictions do not allow lenders to make money from defaults. Financially astute obligors who had reached time step 96 without a default

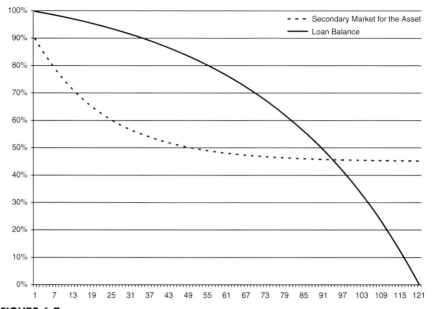

FIGURE 6.7

Loss amortization–depreciation curves.

would most likely not default after that since they could simply sell the asset in the open market and pay off the loan balance in full. In reality, though, very few obligors are clever enough to manage their equity in the asset so skillfully, and many defaults are in fact seen after the point at which credit losses would theoretically be negative.

However, for purposes of basic cash flow modeling, the economics of the secondary market, which makes LGD time-dependent, will be ignored. Assume, instead, that you are working with the same information set as a rating agency analyst, to whom LGD is typically given as a constant.

Current Collections (= Available Funds)

From the cash flow section, we are now able to compute *Available Funds* $AF_0(t)$ for each collection period as:

$$AF_0(t) = I(t) + P(t) + R_C(t). \tag{12}$$

Recall from above that $P(t)$ represents principal collections, i.e. the sum of $PP(t)$ and $P_R(t)$.

Principal Due

For each Collection Period, the principal due $P_D(t)$ to bondholders that allows them to remain fully collateralized is thus:

$$P_D(t) = P_R(t) + PP(t) + D(t) \tag{13}$$

Clearly, only the first two components were actually received while defaults must be covered from excess spread.

For liability-side calculations, it is propitious to calculate $C(t)$, cumulative principal due, at the same time as total principal due. $C(t)$ is the cumulative principal due:

$$C(t) = \sum_{t=1}^{t} P_D(t) \tag{14}$$

Ending Pool Balance

The ending pool balance at time t is the initial pool balance at the beginning of time t adjusted by the monthly amortization, i.e., reduced by scheduled principal payments, prepayments and defaults:

$$V(t) = V(t-1) - D(t) - PP(t) - P_R(t) \tag{15}$$

Other Assets of the Trust

In this chapter, we will not discuss other potential sources of cash in the form of reserve accounts, insurance policies, and the like. The discussion of some of these sources is postponed to later chapters.

END-OF-CHAPTER QUESTIONS

1. Describe the desiderata and organization of information for building a cash flow model of a structured finance transaction. Does it make a difference to your answer if the transaction is a repackaging of risky or riskless cash flows? (What is a "riskless" cash flow?)

2. Characterize the differences between the empirical and theoretical "expected loss."

3. What is a logistic function? What is its characteristic shape? Why has it become the accepted norm in describing the pattern of cumulative defaults and losses on static pools? Explain the significance of each element in the formula for the cumulative loss curve provided in this chapter.

4. Characterize the differences between the formulas for estimating defaults and for estimating prepayments in this chapter. What are the limitations of each?

5. How are recoveries treated in the version of the cash flow model introduced in this chapter? What is the limitation of this approach? How much information is lost as a result of using this approach? Would your answer vary by the type of collateral being securitized? How would it do so?

6. Derive the formula for current balances using the formula for the level pay loan amount.

7. Show the formula for the level pay loan amount as the sum of current interest and current principal. Subtracting the interest amount from M gives you an

alternative formulation for the principal portion of the level payment. What is it? Describe the meaning of principal in words, using these two equivalent formulas. Derive the formula for principal given in this book using the balance formula.

8. Explain the meaning of the terms *allocation* and *distribution* in simple English. Which items in the cash flow summaries relate to liability-side allocation, and which to liability-side distribution?

7

Analysis of Liability-Side Cash Flows

The discussion in chapter 6 regarding the synthesis of expected asset cash flows, including deviations from contractual payments, is an arena where applied intuition and experience can significantly improve transaction efficiency.

Liability analysis is more prosaic. Liabilities are logically determined, and technical facility is less a question of good and bad, more a question of right and wrong, although there is opportunity for skill development in making good transactions better and more efficient. Once the transaction goes to market, the quality of design is revealed. It may turn out to be *optimal*, a perfect fit for the expected lifetime profile of asset cash flows given what is known at closing, where every bondholder is fairly compensated for the risk undertaken. This is very unlikely.

It can also happen that the deal may simply be *feasible*. Not perfect, because the structure favors certain bond holders over others, but it pays off roughly as reflected in pricing. Otherwise, it may be *unfeasible*, i.e. the transaction is inadequately collateralized at closing and some bondholders will suffer. Analysts who reverse-engineer the transaction have no choice in how to reflect payment instructions already set in stone. This is where the question of right and wrong comes into play.

Correct implementation of the payment routines, detailed though consistently under-recognized, is a virtue in a market that fails to consistently apply the algebra of payment routines correctly. The rules must work together for the payment promise to investors to carry a high probability of being met. AAA investors take a AAA risk and have a AAA certainty of repayment, and so on for investors in tranches of any other credit quality. Structuring virtuosity cannot be claimed without first having in place the more fundamental assurances that the payment rules are being properly constructed and followed.

7.1 THE LANGUAGE OF PAY-THROUGH SECURITIES

A liability structure is a set of rules for allocating and distributing cash collected from the assets, where allocation and distribution are separate processes. Loans made to a borrower in the first instance typically specify the timing and amount of interest and principal amounts payable. Certain patterns are common. For example, consumer credits tend to repay in an actuarial amortization pattern, whereas companies often have the benefit of a less stringent, bullet amortization. In contrast to these norms, the most typical payment promise of structured securities is timely interest at the contractual rate and ultimate principal.[1] *Timely interest* means that interest due amounts are formulaic, precisely determined and enforceable. *Ultimate principal*, on the other hand, means just that. The precise arrival times of principal repayments are not specified or enforceable until the legal final maturity to avoid increasing the risk of technical default by over-specifying the behavior of an uncertain cash flow. This characterization describes *pass-through* (single tranche) and *pay-through* (multiple tranche) structures, where by 100% of principal amortization on the asset side is allocable to liability holders each period and all cash collected within the period is deemed available to meet those claims. Please note that revolving structures, whereby principal repaid is reinvested in new assets rather than being distributed to bond holders periodically, are neither pass-through nor pay-through structures. Therefore, they are investment-holding companies in substance, regardless of whether or not they are exempted from the registration requirements of investment-holding companies under the securities laws.

At the heart of liability structures are two intertwined processes: *allocation*, which means setting aside funds for the due amount at the level where it is due, and *distribution*, which means paying the due amount from available cash collections. Strictly speaking, a pass-through structure describes a *participation*, with a wholly symmetrical *allocation* and *distribution* process on either side of the balance sheet. By contrast, *Pay-through* structures evidencing hierarchy of credit tranches typical of structured securities, are characterized by payment speed symmetry and top-down payment priority, but with asymmetrical allocation of principal that favors some investors at the expense of others under a controlled risk-transfer design. *Complex* transaction structures relax the symmetrical payment speeds or top-to-bottom waterfall directionality, or both. These structures are ill-suited to spreadsheet modeling.

The payment logic of all simple pay-through structures can be described with reference to permutations of special terms used to describe the hierarchy of claims in fixed income: *sequential*, *pro rata* and *pari passu pro rata*, where

- *sequential* means serial repayment
- *pari passu* means parallel repayment
- *pro rata* means *partitioned ratably* or in proportion to the invested amount

In structured finance, a rather widespread misunderstanding exists with respect to the difference between *pro rata* and *pari passu pro rata*, where the former is often mistaken for the latter.

TABLE 7.1
Due-paid patterns of pay-through securities

	ALLOCATION	DISTRIBUTION
Sequential	Serial	Serial
Pro rata	Parallel/pro rata	Serial
Pari passu pro rata	Parallel/pro rata	Parallel/pro rata

If principal is allocated (and cash distributed) first to Class A its initial balance is fully allocated, and then to Class B, Classes A and B are said to be sequential. Table 7.1 delineate the allocation-distribution patterns in these two payment regimes.

If, on the other hand, principal is allocated pro rata based on the initial participation percentages of Class A and Class B, respectively, but Class A is nevertheless entitled to receive its allocation prior to Class B, Classes A and B are said to be pro rata.

If principal is allocated pro rata based on the initial Class A and Class B participation percentages and both classes are entitled to receive a pro rata simultaneous distribution, Classes A and B are said to rank pari passu pro rata. Please note that while this pattern may logically exist, it is unlikely that a suitable rationale can be found for partitioning one credit-class into two sub-classes. Much more likely, pari passu pro rata describes interest payment rules within a single credit-class of notes where the sub-classes have staggered maturities and carry different rates reflecting the yield curve. More formal definitions of these terms are given in section 7.2 below.

7.2 THE RAW DEAL: A PSEUDO-MODEL FOR LIABILITIES

This section lays out the algebra of allocation and distribution processes for the simplest of all pay-through structures: the *Raw Deal*.[2] In the Raw Deal, the only sources of credit enhancement are excess spread (*XS*) and subordination, (there are no reserve accounts, triggers, or surety bonds) and the only cash available to pay claims comes from current collections. Deals like this are extremely rare because few investors would be willing to wager exclusively on the payment certainty of current collections without some cushion for unexpected market, credit, or liquidity shortfall events. Our goal is not to replicate actual transactions but to impart mastery of the basic allocation and payment algebra.

The Raw Deal uses the most common principal payment regimes: sequential and pro rata. Formulas for the Raw Deal are based on a fully collateralized transaction with two lasses of bonds, A and B, with monthly payment dates.

Glossary of Liability-Side Terms

Bond structure: Most basically, refers to the principal allocation method inside a structured finance transaction, or alternatively it may refer to the entire set of cash allocation modalities in the waterfall (not just principal) and may further involve the use of enhancements like insurance policies and special allocation mechanisms described at greater length in section 7.5.

Waterfall: Rules found in the prospectus and transaction documents that specify the way in which cash will be distributed to claim-holders in the SPE. Each item in the waterfall is referred to as a *level*. Waterfalls may have any number of levels. The one below has six.

Pari passu: When separate distributions are made at the same level in the waterfall, they are said to be pari passu.

Sequential: When the total principal due to bondholders is allocated in such a way as to retire the entire initial principal balance of a senior class before *any* principal is allocated to a more junior class, the structure is said to be sequential.

Pro rata: When total principal due to bondholders is allocated proportionally, i.e., based on the initial principal balance of each class, the structure is said to be pro rata.

Nomenclature

t = each collection period, from 1 to T (*WAM*); time is always an integer
t_r = number of collection periods between default and recovery
r_A = Class A interest rate (annualized)
r_B = Class B interest rate (annualized)
s_f = servicing fee rate (annualized)
s_r = servicing fee shortfall rate (annualized)
$S(t)$ = servicing fee due at time t
$B_A(t)$ = Class A principal balance *at the end* of time t
$B_B(t)$ = Class B principal balance *at the end* of time t
$I_A(t)$ = Class A interest due with respect to time t
$I_B(t)$ = Class B interest due with respect to time t
$P_A(t)$ = Class A principal due at time t
$P_B(t)$ = Class B principal due at time t
$F_i(t)$ = remaining available funds at time t and level i in the waterfall
$P_D(t)$ = total principal due at time t
$C(t)$ = cumulative principal due at time t
$R(t)$ = residual payment due to SPE stockholders at time t
$R_C(t)$ = recoveries on defaulted receivables at time t
$D(t)$ = defaulted receivable balances at time t
$PP(t)$ = prepaid receivable balances at time t
$P_R(t)$ = regular principal collections at time t
$I(t)$ = interest collections at time t
$V(t)$ = pool balance *at the end* of time t
$V(0) = B_A(0) + B_B(0)$

$$\alpha \equiv \frac{B_A(0)}{V(0)} = \text{advance rate} \tag{1}$$

We will use the following two additional conventions:

- The additional subscript P next to any subscript of a *due* quantity will refer to the amount *paid*, which may be *at most* equal to the amount due;
- The additional subscript S next to any subscript of a *due* quantity will refer to the shortfall, which may be *at most* equal to the amount due.

For instance, $P_{AP}(t)$ refers to *Class A principal paid*, $P_{AS}(t)$ to *Class A principal shortfall*, and so on. This convention applies to all other due quantities like interest and servicing fees. Remember that amounts due, paid and shortfalls are all *nonnegative* quantities and that the *cumulative sum* of all amounts paid during any collection period *must* equal available funds $[F_0(t)]$ for that collection period.

7.3 WATERFALL MODELING

Each item of the waterfall is treated uniformly as a block, and each block has the following four-item structure:

1. Amount due
2. Amount paid
3. Shortfall
4. Remaining available funds

The only exception to this rule occurs at the level of the *residual payment*, which is the amount of current collections remaining after distributions have been effected at more senior level. There is no contractual *residual amount due*. In other words, the residual amount due will always equal the residual amount paid. This also implies that the *residual shortfall amount* and *remaining available funds* are zero at that level. In effect, the residual payment represents the highly-variable *common equity* component of the trust.

The Raw Deal waterfall comprises the following six levels:

1. Servicing fee
2. Class A interest
3. Class B interest
4. Class A principal
5. Class B principal
6. Residual payment

Additional credit enhancement sources like reserve accounts and insurance policies would appear as additional levels in the waterfall.

Required data before entering the waterfall at any time step:

Available funds: $F_0(t) = P(t) + R_C(t) + I(t)$ (from chapter 6)

Total principal due: $P_D(t) = D(t) + P_R(t) + PP(t)$ (from chapter 6)

Starting Class A principal balance: $B_A(t-1)$ $\hspace{2em}$ (2)

Starting Class B principal balance: $B_B(t-1)$ $\hspace{2em}$ (3)

Cumulative principal due: $C(t) = P_D(t) + C(t-1)$ (from chapter 6)

Waterfall Levels (1 to 6)

1. Servicing Fee

$$\text{Servicing fee due: } S(t) = \frac{s_f}{12} V(t-1) + S_S(t-1)\left(1 + \frac{s_r}{12}\right) \hspace{2em} (4)$$

Servicing fee paid: $S_P(t) = Min(F_0(t), S(t))$ $\hspace{2em}$ (5)

Servicing fee shortfall: $S_S(t) = S(t) - S_P(t)$ $\hspace{2em}$ (6)

Remaining available funds: $F_1(t) = F_0(t) - S_P(t)$ $\hspace{2em}$ (7)

2. Class A Interest

$$\text{Class A interest due: } I_A(t) = \frac{r_A}{12} B_A(t-1) + I_{AS}(t-1)\left(1 + \frac{r_A}{12}\right) \hspace{1em} (8)$$

Class A interest paid: $I_{AP}(t) = Min(F_1(t), I_A(t))$ $\hspace{2em}$ (9)

Class A interest shortfall: $I_{AS}(t) = I_A(t) - I_{AP}(t)$ $\hspace{2em}$ (10)

Remaining available funds: $F_2(t) = F_1(t) - I_{AP}(t)$ $\hspace{2em}$ (11)

3. Class B Interest

$$\text{Class B interest due: } I_B(t) = \frac{r_B}{12} B_B(t-1) + I_{BS}(t-1)\left(1 + \frac{r_B}{12}\right) \hspace{1em} (12)$$

Class B interest paid: $I_{BP}(t) = Min(F_2(t), I_B(t))$ $\hspace{2em}$ (13)

Class B interest shortfall: $I_{BS}(t) = I_B(t) - I_{BP}(t)$ $\hspace{2em}$ (14)

Remaining available funds: $F_3(t) = F_2(t) - I_{BP}(t)$ $\hspace{2em}$ (15)

4. Class A Principal

Class A principal due: $P_A(t) = Min(B_A(t-1), P_D(t) + P_{AS}(t-1))$

(sequential pay) $\hspace{2em}$ (16)

Class A principal due: $P_A(t) = Min(B_A(t-1), \alpha P_D(t) + P_{AS}(t-1))$

(pro rata pay) $\hspace{2em}$ (17)

Class A principal paid: $P_{AP}(t) = Min(F_3(t), P_A(t))$ $\hspace{2em}$ (18)

Class A principal shortfall: $P_{AS}(t) = P_A(t) - P_{AP}(t)$ $\hspace{2em}$ (19)

Class A ending principal balance: $B_A(t) = B_A(t-1) - P_{AP}(t)$ $\qquad$ (20)

Remaining available funds: $F_4(t) = F_3(t) - P_{AP}(t)$ $\qquad$ (21)

5. Class B Principal

Class B principal due: $P_B(t) = Min(B_B(t-1), Max(0, C(t) - Max(B_A(0),$

$\quad C(t-1))) + P_{BS}(t-1))$ (sequential pay) $\qquad$ (22)

Class B principal due: $P_B(t) = Min(B_B(t-1), (1-\alpha)P_D(t) + P_{BS}(t-1))$

$\quad$ (pro rata pay) $\qquad$ (23)

Class B principal paid: $P_{BP}(t) = Min(F_4(t), P_B(t))$ $\qquad$ (24)

Class B principal shortfall: $P_{BS}(t) = P_B(t) - P_{BP}(t)$ $\qquad$ (25)

Class B ending principal balance: $B_B(t) = B_B(t-1) - P_{BP}(t)$ $\qquad$ (26)

Remaining available funds: $F_5(t) = F_4(t) - P_{BP}(t)$ $\qquad$ (27)

6. Residual Payment

Residual payment due: $R(t) = F_5(t)$ $\qquad$ (28)

Remaining available funds: $F_6(t) = F_5(t) - R(t) = 0$ $\qquad$ (29)

Note that in this simple structure, the last step is clearly redundant. Remaining available funds at level 5 are always equal to the residual payment due at level 6. In our prototype, residual cash flow belongs to the seller. In an alternative but algebraically equivalent structure, residual cash flow might be certificated (turned into a security) and held on the balance sheet or sold to a third party. More complex structures entail other treatments, for example, remaining available funds at level 5 may be capitalized and due after the other tranches pay down (a Z-bond) or they may revert to one or more other classes (the NAS bond feature).

7.4 SUMMARIZING THE RESULTS

At this point, although the work of building the cash flow engine and capital structure is finished, the *security valuation* step described in section 6.2 will have to wait until chapter 9. Strictly speaking, this is a measurement step related to rating and valuation processes, not to coding liabilities. For valuation purposes, two summary measures turn out to be essential. The first one is the difference between the actual return and the payment promise, measured either as a present value or a yield-to-maturity. The other is the average life of each class of notes, calculated as the sum of principal payments on each class multiplied by the relevant time of payment t and divided by the original class principal balance.

Required Summary Measures:
- Loss on this scenario; or
- Yield to maturity on this scenario; and
- Security average life

7.5 RESERVE ACCOUNTS AND LIQUIDITY FACILITIES

Reserve mechanisms go by many different names depending on mechanical specifics: reserve fund, reserve account, cash account, collateral account, spread account, yield supplement account,[3] etc. The term *reserve fund* here refers to a mechanism for placing, holding, and releasing cash in the transaction, where some or all of those steps may be involved. Recall from chapter 4 that in the BOTE analysis, the correct way to measure the reserve fund's contribution to total *CE* is to include only its initial cash contribution and to include *XS* spread that may be allocated to the reserve fund *as XS* to avoid double-counting. Nevertheless, in modeling a reserve fund, it is necessary to be able to replicate the mechanics of the initial contribution, *XS* capture and growth, as well as controlled release if a fixed target percentage or fixed target amount is used.

Before delving into the algebra of reserve funds, it is appropriate to highlight the distinction between liquidity and credit facilities. Liquidity is cash available to facilitate payment when the need for timing precision in the repayment is high and the likelihood of default is remote or immaterial. Credit is capital that facilitates payment when the certainty of return is quantifiable but not necessarily high and a premium for bearing the risk of payment uncertainty forms an important part of the return to bondholders.

In modeling terms, the difference between a liquidity facility and a credit enhancement facility boils down to the position that reimbursements occupy within the waterfall. Consider the hierarchy of claims in our model transaction:

1. Servicing and other fees (including mono line wrap fees)
2. Class A interest
3. Class B interest
4. Class A principal
5. Class B principal
6. Residual

To build a reserve account, modify the waterfall by inserting the reserve below the principal account of the Class B or, more generally, the lowest class on the hierarchy of claims to benefit from it:

1. Servicing and other fees (including monoline wrap fees)
2. Class A interest
3. Class B interest
4. Class A principal
5. Class B principal

6. *Reserve account draw reimbursements*

7. Residual

In this scheme, the reserve is subordinated to the payment of principal to all classes that benefit from it. Should money in the reserve be drawn, the facility can only be replenished after principal claims from both classes have been met in full. At all times, its current balance accrues interest at the *eligible investment rate*.

This architectural analysis is logically true because credit risk is risk to principal, and the reserve account is positioned below principal allocations. To highlight this point, consider a transaction equipped with a cash collateral account in a waterfall with the following order:

1. Servicing and other fees (including mono line wrap fees)

2. Class A interest

3. Class B interest

4. *Facility draw reimbursements*

5. Class A principal

6. Class B principal

7. Residual

Since draw reimbursements lie above principal allocations, the facility does not provide credit enhancement, but merely delivers liquidity whenever current cash collections are insufficient to pay interest on both classes. In this structure, before any cash can be applied to amortize Class A or B, collections must first be allocated to replenish draws on the facility plus any accrued interest. In that sense, the reserve account in this transaction supplies liquidity, not credit enhancement. Unless the facility is positioned above the level of principal, it is not liquidity in the formal sense. The mere fact that some pool of cash is available to the structure is not a justification for calling it a *liquidity reserve*. This fundamental fact continues to escape many parties, including rating agencies, investors, and financial system regulators.

7.6 IMPLEMENTING RESERVE ACCOUNTS

Inserting reserve account mechanics inside the Raw Deal is relatively easy. In our initial implementation, after Class B principal allocations were made, we were left with the residual amount $F_5(t)$ which simply escaped back to the equity holder. Now, instead of remitting the residual to the issuer, we use it to fulfill the current requirements of the reserve account as follows. First, some nomenclature is in order:

Beginning balance in the reserve account (at month end):	$R_b(t)$
Ending balance in the reserve account (at month end):	$R_e(t)$
Reserve account draw in the current period:	$R_d(t)$
Remaining monthly collections after Class B allocation:	$F_5(t)$
Collection account balance after Class B principal:	$F_6(t)$
Residual amount after draw reimbursements:	$F_7(t)$
Target reserve percentage:	R_p

Target reserve amount:	$R_r(t)$
Reserve contribution amount:	$R_a(t)$
Ending monthly pool balance:	$V(t)$
Eligible investment rate:	r_e

The facility should be able to both reimburse the reserve account for draws and fund it to its target percentage using residual cash collections, thus helping the deal keep up with all mandatory payments. Any shortfall must be made up from cash collected during later periods. To illustrate, enter the following formulas in the waterfall after Class B principal allocations.

$$R_b(t) = R_e(t-1)\left[1 + \frac{r_e}{12}\right] \tag{30}$$

The amount $R_b(t)$ is to be added to current collections. Together, both of these now make up available funds.

Recall that in our basic model, available funds were simply equal to monthly current collections. When available funds are sufficient to pay the current claim at level i, there is no need for a reserve draw. Algebraically, this situation is true when available funds at the current level exceed the beginning balance in the reserve fund for the current period. The difference is equal to remaining collections from the current period. Logically, this means

$$F_6(t) = Max[0, F_5(t) - R_b(t)] \tag{31}$$

When available funds are smaller than the beginning reserve fund balance for the current period the difference is perforce equal to the collection shortfall. The reserve fund needs to make it up if possible. The algebra of this situation is expressed as:

$$R_d(t) = Max[0, R_b(t) - F_5(t)] \tag{32}$$

For a dynamic reserve, the target is expressed as a percentage of the current pool balance:

$$R_r(t) = R_p V(t) \tag{33a}$$

For a static reserve, the target is expressed as a percentage of the initial pool balance:

$$R_r(t) = R_p V(0) \tag{33b}$$

The reserve contribution amount will always be the minimum of the shortfall on the target balance and the residual cash at that level. Note that when the target balance is reached, the reserve contribution amount will appear negative, i.e. cash is released from the reserve account to the issuer.

$$R_a(t) = Min[F_6(t), R_r(t) - R_b(t) + R_d(t)] \tag{34}$$

The ending balance is just a true-up of the initial balance after all current period draws and contributions have been accounted for:

$$R_e(t) = R_b(t) - R_d(t) + R_a(t) \qquad (35)$$

The excess cash flowing through the fully funded reserve is calculated as follows:

$$F_7(t) = F_6(t) - R_a(t)$$

Once these formulas are incorporated into the cash flow model, monthly collections represented by $F_7(t)$ simply flow back to the seller as before.

If the documents stipulate that the facility is to be liquidity to both classes rather than credit enhancement, we would insert the same equations at the higher waterfall position shown above, i.e., after Class B interest due, to reflect the intended purpose of the cash. This would cause the structural feature to behave as a liquidity facility. As stated above, there is no formal difference in the algebra of liquidity and credit facilities save their respective positions within the waterfall, but their utility is fundamentally different. In closing, please keep in mind that the eligible investment rate with respect to liquidity facilities is negative.

7.7 STRESS-BASED RATINGS

All valuation philosophies for structured securities represent a decision to reflect or ignore certain key dimensions of risk, including time, probability, and granularity. The cash flow model that we have just built to examine the impact of time on value can only run one scenario at a time. Analytically, it corresponds to the method described in box (2) in figure 5.3. If all the variances of this transaction come down to this one scenario, then one cash flow run and measures taken from that run will suffice to assign ratings to the tranches.

In reality, one scenario cannot encapsulate all possible states of reality. Cash flow runs must be constructed for all the possible states in which the pool may find itself. How to do this is a philosophical question: are outcomes the result of rolling the dice (a statistical view) or arbitrary interpretation (a stress-based view)? In the latter case, stress scenarios define the rating. Standard and Poor's, and to a certain extent, Fitch Ratings use this method in some types of transactions.

Stress-based ratings are assigned by applying stresses in serial fashion to discover the highest load the security being evaluated can bear. The rating defined by this set of stress scenarios is then assigned to the security. Tranches that pay off when weak stresses are applied, but default under more rigorous stress cases, attract lower ratings. Tranches that can withstand disproportionately more onerous stresses deserve higher ratings. Since the 1970s, Moody's Investors Service has not defined structured ratings in this way. Instead, it claims to assign structured ratings based on a statistical view of credit risk that requires an exploration, via Monte Carlo simulation, of the credit loss distribution and its impact on liability payments. This process is described at length in chapter 9.

Although the stressed-based approach to ratings is tractable and has significant appeal among students of capital-market history owing to the ease with which stress-scenarios may be constructed from historical data, its cardinal drawback is inconsistency. There is no way to ensure that stress severity is properly calibrated so that distances between ratings are internally consistent across different transactions. Furthermore, it is impossible to ensure consistency across asset classes, borrower types, or geographic markets, because each sector requires customized stresses. In short, stressed-based ratings are easy to monitor and reverse-engineer, but impossible to validate.

END-OF-CHAPTER QUESTIONS

1. What is a pass-through security? A pay-through security? An investment-holding company? A corporation? Why do such distinctions in terminology matter in a chapter on liability analysis?

2. Explain, first in words, then mathematically, and finally with respect to their impact on the risk/return features of senior and subordinated tranches, the differences between sequential, pro rata and pari passu pro rata.

3. What is the relationship between the assets and the liabilities on the balance sheet of an SPE?

4. What is the rationale for the convention, in certain transactions, of matching interest inflows to interest outflows and principal inflows to principal outflows, the so-called "specified waterfall?" Please discuss the rationale and the justification for this practice.

5. State the formula for Class B principal due sequential in words and explain its meaning as a string of conditional statements. Change the formula so that it is true for all subordinated tranches that rank sequentially.

6. What is the residual payment? How would you characterize its risk–return features? How would you value it?

7. What is the usefulness of these summary statistics in the cash flow model: scenario loss, yield to maturity, and security average life?

8. Using the formatting concepts and the algebra of assets and liabilities introduced in chapters 6 and 7, build a cash flow model of a transaction with these parameters:

Collateral

Use collateral pool information provided in chapter 6:

$$V(0) = \$30,000,000$$

$$N_0 = 2,000$$

$$WAM = T = 120$$

$$WAC = 12\%$$

$$LGD(t) = 0.5$$

Note: You must calculate the single-loan M (monthly payment) before you can implement the model.

Defaults

Use the logistic curve for $F(t)$ provided in chapter 6, with the following parameters:

$$a = 10\%$$

$$b = 1$$

$$c = 10\%$$

$$t_0 = 55$$

Note: Remember to normalize loan-space defaults

Prepayments

Use the prepayment provided in chapter 6, which has the following parameters:

$$N_P = 400 \ (20\% \text{ expected prepayments})$$

$$t_{OP} = 45$$

Note: Remember that you have to compute parameter a separately.

Liabilities

Use the following parameters to compute liability-side amounts:

$$\alpha = 0.8$$

$$r_A = 7\%$$

$$r_B = 9\%$$

$$s_f = 1\%$$

$$s_r = 20\%$$

9. How would you modify the sequential-pay Class B principal due formula to calculate the amount of monthly principal due on a sequential-pay Class C?

10. Use the BOTE method to find the rating on the Class A and Class B securities in question 8. What additional information does this result give you about the transaction you just modeled?

TABLE 7.2

Sample key spreads for pricing

SPREAD/RATING	5-YEAR	10-YEAR
Aaa/AAA	+10	+25
Aa/AA	+25	+60
A/A	+49	+86
Baa/BBB	+85	+125
Ba/BB	+365	+440
B/B	+505	+595
Caa/CCC	+1600	+1520

11. Additional questions related to the cash flow model from question 8:

a) How high does the collateral default rate have to go before the Class B suffers a reduction of yield? Is it the same in the pro rata and sequential cases? At the collateral default rate where the Class B loses yield, how much yield is lost?

b) The reduction-of-yield method relates the average loss of yield on a security, produced in a Monte Carlo (MC) simulation, to the alphanumeric rating. If the yield reduction obtained at the default rate in question 11a were the result of an MC simulation (average reduction of yield) you could obtain a rating from that number. Find the rating by looking up the reduction of yield (in basis points) in table 9.2. Using the credit spreads in table 7.2 below, adjust the Class B interest rate input to reflect this rating. Is the impact on the Class B rating stable or does it change the rating? What is the significance of question 11b?

c) Given the parameters in question 8 and the outcomes, what is the *seller's* "optimal" Class B size? Why can't you make this the *real* Class B size? In general, given a rating on a security, how do you find the *buyer's* optimal size?

d) How would you adjust the original scenario to analyze a securitization of *subprime autos* with a five-year *WAM*?

e) It turns out that, underlying the collateral are two distinct borrower populations, each with its own characteristic loss curve. How would you factor this intelligence into your analysis?

f) In the scenario where defaults are 22%, the originator/seller/servicer eventually defaults in time step 55 and a backup servicer must step in. Is this a good deal or a bad deal for the backup servicer? Given your answer, can you generalize about pricing for backup servicing?

g) Rating agencies do not model the base case loss curve in cash flow models. In the 1990s, they stressed the loss curve by ramping up losses from 0% to fully loaded over a 6-, 9-, 12-, or 18-month horizon. How much capital did their stress cost the structure in question 8? Is stressing the input assumptions a good idea?

8

Static Analysis of Revolving Structures

The cash flow method for valuing structured securities given in chapters 6–7 is illustrative of a pure plain-vanilla securitization with amortizing assets and a simple two-tranche capital structure. However, in reality the structured finance market is neither pure nor simple. Not every transaction offers the transparency or predictability of the plain-vanilla securitization (PVA).

Beyond term securitizations with amortizing liabilities backed by amortizing assets, there are also master trust structures with amortizing liabilities backed by revolving pools and conduits or warehouses, where by both the assets and liabilities revolve. The assets in an SPE are not always large pools of homogeneous consumer credits. Sometimes, they are consumer loans of different credit quality mixed together. Other times, they are large pools of poorly diversified corporate bonds or loans, the trade credits of a bank's corporate client or the operating revenues of a strategic industry. Very occasionally, they may be backed by intangibles such as royalties and patents. Alternatively, the credit structure may be based on synthetic exposures rather than funded obligations, i.e. *contingent* rights to receive cash flows (or obligations to pay cash flows) under certain adverse credit scenarios. Structured securities have taken the form of bonds, certificates, medium term or money market notes and commercial paper.

These paradigm extensions are the sizzle, and sometimes also the heartbreak of structured finance. Their economic analysis is based on the same structured credit nucleus, the PVA, but usually without pricing appropriately for the incremental risks brought on by relaxing the constraints that define the PVA. The goal of this chapter is merely to strike a compromise between glamour and verisimilitude. In other words, we simply want to depict structured-credit composites visually and explain their microstructure in one or two product types from a simplified, static viewpoint. We postpone guidance on valuation and pricing to the Advanced Part.

8.1 THE STRUCTURE AND ORGANIZATION OF THE SHADOW FINANCIAL SYSTEM

The life cycle of a credit portfolio can be partitioned into three phases: the *ramp-up* or *warehousing* of originations to a threshold pool size; the revolving phase, in which matured loan exposures are replaced with new exposures; and the amortizing phase, where the portfolio has become static and simply pays down. The first two phases tend to take place on the originators' balance sheets or off–balance-sheet in warehousing subsidiaries or vehicles. This life-cycle is depicted in figure 8.1.

The possibility of unbundling has made the financial institutional landscape much more complex, with different entities various degrees, as in shown figure 8.2. The imaginary line that connects them is the global credit supply chain. The segment to left of the operating companies is none other than the *shadow financial system*. PVAs, the

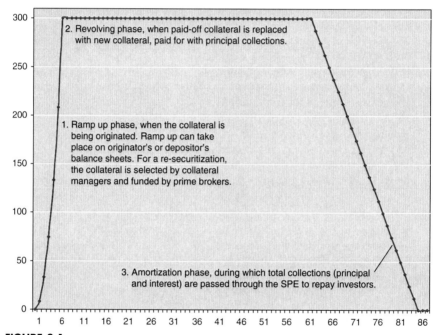

FIGURE 8.1
The credit-portfolio lifecycle.

FIGURE 8.2
How the shadow financial system and the real economy intersect.

value nucleus of the credit portfolio lifecycle, are found on the extreme left, while banks and corporations are located on the extreme right. Structured vehicles at points in between embody different ways of bundling or unbundling assets and evidence different degrees of management discretion. A brief overview of role specialization along this continuum shows the influence of anti-competitive bank strategy. What connects the endpoints of the credit supply chain, invisibly and haphazardly, is the real economy.

Minimal discretion, maximal unbundling

At the far left are the PVAs, which finance only the amortizing phase of amortizing exposures. With the PSA as a comprehensive operational blueprint, management has the least discretion over the PVAs. The PVA as a disposable, brain-dead company is a frequent and predictable source of fee income to banks.

To the immediate right of the PVAs are prefunded transactions, whose risk exposure includes the tail end of the ramp-up and amortization phases but not the early ramp-up or the replacement (revolving) phase. Prefunded structured transactions go to market before the collateral has been completely originated. They enable niche lenders to use a portion of the proceeds of a deal to fund part of the target collateral pool. Under Reg AB in the United States, the maximum allowable prefunded amount is 50% of the total transaction. Cash not used to purchase loans in a portfolio or warehoused in an intermediate SPE must be stored in trust accounts and used to purchase *eligible collateral*, i.e. assets that conform to *criteria* set forth in the indenture to preserve the financial characteristics of the original pool. Reg AB also limits the prefunding period to one year after the closing date, Thereafter, all unused funds must be repaid through the waterfall in one period. Many transactions with prefunding are structured with a money market tranche senior to all the other tranches. It is designed to absorb large prepayments within a one-year time horizon.[1] Compared to the PVA, prefunded deals are riskier. Prefunding may dilute the credit quality of the borrowing base, introduce negative carry or else raise the level of reinvestment risk to investors. Nevertheless, these risks are short-term and finite. With revolving structures, although the sources of risk are identical, their impact is much larger because the transaction is longer-dated.

Limited discretion, partial unbundling

Moving to the right on the continuum are structures catering primarily to banks seeking to partially unbundle their portfolios, primarily for regulatory capital relief, and to nonbanks seeking to become bank-like, whereas PVA-type structures clearly benefit the clients of banks seeking to reduce their cost of funds.[2] Immediately to the right of the Static Pool/Revolving Portfolio divide are collateralized debt obligations (CDOs).[3] The salient process differences between PVA and CDO structuring are outlined in table 8.1. While amortizing CDO structures are historically a small and declining percentage of the CDO market, the quintessential CDO has a three- to five-year revolving period during which collateral substitution is allowed, and after which liabilities begin to amortize. Substitution may be permitted to replace the

TABLE 8.1
ABS and CDO approaches compared

STEP	ABS METHOD	CDO METHOD
1	Assemble the collateral pool. Audit it.	Assemble the collateral pool. Audit it.
2	Estimate the **cumulative credit loss curve** as a percentage of initial principal balance. It is better to derive the loss curve from the two constituent processes: default, recovery (or, loss-given-default).	**Apply the ratings** on each security as an ex ante default measure. If a public rating is not available, choose (in this order of preference) the internal/shadow rating, ratings bootstrapped from bank credit scores, or a haircut rating of another CRA.
3	Analyze the impact of unexpected losses: S&P/Fitch: this is done via stress analysis, applied in the next step. Moody's: impute a functional form to the **distribution function of cumulative credit losses** and a value to its **standard deviation**.	For Moody's, the unexpected loss analysis went missing until 2004.
4	Pool assumed to be well-diversified.	Address correlation issues: S&P/Fitch: **simulate the portfolio. Apply a Copula function** to load the tail risk more fully. Moody's: compute the **diversity score** and use that as the count (N) of securities in the pool. Apply the **Binomial Expansion Theorem (BET)**.
5	Portfolio triggers are inappropriate for a static pool (it winds itself down) but early amortization triggers are put in place occasionally to protect investors against "unknowns" in the data.	Revolving CDOs typically have many triggers, some optional, some mandatory. The purpose is to contain the portfolio risk within the umbrella of certain pre-defined scenarios that are believed to stabilize the payment risk on the liabilities consistent with their initial ratings.
6	Model the structure. Check that it retains the CE required for the target ratings—at least, the ratings on the senior classes.	For S&P and Fitch, steps 4 and 5 are combined. CE required for the target ratings—at least, the ratings on the senior classes. For Moody's, a cash flow model must be run to examine the interaction between spread and risk on cash deals, while a synthetic CDO is treated statically
7	Rate the liabilities.	Rate the liabilities.

maturing collateral, or the controls on discretion may be further relaxed to allow active trading. Limited substitution is only associated with cash flow CDOs. Trading is more often associated with market-value structures, which are much closer to hedge funds than to PVAs. Revolving period purchases, like prefunded transactions, are subject to eligibility criteria. Further to the right are transactions with near-infinite revolving periods. Such structures are designed to continuously purchase collateral unless, or until, such activity is pre-empted by *early amortization* or other triggers controlling the term of operations. This sector produces financing vehicles like Credit Card Master Trusts (CCMT), Asset-Backed Commercial Paper (ABCP) conduits, and Structured Investment Vehicles (SIVs). Note that the revolving nature of these structures keeps set-up costs and related fees (borne by the banks) to a minimum.

True hybrids, some with limited prefunding

To the right of the SPE sector are the true corporate-structured hybrids: limited purpose finance companies that buy to originate or guarantee structured products. Of late, this sector has proven vulnerable to systemic change. The ranks of such companies include government sponsored entities (GSEs) and financial guarantors (mono line insurers). All businesses in this sector are dependent on an institutionalized right to financial arbitrage bestowed on them by regulatory or quasi-regulatory institutions. They self-finance at a regulated cost of funds commensurate with their high investment-grade ratings even when their investment portfolio might be deemed questionable. The quid pro quo for this privilege is that they must carry out a special financial or social policy purpose that serves the goals of their sponsor. For the GSEs, the sponsor is the federal government. For the mono lines, it is the rating agency that bestows its AAA rating upon them.

"Corporation," viewed through a structured finance lens, means unlimited prefunding

Furthest to the right are normal operating companies. Viewed from a radical structured finance perspective, operating companies are just revolving portfolios of assets and liabilities placed inside a weak control structure, bounded by the law at the macro-level but with a high degree of discretion over financial micro-processes, where the maximum allowable amount of prefunding is 100%. It is worth reflecting that banks operated for centuries, and in particular during the era of *haute finance*, as *true hybrids* benefiting from a regulated spread income. In the 1970s, deregulation forced them out of their comfortable habitat into the corporate jungle. It has been a difficult transition for banks. As information specialists, their franchises are being eroded via greater disclosure and greater borrower access to capital through organized markets. Banks have endeavored to recapture some of that regulated spread business by re-inventing themselves inside the shadow banking system.

Finally, it is worth noting that the amorphous commercial mortgage-backed securities (CMBS) market spans the entire analytical spectrum. Its defining feature is not structural, but the fact that its key asset is physical rather than financial. CMBS backed by a statistically large and diverse borrowing base of rental contracts resemble PVAs if the maturity ends within the contract period of the rental agreements, and

CDOs if the contracts roll over before maturity. CMBS backed by a smaller number of buildings exhibit the same types of cash flow and market value credit structures as CDOs. Single property CMBS, where multiple tranches of debt are issued against one operating asset are most similar to single-name corporate debt, i.e. their payment risk cannot be diversified away by structuring.

8.2 MACRO-STRUCTURES OF THE SECONDARY MARKET

This sci-fi-sounding heading, *macro-structures of the secondary market*, refers to the expanded universe of transaction types that have equally sci-fi-sounding abbreviated names. They include several transaction families: (1) in the cash market, the group whose financial properties are measured using empirical data, i.e. ABS, RMBS and CMBS; (2) the partially revolving CDO group whose financial properties are measured using ratings; (3) the infinitely revolving ABCP and SIV conduits and (4), in the synthetic market, Credit Default Swaps (CDS), Credit Linked Notes (CLNs), synthetic CDOs, reference portfolios of credit indices and CPDOs, whose valuations represent a confluence of belief systems from ratings-based approaches to contingent pricing models. These products have come into existence at different points in time and have been evaluated according to different rating methodologies, creating virtually endless opportunities for financial arbitrage.[4] The evolutionary logic within these markets, set forth in figures 8.4 through 8.8, is a mixed calculus of balance sheet deconstruction fueled by the single-minded pursuit of economic and regulatory arbitrage.

Convergence and Cloning

Though it is hard to recall the siloed world of banking from 30 years ago, at the time corporate balance sheets looked (figure 8.3) like an ecology of niche investors. Collateral-based lenders, often with bootstrapped beginnings, clustered in the blue-collar, left-hand of the balance sheet. Lenders on the genteel, aloof, and moneyed right-hand side while large equity investors traded against smaller ones.

Banks were the primary source of debt capital. Structural barriers to entry discouraged competition and kept the cost of capital above where the clearing price would have been in a more competitive market. Contrast figure 8.4, a diagram of the wholesale lender–borrower relationship in a traditional bank-oriented market, with figures 8.5 and 8.6, which show an expanding array of asset-based and wholesale finance options made possible through structuring.

Figure 8.4 is a diagram of bank funding alternatives for a hypothetical XYZ corporation.

Figure 8.5 presents the range of options for XYZ to borrow off-balance-sheet using its collateral. To the left is term securitization of ABS. The dotted box at the bottom of XYZ's asset side represents its intangibles, and dangling below that, an intangibles securitization.[5] To the right are two revolving off-balance-sheet vehicles, a Credit Card Master Trust Structure that provides financing to XYZ (if it is a bank) through the serial issuance of card-backed securities, and an ABCP conduit backed by collateral structured to a prime level. Each box has a different funding strategy: the term

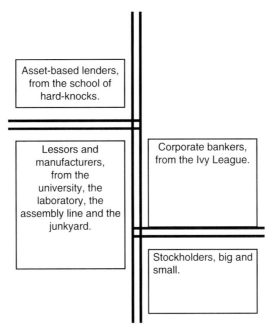

FIGURE 8.3
The ecology of the stratified balance sheet.

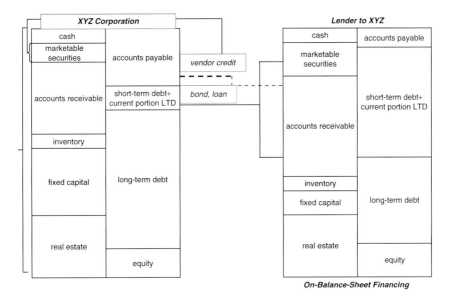

FIGURE 8.4
The on-balance sheet borrowing/leading relationship.

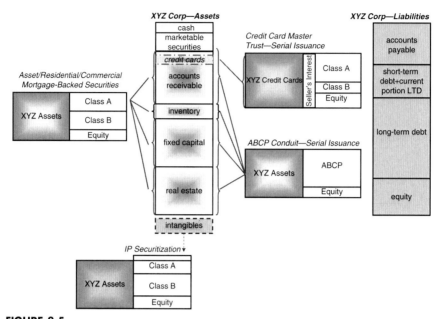

FIGURE 8.5

Off-balance sheet asset-backed financing alternatives.

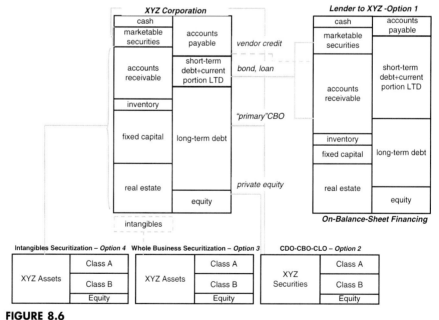

FIGURE 8.6

Off-balance-sheet wholesale financing alternatives.

securitization enables XYZ to capture the maximum benefit of the intangible value of its operations, while credit card ABS and ABCP offer regulatory capital arbitrage and opacity. Intangibles securitization may also involve tax arbitrage.

Figure 8.6 shows two transactions backed by XYZ's expected future operating revenues (options 3 and 4: both *future flow transactions*) and one backed by XYZ's debt in the form of loans, bonds, or other debt obligations bundled with that of other sellers (option 2: *CDO/CLO/CBOs*) in addition to the traditional lending situation (option 1). Significantly, the structured market for wholesale finance does not transform the economics of debt finance for XYZ through informational disclosures. Instead, repackaging can change the pattern of supply and demand by delivering a wider menu of asset flavors to investment channels that only buy highly-rated securities, and hence drive down the cost of debt finance at the margins.

Next, figure 8.7 shows the pattern of market convergence since 2000. Prior to then, the amortizing and revolving structured markets were virtually disconnected except for the occasional take-out securitization or conduit purchase of senior ABS or CDO notes. In the new millennium, arrangers discovered repeatability. Whatever could be repackaged could be depackaged and repackaged again into CDOs. Not just corporate debt, but also ABS, RMBS, CMBS, and other CDOs. The beauty of repeatability was that the models, being static, were insensitive to changes in the level of risk after the rating was assigned. Serial repackaging injected increasing amounts of leverage into capital structures without any impact on ratings and therefore, without any impact on price. With insufficient weight given to the severity of unexpected losses, the free lunch eventually turned into a credit binge.

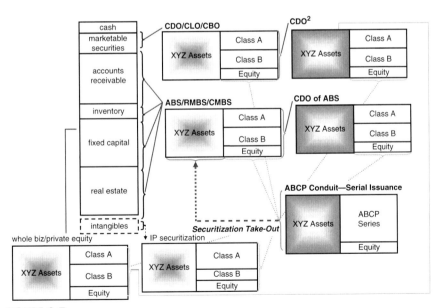

FIGURE 8.7
The art of serial repackaging.

Finally, figure 8.8 shows attempts at market completeness through synthetic replication. Several new types of issuer and product are introduced in this picture. Under the liability side of XYZ are *unfunded CDSs*, structured as bets against a defined credit event (corporate insolvency or downgrade). Entities can buy protection (short) or sell protection (long) against the event. Rather than providing credit risk protection on only one company, portfolios of reference names have also been created.

Unfunded single name or reference portfolios of CDS can also be sold in a funding structure, whereby the proceeds from the sale of CDS-backed notes are used to purchase low-risk securities, which generate interest and principal for the buyer of the notes in addition to the swap premium. This is known as a synthetic CDO. The synthetic CDO can be partially or fully funded. Although the rating measures for cash and synthetic CDOs are much the same, their investors have not always priced securities within the traditional cash securitization framework. Coming to credit derivatives from a trading background, many use contingent pricing methods that have been refined, for example via the use of copula functions, to incorporate inter-asset correlation. The synthetic space inverts the cash paradigm, with a fixed capital structure and flexible price, making it possible to synthetically replicate a long or short position on different gradations of credit risk.

Although there is much to say about the credit derivative market, a full discussion and critique of its assumptions is beyond the scope of this book. Nevertheless, it

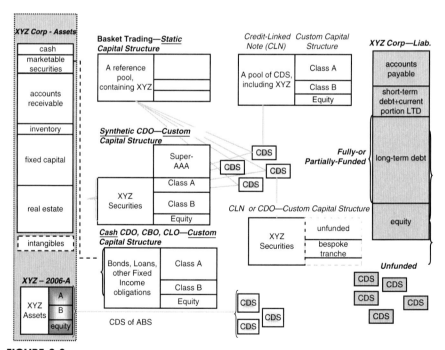

FIGURE 8.8
The synthetic side of structured finance.

is important to note that all synthetic position-taking is ultimately based on the economics of the cash market and the PVA, to which a validly constructed synthetic position must, in the end, converge.

8.3 THE TWO BASIC CCMT STRUCTURES

Most credit card receivable backed securities originate from master trusts (CCMTs), so-called because all of the issuer's receivables are concentrated within a single legal vehicle out of which several series of securities are issued. Each series may come with its own terms, maturity, revolving period length, number of tranches, type of interest rate (fixed or floating), and so on.

Since the receivables belong to a single legal entity, a few options are available to the issuer when it comes to allocating interest collections within the master trust. Two basic structures exist:

- The most common is the *socialist trust*, whereby each series' interest collection allocation is based on its needs, i.e., its average coupon, servicing fee, and allocated default amount, which needs of course do change every month
- Alternatively, in a *capitalist trust*, interest collections are allocated pro rata based on outstanding series balances, i.e., based on their wants, while series-wise excess spread, if any, simply escapes back to the seller

This means that while one series in a capitalist trust may be experiencing early amortization due to a higher average coupon, a lower trust yield, or some combination thereof, another may still be revolving in a (presumably) deteriorating environment. It is to avoid this unwanted phenomenon that the socialist structure was in fact invented. In a socialist trust, all series are thus cross-collateralized and enter early amortization at the same time, if and when they do. An intermediate form also exists, one we have dubbed the "IMF" structure, whereby excess spread remaining in any given series may be allocated to other, needy series should they be running short on cash to pay their expenses.

The main credit protection mechanism for investors in a CCMT is its early amortization feature, which causes the return of principal to investors ahead of schedule should credit performance deteriorate significantly. The mechanics of early amortization are further explained below.

8.4 THE CCMT LIQUIDATION ANALYSIS

Each month, credit card receivables in the trust should generate yield in an amount more than sufficient to pay senior expenses: servicing and trustee fees, and coupon on securities backed by the receivables. After compensating investors and the seller for receivables that have defaulted during the most recent monthly collection period, excess collections should remain, the so-called excess spread (XS). If this excess were to fall to zero, for instance, through a rise in defaults, a decrease in the effective yield of the trust, or some combination thereof, investors would run the risk of principal loss. In that case, their remaining protection would come from whatever form of credit enhancement is available to them. At that time, the process of investor reimbursement would begin using that enhancement. This is the process referred to as *early amortization* within a CCMT.[6]

These considerations are sufficient to motivate, within each CCMT, an early amortization index usually set equal to the quarterly rolling-average value of *XS*. Thus, if the index were to fall below its trigger value, normally zero or close to it, the structure would begin amortizing early according to a preestablished method.

It is important to remember that the receivables in a CCMT can be regarded as forming two logically distinct sets, namely the *investor portion* and the *seller portion*. The investor portion is the amount of trust receivables that correspond dollar-for-dollar to liability balances. The seller portion is simply the difference between the trust's aggregate receivable balance and the investor portion. The seller portion is an analytical mechanism aimed at cushioning the investor portion from noncredit risks, for example, dilution risk, and to guarantee that investors are fully collateralized by receivables at all times. In this context, the seller portion does *not* serve as credit enhancement to the investor portion but, as its name implies, is a co-investment by the seller in its own receivables.

As mentioned above, once the early amortization feature is triggered, monthly principal collections from obligors are no longer reinvested in new receivables but instead allocated to investors, normally in a sequential manner. Two allocation methods are conventional:

1. *Controlled accumulation*, whereby principal collections accumulate in a separate principal account and are returned to investors as a lump sum equal to their original investment.

2. *Controlled amortization*, whereby principal collections are returned as received, but usually in some orderly fashion, e.g., in an amount equal to a specified percentage of the original investment each month or according to some other pre-negotiated formula.

Credit Dynamics of the CCMT

Given the above, our geometric credit analysis of a CCMT begins by asking how much credit enhancement is sufficient to allow senior securities backed by credit card receivables to be repaid in full under an arbitrary stress-scenario that assumes *XS* drops linearly and continuously past its critical value, in essence, a "race to get out" against a backdrop of collateral deterioration, with senior investors reimbursed first from available funds followed by subordinated investors. A credit event or *default* would occur if rising credit losses caused a principal loss on the senior securities after eating through all available credit enhancement.

In other words, the measure of creditworthiness for the senior tranche under this simplistic model is its ability to sustain no principal loss upon liquidation under severely deteriorating credit conditions. Since we have implicitly made *zero* principal loss under an extreme default scenario the measure of credit quality for senior securities inside a CCMT, the meaning of Aaa may be defined via this condition. All other ratings can then be referenced to that Aaa benchmark.

It should be mentioned in passing that credit enhancement within credit card master trusts may take several forms and that all of these contribute to investor protection. Although in some cases, external support may be available, the three main varieties are:

- Subordination
- Cash Collateral Account (CCA) or Collateral Invested Amount (CIA)
- Reserve Account

The Liquidation Analysis

Figure 8.9 depicts an idealized time-line of XS deterioration within a CCMT, where the horizontal axis represents time in years and the vertical axis represents XS as an annualized percentage of the initial investment.

The line of slope $-K$ ($K > 0$) represents the assumed, stressed XS scenario that triggers early amortization upon breaching level X_t. The declining XS trend is assumed to continue unabated until the associated securities are retired in full or suffer a loss of principal.

We must now determine the Aaa credit enhancement requirement for the senior securities, which amounts to finding the level of enhancement at which they experience no principal loss under this assumed stress scenario. Starting from an initial level X_0, XS first breaches the trigger level X_t at time T_1, causing the structure to enter early amortization. At time T_2, XS reaches zero and keeps falling until T_3, at which time it would have reached some hypothetical level $-B$ ($B > 0$).

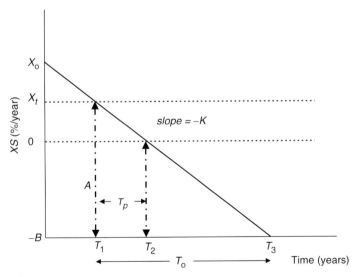

FIGURE 8.9
Sizing AAA-enhancement for a CCMT.

The heart of the liquidation analysis for Class A lies in computing the value of the minimum allowable slope for this spread line. This extreme slope effectively determines how much monthly deterioration can be tolerated within the structure, given its parameters, while still allowing senior security holders to be repaid in full.

Define $T_0 = T_3 - T_1$ and $T_p = T_2 - T_1$.

Now, consider the large triangle with area $\dfrac{A\,T_0}{2}$ shown in figure 8.9, and formed by the vertical line labeled A, the abscissa and the downward-sloping XS line.

As a percentage of the initial invested amount, the trapezoidal area below the zero spread line represents the cash shortfall experienced by security holders between T_2 and T_3 due to deteriorating collateral performance after early amortization begins. Remaining positive XS between X_t and zero will absorb some of this deterioration, but most of the protection will have to come from outside credit enhancement.

Geometrically, the area formed by the small triangle above the $X_t = 0$ line thus represents additional investor protection beyond the theoretically available credit enhancement. As expected, structures with XS trigger levels above zero are stronger, albeit marginally, than those with $X_t = 0$.

Note that, strictly speaking, this formulation is correct for controlled *accumulation* structures only, where the invested amount remains constant during the accumulation period. Controlled *amortization* structures would clearly warrant a reduction in enhancement approximately equal to the difference between the initial invested amount and the average balance outstanding during the amortization phase, times the weighted average interest rate, expressed as a percentage of the initial investment. The amount of this difference could be significant, pointing to possible cost savings to issuers switching from a controlled accumulation to a controlled amortization structure. How investors would acknowledge the difference in their pricing is an open question we cannot address here. However, in our experience the associated cost–benefit analysis is well worth the effort in terms of the embedded value.

Sizing the AAA Credit Enhancement

Referring to Figure 8.9, credit enhancement requirements meeting the full senior tranche retirement condition within a time frame, T_0, can be expressed via the following condition:

$$\frac{A\,T_0}{2} - \frac{X_t\,T_p}{2} = C \tag{1}$$

In equation (1), C is external credit enhancement, which is first made available to senior security holders. Normally, we would want such external enhancement to be liquid so that it is readily available when needed. Subordination, for instance, does not have the liquidity properties possessed by either reserve or cash collateral accounts. Only the crudeness of this model allows us to gloss over these details.

From the functional form of the *XS* line, defining K as the (negative) slope of that line and using similar triangles, we now have:

$$K T_0 = A \tag{2}$$

$$T_p = \frac{X_t T_0}{A} \tag{3}$$

Substituting equations (2) and (3) back into equation (1), we obtain:

$$K \left[T_0^2 - \frac{X_t^2}{K^2} \right] = 2C \tag{4}$$

Rearrangement of equation (4) yields:

$$T_0^2 K^2 - 2CK - X_t^2 = 0 \tag{5}$$

Choosing the positive quadratic root of equation (5), we then have:

$$K = \frac{C}{T_0^2} \left\{ 1 + \sqrt{(1 + (T_0 X_t / C)^2} \right\} \tag{6}$$

Clearly, for senior tranche holders to be repaid in full under a sequential allocation, T_0 has to be such that total principal due under the structure will aggregate to $(1 - S)$, where S is the subordination below the senior tranche. If P is the average total payment rate (i.e., the sum of defaulted receivables and actual principal collections) expressed as a percentage of the initial investment, we have by definition:

$$P T_0 = (1 - S) \tag{7}$$

Alternatively, we could simply assume that subordination is first exhausted, after which external credit enhancement is drawn upon if required. Either way, the enhancement available to Class A is still subordination plus external enhancement in whatever form.

To define P analytically, we boldly assume that principal reimbursements are a constant percentage α of the initial investment, and that defaults simply follow the same pattern as the *XS* line in figure 8.9, i.e., that *XS* deterioration stems exclusively from increasing losses, and not from either decreasing yield or increasing servicing fees. Hence, we can define two new quantities $\overline{R_p}$ and $\overline{R_d}$ as the average principal reimbursement rate and the average default rate, and posit:

$$P = \overline{R_p} + \overline{R_d}$$

where, on the one hand, we set:

$$\overline{R_p} = \alpha$$

and, on the other, linearity of the assumed XS behavior leads to the definition of $\overline{R_d}$:

$$\overline{R_d} = \frac{1}{T_0} \int_0^{T_0} [D_0 + K\,t]\,dt = D_0 + \frac{K\,T_0}{2} \tag{8}$$

In equation (8), we have defined D_0 as the default rate associated with the trigger breach starting point T_1. In other words, D_0 is the default rate at which early amortization begins. In practice, D_0 is defined by reference to the identity:

$$Y - F - D_0 - I = X_t \tag{9}$$

In equation (9), Y, F, and I are the annualized net trust yield, servicing fee, and weighted average security coupon, respectively.

Combining equations (7) and (8) with the definition of $\overline{R_p}$, we have:

$$\left[\alpha + D_0 + \frac{K\,T_0}{2}\right] T_0 = (1 - S) \tag{10}$$

Together, equations (6) and (10) form an implicit system defining X and T_0 in terms of known quantities and parameters, including the value of credit enhancement, C.

Given a known value of C, and assuming all other parameters save T_0 and K, to be known a priori, a normal solution would proceed iteratively. First, one would guess the value T_0 and use it inside equations (10) and (6) to find the corresponding values of K. If the two values differed by more than an agreed upon error, the K obtained from equation (6) would be substituted back into equation (10) and a new value of T_0 thus derived. This new T_0 would be used in equation (6) to obtain a new slope K, and thence a new T_0 via equation (10). This process would continue until convergence of the values of K and T_0 issuing from both equations.

Alternatively, if the stressed loss scenario (K) were assumed known, equation (10) would first be used to find the relevant T_0. The latter would be substituted back into equation (6) which would then be solved iteratively for the value of required external credit enhancement, C. This is the type of procedure normally followed by rating agencies to determine credit enhancement. In general, however, rather than merely external enhancement, total required enhancement is calculated. In this respect, exactly how stressed loss scenarios are defined by the agencies is largely unknown since the former are usually set at levels largely inconsistent with historical experience, master trust or not.

In practical terms, if credit enhancement is known, equations (6) and (10) tell us how much instantaneous XS deterioration can be empirically observed without requiring a re valuation of the creditworthiness of the affected securities, assuming they were rationally rated in the first place. In other words, *excess spread volatility* is how credit card master trusts should be monitored for changes in security value.

A Worked Example

Assume the analyst has the following data for some credit card collateral and a proposed sequential structure:

$S = 5\%$ at closing
$\alpha = 8\%$ per month
$I = 6\%$ per year
$Y = 16\%$ per year
$F = 1.5\%$ per year
$X_t = 1\%$ per year
$K = 1\%$ per month per year

Rearrangement of equation (10) yields the solution T_0:

$$T_0 = \frac{\sqrt{[\alpha + D_0]^2 + 2K[1 - S]} - [\alpha + D_0]}{K} \tag{11}$$

Insertion of the above quantities produces:

$$T_0 = \frac{\sqrt{[0.96 + 0.075]^2 + 2\,(0.12)0.95} - (0.96 + 0.075)}{0.12} = 0.874 \text{ years}$$

Next, equation (6) can be written with C as the only remaining unknown:

$$0.12 = \frac{C}{[0.874]^2}\left\{1 + \sqrt{1 + \left[\frac{0.874\,(0.01)}{C}\right]^2}\right\} \tag{12}$$

Back-substitution easily leads to the required external credit enhancement:

$$C = 4.54\%$$

Hence, total senior credit enhancement would amount to 9.54%, i.e., 5% subordination and 4.54% outside enhancement. By contrast, if our regular principal payment rate assumption dropped to 5% per month instead of 8%, the following would obtain:

$$T_0 = \frac{\sqrt{[0.60 + 0.075]^2 + 2\,(0.12)0.95} - (0.60 + 0.075)}{0.12} = 1.265 \text{ years} \tag{13}$$

An iterative solution using equation (12) would then lead to:

$$C = 9.56\%$$

In this case, total required credit enhancement would be 14.56%. Therefore, while the payment rate has dropped by about 38%, the *outside* required enhancement has more than doubled. These simple calculations demonstrate rather dramatically the sensitivity of credit enhancement levels to principal payment rates.

For example, if we now assume $X_t = 0$, i.e., that the XS trigger level is set to zero, we have from equation (6):

$$C = \frac{K\,T_0^2}{2} \tag{14}$$

Glancing at equation (11), equation (14) shows that to leading order, required outside credit enhancement is related quadratically to the trust's principal payment rate.

It is also instructive to apply the above model to the charge-card master trust. For this type of collateral, empirical data reveal payment rates in the neighborhood of $\alpha = 70\%$ per month, leading to the surprising solution:

$$T_0 = 0.1125 \text{ years}$$

$$C = 0.15\%$$

Hence, total enhancement for this type of transaction would generally be in the range of $S\%$, i.e., consisting almost entirely of subordination, rather than the more normal levels seen above. In effect, these trusts need no credit enhancement at all because investors are reimbursed immediately.

In such cases, however, liquidity rather than credit issues would probably drive the acceptable AAA credit enhancement level. Interestingly, what we have just witnessed first hand is an instance of a phenomenon most analytical models eventually face, i.e. they behave reasonably only over a limited range of inputs. What "reasonable" means here is, of course, the entire issue.

In practice, this situation would be addressed by building another model, one hopefully better suited to the financial circumstances of charge-card issuers.

Reflection on the Model

A stressed default scenario that postulates a continuous, annualized spread compression of 1% per month is severe, yet leads to a fairly reasonable credit enhancement requirement. In essence, we are assuming that XS could actually fall by 12% in a year, something that has never happened in the 50-year history of the credit card industry.[7] Most credit card master trusts are fairly well diversified and unlikely to go through such stress levels under any conceivable recessionary scenario. Stressing for the sake of stressing is not a rational approach.

It is therefore likely that current credit enhancement levels are excessive given the historical record of the credit card industry and the low interest rate environment. But while it may be difficult to fine tune the analysis of capital and risk using this model, a cursory look at credit enhancement levels on existing master trusts tends toward the conclusion that current credit card structures can probably withstand barely imaginable credit environments and still pay off in full.

Although the foregoing analysis is straightforward and gives a consistent directional signal, it is unacceptably flawed in one respect: the credit rating of securities backed by credit card receivables based on a liquidation analysis using a zero default rate has a different meaning from the credit rating of securities based on an average reduction of yield analysis in a Monte Carlo framework. Without a doubt, the combination of using a more punitive framework and the lack of attention to the credit card industry's historical record has led to systematic over-enhancement of securities issued out of credit card master trusts relative to structured securities from other sectors.

An average reduction of yield calculation could be implemented within the CCMT model without much difficulty by drawing K randomly from a presumed probability distribution, and using equations (6) and (10) repeatedly, with the further assumption that all losses would be deemed to occur at T_3. Some of the stressed loss scenarios would obviously give rise to nonzero credit losses on senior securities, but these would be constructed so as to average out to a level consistent with the assigned credit rating. As an inescapable conclusion, the amount of required credit enhancement would settle at levels lower than the corresponding values given by equations (6) and (10), since security losses would have occurred in a few instances.

Does the CCMT Provide Effective Risk Transfer?

Arguments have been put forward that credit card master trusts are *not* effective risk transfer mechanisms since issuers must continuously fund new receivables, even if their credit performance deteriorates, thus undoing the original intent of securitization. But this argument ignores the CCMT structure whereby deterioration caused by high defaults or reductions in net yield triggers early amortization.

What would happen under the feared scenario is that the trust would immediately amortize, and would no longer be allowed to purchase newly minted but fiendish receivables. The bank would have to fund the receivables on-balance sheet or cease funding, effectively exiting the business for the time being by setting the credit limit of each obligor in a portfolio to its current balance, with conceivably horrendous business consequences. The former case would be a business decision to fund but without affecting the securitized investor's risk profile. Although it is a fact that most banks would opt for the first solution, it is not a *requirement* of securitization.

Once a loan is originated, the underlying credit risk never disappears but is simply shifted from one class of investors to another. By shifting the risk of its current receivable exposure from one class of investors to another using structuring, the bank has indeed achieved its objective.

8.5 THE ORIGIN OF THE SYNTHETIC MARKET

The following section is not meant as a comprehensive review of the synthetic market, but rather an attempt to contextualize the emergence of synthetic structured securities and credit derivatives (CDS). Within a few short years, these sectors reached a level of maturity, complexity, and completeness (see figure 8.8) difficult to comprehend without a proper historical perspective. Before delving into the algebra underlying the pricing of credit derivatives, it is a good idea to step back and take stock of how they came to be. Although the underlying idea is simple, it is obfuscated by technical jargon and pricing methods with a lot of math but very little financial insight.

Why do Banks Enter Into Such Transactions?

The rationale underlying the credit derivative market is arbitrage, specifically regulatory arbitrage. This is not surprising since most of Wall Street works on that basis. For example, if 8% is the amount of capital required from a financial institution to hold a certain kind of risky loan or financial asset on its balance sheet, and the securitization of the same asset as part of a pool lowers the requirement to 6%, then it is clear that the extra 2% can be redeployed elsewhere, and that the institution's effective leverage is thereby increased significantly. In the limit, one could conceive of a bank as a mere originator and servicer of assets that have all been securitized. Therefore, the impact of securitization on the bank's stock price is very beneficial and well-worth the heavy transaction costs it may have to pay to implement its securitization program.

One is, of course, tempted to ask why looking at the same assets from another point of view, namely that of the rating agencies, can accomplish such magic. The answer is that U.S. banking regulations are old fashioned and do not recognize the obvious applicability of portfolio risk measurement methods, not to mention other inefficiencies that were built into the process over the years. This is not an indictment of the regulators, for they too recognized that change was sorely needed.

So it came to be that an entire market was created as a rational response to credit traditionalism. Although the Basel II proposals are an attempt to modernize the credit risk measurement process, the intensively political nature of the negotiation process left many irrationalities intact and in some cases produced new ones. The obvious solution, i.e. to rationalize banking regulation and to develop an advanced, internal ratings capability in-house that can also monitor and appraise the work of the rating agencies, is unlikely to happen any time soon.

The Beginning of the Story: The Corporate Bank Loan Market

The early phase of the U.S. ABS markets consisted exclusively of cash transactions whereby a legal sale of assets took place. The buyer was the special purpose vehicle (SPV), which then became the issuer of record thereby replacing the corporation that had originated the assets. This true sale had to be backed up by a legal opinion to that effect in addition to a separate non-consolidation opinion of counsel, although both opinions were usually delivered as one document. In many cases, local laws forced the lender to notify the borrower that his loan was going to be sold to someone else. Of course, from the borrower's standpoint, this sale was a complete non-event since his obligation had not changed at all. However, suspicious borrowers might interpret the sale as the beginning of a harsher collection regime, and who knows what else. In some rare cases, laws actually prevented transactions from going ahead without the prior approval of the borrower.

In the consumer sector, the sale of assets was considered harmless, a mere administrative convenience. Consumers had very little say in the matter, since consumer protection laws are not aimed at this type of operation but more at usury and related issues. By contrast, in the commercial sector the relative power of a single borrower is much greater, and the amounts involved much larger.

For instance, a $100 million syndicated loan is effectively linked to many financial institutions in addition to the lead syndicate manager. Thus if one of the syndicate members attempted to securitize its exposures, and the vast majority of them happened to be pieces of individual syndicates, the bankruptcy of the lead-manager was also a potential problem because of the cash flow mechanics associated with the loan repayments.

In practice, corporate borrowers did not know the identity of syndicate members because the lead-manager was jealously guarding its customers lest another bank steal a march on them. As a result, corporate loan payments were made only to the lead-manager who would then remit pro rata cash flow allocations to all syndicate members. Therefore, the cash flows received and thus securitized by the target bank were effectively funneled through another bank's balance sheet and could be seized or held back should the latter go bankrupt. In such cases, special regulatory dispensations had to be given to the securitizing bank to allow the deal to go forward.

The Rationale Underlying the First Synthetic CDO Transaction

Given the relative power of financial institutions in the U. S., the traditionally open nature of the American body politic, and the attractiveness of securitization from multiple standpoints, these inconvenient legal impediments were quickly overcome and the required dispensations were duly granted. In fact, most corporate documentation now includes clauses that enable the lender to sell the loan without notification as long as the terms remain unchanged. It is understood that the same also applies to consumer loans.

Unfortunately, such accommodations were not so easily reached in other jurisdictions, specifically Europe, where bank secrecy laws are notoriously effective. Switzerland is not the only country where banking is highly sensitive. Most Western European countries have much stricter confidentiality requirements than their American counterparts. Even U.S. branches of European financial institutions tend to conduct business much more secretively than domestic banks. Whereas in the U.S. no one would bat an eye if it were revealed that IBM and Citibank had a credit relationship, in Europe even major corporations fear that the names of their bankers will become public.

The consequences for securitization are severe. To illustrate, suppose that a global Swiss institution wished to securitize its cross-border exposures, where cross-border means the U.S. and Europe, and achieve capital relief in the way already indicated. In general, it will run into a brick wall when attempting to securitize its commercial European loans because the borrowers will simply refuse to give their consent, and the deal will collapse even if the "buyer" of the loan is none other than a brain-dead company. A way had to be found to avoid having to require permission from borrowers to sell their loan. The solution was to sell only the risk associated with the exposure without selling the exposure itself, thereby raising the abstraction one more level and simultaneously achieving the sought-after regulatory capital relief. This metaphysical separation of the risk of the asset from ownership of the asset itself is therefore the origin of the synthetic CDO market.

The first transactions done in this way were inefficient and costly, but the expense was still worth it because so much inefficiency lay at the heart of bank capital rules. Nevertheless, these transactions were the first step on the road to creating today's synthetic markets. Structured securities issued via these transactions had to be given a special name to indicate their special cash flow properties. The name chosen was the "credit linked note" or CLN.

Thus, the creation of the CLN was the first and most original step on the road to a bona fide credit derivative, and for this reason, we need to dig a little deeper into the CLN structure.

8.6 CREDIT LINKED NOTES

The first step in the creation of a CLN transaction is the identification of a reference pool whose principal amount is to be insured against loss from so-called *credit defaults*.[8] Instead of being sold to the SPV, the assets are now simply being *referenced* in order to ascertain whether any one of them has experienced a default during the life of the transaction according to a specific definition, of which three are considered most important: bankruptcy, failure to pay and restructuring.

In addition to the premium owed by one party to the other, the definition of the credit event has been a major cause of disagreement in the credit derivatives industry. Therefore, the standardization of the default definition was the major contribution to the credit derivatives market made by the International Swap Dealers Association (ISDA). It should be noted that the ISDA definitions of default historically have been more restrictive than U.S. rating-agency definitions, which was an impediment to the development of pricing in the market at the outset, since bond ratings are the primary index of corporate bond default propensity referenced by all market players. However, the 2003 ISDA definitions for credit default swaps went a long way toward convergence.

The main idea underlying the CLN-structure was the SPV-bound segregation of risk-free assets in the same dollar amount as those in the reference pool. These assets were then placed inside a SPV and were the basis of the principal protection to the holders of the risky assets. In all cases, the chosen risk-free assets were United States Treasury bonds.

The next step was to issue CLNs backed by the Treasuries in the SPV across the entire capital structure, but with the proviso that they would be liquidated should one or more of the reference assets default over the life of the deal in order to pay for any shortfalls in recoveries on such defaulted asset. In line with convention, any shortfall in principal amount was to be first allocated to the last tranche in the capital structure, then to the one above it, and so forth. The amortization period at the end of the transaction was theoretically made possible by the wholesale liquidation of the Treasuries inside the SPV, although in most cases another defeasance mechanism was used to accomplish the same effect.

From a pricing standpoint, it is logical that Treasuries will earn a relatively low return in comparison to the average yield on the CLN issued out of the SPV. Why else would anyone require a higher return, if not as compensation for the risk of default?

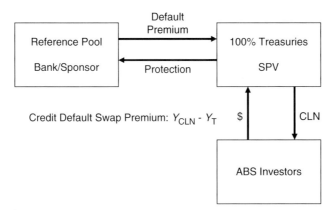

FIGURE 8.10
Basic CLN structure.

Consistent with this logic, the spread between the Treasury yield and the average CLN coupon must represent the fair market value of the risk taken by CLN investors, and therefore, must equal the "insurance" premium the trust needs to collect from the protection buyer. In other words, the bank securitizing its assets under this structure needs to make an annualized but periodic payment equal to the difference between trust assets and CLN requirements. This premium has become the CDS spread for any single-name exposure or, equivalently, the spread on a basket of CDS contracts with respect to a pool of reference obligations.

The steps are summarized in figure 8.10. We have used the labels Y_{CLN} and Y_T to refer to the average yield on the CLNs and the average Treasury yield, respectively.

This transformation is the first and the most important one in order to achieve an understanding of the CDS market. All further synthetic developments have been keyed off the elements of this stage: reliance on agency credit ratings, the basis of the default swap premium, the bypassing of the insurance paradigm, the involvement of ISDA, and the reference pool concept. Each element was pioneered in, and essential to, the CLN structure. Only later were the elements refined and codified into what we now call the credit derivatives market. Seen in this light, the CLN structure represents a major leap forward in achieving a better financial understanding of risk than ever before.

The Second Stage: Partial Funding

It only took a few CLN transactions (one wonders why it even took a single one) for investment bankers to begin to realize that such deals were exceedingly expensive given that the only goal achieved thereby was regulatory arbitrage, which is not, or at least should not be, a core activity of a financial institution.

But, why immobilize such a large amount of Treasury bonds for such a long time? Soon, lawyers and accountants were hard at work trying to find a way to reduce the costs of these transactions. It was not long before someone realized that most of the Treasuries were simply idle and that the vast majority of the reference obligations would never default anyway. In keeping away from the insurance paradigm, bankers had in fact strayed too far into left field and forgotten the basic structure of an insurance company, which is in fact the heart of its profitability: instead of funding the structure 100% with Treasuries, they could accomplish the same objective by operating the way insurers do, i.e. contribute sufficient equity cushion to guarantee the same result in terms of risk and do the rest with leverage.

A BOTE analysis, you may recall, dictates an available credit enhancement approximately five times greater than expected loss for the associated security to be rated **AAA**. If the assets in the reference pool are all investment-grade, the cumulative expected loss might be 2.5% of the pool. Hence, that 12.5% [5 × 2.5%] is apparently sufficient to achieve the AAA-rating objective. Consequently, a relatively small amount of equity capital partitioned across several rated tranches is all that is required to ensure that the unfunded amount would also be rated **AAA** if funded.

But, regulators still required dollar-for-dollar coverage of the reference pool if 100% capital relief was to be achieved. This was the original CLN structure. As a result, the unfunded portion of this new type of CLN demanded some form of insurance coverage should the default experience inside the reference pool move dramatically away from its statistical norm. Remember that the number of discrete assets in a CDO (100+) is nowhere near as large as what one normally sees in a plain-vanilla ABS pool (1,000+). The average synthetic transaction is much more sensitive to a single default event in the reference pool than any cash ABS transaction.

Despite their efforts to make the credit derivatives market a bank-oriented insurance market, the second stage of the credit derivatives market saw insurance companies play a significant role, by offering coverage above the funded debt layers (12.5% in the example above).

Insurance of liabilities had been the exclusive domain of mono line insurance companies, but in this case, many multi-line firms entered the game. The basic strategy of mono line insurers had always been to provide coverage at the investment-grade layer (Baa), their *attachment point*, or above. In the case of the CLN, they attached *above* the **AAA** level, the so-called "super-**AAA**", a key feature of the partially funded synthetic CDO. Since the mono line is ostensibly taking **AAA** risk, premium pricing with respect to the super-**AAA** tranche is very attractive indeed, facilitating unprecedented levels of transaction efficiency. This is shown schematically in figure 8.11.

Partially funded structures made much more sense in Europe than in the U.S., where cash transactions are still the norm. As a result, the synthetic CDO market grew much faster on the other side of the Atlantic. For reasons of regulatory convenience, the bulk of the issuance was centered in places like London and Dublin, which benefited from U.S.-style Anglo-Saxon legal regimes. Soon, European banks were able to take advantage of this technology to hedge their entire book. Not only that: the synthetic structure was cheaper than the cash structure since no true sale was necessary, hence, no true sale opinion. These elements were not wasted on the cost-conscious Europeans, and the market exploded.

However, there is relatively little flexibility in the unadulterated concept of a synthetic CDO, since a reference pool has to be available or located somewhere, and

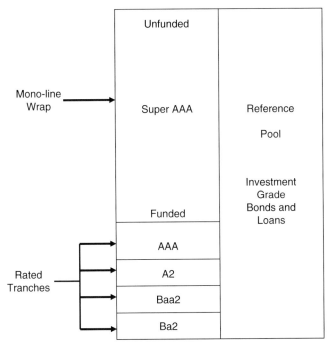

FIGURE 8.11
Partially funded CDO structure.

in many cases, only a single exposure needed to be hedged, which was impossible under the pooling paradigm, not to mention the fact that securitizing institutions had to accumulate a pool of sufficient diversification to benefit from the benevolence of rating agencies and their diversification alchemy. A way forward had to be found. Of course, it was.

The Third Stage: The Single Name CDS and Basket Trades

It was not long before London (mainly) and New York traders figured out that a lucrative business lay in offering individual CDS contracts to corporate customers and financial institutions that had particular needs but lacked a sufficient volume to warrant a fully fledged synthetic CDO.

By 2003, large investment banks had begun providing these services using their own balance sheet and funding ability. They found many willing protection buyers but few sellers. Most of the trading volume originated in the need to remove the risk of the exposure from the protection buyer's balance sheet. The profitability of the trade was based, not on the actual default risk of the associated exposure (an asset-side consideration) but rather its imputed cost with in the alternative funding structure (a liability-side consideration), itself an artifact of the regulatory capital regime. As a result, interesting spreads could be offered to protection sellers.

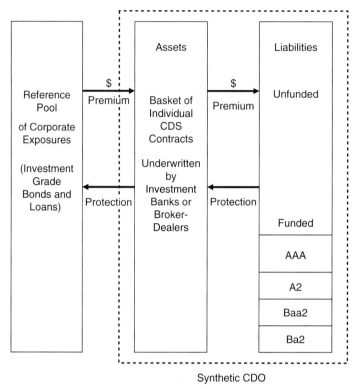

FIGURE 8.12
The CDS basket.

Institutional appetite for this product was practically unlimited, save for the fact that investment banks had limited capital and soon found they were unable to continue offering the single-name CDS products due to insufficient reserves. The solution was obvious: transfer the bank's credit derivative exposure to single names by pooling baskets of such trades into a single structure and sell structured notes that would effectively release their own, scarce capital. This technique resulted in the *basket trades* profiled in figure 8.12.

Under this third structure, instead of requiring a default premium by the bank or financial institution needing capital relief, a pool of individual CDS contracts, each yielding a periodic premium depending on its own reference obligation, constitutes the assets of a novel synthetic CDO. The liabilities are as before, namely a partially funded structure consisting of a few rated tranches across the entire investment spectrum from sub-investment-grade up to AAA. The rest of the capital structure remains unfunded.

Hence, the seller in this case is the investment bank that owns the CDS contracts before consummating the transaction. The structure earns income via the individual premia collected by the protection seller on each CDS contract. Under the same argument that presumably makes an insurance company profitable, i.e., diversification, the subsequent pooling of the CDS contracts into a single structured vehicle should generate arbitrage profits that would be the property of the residual owner, which in this case would be the investment bank.

The notes are used to collateralize the default risk of the reference pool up to the **AAA** rating level and can be liquidated to refund the original lenders or investors should any reference asset experience a credit event. As a corollary, immediately after consummating the deal, the investment bank's balance sheet is now improved, and the bank is free to enter into yet another set of CDS contracts, after which another synthetic CDO will be executed. Note also that the CDS spread or premium income earned by the asset pool is what pays the excess interest on the funded portion of the synthetic CDO. On a monthly basis, if not retained inside the capital structure, any excess CDS premium collections simply escape back to the seller or residual holder.

This structure is more flexible than the first two because the reference obligations can be tailor-made and do not have to represent any physical loan or bond on someone's balance sheet. It is this structural concept that gave rise to Morgan-Stanley's I-TRAXX traded index now owned by Dow Jones & Co, and to the Markit indices.

8.7 CLOSING REMARKS ON THE SYNTHETIC MARKET

The following comments on the synthetic market were written in early 2007 as lecture notes. Much of what they say has already transpired. We decided to include them here as an object lesson for the next credit bubble.

As interesting as this all sounds, and the large spreads earned by participating investment banks notwithstanding, the net impact of the explosive growth of the credit derivatives market over the last few years has been to partition and disseminate credit risk across the capital markets in an uncontrolled manner, with the average regulator at a loss to find it. It is a mathematical theorem that credit risk cannot disappear, but merely be redistributed or reallocated to different parties.

Even though many financial institutions are now claiming to be credit-risk free as a result of having hedged out all of their former credit exposures, the truth is that the same amount of risk as before remains throughout the U.S. financial system, except that now it is virtually impossible for anyone to disentangle the credit mess created by the CDS market. Many financial institutions have purchased liability tranches of synthetic CDOs on the back end, in essence reacquiring credit risk they thought they had unloaded just a few months ago.

How this will all turn out is a matter of pure speculation today, since most protection sellers are largely unprepared for the eventuality of a credit event and liquidity in most CDS tranches is spotty at best. The most likely credit events exist with respect to exposures where no CDS is being offered, and this means that the CDS market provides very little actual benefit to the buyer of protection, despite what regulators might have to say about the matter. The response to the GM debacle that took place in 2006 plainly showed that actual credit events are not seriously contemplated by most CDS market players. In the end, market participants discover their real credit exposure only after the occurrence of actual credit events, and it is a virtual certainty that most of them were unaware that they had these exposures.

In closing, we should like to point out that Regulation AB, which deals primarily with asset-backed securities, specifically excludes most credit derivatives from the definition of a structured security unless the reference pool is part of the same transaction. In general, that is not the case for the credit derivatives market. Only plain-vanilla swaps and similar contracts remain as eligible features of eligible structured transactions. As a result, the next phase of the CDS market is liable to be by far the most exciting.

END-OF-CHAPTER QUESTIONS

1. What do the abbreviations of the revolving transactions in structured finance stand for? What is their profile of risk/return? What is their *raison d'être*?

2. What is prefunding? Is it a form of "revolving?" What is the economic purpose of prefunding?

3. Describe the typology, organization, and capital resources of the Credit Card Master Trust (CCMT). To what degree does it resemble other structured vehicles, and in which respects is it unique?

4. What are the key drivers of risk in credit cards? What are the key structural protections of the CCMT?

5. Table 8.2 shows the terms of credit cards offered in a given market. Choose one card type (1–28) and discuss the CCMT structure you would build around it:

6. Describe the typology, organization, and capital resources of Collateralized Debt Obligations (CDOs). To what degree does a CDO resemble other structured vehicles, and in which respects is it unique?

7. Contrast the differences in the conventions of measuring and managing the risks of ABSs and CDOs.

8. Ratings have been poor predictors of performance of CDOs, ever since they were first invented. Identify some of the factors that contribute to a basis risk between the rating and the actual risk.

9. What is a trigger? Discuss the differences in how triggers are crafted for cash flow and market value CDOs. Why do CDO structures tend to make broader use of triggers, generally, than ABS and RMBS?

10. Describe the typology, organization, and capital resources of synthetic securitizations. What is their economic rationale?

11. Contrast the principal write-down process for fully funded CLNs, described in section 8.5, with the principal amortization process in cash structured transactions described in chapter 7. What does the difference between the two processes (if any) signify?

TABLE 8.2

Terms of credit cards on offer

	INTEREST RATE P.A.	INTEREST FREE	BALANCE TRANSFER	ANNUAL FEE
1	19.99%	55 days	6.99%	$95
2	19.99%	55 days	6.99%	$49
3	19.99%	55 days	6.99%	$395
4	12.99%	55 days	0%	$58
5	19.99%	44 days	7.99%	$30
6	19.99%	55 days	7.99%	$87
7	20.74%	44 days	0%	$95
8	20.74%	55 days	0%	$150
9	11.99%	55 days	0%	$49
10	19.89%	55 days	2.90%	$79
11	12.49%	55 days	0%	$65
12	20.74%	55 days	2.90%	$69
13	20.74%	55 days	2.90%	$119
14	20.74%	55 days	4.90%	$150
15	13.24%	55 days	5.99%	$48
16	19.99%	55 days	5.99%	$24
17	20.74%	55 days	5.99%	$59
18	20.74%	55 days	5.99%	$114
19	20.74%	55 days	5.99%	$200
20	13.99%	55 days	0%	$0 year 1, then $39
21	20.49%	55 days	6.99%	$195
22	20.49%	55 days	6.99%	$395
23	11.89%	55 days	0%	$55
24	12.99%	55 days		$69
25	18.75%		0%	$0
26	14.25%	55 days	0%	$79
27	14.25%	55 days	0%	$89
28	18.99%	55 days	0%	$49

12. Are the ramp-up and revolving period risks associated with non-PVA structures fully addressed by the credit enhancement of structures like nonamortizing CDOs, ABCP conduits and SIVs? How would you answer this question?

9

Monte Carlo Simulation

9.1 WELCOME TO INTERMEDIATE STRUCTURED FINANCE

As discussed in chapter 5, there are competing philosophies on the "correct" method of valuing structured securities, differences that tend to be played out along the dimensions of time, portfolio probability, and granularity. Arguments for or against sensitivity in the treatment of these dimensions tend to cluster around competing "goods" of simplicity versus precision, and fast versus slow. Simple approaches invite more democracy in the rating committee process, demand less management specialization, and reach more market participants; however, some truth is inevitably lost in the process of simplification. Fast means more deals out of the door, and therefore increased income velocity, but places more analytical burden on the secondary market, which may not have the requisite training or information needed to absorb the extra burden; and the failure of the secondary market may give rise to a looming business risk.

As must be abundantly clear, the authors are firm believers in doing the structuring and valuation work with as much up-front technical precision as possible. This means choosing in favor of a valuation framework that is sensitive to time, to portfolio statistics, to statistical sub-structures and, a dimension that currently does not receive sufficient attention, to macro-economic processes outside the microstructure of risk.

Regardless of whether you choose a framework that reflects or suppresses information, structuring and valuation work moves you into the realm of nonlinearity: a world where convoluted liability structures and trade-offs between defaults, prepayments and different costs of carry on securities of different risk grades can turn your intuition upside down. Making risks cheaper can, up to a point, make them safer, while safety in the form of a higher risk premium, paradoxically, can make them riskier. The reason why we do not end the book with chapter 7 is precisely because the unintended consequences of static, scenario-driven structuring can be surprising and potentially destructive.

9.2 MONTE CARLO SIMULATION

Once a cash flow model has been built to express the interest and principal allocations of available funds to each class of securities within the given structure, there remains the relatively straightforward task of assigning credit ratings to them. In the modeled transaction (parameters specified in chapter 7, question 8), these are the Class A and Class B tranches. The combination of the yield curve, credit spreads and average life allows analysts to determine simultaneously the interest rate, or alternatively the price, of the securities as well as their credit rating.

Note that finding a price is clearly a matter of negotiation between buyers and sellers, despite what one might believe concerning the efficiency of capital markets. Thus, although the type of modeling reviewed in this chapter is a fundamental and critical component of the pricing process, it can only reduce the uncertainty band to a reasonable level subject to final negotiation between both sides. Even in a field as mundane as the Treasury market, small differences will exist between the offer and the bid prices of securities. In the case of ABS, i.e. an area with much more variability in cash flows than Treasuries, these differences may be sizable.

9.3 THE MEASURE OF PERFORMANCE IN ABS

As we have mentioned many times before, ABS are issued by special purpose entities that are specifically designed to be bankruptcy-remote, in the sense that temporary insolvency when the principal balance of the liabilities exceeds that of the assets does not cause a credit event per se, and can be corrected in future collection periods with cash flows stemming from the securitized assets. In cases of normal, bankruptcy-prone corporations, insolvency would quickly lead to an actual bankruptcy, since most secured lenders would simply refuse to extend credit to an insolvent entity.

As a result of this legal design improvement, the *default rate* of asset-backed bonds is zero by definition. Consequently, it is only permissible to express the creditworthiness of asset-backed securities in terms of the trust's ability to satisfy the promised yield to bondholders. Thus, ABS are assessed based on the difference between the promised yield, i.e., the nominal coupon, and the yield-to-maturity, computed from the set of cash flows allocated to an ABS security over the life of the transaction. This *reduction of yield* on a class of issued bonds then becomes the central focus of the credit analysis and of the associated Monte Carlo simulation.

The idea underlying a Monte Carlo simulation in structured finance is the exploration of the loss distribution associated with the assets in the pool. Once that distribution is known or assumed, the cash flow universe expected to arise from it can be computed in a straightforward manner owing to the cash flow model built for this purpose, i.e., one that reproduces fairly accurately the dynamics of credit losses *within a single realization* of the pool. Once this model is available, the class-wise reduction of yield associated with each asset-side cash flow stream can be calculated.

In general, no analyst will ever be handed a credit loss distribution on a platter from either theoretical or empirical considerations, and it will thus have to be synthesized or estimated using a combination of intuition and experience. Here, the analyst with 20 years of experience has, or should have, a better "intuition" than one with only two years of experience, although someone with five years of experience will probably do as well as someone with 20.

No theory of what a credit loss distribution ought to be is currently available, although the range of possibilities is clearly not infinite. This is because loss distributions are restricted in the shape they can have. These constraints, along with some basic commonsense and as much loss data as can be obtained, are an analyst's basic weapons in the quest for a reasonable credit loss distribution. How one arrives at such credit loss distributions is the topic of the next section.

9.4 CREDIT LOSS DISTRIBUTION ISSUES

Consider figure 9.1 showing the credit loss distribution for an arbitrary pool of assets.

This particular distribution is normal although only the range (0,8) is shown in figure 9.1. Note that there is no a priori reason why this should be the case. In fact, many people use lognormal or other, more exotic distributions as measures of credit losses. The lognormal distribution has a special epistemological status in finance because it is the distribution of choice in market risk studies. It came to the fore when Case Sprenkle and Fischer Black developed models of option pricing in the early 1960s and 1970s, respectively.

However, there is no reason why credit risk should be lognormally distributed. Any distribution will do, as long as it satisfies some basic properties. For one, the maximum credit loss achievable is obviously 100% since one cannot lose more than one's original investment. Thus, an appropriate credit loss distribution should terminate at 100% and not continue indefinitely as the lognormal distribution and others do. (However, this obvious fact has never seemed to deter credit analysts from using it.) The gamma distribution is yet another candidate-distribution and is often used in the insurance industry when looking at the distribution of claims, the term used in that industry to indicate losses.

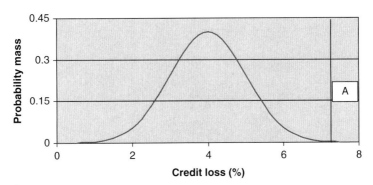

FIGURE 9.1
Credit loss probability distribution.

Choosing a Credit Loss Distribution

As just indicated, credit loss distributions have special properties that reduce the range of possibilities. In addition to the 100% cap, they are usually assumed to lie exclusively on the positive x-axis, i.e., never to extend below zero. However, it is theoretically possible, albeit quite rare, for credit losses to be negative. The apparently sine qua non distributional restriction to *positive* credit loss values touted by most credit analysts in the market is actually bogus and stems from a profound misunderstanding of the nature of credit risk.

There are many circumstances under which a credit loss may be negative. A common one is a situation in which a lender holds collateral as security for a loan that then defaults, allowing the lender to foreclose on the collateral and collect recovery proceeds that exceed the outstanding balance of the loan plus accrued interest. A loan secured by an automobile where the obligor defaults after the positive equity point on the depreciation curve, as illustrated in figure 6.7, would be another such situation. In the U.S., consumer protection laws normally prevent lenders from collecting more than the remaining balance plus accrued interest, thereby preventing a "credit profit" on defaulted loans. However, this may not be the case in non-U.S. markets. It is thus quite possible, although still unlikely, for a lender to benefit from a default and, therefore, for the credit loss distribution to be nonzero for negative values of losses.

To choose a loss distribution, it is helpful to consider the usual suspects in the field and look at their domain of definition. We present four typical choices in table 9.1.

The beta distribution is defined over the required interval, i.e., from 0 to 100%, although it may not have the tail characteristics one might wish around larger values of x. On the other hand, the normal distribution is defined over the entire real axis, and does not satisfy the basic requirement $f(x) \equiv 0$, $x \geq 1$. In practice, the discussion of whether or not $f(x)$ can be nonzero for negative values of its argument is largely academic since most reasonable choices of $f(x)$, normal or not, will leave essentially zero probability mass either below 0 or above 100%. Thus, except in very special circumstances, all of the above distributions are possible candidates for the credit loss distribution of an asset pool.

It will often happen that the chosen distribution will contain parameters that do not map directly to the mean and standard deviation which you will either be given

TABLE 9.1

Properties of common statistical distributions

CREDIT LOSS PROBABILITY DISTRIBUTION FUNCTION $f(x)$	DOMAIN OF x
Normal	$(-\infty, +\infty)$
Lognormal	$(0, +\infty)$
Gamma	$(0, +\infty)$
Beta	$(0, 1)$

or simply assume. In such cases, it will be incumbent upon you to find or work out the values of the particular distribution's parameters that produce the required mean and standard deviation.

For example, assume you have chosen a *beta* distribution as the best representation of the likely range of credit losses to be expected from the pool under consideration. In that case, the challenge would be to find the value of the two beta-distribution parameters α and β required to yield the chosen mean μ and standard deviation σ. To do this, you would simply make use of the following relationships between the beta-distribution parameters and the required results:

$$\mu = \frac{\alpha}{\alpha + \beta}$$

$$\sigma = \sqrt{\frac{\alpha\beta}{(\alpha+\beta)^2(1+\alpha+\beta)}}$$

There are many ways to approach this issue, the most difficult of which is to set up a nonlinear optimization problem and solve it for α and β, given μ and σ. In practice, very little will be gained by doing this and much time will be wasted writing and debugging a code of this sort. Therefore, we recommend a simple trial and error approach to finding these values. In the worst case, you would have learned quite a bit about the behavior of the beta distribution with respect to its parameters.

The Lognormal Distribution

A special comment should be made with respect to the implementation of the lognormal distribution in Excel. For whatever reason, Microsoft requires the input to a *lognormal* random selection statement to be the mean and the standard deviation of the associated *normal* distribution. Remember that if $\ln(x)$ is normally distributed with a mean of μ and standard deviation of σ, then x itself will be lognormally distributed with mean m and standard deviation s. The relationship between the parameters of both distributions is as follows:

$$\mu = \ln\left[\frac{m}{\sqrt{1+\left(\frac{s}{m}\right)^2}}\right]$$

$$\sigma = \sqrt{\ln\left[1+\left(\frac{s}{m}\right)^2\right]}$$

Should you opt for the lognormal distribution, you would be given the values of m and s, and would use the above formulas to convert these given values to the equivalent μ and σ for use inside your Excel formulas. A more sophisticated implementation of the lognormal distribution, using the Box–Muller transformation, is available but lies beyond the scope of this chapter.

The Inverse Distribution Function Method

Selecting random numbers from specified probability distributions is one of the most fundamental operations of statistical analysis. The easiest way to accomplish this is via the Inverse Distribution Function Method (IDFM) described below.

In all instances, the goal will be to select a random sample reflecting a given probability density distribution $f(x)$ defined over the interval $[a, b]$. To do this, remember that the associated cumulative distribution function $F(x)$ is defined by:

$$F(x) = \int_a^x f(y)\,dy \tag{1}$$

By definition we have $F(a) = 0$ and, since $f(x)$ is a probability density function, $F(b) = 1$, i.e., the cumulative distribution function spans the entire range of $f(x)$ over its domain $[0, 1]$. This is shown in figure 9.2.

By reference to equation (1), the inverse of the distribution function $F(x)$ corresponds to the probability mass $f(x)$ which we seek to emulate. Therefore, by choosing a deviate y from a *uniform* distribution on the closed interval $[0, 1]$ and setting $F^{-1}(y) = x$, the resulting x would be distributed as $f(x)$. Thus, the random sampling of *any* distribution comes down to sampling from a uniform probability density function.

For instance, if one wanted to draw a random number x from a *normal* distribution with mean μ and standard deviation σ using Microsoft Excel functions, one would enter the following formula in a spreadsheet, assuming one had first drawn a random

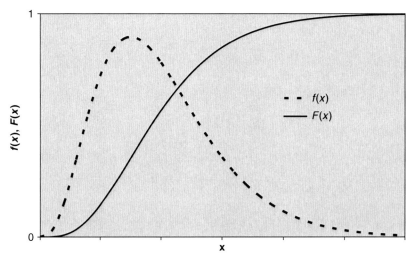

FIGURE 9.2
Inverse distribution function method (IDFM) illustrated.

number, say y, from a uniform probability distribution.

$$x = NORMINV(y, \mu, \sigma)$$

By repeating this operation N times, you would have a sample of N random numbers from the given normal probability distribution assuming the numbers y were *truly* uniformly distributed. Although this may appear trivial via the use of the "Rand" function in Excel, further investigation reveals that sample outputs from Rand are far from uniform.

There will be times when Excel will not have a built-in inverse function to make things easier for you. For example, assume you are given a normalized loss distribution looking very much like the default loss curve $F(t)$[1] from chapter 6 and that you want to draw random numbers from the associated marginal, or density function $f(t)$. To do this, simply set:

$$y \equiv F(t) = \frac{a}{1 + e^{-b(t-t_0)}}$$

To select a *random deviate* from this function, which is not in found in the Excel package, you would have to invert it yourself, leading to:

$$t = t_0 - \frac{\ln(\frac{a}{y} - 1)}{b}$$

By repeatedly drawing y values from a uniform distribution, you would obtain a random sample from the desired distribution. Obviously, you can do this for any given probability density function $f(t)$. Sometimes, you will not be able to invert the given $F(t)$ analytically as we have done with the pseudo loss curve above. In such cases, it will be necessary to find the required inverse function using a numerical root-locus procedure.

9.5 THE STRUCTURED FINANCE CREDIT SCALE

As mentioned above, structured ratings are measures of credit losses that encompass severity (how much do I lose?) as well as frequency (how often do I lose?) via the yield concept. The performance measure is thus the average reduction of yield that investors would experience if credit losses behaved according to the chosen distribution. The average so obtained is then mapped to a letter-grade rating, which is how structured credit ratings are normally communicated to investors. These are the familiar Aaa, Aa1, etc. known to corporate finance analysts, although their meaning is clearly different in structured finance. Table 9.2 shows the standard credit scale in structured finance. Note that scale intervals are logarithmic, not linear.

Interpreting the table, a Aa rating would correspond to an average reduction of yield of about one basis point, while securities bearing A ratings would be associated with average yield reductions of ca. 10 basis points, still an exceedingly small number when one considers that the security yields themselves are in the hundreds

TABLE 9.2

The structured finance rating scale

LETTER GRADE	AVERAGE DIRR (BPS)
Aaa	0.06
Aa1	0.67
Aa2	1.3
Aa3	2.7
A1	5.2
A2	8.9
A3	13
Baa1	19
Baa2	27
Baa3	46
Ba1	72
Ba2	106
Ba3	143
B1	183
B2	231
B3	311
Caa	2,500
Ca	10,000

of basis points. In chapter 13, we describe how to assemble these concepts to assign credit ratings to ABS bonds.

9.6 MONTE CARLO SIMULATION

To compute the average reduction of yield on an ABS bond, we make use of the IDFM random number selection method reviewed above to generate multiple scenarios and hence, credit loss values, from the chosen loss distribution. In each case, the reduction of yield on each class of securities, if any, is computed using a cash flow model. This reduction of yield ($DIRR$) is easily computed from:

$$DIRR \equiv \text{reduction of yield} = [\text{promised yield} - \text{actual yield}]$$

Since the minimum yield attainable is -100%, the maximum reduction of yield $DIRR_{max}$ is:

$$DIRR_{max} = 10,000 + \text{promised yield}$$

For example, in a typical case where the promised yield is 9% (Class B of the cash flow model, chapter 7, question 8), the maximum reduction of yield would be 10,000 + 900 = 10,900 basis points. One hopes this never happens!

The yield-to-maturity (*IRR*) can be calculated using the Excel internal rate of return formula:

$$IRR = 12 \; IRR(\text{cash flows}, E[IRR_{mo}])$$

The reason why multiplication by 12 is required is that yields are normally quoted on a *yearly* basis. Since the output from Excel will be a *monthly* yield, it needs to be annualized. As always, the first cash flow will be (–initial balance), i.e., the size of the initial investment. Thereafter, each monthly cash flow is simply equal to the *sum of interest and principal paid amounts*. For instance, the *monthly* Class A cash flow $F_A(t)$ becomes:

$$F_A(t) = I_{AP}(t) + P_{AP}(t)$$

Note that the quantities on the right of the equal sign have already been computed in the cash flow model from chapter 7. Regardless of when the various interest and principal amounts are received, and regardless of the structure (pro rata, sequential, TAC, etc.), the actual yield will always equal the promised yield as long as sufficient cash is received by the end of the transaction, i.e., the maturity T.

The way to think of the meaning of credit ratings is as follows: suppose the yield *promised* to Class B investors is 9.00% and the average *realized* yield is 8.5%. This means that a Class B investor could expect to suffer a 50 bps yield shortfall on average if he or she held a well-diversified portfolio of such bonds. As can be readily seen from the rating table, in the context of a structured this is a large shortfall that would merit a *non-investment grade* rating. Note also that the *average* yield reduction can be somewhat misleading, since in most cases the yield reduction is zero except in rare cases where it may be quite large. The use of the first distributional moment (average) is an attempt to summarize the entire distribution of credit losses. One could construct more sophisticated measures that would communicate more information about the yield distribution. Whether fixed income investors have the sophistication to demand such measures is an open question.

To see how the IDFM works, suppose that the vertical line labeled A in figure 9.1 represents the available credit enhancement to Class A bondholders. Thus, a zero yield reduction on Class A will occur every time the randomly selected credit loss falls to the left of line A. Credit enhancement may consist of many components, such as subordination, reserve accounts, insurance policies, etc. Therefore, credit ratings happen at the tail of the credit loss distribution and thus will be highly sensitive to the shape of the distribution for extreme loss values. This is why an appropriate choice for the loss distribution is of such paramount importance. Once the final shape of the credit loss distribution is decided, much of the debate surrounding the proper credit rating to be assigned to the associated asset-backed securities becomes moot and self-evident. As a result, the majority of an analyst's work lies in arriving at a proper and reasonable choice for the latter.

Note also that even for lowly-rated securities, most yield reductions arising from the loss distribution will be small to negligible. To obtain a rating, simply add up the total number of simulated *DIRR* values and compute the arithmetic average.

The following is an excerpt from a Visual Basic code that accomplishes the required tasks. The code is shown in bold type:

'Compute the *normal mean* and *standard deviation* as inputs to the Excel formula
'The Expected_Loss and the Standard_Deviation are given
'

Mu = Log(Expected_Loss / Sqr(1 + (Standard_Deviation / Expected_Loss) ^ 2))
Sigma = Sqr(Log(1 + (Standard_Deviation / Expected_Loss) ^ 2))
'

'Perform the Monte Carlo simulation using the Rnd Excel function '
For I = 1 To 5000
'

'Use the IDFM method
'

Loss_Rate = Application.LogInv(Rnd, Mu, Sigma)
Worksheets("Deal").Range("Actual_Loss").Value = Loss_Rate
Application.Calculate
'

Now, assume that cells Class_A_DIRR and Class_B_DIRR contain the reduction of yield computed by your model for Class A and Class B, respectively.
'Cl_A_Yield_Reduction=Cl_A_Yield_Reduction+10000 * Worksheets("Deal").
Cells(Class_A_DIRR).Value
Cl_B_Yield_Reduction = Cl_B_Yield_Reduction+10000 * Worksheets("Deal").
Cells(Class_B_DIRR).Value

The embedded parameters *Expected_Loss* and *Standard_Deviation* can be read into the IDFM routine from the assumptions section of the cash flow model. On output from this portion of the code, the variables *Cl_A_Yield_Reduction* and *Cl_B_Yield_Reduction* contain the sum of all yield reductions from all MC scenarios from 1 to N. You would divide these two quantities by N to compute the average yield reduction and output the result.

9.7 SURETY BONDS

Surety bonds are insurance policies covering the liability side of the SPE balance sheet, and should not be confused with normal insurance policies insuring assets. For instance, if you are an obligor under a mortgage bond and your house burns down, a standard insurance policy issued in your name will help build a new house but will not pay off your mortgage. A surety bond would be equivalent to a policy that would pay off the remaining balance on your mortgage but leave you homeless.

Surety bonds are used in many transactions to make new debt issues more attractive to investors by adding third-party recourse, which boosts the credit rating.

Effectively, the insured securities acquire the rating of the insurer. Model implementation of the mechanics of protection from a surety bond in the structure would proceed as follows:

Define:

α :   random number deviate from a uniform distribution
EDF :   default rate of the monoline insurer commensurate with its rating
X :   boolean variable

For each Monte Carlo simulation, draw one random deviate α as indicated above and set the value of X as follows:

$$X = \begin{cases} 1 , \ \alpha \ > \ EDF \\ 0, \ \alpha \ < \ EDF \end{cases}$$

Now for $t = T$, increment total payments $P_A(T)$ (and $P_B(T)$ if Class B is also insured) via the following formula:

$$P_A(T) = P_A(T) + X \ [B_A(T) + I_{AS}(T)]$$

Thus, any shortfall of principal or interest will be reimbursed by the monoline insurer at the end of the transaction, making investors whole. In cases where the insurer is seen to default, i.e., when $X = 0$, the additional payments will not be made and the wrap will be modeled as effectively nonexistent. Another way to implement a wrap is to increment shortfalls in total payments to the insured classes on a monthly basis from monoline claim payments instead of merely at maturity. In practice, the difference between these two implementations is negligible since interest shortfalls on Class A are usually zero. Note that, to include cases where the Class A is not wrapped, simply set $EDF = 1$.

Please remember that the assignment of the monoline's credit rating to an insured security is erroneous and, in fact, betrays a misunderstanding of the nature of surety bonds. It is obvious that, in practice, the transaction will be at risk only in cases where the trust estate is insufficient to repay investors while, *at the same time*, the monoline insurance company defaults on its promise to pay. Thus, if it can be shown that a perfect negative correlation exists between the need for enhancement and its availability via the wrap, the net result will be that the ABS securities so insured will be able to achieve a higher rating than that of the insurer. On the other hand, if the opposite is true, i.e., if it is the case that the correlation between the cash needs of the trust and the availability of cash through the surety bond is perfectly positive, then the wrap will be effectively useless and the deal will behave as though it were unwrapped. Therefore, the value of a monoline wrap in terms of credit rating hinges on the correlation function between trust credit performance and the fate of the insurer. As serious debates over correlation usually lead nowhere, it is normally assumed that the rating of the insurer and of the security are in fact the same. Nevertheless, the implicit assumption made in doing so is rarely acknowledged.

The foregoing implementation of the wrap in the model unrealistically assumes that complete independence exists between trust defaults and monoline defaults. It could very well be argued that a positive correlation does exist owing to the credit conditions under which a trust might require help, i.e., that market conditions would be such that many other trusts would find themselves in the same position and would all make claims on their surety provider, thus causing the insurer to default due to insufficient funds. As this book goes to print, such scenarios are being tested.

Last but not least, a surety bond is associated with an expense in the form of a premium based on the outstanding principal balance of the insured liabilities and paid out monthly from collections. The premium is usually modeled by increasing the servicing fee by the absolute value of the premium amount since it normally falls ahead of interest due on Classes A and B. In the ideal case, an intermediate waterfall level may be trivially inserted between servicing fees and Class A interest to account explicitly for the surety premium. In practice, this additional effort is usually wasted since most conceivable scenarios will generate sufficient cash to pay both the servicing fee and the surety premium. In any event, a shortfall in either would quickly spell doom for the deal.

END-OF-CHAPTER QUESTIONS

1. Implement a Monte Carlo simulation engine inside the cash flow model (chapter 7, question 8). Which loss distribution did you select, and why?

2. How did you select the input mean and standard deviation (SD) for the default rate? What happens to the *DIRR* outputs when the SD you choose is very large? or very small?

3. Using the same assumptions as in question 1, model the two-tranche transaction using an IDFM based on (a) the beta; (b) the normal; and (c) the gamma distributions. How do the ratings on the A and B classes compare with in these three treatments?

4. Suppose you defined the rating as a probability of default, not a reduction-of-yield. How would you implement this definition in your cash flow model? What numerical benchmarks would you use as a mapping for the ratings?

5. Suppose you defined the rating as a security-level expected loss. How would you implement this definition in your cash flow model? What numerical benchmarks would you use as a mapping for the ratings?

6. Would you expect security ratings produced under the treatments in questions 1, 4, and 5 above to be identical?

10

Introduction to Prepayment Modeling

Note: Much of this chapter's material was provided by Nenad Ilincic. Both main authors would like to hereby acknowledge his substantial contribution to this textbook.

Introduction

The assets underlying most classes of asset-backed securities (ABS) represent the legally enforceable obligations of borrowers to pay back their debt within a certain time. Commonly, the terms of the contract give borrowers the option to pay it off, in full or in part, ahead of schedule. Exercise of this option is commonly referred to as a prepayment. As you already know, asset-backed securities normally return principal to their holders piecewise even under a zero prepayment scenario. Therefore, it is principal amortization in excess of such baseline scenario that we wish to address here.

The reasons for an early payment may be related to the availability of cheaper financing due to a drop in interest rates available to the borrower, or may represent another obligation of the borrower toward the lien-holder of the asset, for example a mandatory repayment of a loan upon the sale of assets. Therefore, the cash flows issuing from asset pools underlying an ABS bond are unpredictable to a certain degree.

Because uncertainty about the timing of cash flow receipt may be a concern to the owner of the security, it is important to try and understand the cash flow behavior of the pool, even if only on a *conditional* basis, i.e., given assumed scenarios for the value of the variables on which those prepayments are known to depend. Such scenarios may relate to changes in the supply and demand for capital, the state of the economy, the impact of changes in fiscal or monetary policy, or endogenous modifications in the general level of risk. State-dependent cash flow modeling allows the owner of the security not only to probe the fate of his investment with respect to movements in key prepayment determinants, but also to hedge his exposure to such movements.

For purposes of this chapter, we treat all cash flows to an ABS investor as coming from one of three sources: interest on the outstanding balance, scheduled principal amortization, and prepayment. Defaulted balances are categorized as a type of prepayment, the so-called *involuntary* prepayments. Since the loans are secured by the underlying property, we assume the lender sustains no loss of principal, only foreshortened interest income. Finally, we ignore other minor sources of cash, such as late fees.

Calculating the amount of interest received is relatively easy as the product of the amount of principal outstanding and the rate (fixed or variable, according to the loan contract) charged against it. Again, only when principal amortization follows the terms of the contract is it referred to as *scheduled* principal. As a reminder, these formulas were provided in chapter 7 for a fixed-rate level pay loan instrument. Thus, the interesting aspect of modeling the cash flow environment is the uncertain loan prepayment behavior. This is why prepayments are the target of significant modeling efforts aimed at developing statistical models to estimate such behavior.

10.1 THE GOAL OF PREPAYMENT MODELING

The purpose of a prepayment model is to estimate future cash flows from prepayments, primarily (defaults and subsequent recoveries may be attempted secondarily) based on the endogenous characteristics of the loan pool and a forecast of exogenous environmental parameters, like interest rates, said to influence prepayments. A prepayment model does not estimate the probability that a given future environment will occur. This is not necessary, as the most important driver, interest rates, can be readily hedged with fixed income instruments. Other variables have manifestly influenced prepayments over the years but may not be as easily hedgeable, for example the level of consumer confidence in the state of the economy. These must be treated by relating them to other variables that can be hedged or must be considered as random, unpredictable influences on prepayment behavior lying outside the model. In this context, model risk refers to the general ability, or inability, of the model to accurately predict the average level of prepayments, given its inputs.

Apart from this risk, the accuracy of the models, as a source of conditional projections, is limited for several reasons, of which the most common are:

- Our knowledge of obligor behavior is imprecise at best
- Prevailing future environmental conditions cannot be completely specified
- The statistics inherent in the finite collateral pool in a particular transaction

From basic statistics, we know that the appropriate measure for the last source of error is inversely proportional to the square root of the number of loans in a pool. For finite pool sizes, cash flows will usually fluctuate randomly from one month to another in a way that probably lies beyond the predictive ability of even the most accurate model. Fortunately, it will normally be the case that in most practical applications, such fluctuations will even out relatively quickly, thus allowing us to regard this phenomenon as a relatively minor source of noise.

Since the predictions of prepayment models are tightly linked to the realization of some future environmental scenario, the output from prepayment models is mostly used to derive necessary hedging strategies. These strategies provide the impetus for taking positions in interest-rate sensitive instruments, allowing the ABS investor to partially or totally hedge away the risk of future interest-rate movements and realize excess return over the risk-free rate, provided of course that the prepayment model is accurate.

10.2 EVOLUTION OF IDEAS IN PREPAYMENT MODELING

In the late 1970s and early 1980s, when the first issues of Residential Mortgage-Backed Securities (RMBS) appeared, issuers and investors noticed different prepayment rates on pools from different mortgage agencies (GNMA versus FHLMC or FNMA), as well as differences among pools of a given collateral type securitized by the same agency. At first, these differences were merely the subject of qualitative analysis. The basic issue was, can we really characterize some pools as prepaying faster than others? Gradually, traders coined a vocabulary to describe the various modalities of MBS pools. Terms like "old pool," "California pool," "FHA experience," etc. came into being to describe prepayment characteristics of pools in the brave new world of MBS. Pools with different prepayment histories came to be priced differently. The Actuarial Division of the Department of Housing and Urban Development had conducted studies of prepayment and default experience on all FHA (Federal Housing Administration, a part of the Department of Housing and Urban Development's Office of Housing) insured mortgages originated as far back as 1957. The results were synthesized into the first model of mortgage prepayment behavior. The profile of prepayments derived from this study is still in use today as a tool for characterizing the prepayment speed of a particular pool by comparing the level of prepayments in relation to seasoning. This model is none other than the PSA curve (Public Securities Association) discussed at the beginning of chapter 5. The PSA is not a true prepayment model for forecasting or hedging purposes.

Several prepayment conventions that survive into the present emerged from this period. Banks invented a *consistency index* based on the standard deviation of monthly prepayments (still in dollar rather than percentage terms) and the length of time the deal had been outstanding to describe the consistency of past prepayments. Contrary to expectation, analytical observations of prepayment patterns indexed by their consistency showed that the higher the previous average prepayment rate the less likely a pool would remain consistent going forward. Apart from reflecting the declining balance of the pool, this phenomenon was also assumed to be the result of a mysterious *convergence to the mean*. It is also the origin of the idea known today as *burnout*.

The next breakthrough in prepayment modeling was a realization that the absolute dollar amount of prepayments was not the best possible measure of the prepayment process. The Single Month Mortality (*SMM*) measure became the replacement benchmark, and was even mistakenly labeled a prepayment *model* when historical prepayment patterns were found to deviate less from the assumption of a constant *SMM* value than from the FHA-experience curve in absolute dollars. The term *SMM* had arisen in the life insurance industry, hence the use of the word *mortality*. Formally, the *SMM* represents the amount of principal reimbursed by obligors, in *excess* of their contractually scheduled amount, during a given collection period as a percentage of the pool's principal balance outstanding at the end of the previous collection period, but reduced by the amount of contractually scheduled principal payments. Scheduled principal amounts appear in the numerator and denominator of the *SMM* definition as follows:

$$SMM(t) = \frac{P(t) - P_s(t)}{B(t-1) - P_s(t)} \qquad (1)$$

In equation (1), we have defined the following parameters:

$P(t)$ = total principal reimbursed by obligors at time t
$P_s(t)$ = scheduled principal reimbursement at time t
$B(t)$ = pool principal balance at time t

Further analysis then demonstrated that observed prepayments varied across other mortgage pool characteristics such as the obligor rate, loan age, geographical location of the property, obligor income, etc. However, these characteristics were not available for the majority of the securitized pools and were difficult to predict or forecast. This provided the motivation for the development of the first and subsequent generations of true prepayment models based on attempts to rationalize the behavior of aggregate pools of borrowers.

The features of a given prepayment model depend on the type of asset under consideration, the amount of information available on borrowers in a particular pool, the purpose of the model, and the degree of precision needed to determine the temporal cash flow sequence. On the other hand, all prepayment models use interest rates as a cardinal input, since most other variables are not nearly as interesting from a hedging perspective. To further explain borrower behavior, a prepayment model can be either *structural*, whereby different sources of prepayments such as refinancing and default are modeled explicitly, or it can embody an approximation theory predicated on the analysis of historical prepayment data. Between the two, structural models, i.e. those which make use of real-world knowledge about borrower behavior, are particularly well suited to situations where historical data are noisy or limited in scope.

With respect to the statistical methods used in prepayment modeling, both parametric and nonparametric models have been devised. Within the latter type, one finds the family of proportional hazard models, while to develop the former, one would need to specify the main sources of prepayment behavior: turnover, refinancing, default and, for residential mortgages, curtailment. In the proportional hazard framework, prepayment factors are supposed to influence prepayments relative to some benchmark loan-cohort, for which the prepayment profile is already either specified or known a priori. Proportional hazard analysis provides for *correction factors* based on loan characteristics and the influence of external variables which act as multipliers of a baseline prepayment curve. Although the ability to establish the underlying factors which drive prepayment decisions is assumed, the parametric forms of the functional relationships between these factors and prepayment probabilities remain unknown. In general, statistical software is used to calculate the optimal "fit" or relationship between a set of arbitrary nonlinear functions that depend on the chosen prepayment factors. These functional forms then turn into multipliers applied to the benchmark prepayment rates.

10.3 THE ANATOMY OF A PREPAYMENT MODEL

Having touched on the origins of the conventions in prepayment modeling, we now turn to our main task: the role of prepayment models in the cash flow modeling and valuation of structured securities. Rather than describing the entire panoply of existing prepayment models, we will focus on the structural type of prepayment models and discuss in more detail the characteristics of such models in some of the major asset classes, such as automobile and home equity loans, as well as residential mortgages where they find their main application.

Prepayment models are normally developed from historical prepayment data whenever such data are available. Thus, within the context of a completely new asset class, the paucity of available data would limit the usefulness and accuracy of prepayment analysis. Therefore, in many cases a blend of statistical techniques and ad hoc methods needs to be brought to bear on the problem in order to have any hope of building a robust and accurate prepayment model.

In general, a prepayment model deals either with loan-level data, where the individual characteristics of each loan are used as inputs, or with pool-level data, whereby loan-level data are aggregated and only averages are used. In the later situation, loan-level data may not be available or else be considered too costly to use either from a computational resource perspective or from the standpoint of the modeling effort that would be required to make proper use of them.

For example, in the residential housing sector, the components of prepayment are normally modeled independently with respect to each influence factor:

1. First, it is assumed that where the interest-rate-bound incentive to prepay is either zero or negligible, the vast majority of prepayments will result from statistical turnover—borrowers moving and selling their house as they do so. It is also possible to estimate the turnover rate based on total housing stocks and existing house sales.

2. Defaults are relatively minor components of prepayments in the RMBS marketplace. Some default data are available on residential mortgage pools, and historical averages may also be used.

3. Curtailments, generally a relatively small factor in RMBS prepayment, may nevertheless become significant with respect to highly seasoned pools.

They can be modeled as residual prepayments once prepayments from other sources have been calculated.

4. As expected, refinancing represents the most volatile prepayment category. When total prepayment rates are high, those stemming from refinancing usually represent the largest component. In most asset classes, the main determinant of refinancing is the difference or *spread* between the rate paid on the loan and the current rate the borrower could obtain in the open market. The ratio of the two rates can also be used. Second, since the refinancing process requires time and money (closing and other fees), the next most important variable influencing refinancing rates is the total amount the borrower could save by refinancing. The latter can be measured in many ways, for instance by loan size, monthly payment amount, owner's equity in the home, etc. Within the parametric modeling framework, the impact of these factors is usually modeled via a response curve, such as the so-called *S*-curve,[1] which translates the refinancing incentive into a prepayment measure (*SMM* or *CPR*—Conditional Prepayment Rate) or a prepayment multiplier as explained above.

For all of the above components, the presence of an aging process is assumed whereby prepayments are seen to ramp up towards a steady-state plateau starting from their initial value at deal origination, which is close to zero in most cases. The aging process needs to be considered because it has been observed that prepayments will be relatively low for any class of borrower immediately after closing. This stems from the commonsense notion that borrowers will not respond to a refinancing incentive, no matter how large it may be, right after taking out a brand new mortgage for which they paid hefty fees, not to mention that either the incentive or the probability of moving for such borrowers is likely to be relatively small.

Seasonality (monthly changes in prepayments over their average value) plays a significant role in the analysis of prepayments arising from turnover, since this effect represents a pattern of prepayments derived from the propensity of borrowers to preferentially change their residence in the summer instead of the winter. In addition, factors such as consumer borrowing needs, automobile model-year release calendar, and even the number of working days in a particular month can affect seasonal trends.

10.4 NON-INTEREST-RATE-SENSITIVE MODELING: AUTOMOBILE

There are different reasons why prepayments with respect to a given collateral pool may not be sensitive to interest rates and these vary by asset class. In some cases, monthly savings from refinancing can, for various reasons, be relatively insignificant compared to those achievable on a mortgage. Second, in some market niches, borrowers may have impaired credit and may not be sensitive to a decrease in interest rates because they cannot obtain new credit at any price. Alternatively, prepayment penalties like those seen in home equity loans may be imposed on the original loan, thus limiting the effective savings to the borrower.

Automobile loans are a classic example of collateral relatively insensitive to changes in interest rates. In general, the reasons for this are as follows:

- Refinancing loans would have to be taken out on pre-owned vehicles, and such loans generally carry higher rates that those on new vehicles.
- Because of depreciation, the initial principal balance of the new loan may exceed the current value of the automobile by a wide margin, forcing the obligor to make an additional downpayment.
- Considering the average balance of these loans, the monthly savings arising from refinancing alone, even for a considerably lower interest rate, are relatively small and commonly will not justify the necessary investment in time and up-front cash.

As a result, in this asset class the determinants of prepayments can be reasonably assumed to be *loan seasoning* and *borrower credit quality*, in addition to the normal seasonality effects on an aggregate basis. Automobile loans are usually originated with terms of 36 to 60 months, although longer maturities have frequently been observed. However, an owner may decide to sell his vehicle and buy a new one before the expiration of the loan, thus prepaying the loan. This normally does not happen immediately after the original purchase but is increasingly the case as the loan matures and obligors switch to more recent model-years. Other sources of prepayments are accidents and thefts, in which cases the insurance company would pay the loan off.

Borrower credit quality for some types of consumer loans is available as a reported credit score, such as those sold by Fair, Isaac & Co. (FICO). In other cases, an implicit score can be deduced from the difference between the loan rate and prevailing interest rates at the time or loan origination, the assumption being that borrowers judged to be poorer credits would be charged higher rates to compensate the lender for the increased risk of default. Here, the measure of credit quality could be the spread between the loan rate and some constant-maturity Treasury rate at origination. The maturity of the Treasury would be chosen to correspond to the loan's maturity. Although this variable has been found to be a significant measure of the ability of borrowers to prepay their loans, it is imperfect due to various promotions, discounts and "points" paid by the borrower.

For an automobile loan, we can use the average spread between the loan rate and that on the relevant constant maturity Treasury (CMT), for example the 5-year CMT rate, at the time of loan origination as a proxy for borrower credit quality. The distribution of this variable among pools of auto-loans from different originators usually turns out to be bi-modal. This seems to suggest the existence of two groups of borrowers. First, those with relatively high creditworthiness, corresponding to low values of the spread parameter and second, those with low creditworthiness corresponding to a relatively higher spread. Thus, two separate prepayment submodels should be fitted to each of these two groups of borrowers.

Two separate issues determine the propensity to prepay as a function of credit quality. On the one hand, higher quality borrowers have the means to refinance their loans, even if it requires an additional payment. In the case of auto-loans, they are more likely to buy a new vehicle before the maturity of the loan. On the other, some of the lower credit quality borrowers undergo something called "credit curing," i.e., a revaluation of the obligor's credit quality after a certain time interval during which they meet their financial obligations regularly. Typical examples are home-equity and subprime mortgage loans. Herein, we will not deal explicitly with the credit curing effect since we do not break prepayment rates down into their various components. In addition, refinancing based on credit curing is not normally offered by auto-loan originators.

An auto-loan prepayment model may be developed within the *SMM* framework, the basic measure of prepayments defined by equation (1). Alternatively, another widely used measure for modeling purposes is the conditional prepayment rate (*CPR*), which is simply an annualized measure derived from the *SMM* as follows:

$$CPR = 1 - (1 - SMM)^{12} \tag{2}$$

Defining s_i as *SMM* for month i, the prepayment probability or odds ratio can be computed as:

$$z_i = \frac{s_i}{1 - s_i} \tag{3}$$

This formulation broadens the range of the variable to be modeled. To linearize the model, the log-odds ratio is calculated via:

$$x_i = \ln z_i \tag{4}$$

Assume that after some trial and error, we feel confident in postulating the following polynomial expression for x_i as cubically related to age A and linearly to credit quality C via the following form:

$$x_i = \alpha + \beta_1 C + \beta_2 A + \beta_3 A^2 + \beta_4 A^3 \tag{5}$$

Next, given prepayment data as a function of age and credit quality, we can use least-squares regression to determine the value of the free parameters.

It is important to emphasize the linearity of equation (5). To an observer not familiar with numerical methods, it may not appear so for, after all, equation (5) is certainly nonlinear with respect to obligor age taken alone. But age is known, whereas the free parameters α and β_i, $i \in [1, 4]$ are what needs to be determined. Thus, equation (5) is linear in its unknown parameters. Please note that linearity in this sense is not universally justifiable in the context of prepayment modeling, but when it is applicable, model calibration is greatly facilitated.

After having fully specified basic model parameters using average prepayment data, we can introduce the seasonality multiplier by examining the monthly prepayment rates. These multipliers represent the average monthly differences in prepayment rates regardless of the value of the other intrinsic variables, in this case credit quality and age.

In the automobile sector, the most widely used measure of prepayment behavior is the absolute prepayment speed (ABS). The latter measures the principal balance leaving the pool due to prepayments on a monthly basis, but this time as a percentage of the *original* pool balance. The reason for a different definition from that used in mortgage assets is that historically speaking, the automobile prepayment curve turns out to remain relatively flat when measured using the ABS metric, and the easiest behavior to model is obviously a curve with vanishing slope. Naturally, constant ABS prepayment rates lack seasonality. Any such influence factor would presumably be a pattern seen in empirical data and incorporated into the model.

As an illustration of automobile ABS prepayment model projections versus synthetic data, consider figure 10.1. Despite the substantial monthly variation in prepayments, the geometrically averaged empirical CPR rates are fitted quite well. Note that, measured in CPR terms, prepayments clearly increase with age and that, although this is not apparent from the data due to the large dispersion in data points, model driven seasonality is obvious. Most likely, the monthly dispersion in the observed prepayment rates increases markedly toward the end of the deal due to the small percentage of principal outstanding at that time. When plotted in ABS units, model prepayment rates are invariant except for an initial, fairly short seasoning period in addition to the aforementioned acceleration of prepayments toward the maturity of the pool.

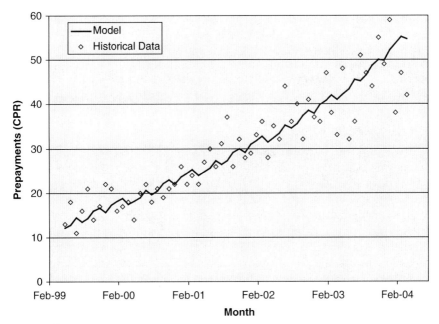

FIGURE 10.1

Hypothetical auto ABS prepayment rates.

10.5 INTEREST-RATE-SENSITIVE MODELING: HOME EQUITY

Aside from residential mortgages, home equity loans (HEL) currently represent the largest category of asset-backed securities in the US generally considered a separate market. At present, more than 90% of HEL represent first liens on the associated property. Unlike loans with identical borrower characteristics used to purchase new homes that fall in a special subprime residential mortgage category, HEL are used almost exclusively for refinancing purposes. In many cases, additional equity is financed simultaneously and used for debt consolidation, home improvements and other home-related purposes. This profile represents a significant change from the situation that prevailed 10 to 15 years ago, at a time when the vast majority of HEL represented second liens on property. The latter type of loan is still originated and securitized but constitutes a minority of the home-equity universe. Home improvement loans (HIL) form a distinct category. Thus today, HEL mostly refer to senior-lien positions with respect to borrowers with impaired credit history or high debt-to-income (DTI) ratios that make them ineligible for a loan qualifying under the guidelines of mortgage agencies like FNMA or GNMA.

The majority of HEL have a fixed-rate period, from two to five years in length, followed by a much longer floating-rate period. Interest unpaid during the latter period is added to remaining principal and paid off during the floating-rate period. Home equity lines of credit (HELOC) are open-ended, revolving loans carrying floating rates. As a result, they have a structure similar to credit card loans and will not be included in this discussion.

The prepayment rates of HEL are much more stable than those of residential mortgages, resulting in a lower negative convexity for the associated ABS transactions. This is mainly due to the lower refinancing opportunities of borrowers with impaired credit, i.e., those that form the bulk of the home-equity universe. It is generally estimated that interest rates must decrease by 200 to 300 bps to cause the refinancing of home equity loans to increase significantly, compared to the mere 25 to 50 bps necessary to achieve the same effect in residential mortgages.

A Primer on Home Equity Loans

For the securitized universe originated between 1995 and 2000, HEL were characterized by median original principal balances around $40,000. The loan-to-value ratio (LTV) was relatively high (about 74%) and the rate paid by the borrower was higher than for residential mortgage loans originated during the same time period. In general, for reasons indicated above, FICO scores associated with HEL are lower than those on residential mortgages. However, the lack of original FICO score data on older transactions has decreased the utility of this variable within the context of prepayment modeling, an area normally requiring a relatively long historical database. The variability in credit quality can be high within the same HEL pool, which can mean large differences in involuntary prepayment behavior (defaults) between two deals with the same average pool characteristics. Second, since refinancing opportunities also depend on credit quality, differences in prepayment speeds due to refinancing based on the actual credit score distribution will generally obtain. This also means that no single threshold rate is likely to trigger a massive refinancing of the loans in a given pool.

Over the years, originators have developed their own rating systems for HEL borrowers based on the letters A to D. However, in contrast to the world of prime obligors, even A-class borrowers in this asset class may have experienced prior credit problems like bankruptcy. Normally however, their credit history post-bankruptcy is unblemished. This type of credit profile is tolerated because US law allows a bankruptcy petition only once every seven years, thus giving lenders powerful leverage over a recalcitrant borrower who may not declare bankruptcy again for a few years. Unfortunately, the specific underwriting criteria corresponding to each letter-grade credit category (A to D) vary from one issuer to another and thus do not represent a useful feature for modeling purposes unless they can be explicitly taken into account in the model.

An alternative to FICO scores or the above alphabetical classification is the credit spread. In a manner similar to the automobile asset class reviewed in the last section, credit spreads can also serve as a measure of credit quality. For example, the credit spread could be defined as the difference between the gross obligor coupon and the prevailing 30-year mortgage rate at the time of origination. Interestingly, given the relative absence of real interest-rate incentive owing to the floating-rate nature of the loan, a paradoxical phenomenon is observed. Loans exhibiting higher credit spreads, and therefore representing poorer credit, can prepay 30 to 40% faster than those with comparably lower spreads. The most likely reason for this unusual type of behavior is credit curing. By this we mean that often, low credit score borrowers can qualify for a new loan at a lower rate once they have maintained their account current for a certain number of months, usually 12 to 18.

Second in importance is the effect of LTV on prepayment rates. Borrowers with lower LTV ratios are more likely than those with higher LTV ratios to mortgage the same property even further, or else refinance into a larger loan. In addition, since their recovery percentage is higher due to the lower LTV ratio, such borrowers can usually obtain credit under better terms. Note that there exists a special subclass of home equity borrower consisting of loans with LTV ratios exceeding 100%. Such borrowers display a very different refinancing response and aging function, and their loans are generally subject to much lower levels of average prepayments.

Unlike residential mortgages, home equity loans normally retain their sensitivity to interest rates even when refinancing would actually cost the borrower more in interest expense. In such cases, the prepayment option is said to be *out of the money*. The reason is that these borrowers may have other outstanding debt, such as credit cards, on which they pay interest rates even higher than those on home equity loans. Thus, it may make sense for them to take out a new loan at a higher rate than the old one, as long as the average interest expense is reduced when outstanding debt is refunded via this form of refinancing.

Thirty-year loans generally prepay faster than 15-year loans given the same rate incentive because interest-rate savings are higher on longer-dated loans, since the interest payment represents a higher proportion of the monthly payment on these loans. With respect to seasoned loans however, differences in prepayment speeds tend to disappear. Since equity builds up relatively fast on a 15-year mortgage loan, these borrowers have easier access to credit than their 30-year colleagues, resulting in an effectively higher prepayment rate from the refinancing process. "Balloon" HEL prepay faster than both 30- and 15-year mortgage loans. A balloon loan requires a large, final payment at maturity because it does not amortize down to zero by its stated maturity date. The reason why such loans may be attractive is that monthly payments are consequently smaller, and the borrower expects that he will be in a position to refinance the remaining balance at maturity providing his credit record still meets the lender's guidelines. Although this is risky from the obligor's standpoint, it is often done.

In addition, loan age is an important determinant of prepayment rates. After an initial ramp-up phase reaching a plateau around 24 to 36 months post closing, aggregate prepayment rates tend to decline, due to burnout, after approximately 40 months. Credit losses are also a function of loan age. They tend to be low during the first year, increase throughout years two and three, peak around year three after closing, and decline thereafter. Apart from expected differences across issuers, credit losses also depend on the year the loans were originated, the so-called "vintage" year. Mainly, this is due to changes in underwriting criteria and general macroeconomic conditions affecting all obligors simultaneously. Thus, credit losses are cyclical in nature.

Another factor affecting prepayments is the possible imposition of a penalty upon prepayment for a certain length of time after origination. The amount of such penalties obviously varies from issuer to issuer, but in general they would severely depress voluntary prepayments during the penalty period, usually three to five years.

Given the above prepayment influence factors in the home equity asset class, prepayment models for such collateral are more involved. In addition to the standard impact of interest-rate variations, prepayment models usually incorporate path dependence, for example the difference in current pool prepayment behavior due to the relative depletion of borrowers ready, willing, and able to refinance. Thus, as a rule, inputs to HEL prepayment models are *age*, *borrower credit quality*, LTV, *loan type*, and *interest rate*.

Borrower credit quality and LTV are determinants of prepayments because they signify the ability of the borrower to incur new debt should interest rates fall. Although FICO scores are generally recognized as the most applicable measure of borrower credit quality in this asset class, they were unfortunately not widely reported until recently. As a result, models still tend to use the spread between pool's WAC and 30-year Treasury at origination as a surrogate measure. The type of loan means whether it is a plain-vanilla 15- or 30-year, adjustable rate, but mostly with a two- or three-year fixed-rate period, or a balloon loan. As can be expected, loans with prepayment penalties normally exhibit a sharp increase in prepayments at the end of the penalty period which, as indicated above, is usually three to five years from origination. By way of example, prepayment penalties can decrease prepayment rates by 10 or more CPR units compared to otherwise identical pools without the penalty.

The Drivers of HEL Prepayment Speeds

The HEL prepayment profile is characterized by higher baseline speeds by 20 to 30 CPR units for seasoned loans, which is about three times the residential mortgage turnover rate. They also exhibit faster seasoning, with ramps of 12 to 15 months compared to the 24 months or more seen within residential collateral. Therefore, this enhanced seasoning behavior has been reflected in the seasoning profile of the standard prepayment curve (HEP) for this type of collateral whereby a 10-month seasoning ramp is assumed.

To some degree, the aging characteristics of HEL and manufactured housing loans are captured by the standard HEP prepayment curve shown in figure 10.2. 100% HEP is equivalent to 0 CPR at origination, increasing to 20 CPR at month 10, and staying at that level until maturity.

Formally speaking, prepayments may be partitioned into five distinct components, the sum of which is the observed aggregate prepayment rate. These are:

1. Turnover
2. Credit-driven refinancing
3. Rate-driven refinancing
4. Default
5. Payoff

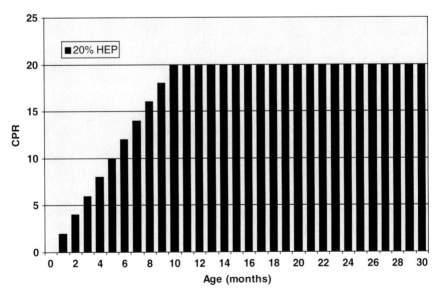

FIGURE 10.2
Home equity loans prepayment curve (HEP).

Turnover

Turnover behavior is thought to depend on the overall housing turnover rate, the relative mobility of the obligors, the position on the seasoning curve and a lock-in effect.

The overall housing turnover rate is usually modeled as a percentage of existing homes sold each year, computed as the ratio of total existing unit-home sales over the total number of existing single-family homes. Historically, this ratio has averaged 5–7%. It is normally reported by the National Association of Realtors and is a function of the overall state of the economy and relative interest rates. Relative mobility characterizes the potentially impaired mobility of HEL borrowers stemming from their generally lower credit quality compared to normal mortgage holders and to the fact that they have just taken on new debt. With respect to turnover, this situation also causes a milder ramp-up of the seasoning curve. Lock-in refers to the reduced inclination of borrowers to move when interest rates rise. The turnover portion of aggregate prepayments is on the order of 6% per year.

Credit-Driven Refinancing

Credit-driven refinancing occurs because the eventually improved credit quality of the borrowers, caused by the timely repayment of home equity loans by borrowers with previously impaired credit histories, enables them to gain access to new credit at lower interest rates even in an otherwise neutral rate environment. This incentive can be substantial. By way of comparison, the spread difference between the A and B categories of obligors can exceed 100 bps, that between A and C can reach 250 bps, while D obligors pay around 400 bps more than A borrowers. Second, borrowers moving up in credit quality are able to raise their permitted LTV, thus giving them an additional incentive to refinance. Historically, credit-driven refinancing peaks between months 12 and 15 at speeds of about 20 to 25 CPR and declines thereafter. In addition, an increase in interest rates can lead to a reduction in credit-based refinancing because it partially nullifies the incentive stemming from improvements in average borrower credit quality. Interestingly, borrowers rated C and D according to the originator's nomenclature actually prepay faster than those rated A. As can be expected, higher principal balance loans will prepay faster than relatively lower principal balance loans because of the larger savings that can be realized on the larger loans. Further, the ever-present fixed costs of refinancing are easier to absorb and justify when monthly dollar savings are higher.

Due to the impact of credit seasoning, the overall baseline prepayment speeds of home equity loans range from 20 to 25 CPR. Remember that baseline speeds are those that obtain in the absence of an interest-rate-driven refinancing incentive. This number would be lower for loans equipped with prepayment penalties and for new originations. Total prepayment speeds of HEL rarely exceed 40 CPR.

Rate-Driven Refinancing

With respect to interest rates, it can be said that HEL are less sensitive to this factor than residential mortgage loans. One of the reasons is that fixed refinancing costs represent a higher percentage of the balance of the generally smaller balances prevailing within this asset class. In addition, as mentioned above, the increase in prepayments due to a reduction in interest rate is proportional to the current average credit quality of the borrowers. This phenomenon results from both improved access to credit by higher quality borrowers as well as from a level of financial sophistication that can vary over a span of years.

HEL also exhibit another source of prepayment called cash-out refinancing. This happens in the absence of rate incentive and results from the borrower's accumulation of equity in the home. Borrowers with substantial trapped equity may then decide to take out a new, larger loan, hence prepaying the existing one, even if the rate on the new loan is no better than that on the existing one. Sometimes the new debt is used for debt consolidation, home improvements, and similar purposes. If rates on such debt are higher than the rate on the prospective HEL, the overall blended rate may still be lower, thus justifying replacing the old debt with the new HEL.

Defaults

The default rates on HEL are substantially higher than those on prime residential mortgages due to the generally weaker credit of the borrowers. Because of the high average loan-to-value (LTV) ratios, in some cases defaults will result in losses to the lender or investor depending on the accumulated equity in the home as well as market conditions at the time of liquidation. Defaults represent an involuntary prepayment of the loans and can be a significant percentage of total prepayments under certain conditions; for example, when a recession would increase the default rate while simultaneously suppressing voluntary prepayment rates.

Data Considerations

We may safely assume that future loan and pool information will keep increasing. Recently, the increased availability of information has been brought about by investor concerns over the exact behavior and nature of their investments. This appears to be a trend, not a fad.

In the home equity sector, loan-level data are generally available. Although this is a clear advantage with respect to designing accurate prepayment models, it does require data aggregation to be done in a way that does not destroy valuable borrower-level information. For instance, at the pool level one can calculate *SMM* by comparing outstanding balances at the beginning of each month while, at the loan level, the obligor is either outstanding or has paid-off. Therefore, one needs to calculate aggregate *SMM* using an alternative method. Normally, this is done by grouping the loans into cohorts based on origination period, coupon, and loan type.

10.6 AN IMPORTANT ASSET CLASS: RESIDENTIAL MORTGAGES

To date, the most sophisticated and complex prepayment models have been applied to residential mortgages. Apart from the size of the market, which by itself definitely warrants the efforts expended to design accurate models, the prepayment characteristics of residential mortgages exhibit many different features and dependencies that need to be incorporated into a model in order to obtain realistic conditional prepayment predictions.

As mentioned above, the option available to the borrower or "mortgagor" to prepay his or her loan at any time, and in most cases without incurring any penalty, unlike what was generally true of home equity loans, lies at the heart of prepayment uncertainty. Modeling the exercise of this prepayment option as a financially efficient process, however, yields poor results as far as prepayment projections are concerned. One reason for this is the randomness of prepayment events. For example, from a phenomenological viewpoint a group of borrowers in very similar socioeconomic conditions and carrying the same relative percentage of mortgage debt will not prepay all at once, as would be dictated via reliance on efficient option exercise theory. In effect, this process somewhat resembles what happens in radioactive decay. Even though all isotopic nuclei are considered identical, they will still decay at a given, fixed unit-rate rather than all at once. As far as we can tell, the identity of the nuclei that actually decay is random. Of course, in that case, it really does not matter which one decays since they are by definition identical. This "sameness" is clearly not applicable to prepayment modeling.

From the modeling standpoint, there is however another dimension to such apparent randomness. Due to the limited amount of information available on borrowers, deterministic (non-random) differences do exist among them that, coupled with the very real soft and hard costs of refinancing, will cause delays in borrower prepayments that could be rationalized were this additional information made available. The effect of refinancing costs is clearly visible when one compares the rate-based incentive necessary to produce a refinancing trend. Whereas it was formerly thought that a full 200 bps decrease in interest rates was needed to produce a prepayment wave during which prepayment rates would increase from about 6 or 7 CPR to 30 or 40, with the recent decline in refinancing costs, the increase in Internet-based solicitations, and savvier borrowers, the required interest-rate decrease is now believed to be on the order of 50 bps. In addition, with closing costs currently standing at around $2,500, although nominally without a penalty, the exercise of the prepayment option still represents a sizable investment on the part of the borrower.

As with HEL, we can distinguish four main factors affecting the aggregate prepayment rate of residential mortgages:

1. Turnover
2. Rate refinancing
3. Curtailment
4. Default

We now examine each of these separately:

Turnover

Housing turnover, representing prepayments from sales of existing housing stock, is the most stable component of prepayment in that it is only weakly sensitive to change in the level of interest rates. Sales occur mostly due to changes in borrower

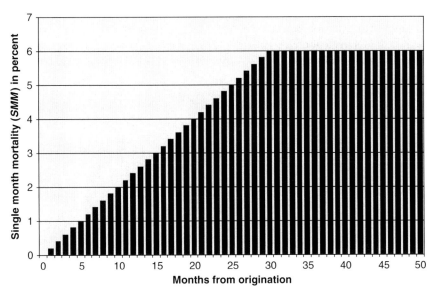

FIGURE 10.3
The PSA prepayment profile.

circumstances, like relocation, marriage, an increase in family size, older children leaving the home, etc. It is the historical average of this component which is, in fact, captured by the PSA curve shown in figure 10.3.

Today's turnover is closer to 150% PSA or even higher for some collateral types. In general, pool turnover will be determined by the state of the economy, fiscal, and monetary policy in the respective jurisdiction, and relative mobility compared to the general population. In addition, turnover is also subject to seasoning and the lock-in effect mentioned above. You will recall that the latter factor measures the reluctance of borrowers to move because prevailing rates are higher than what they are paying on their existing mortgage. As a result, a borrower who would otherwise move right away may hold off until rates ease up somewhat.

The temporal variability in turnover is influenced by a few factors, the most prominent of which are:

1. Aging
2. Lock-in
3. Price appreciation (i.e., a decrease in LTV)
4. Seasonality

Although the first three have already been discussed, a few comments are appropriate concerning the last. Turnover seasonality is the result of weather, vacation schedules, and the school year. Thus, homeowners are much more likely to move during the summer and early fall, when schools are not in session, and least likely to move in the winter and early spring due to weather conditions. In general, housing turnover rates observed during peak months, like August, exceed the same figures during trough

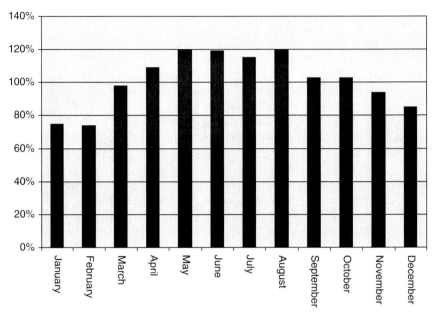

FIGURE 10.4
Seasonal variation in housing turnover.

months like January by almost a two-to-one ratio. A typical profile of the observed seasonality in housing sales is presented in figure 10.4.

Note that, recently, the amount of cash-out refinancing has increased. Such transactions are akin to turnover in the sense that they are not as sensitive to changes in interest rates. In effect, some homeowners are ready to refinance into a higher rate to extract the equity accumulated in their home. As was the case with the HEL asset class, this could also make economic sense when the amount of equity withdrawn is used to pay off other, higher-interest-rate debt.

Rate Refinancing

In general, the interest-rate-based refinancing profile of residential mortgage loans can be modeled using a response curve. The most popular such response function is the logistic curve. As shown in figure 10.5, the S-curve yields the instantaneous prepayment rate, measured in terms of CPR, PSA or *SMM*, as a function of the financial incentive to prepay. The latter is generally either the *difference* between the interest rate on the existing mortgage and the rate available to the same borrower in the market, or the *ratio* of these two rates.

> **A Primer on the S-Curve as Applied to Prepayment Analysis**
>
> On the far left of the x-axis, any prepayment impact stems from the fact that some borrowers are insensitive to the negative incentive because their goal is to take equity

out of their home. This can be done either by taking a HEL or by refinancing the entire first mortgage. If HEL rates are significantly higher than those available on first mortgage loans, as is usually the case, the borrower would benefit economically by refinancing the existing mortgage to take out equity. As current interest rates increase further, the attractiveness of refinancing for any reason decreases accordingly, hence the asymptotic decay of the corresponding prepayment rate toward zero as the rate incentive becomes increasingly negative. On the positive side, historical observations show that prepayments tend to increase markedly once a certain threshold level is attained. This point corresponds to the elbow of the curve shown in figure 10.5. For very large positive incentives, a saturation point is reached whereby all borrowers able and willing to refinance have already done so, hence larger incentives do not lead to measurably higher refinancing rates.

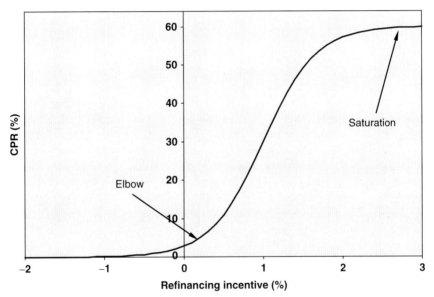

FIGURE 10.5

A typical *S*-curve profile.

In addition to the above interest-rate-based incentive, it is believed that this component of prepayments is influenced by the following attributes, measured as aggregate:

1. Loan size
2. Media effect
3. Cash-out (decrease in LTV)
4. Burnout
5. Shape of the yield curve (hybrid and other alternatives)

Loan size influences prepayments because the monetary reward from refinancing (i.e., the reduction in monthly payment) is proportional to loan size. As the costs of refinancing have a significant fixed component, consisting for example of various fees, as well as intangible costs in terms of time and effort, borrowers refinancing a larger loan would be able to recuperate such costs over a shorter time period, thus making them more likely to undertake the refinancing in the first place.

The "media effect" reflects increased media reporting of historically low mortgage rates when they occur, making borrowers more aware of them and therefore more likely to take advantage of the perceived opportunity to refinance their mortgages.

Cash-outs as source of prepayments have become more prominent in the last 10 years as a steady rise in home prices has decreased the borrowers' LTV ratio much faster than via scheduled amortization, thus tempting some borrowers into assuming new debt as a mechanism for tapping into the accumulated equity in their homes.

What is the Right Measure of Prepayment Incentive?

The difference between existing and current market mortgage rates is usually not the best proxy to measure the incentive to refinance. This is because, in practice, most borrowers make their refinancing decision based on the corresponding reduction in monthly payments versus the refinancing costs per se, and the ratio of the two rates is a better reflection of the difference in monthly payments. In addition, when the original loan rate carried a premium versus the then-available market rate, for instance due to the borrower's impaired credit profile or a lower FICO score, it would be more realistic, *ceteris paribus*, to measure the incentive against the current market rate plus the same premium. In other words, a proper measure of the refinancing incentive has to take into account the fact that some loans in a given pool have a higher coupon than others in the same pool, originated at the same time and under the same conditions, due to extraneous factors like the borrower's credit quality, or the probability of a loss in the event of default through a relatively high LTV, for example.

Yield Curve Plays

Although this is probably a secondary factor in our modeling effort, it should be mentioned that depending on the shape of the yield curve at the time of the refinancing decision, borrowers could refinance at shorter maturities, thus defeating a model that would have based its predictions on the longer end of the curve. Today's borrowers have a wider array of choices than ever before when it comes to refinancing. Whereas traditionally, only 15-year and balloon mortgages were available to make a play on the yield curve, obligors now must increasingly ponder the potential benefits and disadvantages of adjustable-rate and hybrid mortgages. In particular, hybrid mortgages have gained popularity over the last 10 to 15 years. In addition to exhibiting fixed interest rates for the first few years, rates on these loans are thereafter reset annually based on market rates at the time of reset.

Seasonality

The seasonal component of refinancing is small compared to the turnover season-ality, and is mostly due to the effect of a different number of working days in a particular month.

Burnout and Media Impact

In this major asset class, it is not realistic to assume a simple, linear prepayment model like the one described by equation (4) in the automotive sector. This is because in residential mortgages, in addition to the standard rate-based impact, we are faced with two extraneous influence factors, not encountered in the auto sector, that independently cause path-dependence in prepayment rates. By this we mean that prepayments at any given time depend not only on the current age of the loans and on interest rates, but also on the history of prepayment behavior and on that of interest rates since origination. These two effects are known as *media* and *burnout*.

Media

Let us first consider the more benign media effect. It has been noticed that when mortgage interest rates fall to their historic lows, media attention increases prepayment rates over what would be normally be expected from loans with equivalent characteristics subjected to the same rate-incentive, hence the label "media" effect. The strength of this effect can be modeled via an exponential function of the time span during which rates have hovered around their historic lows as well as from the spread between the existing mortgage rates and currently available rates.

Burnout

A more interesting and challenging phenomenon is burnout, which is related to changes in the composition of the borrower pool. As a result of previous refinancings, borrowers most eager and able to refinance have left the pool, leaving only those less able to refinance. Should rates drop once again to levels already tested by the same pool, refinancing speeds will be significantly lower the second time because remaining borrowers will presumably be more resistant to the rate-based incentive, or else they would have refinanced the first time around. Thus, depending on the path interest rates have followed till the present day, which path implicitly explains the current pool composition, prepayment levels will vary given identical rate-based incentives. In passing, note that a standard Markov process would fail to take this phenomenon into account since it implicitly assumes the absence of any path dependency in the modeled stochastic variable.

One way to model burnout is to posit the existence of several groups of homogenous borrowers, which groups may be defined based on loan-level data whereby individual loans are aggregated based on similar characteristics. This procedure also saves time compared to modeling prepayments at the individual loan level. In this case, burnout is modeled in a natural and intuitive manner, i.e., pool cohorts exhibiting higher prepayment levels would be depleted earlier, resulting in diminished prepayments on the remaining cohort of outstanding loans. In such models, pool compositions are updated monthly from loan-level data. If loan-level data are not available, we may infer a property distribution based on collateral information and partition the pool into groups that way. In this case, the modeling of burnout would be done identically. This method, known as 'Active-Passive Decomposition', has the major advantage of obviating the explicit modeling of burnout itself. It also results in prepayments being modeled as path-independent rather than path-dependent. It should be noted that within the context of such models, one can recover the current pool composition purely based on aging and pool factor.

In order to calculate future prepayment speeds, we would proceed as follows. First, the pool is partitioned into two groups of borrowers, and the current pool composition is broken out by group. Next, future interest-rate states of the world are generated according to some assumed stochastic process. Owing to the different borrower characteristics within each group, the model then allows the computation of remaining borrower composition within each group given each world-state. Thus, when valuing the securities using multiple interest-rate scenarios, this method enables the use of more efficient pricing schemes, such as binary trees and grids, instead of standard Monte Carlo techniques.

However, the advantage of the latter method decreases markedly once the presence of more than two borrower groups is posited. Substates of the world become more and more numerous, increasing modeling demands in terms of CPU time and memory requirements. Further, mortgage liability structures that contain time-dependent bonds, such as the CMO or senior/subordinated structures, will still necessitate recourse to standard Monte Carlo methods, thus negating the advantage of the above decomposition method.

Lastly, when modeling prepayments using loan-level data, the goal will be to compute monthly prepayment *SMM* vectors for each loan. Despite the fact that one would normally expect a loan to prepay in full, amortizing each loan individually enables one to arrive at a natural model of burnout. In addition, this method directly accounts for changes in borrower composition in terms of loan size and coupon distribution.

Seasoning

Refinancing seasoning happens much more quickly than that seen with respect to turnover. For example, loans that have between 16 and 24 months of history can already be considered fully seasoned for purposes of rate refinancing modeling.

Although such seasoning is normally inexorable, macro-economic conditions can sometimes reverse a trend. For example, it is clear that given the proper financial incentive, the main practical obstacles to prepayment are lack of equity in the home and a weak credit history, both of which can improve over time, leading to increased propensity to prepay and thus to pool rejuvenation. An LTV change for instance, representing the effect of house appreciation and principal pay-down, has a strong effect on the borrowers' ability and willingness to refinance. House appreciation well in excess of the inflation rate in recent years goes a long way toward explaining the high refinancing rates seen on collateral that would normally have been past the period where burnout would prevail. This is the counter effect to burnout.

Curtailments

Curtailments and payoffs represent additional principal payments above the monthly minimum amount made by some borrowers either as a form of savings or to invest a windfall profit from inheritance or some other extraneous source. This source of prepayment, although negligible on new pools, may nevertheless constitute a substantial source of prepayment with respect to older pools when outstanding amounts are relatively small. Curtailments are usually modeled by difference, i.e., as what remains from total prepayments after turnover, rate refinancing, and defaults have been taken into account.

Treatment of Defaults

Defaults are frequently modeled using prior historical default experience reflected in the Standard Default Assumption (SDA) curve given as figure 10.6. This model is based on commonsense assumptions positing that default rates will remain relatively small immediately after origination, since borrowers likely to default would presumably have been unable to obtain a loan that would place them in the target pool. Defaults then gradually ramp-up until 30 months after origination, after which they are assumed to remain constant for next 30 months. Next, a steep downward slope in defaults is usually observed, after which defaults are assumed to remain relatively low for the remainder of the pool's lifetime. The low default rates during the latter part of the transaction stem from the fact that, rather than default, normal house appreciation will usually enable borrowers facing financial difficulties to sell the property in order to repay the original loan without any impact on their credit history.

Due to the prevailing mechanics of default declaration within MBS, normally dictating that defaults are only recognized at liquidation, and because foreclosures are assumed to last approximately 12 months from the time the process is initiated, defaults during the last 12 months of a loan's term are usually set to zero. The SDA curve represents a relatively reasonable model for 30-year mortgage pools under normal circumstances since it was developed based on historical experience of such collateral.

Other Characteristics that Influence Mortgage Prepayment

The other loan characteristics known to influence prepayment rates are loan size, geographical distribution, loan purpose, the amount of points paid at origination, and the borrower's DTI ratio. Factors such as home price appreciation, the overall level of turnover, and the lender's underwriting policies are also known to influence prepayments, but are not used as inputs by the majority of prepayment models.

However, the usefulness of some of this information may be limited because of the difficulties in forecasting future values. For instance, even if we assumed that borrower FICO scores, as they evolve over time, would enable us to refine

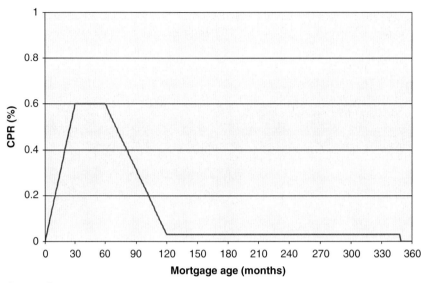

FIGURE 10.6
The SDA default curve.

our prepayment predictions, in the absence of updated FICO score information on borrowers it is difficult to make good on this promise to update our forecast. Another example is the prepayment characteristics of HEL from different originators. With respect to this factor, the problem is not simply that the magnitude of the impact is difficult to quantify. Even if it was shown to be relatively stable on past transactions, there is no guarantee that it will remain at this level for newly originated loans or that it will remain relevant at all, since some key elements of the originator's business strategy may change so as to render past experience well-nigh useless.

Second, and more importantly, prepayment modeling for valuation purposes requires the examination of different scenarios affecting the variables that influence prepayments. The development of such scenarios is impossible without first developing a fairly consistent and workable model of the behavior of the underlying variables.

Correlations and Hidden Variables

A special problem within prepayment modeling is the possibility of correlation between the explanatory variables. For example, borrowers taking on high LTV debt tend to exhibit somewhat lower FICO scores than borrowers with loans of average LTV ratios. Clearly, this poses a difficulty when trying to model the separate prepayment impacts of LTV and FICO score.

Similarly, is has been observed that pools with larger average loan size prepay faster than pools with relatively smaller average loan sizes. At the pool level, a more rapid prepayment rate by borrowers with larger loans will leave loans in the pool that would have lower loan balances, and thus would prepay more slowly in the future. This is exactly what we mean by the term burnout. However, in the absence of constantly updated loan size information, it is difficult to model burnout by tracking evolution of loan size distribution in a pool. Thus, correlation effects, and other, currently unused variables may offer an analytical solution to some of the aspects of prepayment modeling that are now handled synthetically.

Prepayment Characteristics of Different Loan Types

The reasons for the different prepayment behavior of various mortgage types have to do with borrower self-selection as well as with the particular characteristics of the loan. For example, balloon mortgages generally display faster prepayment rates, especially as the balloon date nears, because the borrower needs to find a source of repayment for his loan.

Hybrid loans prepay faster and exhibit a spike in prepayments around the first reset date. The reason is that borrowers sometimes target certain time horizons, after which they plan to move or trade up. Second, borrowers are generally risk-averse and thus wish to avoid the risk related to the resetting of their mortgage interest rate every year after the first reset date, otherwise they would have taken out a one-year resetting, adjustable-rate mortgage in the first place. Therefore, they tend to prepay around the first reset date.

In addition, some hybrid-loan borrowers, the so called "qualifiers," use the lower monthly payments on their adjustable-rate or hybrid mortgage to qualify for a larger loan. Currently, it is not clear whether these borrowers would necessarily exhibit a higher refinancing rate.

Loan size influences prepayments because dollar savings resulting from refinancing at the same incentive level are proportional to the loan amount. Second, refinancing costs consist of fixed costs and variable costs proportional to the loan amount. Therefore, for a larger loan the fixed costs are easier to absorb and justify. Next, borrowers with smaller loan balances clearly represent a segment with smaller gross incomes and are therefore less likely to obtain favorable loan terms in a future refinancing.

Last but not least, loans with prepayment penalties are attractive to borrowers wishing to reduce their nominal rate by 15 to 25 bps. Of note is that this type of penalty does not apply to sales of the home. As expected, prepayments on such collateral start increasing immediately after the expiration of the prepayment penalty period, which is normally five years in length.

Short-Term Prepayment Predictions

The short-term forecasting accuracy of residential prepayment models can be improved using the Mortgage Bankers Association's (MBA) Refinancing, Purchase and Market Indices as well as the autocorrelation spectrum of pool prepayments. The MBA Refinancing Index is an especially good short-term indicator of mortgage prepayments. For a particular pool, significant autocorrelation in prepayment rates exists, meaning that pools that prepay at speeds below average are more likely to continue such idiosyncratic behavior, at least in the short run. Thus, even if we do not know the reasons underlying the relatively low prepayment speeds on these pools, using the discrepancy between the model's predictions and recent history can improve the model's predictive ability in the near term.

As much as feasible, borrowers will time their prepayment to catch the trough in what they perceive as an interest-rate cycle. However, when interest rates reach historical lows and large prepayment waves occur due to increased media attention (see "Media" above), surges in prepayments will actually occur after interest rates have in fact started moving in the opposite direction because a large number of borrowers may be trying to lock-in their rate before rates move against them even further. This timing effect can be significant and needs to be accounted for in short-term prepayment forecasting.

Data Availability

The availability of data on mortgage pools has increased greatly in recent years. For example, in 2003 both Freddie Mac (FHLMC) and Fannie Mae (FNMA) (the two major issuers of pooled mortgage loans in the US) started publishing average LTV and credit scores similar to FICO scores on borrowers in their pools. Apart from pool averages, minima and maxima with respect to certain loan characteristics are now also available by quartile. On the other hand, for mortgages not securitized by the three main agencies (i.e., Freddie Mac, Fannie Mae and Ginnie Mae (GNMA)) a plethora of loan-level data are available.

10.7 ADVANCING THE STATE OF PREPAYMENT ANALYSIS

The increased use of loan-level information makes sense for collateral whose prepayment rate depends on interest rates or for modeling the default behavior of risky collateral. Mortgage and other mortgage-like consumer asset classes, such as home equity and manufactured housing loans, exhibiting a wide range of historical prepayment speeds because of the size of their respective markets, certainly warrant the extended modeling effort. The nonagency mortgage market consists of subsectors like jumbo, conforming balance Alt-A, nonconforming balance Alt-A, etc., and has developed rapidly. A large amount of information is now available on the underlying collateral at the loan level. As historical data on prepayment accumulate it will be possible to develop prepayment models based on more detailed knowledge of pool composition.

Simultaneously, computational limitations on processing larger amounts of data have been reduced gradually. The computational requirements of loan-level analysis are extensive, especially in the area of Option Adjusted Spread (OAS) calculation. For example, considering a whole-loan transaction consisting of 10,000 loans, using 512 interest-rate paths, a prepayment model would be invoked 921,600,000 times ($10,000 \times 512 \times 3$ scenarios $\times 360$ amortization months) to compute the OAS of a single bond.

New prepayment models will increasingly rely on monthly updates to borrower home equity because this latter quantity is seen as the key determinant of the propensity to prepay. In addition, other market and econometric variables known to influence prepayments, and that may be hedged through a combination of financial instruments, should eventually be incorporated inside a prepayment model. For example, assuming a known correlation between unemployment rate and the slope of the yield curve and given an interest-rate path, we can calculate future, expected unemployment rates based on yield curve slopes during subsequent periods, and then use those rates to adjust the housing turnover rate since high unemployment leads to a decreased propensity to move or upgrade to a larger home.

A special area of significance with respect to prepayment modeling is the measurement of the actual prepayment incentive and the modeling of mortgage rates. Recently, mortgagors have been faced with an ever-widening array of mortgage products into which to refinance. In addition to the traditional 30-year fixed-rate and 15-year fixed-rate mortgage product, prepayment penalty, adjustable-rate and hybrid loans with fixed-rate periods of different lengths linked to Treasury or LIBOR rates have now become available.

Further, the mortgage rates available to different borrower categories are not identical. Due to yield curve effects, 15-year mortgage rates are typically 30 to 50 bps lower than 30-year rates. Jumbo rates are 10 to 25 bps higher than those available on conforming mortgages and Alt-A rates are higher still. Clearly, differences will vary over time depending on market conditions. In addition, each such rate must be calculated going forward in a manner consistent with the assumed behavior of the yield curve. Generally, past behavior is used to derive a model that enables rates to be computed going forward.

Thus, two issues are of paramount importance when contemplating the modeling of the refinancing incentive:

1. Borrowers are now considering several different available rates with which to execute their refinancing option.
2. They may refinance into a different product than the one they currently have.

Last but not least, the interest rates on these products are not only different, but they are also imperfectly correlated and thus need to be modeled differently. As well as the continuing innovation in the mortgage markets, this rate complexity will make it increasingly necessary to develop more sophisticated and comprehensive prepayment models.

10.8 RMBS: OPTION ADJUSTED SPREAD ANALYSIS

Finance answers the two fundamental valuation questions with respect to cash: how much and when? Consequently, in a world without credit risk, which is largely the case within RMBS, the focus of *value* analysis must shift to liquidity considerations. Essentially, RMBS investors are betting on the yield curve and are not at all focused on the ultimate return of their principal which they consider quasi-certain, at least until now. For an entirely different set of reasons, the precise timing of such return is what worries them. In other words, whereas in most ABS asset classes one's attention and time is spent mainly addressing credit risk (how much), the world of RMBS revolves around the timing of cash flows to bondholders (when). This timing is uncertain because of the legally enforceable ability of consumers to refinance their residential mortgage at any time without incurring a penalty. Consequently, RMBS analysis has been reduced to prepayment forecasting, the latter being determined in large measure by the volatility of interest rates around their initial value. Moreover, since most RMBS analysts learned their craft in an interest-rate-sensitive environment, they have not learned techniques for the valuation of credit-sensitive instruments. Hence, the siloing of analytical skills across interest-sensitive and credit-sensitive domains has been pervasive.

We can only engage in a brief overview of the field of option-adjusted spread (OAS) analysis. Entire financial careers have been, and are being devoted to this arcane topic and we simply cannot do justice to the wealth of available techniques in a few pages, nor is it our intention to do so. Nevertheless, it is highly instructive to present the basic concepts and issues found within the OAS methodology in a logical sequence, if only as an impetus to further study and research.

The Basis of OAS Analysis

Recall from basic fixed income mathematics that the price P of a bond can be obtained as the net present value of its cash flows C_i, $i \in [1, n]$ discounted at some rate r usually given by prevailing interest rates:

$$P = \sum_{i=1}^{n} \frac{C_i}{(1+r)^i} \tag{6}$$

If the discount rate r is equal to the nominal or *stated* coupon y on the bond, the price will equal par, or 100%. If the discount rate is less than y, the bond will be valued above par and vice versa in the case $r > y$. This means that should prevailing interest rates increase, the nominally promised cash flows are worth relatively less since higher rates are available elsewhere, and consequently investors will demand equal yields as a precondition to purchasing existing bonds in the secondary market. In other words, once rates rise, the added discount in the denominator of equation (6) will reduce P below par and the bonds will perforce sell for less than 100% of their face amount. Obviously, the opposite situation will obtain if rates decrease. This state of affairs is shown as the solid line in figure 10.7. In all cases however, the cash flow numerators in equation (6) remain unchanged since borrowers under a standard fixed income instrument will in general never prepay their debt ahead of scheduled maturity.[2]

Now, consider the possibility that, because of the aforementioned penalty-free ability of obligors to prepay their mortgage to refinance at a lower rate, as a result of a job change or for some other reason, the originally promised cash flows are different from what was originally anticipated. In a case where interest rates have come down, prompting many consumers to prepay their debt and refinance it outside the original transaction, it follows from equation (6) that some of the numerator cash flows C_i, namely those close to the average date of prepayment, will be higher than their original values, and vice versa for later cash flows since the sum of principal cash

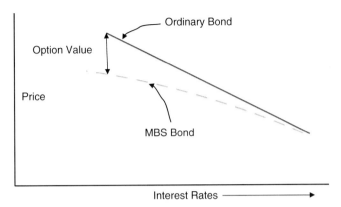

FIGURE 10.7
The basis of OAS analysis.

flows is identical in all cases. By the same reasoning, the total amount of interest paid by all obligors will decrease since they will be paying collectively less total interest at the stated rate due to the prepayment. As we shall see in chapter 11, protecting IO investors in such cases is what the PAC bond is in fact designed to do.

The problem with this situation, and hence the entire basis underlying the need for OAS analysis, is that investors will receive their principal ahead of what would have happened had the obligors not been able to prepay their original obligation in an obviously deteriorating (i.e., lower rate) environment compared to the situation prevailing at issuance. Consequently, investors are faced with having to reinvest more cash than they had anticipated at a rate that will clearly turn out to be lower than the one they are now receiving. Even worse, the converse of this case (i.e., a rising rate environment) in no way compensates them for their disadvantage vis-à-vis decreasing rates, since in that case they would be receiving their principal relatively later and would be unable to take advantage of higher prevailing rates.

In other words, since under both rising- and decreasing-rate scenarios they will be "losing" yield, investors will obviously demand some form of compensation from borrowers. This situation is shown as the dotted line in figure 10.7 whereby the RMBS price cannot rise as fast as the bond without the prepayment option (non-callable) if interest rates have fallen from where they stood at issuance, and thus prepayments are expected to increase further as consumers wise up. Note how different this is from the situation facing an ABS investor within credit-risk-prone asset classes, one usually happy to receive her principal back in full and whose investment profile will typically include a credit risk premium that will commonly overwhelm the prepayment premium.

The sloping behavior of the RMBS bond versus that of the corresponding plain-vanilla bond is referred to as its *convexity*. Because the slope of the RMBS pricing curve itself decreases as rates fall further, we normally refer to such convexity as *negative* by reference to the quadratic equation $ax^2 + bx + c$ in which $a < 0$, indicating a curve with a maximum instead of a minimum. By contrast, although we have not shown it explicitly in figure 10.7, plain-vanilla bonds and Treasuries display positive convexity since their price rises with a slope that itself both increases as rates decreases and decreases as rates increase versus the original rate environment. It is therefore possible to classify RMBS bonds by reference to their convexity properties, i.e., depending on whether they are more (positively) or less (negatively) convex than standard bonds.

Finally, the compensation sought and received by investors for this undesired behavior is reflected in a lower price for the RMBS bond as compared to that of a fixed income instrument of equal stated yield, but without an embedded prepayment option. This negative price difference, expressed as a basis point yield spread, is what we call the option adjusted spread (OAS), or the bond's *convexity cost.*

10.9 DURATION AND CONVEXITY MEASURES

We have just seen that RMBS bonds are subject to a price-yield performance markedly different from that of normal fixed-income instruments lacking prepayment options. Understandably, investors would like the ability to express the lower price they pay for such uncertain performance via easily understandable parameters that can measure the rate of change of the RMBS price when subjected to rate environments different from the one prevailing at issuance. This is how they can be better informed as to what will happen to their collateral when rates move unexpectedly. For instance, should interest rates fall by 100 bps, what would happen to the price of the RMBS they now hold? Even granted that, as we saw in figure 10.7, RMBS prices would increase at rates lower than those of non-callable bonds should rates fall further, is the sensitivity of price to declining rates relatively stable or are we potentially standing on the edge of a cliff?

Duration

The most obvious such metric is the first derivative of price with respect to yield. In effect, we are asking about the slope of the dotted line in figure 10.7. This measure has been given the unfortunate name "duration" D, even though this naming convention leads to immediate confusion with a time measure (see Appendix below). It should be noted however, that longer-dated bonds also have higher durations, and vice versa. But despite this more intuitive, time-related notion of duration, the latter has nothing to do with time and can be defined as follows:

$$D \equiv \frac{\partial P}{\partial r} \qquad (7)$$

In equation (7), the quantity r is defined as the bond's periodic yield to maturity or simply yield. As stated above, in circumstances where the cash flows C_i are independent of interest rates, the duration D of the bond, may be written as:

$$D \equiv \frac{\partial P}{\partial r} = \frac{-1}{(1+r)} \sum_{i=1}^{n} \frac{i C_i}{(1+r)^i} \qquad (8)$$

Note from equation (8) that duration is algebraically negative for normal bonds, which indicates the known inverse relationship between yield and price changes. However, despite this negativity, duration is usually stated as a positive value measured in years and equal to the number of basis points by which a bond will appreciate given a 100 bps decline in rates, and vice versa for rising rates. For example, five-year duration means that if rates should decline by 1%, the bond's price would rise by 5% and vice versa. Some practitioners also use a standardized percentile system whereby the last situation would be described as "5% duration." These definitions are as unfortunate as they are non-intuitive.

Conversely, in instances where C_i are dependent on prepayment rates and hence on interest rates, i.e., we have $C_i(r)$, duration is no longer given by the right-hand side of equation (8). Rather, we must go back to the middle term and include the new cash flow dependence on yield:

$$D = \sum_{i=1}^{n} \frac{(1+r)^i \frac{\partial C_i(r)}{\partial r} - i(1+r)^{i-1} C_i(r)}{(1+r)^{2i}} \qquad (9)^3$$

As a rule, the acceleration of cash flows stemming from a reduction in the level of interest rates vis-à-vis their original benchmark, and thus from a corresponding increase in prepayment rates, also increases the absolute value of duration since in general, the condition

$$\frac{\partial C_i(r)}{\partial r} \leq 0$$

will hold for all values of r in some target range. Although other, derived measures of duration are used, such as Macaulay or modified duration, they all express the same basic concept.

Convexity

The second measure of significance in RMBS analysis is the second derivative of price with respect to yield, aptly named convexity K. It is normally defined as follows:

$$K \equiv \frac{\partial^2 P}{\partial r^2} \qquad (10)$$

In the case of a non-callable bond, equation (10) leads to the analogue of equation (8):

$$K \equiv \frac{\partial^2 P}{\partial r^2} = \frac{\partial D}{\partial r} = \frac{1}{(1+r)^2} \sum_{i=1}^{n} \frac{(i+i^2) C_i}{(1+r)^i} \qquad (11)$$

The derivation of the relationship corresponding to equation (9) for convexity is left as an exercise.

Fundamentally, convexity expresses the basic nonlinearity of the price yield curve since bonds with prices linearly related to yields have zero convexity. As already indicated, RMBS bonds will normally exhibit negative convexity while Treasury bonds will be positively convex. Higher convexity bonds are more sensitive to rate changes than lower convexity bonds. This undesirable behavior can be significant in the context of hedge fund analysis. Unfortunately, we cannot enter into details at this point (see chapter 24 below).

The Cost of Convexity

As demonstrated in the last section, investors will be unwilling to pay the same price for any given nominal or stated spread on an RMBS because of the associated prepayment option. They feel, and rightly so, that their stated spread is at risk versus that of an equally yielding but non-callable bond, and the difference between what they should pay and what they are willing pay is referred to as the bond's OAS. Note that we could also view the situation in option-theoretic terms by stating that the bondholder has effectively sold a group of borrowers the option to prepay their investment. Therefore, the investors can be regarded as being short such prepayment options. The negative sign associated with this short position can thus "explain" the price difference between the RMBS and the plain-vanilla bond.

Clearly, the collective cost of the short positions will be different for bonds with different stated yields since the prepayment options will be *in the money* at different rates for different mortgage coupon rates. As a result, we find that the OAS is different across the entire Treasury curve rather than being unique throughout. This further complicates the investment landscape and creates confusion. To help clear up such confusion and enable investors to visualize the global impact of convexity, investment banks often produce in graphical form the cost of bond convexity over a wide range of interest rates. Such a graph is reproduced roughly in figure 10.8.

This cost can also be viewed as the risk premium demanded by investors versus what they would require from a normal, non-callable bond. It can be calculated by comparing on a static basis the yield spread versus Treasury bonds of equal

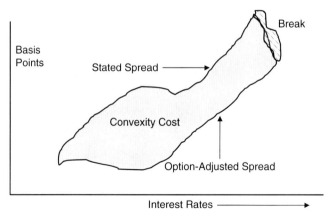

FIGURE 10.8
Embedded cost of convexity in RMBS investment.

average life to the situation where prepayments are allowed to vary with a series of interest-rate scenarios in combination with a prepayment model producing the associated cash flows. A spread is labeled *static* when it is computed by means of a single prepayment scenario, usually termed the *base case*, resulting in a single average life value at which the RMBS spread is read off the prevailing yield curve for such instruments.

By contrast, the OAS model (see "The Modeling of OAS" below) spawns a sequence of interest-rate paths, each of which produces its own set of cash flows, and hence its own average life for each security given the deal's bond structure. Using the associated spread will normally never result in the price for which the bond currently sells. In order to match the computed and actual bond prices, it will be necessary to discount the model-computed cash flows by an additional amount, which amount is always measured in basis points (bps). This amount is the OAS.

10.10 THE MODELING OF OAS

Although producing the spread difference referred to as the OAS is not theoretically complicated, it is quite involved numerically and involves many aspects of statistical analysis. Herein, we review briefly the main highlights of all OAS models and indicate the most glaring analytical pitfalls that should act as cautionary tales for investors relying on such models in order to make judicious choices.

An OAS model consists of three main building blocks:

1. An interest-rate model (see below) used to generate a reasonable set of rate paths that will be inputs to the next block. Rate paths will need to be as long as the longest maturity of any loan in the RMBS pool.

2. A prepayment-rate model using rate paths produced in Step 1, and outputting cash flows derived therefrom. As indicated above, prepayment models are *conditional* in the sense that they attempt to predict prepayment rates given interest rates and other driver variables, instead of trying to predict these independent variables themselves.

3. A cash flow model able to combine the prepayment rates from Step 2 and compute the OAS spreads by reference to market bond prices and the yield curve. Schematically, the OAS methodology can be visualized as shown in figure 10.9

When we speak of OAS analysis, we enter a world filled with slippery slopes, half-truths and innuendos. This is not to say that OAS modeling has no place in finance, quite the contrary. In fact, despite its shortcomings OAS analysis is probably the best one can do given the current state of prepayment knowledge. But this pat on the back should never obscure the plain fact that much of the resulting output is groundless and must be taken with a grain, if not an entire bucket, of salt. Nevertheless, it is instructive to examine the above components a little more deeply to extract some clues as to how to proceed.

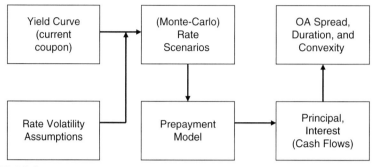

FIGURE 10.9
The derivation of option-adjusted spread via OAS modeling.

The Interest-Rate Model

When we talk about an interest-rate model, we are specifically referring to a short-rate model whose sole output is the instantaneous rate of interest, often the one-month LIBOR rate. There are many such models in the literature, but most of them are based on the work of Oldrich Vasicek. The one we prefer is the Cox–Ingersoll–Ross (CIR) model, one of the many subsequent incarnations of the original Vasicek model published in 1977.

Note that the use of any other model is acceptable, and we encourage credit analysts to use the model they know best. All short-rate models can be made to produce comparable outputs. The difference in their predictive accuracy is negligible compared to the average error they produce.

The CIR Short-Rate Model

Within the CIR model, the short-rate increment dr is estimated using:

$$dr = \mu (r_0 - r) dt + \sigma \sqrt{r} dz \tag{12}$$

It should first be mentioned that the main innovation in both the CIR and Vasicek models comes about via a steady-state mean short rate r_0 rather than through the term $\mu\, dt$, which was symptomatic of previous modeling efforts. As can readily be seen, for all values of r satisfying $r > r_0$, the increment dr would on average satisfy $dr < 0$ and hence the rate r would tend to be brought back closer to r_0, and vice versa in the opposite case. Thus, the value r_0 acts as an "attractor" in yield space. The dynamic sequence of short rates r regards the line $r = r_0$ more or less as a limit cycle of the system. The ratio σ/μ then determines how closely the current rate hugs this limit cycle.

We can therefore expect that, much of the time, the model will force interest rates to oscillate around r_0 (i.e. the mean short rate in equation (12)) while still allowing rate excursions dictated by the value of volatility σ. In addition, the term $\sqrt{r}$ was added to recognize the fact that absolute rate-volatility tends to increase when rates

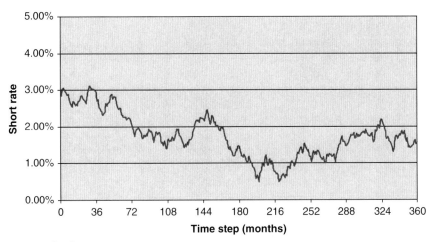

FIGURE 10.10
Typical short rate sequence from the CIR model.

are relatively high and vice versa. The Vasicek model simply omits the square root term but preserves the basic limiting intuition.

The essence of the CIR model is its mean-reversion feature, captured by the value of r_0, and thus requires that a reasonable estimate for that quantity exists already. Figure 10.10 shows a typical short-rate sequence arising from the CIR model, whereby the limit cycle was set at $r_0 = 0.02$ and where the initial rate $r(0) = 0.03$. For this run, we set short-rate volatility $\sigma = 0.10\%$.

As stated before, as long as rates remain within the realm of the possible, any short-rate model may be used.

The Basic Prepayment Model

Prepayment modeling is an art and a science, as well as being very time-consuming. We do not intend to go into details, but seek merely to highlight the main drivers of all such models. We introduce a basic form of prepayment model consisting of Brownian motion coupled with an inverse rate driver and a burnout factor. As a result, single-month mortality can be represented as follows:

$$SMM(t) = e^{-at}\left[\alpha_0 + \beta_0\left(\frac{K}{r(t)} - 1\right)\right] + \sigma\, dz \qquad (13)$$

In equation (13), we have defined the relevant parameters as follows:

t $=$ time (months)
$SMM(t)$ $=$ single month mortality at time t
$r(t)$ $=$ CIR short-rate model output
K $=$ $r(t_0)$ (calibration variable)

$r(t_0)$ = short rate on the closing date of the target transaction
α_0 = base prepayment rate
β_0 = interest-rate effect multiplier
a = burnout rate
dz = Wiener process
σ = volatility of prepayment rates

The variable K is simply a calibration variable introduced in order to force the initial prepayment rates to be close to the base rate. We do this because we expect that in the initial stages of the transaction obligors will lack the incentive to refinance their mortgage or indebtedness because interest rates will tend to hover around the value at which the loan was issued, which is likely to be in the neighborhood of $r(t_0)$ in most cases. In other words, as stated above when current rates are near their closing value obligors will have neither the financial incentive nor the wherewithal to repay their loan immediately. We recognize this fact via $K = r(t_0)$, leading to the condition $K/r(t) - 1 \approx 0$ in the first few years of a transaction.

The implementation of this prepayment model merely amounts to the insertion of equation (13) into the dynamics of the transaction as represented inside the cash model (see the next sub-section). In essence, we are modulating the conditional prepayment rate $SMM(t)$ to the extent it is different from its formerly constant value α_0, the base prepayment rate. As an illustration, figure 10.11 shows a path of single month mortalities produced by the our basic prepayment model.

In actual implementations, it is customary to impose a cap and a floor on the value $SMM(t)$ can assume, to avoid either negative prepayment rates or rates that have never been experienced.

Although admittedly simplistic, the above model nevertheless tries to recognize explicitly the interest-rate component of prepayment, which is of prime importance,

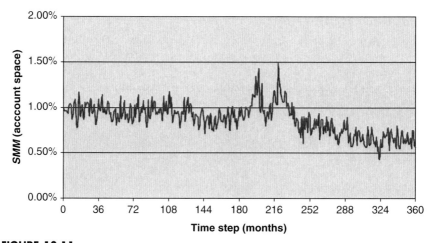

FIGURE 10.11
Typical SMM sequence for prepayment model equation (13).

as well as its burnout feature, itself a relatively recent addition to formal prepayment models. The stochasticity of prepayment rates is also included via a standard Wiener process.

The Cash Flow Model

This portion of the OAS methodology consists of applying principal and interest cash flows to the various classes of bonds that make up the structure of the transaction under review. Although this is a vast topic, a fairly comprehensive introduction was already given in chapter 7. Readers should refer to that chapter for further details on the cash flow modeling of structured liabilities. We should stress that an OAS model needs to be able to compute the average life t_A^a of a bond according to its formal definition, and not by assuming an amortization schedule a priori:

$$t_A^a = \frac{1}{P_A^0} \int_0^T t \, dp_A \tag{14}$$

In equation (14), we have defined dp_A as the actual amortization schedule for the Class A bond resulting from the application of principal and interest cash flows produced by the prepayment model under the current Monte Carlo scenario, and P_A^0 as its initial principal balance. A corresponding definition applies to all classes of bonds.

Closing Remarks

In closing, it would be disingenuous on our part to leave unsaid the considerable level of guesswork involved in computing the OAS of an RMBS security. Apart from interest-rate volatility and other critical assumptions, a financial analyst wishing to calculate OAS must make a variety of choices with respect to future rate scenarios and the coefficients affecting the drivers of prepayments based solely on past performance. Interest-rate prediction being what it is, the best that can be obtained from an OAS analysis is an idea of the range of yield performance likely to be encountered over the life of the bond.

As far as the precise yield that the investor will experience is concerned, nothing specific can or should be said. Unfortunately, this has never stopped marketing claims to the contrary. A sober assessment of any contemplated investment should be the rule rather than the exception.

END-OF-CHAPTER QUESTIONS

1. Derive the monthly series of $SMM(t)$ that results from table 10.1, representing monthly cash flows from an arbitrary mortgage pool.
2. Assume that the prepayment history of a particular pool is given (in terms of PSA) for the first 12 months after the loans were originated as: 186 PSA,

TABLE 10.1
Hypothetical cash flow run

OUTSTANDING PRINCIPAL	INTEREST	PAYMENT	SCHEDULED PRINCIPAL	PREPAYMENTS
$200,000,000.00	$1,075,000.00	$ 2,002,300.00	$ 182,566.72	$ 744,733.28
$199,072,700.00	$1,070,015.76	$ 1,341,231.00	$ 187,550.96	$ 83,664.28
$198,801,484.76	$1,068,557.98	$ 1,257,566.72	$ 189,008.74	$ (0.00)
$198,612,476.02	$1,067,542.06	$ 3,058,472.00	$ 190,024.66	$ 1,800,905.28
$196,621,546.08	$1,056,840.81	$ 4,256,878.00	$ 200,725.91	$ 2,999,311.28
$193,421,508.89	$1,039,640.61	$ 4,875,600.00	$ 217,926.11	$ 3,618,033.28
$189,585,549.50	$1,019,022.33	$ 1,257,566.72	$ 238,544.39	$ (0.00)
$189,347,005.11	$1,017,740.15	$ 8,810,295.00	$ 239,826.57	$ 7,552,728.28
$181,554,450.26	$ 975,855.17	$ 5,013,274.00	$ 281,711.55	$ 3,755,707.28
$177,517,031.43	$ 954,154.04	$ 4,826,137.00	$ 303,412.68	$ 3,568,570.28
$173,645,048.48	$ 933,342.14	$ 5,931,508.00	$ 324,224.59	$ 4,673,941.28
$168,646,882.61	$ 906,476.99	$ 6,682,362.00	$ 351,089.73	$ 5,424,795.28
$162,870,997.61	$ 875,431.61	$ 9,056,238.00	$ 382,135.11	$ 7,798,671.28
$154,690,191.22	$ 831,459.78	$ 7,720,367.00	$ 426,106.95	$ 6,462,800.28
$147,801,284.00	$ 794,431.90	$ 6,923,014.00	$ 463,134.82	$ 5,665,447.28
$141,672,701.90	$ 761,490.77	$ 8,083,924.00	$ 496,075.95	$ 6,826,357.28
$134,350,268.67	$ 722,132.69	$10,230,559.00	$ 535,434.03	$ 8,972,992.28
$124,841,842.37	$ 671,024.90	$ 9,873,563.00	$ 586,541.82	$ 8,615,996.28

The cash flow comes from a mortgage pool with weighted average maturity of 360 months and mortgage interest rate of 6.45%.

122 PSA, 241 PSA, 177 PSA, 135 PSA, 111 PSA, 98 PSA, 86 PSA, 122 PSA, 131 PSA, 129 PSA, 144 PSA. What is the arithmetic average of prepayments on this pool in terms of the *SMM* prepayment measure?

3. Using table 10.2 calculate the total single-month mortality prepayment rate that results if voluntary prepayments and defaults are as shown in table 10.2.

TABLE 10.2

TIME	PREPAYMENTS	DEFAULTS
Month 10	92 PSA	120 PSA
Month 11	110 PSA	140 PSA
Month 12	114 PSA	220 PSA
Month 13	124 PSA	185 PSA
Month 14	139 PSA	170 PSA
Month 15	142 PSA	175 PSA

4. How would prepayment patterns for auto loans be different in a country where average auto loan payments were a higher percentage of disposable income than they are in the U.S.?
5. What causes seasonality patterns in turnover and refinancing behavior of mortgage borrowers? How about in the behavior of auto-loan borrowers?
6. Explain the phenomenon of burnout and various ways to model it. What are the strengths and weaknesses of each of these different methods? Under what conditions may we be able to neglect burnout?
7. Explain how the changes in macroeconomic conditions shown in table 10.3 would affect the prepayment rate of fixed-rate mortgages.

TABLE 10.3

EFFECT
1. General decrease in interest rates
2. Acceleration in home prices appreciation
3. Worsening credit situation of borrowers
4. Flattening of the yield curve, with long rates constant
5. Economic recession

8. Calculate the default rate (in *SMM* units) of a pool if monthly defaults are given as the following percentages of the SDA profile in figure 10.6 for the first 12 months of the pool's life: 100% SDA, 120% SDA, 99% SDA, 110% SDA, 125% SDA, 130% SDA, 135% SDA, 120% SDA, 170% SDA, 175% SDA, 225% SDA, 250% SDA.
9. The term *prepayment risk* is sometimes confused with *reinvestment risk*. Please define the meaning and the funding impact of each type of risk.
10. The chapter refers to hedging against the interest rate shifts that can motivate borrowers to refinance certain types of loans (strategic prepayment). How can a portfolio manager use hedging to mitigate the portfolio impacts of strategic prepayment in an environment of declining interest rates? What are the limitations of hedging under those circumstances? Where possible, illustrate your argument with a numerical example.
11. Average life under principal shortfalls.
    - Derive the parity condition that links the average life of the pool to that of the associated liabilities.
    - What periodic cash flow environment ensures that the parity condition will hold for a given deal realization?
    - Define the average life of a pool of assets. Define the average life of a liability tranche associated to any asset pool.

- Derive a modified version of the parity condition for cases whereby the aggregate asset and aggregate liability amortization are not always equal at each time step under one particular transaction realization.
- Under which scenario does this formula no longer apply?

APPENDIX: DURATION AND AVERAGE LIFE

Introduction

Despite the fact that the concepts of *duration* and *average life* could not be more different from each other than they already are, there appears to exist widespread confusion in the mind of many practitioners as to a possible relationship between them, a confusion that sometimes takes the form of outright identification. For some, duration even seems to stand for another way of expressing the idea of average life. The following paragraphs are intended to dispel as much of that confusion as possible, hopefully without introducing more.

To begin with, one could not be faulted for believing that the two concepts are in fact one and the same. After all, the word "duration" certainly connotes a time determination, and so does "life". What else but time could there be in the idea of "duration"? On the other hand, mathematically speaking the situation could not be clearer. Duration is an attempt to measure the sensitivity of the price of a bond to instantaneous changes in interest rates, while average life speaks of the "average" maturity of a stream of principal payments extending over possibly many years. Thus in the concept of duration, time per se is absent, whereas it is of the essence when computing average life since it represents the sole integration variable. In other words, duration is a *local* concept, while average life is a *global* concept.

In addition, and more importantly, duration involves total cash flow received by bondholders whereas average life solely addresses flows allocated to principal. Yet there remains a lingering belief in many quarters as to their putative kinship. Why is that? Contrary to all mathematical notions, not to mention commonsense, why do so many people still harbor the secret intuition that they are somehow connected? The answer is quite simple: they are.

The Connection between Average Life and Duration

Ostensibly, the story of duration begins in 1938, the year in which Frederick Macaulay introduced the first attempt to characterize the volatility of bond prices with respect to interest rates. By using the word *duration* to refer to his concept, he could perhaps be regarded as the man most responsible for the confusion that now exists. Yet, to pass judgment so hastily on one of the few people who ever tried to bring clarity to Wall Street would be to commit a grave error. His original formulation eventually acquired the label *Macaulay duration* and still constitutes the basic intuition underlying duration in the capital markets. In the standard case of a plain-vanilla corporate bond, one not subject to the sort of call risk that affects mortgage-backed securities for instance, it ran as follows:

$$D_M \equiv \frac{\sum_{i=1}^{T} \frac{t_i C_i}{(1+r)^{t_i}}}{\sum_{i=1}^{T} \frac{C_i}{(1+r)^{t_i}}} \qquad (A.1)$$

In the above relationship, we have defined the following quantities:

D_M = Macaulay duration
T = stated maturity of the bond
i = integer time index with $i \in [1, T]$ (i.e., $t_1 = 1$, etc.)
C_i = total cash flow received during period t_i
r = periodic discount rate of interest

Although Macaulay probably did not have calculus in mind when he devised equation (A.1), analytically minded readers will immediately recognize the denominator as corresponding to the definition of the value V_0 of a bond as of $t = 0$ and expected to receive T cash flows at future times $t_i, i \in [1, T]$, while the numerator looks suspiciously like the first derivative of the denominator with respect to yield r. Yet, Macaulay did not propose equation (A.1) by backing out of a rigorous mathematical derivation. Instead, he was operating on pure instinct.

As you can see, save for the missing minus sign in the numerator and a factor $(1+r)$ in the denominator, the definition of D_M given by equation (A.1) is simply a modified version of the more modern formulation of duration which, not surprisingly perhaps, came to be known as *modified duration*, or duration tout court:

$$D(r) \equiv -\frac{1}{V_0} \frac{\partial V_0(r)}{\partial r} \qquad (A.2)$$

In the equation (A.2), $V(r)$ is the fair market value of the bond at some time, and without loss of generality, we have defined $V_0(r)$ as its fair market value at $t = 0$. In any event, the current time can always be normalized to zero. In essence, practitioners simply filled in the elements of the definition of first derivative that were missing from Macaulay's original insight.

As you may already know, there are many practical reasons why the value of a bond might fall or rise with interest rates in ways that would falsify the result obtained using equation (A.2), which factors go beyond the simple logic of equation (A.1). We reiterate that equation (A.2) merely addresses the standard case where risk-free cash flows are received and where investors simply look to the opportunity cost of alternative, current investments to value an existing plain-vanilla bond.

In our treatment, we thus fully abstract from these various real-life effects and consider the impact of interest-rate fluctuations on a pure cash flow stream in a totally fluid environment. Far from being unimportant, this case is actually the way most financial analysts are first introduced to duration within an academic setting.

By contrast, the canonical definition of average life t^a reproduced here for the sake of argument, goes as follows:

$$t^a \equiv \frac{1}{P_0} \int_0^T t \, dp(t) \qquad (A.3)$$

In equation (A.3),we have defined the following additional quantities:

$p(t)$ = principal balance of the bond outstanding at time t
$dp(t)$ = amortization schedule for the bond from $t - dt$ to t

As always, we postulate the following two boundary conditions:

$$p(0) \equiv P_0 \qquad (A.4a)$$

$$p(T) = 0 \qquad (A.4b)$$

In the absence of any information to the contrary, it is customary to assume a fair market, which implies that price and value are numerically identical, leading to:

$$P_0 = V_0 \qquad (A.5)$$

Now, recall our fundamental cash flow balance equation for the plain-vanilla bond, from which we can also derive the principal balance schedule $p(t)$:

$$f(t) dt = r p(t) dt - dp(t) \qquad (A.6)$$

In equation (A.6), variable $f(t)$ represents the total cash received by bondholders, which is then partitioned into principal and interest allocations.

The next step is to transform the basic definition for the value of a plain-vanilla bond usually conceived as a discrete sum of payments made over the T periods into an integral from zero to maturity:

$$V_0 = \int_0^T f(t) e^{-rt} \, dt \qquad (A.7)$$

This "passing to the limit" will enable us to manipulate the above relations more easily. In doing so, $f(t) dt$ takes the place of the discrete payments C_i shown in (A.1) while the factor $(1+r)$ in the denominator is simply the first term of the Taylor-series expansion of e^{-r}. Applying definition (A.2) to equation (A.7) leads to:

$$D(r) = -\frac{1}{V_0} \frac{\partial}{\partial r} \left[\int_0^T f(t) e^{-rt} \, dt \right] = \frac{1}{V_0} \int_0^T t f(t) e^{-rt} \, dt \qquad (A.8)$$

In deriving the last identity, we can take the differential operator inside the integral sign without recourse to Leibniz's rule because r and t are independent variables.

Now, substitute equation (A.6) inside equation (A.8) to obtain:

$$D(r) = \frac{1}{V_0} \int_0^T t e^{-rt} [r p(t) dt - dp(t)] = \int_0^T r t p(t) e^{-rt} dt - \int_0^T t e^{-rt} dp(t) \quad \text{(A.9)}$$

Next, we use integration by parts on the second term on the right of equation (A.9). As usual, we have:

$$u = t e^{-rt}, \, du = (e^{-rt} - r t e^{-rt}) dt \quad \text{(A.10a)}$$

$$dv = dp(t), \, v = p(t) \quad \text{(A.10b)}$$

The mechanics of integration by parts quickly yield:

$$D(r) = \frac{1}{V_0} \left[-t e^{-rt} p(t) \Big|_0^T + \int_0^T p(t) (1 - rt) e^{-rt} dt + \int_0^T r t p(t) e^{-rt} dt \right] \quad \text{(A.11)}$$

Applying boundary conditions given as equation (A.4) and effecting the obvious cancellation inside equation (A.11), we finally obtain:

$$D(r) = \frac{1}{V_0} \int_0^T p(t) e^{-rt} dt \quad \text{(A.12)}$$

Now, making use of our fair value condition given as equation (A.5) we can write:

$$D(r) = \frac{1}{P_0} \int_0^T p(t) e^{-rt} dt \quad \text{(A.13)}$$

Glancing at the definition given as equation (A.3), we note that average life can be rewritten under a Riemann framework instead of the above Lebesgue formulation:

$$t^a = \frac{1}{P_0} \int_0^T p(t) dt \quad \text{(A.14)}$$

Equations (A.13) and (A.14) should provide ample motivation for the following definition of average life as the transcendental limit of duration in the case of vanishing yield:

$$t^a \equiv \lim_{r \to 0} D(r) \quad \text{(A.15)}$$

As can readily be seen, there does indeed exist an intimate relationship between these two seemingly disparate concepts. This relationship, which remains for the most part hidden in the background of our calculations, is precisely what gives rise both to the prevailing confusion about duration and average life and to the intuition that they are "the same". In fact, the transcendence of average life vis-à-vis duration is why Macaulay himself was led to his brilliant intuition.

A Few Practical Examples

Example 1: Straight-line Amortizing Bond

Our first example is more of a reality check than anything else. To see whether our new, transcendental definition for average life makes any sense, we wish to use equations (A.13) and (A.15) to compute explicitly the duration and average life of a bond with initial principal balance P_0 and amortizing in a straight-line pattern across the interval $t \in [0, T]$.

In this simple case, the use of equation (A.15) to compute t^a is clearly superfluous since triangulation quickly leads to the well-known result:

$$t^a = \frac{T}{2} \tag{A.16}$$

The goal of this exercise is to verify that equation (A.15) reproduces the known result (A.16).

We first write down the amortization schedule for the bond, ensuring further that it satisfies boundary conditions (A.4):

$$p(t) = P_0 \left(1 - \frac{t}{T} \right) \tag{A.17}$$

Substituting equation (A.17) into equation (A.13), we readily obtain:

$$D(r) = \frac{1}{P_0} \int_0^T P_0 \left(1 - \frac{t}{T} \right) e^{-rt} dt = \int_0^T \left(1 - \frac{t}{T} \right) e^{-rt} \, dt \tag{A.18}$$

Skipping the trivial algebra, we get:

$$D(r) = -\left. \frac{e^{-rt}}{r} \right|_0^T - \frac{1}{T} \left\{ -\frac{e^{-rt}}{r} \left(t + \frac{1}{r} \right) \right\} \Big|_0^T$$

$$D(r) = \frac{1}{r} \left(1 - e^{-rT} \right) + \frac{1}{T} \left\{ \frac{e^{-rT}}{r} \left(T + \frac{1}{r} \right) - \frac{1}{r^2} \right\} \tag{A.19}$$

Equation (A.19) is our formula for duration. Whether or not it is correct cannot be decided right now, but let's see if it leads to the known result (A.16) for average life.

We cannot simply substitute the limit $r = 0$ inside equation (A.19) because of the obvious pole singularities. Instead, we need to expand the factor e^{-rT} into its Taylor-series and let r approach its vanishing limit that way. High-school calculus lets us write:

$$e^{-rT} = 1 - rT + \frac{(rT)^2}{2} - \frac{(rT)^3}{6} + \ldots \ldots \tag{A.20}$$

Note that, in equation (A.20), the neglected terms are all of quartic or higher order and will not play a leading role in our derivation. Next, expansion of equation (A.19) gives us:

$$D(r) = \frac{1}{r} - \frac{e^{-rT}}{r} + \frac{e^{-rT}}{r} + \frac{1}{r^2 T}\left[e^{-rT} - 1\right] \qquad (A.21)$$

After canceling the middle two terms, insertion of equation (A.20) into equation (A.21) yields:

$$D(r) = \frac{1}{r} + \frac{1}{r^2 T}\left[1 - rT + \frac{r^2 T^2}{2} - \frac{r^3 T^3}{6} - 1 + \ldots\ldots\right] \qquad (A.22)$$

Collecting terms, we have:

$$D(r) = \frac{T}{2} - \frac{rT^2}{6} + \ldots\ldots \qquad (A.23)$$

As advertised, in the limit of vanishing yield we obtain:

$$t^a = \lim_{r \to 0}\left[\frac{T}{2} - \frac{rT^2}{6} + \ldots\ldots\right] \to \frac{T}{2} \quad QED$$

Example 2: Laplace Transform Formulation

As we just saw, in a simple case equation (A.15) enabled us to recover the well-known average-life result for a straight-line amortizing bond. Now, let's see what it can do with a situation that is perhaps less intuitive than the previous one, namely the case of a bond with infinite maturity and an unusual amortization profile. Specifically, we wish to compute the duration and average life of a security with the following principal balance schedule:

$$p(t) = P_0\, e^{-\alpha t}\left[1 + \sin\left(\omega t\right)\right], \ p(\infty) \to 0 \qquad (A.24)$$

Figure 10.12 shows a typical pattern produced by equation (A.24). This type of profile could arise, for instance, in the case of a graduated-payment student loan in which the initial total payment made would be insufficient to pay even the interest on the loan when due, thus causing negative amortization to take place, but soon followed by higher payments that would let the principal amortize, and so on. Whether this is realistic or not is not at issue here.

According to equation (A.13), we need to extend the upper integration limit to infinity, thus reproducing the canonical definition of the Laplace transform of the principal balance schedule $L(p(t))$. Therefore, in general we can redefine modified duration as the normalized Laplace transform of $p(t)$ as follows:

$$D(r) \equiv \frac{1}{P_0} L(p(t)) \qquad (A.25)$$

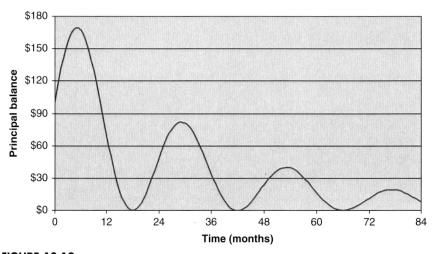

FIGURE 10.12
Amortization schedule of an exponentially decaying sinusoidal bond.

The Laplace transform of cash flow stream in equation (A.24) can be looked up in any mathematical handbook, and we obtain:

$$L(p(t)) = P_0 \left\{ \frac{1}{r+\alpha} + \frac{\omega}{(r+\alpha)^2 + \omega^2} \right\} \tag{A.26}$$

Equation (A.26) yields modified duration directly, while average life simply drops out as:

$$t^a = \lim_{r \to 0} \left\{ \frac{1}{r+\alpha} + \frac{\omega}{(r+\alpha)^2 + \omega^2} \right\} = \frac{1}{\alpha} + \frac{\omega}{\alpha^2 + \omega^2} \tag{A.27}$$

It is probably fair to say that equations (A.26) and (A.27) are not intuitive and could not have been "guessed" by just glancing at the cash flow stream in equation (A.24). Therefore, the above Laplace transform formulation of duration offers an appealing extension of the latter concept to cases like perpetual bonds and to other pathological situations with no obvious answer.

We can extend the above Laplace transform definition to convexity $C(r)$ in a simple manner by noticing that the latter quantity may be defined as follows:

$$C(r) = \frac{\partial D(r)}{\partial r} = \frac{\partial}{\partial r} \left[\frac{1}{P_0} L(p(t)) \right]$$

From one of the well-known properties of Laplace transforms, we can readily write:

$$C(r) \equiv -\frac{1}{P_0} L(tp(t)) \tag{A.28}$$

In the case of bonds paying discrete cash flows, it is clear that duration can be expressed as a sum of terms with the factor $z \equiv (1+r)$ in the denominator. Assuming a bond with principal balance $p(n)$ at time n, our equivalent definition of duration gives us:

$$D_d(r) = \frac{1}{P_0} \sum_{n=0}^{\infty} p(n)z^{-n} \qquad (A.29)$$

However, the summation on the right of equation (A.29) is none other than the unilateral Z-transform of an infinite sequence of real numbers and is normally labeled $Z[p(n)]$. In other words, in the case of discrete bonds, duration can be generalized as the normalized Z-transform of the bond's principal balance schedule:

$$D_d(r) \equiv \frac{1}{P_0} Z[p(n)] \qquad (A.30)$$

By strict analogy with the continuous case and using the basic properties of Z-transforms, discrete bond convexity drops out immediately as:

$$C_d(r) \equiv -\frac{1}{P_0} Z[np(n)] \qquad (A.31)$$

Example 4: Duration formula for the plain-vanilla ABS bond

Let us use our new-found knowledge to compute the duration of our plain-vanilla bond defined via the relationship:

$$p(t) \equiv \begin{cases} \frac{M}{r_0}\left[1 - e^{r_0(t-T)}\right], 0 \le t \le T \\ 0, t \ge T \end{cases}$$

From the above definition, we can readily write down:

$$D(r) = \frac{M}{r_0 P_0} \left\{ \int_0^T e^{-rt}\,dt - \int_0^T e^{r_0(t-T)-rt}\,dt \right\}$$

Skipping the trivial algebra again, we obtain:

$$D(r) = \frac{1}{1 - e^{-r_0 T}} \left\{ \frac{1 - e^{-rT}}{r} + \frac{e^{-r_0 T} - e^{-rT}}{(r_0 - r)} \right\} \qquad (A.32)$$

Now, assume the following data:

$r_0 = 0.12$ APR
$T = 5$ years
$r = 0.10$ APR

Direct substitution yields:

$$D(0.1) = \frac{1}{0.4512}\left\{ \frac{1 - 0.6065}{0.1} + \frac{(0.5488 - 0.6065)}{0.02} \right\} = 2.22(1.045) = 2.32\ yrs$$

As a reality check, duration for the case $r = 0.14$ yields:

$$D(0.14) = \frac{1}{0.4512} \left\{ \frac{1 - 0.4966}{0.14} - \frac{(0.5488 - 0.4966)}{0.02} \right\} = 2.22 (0.985) = 2.18 \text{ yrs}$$

Example 5: First-order Taylor-series expansion and bond price prediction

The computation of duration and convexity enables us to make interesting predictions for bonds in the secondary market. For example, suppose a bond is now selling for 105.5 in a market where the current interest rate r_c is 10%. What it would sell for if interest rates jumped up 200 bps? To answer this question, let's expand the market value of the bond about the current value of 105.5 as a first-order Taylor-series:

$$V(r_c + \Delta r) = V_{r_c} [1 - D(r_c) \Delta r]$$

Given the above data, the predicted market price of the bond after a 200 bps rise would be:

$$V(12\%) = 105.5 [1 - 2.32 (0.02)] = 100.60$$

Example 6: Second-order Taylor-series expansion and bond price prediction

As a last example, suppose we wish to refine the estimate in example 5 using convexity, and assume that duration and convexity satisfy the following relationship:

$$\frac{C(r_c)}{D(r_c)} = -\frac{1}{r_c} \tag{A.33}$$

Now, expand the value of the bond into a second-order Taylor-series using normalized duration and convexity as follows:

$$V(r_c + \Delta r) = V_{r_c} \left[1 - D(r_c) \Delta r - \frac{1}{2} C(r_c) \Delta r^2 \right] \tag{A.34}$$

Substitution of equation (A.33) into equation (A.34) using the data from example 5 readily yields:

$$C(r_c) = -10 D(r_c)$$

$$V(12\%) = 105.5 \left[1 - 2.32 (0.02) + \frac{1}{2} 23.2 (0.02)^2 \right] = 101.09$$

As you can see, the availability of duration and convexity for all possible bonds affords us much flexibility in making markets in the ABS space. Similar calculations can be performed with respect to the discrete version of the duration and convexity formulas. We leave them as exercises.

BIBLIOGRAPHY

A Primer on Securitization, Leon T. Kendall, Michael J. Fishman, The MIT Press, 2000.

Advances in the Valuation and Management of Mortgage-Backed Securities, Frank J. Fabozzi, Ed., Frank J. Fabozzi Associates, 1998.

Securitization of Credit—Inside the New Technology of Finance, James A. Rosenthal, Juan M. Ocampo, John Wiley & Sons, Inc., 1988.

Investing in Asset-Backed Securities, Frank J. Fabozzi, Ed., Frank J. Fabozzi Associates, 2000.

The Handbook of Mortgage-Backed Securities, 5th edition, Frank J. Fabozzi, Ed., Frank J. Fabozzi Associates, 2001.

"Active-Passive Decomposition in Burnout Modeling", Alexander Levin, *The Journal of Fixed Income*, March 2001.

"Anatomy of Prepayments", Lakhbir S. Hayre, Sharad Chaudhary, and Robert A. Young, *The Journal of Fixed Income*, June 2000.

Salomon Smith Barney Guide to Mortgage-backed and Asset-backed Securities, Lakhbir Hayre, Ed., John Wiley & Sons, Inc., 2001.

11

PACs

The Planned Amortization Class (PAC) is a fairly common, well-understood structural feature of mortgage-backed and some auto-loan backed structured financings. By their nature, PACs are more difficult to use in high-credit-loss than in low-credit-loss environments like RMBS backed by prime collateral. In addition, as a play on interest rates, PACs are unlikely to be attractive in environments where interest-rate related cash flow sensitivity is weak, which is the case for most liquid classes of ABS. In the next few paragraphs, we discuss the philosophy of the PAC and its mechanics as they relate to prepayment protection.

11.1 THE PHILOSOPHY OF THE PAC

The PAC was conceived to give prepayment protection to certain classes of investors who would suffer either yield erosion or a relatively less favorable set of reinvestment opportunities should prepayment speeds severely exceed historical norms. Such risks may arise under different scenarios, but the most interesting is probably that facing the purchaser of an interest-only (IO) class in a pool of mortgages. Since the buyer's cash flows stem exclusively from collateral interest collections it is conceivable that the entire pool might prepay on day one, in which case interest cash flows would be zero. In that case, the return on the IO would be -100%, i.e., the buyer would lose his entire investment. Furthermore, this case would not result from any default or credit event, and would occur regardless of the fact that the IO might have been rated Aaa by a rating agency. The flip side of this argument would obviously apply to a principal-only (PO) security buyer who would also receive all cash flows on day one, and therefore realize an unexpected windfall from this extreme prepayment speed.

Albeit such cases are rather academic, the point is that an investor potentially exposed to such high return volatility will usually demand some modicum of downside protection. Someone might retort that the IO downside risk is compensated by the "opportunity" of perhaps an equally probable, but lower than expected prepayment speed, in which case the IO buyer would receive the windfall gain instead of the PO buyer. Unfortunately, given the predictive power of most prepayment models, which are essentially interest rate forecasting models,[1] coupled with the fact that the Wall Street fear index usually exceeds its greed index by an order of magnitude, this argument is unlikely to be comfort investors considering a purchase.

Although IO buyers are fully aware that their investment entails prepayment risk, over the years they have become comfortable with risk within a certain universe of prepayments based on historical evidence with similar collateral. Even though the price of the IO was negotiated freely between buyer and seller based on their relative views on prepayments, these views were heavily conditioned by contemporary and historical interest rate volatility patterns. If interest-rate volatility were to take the pool outside the prepayment universe initially contemplated, the IO buyer would be exposed to losses without recourse.

In other words, risk aversion introduces an asymmetry in the risk perception of an otherwise risk-neutral pricing scenario. As a result, even assuming equal low and high prepayment speed probability mass on either side of the pricing curve, IO investors nevertheless require more security against excessively high prepayment speeds. Achieving this security is what the PAC is designed to do.

Bear in mind that the PAC mechanism is not supposed to remove *all* downside risk from the IO, just that portion of the at risk that could arise from prepayment speeds in excess of most conceivable historical norms. In the end, nothing can save an IO buyer from the cash flow consequences of a doomsday scenario.

11.2 THE MECHANICS OF THE PAC

The basic technique at the heart of the PAC is the partitioning of the pool's outstanding principal balance $B(t)$ into two components: the PAC [$P(t)$] and the companion class [$C(t)$]. At all times the following condition holds:

$$B(t) = P(t) + C(t) \tag{1}$$

Assuming cash to be always available for distribution, the IO buyer would receive the following periodic allocation $F(t)$, where t measures the number of payment periods:

$$F(t) = rP(t-1), 0 < r \le R \tag{2}$$

In equation (2), r is the IO periodic rate and R is usually much smaller than the pool's weighted average coupon. The next step is the crucial element of the PAC concept.

Based on prepayment speeds considered high given historical norms, a PAC schedule $S(t)$ is established at closing. The schedule $S(t)$ may be derived in a number of different and equally valid ways, but for our purposes we can assume that it represents some fixed percentage α of the pool's outstanding principal balance under an extreme historical prepayment scenario, which we label $B^h(t)$. In other words $S(t)$ is mainly computed based on the highest historical prepayment speed seen on similar collateral over a comparable period and the amount of cushion may therefore be conveniently defined as $1 - \alpha$.

Once the ratio $\alpha = \frac{S(t)}{B^h(t)}$ is agreed upon, the IO price is negotiated between buyer and seller solely based on cash flows allocated to the PAC component.

Finally, the PAC balance $P(t)$ required as input to equation (2) is computed for each period according to the following scheme. First, the companion class balance $C(t)$ is calculated from:

$$C(t) = Max[0, (1 - \alpha)B(t) - Max[0, S(t) - \alpha B(t)]] \qquad (3)$$

Then, the PAC balance $P(t)$ is computed from equation (1).

Since IO cash flows are based on $P(t)$ only, this technique exposes investors to the following three prepayment regimes:

1. For prepayment speeds between zero and those such that $B(t) \geq \frac{S(t)}{\alpha}$, we have $P(t) = \alpha B(t)$. In such cases, the IO holder is taking prepayment risk within the universe originally contemplated and is receiving an expected return presumably in line with such risks.

2. For prepayment speeds such that $B(t) \leq \frac{S(t)}{\alpha}$ and $C(t) > 0$, we have $P(t) = S(t)$. This is the PAC's chief prepayment protection feature. In essence, over a range of prepayment speeds in excess of historical norms, the IO buyer is assured of a known principal balance schedule for purposes of IO cash flow allocation. Obviously, this range depends entirely on the value of α. Traditionally, this region of prepayment speeds has been referred to as the "PAC structuring band," or "PAC range." We will henceforth adhere to this naming convention.

3. For prepayment speeds such that $B(t) \leq \frac{S(t)}{\alpha}$ and $C(t) = 0$, we have $P(t) = B(t)$. In other words, in this case IO investors suffer a dollar for dollar reduction in the basis of their cash flow allocation formula. This regime would be considered extreme by any measure and completely outside even the highest conceivable prepayment speeds.

It can be readily seen that equations (1) and (3) meet the above requirements. For instance, under the first regime, equation (3) yields:

$$C(t) = (1 - \alpha)B(t) \qquad (4)$$

Insertion of equation (4) into equation (1) then gives:

$$P(t) = B(t) - (1 - \alpha)B(t) = \alpha B(t)$$

Under the second regime, we have from equation (3):

$$C(t) = (1 - \alpha)B(t) - (S(t) - \alpha B(t)) = B(t) - S(t) \qquad (5)$$

Insertion of equation (5) into equation (1) now yields:

$$P(t) = B(t) - (B(t) - S(t)) = S(t)$$

Finally, under the third regime equation (2) leads to:

$$C(t) = 0 \qquad\qquad (6)$$

Insertion of equation (6) into equation (1) produces:

$$P(t) = B(t) - 0 = B(t)$$

As mentioned earlier, the value of α dictates the amount of downside protection the investor will receive, i.e. while prepayment speeds are within the PAC structuring band, since the companion class is nominally sized as $(1 - \alpha)B(t)$. Thus, the lower the α, the higher the corresponding PAC band defined by $0 < C(t) \le (1 - \alpha)B(t)$. Clearly, a smaller α is compensated by a lower price for the IO, and vice versa.

Note that, since many investors may have prepayment views quite different from historical norms, arbitrage profits are definitely possible. In addition, the credit risk of the IO would only enter the fray should there be insufficient cash to make the promised payment to IO holders per equation (2) perhaps as a result of high defaults or delinquencies. In certain asset classes, for instance autos, the probability that this will happen may in fact be significant. Such IO buyers would need to consider credit risk as well as market risk. However, in most cases IO investors will be betting indirectly and exclusively on interest rates via the pool's prepayment behavior. Needless to say, doing this is inherently risky.

In conclusion, although PACs are a viable market risk protection mechanism available to investors especially vulnerable to prepayment risk, they can sometimes distract investor attention from credit risk. Those accustomed to thinking of PACs in a traditional mortgage-backed context may be lulled into a false sense of security and might be surprised to find that ABS PACs can display unexpected credit-linked features that should have some influence on pricing once they are properly assessed. As always in finance, the extension of a concept successful in one framework to a completely different environment should initially be viewed with skepticism.

In general, however, when an investor purchases a standard PAC bond rather than a PAC IO (i.e., a bond that includes both interest and principal components), the amount of prepayment protection over the PAC range might be critical since that investor may in fact be looking to duration-match a specific liability on his balance sheet, and thus would be highly concerned about reinvestment risk protection. In that case, investing in a PAC might make perfect sense. Conversely, another investor merely hungry for raw return might purchase the corresponding companion class and, given its structural imperatives, receive an attractive yield incentive to do so. Thus, although the practical utility of a PAC IO may have been oversold, that of standard PAC and companion bonds is significant.

Let us now take a few moments to see how the structure of the PAC reduces the duration impact of interest rate volatility for an investor. Recall from basic fixed income arithmetic that the price P of a bond may be set equal to the discounted present value of the cash flows $C_t, t \in [1, T]$ to which its holder is entitled over the remaining life of the bond:

$$P = \sum_{t=1}^{T} \frac{C_t}{(1+r)^t} \qquad (7)$$

In equation (7), the quantity r is defined as the bond's periodic yield to maturity, or simply yield, which, as is well known, is a critical parameter in pricing any type of fixed income security. In circumstances where the cash flows C_t are independent of interest rates (which describes much of corporate finance) the duration D of the bond defined as the first derivative of its price with respect to yield may simply be written as:

$$D \equiv \frac{\partial P}{\partial r} = \frac{-1}{(1+r)} \sum_{t=1}^{T} \frac{t\,C_t}{(1+r)^t} \qquad (8)$$

Conversely, in instances where the cash flows C_t are dependent on prepayment rates and hence on interest rates, cash flows are represented as $C_t(r)$ and duration is no longer given by equation (8). Rather, we must extend the definition to include such cash flow dependence on yield:[2]

$$D = \sum_{t=1}^{T} \frac{(1+r)^t \frac{\partial C_t(r)}{\partial r} - t\,(1+r)^{t-1}\,C_t(r)}{(1+r)^{2t}} \qquad (9)$$

As a rule, the acceleration of cash flows stemming from a reduction in the level of interest rates vis-à-vis their original benchmark, and from a corresponding increase in prepayment rates, also increases the absolute value of duration because, in general, the condition $\frac{\partial C_t(r)}{\partial r} \leq 0$ will hold for values of r (see figure 11.1) in the relevant range. Normal PAC buyers will usually be more interested in cash flow stability than capital gains, and so will seek reassurance that $\frac{\partial C_t(t)}{\partial r}$ is fairly benign over the same

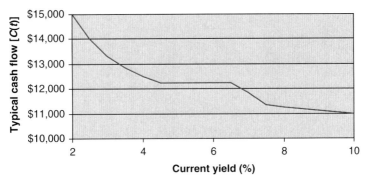

FIGURE 11.1
Interest-rate sensitivity of PAC cash flows.

range. The opportunity for gains will usually reside in the PAC band where, as we shall see shortly, the condition $\frac{\partial C_t(r)}{\partial r} = 0$ holds throughout.

The good news about PAC investing is that although the absolute prediction of prepayment rates is notoriously inaccurate, being indirect interest rate forecasts, conditional prepayment models provide respectable results over a wide range of yields. Some investment banking firms have developed fairly reliable models of conditional prepayment behavior, and their outputs are thus important inputs to structured bond pricing models.

Being the result of statistical analyses, these yield-dependent cash flows will be given as point-sets rather than continuous functions, and will therefore be at best piecewise continuous in r. In order to compute first- and higher-order derivatives, however, continuity of the approximations to $C_t(r)$ and of its derivatives will be paramount. In practice, the calculation of derivatives beyond $\frac{\partial^2 C_t(r)}{\partial r^2}$, needed to compute the bond's convexity, will usually not be necessary.

For example, consider figure 11.1 as the output of some conditional prepayment model giving the interest-rate sensitivity of some arbitrary cash flow $C_t(r)$ accruing to the owner of a PAC bond.

As expected, an investor would experience little price volatility solely from the time-dependent distribution of cash flows in an improving (decreasing) interest-rate environment. As was shown above, the PAC band corresponds approximately to the yield range $r \in [4.5\%, 6.5\%]$ and is therefore the range of prepayment speeds during which the companion class would be eaten away to protect the PAC.

Finally, one could make the game more interesting by subpartitioning a standard PAC bond into a sequential array of sub-PACs, thus adding further effective prepayment protection to holders of the senior-most tranches in the sequence (see section 11.4 below). This super-protection would stem from the fact that, for a given single-month mortality path, the senior tranches in the sequence would have relatively more time to be paid off according to their original schedule, despite the existence of prepayment rates above the upper limit of the PAC band before the exhaustion of the companion class. Therefore, in a dynamic sense, the subordination of the junior sequential sub-tranches in a multi-tranche PAC effectively creates enhanced prepayment protection for the senior sub-tranches vis-à-vis the standard PAC. The protection from subordination is especially meaningful since, from a prepayment standpoint, the most predictable part of a transaction's prepayment history is its initial phase. In practice, the optimization of a PAC structure is largely a matter of interest-rate speculation, i.e. more art than science.

11.3 AN EXAMPLE OF PAC MECHANICS

To illustrate PAC mechanics and further clarify the PAC IO concept, let us work through a simple and admittedly somewhat unrealistic example.

Consider figure 11.2, showing three possible amortization scenarios of a $10,000 pool. The top curve represents zero prepayment speeds, the middle curve the base case prepayment scenario given historical norms and expected interest rates, while

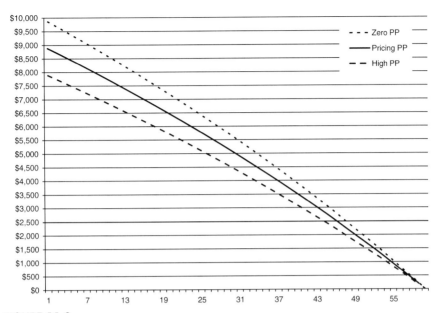

FIGURE 11.2
Amortization at low, base, and high prepayment speeds.

the bottom curve represents the highest observed prepayment rates over a comparable period in this asset class. As explained earlier, the PAC will be priced based on the middle curve.

Now assume the following pricing parameters:

R:	10% (APR)
r:	5% (APR)
α:	see below
WAM:	60 months
Pricing yield:	12% (APR)

Starting from the these parameters, we can derive the price of the IO as the net present value of base case cash flows discounted at 12% annually, yielding a basic price of:

IO price ($\alpha = 0.8$): $810.39
IO price ($\alpha = 0.9$): $911.69

Essentially, an IO strip of 5% is being structured into this transaction with either a 20% or a 10% downside cushion against excessive prepayments. The question now is, what will happen to the return on the IO under various prepayment speeds? The 12% return on this investment will be realized only if prepayments cause the pool to amortize exactly according to the "pricing PP" curve in figure 11.2. This is clearly unlikely despite our best efforts, not to mention theoretically impossible.

TABLE 11.1

Distribution of returns on a PAC IO with 20% and 10% companions at different prepayment ppeeds

| | IO STRIP RETURNS (%) | |
| | δ PARAMETER | |
PP SPEEDS	$\alpha = 0.8$	$\alpha = 0.9$
1.000	18.49	18.49
0.975	16.90	16.90
0.950	15.29	15.29
0.925	13.65	13.65
0.900	12.00	12.00
0.875	10.32	10.32
0.850	8.62	8.62
0.825	6.90	6.90
0.800	5.14	5.14
0.775	5.14	5.14
0.750	5.14	5.14
0.725	5.14	5.14
0.700	5.14	3.56
0.675	5.14	1.55
0.650	5.14	−0.50
0.625	3.81	−2.60
0.600	1.55	−4.74
0.575	−0.76	−6.93
0.550	−3.13	−9.18
0.525	−5.56	11.49
0.500	−8.05	−13.87

Before buying, the IO investor will usually want to see the distribution of returns across the entire spectrum of prepayment speeds and attach probability estimates to such scenarios. We present this distribution in table 11.1 for a range of prepayment speeds measured by a single parameter δ. For ease of understanding, we have defined zero prepayment as $\delta = 1$, corresponding to the maximum return achievable on this investment. For pricing purposes, we assumed $\delta = 0.9$ while the PAC schedule $S(t)$ was defined using $\delta = 0.8$. In passing, recall from chapter 6 that in the world of prepayment modeling, defaults are counted as involuntary prepayments.

As expected, the IO with $\alpha = 0.8$ is afforded a wider protection band compared to the holder of the second IO with a 10% cushion. Also, note that both IO holders are exposed to the same returns up to prepayment speeds corresponding to the beginning of the PAC structuring band, i.e., for $\delta = 0.8$.

Although this analysis can form the basis of a purchase in some sense, it is usually more informative to investigate risk-adjusted returns in both cases. We postulated a

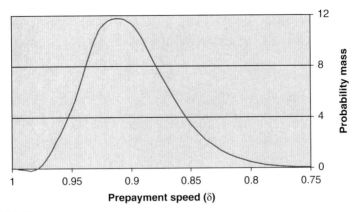

FIGURE 11.3
Prepayment probability distribution.

distribution of prepayment speeds using the parameter δ. Now, assume prepayments are ruled by a gamma process defined by a distribution function $F(\delta)$, with a mean $E(\delta) = 0.9$ and a standard deviation such that $F^{-1}(0.99) = 0.8$. In other words, we assume that the prepayment speed used as a basis for the schedule $S(t)$ exceeds 99% of all historical experience. The resulting probability distribution is shown in figure 11.3.

Not surprisingly, when the risk-adjusted return is computed for the first and the second IO, one finds essentially the same value (ca. 12%) in both cases. Although it is true that the first IO had significantly more downside protection than the second IO on a probabilistic and historical basis this extra cushion amounts to precious little.

Finally, it should be noted that ABS investment bankers, as opposed to MBS players, have shown much creativity in defining PAC schedules for IO cash flow allocation purposes. Unfortunately, it cannot be said that IO classes in ABS have met with the same degree of success they generally enjoy in MBS. To be sure, incremental credit risk is a factor, but ABS investors also have yet to develop the confidence required to push the design envelope to a level of sophistication whereby the special features of the PAC could emerge and reach maturity. Until that day, PAC IO classes will largely remain marginal features of ABS transactions.

11.4 VARIETIES OF PAC EXPERIENCE

As we saw earlier, the fundamental idea behind the PAC is the partitioning of the outstanding principal balance in the trust into two logically distinct sets, the PAC and companion portions, respectively. This is done in order to provide the PAC with a cushion in the event prepayments speeds exceed all conceivable norms, resulting in a potentially severe loss to holders of certain classes of securities. A prime example of such securities is the PAC IO.

To demonstrate the basic mechanics of the PAC IO, we started by defining the amount of this cushion as $(1 - \alpha)$, where α was chosen arbitrarily. As a result, we were able to conveniently define the PAC schedule via:

$$\alpha = \frac{S(t)}{B^h(t)} \qquad (10)$$

To calculate the schedule $S(t)$, we used an amortization schedule $B^h(t)$ originating from a severe prepayment environment by historical standards. We were then able to easily compute the time-dependent balance associated with both portions of the pool, from which the cash flows accruing to the PAC IO could be calculated.

Nevertheless, our initial discussion left out the manner in which total principal due $P_d(t)$ should be allocated between PAC and companion classes. Regardless of the principal allocation method used, the variable $P_d(t)$ is the reference for allocation to all tranches inside the deal. In chapter 7, we reviewed both the pro rata and sequential methods of allocating $P_d(t)$ and pointed out that these two modes represented opposite ends of the allocation spectrum, assuming one ignores the reverse-sequential allocation scheme as unrealistic.

Consequently, it would be natural to wonder whether the PAC formulas derived earlier are the *only* PAC mechanical possibilities, or if there is such a thing as a "pro rata PAC" and a "sequential PAC." The answer to this last question will turn out to be a resounding yes.

The following discussion progresses from PAC mechanics and extends the PAC concept to more than a single PAC tranche, i.e., to the so-called PAC Group.

The Distinction between Pro Rata and Sequential PAC Tranches

Recall the principal balance of the PAC companion class $[C(t)]$ given by equation (3):

$$C(t) = Max[0, (1 - \alpha)B(t) - Max[0, S(t) - \alpha B(t)]] \qquad (11)$$

To use equation (11), we defined $B(t)$ as the pool's outstanding principal balance at the end of time step t.

Recall that on each payment date, the sum of the PAC $[P(t)]$ and companion portions is by definition equal to the current pool balance $B(t)$, so that, at each time step the following condition holds:

$$P(t) + C(t) = B(t) \qquad (12)$$

Recall also that, within the range of expected prepayment speeds corresponding to the entire universe of historical experience seen on similar or comparable collateral, we could use equation (11) and compute $C(t)$ as:

$$C(t) = (1 - \alpha)B(t) \qquad (13)$$

Under such conditions, and assuming sufficient funds are on hand to make the associated payments, the following allocations are implied by the last two equations:

$$P(t) = P(t-1) - \alpha P_d(t) \tag{14}$$

$$C(t) = C(t-1) - (1-\alpha)P_d(t) \tag{15}$$

Equations (14) and (15) show clearly that we have created a pro rata PAC. This is the case of greatest interest by far, and the main reason why we used it as the paradigmatic PAC. Why is this true?

Simply because the average PAC investor is looking for protection against excessive prepayment speeds and is not interested in shortening the average life of the tranche at the basis of the cash flow stream by choosing a sequential principal allocation regime. Since prepayment speeds are unknown a priori, it is thought far better to begin with the most conservative allocation regime. Because preventing excessive reimbursements is precisely the rationale for the PAC, the pro rata PAC is preferred because in that case the companion class absorbs some of the pool's amortization at all times, not just when the schedule $S(t)$ becomes relevant, or so it would seem. But, is there trouble in paradise?

Consider what happens when prepayments dynamics follow the expected case. To begin with, ask yourself approximately when prepayment speeds can be expected to reach abnormal levels: at the beginning, the middle, or the end of the deal? Prepayment speeds are much more likely to exceed the statistical historical universe during the middle rather than either at the beginning or the end of the deal, albeit for different reasons. How is this so?

At the beginning of the deal consumers are faced with precious little rationale for prepaying. On the one hand, interest rates are most likely just about where they were when their mortgage loan was made. On the other, they have just paid closing and other fees and are in no financial shape to refinance. As a result, prepayments at the beginning of the transaction are likely to be small-to-insignificant at best. Conversely, at the end of the deal those that could have been encouraged to prepay are already gone, while others are too stubborn or uninformed to do so. As a result, prepayment speeds toward the end of the deal are also likely to be low. This leaves us with the middle portion of the deal where the majority of the action will most probably take place, if and when it does. Bear in mind that the *end* can only be seen *as* the end because of what happened in the *middle*. Thus, forecasting low prepayment activity at the end of a transaction is a trivial matter since it is a self-fulfilling prophecy.

But if the foregoing analysis is correct, investors in PAC IO tranches that amortize right away under a sequential regime would experience greater cash flow certainty than those accruing to a pro rata PAC buyer operating as previously shown. Clearly the cash flow, and hence the dollar price, of a sequential PAC IO will decrease more than that of a pro rata PAC IO pegged off a PAC with an identical starting balance. However, for the reason just elicited, the region of uncertainty around the yield will objectively decrease as well. Thus, ceteris paribus, sequential PAC IO tranches should cost more than pro rata PAC IO tranches or price at lower yields.

For the sake of completeness and clarity, consider the following allocation formulas equivalent to equations (2) and (3) for the case of a sequential PAC:

$$C(t) = Max\,[0, C(t-1) - Max\,[0, S(t) - P(t-1) + P_d(t)]] \qquad (16)$$

$$P(t) = B(t) - C(t) \qquad (17)$$

To see how these formulas behave with respect to the PAC bond, note that under most circumstances the principal balance of the PAC will be computed via:

$$P(t) = Max\,[S(t), P(t-1) - P_d(t)]$$

The idea underlying equations (16) and (17) is that once the pool's actual amortization schedule exceeds the preestablished schedule $S(t)$ at time step t, the difference needs to be absorbed by the companion portion $C(t)$ until the latter is reduced to zero via excessive prepayments. Until schedule $S(t)$ catches up to the pool's current balance $B(t)$, the PAC principal balance will remain equal to $S(t)$ for as long as the companion class is still outstanding. This is precisely how the protection mechanism works on behalf of PAC IO investors.

The Notion of a PAC Group

Suppose now that you wanted to combine the advantages of a pro rata PAC with those of a sequential PAC, perhaps in order to create an entire universe of PAC-style securities that allows investors to take a broad array of views on prepayment speeds.

You could do this easily by subdividing the originally monolithic PAC portion $P(t)$ of a pro rata PAC into a finite series of smaller PAC bonds, and then allocating principal sequentially within this ensemble. Investors could select the tranche they felt afforded them the highest return given their current view on future prepayments. If you had been the first one to do this, you would have given birth to the concept of the "PAC Group."

The PAC Group allocation formulas are self-evident once the basic PAC mechanics (which, by now, ought to be second nature to you) are understood. First, redefine the principal balance of the PAC portion as the sum of its n sub-PAC components as follows:

$$P(t) = \sum_{i=1}^{n} p_i(t) \qquad (18)$$

While the formula for computing the companion class balance $C(t)$ remains unaffected, the time-dependent balances of the sub-PAC bonds can be computed using the standard sequential scheme.

To illustrate, consider the first prepayment regime highlighted as equation (4), which covers the vast majority of actual cases. In that situation, allocate the total amount $\alpha P_d(t)$ to the PAC Group. For argument's sake, define the Group's allocated principal amount $P_G(t)$ in the same way, i.e.:

$$P_G(t) = \alpha P_d(t) \tag{19}$$

Next, allocate principal sequentially within the Group in the following manner:

$$p_i(t) = Max[0, p_i(t-1) - P_G(t)], \ i \in [1, n] \tag{20}$$

$$P_G(t) = P_G(t) - \{p_i(t-1) - p_i(t)\}, \ i \in [1, n] \tag{21}$$

Note that the cash required to effect these distributions is always presumed to be available. In a credit-risk situation, one would be forced to consider shortfall quantities in order to keep track of the principal balance of each sub-PAC tranche. Please note that formalism (19) assumes that (20) and (21) are implemented within a loop where by both statements are executed for the same index i before moving onto the next.

11.5 CONCLUDING REMARKS

Needless to say, the number of PAC variations available to a deal is nearly infinite and limited only by the imagination of the analyst. The type of prepayment forecast consistent with any given sub-PAC, and the consistency between such forecasts, would be an interesting research area if prepayment modeling had even half the appeal it once had.

One could further expand on the approaches provided herein and create increasingly more complex pool partitioning schemata, up to and including the partitioning of the companion class. However, what matter most to a serious study of PAC bonds are the relationships that exist between the various principal allocation methods and the different types of PAC tranches. Mastery of the algebra underlying these relationships will make products like Z- and accretion directed bonds, the strange beasts that appeared many years ago in the world of collateralized mortgage obligations, much more intuitively obvious. Such products tend to make more sense on the job, i.e. while devising actual payment schedules with respect to live transactions. Theory for the sake of theory is always a mistake.

END-OF-CHAPTER QUESTIONS

1. Definitions:

    a. What does PAC stand for?
    b. What does TAC stand for?
    c. How is the P in PAC implemented, and where can you find it?
    d. Why would anyone buy a PAC bond?
    e. PAC bonds usually come in pairs. Please name the two members of the pair.
    f. What types of risk is the PAC designed to address?
    g. What is a PAC IO?

    h. What types of risk faces the holder of an IO in general?

    i. How does one define the PAC bond? How does the PAC bond address the risk of the PAC IO holder?

    j. Derive the equation for the time-dependent principal balance of the second member of the PAC pair?

    k. How are the two members of the pair related to the pool balance?

    l. How do the plan in the PAC and the two constituents interact?

    m. What is the PAC band, and how is it defined?

    n. Under how many prepayment regimes can a PAC conceivably operate?

    o. Describe each prepayment regime that you have identified, and discuss its impact on the PAC bond.

    p. What happens to the cash flows allocated to the PAC bondholder when prepayments fall within the PAC band?

    q. How does the PAC band affect the current duration of a mortgage-backed security?

    r. Are prepayment speeds outside the PAC band commonly seen?

    s. Does the standard PAC have a pro rata or a sequential payment regime? Explain your answer.

    t. Are there other types of PAC beyond the plain-vanilla ones?

    u. What is a PAC Group? What is the idea behind a PAC Group? Why would anyone conceive such an animal?

    v. Develop a formula for the second member of the PAC Group similar to the one you derived earlier with respect to the ordinary PAC concept.

    w. How are PAC Groups linked to the prepayment dynamics of structured pools?

2. What is the economic usefulness of CMO structures described in this chapter: PACs, PAC IOs, PAC Groups? What are the limits to the usefulness of such structures? What is the difference between a PAC and a TAC? Based on your definition, which of the two should be more costly to the investor?

3. This chapter discusses Interest-Only securities (IOs) in the context of PAC IOs. How do IOs work? Contrast the economics of IOs with that of Principal-Only securities (POs).

4. Imagine that a pool of fixed rate loans or bonds is stripped into interest-only and principal-only cash flows, which are then repackaged as IOs and POs, respectively, and that these securities are purchased by a new investor. Would the aggregate price the new investor pays be equal to the financing cost of the original pool? Should these prices be identical?

5. Discuss prepayment dynamics in the context of mortgage-backed securities for the length of an entire transaction. Contrast this discussion with the prepayment dynamics of automobile-loan-backed securities for the length of an entire transaction. Contrast prepayments within MBS and ABS in general.

6. Contingent pricing theory holds that the fair value of an option (call or put) on uncertain cash flows is a function of its intrinsic value plus the price of

uncertainty at the time the option's price is computed. The Black–Scholes theorem defines the price of uncertainty c as the mean value of the distribution of stock prices in excess of the returns over the risk free rate across a given term structure, i.e.,

$$c = S \cdot N(d_1) - e^{-r_f T} X \cdot N(d_2),$$

where

$$d_1 = \left[\frac{\ln(S/X) + (r_f + \frac{\sigma^2}{2}) \cdot T}{\sigma \sqrt{T}} \right] \text{ and } d_2 = \left[\frac{\ln(S/X) + (r_f - \frac{\sigma^2}{2}) \cdot T}{\sigma \sqrt{T}} \right] \text{ respectively,}$$

with $N(d_1)$ and $N(d_2)$ representing the weighted average probability of the values of S (the spot price of the stock) and X (the exercise price of the option). Could contingent pricing theory be used to value a PAC? How would the price obtained by using contingent pricing compare to the valuation obtained via credit valuation? Explain your answers. Which approach is to be preferred, and why?

7. Chapter 10 offers two approximations to pricing bonds in the secondary market (equations 8 and 9). What is the difference between them? Why is equation (9) of specific relevance to this chapter, which discusses the *internal hedging* of prepayment risk?

8. What is a Z-bond? What is an accretion-directed bond? Explain its structural features in terms of concepts already introduced in this chapter.

9. Quantitative analysis of RMBS:

    a. Define, formally, the concept of duration with respect to a security.
    b. How are *duration* and *average life* different?
    c. Why are their meanings frequently confused in practice?
    d. Define convexity formally.
    e. Starting from the formal definition of the price P of a bond $P = \sum_{i=1}^{n} \frac{C_i}{(1+r)^i}$ and the above definition of duration, derive the analytical formula for duration in the case of a noncallable bond, such as a plain-vanilla corporate bond for instance.
    f. What is call risk?
    g. What is the largest risk faced by the holder of an MBS insured by a U.S. GSE such as FNMA?
    h. Why do the holders of mortgage-backed securities hold more call risk than those holding plain-vanilla corporate bonds?
    i. Should people with more call risk pay more or less for the privilege of holding this type of bond than for holding a bond with less call risk?
    j. Why do we say that the convexity of an MBS is negative?

k. Show that the duration of a bond with call risk can be generally expressed as follows

$$D = \sum_{i=1}^{n} \frac{(1+r)^i \frac{\partial C_i(r)}{\partial r} - i(1+r)^{i-1} C_i(r)}{(1+r)^{2i}}.$$

In the last relationship, $C_i(r)$ generally expresses the way cash flows to the bondholder will vary with changes in interest rates.

l. Derive an analytical formula for the convexity of a plain-vanilla corporate bond.

m. What is the standard measure used to express the cost of convexity in MBS analysis?

n. What is the difference between prepayment risk and reinvestment risk?

o. Name a cash flow allocation feature commonly seen in RMBS transactions, and aimed at protecting investors from the prepayment risk due to the excessive prepayment speed of the underlying pool of mortgages.

p. Name a cash flow allocation feature commonly seen in RMBS transactions, aimed at protecting investors from the reinvestment risk due to the excessive prepayment speed of the underlying pool of mortgages.

q. Identify the three main components of an OAS (Option-Adjusted Spread) model.

r. What variables are likely to affect the speed with which obligors prepay their mortgage in full, or partially? Justify your answers.

12

Intermediate Cash Flow Modeling

This chapter focuses on enabling the intricacies of cash flow modeling of real transactions. The first section lists the formal and functional elements that belong in a "best practice" cash flow model built from scratch. The second section presents an intuitive approach to the cash flow modeling of waterfalls within a web-based software system called the Waterfall Editor™. As a natural dealing language for communicating and valuing transactions with different structural features, it is a useful tool for structurers wishing to go beyond the two-tranche structure of chapters 6 and 7.

12.1 MODEL DESIDERATA: INTERMEDIATE LEVEL

The hallmark of an analyst with intermediate-level structuring proficiency is the ability to transcend script knowledge and demonstrate for script sophistication. The evidence for script sophistication is the ability to carry out certain standard modeling tasks to ensure model integrity. Some are related to error checking and-minimizing characteristics that have nothing to do with the accuracy of the model. These we call *formal features*. Others relate to the ability of the modeler to capture the financial essence of the transaction and are called *approximation features*. The minimum set of formal and approximation features that a cash flow model must have for structuring and valuation work at an intermediate level of sophistication are listed below.

Formal Features

1. A spreadsheet is still acceptable as long as it can be accompanied by a set of Visual Basic macros beneath the top layer.
2. The model should be self-contained and have all inputs and outputs labeled differently for ease of recognition.
3. The labels should appear in one language only. It does not have to be English!

4. The names of all assumptions, inputs, and outputs should never be abbreviated. No jargon should be used anywhere unless defined in full in the assumptions, and followed by the abbreviation or jargon expression (e.g., *WAC* or Weighted Average Coupon).

5. The use of color should be minimized, except as indicated below; graphs with multiple lines should reserve one color for each line. Remember that many printers often show the colors differently.

6. The assumptions should be shown on a separate sheet and linked to the main sheet that holds the cash flow engine.

7. All parameters or assumptions that never change should be eliminated from the code and hard-coded inside the cells. (This should never happen, but if a value does not change, it is not really an assumption, is it?)

8. Key inputs and outputs should be separated but still shown on the same sheet in horizontal fashion, i.e., the outputs should be arrayed to the *right* of the inputs.

9. All assumptions should be partitioned logically. For instance, all asset-side assumptions should be together, all loss curve assumptions should be grouped together, etc.

10. Formatting delimiters, such as outlines and boxes are properly used to indicate when a group of assumptions begins and an other one ends.

11. Cells that show third-party assumptions and scales (e.g., credit ratings), ought to be entered in cells that are locked for entry unless a password is given to the user.

12. The status of the cell entry (whether it is an output or an input) should be readily apparent not only from the label of the cell but also from its color or shading, or otherwise.

13. Cells allowing the user to enter assumptions with Boolean or multiple-choice answers (e.g., pro rata, sequential, PAC, TAC) should be annotated to show the range of possibilities. The annotation is a feature in newer versions of Excel.

14. If key rates in the model are applied more frequently than annually, but are expressed as an annual percentages, the periodicity (12 for monthly, 4 for quarterly, etc) should also be recorded as an assumption and implemented in the cash flow engine calculations. This way, the right results can be obtained without modifying the main sheet.

15. There should be no hard-coded numbers in the main sheet.[1]

16. Time, as the most important variable, should be the first column of the cash flow engine in the main spreadsheet. Note that when counting time, 1, 2, or 3 does not mean 1 month, 2 months, or 3 months. The numbers are merely labels for time steps and, as such, are all nondimensional.

17. The screen should be able to be partitioned vertically so that time always shows up to the left of the other arguments no matter how far to the right you scroll,

and so that the column titles always appear at the top of the screen no matter how far down you scroll.

18. Column labels should be bolded text. Column labels for groups of related columns should be bolded in a font one point larger than the items in the associated group.

19. Unless a compelling reason exists to do otherwise, the numbers or letters in all columns should be centered, not left- or right-justified.

20. All variables should be formatted in their natural units. For instance, dollars should have dollar signs, Euros should have their appropriate sign, and accounts or other nondimensional variables should have an appropriate number of decimal places.

21. All dollar values should show whole dollar amounts only (no cents) unless the model is being debugged.

22. Percentage-based variables, such as rates, should be shown as such, not as decimals.

23. The number of decimal places should be selected so as to reveal some change in every row of the sheet. For example if the value in the first row is 1,500.24 and the value in the second row is 1,500.27, then *two* decimal places are required, not one or zero.

24. All values below the threshold of 1/10,000 should be formatted scientifically, e.g., 2.503 E^{-4}.

25. The unit associated with a value should be shown attached to the number inside the cell as much as possible, e.g., "months", "%" or "€." If this is impossible, it should be shown once at the top of the column. The scientific practice of only using nondimensional values everywhere is not a good idea in cash flow modeling, but occasionally it is acceptable to clear up clutter.

26. The formulas themselves should never express rates as percentages, only in decimal form. (This means, never divide by 100 inside the formulas.)

27. Abbreviations should follow the English convention, not the French (e.g., *balance* should be abbreviated as **Bal**, not **Bce**, and so on.) using the same number of characters, regardless of the original number of letters (e.g., if *balance* is Bal, then *secondary* should be Sec.) To avoid ambiguities, use more letters. Any skipped letters, no matter how many, should be replaced by a single apostrophe (e.g., *balance* would become Bal'ce, though this is awkward).

28. All tabs and sheets should be labeled with commonsense names that indicate their function, not Sheet1, Sheet2, etc.

29. All sets of columns that pertain to the same topic, such as losses or prepayments, should be grouped together and made into a distinct unit via outlining or some other method that makes them easy to recognize.

30. The cash flow engine itself, including assets and liabilities, should be treated as a distinct unit and presented on the main sheet, not spread out over many sheets.

31. At least one column of empty space should separate assets from liabilities in any cash flow engine. The column used for separation should be formatted differently from the columns showing cash flow activity.

32. All calculations that are subsidiary to the main cash flow engine, like average life or yield, should be performed on a separate sheet so as not to clutter the main sheet with nonessential work.

33. When running a Visual Basic macro for intermediate calculations, new spreadsheets should be created on the fly using VBE, and deleted upon exit so that the main model remains clear of any junk and scratch data.

34. The model should be equipped with a "Close Model" macro function that restores the assumptions either to the current ones, or to some default values so that any subsequent user may recognize cell entries as described in any user manual or by others.

35. Graphs should be created in separate sheets and deleted upon request or when running the "Close Model" macro function. No graph should exist when the model is opened for the first time.

36. All tables and graphs should be labeled and titled appropriately, either on the fly or hard-coded.

37. The x-axis on any graph should be the independent variable, while the y-axis should be reserved for the dependent variable or variables. Avoid three-dimensional graphs as much as possible; they do not display very well in two dimensions.

38. All schedules and required strings of numbers, for instance as required to model a Planned Amortization Class or a Targeted Amortization Class, should be entered on the assumption sheet away from the basic set of deal assumptions.

39. No extraneous comment should be appended inside the model itself. Things like "here I divide by 12" or "only for subprime deals" do not have a place in serious modeling efforts.

40. Lists that are longer than 200 items should always be shown vertically, and we recommend that all lists should be shown vertically anyway.

41. When running Monte Carlo scenarios, a running count of where the simulation is at any point in time should be displayed to the user, to pick up infinite loops and other counts.

Approximation Features

1. The modeler should understand the meaning of compounding and past-due amounts and be able to enter the correct Excel formulas representing compounding at different current and past-due rates.

2. The modeler should be able to implement the two most fundamental principal allocation modes, pro rata and sequential, inside the model simultaneously and use a switch to select from both.

3. The modeler should understand the concept of a shortfall, principal or interest, and be able to implement the same inside the spreadsheet model.

4. The modeler must be able to compute the asset-side cash flows that would result with respect to a pool with a certain number of delinquent loans, instead of using the default paradigm whereby all loans are either current or defaulted. This will be useful at the advanced modeling level.

5. The model should work independently for assets and liabilities, since these are two independent aspects of a corporation or structured transaction.

6. The modeler should be able to build a two-class structure with a reserve or spread account, delayed recoveries, and analytically given prepayment, recovery, and credit-loss routines.

7. The modeler should be able to introduce an asset- or liability-based trigger that allows the deal to switch from pro rata to sequential upon a breach.

8. The modeler should be able to compute the yield and the average life of any security and the return on equity for any transaction without the use of the Excel IRR function (for yield), i.e. via a brute-force root locus approach.

9. The modeler should be able to compute the credit rating of any security using either the Moody's (cash-flow based) or the S&P method (liquidation-based).

10. The modeler should be able to embed a table lookup function in the model, to output the ratings using letter grades, default rates (S&P), and average reductions of yield (Moody's).

11. The modeler should be able to incorporate the presence of a counterparty guarantee on a transaction and show the resulting improvement in the rating of the related securities compared to the unwrapped structure.

12. The modeler should be able to implement the inverse distribution function method using the built-in Excel method and the appropriate distribution function.

13. The modeler should be able to show graphically the key dynamic elements of the cash flow analysis: the pool's actual and theoretical amortization schedules, the security's theoretical and actual amortization schedules in either the pro rata or sequential mode, the loss curve, the prepayment curve, and the recovery model using dynamic graphs tied to the Excel formulas.

14. The modeler should be able to perform a sensitivity analysis on transaction parameters, i.e., advance rate, reserve account size, eligible investment rate, etc., and show a table indicating how each variable affects the credit ratings of the classes and the return on equity to the sponsors.

15. The modeler should be able to implement a portable random number generator from scratch, not simply using Rand from Excel.

16. The modeler should be able to show graphically the entire distribution of yield reductions on a given class of security and the distribution of returns on equity.

17. The modeler should be able to read values from external spreadsheets and bring them into Visual Basic for later use, and export any output to either the main model sheet or to an external sheet.

18. The modeler should be able to link a Word document containing tables with data drawn from the model, that can be updated dynamically if the output

credit ratings or other parameters change. This allows efficient communication to consumers of the model.

19. The modeler should be able to demonstrate via a histogram that the theoretical loss distribution has been respected inside the Monte Carlo implementation, and that resulting losses are indeed distributed as intended.

20. The cash flow engine should make minimal use of built-in Excel functions or subroutine calls, and substitute fundamental formulas wherever possible. This goal may be impossible in some distribution functions, but the rest of the code should be as self-contained as possible, to improve portability to other machines and minimize operating system conflicts.

21. The model should be able to conduct a Monte Carlo simulation using a selection of a few standard distribution functions, like the normal, lognormal, and gamma distributions.

22. The model should have the ability to include continuous cumulative distribution functions that can be integrated, using the simple Euler method, to obtain marginal contributions with respect to defaults, losses, revenues, expenses, etc.

23. The model should have check cells, which indicate via a Boolean result (TRUE or FALSE) if the model is behaving as expected. For instance, if the pool is amortizing, the ending balance at the end of the deal, say time T, should be zero. So one cell should indicate if the balance at time T is indeed zero and if so, the result should evaluate to TRUE. These can also make life very simple when looking for a bug.

24. It is important to build the cash flow model to have the standard set of approximating features; in simple deals where certain features are unused, the columns or rows should output empty or null results, not **NA#** or **NUM**.

12.2 INTRODUCTION TO WATERFALL SCRIPTING

In what remains of this chapter, we introduce the Waterfall Editor (WFE), a flexible, extensible solution that embodies the desiderata spelled out in 12.1 and permits free-form scripting. WFE mimics the language of dealing: it is organized to parse the deep structure of deals into modular, recombinant structures.

Utility Bar: Structure and Application

Figure 12.1 shows the WFE home page interface and two main menus, **Utility Bar** and **Syntax Bar**. **Utility Bar** hosts the program-level controls while **Syntax Bar** hosts the programming language elements and their associated operations.

Utility Bar controls the four main operations of WFE:

1. File management commands are found in **File**
2. Variable-management commands are found in **Tools**
3. Debugging/executing commands are found in **Run**
4. Information and self-correcting feedback are obtained via **Help**

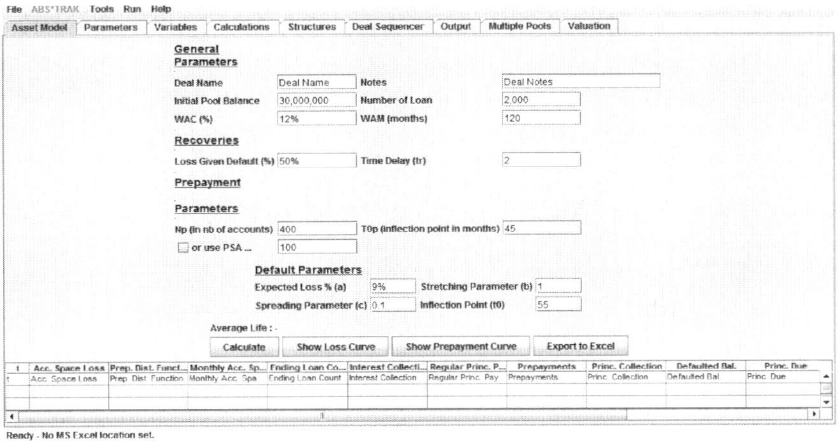

FIGURE 12.1
Utility bar (top) and asset model interface.

1. File Menu

The *File* menu enables the creation, storage and re-use of deal files. It is organized as follows:

File	Tools	Run	Help
New Empty Deal			
ABS Deal Wizard			
CDO Deal Wizard			
Load (XML)			
Save As (XML)			
Save (XML)			
Load (Binary)			
Load as URL (Binary)			
Save As (Binary)			
[Last Opened File]			

Select *New Empty Deal* to set up a new liability structure manually. This option gives the modeler total freedom to design the method of cash flow allocation and distribution ("due-pay"). It should be selected for modeling non-standard write-down/write-up payment logic that departs from equilibrium waterfall logic[2] and cannot be cloned from an existing deal.

ABS Deal Wizard and *CDO Deal Wizard* are templates for coding liability structures with typical features from ABS, RMBS and CDO sectors. On the dropdown menu, the modeler declares and initializes basic transactional features: reserve funds, spread accounts, yield-supplement accounts and servicer fee class/sub-class structures. *Deal Wizard* automatically generates the programming code linking the objects together using the equilibrium logic's due-pay mechanisms. Use of *Deal Wizard* reduces production time and minimizes coding error.

Load (XML), Load as URL (Binary) and *Load (Binary)* may be the best way to code existing deals from existing transactions in an XML or Binary library using cloning tools. Their files can be modified as required and saved under an appropriate name using *Save As (XML)* or *Save As (Binary)*.

2. Tools Menu

The **Tools** menu relates to the use and management inside the WFE environment of externally produced cash flow vectors. Its menu structure is displayed below:

File	Tools	Run	Help
	Load Assets Vector		
	Load Assets Vector from URL		
	Save Values in Memory		
	Restore Previous Variables		
	Add Tranche		
	Rename Tranche		
	Remove Tranche		
	Add Servicer		
	Create Scheduled Calculation		
	Build from Web-based Data Provider		

Load Assets Vector uploads cash flows stored in CSV format and *Load Assets Vector from URL* uploads CSV files from a URL. *Save Values in Memory* is used for debugging: it hold the values of a current run in memory for future use. *Restore Previous Variables* retrieves values stored using the *Save* tool. *Add Tranche, Rename Tranche*, and *Remove Tranche* permit modification of an existing transaction or of a template created with a deal wizard. *Add Servicer* allows backup or multiple servicers fees to be reflected in the waterfall. *Create Scheduled Calculation* allows the user to build and deploy schedules to capture time-dependent events like notional amortization schedules or step-up and lock-out triggers. *Build from Web-based Data Service Provider* allows WFE to be coded automatically from deals in cash flow simulator engines fed by their web-based data providers.

3. Run Menu

Run Menu is the workhorse menu in WFE for running and debugging liabilities. It features the following commands:

File	Tools	Run	Help
		Run the Deal using the Asset Model	
		Run the Deal using the Uploaded Vectors	
		Run the Deal up to a Period	
		Debug the Sequencer	
		Debug the selected Structure	
		Debug the selected Calculation	

Run the Deal using the Asset Model applies when the asset cash flows of the deal are produced inside the WFE asset model. Details on the use of the Asset Model are provided in the first section of **Syntax Bar** below. *Run the Deal using the Uploaded Vectors* is meant for transactions whose cash flow input vectors are created in an external model and uploaded via *Tools* (see Tools Menu above) All *Run* commands execute the code. *Run the Deal* commands also launch an output window where the results can be reviewed provisionally. Selection of outputs for review and export into an Excel spreadsheet is done via **Syntax Bar**/*Output*. To view the code that has been executed following a *Debug* command, go to the adjacent *Help* command and select Show Console Window.

Run the Deal up to a Period allows the user to examine the outputs of particular periods. This is useful for checking that the model is correctly processing data. It is particularly helpful for spot-checking the outputs at critical transaction times. Examples of critical times are the period when principal due in a sequential-allocation structure switches from one tranche to the next, or when triggers are breached.

Debug the Sequencer, Debug the Selected Structure and *Debug the Selected Calculation* isolate certain parts of the Waterfall Syntax for debugging and testing. The main syntactical forms of Waterfall Syntax, **Variables, Calculations**, **Structures**, and **Sequencer**, are presented in **Syntax Bar**.

4. Help Menu

File	Tools	Run	Help
			About Waterfall Editor
			Show Console Window
			Show Output Window
			Logging Enabled
			Set MS Excel Location

About Waterfall Editor will host the finished version of this manual. *Show Console Window* opens the debugging console so the executed code may be viewed and debugged. *Show Output Window* opens a window to view the selected outputs of a transaction run. *Logging Enabled* logs the run for console display and debugging. It can be deactivated for time-consuming tasks like *full run, valuation*, and *multiple pool run*. *Set MS Excel Location* is for choosing the target location in which to save the Excel spreadsheet version of cash flows exported from WFE.

Syntax Bar: Structure and Application

Syntax Bar is where programming language elements and their associated operations are hosted. It can be seen in Figure 12.1, directly under the **Utility Bar**.

The programming elements in **Syntax Bar** are partitioned into eight tabs:

1. **Asset Model** is the cash flow engine that supplies cash flow vectors inside WFE.
2. **Parameters** (deal constants) store the transaction's key rates.

3. **Variables** (deal elements influenced by time) hold the values of flows, stocks, and certain payment rules.

4. **Calculations** (deal formulas) express the meanings of Variables algebraically.

5. **Structures** (deal sub-structures) link **Variables** in accordance with payment rules (waterfall logic).

6. **Deal Sequencer** (the deal waterfall) is the deal's execution logic.

7. **Output** is the command to view the outputs.

8. **Multiple Pools** assigns Waterfalls to transactions consisting of multiple pools or pool groups, and in which cross-collateralization usually requires custom tailoring.

9. **Valuation** computes the rating and fair market value of each tranche using a proprietary nonlinear convergence routine.

1. Asset Model Interface

Asset Model is a user-friendly template for building cash flows inside WFE when external cash flow vectors are not used. It provides an *average loan* analysis for level-pay instruments. Defaults follow an assumed logistic curve in which the last data point is equal to the Expected Loss in account-space, i.e. the way it was done in chapter 6. This curve can be modulated to fit different types of collateral and different degrees of borrower quality. Prepayments are assumed to follow the PSA model's characteristic curve but expressed as a percentage of initial ("CIPR" or Constant Initial Prepayment Rate) rather than declining balance ("CPR" or Conditional Prepayment Rate).

The dropdown menu for **Asset Model** prompts for the following deal parameters:

a. *General Parameters*: **Deal Name** and **Deal Notes**; **Initial Pool Balance** (currency), **Number of Loans** (count); **Weighted Average Coupon** (%) or **WAC**, and **Weighted Average Maturity** (months) or **WAM**.

b. *Default Parameters*: **Expected Default** (% initial balance), **Stretching Parameter (b)**, **Spreading Parameter (c)**, and **Default Curve Inflection Point (t_0)**.

c. *Recoveries*: **Loss Given Default** (%), **Time Delay** (lag between default and recovery in months).

d. *Prepayment Parameters*: **Number of Prepaying Loans (Np)** and Prepayment Curve Inflection Point (T_{0p}). Alternatively, enter the **PSA** speed and WFE will automatically convert CPR to CIPR.[1]

These parameters are stored for general use. Rates quoted on an annual basis (e.g., coupon) are input such. Whenever the rate required for the calculation has a different frequency (e.g., payment frequency is monthly) this information will be captured on the appropriate page and automatically converted. **The Pool Average Life (AL)** is automatically calculated.

> Snapshots of asset cash flows, as well as default and prepayment curves can be obtained as pop-up windows by pressing *Calculate, Show Loss Curve* and *Show*

Prepayment Curve buttons. Asset cash flows can be exported to a spreadsheet by pressing *Export to Excel*.

2. Parameters

Parameters (figure 12.2) is where the key parametric values in the transaction are added, named, assigned values and deleted. Defined parameters are objects of the Waterfall Syntax. This means they have a fixed name and value.

Add a Parameter: Press the **Add** button on the left, under **Syntax Bar**. An unassigned parameter will appear in the parameter editor (**Parameter List**) underneath the Add and Delete buttons.

Assign a Name, Value to the Parameter: Highlight the new, unassigned parameter. Type its target name in the text box **Parameter Name**, its target value in the text box below, and press **Enter/Return**. The name is successfully assigned when the name change takes effect. Highlight the newly named variable to ensure the new value has been properly assigned.

Delete a Parameter: Highlight the target parameter and press the **Delete** button. When prompted by the text box (*Do you really want to delete this Parameter?*), press the **Yes** button.

Since WFE is a tool for scripting and editing Waterfalls, most parameters in the Parameters page will naturally relate to the liability side. However, five asset-side parameters are supplied by default and appear in the Parameter Editor. These constitute the minimum set needed to compute asset cash flows (**Initial Pool Balance**,

FIGURE 12.2
Parameters page, *WAM* is 360.

WAM, **Pool Average Life**, and **WAC**) as well as a floating-point precision parameter (**Precision**). Although this minimum set should not vary significantly from deal to deal, the parametric values must match those of each target transaction. If **Asset Model** is the source of the asset cash flows, asset-side parameters will be imported automatically from the interface.

When a transaction is created in *New Empty Deal*, liability-side parameters are manually created and populated. When created in *New Deal Wizard*, liability-side parameters are automatically generated at the time the structural features are specified, although values are not automatically assigned. These will need to be assigned on the **Parameters** page. Deals cloned from existing deals will inherit their liability-side parameters and values from the source transaction. They can be updated or changed manually.

Note: changes to the structure may affect other non-parameter objects that will need to be handled in accordance with their properties and Waterfall Syntax.

3. Variables

Variables (figure 12.3) is the input page for dimensioning transactional value elements that change with time: flows, stocks and payment rules. The main property of a variable is its value. It may also be a formula (which may have an initial value) or a vector.

At the time a variable is named, it is only a stored element, not an object in Waterfall Syntax. It becomes an object only after being initialized as one of three object types on the variables page:

a. a *default value* (typically its value at the closing);

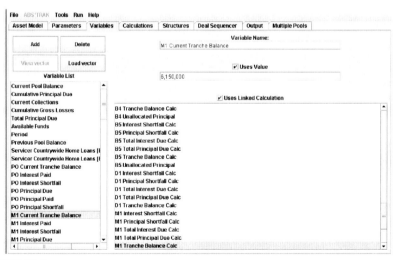

FIGURE 12.3a

M1 Tranche variable initialized at $6.15 million, linked to a balance calculation.

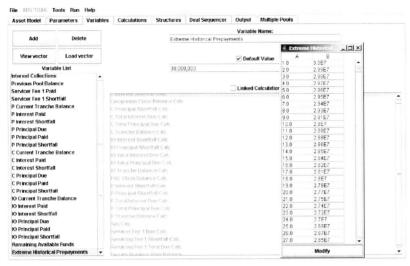

FIGURE 12.3b
Extreme historical prepayments vector (*View Vector*).

   b. a *linked calculation*, a property that expresses its relationship to other variables or raw amounts; or

   c. a *vector* imported from outside the WFE environment.

The process of initializing a variable linked to a calculation starts on the **Calculations** page, the subject of the next section. Initializing is a two-step process distributed across two pages:

1. *Define* the **Calculation** on the **Calculations** page by selecting the required elements from the Variable and Calculation editors (see next section)

2. *Create* the **Variable** on the **Variables** page and link it to the corresponding formula in the *Linked Calculation* section to initialize it.

The key variables will vary from transaction to transaction in accordance with the design of the capital structure. In the simplest case, three classes of variable must be created to run a waterfall: **Available Funds**, **Total Principal Due**, **Current Pool Balance**. Subroutines for handling variables resemble those for parameter handling:

Add a Variable: Press the **Add** button on the left, under the **Syntax Bar**. An unassigned parameter will appear in **Variable Editor**.

Assign a Name, Value to the Variable: Highlight the new, unassigned variable. Type its target name in the text box **Variable Name**. The name is successfully assigned when the name change takes effect in the Editor.

Select the format: for a **Default Value** or **Linked Calculation**, or both, check the appropriate boxes and type the target value in the associated text box; for a Vector, press *Load Vector* and browse for the target CSV file containing the vector. Then, press *Enter/Return* on the keyboard. Re-highlight the newly named variable or *View Variable* to check that the value or values have been properly assigned.

Delete a Variable or Vector: To delete a variable, highlight and press *Delete*. *Del. Vector* removes the vector associated with a variable. When prompted by the text box ("Do you really want to delete this Parameter?") press the Yes button. *Clean var.* removes all unused parameters and variables.

4. Calculations

The **Calculations** page (figure 12.4) is where the logical and arithmetic properties of transaction variables are defined. In the overall sequence of coding steps, the **Calculation** needs to be defined before the variable can become an object in Waterfall Syntax.

   Calculations are created and defined using the **Tree Editing Tools**. Their relationships to other waterfalls are defined using **Node Properties**. Thumbnail descriptions of the Tree Editing Tools and Node Properties are provided in tables 12.1 and 12.2. Following are some common routines involving calculations:

   a. *Icon Creation*: In the upper left-hand corner, press *New*. This creates a **Calculation Node** icon. Name it by placing the cursor on the name box and typing the new name. Be sure to append the name with **Calc** to distinguish it from a Variable. Press enter to make sure the name change takes effect.

   b. *Properties*: Highlight the **Calculation Node** and select a **Calculation Method** that correctly describes the arithmetic or logical relationship between the elements inside the Node.

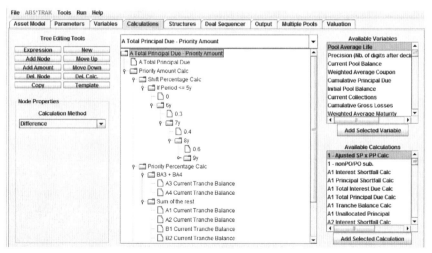

FIGURE 12.4
Example of Tranche A principal due; priority amount calculation.

TABLE 12.1

Tree editing tools

TOOL	OPERATION
Expression	Launches a name box to hold an ad hoc mathematical string
Add Node	Launches a Node substructure to the Calculation. As before, name it by placing the cursor on the name box, type the new name; press enter.
Add Amount	Launches a Leaf substructure containing a raw amount. Change the value as you would change a name.
Del. Node	Deletes Nodes, not Calculations.
Copy	Clones selected Calculation elsewhere on the **Calculation** page.
New	Launches a new Calculation.
Move Up	Moves a sub-structure in the Calculation up the trunk-line.
Move Down	Moves a sub-structure in the Calculation down the trunk-line.
Delete Calc	Deletes Calculations, not Nodes.
Template	Clones the current calculation onto another tranche.

TABLE 12.2

Node properties

METHOD	OPERATOR	EXAMPLE
Sum	Arithmetic	Servicer Fee Due (current + past-due terms)
Difference	Arithmetic	Servicer Fee Shortfall (due–paid terms)
Product	Arithmetic	Current Servicer Fee Due (balance × year fee)
Quotient	Arithmetic	Monthly Rate (year fee/12)
Maximum	Arithmetic	B Tranche Principal Due (maximum of 0, Cumulative Principal Due – ...)
Minimum	Arithmetic	Servicer Fee Paid (minimum of Available Funds, Servicer Fee Due)
Branching	Logical	Boolean calculation
Condition – 2 Vars	Logical	If Period > Step Down Date
Condition – 1 Var	Logical	If Period > Maturity

Calculations' main property is their *Calculation Method*, with nine possible arithmetic operators

   c. *Reverse-Parse*: Each **Calculation Node** may contain branches with multiple Nodes and leaves. Reverse-parse the formula using the other **Tree Editing Tools**, so called because they control the branches and leaves of the structure. Find the required deal elements to express the Calculation from the **Available Variables** and **Available Calculations** editors on the right of the page. "Available" means that the deal elements have already been created and can be found in the deal file. Repeat the process of branching and assigning properties until the Calculation is completed.

d. *Test and Debug* the **Calculation** using **Syntax Bar/*Run/Debug* the selected Calculation**.

5. Structures

Structures (figure 12.5) is where waterfall mechanics are translated into WFE subroutines. It is important to remember that the term **Structure** in WFE does not refer to the capital structure[2] as the term is commonly used in natural language. In WFE, the capital structure is implemented via the **Sequencer**.

Structure means the substructures that allocate and distribute cash running through the structure. These sub-structures, whose mechanisms are invisible to the non-modeler, are a battleground for the conquest and capture of excess spread. Every capital structure is composed of two **Primary Structures**: a mechanism for allocating cash and a separate for distributing it.

Structures can use implicit allocation methods, whereby the instructions are conveyed by words like *pro rata, pari passu pro rata*, and *sequential*; or they can use subroutines with explicit payment instructions. Implicit allocation methods are those found in the equilibrium waterfall logic, while explicit allocation methods deviate from the equilibrium either by altering the payment rules that apply to the liabilities given the pool's amortization schedule, or by reversing the normal, downward directional flow of cash. Such transactions are referred to as *complex*, in contrast to *simple* transactions like pass-through or pay-through structures.

The mechanics of simple transactions observe the following conventions:

a. Due amounts on credit tranches (**Principal Due**) are allocated in accordance with their *pro rata, pari passu pro rata* or *sequential* properties;

b. Due amounts on liquidity tranches (**Fees and Interest Due**) are allocated across all liquidity tranches *pari passu pro rata*;

FIGURE 12.5a
Principal allocation in a simple transaction.

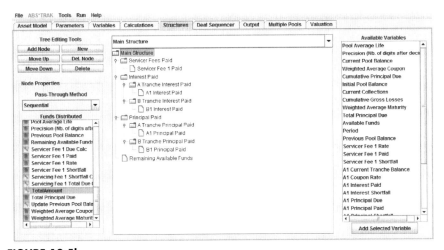

FIGURE 12.5b
Principal distribution for the transaction in figure 12.5a.

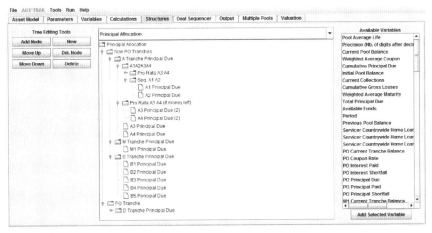

FIGURE 12.5c
Principal Allocation for a complex RMBS transaction.

    c. Distribution (**Fees, Interest, Principal Paid**) amounts are paid *sequentially* across credit tranches and *pari passu pro rata* across liquidity tranches, the same as for due amounts on liquidity tranches.

Structures are stacks of **Variables** reverse-parsed from **Nodes** and **Leaves** using the **Tree Editing Tools**: *Add Node, Delete Node, Delete [Structure], Move Up, Move Down and Copy*.

The precise sequencing to initialize a **Structure** is as follows:

a. *Icon Creation*: Press **New Structure** to the right of the Structure Editor in the page center. This creates a Structure Node icon. Name it by placing the cursor on the name box and typing the new name.

b. *Properties*: Assign properties to the **Structure Node** using methods supplied in the **Node Properties** frame under **Tree Editing Tools**. Structures have characteristic **Pass-Through Methods** (operators) and **Pass-Through Variables**.

> **Payment Methods**: Structures that allocate or distribute funds use a **Pass-Through Method**. To set the logic of the structure, highlight one of the eight methods provided in WFE: *Allocate to a Variable, Pro Rata, Pro Rata Pari Passu, Pro Rata Specified, Pro Rata Specified Dynamic, Sequential, Conditional—1 Variable*, and *Conditional—2 Variables*.

> **Flow Objects**: Highlight the Object, which will be a **Pass-Through Variable** or a **Calculation**. If the required element does not appear in the **Pass-Through Variable** or **Due Calculation** libraries, it can be supplemented from the **Available Variables Library** on the right side of the page.

c. *Reverse-Parse*: Reverse-parse the internal cash flow mechanics of the structure by creating **Branches** to hold the operations of process sub-structures, which may be a **Node** (composite of variables) or **Leaf** (single variable acted upon by a calculation). The reverse-parsing process for a Leaf is analogous to that of a Node (see step 2) but with these minor syntactical modifications:

   i Use **Tree Editing Tools** to add a **Variable Node**;
   ii Under **Variable Properties**, select the **Payment Method** to set the payment logic and highlight the **Flow Object**;
   iii Using the **Variable Editor**, inject the Node with the Variable associated with the payment item; this is a leaf;
   iv While the leaf is highlighted, select the correct **Flow Method** and **Due Calculation** in the **Variable Property** box.
   v Repeat this process until the Structure is completed.

d. Test and debug the completed **Structure** using the **Utility Bar/*Run/Debug the selected Structure*** command.

6. Deal Sequencer

Deal Sequencer (figures 12.6a-c) is the WFE object that most closely corresponds to the deal's *capital structure*. However, the abstraction level in Waterfall Syntax gives Deal Sequencer additional flexibility far beyond intuition. Waterfall Syntax allows the **Deal Sequencer** to combine and array **Structures** created out of transaction **Variables** with unbounded freedom. These activities take place on the **Deal Sequencer** page.

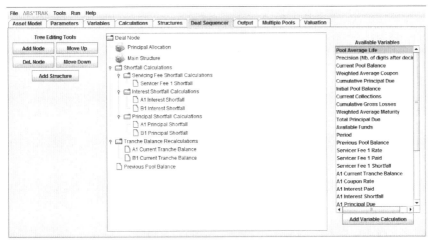

FIGURE 12.6a
Deal Sequencer for a simple transaction.

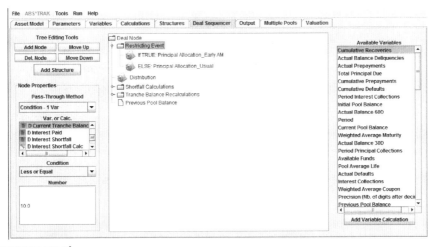

FIGURE 12.6b
One-variable conditional statement (if–else) inside deal sequencer.

Sequencing objects in **Deal Sequencer** is the easiest coding task *mechanically* but the most challenging *conceptually*. The transaction is sequenced by adding existing nodes and leaves, as follows:

a. *Initialize*: Place the Cursor on **Deal Node** appearing at the top of the trunk-line. The main property of a **Deal Node** is its **Pass-Through Method**. When cash flows can only flow according to one path (one waterfall) the Method is *Sequential*. When the **Pass-Through Method** is contingent on certain variable values being true, it is said to be *Conditional*. Select the correct property

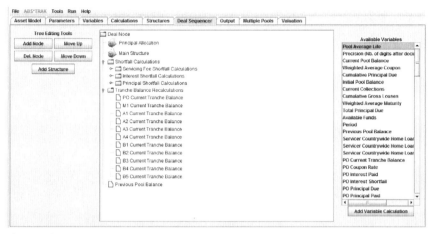

FIGURE 12.6c
Deal sequencer for a complex RMBS transaction.

(the default setting is *Sequential*) and continue to build the sequencer by adding nodes and leaves, from top to bottom.

A simple transaction typically leads off from the **Deal Node** with two **Structure Nodes**, one for each **Primary Structure**, which have a unique **Node Property**, *Pass Through from a Variable*, and take an object, *Pass-Through Variable*.

b. *Stack* or *Reverse-Parse*: Create a **Structure Node** with *Add Structure* in **Tree Editing Tools**; immediately afterwards select the appropriate **Structure** from **Structures Editor** and associated **Pass-Through Variable** from **Pass-Through Variable Editor**. In complex transactions, the **Deal Node** may hold a conditional statement or grouping of variables rather than a **Structure**.

To group variables, *Add Node* and import the variables from **Variables Editor**. To create a conditional statement, press *Add Node*, then name the node so that the *If statement* is easily recognized. Select the correct conditional property from **Node Properties**. Finish the conditional statement by selecting a variable (or variables) and assigning the correct raw amount (if any).

Add Calculations via **Tree Editing Tools** *Add Node, Del. Node* that complete the transaction and pass properties to them as above. Adjust the node order of **Deal Sequencer** *Move Up*, and *Move Down* until the trunk-line is accurate and complete.

The terminal object is the ***Previous Pool Balance Variable***, a **Leaf** whose Linked Calculation connects the *balance in advance* at time $t-1$ to the *balance in arrears* at t, for all time steps t, so the balance can amortize and the transaction can terminate.

c. Test and debug the completed **Deal Sequencer** using the **Utility Bar**/***Run***/ ***Debug the Sequencer*** command.

Figures 12.6a-c illustrate the sequencer for a hypothetical deal, the conditional statement, and the sequencer for an actual RMBS transaction.

7. Output

The **Syntax Bar/Run** commands execute the code and launch the **Deal Output Window** (figure 12.7) where the results can be reviewed. The selection and array of outputs for display take place on the *Output* page of **Syntax Bar**.

A comprehensive list of available transaction variables appears in Output Editor, on the left side of the window. The array of selected variables appears on the right side of the page. The order can be changed by highlighting the variable and using the *Move Up, Move Down* or *Remove* buttons. To move a variable from the bottom to the top: highlight it and hit the *Move Down* button twice.

8. Multiple-Pool Transactions

Some transaction types, notably in RMBS, are backed by multiple pools of assets that are not fully cross-collateralized but grouped into separate capital structures (*group waterfall*) and linked at the bottom of the capital structure (*common waterfall*). To model the cash flows within such transactions, it is necessary to link the separate waterfalls to their related pool and create a joint interface at the point when the various pools become cross-collateralized (figure 12.8).

In WFE, the required group waterfalls and the common waterfall are first individually built in accordance with the Waterfall Syntax. In addition, the common waterfall needs additional parameters for mapping each tranche to the right group. For example, if you want to map a tranche A1B to Group 1, you would have to create the parameter "A1B GROUP MAP" with the value 1. If you did not want Group 1 to share in remaining funds within the common waterfall, you would have to add the parameter "SHARED GROUP" with the value 0 in the Group 1 Waterfall.

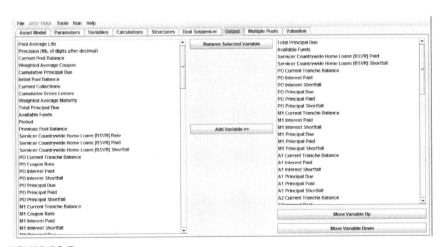

FIGURE 12.7
Output for simple transaction.

FIGURE 12.8a
Linking the waterfalls to related pools and a common waterfall.

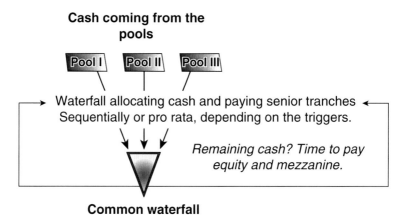

FIGURE 12.8b
Integration of the cash flows into a common waterfall.

The multiple pool interface is shown in Figure 12.8a, while the mapping of the groups to the common waterfall is shown in Figure 12.8b.

To display output variables from the common group, it is necessary to create tranche variables from the group waterfall separately for the common waterfall. These will be automatically updated in the cash flow runs.

9. Valuation

The **Valuation** tab computes the ratings of each tranche through a Monte Carlo simulation described in chapter 9 which drives a nonlinear convergence technique able to compute a unique rating on each tranche via matching input and output tranche interest rates for a pool specified within the WFE Asset Model and a capital structure specified in WFE. Chapter 13 offers more detail on the technique itself.

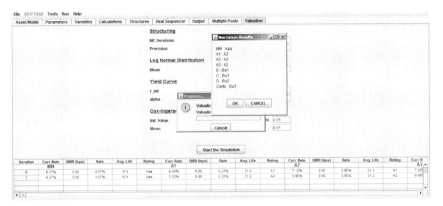

FIGURE 12.9
The valuation input screen in WFE

The input screen is presented in figure 12.9 and the main input variables are as follows:

- a. *Structuring*: the data fields include MC Iterations (number of simulations), Precision (error precision), Relaxation Factor used to modify the tranche-rating update rule, NL Iterations Max. (maximum number of iterations);
- b. *Lognormal Distribution*: mean and standard deviation of losses;
- c. *Yield Curve*: user-specified fixed-rate yield curve model;
- d. *Cox–Ingersoll–Ross Model*: short-rate model used to value floating-rate tranches.

12.3 WATERFALL LEXICON

Waterfall Grammar is a special dealing-language that reflects financial intention with precise mechanical instructions and unifies the processes of structuring and valuation into a monolithic framework by using special terms (**Waterfall Lexicon**) and operating rules (**Waterfall Syntax**).

This section begins with a catalogue of the **Waterfall Lexicon**, then proceeds to answer the paradigm question: *What is Reverse-Parsing?*

At the highest level of WFE functionality is its structure of global commands activated by the **Utility Bar**, described above.

The second level of functionality is the structure of programming and compiling commands activated by **Syntax Bar**, described above. **Asset Model** and **Multiple Pools** offer optional asset-making interfaces while **Parameters**, **Variables**, **Calculations**, **Structures**, and **Deal Sequencer** define the elements in the deal. Deal elements are the financial or programming building blocks required to implement a waterfall. Syntactically they are objects with names and associated properties.

Ready-made or custom-made, they are graphically depicted in WFE as icons that can be:

1. *Activated* from an **Editor** that matches their type;
2. Named or re-named in a **Name Box**;
3. Reverse-parsed via **Tools** and **Methods** to make a higher-order deal element; and
4. Stored in an **Editor** to match the new Element-type.

TABLE 12.3

Node properties

DEAL ELEMENT	EDITOR	TOOLS	ICON	ICON PROPERTIES
Parameters	Parameter List	Parameter Name	Leaf/-	Default Value
Variables	Variable List	Add, Delete Load/ View Vector Variable Name	Leaf/-	Default Value Linked Calc. Vector
Calculations	Available Variables Available Calc.	Tree Editing Tools	Node/Calc[4]	Calculation Method
Structures	Available Variables	Tree Editing Tools	Node/-	*Node Properties* PT Method
			Leaf/-	*Variable Properties* PT Method
Deal Sequencer	Structure PT Object	Tree Editing Tools	Structure/-	*Structure Properties* PT Method
	Available Calc. PT Object		Node/-	*Node Properties* PT Method (Var/Calc)
	Available Variables PT Object		Leaf/-	*Variable Properties* Payment Method

Appending the ***Calculation*** with ***Calc*** distinguishes it from a ***Variable*** but makes it polymorphic: an *operand* in a structure and an *operator* on a variable. Although a ***Calc*** has only a transitory financial meaning in the context of the transaction, some ***Calculations*** provide important measures of performance, like *Shortfall Calcs*. In the end, a deal element's financial meaning boils down to modeling and measurement conventions of the user group.

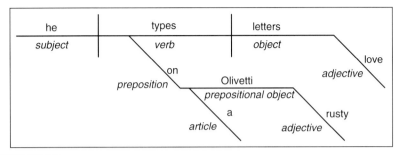

FIGURE 12.10
The parsing of "He types love letters on a rusty Olivetti."

Deal Elements

A deal element is an object. Its type is determined by the page where it is initialized. Each deal element has its own **Editors**, **Tools** and **Methods**, but the modular design of WFE means a high degree of similarity from page to page. For example, **Editors** typically appear on the left- (called *List) or right-hand side (called Available*) of the page. **Tools** typically appear at the top-left side. **Methods**, by which deal elements acquire their properties, typically appear at the bottom-left. The **Name Box** appears in the center. On the **Variables**, **Calculations**, **Structures**, and **Deal Sequencer** pages, deal elements are displayed as icons in a graphical interface that shows their relational properties to other elements using **Tree/Branch/Leaf** format (table 12.3).

Reverse-Parsing

We tend to think of the capital structure of ABS transactions as a parsing of the asset cash flows being securitized. But with non-recourse debt, a glimpse at the structure or even a careful reading of the waterfall is insufficient to form a well-reasoned value opinion. Unlike corporate debt, structured securiy valuation is intensively statistical. Only by simulating asset performance under a wide variety of macroeconomic environments can the analyst begin to move toward an approximation of security value.

If the capital structure is understood as a pattern of parsed asset cash flows, it can be modeled as a process of *reverse-parsing* and linking cash flows to allocation rules to express the deal's value proposition. Only in this way can the impact of different macro-economic states on asset value at different levels in the capital structure be measured precisely. The term *parse* brings to mind the division of a sentence into its component parts by placing the main syntactical objects (S–V–O) or (S–V) on the trunk-line and branching the dependent parts of speech in accordance with their sub-structures below the main structure (figure 12.10). By reverse-parsing, we mean the analysis of a sentence in reverse order by first creating its sub-structures and then synthesizing them.

13

Nonlinear Convergence

Finishing the Excel-based cash flow model and its enhancements takes you a long way toward the completion of a valuation engine. However, you have really only built the linear portion of what is required to analyze transaction. What remains is to tackle the deal's nonlinear aspect, its so-called yield or "original time" level. This is necessary to ensure that the structure is self-consistent and does not contain arbitrary yield assumptions that introduce spurious elements of risk or cushion into the analysis. Thus, even before embarking on the full analytical conceptualization of the cash flow modeling problem in the Advanced Part, the nontrivial task of yield-space convergence needs to be addressed. After completing that step, you will be in possession, at least theoretically, of the full skill set required to properly value structured securities without the crutch of credit agency ratings. But, as usual, what you do with those skills is up to you.

Today the structuring methods used on Wall Street ignore the essentially nonlinear aspect of structured securities. The reason nonlinearity is ignored is the professional deformation that equates structured securities with corporate bonds. Their equivalence is enabled via a linearization made possible by the magic of credit ratings. In truth, the equivalence only works because no one has cared to challenge the shaky opinions of traditional rating agencies, at least until now. The problem of intrinsic nonlinearity cannot be wished away or "solved" by substituting one's own credit opinion for that of a rating agency analyst. The person who does this only demonstrates a lack of understanding of structured finance. The resolution lies not in substituting one unjustifiable prejudice for another equally bad one, but by eliminating prejudice altogether.

Happily, sophisticated analysis does not involve higher-level concepts, only progressive refinements of concepts embedded in the cash flow model already built. To be sure, you will be forced to graduate from spreadsheet modeling to environments like VBA or C++. Not only will this progression help you better conceptualize the deal, but you speed of execution will be greatly enhanced. The limitations of Excel are now patent with respect to loan-by-loan analysis, not to mention the mental contortions required to implement ordinary deal features like triggers.

13.1 THE NONLINEAR LOOP

The uppermost level with respect to deal analysis brings it to self-consistent closure via yield space iteration, which results in finding a unique fixed point called the *Value* of the deal. Although the existence of this fixed point will be discussed fully in chapter 22, suffice it to say here that the difference between deals and non-deals lies in the unique ability of the former to achieve convergence. All properly structured deals will come together in yield space and converge onto a set of consistent risk-interest-rate combinations from some initial guess. The reason one needs to guess the rates at the outset is that risk, and hence ratings, are based on average reductions of yield from the original coupon promise to bondholders. In turn, that promise is heavily dependent on the risk taken, which is to say on the credit rating of the target securities. However, the rating itself is precisely what we are trying to determine in order to ascertain the risk. Nonlinearity comes about because interest rates are determined by ratings, and vice versa. Thus, at the outset we can only guess at rates that hopefully will result in average yield reductions compatible with the very same rates.

The probability with which one can readily intuit or guess a set of rates that will, on output from a lengthy Monte Carlo simulation, reproduce the same rates to within a small error bound is zero. Therefore, the nonlinear loop consists of the feedback mechanism that successively updates the rate vector, allowing a feasible transaction to converge onto a set of consistent tranche-wise rates. As always with nonlinear problems, there is no guarantee that this will happen for all initial rate-vectors. Familiarity with the asset class and the macro-economic environment is thus of paramount importance to ensure convergence.

13.2 THE YIELD CURVE MODEL

In what follows, you will be called upon to use a yield curve model. It can be either something you have concocted yourself or something you have literally lifted from a financial publication. We disclose one such model as equations (39) and (40) in chapter 22. Although it is sufficient for our academic purposes, we are not endorsing it by any means. You may prefer to build your own yield curve model from empirical data. In all cases, the yield curve can be conceptualized as follows:

$$\text{yield} = \text{risk-free rate} + \text{credit spread} + \text{liquidity spread}$$

Equation (39) of chapter 22 contains only the first two components on the right. The reason for omitting the third term is that the liquidity spread is really a "fudge" factor aimed at explaining why yields at the same rating level are different. In effect, the integrated *average* liquidity spread is normally zero by construction, since the yield curve is constructed using total yield data that already include the combined credit and liquidity effects. The net result is conceived as representing the credit spread

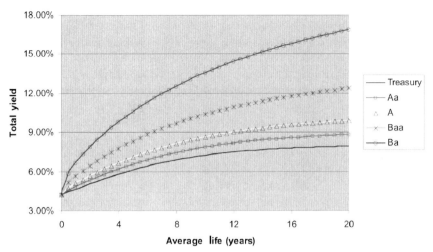

FIGURE 13.1
Yield curve and yield spreads.

only and liquidity has averaged out to zero, by construction. In other words, liquidity is effectively a measure of the negotiating positions and strengths of both parties in a given trade. In that sense, it is nonanalytic.

As discussed at greater length in chapters 5, 7 and 9, there are two inputs to a yield curve model as used in structured finance:

1. Average life
2. Reduction of yield (risk level of the security)

A typical set of yield-spread curves for various levels of risk is given in figure 13.1.

13.3 THE REDUCTION OF YIELD SCALE

In order to assign the familiar letter-grade ratings to structured securities that are understood by the capital markets, a correspondence mapping between the reductions of yield and the alphabetical ratings is required. But always remember that knowledge of this scale is not necessary to achieve closure and value the securities, since the yield curve model alone is sufficient to derive the final, converged rate-vector.

Since we have used the yield curve as an integral part of the valuation exercise, the letter-grade ratings are superfluous; the only reason for using them was to compute interest rates in the first instance. On output from the analysis, the structured securities we have valued will already have interest rates assigned to them as part of the solution procedure. Since letter-grade ratings are no longer necessary, this also means that rating agencies are no longer necessary. This is possible because we have resolved the nonlinearity embedded in the valuation problem with numerical benchmarks and a convergence routine, without the crutch of rating agencies. One such benchmark is the standard reduction-of-yield scale given in table 9.2. Please note that the particular values on the scale are irrelevant to the analysis. Any fixed set of monotonically increasing numbers could be used as long as the logarithmic nature of the scale is respected.

To assign a letter grade to the securities, look up the average of the outputs for each tranche of a fully converged Monte Carlo simulation, and compare these to the points on the scale. For example, a tranche that achieved an average reduction of yield of 6 basis points would be assigned an alphabetical credit rating of A2 since, according to table 9.2, 6 is between 5.2 and 8.9. Any reduction of yield between 0 and 0.06 bps warrants the highest rating category available , i.e. Aaa. To fine-tune the structuring so as not to give away value to the buyer by structuring the tranche above the midpoint or to the seller by structuring the tranche below the midpoint, it is necessary to match the average reduction of yield on the tranches to the midpoint indicated in the right-hand column, working down the capital structure beginning with the most senior class.

We should note that Standard & Poor's and Fitch Rating Services do not subscribe to the DIRR scale, nor do they agree that there is any nonlinear problem involved in rating structured securities. For that matter, Moody's also does not recognize this key issue despite the fact that they themselves introduced the average reduction of yield method in the 1980s. S&P and Fitch still opine on structured credit quality from within the paradigm of corporate finance and are a long way from abandoning what seems to "work" so well. It is a foregone conclusion that, as a result of this basic lack of understanding of the structured rating process, gross inefficiencies have crept into the analysis of hundreds of transactions, and that a vast array of opportunities for credit arbitrage exists.

13.4 THE STEP-BY-STEP NONLINEAR METHOD

Referring to figure 13.2, proceed as follows:

1. Determine an initial set of input rates from either a prior proxy-transaction or from a BOTE analysis of the target transaction as demonstrated in chapter 4. In the case of our target, two-tranche transaction, let us refer to the set of provisional interest rates as $r_A(n)$ and $r_B(n)$, respectively, where $n \in [0, N]$, is always an integer and where the initial rate-vector is defined by $n = 0$. Our main task now is to update the two tranche-rates inside a converging process.

2. Proceed with one complete Monte Carlo (MC) simulation consisting of a set of at least 2,500 scenarios, each represents a single transaction realization under a simulated macro-economic environment. As indicated in chapter 9, these environments are selected using the inverse distribution function method based on some given probability density function. The most popular candidate-distribution is the lognormal distribution described elsewhere. Each MC scenario is differentiated by having its own random deviate taken from the said distribution. Across the entire sample of 2,500 scenarios, it is a virtual certainty that the entire domain of the distribution will have been sampled.

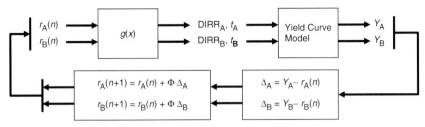

Φ = Relaxation factor (over or under)

FIGURE 13.2
Nonlinear valuation.

In chapter 7, the macro-economic distribution is simulated via the cumulative credit loss rate distribution function assumed to be highly correlated to macro-economic conditions. Before going through a MC scenario, select one random deviate from the given lognormal distribution so you can look at what happens to each tranche under the associated loss rate. This is the process we have shown as $g(x)$ in figure 13.2.

3. On output from each MC scenario, compute the average life and the reduction of yield, if any, of each liability tranche in the deal. If the tranche balance did not pay down to zero, the resulting average life must be ignored, since in those cases it would be theoretically infinite. Sum the yield reductions and average lives thus obtained.

4. Once the initial MC simulation terminates, compute the average yield reduction and the weighted average life of each tranche. The weighted average life is defined as the arithmetic mean of all finite average lives. Define the tranche-wise average yield reductions as $DIRR_A$ and $DIRR_B$, and the weighted average lives as t_A and t_B, respectively.

5. Invoke the yield curve model you have built to calculate the yield corresponding to the inputs from step 4. Label the yields thus produced Y_A and Y_B, respectively.

6. Compute the tranche-wise raw differences between the input yields for $r_A(n)$ and $r_B(n)$ and the output yields just calculated via $\Delta_A = Y_A - r_A(n)$ and the equivalent formula for Class B.

7. Compute the new rates $r_A(n+1)$ and $r_B(n+1)$ via the successive over- or under-relaxation formulas $r_A(n+1) = r_A(n) + \Phi \Delta_A$; and the equivalent formula for Class B. The relaxation factor Φ is normally tranche-dependent, but we ignore this second-order detail and select a value of order one as the unique Φ for both classes. In general, you will be forced to under-relax (SUR) higher alphabetic-denomination classes while lower denominated classes will normally withstand successive over-relaxation (SOR). Begin with $\Phi = 1$, but remain open to the possibility of having to modify it if the solution converges too slowly. Only trial and error can tell you what the optimum relaxation factor should be. More complicated transactions will more than test the limits of your ability to intuit such factors.

8. Repeat steps 2 through 7 as long as necessary to reduce the weighted average difference between two successive rate-iterates to within a target error margin, usually 0.5% or less. As weights, use the initial tranche balances.

9. Once the solution has converged in yield space, use the above letter-grade rating scale to convert the final reductions of yield to letters if you should ever need or want them. Display the final yield, the average life and the letter-grade credit rating of each tranche on a separate part of your spreadsheet.

If the structure does not converge, it is because you have either assumed initial rates outside the basin of attraction of the nonlinear function $g(x)$, or else your structure is ill-posed. In that case, to achieve convergence you may have to reduce the standard deviation of the cumulative loss distribution (which would be tantamount to selecting a pool with a lower loss variance), or otherwise change the structure until the transaction becomes feasible. The proper method is to focus on the right side of the SPV balance sheet since the performance of the assets is not something you can change unless you can somehow influence pool composition. By contrast, the bond structure and other transactional features are completely within the purview of structured analysis. Therefore, it is in that domain that you should look for an acceptable resolution to the divergence question.

In a learning setting, where asset parameters are hypothetical, there is nothing wrong with changing their assumed performance universe. But in the real world this is not the case, so beware of facile, wishful-thinking solutions to difficult structuring problems. The last thing you ought to do is bypass this process in the hope of gaining a dealing advantage. Many others have tried to do this before using various stratagems, and they ultimately failed.

Part II

$\triangleright$

Advanced Structured Analysis

The following 11 chapters make up the Advanced Part of this text. As such, the exploration of the concepts and ideas described therein should only be undertaken once the student has sufficiently mastered the material that precedes it. To begin here right away, perhaps aiming to forego foundational stages and becoming an "expert" in no time, is naïve and in the end will most likely result in having to go back to those early chapters anyway. If a career in structured finance is what you are truly looking for, and we sincerely hope that it is, there is nothing wrong with practicing the art of going slowly. Rest assured that the breadth of your fundamental understanding of the field and your ability to execute deals quickly and efficiently can only be strengthened by learning how to walk before trying to run.

Chapters 14 through 22 take you in detail through a single, nonrevolving securitization from conception to closing, including valuation, pricing, and ratings. It is only when you understand a transaction in all its moving parts that you will ever be able to tackle every other deal in a similar way. Chapter 23 is a relatively complete, and yet far from comprehensive introduction to revolving periods and their idiosyncrasies. Finally, chapter 24 is a collection of topics peripheral to structured security valuation but lying beyond the scope of the target deal.

In completing the first nine chapters of the Advanced Part, both main authors benefited from the considerable programming and analytical support provided by Mr. Michael Spencer, a former student of ours. His painstaking efforts in writing, debugging, and running the intricate nonlinear code implementing the security valuation algorithm described below, made the task of writing the text that much easier. We remain eternally grateful for his contribution, especially one made under the pressure-cooker atmosphere that invariably surrounds a job on Wall Street.

In addition, one of us (SR) would like to highlight and acknowledge the inspiration and leadership provided by two special individuals who unknowingly and significantly contributed to the making of this textbook.

First, Dr. Wolfgang Kollmann, former professor of numerical methods and turbulence theory at the Von Karman Institute for Fluid Dynamics in Brussels, Belgium, and now Professor of Mechanical and Aeronautical Engineering at the University of California, Davis. It was sheer luck to be exposed to such utter brilliance, impeccable technique, and total integrity just when it was most needed.

Last, but certainly not least, *The Dao of Dealing* could never have seen the light of day but for the steadfast encouragement and keen insights supplied in absentia by Martin Heidegger, a philosopher no longer in need of an introduction. The magnitude of the debt structured finance owes him is only now starting to dawn on the rest of us.

INTRODUCTORY PREAMBLE

For better and for worse, we are about to move on from the framework that has apparently stood us in good stead thus far in order to embark on a journey into fine-grained cash flow modeling techniques, one that will compel us to have recourse to more powerful and flexible valuation environments. This does not mean that our previous efforts were somehow wrong or misguided, for anything that enables you to organize your thoughts and allow the deal to reveal itself is by definition right. However, as has already been made abundantly clear, the nature of structured finance is such that the basic limitations of spreadsheet software quickly become major impediments to serious analysis.

We would be doing great harm to a transaction were we to ignore its special properties just because they are too complex or even impossible to represent using the basic tools at our disposal. Why do complicated structural features even exist if no one is given any tangible credit for them? When this happens, and it happens a lot, reality is thrown out the window and what remains can in no meaningful way correspond to the construct we have come to know as a deal. The upshot is either irrational exuberance of the *laissez les bons temps rouler* variety or built-in conservatism in the form of over-enhancement. More often than not, the loser is the sponsor, the only party that commonly does not have the ability on its own to separate the wheat from the chaff.

For example, how are we to gauge the effectiveness of a delinquency trigger linked to excess spread trapping if no effort is ever made to model the trigger in concert with the implicit pool delinquency-structure? How can the risk taken by a PAC IO holder be measured if prepayments are mainly afterthoughts never to be integrated into the formalism? How can the dynamics of credit losses come to influence structural design if credit risk is misapprehended as a static phenomenon? Unfortunately, these and other questions must remain largely unanswered under our initial analytical framework. In other words, we do not make a transition to more intricate cash flow environments because we have more time on our hands, but simply because we have no choice in the matter.

Over the course of the next nine chapters, we will introduce one by one the sequence of steps involved in doing a deal at the advanced level and will be featuring a set of core numerical methods along the way. In essence, we want to formalize properly what ought to be called *financial engineering* if this label were not already overworked and overrated. Today, what appears under this rubric is usually an obsession with a single differential equation whose solution is supposed to provide mystical wisdom whatever the situation. In truth, today's best-trained financial engineers commonly have no systematic way to proceed with respect to even the most plain-vanilla prospectus. Unfortunately, this is the perennial dilemma facing those with ready-made solutions looking for problems.

In contrast to "*The Analysis of Structured Securities*" (OUP, 2003), where we presented similar material in an admittedly hodge-podge manner, here we will be building a single transaction from the ground up, highlighting appropriate portions of code when warranted and presenting just enough theory to guide the student without overwhelming him or her. Although the methods outlined and demonstrated below are but a subset of a seasoned structured analyst's toolkit, time spent becoming adept at using them will be well worth the effort, as they will come up repeatedly in a variety of contexts across the entire credit spectrum.

At first blush, the analysis of a single transaction might seem overly restrictive and specialized when compared to the immense structural variety presently found in the wide world of structured finance. Understandably, time-conscious readers may fear becoming "*one-trick ponies*". Should you think so, think again, for what we are after is not this or that particular deal but simply *deal-hood*, the essence of dealing. More specifically, we are looking for what must always be present in a deal *as such*, of which the target transaction is but a randomly chosen example from the *whole*. Understanding what makes an amorphous blob into a *thing* with basic integrity, is the summit we must climb. Rather than a lengthy tutorial on subprime auto-loan backed structured securities, what follows should be construed as the prototype of what essential dealing really means. Thus, our job here is to investigate deals as such and as a whole. Most likely, this will be your toughest assignment, the one that has been delayed the longest. Undoubtedly, it will be your loneliest wandering.

To some of you, our approach will look and feel suspiciously like philosophy, and this is not a coincidence. It is how it must be, because the relationship between philosophy and the positive sciences[1] is identical to that prevailing between finance and the *positive* businesses. Philosophy enables the positive sciences and gives them empirical validity and reality, and finance does the same to the entire universe of physical processes we normally associate with a *real* business. This is what Hegel meant when he referred to philosophy as "die verkehrte Welt",[2] the inverted world, for only on the basis of a negative philosophical grounding can something positive ever come to exist.

Seen radically and philosophically, the objects of physics are identical to those of chemistry, computer science and yes, of finance too. Any recognizable business endeavor is primarily grounded in finance regardless of its specific object, i.e., finance is the *philosophy* of business. Thus, at bottom *every* company is a *finance* company. Consequently, oblivion of the truth of finance soon spells the doom of any firm just as surely as a science forgetful of its own philosophical underpinnings quickly becomes mired in platitudes. Bluntly put, one does not mess with finance. This *conditio sine qua non* is precisely what gives the latter its unique and a priori status within the realm of worldly pursuits, and what allows us to look at deals in a way that fully abstracts from their specifics.

What keeps finance locked inside a purportedly unavoidable cycle of boom and bust is that its most original and metaphysical essence has long remained unrecognizable, and hence unrecognized, most of all by those directly engaged in it.

It is not so much that finance has been misunderstood, for to *misunderstand* something, you first have to *understand* it. Unfortunately, just as the average physicist is ignorant of the intensely philosophical outlook of his illustrious predecessors and brethren, the average financial analyst simply takes his field for granted, as a no-brainer. In fact, it is the very self-evidence of our profession, the commonplace notion that it can be practiced by anyone with an IQ above room temperature, which is questionable. Perhaps all of us ought to look in the mirror and ask whether we proceed in this way because deals are so obviously there for the mere taking or, on the contrary, so we can more easily turn our backs on finance.

Analysts hoping to value securities without first grasping philosophy are like people trying to fathom baseball without understanding pitching. At best, they provide great amusement for those who actually do. As you are about to discover, valuation is nothing but applied philosophy and any attempt at bypassing the latter will, sooner or later, spell the demise of your deals.

14

The Dao of Dealing

无为而为

14.1 THE BASIC PROBLEM OF STRUCTURED ANALYSIS

Before setting out on our great trek along the horizon of valuation, it is perhaps propitious to ask what finance is all about. After all, the central challenge before us is how to define a deal in a more fundamental way than ever before. The pivotal question, in fact the *only* question in finance, is the question of the deal: what is a deal? Regrettably, this question has yet to be posed, let alone answered.

The first step on the way to a meaningful reflection is to interrogate your own self about the issue without prejudgment. Have you ever seen a deal? Have you ever seen a bond? Why yes, you might reply, and perhaps pick up a prospectus on a table somewhere in your office and say *this* is a deal. No, it is not. A prospectus is just a piece of paper and is, at best, the representation of a deal. It is no more a deal than the picture of an airplane is an airplane.

But wait, let's back up one step. What is a loan? Is it a piece of paper? It seems we are back to the prospectus argument. In fact, a loan is a legally enforceable promise to pay, which is what a bond also means. However, a promise is not something you can touch; it is not physical, but metaphysical. In other words, loans do not exist in the same way houses do. However, they must exist in some way must they not? Which way is that? And once you know that *way*, is it of a lesser *nature* than that of houses?

Now, structured finance is all about loans and bonds, i.e., it is about things that don't *really* exist. But if structured finance is about things that don't really exist, maybe structured finance itself does not really exist. Something seems completely goofy here and yet nothing we have said so far has been wrong, or even an exaggeration.

The result of these obvious considerations is that the reality of finance is of a different sort than that of a cup or a knife. Yet, both cups and deals must have at least some basic features in common, features that enable us to call both of them *some-thing*. Cups must be *there* in some original and fundamental way, a way in which deals can also be there. After reflecting on this for a while, it should dawn upon you that the universal *being-there* character of both deals and cups could only rest in our ability to relate to them a priori, i.e., prior to any empirical verification. In fact, it is solely based on this type of original intuition that knowable deals and cups can ever be empirically encountered. Yet in our daily lives, we remain entirely unaware of this phenomenon because it is, in truth, why the world makes any sense at all. Otherwise, we would see utter chaos, literally nothing. It is precisely the fact that the world makes sense to us, its self-evidence, that constitutes the basic and unavoidable problem of knowledge and that, therefore, requires an explanation. In essence, the problem is that there is no problem.

This is so obvious if you just think about it for a second. You really need to *know* a cup before you can *see* a cup, and vice versa. You need to *relate* to the cup in a primordial way before you can start presupposing that what you are seeing before you is in fact *some-thing* and not *no-thing*, before you can begin to investigate that cup. If you did not already possess a unified pre-understanding of the concept *cup*, no actual cup could ever be built because it is not possible to conceive of objects piecemeal, statistically. The conceptualization process leading to the cup, its *idea* must have a unitary nature, and this means that you can only think of a cup as a manifold totality if you are ever to encounter one. The *real* cup is the one you must have in your head from the word go, not the other way around. If you simply assume, as most people do, that the physical cup precedes the metaphysical cup, you have ipso facto assumed the problem away. Does this ring a bell?

Consequently, the original way to conceive of cups, knives, and structured securities must be as a nexus of relationships. The sheer relatedness of a deal is what forms its substance and reality. Because what is real in a transaction consists exclusively of such relationships, valuation simply amounts to representing them, as they are known to exist *in advance* without taking shortcuts or conveniently ignoring features because they are *too complicated* to handle.

The Ontic Nature of Assets versus the Ontological Nature of Liabilities

As you will know by now, a deal always involves a special purpose vehicle (SPV) that serves as the legal construct within which it will exist, no matter how it does so. Formally speaking, the SPV is a corporation. Even if it pays no taxes, it has all the hallmarks of corporate existence, i.e., a balance sheet, a cash flow statement, and many more things we ascribe to the careful work of lawyers and accountants. In this context, doing a deal can be succinctly described as a *de-construction* of both sides of the SPV balance sheet, thereby creating a world where each of them can live, which means interact with, and relate to the other in real time.

It is at this point that a second basic observation forces itself upon us. It boils down to noticing the fundamental difference between the assets and the liabilities at the level where they must live. On the one hand, bonds are mere logical devices. As far as their economic being is concerned, they are completely circumscribed by the prospectus. Because their existence is strictly logical, they are said to be *ontological* objects. This must be true since a financial bond is nothing but evidence of some simple, metaphysical relationship between two parties. As a result, bonds can be described as pure concepts of which absolute knowledge is feasible, i.e., logic alone exhausts the ontology of a bond. Since ontological constructs are not bound by linear time, this also means that bonds are a piece of *eternity*. Consequently, uncertainty cannot exist with respect to liabilities. If transaction rules are followed properly, bondholders can have perfect knowledge of what will happen to whatever cash flows through their deal. The crux of the analysis lies in noticing that if that were true of the assets as well, structured finance would amount to an exercise in riskless logic. Unfortunately, it is not.

It should come as no surprise to hear that the reality of a deal's assets is different from that of its liabilities. The range of relationships *intended* by assets can never be represented exhaustively since what is true for them is far more involved than what could ever be written down in a prospectus or expressed via a few logical statements. Even in the best case, it can only be suggested.[3] Thus, to express the fact that unlike liabilities, assets are not given a priori as pure concepts, but instead consist of a complex web of hidden and in many cases unknowable relationships, we say they are *ontic* objects. Although the truth of liabilities begins and ends with the prospectus, that of the assets does not.

Is there a problem here? Yes, there is. The problem is that since in the final analysis a model is exclusively a logical device, within this context ontic objects can only be *represented* via their *transformation* into ontological objects bound to fall short of the mark at some level. If assets are to be handled ontologically, they too must eventually be reduced to pure logic, and there lies the rub. In other words, the basic problem of finance is the ontological characterization of assets, not liabilities. Therefore, serious structured analysis is asset- not liability-focused

Structured finance is not difficult because it talks about bonds, for they are comparatively trivial. Rather, it is complicated because the proper representation of the assets is not given in advance through logic alone. However, to do it well, one necessarily has to know what matters and what does not, i.e., what must be explicitly modeled and what can be explicitly ignored at the level of acceptable precision. As a result, any asset conceptualization regime needs to proceed in a reductive and essentially *negative* direction whereby an appropriate ontological reduction of the assets is attempted through the nonarbitrary selection of a manifold relationship thought to endure. In our search for assets as ontological constructs, we are thus looking for *conservation laws* since they alone stand outside linear time. In short, what matters is what lasts, for that is what is *true*.

Given that asset description is perforce incomplete, there must be better and worse ontological reductions of the same deal. In fact, the real measure of our analytical sophistication lies in the way we are able to discover the enduring, formal, and hence mathematical structures underlying asset pools. Although there is no failsafe or step-wise method to discover such basic schemas, we do not have to start from scratch because we have at our disposal a panoply of pre-existing, logical patterns that became paradigmatic themes within various, not necessarily financial contexts. Such formal ontological structures must be brought to bear on asset analysis.

In doing this, remember that the first step of any rigorous analysis is always intuitive, i.e., it cannot be conveyed externally in words but only experienced internally as thoughts. Watching other people do deals from the dugout amounts to nothing. In fact, it amounts to less than nothing, for it gives you the false impression that you actually know something. There is no substitute for direct interaction with a live deal, and reading this book is no exception. No matter how skilled you ever become at retracing the steps described below, it would no more teach you the Dao of Dealing than listening to Beethoven would make you a great composer.

Failing the moral sanction that must inevitably operate in finance due to its ontological character, we need to become conscious of how it can and must become a science, which boils down to answering the question about the essence of finance. What you are about to read is a framework to do so, that is all. It can never tell you how to proceed physically, only metaphysically. In each particular case, the situation will be slightly different and the deal will have to come together in its own way. How will you know what that is? The simple answer is that you don't have to *know* because the deal itself will tell you, if only you would listen.

14.2 A FRAMEWORK FOR FINANCIAL ENGINEERING

The way of the deal is nothing earth-shattering. It is the way of all things, and finance is no exception. In the East, it is called the "Dao," in the Middle East the "Tariqa," and in the West *metaphysics*. In all cases, what is intended is the same, i.e., the nonlogical process via which objects, things can come alive, can *exist* as beings, as things. The same way the trial is the unit of law and the inning that of baseball, the deal is the *unit* of finance. If we *do not* have a deal, then in some sense we have *nothing*. If we *do* have a deal, then in some sense we have *everything*. The theory of finance is deal theory and nothing else.

To capitalize on this, what must first be understood is that deals may only come together within freedom space, a sui generis abstract space. If you ever want to grasp the Dao of Dealing, you will eventually have to become comfortable with such abstractions. Freedom space is not new. It is the space of *degrees of freedom* engineers and statisticians talk about all day long. In fact, it has practically become second nature to them, and so it will to you one day. Freedom space sits above yield space and enables it essentially, i.e., out of itself. To make any sense, dealing must be conceived primarily as a process taking place in this realm in the arc-like manner shown in figure 14.1.

Before delving into the Dao any further however, you need to hold onto the notion that this arc is merely an arbitrary sample taken from an infinite sequence, whereby each represents but a single realization within the eternity of the deal. The meaning of nonlinearity is specifically the way something can exist self-identically, i.e., repeating itself ad infinitum. Indeed, it is *eternity* itself conceived metaphysically and therefore, cyclically. Since every phase is isomorphic to the prior and successive one, the detailed description of a single unit is both sufficient and necessary to grasp the whole.

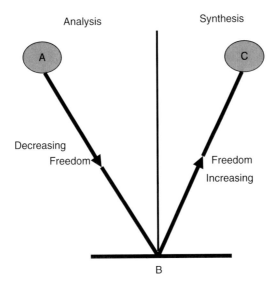

FIGURE 14.1

The three moments of essential dealing.

To help us describe the mechanics of the Dao, we have identified three specific positions along the arc. These are the analogues of the negative and positive determinations at the heart of all logical constructs. They are the stages of *deal-hood*. Better still, because they do not reference a linear temporal sequence, they can be traversed in any manner. In other words, the process of essential dealing is intrinsically nonlinear. In most cases, seasoned practitioners will be shuttling back and forth in some seemingly irrational fashion that will look like sheer madness, at least when observed by outsiders. As Napoleon was fond of saying "gentlemen, a field of glory is not a pretty sight!"

The first step in this process is fundamentally *negative*. This is because the basic structures underlying the assets must be literally extracted out of the primordial soup that makes up the *world*. From such original data, invariant relationships must be discovered among the deal's components. Here, we are looking for things that do *not* change as opposed to those that do. As already highlighted, looking for invariant relationships among the deal's constituents is what we mean by the negative character of asset modeling. Such negativity is the essential core out of which something positive will eventually emerge.

In terms of freedom, the associated negative–positive duality is inextricably linked to the negative and positive aspects of freedom already known to you. A deal can only exist positively (i.e., *as* a deal) once it has been pulled out of nothingness through intuition. The difficult aspect of dealing is not to converge onto a deal as a positive object, for that is relatively straightforward, but rather how to extract it out of thin air in the first place. Thereafter, letting the deal unfold out of itself becomes a routine matter.

14.3 THE MOMENTOUS TRINITY OF DEAL-HOOD

In order to clarify and concretize what must seem like a rather weird and incomprehensible technique, we will organize our treatment according to the three special positions already identified along the arc and known as the *moments* of essential dealing.

For purposes of demonstration we discuss linearly (i.e., in sequence) what is essentially a nonlinear process. In practice, the arrows in figure 14.1 may be traversed back and forth at will and, most definitely, at random. Again, by the word *moment* we do not mean a moment in time, but rather a determination in freedom space akin to the Latin form *momentum*. Essential dealing consists in traveling both sides of the arc within a process whose linear-temporal succession is irrelevant. Mastering this process is the key to structured financial analysis.

Traversing the Arc

To begin with, the deal must be extracted out of the immediacy of the now as a set of metastructures corresponding to concepts like transition matrices, cash flow transfer functions, copulas, correlation structures, and the like. At this stage, each subunit or *block* is still largely undetermined, i.e., free in the negative sense. Dealing per se can now begin in earnest via a two-fold deconstructive–constructive process.

On the left -hand side of the arc, the degrees of freedom available to the block must be brought to zero. Following Heidegger, this is the process we call *de-struktion* in order not to confuse it with the ordinary, linear concept of destruction. De-struktion should not be thought of as a destructive process, but on the contrary, as one of taking apart, *de-constructing* the block, and of defining its mathematical relationships. Going down the arc is the colloquial name we give to the mathematization of the complete set of structural relationships relevant to a given deal.

On the other side, the process of de-struktion is reversed and gives rise to *con-struktion*. This refers to the successive building up of the deal's positive characterizations via the linking of deterministic structures, i.e., structures with zero freedom. In this manner, a deal can emerge as a positive object characterized by a preconceived ensemble of ontological relationships.

Any attempt to bypass or skip Moment B (determinism) is bound to fail since it must inevitably result in a situation whereby cash flow is either undefined or unallocated. When this happens, so do questions like "what happens here?" or "how do I get that number?" These and similar questions are symptomatic of a failure to traverse Moment B. In other words, the deal then becomes *impossible* to model, or so we believe. Therefore, the sole possible avenue is the full de-struktion of each block. Only then can it be appropriately inserted inside deal-related linkages.

Now, let us examine the deal's moments one by one.

Moment A (World)

The deal's first moment refers to the situation, present in every deal, whereby all substructures involved in its world have been provisionally preconceptualized.

In this way, they can become analytical objects amenable to logical analysis, i.e., using mathematics. These blocks will soon become the agents, the actors in the deal.

As mentioned above, blocks must be extracted from the ontic world via the ontologically restrictive process we discussed earlier. This is why we call world-creation a *reduction*, a limiting of what is first possible from the undifferentiated unity primarily given to us. For example, to decide whether the use of Markov chains will be appropriate and if so, in which specific ways (e.g., continuous or discrete time, continuous or discrete obligors, and so forth). Each deal lives in its own world consisting of such ontological substructures. When doing a deal, the pre-conceptual world will usually be given in the form of a prospectus. In other words, and with all apologies to lawyers, the prospectus is really nothing.

A deal found at Moment A is trivially free in the sense that its structures have not been related to each other in the way they must to let it come to life. Accordingly, it is still pure potential, pure possibility. The deal is free, and yet that word is somehow misleading because it does not properly convey the fact that such freedom really amounts to nothing. It is the freedom of an amorphous blob, the careless freedom of the adolescent; the "I can do anything I want" type of freedom, the world-hood moment of essential dealing. Not surprisingly, this is the most difficult task to master, since it cannot be taught in the usual sense. It is, as they say, a priori and why we can state that reading 10,000 prospectuses will teach you no more about the essence of dealing than watching the same number of games at Yankee stadium will about that of baseball. As a result, Moment A is where the word *experience* takes on a brand new meaning.

In structured finance, we call this the moment of *negative* freedom for reasons that should be obvious by now. Without first assembling its world in this manner, the deal must remain forever hidden, concealed. If it can ever be brought out of concealment as a positively free object, it will have to go through the very negation of that negative freedom, the process leading to Moment B.

Moment B (Ground)

As already mentioned, the path down the arc is one whereby freedom is systematically restricted until complete logical certainty is achieved. It is the point toward which everything converges and from which everything emerges. In one word, it is the *ground* of the deal. In common, everyday language, the reductive path lying to the left of ground, and taking place in freedom space, is referred to as *analysis*. In philosophical terms, ground is the *reason* of the deal, the thing that "is" for its own sake. When someone says, "I didn't have a choice," what he really means is that he had reached his own-most ground. On the contrary, that was precisely the moment when he *did* have a choice.

This is the moment at which the internal structure of the building blocks elucidated at Moment A has been described, to the extent that vagueness and indeterminacy are completely eliminated in a way commensurate with the depth of the deal's prevailing paradigm. For instance, random number generators, if any are present, are formally specified so that the output sequence is in fact known with certainty. As you know, there are no truly *random* numbers inside computing machines, only pseudo-random numbers. Likewise, all other substructures are defined in excruciating detail, leaving no room for arbitrariness and the garden-variety shortcuts commonly seen in cash flow modeling.

Along the arc, analysts will usually be called upon to make use of the full spectrum of cash flow modeling skills at their disposal to sort out the leaks and financial inconsistencies that plague the vast majority of cash flow models. This is where stochastic calculus and statistical methods enter the fray. Owing to this criticality, the explication of the deal's analytical phase will form the bulk of the next 10 chapters.

Once Moment B is reached, nothing has been left to chance. Since the deal's world-hood relationships have been completely determined down to the last available detail, we call this moment *determinism*, the point of zero freedom. It is only at that moment that one is potentially in complete control of the deal. We say *potentially* because the deal has yet to be fully articulated as a living organism. In other words, the deal qua deal is still dead, and bringing it to life is the task that will occupy us going up the arc. To be sure, in professional terms Moment B is deal-hood's most demanding moment, the one that reveals the difference between amateurs and professionals and the main reason why you should read the rest of this book.

At first blush, this downward process might be viewed by some as the most difficult part of doing deals, where you earn your keep as an analyst. On the other hand, since it is completely teachable, analysis is in fact rather straightforward once you start digging into and losing yourself in actual transactions.

Finally, when viewed at this precise point in linear time, literally in suspended animation, the deal looks like an assembly line, i.e., a series of blocks or subroutines waiting to be linked into a unique and objective structure we will come to regard as *real*. Once this is done, we have finally reached Moment C, where the deal lives.

Moment C (Life)

When the deal has been so reduced to a set of building blocks with fully determinate inputs and outputs, we can start moving up the arc toward the third stage where the deal can exist as truly free. At that moment, the analyst has the deal fully under control, one that displays the hallmarks of positive freedom, the *freedom-for* of lawfulness. This is the freedom of the chess grandmaster, of the professional basketball player expressing the paradoxical notion that only under complete self-control can anything be said to be actually free.

Witness the so-called *free markets* everybody swears by, i.e., those that contain more regulation than anyone could ever dream of. Why do we call them free? Because you can do whatever you want? No, quite the opposite; we call them free specifically because the intended freedom is precisely not the carefree, laissez-faire freedom of the teenager to break windows. Rather, it is the more real and meaningful freedom that can only be achieved through knowledge[4] instead of smoke and mirrors. This is the meaning of *positive* in positive freedom.

As mentioned earlier, this phase consists primarily of linking, first in time and obligor domain and then in their manifold unity, the deal's building blocks created while reaching Moment B. This is the process we call *synthesis*. Hence it becomes clear how analysis and synthesis are inextricably intertwined and in fact, are both necessary corollaries of each other if a deal *as such* is to emerge.

Carrying this out first implies thorough knowledge of deal mechanics as presented in the prospectus and elsewhere. However, it also requires complete familiarity with the asset class. Although by no means as involved as the analytical road down to Moment B, the path up to Moment C is how the deal finally comes together as a living, breathing organism that comes out of itself for itself. This is the stage where assets and liabilities merge, giving the deal its own voice, where triggers can be inserted and analyzed in situ instead of being arbitrarily valued at 50 bps in the silly hope of pacifying irate investment bankers.

The first step in this process usually amounts to time-domain resolution, the ubiquitous time loop whereby every Monte Carlo scenario is precisely specified from Closing to Legal Final Maturity. Embedded inside this loop is the asset loop cycling through a pre-given ensemble of dependent or independent exposures and in which deterministic cash flows can be computed. Indeed, this is where the deal achieves full articulation, and is allowed for the first time to show itself coherently *as* a deal. In doing so, each collection period is specifically modeled while the process of investor reimbursement is linked to that of obligor repayment. Macro-economic abstraction is then overlain, wrapping the time loop inside its own, yet-more-abstract loop driven by the complete credit loss distribution. Only when this is accomplished is a structured analyst finally in a position to explore the deal's possibility range within which valuation can finally be carried out.

In short, Moment C shows explicitly how the deal is relationally held as a manifold unity and allowed to reach its own-most primary market unfolding via a nonlinear yield-convergence process in which it comes together in a self-consistent and well-posed manner.

This is crystal clear right? Yeah, right!

14.4 THE DAO OF DEALING AND THE LEGAL TRADITION

As odd as this may seem, it is our sincere hope that legally minded financial professionals will one day read this chapter and recognize in it something strangely familiar, something they in fact already know. Because it belongs squarely within their own tradition, perhaps they would then embrace structured analysis in a meaningful way as *the* financial paradigm.

If you think about it for a moment, it would be truly amazing if the approach we have so painstakingly deconstructed had nothing whatsoever to do with the ordinary world, the *everydayness* of our lives. For in that case, structured finance would belong to an alien genus; it would be some uncanny process knowable only to the elite, those living within Wall Street's Forbidden City. In fact, what we have explicitly formalized and labeled "The Dao of Dealing" is nothing more than a plain-vanilla decision-making process, one about which the Anglo-Saxon legal tradition has much to say, and in which it has been more successful than most of its rivals. This sidebar is intended to show how these two seemingly disparate paths are intimately related and, in fact, identical once viewed from the proper perspective. Our silent agenda is to make lawyers feel just as much at home with the mathematics of structured finance as they are with the minutiae of legal analysis.

Aristotelian Preamble

The analytics involved in our left-hand conceptualization of the Dao of Dealing, the steps leading from World to Ground, go back to ancient Greece and most particularly to Aristotle's Nicomachean[5] Ethics. It is there that we find, for the first time perhaps, a precise formalization of decision-making akin to what you have read in the last section. This should not surprise you since most of our concepts come from Aristotle anyway. Obviously, the great philosopher was not thinking about finance when he laid down his opinion on the state of affairs with respect to proper deliberation. Besides, as we all know, he thought very little of financial men. However, his description was original and powerful enough to survive to this day and be applicable to a field he would most likely have thought unworthy of consideration. Now, there is no point rehashing a well-known Western philosophical classic in a textbook on finance, but drawing a useful parallel between two apparently alien methods still requires us to go back to a point in time where they were, in fact, the same.

Phronesis as Proper Deliberation

In the above work, Aristotle lays out a paradigmatic deliberative process he designates via the label "Φρονησις" (Phronesis). The latter technique is later differentiated from, and contrasted with "Σοφια" (Sophia), an expression you will recognize as more or less meaning *wisdom*. In the end, Σοφια will prevail over Φρονησις as a maxim for human existence, but not yet.

Aristotle describes the structure of Φρονησις as a procedure via which alternatives are eliminated systematically within a dialectical sequence leading to an endpoint. In essence, it is a deconstructive process similar to what happens on the left side of figure 14.1. The sequence is not haphazard, but possesses a pre-established purpose, a goal he calls τέλος (telos). Otherwise, there is no way to guarantee that the process will ever terminate. Thus, logically speaking once you say "yes," you cannot turn around and say, "no" because you are losing the argument, i.e., explicitly changing your mind is not allowed. This is what we mean when we say that someone is arguing *honestly*. The endpoint of the sequence is the έσχατον (eschaton), its outermost limit.

Within Φρονησις, it is shown that we are bound to reach such a point because, to use a more modern formulation, of the lack of *data* or more generally, because *grounds* are missing. When we do reach this limit, we face a choice that by definition must be binary in nature since it involves ignorance of consequences. This is the decision point properly conceived, what we normally call an *executive decision*. Otherwise, this stage would not be the έσχατον and additional facts could be brought to bear to dig a little further down the analytical scale. Thus, the έσχατον is the place where additional conceptualization is deemed impossible because of insufficient information. If this were not the case, no decision would be necessary and the whole thing could be reduced to an exercise in riskless logic. In passing, logic is what computers do, and why they never make *decisions* in the original sense of the word.

If you think about it, this is quite intuitive. A human, deliberative process always reaches a finite endpoint because it eventually places the deliberator himself in question. Unlike what is true in physics, it is not possible to experiment with oneself in an attempt to reach an ideal limit, regarded here as perfection (αρετη), by trial and error. Everything we do in life stems from a chain of reasoning sustainable only because it keeps providing something for the sake of which we continue deliberating. Obviously, this chain must eventually come to a point where we can no longer find grounds, i.e., a rationale *for the sake of which* we choose one alternative over the other. Consequently, the limit-character of the εσχατον rests on the singular notion that whatever we actually carry out is done simply *for its own sake*, i.e., without any direct logical connection as to consequences. That point is the essential reason for the decision, its ultimate *ground*. It is critical to be aware of the fact that the ground always points back to the deliberator him- or herself. Thus, the key concept applicable to Φρονησις is self-reference, i.e., the impossibility of taking oneself out of the process in the way we can within the region of natural objects.

In metaphysical terms, reaching the εσχατον is equivalent to standing on the surface of a conceptual and multidimensional sphere that cannot be penetrated or taken apart any further. This sphere consists of the nexus of unknown possibilities that will reveal themselves once the decision is actually made. Because what can no longer be divided is usually termed *atomic*, the limit point of Φρονησις is also its atomic point. Throughout, it must always be recognized that the atom is not *empty* as we are wont to say, but simply that our current state of knowledge prevents us from reaching definite conclusions as to what is lurking inside the surface of the sphere. The atomic point is thus never final, but always provisional, pending further knowledge. Therefore, Φρονησις is by definition an asymptotic process, an idea to which we will have occasion to return when discussing security valuation in chapter 22.

The decision space is binary because, at the limit, we are always faced with irretrievable action, i.e., Φρονησις owes its binomial essence to the fact that the arrow of time involves a one-way street.[6] One cannot take back what one does, only what someone else does. Since the upshot of Φρονησις is human action, the essence of action is seen to lie in the binary nature of the choices we make. This is what *risk* is all about, for if the sequence never terminates there is no εσχατον and risk has thereby vanished. The fact that the atom still harbors the source of its own emerging possibilities is the reason why one must constantly adapt to such self-revelation. As you may have already surmised, the efficiency and responsiveness of the adaptation process in each case is thus the essence of *risk management*.

By now, it should be obvious that risk and freedom are inseparable and that a rock falling from a cliff is risk-free. In addition, how to manage risk rather than eliminate it should also have become clear, for risk elimination simply amounts to doing nothing. As you can see, risk is just the mode of intrinsic nonlinearity with which many of you are already familiar.

As a result, upon reaching the eschatological[7] or limit point, we come face to face with an either-or decision space whereby one option is always the logical negation of the other. It is not binary out of some whim or fancy, but simply because by definition the situation cannot be further analyzed and the space of possibilities has to come down to "do it" or "don't do it." The word Aristotle uses to describe this aspect of the ἐσχατον is στοχαστυκη (stochastic). Therefore, the essence of *stochasticity*, a notion that has of late acquired quasi-mythic status in finance, is the impossibility to take your self out, i.e., to smooth the process via trial and error whereby the decision space could be regarded as continuously varying, as statistical. Thus *stochastic* and *statistical* are to be rightly regarded as counter-concepts.

For Aristotle, the self-referential property peculiar to human decision processes is the main distinction between physics and ethics. Said differently, although there is no *risk* in physics, a fork always lies at the end of the human road. In addition, please note that this fork is different in character from the usual concept of linear discontinuity inside functional analysis since a discontinuous function still has only one value of y for every value of x, otherwise it is not a function. Here, no matter how close to the ἐσχατον we eventually come, the process remains essentially bifurcated. It is therefore a fundamentally different process from what we normally encounter within ordinary calculus.

Stochasticity: Ethics versus Physics

In the above description, some of you will already have recognized the original idea underlying the Wiener process, the heart of stochastic calculus. This is why, for instance, the canonical stochastic differential dz is not like the linear time differential dt or some other infinitesimal quantity that might be taken from ordinary calculus. It cannot be analyzed as a simple limit arising from a continuous function but must be dealt with on its own terms.

Consequently, to begin a disquisition on stochastic calculus with the well-known relationship $\Delta z = \varepsilon \sqrt{\Delta t}$, as if this were completely self-evident,[8] is to guarantee that the student will never understand, assuming of course that the goal of education is understanding in the first place. What is amazing is that the fundamental structure behind stochastic calculus goes back to Aristotle. The difference is that when you read his exposition of the matter, you actually know what you are talking about when uttering the word *stochastic* before a usually befuddled audience. Even after more than 23 centuries, the depth of his thought is barely thinkable.

To grasp the stochastic horizon fully, it is paramount to becoming conscious of the fact that the two-fold nature of stochasticity is inherently different from that of logic, i.e., what matters here is that there are not two choices in Φρονησις in the same way there are two banks of the River Seine. Rather, what should have emerged from the foregoing is the *irreversibility* of stochasticity compared to the *reversibility* of logic. The crux of the argument is precisely the notion that self-reflexivity and irreversibility are merely two faces of the same metaphysical coin. By contrast, both sides of the Seine are at bottom indistinguishable from each other and can be so regarded without any loss of generality. In other words, *symmetry* is the hallmark of *linearity* and *asymmetry* that of *stochasticity*.

This irreversibility is what truly constitutes the *arrow of time* mentioned earlier, something that otherwise remains mysterious and inexplicable. Hence, the incompleteness of our dataset is the fabric that makes up the intrinsic directionality of temporality. Time flows in one direction only because any man-made conceptualization regime remains finite and therefore, contains a basic and unavoidable indeterminacy that serves to bound a region within which "freedom reigns" so to speak. In the final analysis, the irreversibility of original time is the sole justification for the existence of essential freedom, for logical time can indeed flow both ways. Since in finance, the implicit orientation of original time is ultimately experienced as yield, it becomes clear why the latter must be nonlinear.

To understand stochasticity as most students do, i.e., via statements like "the stock can move up x% with a 50% probability or down x% with a 50% probability," and so on ad infinitum, is to understand nothing at all. In fact, it misses the point entirely, which is that a statement of this kind can only hold in a factical sense within an instant of linear time with zero measure, after which the inherent self-reflexivity, or feedback, present in the system spontaneously modifies the probability space associated with further outcomes. As long as feedback is missing from a theoretical scheme purporting to *explain* the behavior of financial variables, there is no way it can ever reconcile the seemingly random meanderings of markets. Without feedback, one never even has a chance to fathom why, in the observed evolution of a stock, there can be such things as *support* and *resistance* levels, two well-documented phenomena relevant to technical analysis. When the results of a model fail to agree with empirical data, we strongly suggest that it is the model, instead of the truth, that needs to be jettisoned.

Stochastic calculus is not something subversive invented by insidious Europeans to make the lives of American financial analysts miserable. It is just a part of our basic, daily life of action. Unfortunately, judging from the mountains of literature on the topic, it is a good bet that most financial analysts have yet to come to grips with the simplicity and everydayness of stochasticity. In short, whereas ordinary calculus is applicable to physics, stochastic calculus holds sway within the ethics of human action.

The Anglo-Saxon Trial System and the Dao of Dealing

Is it conceivable that we have surreptitiously led you astray by spouting a bunch of idiotic nonsense on ancient philosophy? In other words, is all this Greek to you? Actually, being led down the primrose path is a definite possibility on Wall Street, but not this time. What you are about to discover, is that the Anglo-Saxon legal tradition is merely an institutionalized form of Φρονησις that also includes an arbiter, normally called a judge, to ensure that the aforementioned logical sequence eventually comes to its proper limit. Remember that in French, a trial is called a "procès," which simply means a process. Let's talk about this process a little and draw some useful parallels with the Dao of Dealing.

Instead of Φρονησις, the legal process is called *pleading*, by far the greatest contribution British culture has ever made to the legal tradition. When the endpoint is attained within pleading, the process is said to have reached the issue (*exitus*). In the law-French applicable to the English medieval (1066+) period, the word issue meant exit. It was called the issue because no one was allowed to leave the courtroom until that point was reached. The issue is obviously the ἔσχατον, the central question upon which the trial shall be decided. It was always binary and its resolution amounted to the famous guilty or not-guilty verdict. As every lawyer knows, back in the thirteenth century the issue was rarely sorted out in the same courtroom but, more often than not, was taken up within another, local court system known as *nisi prius*. The latter term was used because the action taken upon such verdict was *nisi* (unless), i.e., final and irretrievable unless something could be further adduced beforehand (*prius*) in the local court. What was physically irretrievable of course was what could be done to the defendant upon guilt, i.e., the sentence. In addition, because the trial system was grounded in stochasticity, statistical certainty could not be allowed to play any part in the verdict, hence jury unanimity was a *conditio sine qua non*. In other words, *maybe* was not an acceptable outcome.

Note that, strictly speaking, the foregoing was really meant to apply to criminal cases whereby the action was indeed irretrievable since, in most cases of interest, the punishment for guilt was death or torture. By contrast, for this very reason civil actions operate under a statistical,[9] not a stochastic principle. It is crucial to understand that the issue-bound decision space cannot be guilty or innocent. Such characterization falls short of the very essence of the process since *innocence* is clearly not the logical negation of guilt.[10] To guarantee that the process would eventually terminate, the number of possible moves was limited to four[11] and as hinted earlier, a lawyer could not deny prior pleadings. In most cases, only a few moves were required to reach the issue.

The *nisi prius* system is what we now call the *jury phase* of the trial, where the situation, the *life* of the defendant is the subject matter, and where that life is reconstructed in a way supposed to let the truth emerge. This phase is effectively the right-hand side of figure 14.1. The theory is that it is possible to arrive at just, or true, decisions because the pleading process is grounded. In other words, trials are merely re-enactments of the freedom arc in figure 14.1 whereby the issue corresponds to the grounds of the trial, enabling the jury to tell the truth (*vere dictum*), i.e., to reach the verdict. Absent grounds, it is accepted that the truth of the trial cannot be found. Of course, in no way does this imply that grounds are unique, but to the extent they are, *justice* should prevail. As you can see, this is not exactly a guarantee, but for that matter, neither is a credit rating, and yet most investors believe it amounts to the same thing.

Uniqueness and Civil Actions

Legal aficionados might be wondering whether, as the foregoing treatment applies strictly to criminal cases, we could in fact do away with the binary concept of uniqueness with respect to civil actions and stick to *physics*. Unfortunately, even within the statistical framework appropriate to them, the specter of uniqueness looms large within civil actions and still provides an essential determination.

Civil actions at law can be fundamentally partitioned into real and personal. Legal textbooks define real actions as those intended to recover real property, or *realty*, while personal actions are aimed at recovering personal property or *personalty*, mainly *goods and chattels*. So far, we have made eminent sense and yet have said absolutely nothing, for the obvious problem is how one ought to characterize the essence of realty as opposed to that of personalty. To do so, perhaps we could take our cue from public opinion and *define* realty as real estate and personalty as everything else. As a result, the crux of the issue would appear to be the definition of realty, while personalty simply means *non-realty*. Although we could eventually make progress in this way, a more fruitful approach lies in asking whether realty is just an instance of real estate or conversely, whether real estate might not simply represent the most common formation of realty. The second is the case.

To begin with, a cup is just as *real* as a house, and yet we call the former personalty and the latter realty. In other words, physics will not help us solve this riddle. More to the point, why do lawyers assign realty status to houses, and none to cups? Are they blind? If you think so, it is only because we have yet to define the essence of *legal* reality. Once we do, the fog suddenly lifts and everything makes sense.

So what is that, the essence of reality for a lawyer? Incredibly, it is uniqueness and nothing else. What is *real* in realty is just the relative uniqueness or nonuniqueness of the subject matter. In equitable terms, this means that the operative demarcation between realty and personalty is the fact that specific performance is the only possible remedy for realty, but that money damages will suffice in the case of personalty. Now what in Heaven's name does this mean? The following hypothetical example should make it clear how, in both the law and structured finance, the essence of reality is uniqueness.

Suppose you hire Luciano Pavarotti to sing in your opera, and he DK's you two days before the opening curtain. You scramble like mad and manage to locate Placido Domingo to replace him. Are ticket-holders entitled to a refund? The answer is clearly yes, but why? Because Pavarotti's voice is unique, that's all. People who paid $150 to listen are presumed to have done so to hear Luciano, not Placido. In other words, Pavarotti and Domingo are *not the same*. As opera house manager, you would be entitled to *specific performance* (no pun intended) in this case, an equitable remedy that could force Pavarotti to sing on some other day when he is feeling better. The obvious fact that it would be bad business practice to sue your leading man is irrelevant to this theoretical discussion. By contrast, mere *performance* would mean that Pavarotti simply owed you the net profit you would have demonstrably made from his appearance, i.e., money damages alone would be sufficient redress to cure the breach.

Now you can easily see why real estate is a form of realty, for an acre of land in Ohio is *not the same* as an acre of land in New Jersey, as citizens of those two great States would no doubt confirm without hesitation. Your house is not just a *house*; it is a *home*. It has unique status in your eyes, which is what you mean when you say, "there's no place like home." By contrast, even in your own opinion a pencil is not so privileged. Any other pencil will do and that is why it is personalty, and not realty. If you could somehow prove that *your* pencil was unique, you could presumably initiate a real action to recover it, and not either some other pencil or its monetary equivalent. In that case, money damages would not suffice as a form of compensation. Therefore, here too uniqueness defines the essence of reality. To *define* personal actions as those for the recovery of *goods and chattels* is to confuse matters hopelessly because it is plain as day that a house is also a good, at least as far as economics is concerned. The purpose of academic life is not to learn laundry lists by heart but, on the contrary, to be able to reason from the ground up.

Although this sounds simple in theory, many practical complications are hiding underneath the covers. For example, who decides what is unique, and what is not? According to what we just laid out, uniqueness seems to lie in the eye of the beholder. But in that case, there would be no such thing as a personal action, since everyone could simply state that *their* pencil was in fact one of a kind. The reason why realty has come to mean real estate (land, buildings, etc.) is that general agreement seems to exist as to the uniqueness of real estate, but not as to that of pencils. Apparently, agreement has much to do with reality. Agreed, but does it help us in any way to know that? Yes, it does, but not yet, not yet.

The Eternal Recurrence of the Same: Deals and Trials

We can now understand how the process involved in a trial must consist of two distinct legs separated by ground and further, that the analytical leg is intimately tied to the respective pleading abilities of the opposing lawyers. Instead of *Analyst versus the World* in 15 conference calls, what we have here is *Lawyer X versus Lawyer Y* in a few metaphysical jabs and uppercuts. If Lawyer X can move the issue in his or her direction ever so slightly, the truth of the trial might be reached alright, but still remain dissonant with the fundamental intent (τέλος) of the procedure. From this vantage point, it can easily be seen how, in finance, an improper analytical procedure, even one based on flawless data, can lead to faulty valuation despite the fact that every rule has been followed precisely. In other words, the point is not to do the thing right, but to do the right thing.

By its very nature, the eschatological process at the heart of a deal or trial is required to push as far as it can before reaching its atomic point, for otherwise the uniqueness of the equity thereby realized might be in jeopardy. The deeper the analysis, the smaller will be the atomic sphere, and thus the lower the probability that an injustice will be committed. It is in this way that the asymptotic nature of either valuation or justice reveals itself to the analyst or lawyer as the case may be. The intimate relationship between uniqueness and *alue* is further discussed in chapter 22.

> The English word "jeopardy" (*jeu parti*) was originally a chess term that meant a set problem with even odds. It was taken over by the legal profession to indicate a bypassing of normal pleadings whereby both lawyers agreed at the outset to stake the outcome of the trial on a pre-established question to be handed over to the *nisi prius* court. This was commonly done when the odds of the verdict were reckoned to be even. Such an agreement was then said to place the outcome *in jeopardy*.

In structured finance, placing the deal in jeopardy simply means bypassing the analytical phase involved in valuation via unjustifiable, albeit always convenient, reliance on some assumed and groundless mathematical model taken over from another field. This should definitely sound familiar.

In this rather impromptu section, we have sought to highlight the fact that the Anglo-American legal tradition and the Dao of Dealing are based on the very same process, one supposed to lead to the truth of their respective phenomenon via ground. By analogy with their own field, lawyers already familiar with the trial system are therefore particularly well positioned to understand structured finance from the inside.

Is the Dao of Dealing so mysterious after all?

14.5 THE ESSENTIALLY NONLINEAR NATURE OF STRUCTURED FINANCIAL ANALYSIS

Right now, you may be wondering what this can possibly have to do with structured finance. You should always remain open to the possibility that the foregoing was nonsense and hogwash at best. If you are having such doubts, you are on the right track. Maybe you should also ask yourself whether you *know logically* that the sun will rise tomorrow. The obvious answer is that you do not, yet you seem to go on happily as if you did. Can a world really be based on such secure uncertainties? Is there a sane way out of this? Could it be that the only thing we can know for sure is our lack of certainty?

It is only when you start questioning in this way that you begin to fathom the meaning of nonlinearity. The core of structured finance lies in just such an abstraction, one that restores the deal to its primal unity and lets it exist as self-identical.

Nonlinearity in Structured Finance

Recall how, in corporate finance, the probability of default was the appropriate measure of creditworthiness. Historically, this came about because corporations were primarily intended to be going concerns, entities that would last forever. In turn, this pretense to *eternal life* arose as a direct consequence of the extortionate taxation policies practiced by most European rulers. Therefore, it happened that corporate death was *the* event to be avoided at all costs since physical death was the main taxation mechanism. As a result, bankruptcy became the doomsday event in the life of a corporation and thus the rationale for any serious corporate credit analysis.

Enter structured finance, a seemingly magical procedure specifically designed to obviate default per se by allowing securities to be issued out of special-purpose vehicles with zero default rate. Obviously, the fact that the default rate of a structured security is zero by design cannot imply that its credit rating is always *Aaa*. But it does mean that some other measure of creditworthiness needs to be brought in to handle the situation. As we saw earlier, this alternative measure turned out to be the average reduction of yield from the original promise that investors holding a diversified portfolio of similar securities would experience over the range of cash flow possibilities potentially arising from the behavior of comparable assets. Once the ergodic hypothesis (see "The Ergodic Hypothesis and Monte Carlo Simulation" below) was invoked to link this hypothetical portfolio to the specific transaction under review, the analysis acquired an empirical character that had, or should have had, meaning for investors. Hence, by computing this average yield reduction tranche-wise, we were able to assign a meaningful credit rating to any structured security issued out of an SPV. So, are we back in business now? No, we are not. What's the problem?

For starters, the problem is precisely that no one seems to realize that there is a problem. Most structured analysts simply go on as if the linear approach actually made sense. Briefly, the problem is the proverbial "chicken and the egg" issue. To know the reduction of yield from the original promise, we obviously have to know the promise itself. But to know the latter, we need to know the bond's credit rating, since yields are directly, albeit sluggishly, determined by credit spreads in concert with the yield curve. However, to know the credit spread, we need to know the credit rating, which is precisely what we are trying to find in the first place. We seem to be moving in a circle. In fact, this circle is how nonlinearity is commonly understood.

In mathematical terms, a nonlinear problem is one whereby the solution is itself part of what we need to know to find it, i.e., the input data. As a result, an iterative solution is always required. Strangely enough, quite involuntarily, we seem to have created nonlinearity out of thin air and made life much more difficult than it really needs to be. Why not assume the promise known and compute credit ratings in one step, i.e., linearly? The answer is that this would never work since the output rates would in general never match the input rates. You would be talking from both sides of your mouth at the same time and your credit ratings would be inconsistent at best. Does this describe anyone you know?

Closer investigation reveals that the nonlinearity we have apparently imported into the analysis from the outside was there all along. In truth, we understand the ontic, empirical world nonlinearly to begin with. When we conceive or interpret a deal, every one of its relationships is always tightly linked to every other one within the nonlinear immediacy of the *now*, the latter being essentially bound up with our own understanding of the situation. For us, the deal either exists as a unity or simply does not exist. The world as given to our understanding is already nonlinear. Therefore, it is linearity, rather than nonlinearity, that requires an explanation.

As a direct consequence of this, we find that nonlinearity cannot be avoided if a deal is to emerge out of the primordial togetherness of the immediate. Nonlinearity strikes at the heart, the essence of finance. If you think about it, this makes perfect sense, for how else is a deal supposed to emerge from nothing if not as self-identical? This is not a special case we have just concocted to muddle and hopelessly confuse the issue. This is not how it *could* be; this is how it *is* at the very moment you are reading this passage for that is what makes *reading* possible.

Cybernetics and Finance

When we experience deals as wholes, we effectively create for ourselves a horizon against which we can project the deal, enabling it to remain equal to itself. This projective horizon is the basic intuitive notion that enables us to grasp the objects constructed via unmediated, hence intuitive understanding, a notion that allows us to *stand under* the deal and let it emerge as a deal; it is what we called *original time*.

In finance, original time is given a different name lest we confuse it with ordinary, linear time. What remains true, however, is that original time is the way we really understand deals, it is how we *speak* of deals. More precisely, it is how deals speak to us, their λογος. What do we call original time in finance? Yield of course. In essence, yield is the *meaning* of time in the deal.

What is finance? Quite simply, it is the algebra of original time.

This conclusion is unavoidable if you consider the relationship that defines the yield r of an investment I_0 expected to produce N cash flows C_i, $i \in [1, N]$:

$$I_0 = \sum_{i=1}^{N} \frac{C_i}{(1+r)^i}$$

This formula says that yield is what makes an amount *now* equal to itself in the *future*. Not surprisingly, yield is intrinsically nonlinear in import because nonlinearity is what makes self-identity possible in the first place. Another way of expressing the same notion is to note that yield and *Value* are always inversely or *negatively*, related to each other. When yield goes up, *Value* goes down and vice versa. Thus, it is easily seen how yield is a positive concept that is grasped negatively.

The upshot from such basic considerations is that the deal's final abstraction must be cybernetic, i.e., a negation of linear time ultimately leading to the construction of a manifold unity as original time. To let the deal come together in this manner, it is necessary to wrap it inside a mechanism operating outside linear time, and this is accomplished by linking assets and liabilities in a way enabling its negation. For this reason, nonlinearity operates at the level of yield. The nonlinear aspect of structured security valuation is fundamental and cannot be eliminated, assumed away, or even circumvented. Because it is routinely ignored, deals that make no sense at all see the light of day every day. The recognition of the intrinsic nonlinearity at the core of structured finance is what this book is really all about.

14.6 OPEN AND CLOSED STRUCTURES

By linking liability interest rates to their corresponding credit ratings via the yield curve acting as an anchor, we can achieve self-consistent convergence. Indeed, such self-consistency is how we can determine whether the deal has been properly posed at all. The well posed-ness problem discussed in "*The Analysis of Structured Securities*" (OUP, 2003) now naturally arises from this procedure. In cases where convergence is achievable, the deal organically reveals itself as holistic and produces the fair value of its liability tranches as a byproduct. The mechanics involved in doing this will form the bulk of chapter 22.

Open Structures

In the previous two sections, we highlighted the fact that the logical construct achieved at Moment C was not yet the deal itself since it still lacked the basic nonlinearity we knew to be operative and symptomatic of its essential nature. As we now see, the upshot of going down the arc and back up again is a set of deterministic

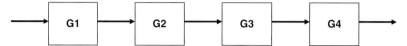

FIGURE 14.2
The open deal structure.

block-structures tightly linked to produce the schematization that becomes the deal's original conception. When this is done, the structure is termed *open* and can be conceptualized as shown in figure 14.2. In this hypothetical case, the deal consists of four blocks (G1 through G4). Actual transactions will usually have many more. Open structures are just linear versions of deals and hence highly misleading.

Interestingly, an open structure is how we conduct local analysis, the process of answering questions like "how bad can it get out there?" and of *solving* such problems.

In other words, in structured finance local analysis is the name we give to worst-case scenario analysis or *stress testing*. Admittedly, this is a very primitive way to either structure transactions or perform the initial credit analysis. Yet, it is still the method of choice on Wall Street.

However, once the deal has been restored to its primordial nonlinearity via the closed loop technique outlined earlier, linear analysis is the way deals can be monitored since tranche interest rates are now known. Thus, open structures find their usefulness in the *secondary*, not the *primary* market.

Closed Structures

By contrast, to synthesize deals in the primary market and let them reveal themselves as such, input and output rates must be linked together within a cybernetic framework. This process effectively *closes* the structure, which now appears as shown in figure 14.3. A closed structure is nothing but a nonlinear version of an open structure.

The control block (C) inserted into the process is critical in letting the deal come together because it provides the mathematical mechanism via which ill-posed transactions can show themselves out of themselves. The associated feedback loop generates the basic yield signal that allows nondeals to *blow up* before your very eyes rather than remain on the table as adequately capitalized. Properly designed,

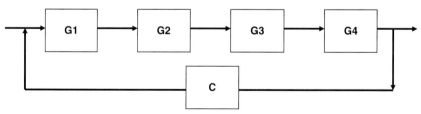

FIGURE 14.3
The closed deal structure.

this loop keeps the deal under control and allows deficient structures to be ferreted out.

14.7 THE CONTROL LOOP IN YIELD SPACE

Primary market valuation mechanics can be visualized schematically as shown in figure 14.4.

1. Tranche-wise interest rates are initially estimated and inserted into the formalism. This can be done in many ways, and the back-of-the-envelope method (BOTE) discussed in previous chapters is just one of them.

2. A Monte Carlo simulation is executed, resulting in a new set of liability credit ratings via the weighted average life of each tranche or sub-tranche and its average reduction of yield experienced over the entire range of macro-economic realizations.

3. From the new credit ratings, provisional yields can be inferred from an empirical or theoretical yield curve.

4. Such provisional yields are fed to a relaxation mechanism that produces tranche-wise updates to the initial rate vector derived in item 1. The relaxation engine is designed to control this process and ensure a smooth convergence provided the deal is well posed. This step constitutes the feedback loop.

5. Sequence 1 through 4 is carried out iteratively until either convergence is achieved (well-posed structure) or the deal simply blows up (ill-posed structure). The latter two concepts are further discussed in chapter 22. Only a few nonlinear trials are normally required for convergence. In addition, total CPU time can be further reduced through educated guesses based on prior experience with similar transactions.

As you can imagine, even though only a handful of nonlinear iterates are involved, a significant amount of number crunching has taken place by the time the deal converges. Each Monte Carlo simulation itself consists of thousands of individual scenarios, each representing one complete deal realization that may span 25 years of monthly cash flows computed from the thousands of individual obligors in the pool. Revolving structures, fully discussed but not treated in this work, are even more demanding in terms of overhead and peripheral computations.

FIGURE 14.4
The control loop in yield space.

The CPU requirements of structured finance are significant and should not be underestimated. The computation of a single monthly set of cash flows, especially inside a revolving pool, may take noticeable CPU time on a desktop machine. Serious structured analysis requires considerable programming talent. A compiled language like Microsoft VB, Java or C++ is recommended if a structurally optimized transaction is desired.

14.8 DOING DEALS IN CODE

Over the last few pages, we have been referring to the many levels of resolution that a structured analyst needs to address specifically. At this point, it is appropriate to give an idea of the task that looms ahead if only as a guide to the next 10 chapters.

No matter what the asset class turns out to be, analysts will be required to understand the deal in advance and to anticipate the way its formal structures will eventually coalesce. We have found that, in the main, students usually fail in not being sufficiently conscious of how the deal is to come together as a whole and become embroiled in minutiae trying to go about it one step at a time. This will not work.

What *will* work is to conceptualize deals *as such* from the very beginning, with all their moving parts, and to work on each one separately as part of a master plan. A written blueprint for the deal needs to exist, if not on paper, then at least in your head. In terms of both time-saving and bug-fixing, the usefulness of creating a flowchart can never be over-emphasized.

In general, a properly designed structure should look like figure 14.2. It is unlikely that you will be able to reach closure if you simply set off on a random journey without the end of the road being clearly in your sights. We highly recommend that you draw a similar block diagram before writing a single line of code. You can rest assured this will be time well spent.

The Deal's Nested Loop Structure

A list of the various resolution levels you will encounter in your meanderings through the primary structured markets is something you should always keep in mind. For illustration purposes only, table 14.1 shows a rough nomenclature of such levels and a typical upper bound for each one. The product of these figures is a measure of the CPU effort required.

The flow of information inside code is what the analyst needs to keep in mind at all times if he is ever to converge on a deal. There are no shortcuts to doing this. As far as we know, practice is the only method that has ever worked. In part, this is why this process will keep us busy for the next 300 pages.

For each nonlinear, iterative pass, the code will navigate through the steps shown in figure 14.5. This is the way your code ought to be conceptualized and constructed. You will discover that the combinatorial possibilities will quickly overwhelm your ability to reduce errors if you attempt to write even a benign nonlinear code without a flowchart diagram. The flow pattern shown in figure 14.5 has been thoroughly tested and leads to a minimal amount of debugging time.

TABLE 14.1
Resolution levels in structured finance

ITEM	UPPER BOUND
***Optimization Level* (not treated)**	**Structure**
Design parameter	500
Deal Level	**SPV**
Original time (yield)	10
Monte Carlo (macro-economic)	5,000
Linear time	360
Asset Level	**Loans**
Obligors (micro-economic)	2,500
Delinquency status	7
Randomness	2
Liability Level	**Tranches**
Waterfall	1
Group (structural)	3
Tranches (credit)	10
Sub-tranches (liquidity)	5
Principal and interest	2

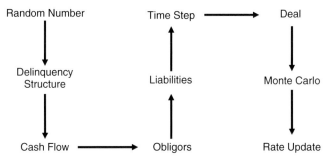

FIGURE 14.5
Information flow in transaction analysis.

14.9 THE ERGODIC HYPOTHESIS AND MONTE CARLO SIMULATION

The analysis of structured securities relies heavily on Monte Carlo analysis, which amounts to little more than the formal randomization of specific parameters within a transaction's ontological structure. There is nothing wrong with this, but it is certainly not the only way to evaluate the credit quality of an investment.

The reason why Monte Carlo simulation is especially appropriate to structured analysis is that it would clearly be foolish to base an investment on specific outcomes within an uncertain world. In other words, the fundamental rationale underlying Monte Carlo simulation is ignorance of the future, a very safe bet indeed. Any deterministic framework would be trivial since precise foreknowledge of future events would result in either no deal at all or in a guaranteed *Aaa* rating. A Treasury bond is not an investment; it is a way to hold cash, i.e., the word *investment* implies finite risk. Because of this uncertainty, we have no choice but to have recourse to statistics. This is not a *problem* of financial analysis. Rather, it is its greatest *opportunity*.

Given this innocent conclusion, what is the logical relationship between the machine-resident Monte Carlo simulation and empirical reality? In other words, how do we know that our Monte Carlo simulation has anything to do with the specific exposure we own or wish to own? If Monte Carlo analysis merely yields the ensemble-behavior of a well-diversified portfolio of similar transactions and the average reduction of yield on such a portfolio is the measure of credit quality for the target transaction, the obvious objection to this apparently flawless technique is that we do not own "a well-diversified portfolio of similar transactions" but rather only this *one* deal. If an investor happens to own the only transaction in the hypothetical portfolio which actually collapses, it will not do him much good to be told that the real problem was not that he owned a bad structured security, but rather that he did not own a sufficient number of them; because if he had purchased a *well-diversified portfolio of similar transactions* he would be doing just fine.

Thus, there is definitely an act of will involved in believing that a Monte Carlo simulation based on averages over ensembles is signaling anything empirical about a particular deal over its future life. In physics, this dogma has in fact been given the strange name of *ergodic hypothesis*. If you accept this hypothesis as true, and most people do, eventually although not directly, it follows that ensemble averages will be equivalent to time averages and thus that the information from a Monte Carlo simulation can be used to infer something empirically valid about one's own deal. In chapter 16, we show how this critical assumption is intimately tied to the theoretical framework underlying Markov chains.

By looking at what happens to an ensemble, i.e., a collection of transactions similar to yours, you can make an empirical statement about your deal if, in addition, you trust in the ergodic hypothesis. As an investor, when you purchase a structured security, you must nevertheless remain conscious of the fact that your blind faith in the ergodic hypothesis is embedded in your implicit acceptance of the aforementioned yield-reduction measure as the basis of its credit quality. However, please do not forget that a *hypothesis* is just a well-formed mathematical proposition that has been neither logically proved nor disproved. This being said, you should probably look for a culprit elsewhere when something goes very wrong with your deal.

The real problem in structured finance is not that the ergodic hypothesis is somehow involved, but that the initial valuation is never updated. In short, the passage of time and the optionality inherent in most structured securities result in a significant modification of the universe of possibilities still compatible with the transaction, a universe we need to keep up with if the deal is to be priced consistently. As we demonstrated in "*The Analysis of Structured Securities*" (OUP, 2003) using an admittedly simplistic, yet realistic model, it is virtually impossible for structured ratings to remain unchanged as time passes, unlike what normally happens in corporate finance. The reason why corporate ratings do change in practice has nothing to do with the fundamental premise at the heart of corporate analysis, which is that they should not. In other words, corporate ratings are conceived stochastically, i.e., as *right* or *wrong*. By contrast, credit ratings in structured finance, far from being static, are dynamic by their very nature. Once the pool starts revealing itself, the drivers of any updated Monte Carlo simulation will perforce change and invariably result in modified tranche credit ratings if the latter are computed as average yield reductions. Whether the associated letter-grade ratings also change is a completely different issue.

The mistake is not that a statistical analysis is performed at the outset, for one can really do nothing else. Rather, the problem is that this is done only once. In most cases, the statistical variance corresponding to the parametric range still consistent with new servicer data will begin to decrease as the pool amortizes. Consequently, uncertainty about future events will telescope to zero as well, and the transaction will ultimately be known with limiting unit probability-measure to either fail to deliver on its promise to some extent, or else pay off entirely. Such limiting coalescence will give rise to distributional convergence and hence, determinism, long before the pool has in fact paid down to zero. Over time, the increasingly certain valuation made possible by this telescoping process will provide a plethora of arbitrage opportunities for those watching it unfold.

Thus, sophisticated structured analysis is an ongoing affair requiring a new look every time data are made available via servicer reports. Only then can you be assured that valuations, and hence credit ratings, remain trustworthy.

14.10 CYBERNETICS: THE DIALECTICS OF DURATION

Cybernetics, what's that? It sounds like something from Hollywood does it not? The American mathematician Norbert Wiener (see Appendix) coined the specific technical use of this term in the late 1940s in a landmark monograph of the same name after a stint as a consultant to the U.S. Navy. That something so obvious and intuitive to any sailor should require a scientist of Wiener's caliber to become an accepted notion is truly amazing, for the concept itself goes back as far as Greek antiquity, and means *governance* in the sense of control, i.e., of management. Cybernetics is the way something can exist as freedom under control. As we saw earlier, this is the freedom of the right-hand side of the arc, the positive freedom; hence the expression *positive control*. What is difficult to grasp is that positive freedom has its origin in negative freedom. The two concepts are always inextricably intertwined via the notion of original time, which for us is nothing but yield. If you know this inside out, you know all there is to know about finance.

The phenomenon of essential dealing has its own nonlinear logic, one we sought to highlight via dealing's fundamental moments inside freedom space. But through it all, what should have become clear is how deals can be assembled, literally extracted out of nothingness, eventually to achieve full expression as freedom under control. The arcing process described above enabled us to hold the cybernetic nature of deal-hood tightly in view, to conceive it as a feedback loop merging assets and liabilities into a manifold unity, a deal via which linear time was forcibly negated. From that moment on, the deal lived as a synthetic organism and could only be understood and conceptualized as such.

Solely when held out to its own intrinsic and original possibility can a deal truly be said to exist, to live. Far from remaining silent, the deal beckons you to dealing from the very depth of your soul.

Ladies and Gentlemen,

Shall we Deal?

APPENDIX: *In Memoriam*

Norbert Wiener (1894–1964)

Norbert Wiener was a maverick and unconventional mathematician. However, it is the significance of his contributions to statistics, probability theory, and random processes, and hence to financial analysis, that compel us to briefly recount his brilliant and unorthodox career in an attempt to add even more color to this already colorful genius. Although he gave his name to the basic stochastic process most finance students have come to know, as well as to the Wiener–Hopf factorization method, a critically useful tool in the solution of many practical problems of engineering and physics, it is his founding of modern cybernetics that ought to be regarded by financial analysts as far more momentous.

Norbert Wiener was born in Columbia, Missouri on November 26, 1894, the first child of Leo and Bertha Wiener (née Kahn). Leo, ethnically Russian, was later to become Professor of Slavic Languages at Harvard University and was to remain the central influence on his son's life. After first studying medicine at the University of Warsaw, he had become dissatisfied with that profession and had left Poland to study engineering in Berlin. Regrettably, Leo found no more solace in the latter topic than in medicine and quickly left Germany to immigrate to the United States by way of England. After many small factory jobs, he eventually started teaching modern languages at the University of Missouri. Having lost out politically in a departmental shuffle, he moved to Boston shortly after Norbert's birth.

Leo was a polymath and an amateur mathematician. Although he never used his mathematical skills professionally, he constantly tried to instill his love for the field into his son, who unfortunately did very poorly in arithmetic. As a result, Wiener *père* switched to algebra where the boy immediately excelled. It was around that time that Leo basically took over Norbert's education until age nine, at which time the boy was sent back to high school, albeit one sufficiently progressive to let him graduate at age 11. A voracious reader, he immediately entered Tufts and graduated at 14 with a degree in mathematics. He then went on to Harvard to begin graduate studies in zoology (yes, you heard right!). That did not go well and he soon left Harvard for Cornell's philosophy department with a full scholarship. But still he was unhappy, forcing Leo to arrange, after an unsuccessful first year, to bring him back to Harvard to continue philosophy, in particular mathematical philosophy under Edward Huntington. He was awarded a Ph.D. from Harvard at 18 with a thesis in mathematical logic and was finally done with having to prove himself. At last, Wiener *fils* could start flexing his intellectual muscles.

He left Boston for Cambridge University on a post-doctorate fellowship under Bertrand Russell and attended lectures by Geoffrey Hardy, an encounter that was to remain a driving force for the rest of his life. He then went on to Göttingen to work under Hilbert and Edmund Landau. As World War II loomed, Wiener accepted Veblen's invitation to join the Aberdeen Proving Ground (Maryland) and soon after the war was appointed to MIT's mathematics department. He remained there until his death at age 70.

His first technical focus had been Brownian motion, a field that eventually led him to define and investigate more general stochastic processes, those that now bear his name. Another passion of his was Fourier integrals and transforms, an obsession that gave rise to the celebrated Wiener–Hopf factorization method. Interestingly enough, it was based on his World War II anti-aircraft fire control consulting work that he made his most remembered and significant contribution to true mathematical analysis, one that eventually crystallized into the epoch-making 1948 monograph *Cybernetics*, a term he himself coined although he had really borrowed it from Plato.

Wiener was a highly intuitive and inquisitive mind, always conscious of the limits of mathematical analysis, something Hardy had drilled into his young protégé back in Cambridge. In his thinking about fire control, he conceived of the gunnery operator as an integral part of the system that could lead to systematic stability if handled properly. In essence, more than any other mathematician in recent times, he took us away from linear thinking into nonlinearity, where the truth holds sway. Wiener made terms like feedback control, homeostasis, transfer function, and stability into household words, thereby laying the foundations of much of modern computer science. His greatest philosophical contribution is perhaps the way he taught the rest of us how to think in information-theoretic terms, the implications of which are only now starting to dawn upon finance.

It would however be naïve to expect superhuman perfection from someone like Wiener. Like the rest of us, he too had his shortcomings and failures. Yet, his legendary charisma and the breadth of his mathematical insights were usually more than sufficient to mollify even the most ardent critic. Besides, he had a singular, exceedingly rare ability on Wall Street: he never took himself seriously.

15

Data Analysis

"He hath indeed better bettered expectation of me than you must expect of me to tell you how."

William Shakespeare, *Much Ado About Nothing*

In order to analyze structured transactions properly, you will be repeatedly called upon to request static pool data from both prospective and seasoned issuers in various asset classes. What follows is a review of the steps you will most likely need to go through, or at least should go through in processing these data with a view toward using the results inside the loan-by-loan, Monte Carlo based cash flow model that will be discussed over the next few chapters. In order to concretize the following discussion, we present the analysis in the single case of the target transaction (automobiles), although the process is relatively similar in the mortgage-backed arena as well in all other amortizing asset classes. Should the data universe within some exotic asset class be markedly different from what we outline below, the sequence would remain the same. Therefore, time spent learning data analysis techniques appropriate to automobile asset backed securities will serve you well in many other asset classes.

15.1 STATIC POOL DATA

The loan-wise nomenclature shown in Table 15.1 will be used throughout this and the remaining chapters to label individual data elements within static pools. Please remember that the periodic rate may be computed from the APR by dividing the latter by the number of periods in one year. For monthly data, which is the most common situation, this number will be 12.

In what follows, we implicitly assume that the loans to be securitized already exist on the balance sheet of some issuer. Although this may seem like a benign assumption,

TABLE 15.1

Auto ABS data dictionary

VARIABLE NAME (UNIT)	SYMBOL
Initial balance ($)	P_0
Current balance ($)	P_c
Periodic percentage rate (%)	r
Original term (months)	T
Remaining term (months)	T_r
Seasoning (months)	t_s
Periodic payment ($)	M
Delinquency status (#)	D
Origination state	S_o
Origination date	t_l
Model year of vehicle	Y
Make of vehicle	M_v
Wholesale vehicle value at origination ($)	W_0
Credit score	S

in fact many deals are now executed in a "future flow" context, i.e., whereby all or a large portion of the receivables that are the subject matter of the deal will have to be created from future originations. This is not the place to debate whether this type of transaction can still be labeled a true securitization. However, strictly speaking the securitization of *receivables* presupposes that such receivables exist. If they do not, the analyst will somehow be forced to use proxies such as comparable portfolios from competitors in the same market or, in the worst case, will simply synthesize as accurately as possible an entire pool from the prospective issuer's credit policy manual, an unpleasant and tedious task at best.

A typical issuer should have much more information available that can be reasonably utilized within even sophisticated Monte Carlo simulations. As we shall see later, most personal data on obligors and their economic situation will be lost when inserted inside a Markov chain analytical framework. The vehicles themselves will normally be described in much more detail than can reasonably be handled. In the end, the more orthogonal the information used in value determination, the more stable and accurate such judgments will be. Over time, you will learn how to distill your requests down to the set you can reasonably use, enabling all your results to be compared directly.

Table 15.2 is a sample from the minimum set we recommend for the analysis of auto ABS transactions. The data elements below were gleaned from an actual automobile ABS transaction that paid off long ago. Should you find that your issuer does not have access to this minimal set, you would have to make reasonable assumptions with respect to missing variables or else obtain them from other sources. However, in practice the inability of any issuer to produce, on demand, the data in

TABLE 15.2

Data extract from a typical auto ABS transaction

ID	P_0	P_c	r	T_r	D	t_l	S_o	Y	M_v	W_0	S
1	$24,699.86	$21,689.56	18.47%	65	0	06/06/98	FL	1996	Chevrolet	$17,242.20	703
2	$21,601.63	$20,234.22	14.72%	68	0	06/08/98	CA	1997	Volvo	$16,015.64	587
3	$22,431.34	$20,237.17	17.40%	69	0	06/16/98	OH	1995	Chevrolet	$15,624.92	534
4	$17,212.13	$15,075.50	17.12%	56	1	06/10/98	CO	1995	Mercury	$11,460.68	569
5	$17,435.06	$15,049.30	13.46%	54	0	04/27/98	CO	1997	Volvo	$13,309.18	571
6	$25,945.32	$23,869.40	16.50%	55	0	04/05/98	MD	1995	Ford	$18,186.49	538
7	$12,252.32	$10,562.76	18.52%	51	1	05/06/98	FL	1998	Mercury	$8,264.29	577
8	$25,693.03	$22,911.39	17.09%	57	0	04/19/98	MD	1997	Mazda	$19,525.74	563
9	$26,660.82	$22,759.29	19.26%	57	0	04/20/98	NJ	1997	Mercury	$19,960.67	535
10	$24,762.68	$21,275.21	18.71%	52	0	04/03/98	MS	1995	Chevrolet	$16,283.30	620
11	$12,816.35	$12,016.20	17.84%	70	0	05/11/98	OR	1996	Ford	$10,397.09	723
12	$19,452.59	$17,728.29	17.05%	64	0	04/23/98	MI	1995	Nissan	$14,387.53	517
13	$27,527.15	$24,271.48	13.42%	70	0	05/25/98	TX	1996	Volvo	$20,942.71	557
14	$26,228.64	$24,632.47	13.84%	71	0	05/11/98	NJ	1998	Mazda	$19,804.27	713
15	$18,723.65	$17,414.41	17.32%	61	0	05/25/98	CA	1998	Chevrolet	$13,907.74	529
16	$29,315.16	$25,254.98	16.76%	66	0	06/12/98	OK	1998	Subaru	$18,970.41	651
17	$27,686.03	$24,178.92	14.60%	66	0	04/19/98	CT	1996	Mazda	$19,641.93	556
18	$13,012.26	$11,233.53	18.14%	68	0	04/20/98	CA	1998	Toyota	$8,852.93	575
19	$29,092.02	$25,768.20	17.63%	64	0	06/24/98	CA	1995	Subaru	$20,255.05	677
20	$18,552.34	$17,347.04	19.90%	58	0	04/12/98	CO	1997	Toyota	$14,872.64	562
21	$21,447.63	$18,360.68	15.69%	64	0	05/12/98	NJ	1996	Chevrolet	$14,246.26	570
22	$25,808.01	$24,002.37	13.13%	67	1	06/27/98	FL	1996	Pontiac	$20,124.11	609
23	$12,963.08	$11,221.52	18.69%	67	0	05/02/98	CT	1996	Mercury	$9,532.85	664
24	$22,664.25	$19,944.82	18.43%	51	0	04/13/98	MI	1998	Pontiac	$16,175.02	649
25	$20,436.60	$18,230.53	16.75%	63	0	04/01/98	CO	1995	Volvo	$14,956.89	727

Table 15.2 should raise serious questions as to its ability to enter the securitization market.

General Remarks on the Minimum ABS Data Set

An obvious missing data element in the Table 15.2 is the original loan term (see below), a value usually close to its remaining term but which can also be quite different, for instance in pools purchased from third parties prior to being securitized. Note that some of these elements will be used in chapter 17 for recovery modeling purposes while others will not be used at all in the simplified treatment presented in this text.

For example, the State of origination (S_o) may have no bearing on the deal perhaps because all the origination States in your transaction treat obligors the same way in the event of default. As you know, for a *variable* to have explanatory power, it must actually *vary* across the obligor base. On the other hand, some jurisdictions may impose restrictions on servicers with respect to the handling of delinquent accounts that limit or constrain the universe of collection actions and thus reduce or even eliminate the associated vehicle's recovery potential. Special obligor-friendly jurisdictions may also exist where loss given default will be highly correlated to default events. As a result, we recommend leaving this variable in the set just in case it later becomes relevant.

In addition, loans placed into a securitization pool may already be delinquent, although standard transaction covenants usually limit delinquencies to 30 days or less. In any event, knowledge of a loan's delinquency status will be relevant when computing trust cash flows from a set of nonstationary Markov transition matrices, a process we fully describe in chapter 16.

For future reference, figures 15.1, 15.2 and 15.3 show the three main distributions of interest in the analysis of an automobile loan pool, i.e., the remaining outstanding principal balance P_c, the annualized interest rate APR and the remaining term T_r. They were produced from the full dataset associated with the target transaction.

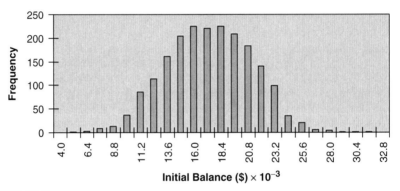

FIGURE 15.1
Principal balance distribution in the pool.

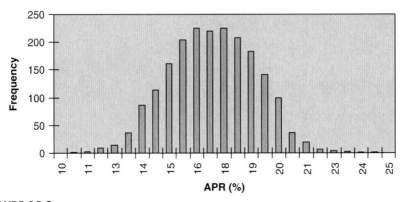

FIGURE 15.2
Interest rate distribution in the pool.

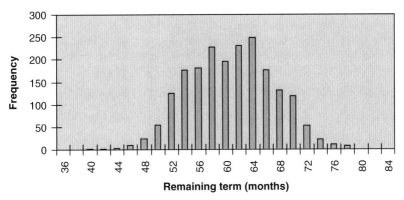

FIGURE 15.3
Remaining term distribution in the pool.

Calculation of Subsidiary Data Elements

Although the dataset in table 15.2 represents the raw data needed to analyze auto-loan backed ABS transactions at a relatively high level of approximation, we will also need to compute two derived quantities, namely the loan's seasoning (t_s) and its initial term (T). In the case of fixed-rate loans, these can be derived from the above dataset as follows.

First, the obligor's monthly payment can be calculated thus:

$$M = \frac{r P_c}{1 - (1 + r)^{-T_r}} \tag{1}$$

Next, the basic equation for a current, amortizing, fixed-rate loan reviewed in "*The Analysis of Structured Securities*" (OUP, 2003) leads to the following equation for the initial loan term:

$$T = \frac{\ln[1/\alpha]}{\ln[1 + r]} \tag{2}$$

In equation (2), we have defined:

$$\alpha = 1 - \frac{r P_0}{M}$$

Finally, from the defining relation for seasoning, we have:

$$t_s = T - T_r \tag{3}$$

Please note that in many applications, T will be given as an integer and produce integer-valued loan seasonings. There is however no reason why, in general, seasoning should be an integer within Markov-chain-based computations. In practice, the issuer will invariably deliver the remaining term T_r as an integer. Therefore, if we allow initial terms to be computed as real quantities, real-valued loan seasonings will result. If the loan is performing as expected, the above calculations will automatically yield T as an integer.

Exercise 15.1

Using L'Hôpital's rule, show that in the limit $r \to 0$, the amortization schedule $p(t)$ of a level pay loan is given by:

$$p(t) = P_0\left[1 - \frac{t}{T}\right], \quad P_0 \equiv p(0)$$

Adjustment for Delinquent Loans

As noted above, strictly speaking, the foregoing equations are valid solely for nondelinquent loans. In certain jurisdictions, Australia for example, the meaning of delinquency is different and a 30-day delinquency actually corresponds to a 60-day actuarially based delinquency. However, save for such pathologies, it is expected that structured pools will contain either current or 30-day delinquent loans.

In standard cases, one should proceed as follows. Since an account delinquent by one month shows up merely as a mismatch between P_c and T_r, we simply increase T_r by one before applying the formulas above. The loan's seasoning t_s also needs to be increased by 1 to reflect the physical situation. This is best accomplished by using the original T_r in the equation for t_s.

In essence, we are saying that the current balance of a 30-day delinquent account is higher by one principal payment than it would have been had the payment been made on schedule. Therefore, the remaining term that would match the initial balance should be one more than the value reported by the servicer, which is normally based on the original amortization schedule. This simple method can obviously be extended to accounts that are more than a single month delinquent but as explained above, it will be rare for this type of situation to exist in a structured pool.

The analysis of delinquencies within static pool data can be extended further by inquiring into the credit policy of the seller to determine the cash flow mechanism whereby a severely delinquent loan has been made eligible via a partial cure or a so-called payment holiday.. The risk of moral hazard is real and should never be either discounted as minimal or simply ignored. Unfortunately, such considerations are beyond the scope of this text.

15.2 STATIC POOL LOSS CURVES

Recall from previous chapters how our steadfast friend the logistic curve was chosen as the generic static pool loss curve. This was done because this functional form was easy to handle and possessed an intuitive appeal difficult to reproduce elsewhere. Now that we have introduced seasoning into the game, we need to modify the basic logistic equation in order to allow loan seasoning to have the impact on obligor behavior it is known to have. Although, in general, seasoning tends to be relatively small compared to a loan's remaining term, it is not the case when portfolios are bought and sold. Given the consolidation environment recently seen in the banking industry, relatively large pool seasonings may start showing up.

To take seasoning into account, modify the basic loss curve relationship as follows:

$$F(t) = \frac{M_p(n)m(L_e)}{1 + be^{-c(t - t_0 + t_s)}} \tag{4}$$

In equation (4), we have defined the following additional quantities:

t = time measured as an integer
M_p = macro-economic modulation parameter
m = micro-economic modulation parameter
L_e = gross expected credit loss for the pool over its life
n = Monte Carlo simulation index
t_0 = inflexion point on the loss curve (obtained from loss data)
b = convenience parameter used sometimes to adjust the curve to fit data
c = loss curve spreading parameter

Although we will come back to equation (4) in chapter 16, we would now like to make additional remarks on the motivation for our choice of the logistic curve as the generic loss curve, and on other data issues related to loss curve constructions and their analytical use.

The first thing to notice is that, strictly speaking, the above curve is not a loss curve but simply has the same functional form. The reason for this is that since we will be reproducing the dynamics of static pools using Markov transition matrices and their formalism, it makes sense to begin with a form that has the ability to faithfully describe such dynamics. Second, equation (4) is meant to represent the pool's *gross* loss behavior, not its *net* loss behavior. Doing this enables us to treat recoveries separately, which is something we need to do if we want to let the variety of automobile makes and models found in any given pool influence its loss behavior. Further, net loss curves are often nonmonotonic, i.e., they don't always rise. This creates analytical inconsistencies when attempting to use them inside Markov chains. The use of gross loss curves is a neat way to use smooth functional forms throughout, thereby simplifying the analysis.

It might be surprising to some that we should be able to represent all static pools within a single functional paradigm. In fact, the logistic curve carries within itself the freedom required to model accurately the vast majority of structured pools. How can this be?

To see this, note that in terms of credit losses, a static pool will generally behave as drawn in figure 15.4. The related curve can be conceived as consisting of three distinct segments separated by the black vertical lines in figure 15.4. To the left of the first line, very little loss has occurred because the pool's ultimate delinquency structure is still building up. Between the two lines, we find the bulk of credit losses. This is where the pool truly reveals itself as either good or bad. Finally, to the right of the second line, the pool's loss history has fully run its course and except for a few

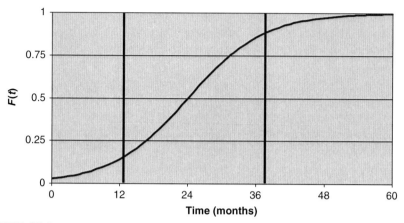

FIGURE 15.4
Static pool loss curve.

laggards, the pool is no longer experiencing significant losses. By then, it has clearly amortized considerably and credit risk has all but disappeared.

Should this be surprising? In essence, the pool's loss history is basically made up of a linear segment sandwiched between two horizontal segments where not much happens. No matter what the pool looks like to begin with, it must have this behavioral structure since losses need to occur somewhere and they certainly won't occur when the pool has amortized to 10% of its original balance. In other words, there is nothing magical in the fact that static pool loss curves look like figure 15.4, for that generic shape is fundamentally built into the process from the outset.

Since the logistic curve, analytically speaking, consists of the same three segments, it is the perfect candidate for loss curve modeling. We did not impose this curve ad hoc as the paradigm of gross loss behavior. Rather, the loss dynamics already built-in to the process itself told us what to do. This is nothing new; it is the way it always works. Analysts do not have to search far and wide for suitable, generic loss curves because the required behavior will already be contained in the physics of the process. The difficulty, of course, was to know beforehand that the logistic curve had the sought-after property.

Frequently Asked Questions

1. What if I don't have enough data to build a loss curve, or any data at all?

Although this will be far less common in structured finance than in corporate finance, it will happen. The easiest way to handle this issue is to select a suitable proxy for the issuer in question. It is basically impossible to find a situation where a two-year-old company was founded by junior people with no prior experience. In most cases, the predecessor company's loss curve will be a good basis for the new entrant's curve. Please remember that in building loss curves within the Markov transition matrix context, the ultimate loss doesn't matter because losses are a priori unknown.

What does matter is the temporal dynamics of loss behavior. In other words, one does not have to be right as far as the absolute value of gross loss is concerned but merely with respect to the shape of the loss curve. Betting on the invariance of a curve's shape instead of its ultimate value is much safer than you might think.

2. If I have a partial loss curve, how many data points do I need to use it safely?

The answer to this question is directly tied to the model you are using. Given that equation (4) contains an inflexion point t_0, it is a safe bet that if you are given actual data points beyond the curve's inflexion point, the errors you will be making will be relatively small. In statistical language, we might say that the standard error of regression parameters with respect to equation (4) will be acceptable if the number of data points N_d satisfies $N_d \geq t_0$. Now, it would be dangerous to declare victory too soon since different issuers may give rise to markedly different loss curves. However, once the inflexion point is behind you, you can start making fairly accurate judgments as to the ultimate shape of the curve.

3. If I want to, can I use a different functional form to model credit losses?

Of course you can. There is nothing sacred about the logistic curve. In fact, if you don't feel comfortable with our choice, by all means pick something you like and understand. It is far better to use a simple model you understand well than to use a more complicated one in the hope of appearing more knowledgeable, or merely because it is the "right" thing to do. What you know is what you should use.

4. Can I assume instead that losses occur uniformly over the life of the pool?

A thousand times no! This is a big mistake. Front-loading and back-loading losses are also costly mistakes. These assumptions are no better than assuming loss uniformity.

As we highlighted in *"The Analysis of Structured Securities"* (OUP, 2003), in order to use Markov transition matrices in the analysis of structured pools, we need to ensure that the operative delinquency dynamics of actual pools are fairly and nonarbitrarily reflected in the mechanics of credit losses inherent in the formalism. As described therein, micro- and macro-economic levels of analysis generally need to be considered for us to have a reasonable assurance that this has been done.

Data and the Two Levels of Structured Analysis

In the next two sections, we show how to use portfolio data to first derive a representative empirical value for the most important quantity in credit analysis, the expected loss, and to compute large deviations from the asymptotically normal loss distribution stemming from microdynamics, deviations that in turn, are caused by macro-economic disturbances.

The basic principle remains the same, i.e., the reason why credit enhancement is required is not to protect investors against the micro-dynamics of structured pools, but against their macro-dynamics. Diversification alone can provide a relatively high level of assurance that investors will not suffer a credit loss simply because of statistical behavior with respect to large pools of homogeneous obligors. As a rule, structured securities are backed by thousands of individual and granular loans, the default of any one of which has no impact on fixed income investor reimbursement. Statistical behavior is quite predictable in this range and one can be highly confident that if securities default, it is not because a "10-sigma" event has occurred, but rather because macro-economic forces, to which all obligors are subject simultaneously, have shifted the playing field under our feet.

To do this well, it will be propitious to clearly separate the micro and macro levels of analysis in order to witness how a nominally normal distribution (micro-economic) becomes skewed and begins to generate abnormal events (macro-economic), i.e., those that lead to investor losses.

15.3 CALCULATING EXPECTED LOSS FROM PORTFOLIO DATA (MICRO-ECONOMIC DISTRIBUTION)

When starting to work on a transaction, in addition to potentially crucial static pool data, the analyst will normally have access to portfolio data as well, which are nothing but the same data reformatted. In fact, it is static pool data that are uncanny among issuers, not portfolio data. Portfolio data analysis is just as important, if not more, than the determination of the shape of a loss curve because it will end up driving the entire loss process via the expected loss parameter and the macro-economic modulation that will later be imposed on these data.

To begin with, analysts will request and normally receive specifically constructed loan samples extracted from the issuer's managed portfolio or. equivalently, from its balance sheet. How the sample is to be constructed will be described shortly. Such samples will generally look like table 15.3 where we use a 100-loan sample merely for calculational convenience.

A sample like table 15.3 is built as follows. First, the issuer selects an initial period (t_1) and a final period (t_2) separated by a time span large enough to be meaningful and to allow the loss process to reveal itself. This will usually be one year or some other interval dictated by portfolio size and maturity, although credit experience will usually indicate an adequate time span. Next, a large sample of current loans at time t_1 is randomly selected from the same universe as those to be securitized and their principal balance noted. The fact that the loans in the sample will not be in the target pool is irrelevant. After $t_2 - t_1$ has elapsed, the actual delinquency status of the same loans is noted.

Current Balance

This is the principal balance of the loan at the original time t_1, not the final time t_2. The relationship between current balance and recovery percentage is discussed under "Recoveries" below. This is an area where many mistakes are made.

Credit Scores (FICO)

FICO scores[1] at t_1 can easily be obtained from the issuer. In the worst case, the analyst can use the loan's closing date FICO score, assuming the issuer uses credit scoring in making underwriting decisions. If the originator does not use credit scoring, this variable is not used. Credit scores from past periods can also be purchased from the

TABLE 15.3

Loan sample from an issuer's credit portfolio

ID	CURRENT BALANCE	FICO	DEFAULT STATUS	LGD
1	$34,271	626	0	53.2%
2	$40,831	646	0	45.3%
3	$26,549	590	0	54.7%
4	$34,492	652	0	44.2%
5	$40,644	512	0	49.7%
6	$41,240	685	0	45.2%
7	$33,820	568	0	57.5%
8	$36,504	695	0	56.9%
9	$44,158	505	0	43.7%
10	$40,306	665	1	50.4%
11	$29,499	682	0	43.3%
12	$36,817	530	0	46.8%
13	$44,346	527	0	55.4%
14	$33,375	659	0	52.8%
15	$27,401	540	0	46.3%
16	$40,460	642	0	46.7%
17	$40,971	534	0	52.5%
18	$40,953	647	0	54.9%
19	$32,180	534	0	57.8%
20	$39,397	506	1	45.6%
21	$34,797	520	0	55.9%
22	$43,694	596	0	46.4%
23	$32,861	581	0	42.6%
24	$27,582	527	0	40.8%
25	$32,074	646	0	43.4%
26	$38,421	526	0	56.8%
27	$42,165	563	0	56.6%
28	$43,017	646	0	57.7%
29	$37,824	597	0	46.6%
30	$31,922	649	0	49.7%
31	$44,016	569	1	59.4%
32	$28,967	670	0	54.0%
33	$35,343	552	0	48.6%
34	$31,892	584	0	52.9%
35	$37,501	537	0	40.9%
36	$27,034	596	0	59.0%
37	$35,889	660	0	45.9%
38	$29,162	652	0	41.2%
39	$44,875	633	0	48.9%

continues to next page

TABLE 15.3

continued from previous page

ID	CURRENT BALANCE	FICO	DEFAULT STATUS	*LGD*
40	$40,759	659	0	49.9%
41	$32,471	617	0	40.6%
42	$40,887	612	0	59.5%
43	$25,152	518	0	47.8%
44	$32,817	654	0	45.5%
45	$29,068	626	1	56.8%
46	$27,548	669	0	56.5%
47	$29,011	674	0	41.0%
48	$39,957	613	0	41.6%
49	$34,868	520	0	50.2%
50	$39,162	691	0	44.9%
51	$44,899	618	0	57.0%
52	$30,287	538	0	47.4%
53	$29,446	574	0	48.6%
54	$26,372	522	0	40.9%
55	$40,292	674	0	59.2%
56	$26,025	690	1	46.1%
57	$33,593	587	0	47.1%
58	$36,997	567	0	41.6%
59	$44,973	577	0	58.3%
60	$32,261	614	0	53.1%
61	$36,497	507	0	44.4%
62	$29,579	550	0	45.1%
63	$37,613	589	0	42.0%
64	$37,994	690	0	57.9%
65	$42,386	589	0	57.8%
66	$28,572	586	0	59.4%
67	$34,625	663	0	40.1%
68	$44,446	600	0	44.4%
69	$28,689	504	0	54.2%
70	$41,493	539	0	40.2%
71	$39,132	658	0	52.4%
72	$41,283	629	0	50.4%
73	$35,838	575	0	40.4%
74	$31,048	568	1	57.9%
75	$34,211	542	0	54.7%
76	$27,780	656	0	59.5%
77	$39,920	533	0	54.3%
78	$43,557	651	0	51.9%

continues to next page

TABLE 15.3

continued from previous page

ID	CURRENT BALANCE	FICO	DEFAULT STATUS	*LGD*
79	$27,416	624	0	60.0%
80	$39,419	630	0	59.5%
81	$33,128	696	0	53.4%
82	$41,312	647	1	54.4%
83	$28,738	696	0	53.7%
84	$40,742	529	0	48.5%
85	$39,697	620	0	55.4%
86	$26,804	590	0	54.6%
87	$34,158	661	0	41.9%
88	$32,755	679	0	54.6%
89	$34,954	582	0	58.9%
90	$41,952	526	0	58.0%
91	$26,217	688	0	51.7%
92	$29,696	550	0	59.1%
93	$44,105	506	0	54.4%
94	$35,033	506	0	58.5%
95	$43,988	557	0	53.5%
96	$42,717	676	0	50.5%
97	$40,432	563	1	58.5%
98	$44,039	542	0	45.4%
99	$42,851	511	0	43.3%
100	$33,052	668	0	55.9%

three major U.S. credit bureaus. Since the use of credit scoring has become widespread among finance companies, you should expect that this data element will usually be available.

Default Status

The assignment of a default status to each loan is done as follows. First, partition the loans into three disjoint categories. Those that are mildly delinquent, usually from zero to a maximum of 40 days past due, are assigned a default status of zero. The upper bound is usually sharp, in that most people will keep making their loan payments until they have run out of cash. Although one can always be found, the empirical determination of the upper delinquency bound appropriate to a zero status is beyond the scope of this text.

Next, a special category is created in which we place loans found more delinquent at time t_2 than the upper bound allowable for zero status but less than the lower bound for default. Such loans are assigned a default status of 0.5. The remaining loans are assigned a default status of 1.0. The lower bound for unit status will normally be lower than the official credit policy of the issuer since the latter is simply an arbitrary boundary without economic significance. In the automobile asset class, loans that are more than 75 days past due should usually be considered economically defaulted and thus eligible for unit status. However, there is clearly room for a judgment call here.

The next step is to eliminate from the sample all the loans with default status 0.5. At this point you are left with a smaller sample of loans with default status equal to either 0 or 1.0. Select 100 loans or more at random from the latter sample to end up with something like table 15.3.

Recoveries (Loss Given Default)

The determination of loss given default (LGD) must be split into two steps, one for unit-status loans and the other for zero-status loans. We take these up below:

1. Loans that defaulted (Status $= 1$)

Recoveries $(1 - LGD)$ on loans from obligors with unit status must be calculated as a percentage of the loan's principal balance at time t_1. Such data should be available if t_1 and t_2 are selected long enough in the past for the issuer to have foreclosed on all defaulted loans in the original random sample. If issuer data are provided only as a percentage of the loan's principal balance at the time of default, gross up recoveries by any normal amortization experienced between t_1 and t_2.

Some might argue that loan recoveries should be computed as a percentage of the balance at the time of default (i.e. t_2). Leaving aside for the moment the obvious objection that, owing to both our default status definition and the cumulative nature of default status assignment, such loans did not really default at time t_2 except in rare instances, doing this ignores the plain fact that loans will be securitized at t_1, not t_2. If you still have problems conceptualizing this method, just think of any amortization between t_1 and t_2 as a "mini" default with 100% recovery. Finally, please do not forget the time-value of money.

2. Loans that did not default (Status $= 0$)

For loans with zero status the analyst needs to estimate putative recoveries from wholesale data on similar vehicles by conservatively assuming a hypothetical default occurring at t_2. Even if it is true that LGD means loss "given" default, this arbitrary label should not obscure the fact that LGD can be calculated for *all* loans, not simply those that happened to have defaulted during the year. Although it is obviously tempting to ask issuers to do it, analysts need to do this in-house.

The reason is simple. Issuers tend to be optimistic when computing recoveries on nondefaulted loans since they realize the credit enhancement value of strong recoveries. By researching and obtaining proprietary raw data on the largest (i.e., *nondefaulted*) portion of the issuer's portfolio, analysts may better judge to what extent recoveries have been exaggerated. Perish the thought that they have not been.

Expected Loss Calculation

Once this considerable amount of work has been done, portfolio analysis can begin in earnest. Using Monte Carlo simulation, the basic idea is to generate a sequence of sample portfolios with the same statistical characteristics as the given one, thereby generating a sequence of corresponding gross loss rates that will form a distribution.

Exercise 15.2

Assume that, in general, credit loss L is given by the following familiar relation:

$$L = LEE \ X \ LGD \qquad (5)$$

In equation (5), we have defined the usual quantities:

$$LEE = \text{loan equivalent exposure}$$
$$X = \text{default status indicator}$$
$$LGD = \text{loss given default}$$

Assume also that an expectation operator $E[x] \equiv \overline{x}$ can be defined as follows:

$$E[x] = \frac{1}{n} \sum_{i=1}^{n} x_i$$

Then, show via Taylor-series expansion of equation (5) that, to first order and for a known value of LEE, the formulas for the exposure-level expected loss (μ) and standard deviation of loss (σ) are given by:

$$\mu = LEE \ \overline{X} \ \overline{LGD} \qquad (6)$$

$$\sigma = LEE \ \sqrt{\overline{LGD}^2 \ \sigma_X^2 + \overline{X}^2 \ \sigma_{LGD}^2 + 2 \overline{X} \ \overline{LGD} \ Cov(X, LGD)} \qquad (7)$$

In equation (7), we have defined the usual statistical quantities:

$$\sigma_X^2 = E\left[(X - \overline{X})^2\right]$$

$$\sigma_{LGD}^2 = E\left[(LGD - \overline{LGD})^2\right]$$

$$Cov[X, LGD] = E\left[(X - \overline{X})(LGD - \overline{LGD})\right]$$

Note: These relationships in no way require that X be a binary variable.

Thanks to the central limit theorem, the resulting distribution will be approximately normal. Next, using the well-known analytical formula for the average life of the given pool, we will derive a representative value for L_e, the mean sample loss for the pool. At this time, please recall that the sample given in table 15.3 had a default rate of 8% since eight loans out of 100 defaulted over the one-year time horizon.

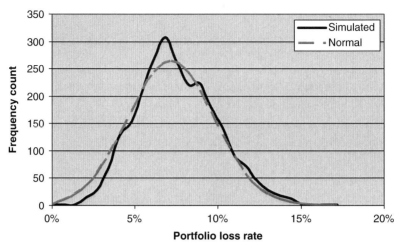

FIGURE 15.5
The micro-economic loos distribution from a sample portfolio.

The procedure to compute the mean sample credit loss is straightforward. Simply enter the above sample portfolio into a Monte Carlo simulation engine and generate repeated loan samples using any random number generator. The micro-loss distribution will emerge naturally from this process. Since we are interested in the gross credit loss micro-distribution, recoveries may be set to zero for this exercise. In terms of statistical accuracy, the VBA-resident uniform random number generator (RND) is usually sufficient for this purpose although more sophisticated methods of uniform deviate generation are certainly welcome and are discussed in chapter 18.

As an example of this procedure, exhibit 15.1 shows a VBA code section calculating a typical micro-loss distribution from the above 100-loan portfolio. Figure 15.5 shows the resulting normal distribution after 2,500 sample portfolios were generated via Monte Carlo simulation.

Exhibit 15.1 Synthesizing Micro-Economic Loss Distributions

```
Sub main()

Dim Loan_ID(1 To 100) As Integer, Current_Loan_Balance(1 To 100) As Double
Dim Default_Status(1 To 100) , LGD(1 To 100) As Double
Dim Mean_Loss As Double, Loss_Standard_Deviation As Double
Dim Number_of_Scenarios , Number_of_Loans As Integer
Dim Scratch , Total_Portfolio_Balance , Scenario_Loss(1 To 2500) As Double
Dim i , j As Integer, Average_Default_Rate , FICO_Score(1 To 100) As Double
'
' Read the loans into the code from Excel
'
```

```
Number_of_Loans = 100
For i = 1 To Number_of_Loans
Loan_ID(i) = Range("Loan_ID").Cells(i, 1).Value
Current_Loan_Balance(i) = Range("Loan_ID").Cells(i, 2).Value
FICO_Score(i) = Range("Loan_ID").Cells(i, 3).Value
Default_Status(i) = Range("Loan_I
D").Cells(i, 4).Value
LGD(i) = Range("Loan_ID").Cells(i, 5).Value
Next i
'

Synthesis of the micro-economic gross credit loss distribution from a sample of loans
'

Compute the average default rate for the portfolio and the total sample balance
'


Scratch = 0
Total_Portfolio_Balance = 0

For i = 1 To Number_of_Loans
Scratch = Scratch + Default_Status(i)
Total_Portfolio_Balance = Total_Portfolio_Balance + Current_Loan_Balance(i)
Next i
Average_Default_Rate = Scratch / Number_of_Loans
'

' Proceed with the Monte Carlo simulation
'

Number_of_Scenarios = 2500
For i = 1 To Number_of_Scenarios
Scenario_Loss(i) = 0
For j = 1 To Number_of_Loans
Scenario_Loss(i) = Scenario_Loss(i) - (Rnd <= Average_Default_Rate) *
Current_Loan_Balance(j)
Next j
Scenario_Loss(i) = Scenario_Loss(i) / Total_Portfolio_Balance
'

' Output for graph display
'

Range("Loss_Scenario_Vector").Cells(i, 1).Value = Scenario_Loss(i)
Next i
'

' Compute the mean portfolio credit loss
'

Mean_Loss = 0
For i = 1 To Number_of_Scenarios
Mean_Loss = Mean_Loss + Scenario_Loss(i)
Next i
Mean_Loss = Mean_Loss / Number_of_Scenarios
Range("Mean_Loss").Value = Mean_Loss
```

continues to next page

```
continued from previous page
'
' Compute the standard deviation of portfolio credit losses
'
Scratch = 0
For i = 1 To Number_of_Scenarios
Scratch = Scratch + (Scenario_Loss(i) - Mean_Loss) ^ 2
Next i
Loss_Standard_Deviation = Sqr(Scratch / Number_of_Scenarios)
Range("Sigma_Loss").Value = Loss_Standard_Deviation
```

The fit between figure 15.5 and the associated normal is quite convincing, although there are still doubts as to what the micro-economic loss distribution's shape is really saying to us. The largest source of fitting error is in fact the quality of the Excel-resident uniform random number generator (RND), something we pointed out repeatedly when discussing the topic of random number generation in "*The Analysis of Structured Securities*" (OUP, 2003).

Were one to use the low discrepancy sequence method reviewed in chapter 18, the fit would be essentially perfect. Increasing the number of Monte Carlo scenarios does help a bit, but the point here is to notice that from micro-dynamics alone, the sample portfolio does behave in accordance with the central limit theorem. This should come as no surprise.

Although a few inquisitive readers might argue that some, as of yet unspecified, distribution gives a better fit, this is meaningless unless one specifies the distribution in question. From among the 17 or so known analytical distributions we have investigated, none gives a closer fit to the empirical distribution than the corresponding normal distribution.

Using FICO Scores instead of Default Status Codes

As you will have noticed already, the above sample of 100 loans contains another important source of valuable information on the creditworthiness of the obligors in the issuer's portfolio: credit scores. In most cases, Fair, Isaac & Co. is the corporation that commercially supplies such scores, especially in the auto sector. This is not an advertisement for this company, but simply a fact. In what follows we assume that either a FICO score or one produced by any other commercial vendor is available for each obligor in the sample.

Instead of using the default status as was done before, we can use the scores directly by transforming them into an average default rate for the portfolio in a manner analogous to what we did with the default status. This enables us to repeat the same exercise using potentially more accurate information.

Admittedly, nothing beats actual empirical evidence from an issuer's portfolio, but there are situations where the credit-scoring method is inevitable. The three most common such instances are:

1. The target issuer might be too unseasoned to have defaulted loans in sufficient numbers to give statistical credibility to the above status code method.

2. Even when sufficient empirical default data exist, FICO scores may be more recent and provide a better read on the loss potential symptomatic of the target portfolio.

3. The probability that fraud will take place when issuers deliver their credit scores to the analyst is reduced since most of them do not know how to transform such scores into default probabilities, and thus are less likely to manipulate the process. As far as they know, a higher score is better than a lower score, and that is pretty well the end of it. In a nutshell, the quality of the FICO information might be superlative compared to that handed over by the issuer with respect to defaulted loans.

To use the credit-score method to determine the mean sample loss, proceed as follows. First, find out from FICO itself how to turn their score into an expected default rate. This can always be done because commercial scores are well documented. For the sake of argument, pretend that a mapping function transforming the score into a one-year expected default frequency can be found.

After some normalization, assume we have synthesized the following complementary logistic map. For an obligor with FICO score S_i, the one-year default probability P_i can be expressed as:

$$P_i = \frac{0.08\, e^{-0.15\left(\frac{S_i}{50}-24\right)}}{1 + e^{-0.15\left(\frac{S_i}{50}-24\right)}} \tag{8}$$

Next, go through the sample and convert the given score into a default probability using equation (8) on each obligor. In practice, you would most likely not have to derive the equivalent of equation (8) since the issuer or FICO itself would make expected obligor-wise default probabilities available to you.

The sample default rate we will use (P_D) is the arithmetic[2] mean default rate derived from the FICO scores of the N loans in the given sample:

$$P_D = \frac{1}{N} \sum_{i=1}^{N} P_i$$

Now, redo the same exercise as above using the FICO-score derived sample default rate. Equation (8) leads to $P_D = 6.85\%$ and using this value inside our Monte Carlo formalism, we obtained the normal distribution in figure 15.6. Exhibit 15.2 is the short code section implementing the mapping from credit scores to default rate and the calculation of the average default rate.

Not surprisingly, the results are also normal except that the mean sample loss (6.84%) is now more in line with expectations from the FICO-average default rate. In a nutshell, the micro-loss distribution is to all intents and purposes normal and can be regarded as such. In practice, portfolios consisting of thousands of loans only reinforce our expectations of normality at the micro-level and act to further reduce the micro-loss distribution variance down to an extremely low level. Recall that the distributions given here are only valid for 100-loan samples, far fewer than what can

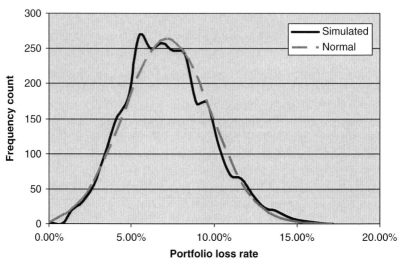

FIGURE 15.6
The FICO-derived micro-economic loss distribution.

be found in even the smallest auto-loan securitization. The situation that prevails with respect to the CDO universe is very different.

The Net Loss Distribution

If the net loss distribution is needed, simply multiply the current balance by its corresponding loss given default before aggregating losses in the sampling distribution. Losses given default are included in table 15.3 but, as we indicated above, you can also compute them from vehicle depreciation data in concert with raw issuer data. The net loss distribution is more intuitive for those using the back of the envelope approach since it allows you to compare credit enhancement to losses directly.

Exhibit 15.2: Computing the FICO-Derived Arithmetically Averaged Default Rate for the Sample Portfolio

Scratch = 0

For i = 1 To Number_of_Loans

A = 0.08 * Exp(-0.15 * (FICO_Score(i) / 50 - 24))
B = (1 + Exp(-0.15 * (FICO_Score(i) / 50 - 24)))
Default_Probability(i) = A / B
Scratch = Scratch + Default_Probability(i)

Next i

Average_Default_Rate = Scratch / Number_of_Loans

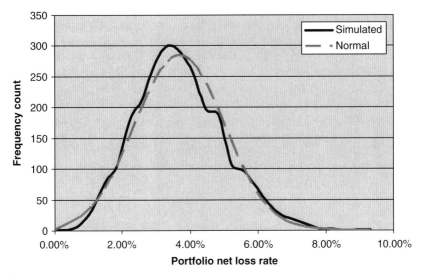

FIGURE 15.7
The FICO-derived micro-economic net loss distribution.

At the advanced level, it is not necessary to derive the net loss distribution since it will naturally drop out of the analysis. Figure 15.7 is what results from using FICO scores as in the last exercise, but this time also multiplying by loss given default.

The mean loss rate of this net loss distribution is 3.51%, in line with defaulted loan recoveries of approximately 50% (see table 15.3).

The Static Pool Expected Loss Value

So far, we have concentrated our efforts on the sample of given loans from the issuer's managed portfolio and have obtained the mean loss value using two different methods. One or the other of these methods will always be available to the analyst. We now need to finish the job and compute the expected, gross static pool loss for the target deal, i.e., the subject of the prospective securitization (figure 15.7). What we have obtained thus far is an average synthetic value representative of the managed portfolio, but which does not reflect the specific characteristics of the target pool.

Doing this is straightforward and accomplished via the asset-based average life formula. Recall that the average life t^a of an amortizing loan paying down according to its terms, with maturity T and periodic interest rate r was given by the following relationship:

$$t^a = \frac{T}{1 - (1 + r)^{-T}} - \frac{1}{\ln(1 + r)}$$

To compute a preliminary value for expected loss, first compute the target pool's average life under a no-prepayment, no-default scenario using the definitions:

$$T = WAM$$

$$r = \frac{WAC}{12}$$

Using the above 25-loan sample for the sake of argument, we have a weighted average maturity of 62.16 months and a weighted average periodic coupon of 1.39%. This was computed by dividing the weighted average APR (16.65%) by 12. Direct substitution then leads to:

$$t^a = \frac{62.16}{1 - (1.0139)^{-62.16}} - \frac{1}{\ln(1.0139)} \approx 35.47 \text{ mths} = 2.95 \text{ years}$$

In general, the normal course of prepayments and defaults will take away from this theoretical maximum. To estimate by how much, simply look at past pools from the target issuer as well as from other issuers. The latter procedure is acceptable since the default process is fairly consistent across issuers in the same market. Assessing future prepayments is an obviously difficult task, but the ratio of theoretical to actual pool average life is remarkably stable, much more so than the dynamics of either defaults or prepayments. Thus, in practice, estimating asset average life does not involve significant errors compared with those made in the remainder of the analysis.

We find that actual average lives are 10% to 15% short of their theoretical maximum. Taking the larger figure for demonstration purposes, we would estimate the average life of this asset pool t_e^a as:

$$t_e^a = 0.85(2.95) = 2.51 \text{ years}$$

Finally, using the FICO-derived one-year mean loss value computed above (6.84%), we can easily estimate the gross expected loss for this auto pool:

$$L_e = 2.51(6.84) = 17.37\%$$

Remember that the average life of a pool is defined as a hypothetical period over which assets would be theoretically outstanding at their initial balance, and this is precisely the basis for the default study undertaken above using portfolio data. Therefore, by using the one-year default history for the portfolio as a whole along with the specific parameters of the target pool, we obtain an expected loss value far more representative than what would obtain by simply using any one value from prior deals or via some other, indefensible crystal ball.

The political use of expected loss in the way rating agencies are wont to doing is a nonstarter since there is no theoretical justification for any specific value. The above procedure can be rigorously implemented in 95% of all cases, at least for issuers that can supply one year of portfolio data or more. It is difficult to imagine a case where securitization candidates would have fewer than 12 months of data to offer.

The net expected loss L_e^n is calculated similarly, i.e., using the net loss from the identical computation (3.51%):

$$L_e^n = 2.51\,(3.51) = 8.81\%$$

Normally, we use gross pool losses to perform the Markov chain micro-calibration. We fully discuss this critical procedure in chapter 16.

15.4 ESTIMATING THE MACRO-ECONOMIC LOSS
DISTRIBUTION PARAMETERS

Economically speaking, we have now come to the most important and yet, the most neglected aspect of deal analysis: macro-economics. As we have said so many times before, on the basis of micro-dynamics alone, most transactions could simply close at par completely unenhanced. This is because the central limit theorem, which effectively rules the risk universe within which micro-losses play themselves out, will indicate that the deal is highly creditworthy even without external or optical credit enhancement.

In other words, the reason why deals need additional credit enhancement beyond what is already present in the unenhanced situation is not to counter fiendish but unsuspected correlation among the assets in the pool, for in that case we could make rather convincing arguments that the assets are truly independent. Instead, enhancement is needed because pool assets are linked to a macro-economy that causes indirect correlation to exist among them. In fact, this correlation is what produces loss scenarios essentially excluded based solely on micro-dynamics. Therefore, the way to handle this phenomenon numerically is not to create artificial inter-asset correlation, as if that somehow could adequately stress the portfolio, but to explicitly introduce a suitable macro-economic index as a driver of loss behavior.

We maintain that this aspect of the analysis is *neglected* not because no one has yet come to grips with macro-economics, quite the contrary, but simply because far too little attention has been and is being paid to the creation of a nonarbitrary framework for doing so. The essential conflict here is not between right or wrong, since no one can prove a priori that something will or will not happen, but more between consistent and inconsistent analyses. As usual, rating agencies did not have to face this problem because what they decided has the status of the Oracle at Delphi among the Ancient Greeks. In effect, as things now stand the required credit enhancement in the majority of ABS transactions is implicitly decided beforehand via an arbitrary stress ratio that is neither challengeable nor, for that matter, challenged.

In the vast majority of cases, the last transaction by the same issuer provides the benchmark for the current deal. Issues of pool characteristics and their specific impact on enhancement values are neither discussed nor resolved. It is not sufficient to casually remark that the credit environment is riskier, thereby concluding that the additional risk is worth 50 bps. Maybe it is worth 45 or 75 bps, maybe nothing. Who knows? Risk analysis by decree is anathema and inconceivable in any other field and yet, in structured finance, it is the state of the art.

In our previous book (*The Analysis of Structured Securities*, OUP, 2003), we discussed in detail how to construct a nonarbitrary macro-index distribution and use it as a driver of a macro-economic analysis within a Markov transition matrix context. Consequently, our main goal here is not to rehash the politics or economics of avoiding arbitrariness, but simply to demonstrate a simple way to implement the chosen distribution in a specific case via the use of copula functions.

It is however worthwhile reiterating that the most glaring pitfall within structured analysis is the inability to achieve transparency at the macro-economic level. As we showed in the above monograph, all decisions leading to the synthesis of macro-economic distributions need to be openly debated and take place within a self-consistent framework that does not dictate credit enhancement by fiat. Contrary to popular belief, serious credit analysis in no way requires prescient knowledge of the future.

Macro-Economic Losses via the Clayton Copula

As discussed above, the principle underlying the entire macro-economic analysis is the linking of formally independent obligors to a unique and independent macro-economic index deemed a reasonable proxy for the chief credit loss driver in the asset pool under consideration. In the auto sector, unemployment and GNP (Gross National Product) growth per capita are two likely candidates for this task. Data on both indices abound on the Internet and elsewhere. Remember that the linkage to the macro-driver is accomplished separately for each obligor in the pool. This is different from an asset-wise correlation dictated by some given correlation matrix. As mentioned above, it is widely held that inter-asset correlation is not an appropriate representation of the process that describes the physics of credit losses in the field.

There is more than one way to relate nominally independent assets to an index and we do not favor any one method over any other. However, the recent popularity of the copula function approach makes it an attractive candidate for an introductory text. In a 2002 paper, Schönbucher[3] describes a straightforward implementation algorithm for the generalized copula framework based on the Laplace transform of macro-economic density functions. In structured finance, the Laplace transform formalism is a highly propitious approach, and one to which we will return in chapter 18. In this case, it provides a ready-made solution to the problem of correlating independent assets to a single macro-index. In what follows, we review just enough theory to justify our VBA implementation. Interested readers should consult Schönbucher's excellent paper for further results and consequences.

What Are Copulas?

The word "copula" means a link or a relationship, and so a copula function is a linking function, in this case the linking of the assets to the macro-index. By saying that, we have obviously not said very much since there are many ways to link things together. Philosophically, it works as follows.

Assume that by looking through your crystal ball or using publicly available data, you have been able to determine that the cumulative distribution function of the macro-economic index in question (y) is accurately described by a known functional form $F(y)$ which can be specified by a finite set of parameters and further, that it can be integrated over the semi-infinite index domain $[0, \infty)$. Next, recall the basic definition of the density function $f(y)$ of a statistical variable:

$$dF(y) = f(y)\, dy \tag{10}$$

From the definition of the Laplace transform (see chapter 18) $g(s)$ of a given function $f(y)$ we have:

$$g(s) \equiv \int_0^\infty e^{-sy} f(y)\, dy = \int_0^\infty e^{-sy}\, dF(y) \tag{11}$$

You will recall that the function $g(s)$ is an algebraic function of the transform variable s.

Next, select a group of N nominally independent uniform random variables $u_i, i \in [1, N]$ and transform them into a new set of $x_i, i \in [1, N]$ variables via the modulation:

$$x_i = g\left(-\frac{1}{y}\ln(u_i)\right) \tag{12}$$

It is claimed that the variables x_i are correlated with the macro-economic index in some specific manner while still being independent of each other. Does this make sense or is there some sort of "magic" at play here?

To see how this works and to understand the mechanics of copula correlation, simply introduce the right-hand side of equation (12) into the right-hand side of equation (11) to yield:

$$g\left(-\frac{1}{y}\ln(u)\right) = \int_0^\infty e^{-[-\frac{1}{y}\ln(u)y]} f(y)\, dy = \int_0^\infty u f(y)\, dy \tag{13}$$

The right-hand side of equation (13) demonstrates that, in effect, we are merely convoluting the original, uniformly distributed and independent variables u_i with the macro-index density function $f(y)$. In other words, the correlation process amounts to the shifting up and down of the u_i according to the behavior of $f(y)$. Since the density function integrates to unity and the independent u_i variables are uniformly distributed to begin with, this shifting process does not change the latter property and we are left with a set of variables that have been modulated, or correlated, in synchronization with the density $f(y)$.

For instance, whereas before only one of the u_i was potentially below the average default threshold, because of the downward shift there might now be two, three or more u_i that meet the default criterion and that will cause their associated exposures to default.

It works the other way too, i.e., whereby formerly two or three u_i were below the threshold and resulted in a relatively high loss rate, now the upwards shifting might prevent one or both of the exposures to default and the portfolio loss would decrease accordingly. The net result is that, in the correlated version, both high and low loss scenarios are more frequent, i.e., the distribution "spreads" out from both sides of the mean as compared to the formerly normal distribution that obtained in the independent case. Since loss rates are bounded from below by zero and from above by 100%, in other words because there is more wiggle room up than down, the upshot is that we see a net positive skew that transforms the Gaussian micro-distribution into a macro-distribution that looks very much like a gamma or a lognormal density function.

In passing, under the current model, we are excluding cases where recoveries are greater than 100%, thereby preventing net credit losses from ever being negative. Although this is probably the right thing to do in an asset class like autos, there is no theoretical reason why recoveries cannot exceed 100%. In the United States, as a matter of law most jurisdictions will prevent recoveries beyond the defaulted amount plus accrued interest. However, this does not mean that actual, economic recoveries may not exceed the amount in question. Analysts who believe that net credit losses can never be negative, and thus always use net loss distributions that begin at zero for modeling purposes, have probably never worked in a real bank.

In many countries consumer protection laws are still elusive concepts. Nothing prevents such lenders from foreclosing on collateral and keeping the entire proceeds of the sale. Even in the United States, various repossession and "processing" fees can be tacked on, effectively allowing lenders to keep whatever the collateral yields at auction. In other asset classes and jurisdictions, lenders sometimes control both ends of the deal and actually look forward to a default that enables them to enhance their nominally low, fixed return into an equity-like return when the borrower thought he was made a loan. Thus, economic credit losses are not defined over the interval [0, 1] as is commonly thought, but over the larger interval $(-\infty, 1]$. In other words, although one can only lose at most 100% of one's investment, there is no reason why net gains from default events cannot happen. The fact that negative credit losses are, practically speaking, negligible is irrelevant to this theoretical argument. As a matter of fact, they do happen. A paradigm example would be an aircraft lease portfolio transaction whereby the servicer repossessed an asset following lessee default, confiscated the latter's security deposit and then went on to immediately re-lease the airplane without missing a beat. From the deal's standpoint, the confiscated security deposit that until then had to be treated as trust funds, and thus excluded from SPV assets, would look like negative credit losses.

Implementation Using the Gamma Macro-Economic Index Density Function

As far as the copula method is concerned, so long as we can find density functions that integrate to tractable algebraic Laplace transform-functions $g(s)$, we can synthesize a series of copula functions linked to various macro-index distributions. The standard gamma density function happens to yield a particularly simple functional form for $g(s)$ that has been associated with the name of Clayton.

Specifically, we need to write down the formal definitions of the standard gamma density function and of its Laplace transform, respectively,[4] as follows:

$$f(y) = \frac{y^{\gamma-1} e^{-y}}{\Gamma(\gamma)} \tag{14}$$

$$g(s) = (1+s)^{-\gamma} \tag{15}$$

As outlined above, copula function implementation simply amounts to repeatedly cycling through equations (12) and (15) using different values of y chosen at random and independently of the uniform random numbers selected for the individual assets in the sample portfolio.

At this point, we want to discuss two issues pertaining to the standard gamma function at the heart of equation (15):

1. The parameter γ is a shape parameter for the standard gamma distribution. This means that choosing different values for γ will result in various aspect ratios for the density function. The selection of γ can obviously not be made a priori in a vacuum but, as explained in chapter 20 of "*The Analysis of Structured Securities*" (OUP, 2003), this choice must be related to the actual macro-economic data underlying the macro-analysis. This is what, in fact, gives the procedure its empirical meaning. If the data in question do not fit a gamma distribution, you are not to insist that the data are wrong, but either to find another copula that relates the uniform variables to the one that does fit or to simply abandon the copula framework altogether. Stubbornness in using a given functional form because one knows how to implement it does not amount to consistency, but to plain irresponsibility. What needs to be consistent is the approach, not the result of the approach. The good news here is that macro-economic data do not usually dictate one distribution over another very convincingly, and one can usually talk oneself into a gamma distribution in most cases without running the risk of being accused of cheating.

2. Micro- and macro-economic analyses are clearly dependent since both are descriptions of the same underlying reality. In essence, the unspoken but implicit assumption at the heart of the above micro-analysis was that the sample results we were given were somehow obtained under average macro-conditions and therefore, that the default rate computed at that time would be the one that would obtain in such average cases. Clearly, this is never empirically true, since what does it mean to experience "average" conditions? The economy never hangs out anywhere very long. The meaning of average conditions is rather what would happen if we repeated the same experiment many times under identical starting conditions, and this is never going to happen. Consequently, the macro-analysis must be forward looking and must ask about the possible range of macro-indices the deal could potentially experience over its lifetime. As outlined above, the ergodic hypothesis then takes over and allows us to make empirically derived statements about the target deal even if we recognize that this particular transaction will in reality

be exposed to various macro-economic regimes. Thus, the object of the macro-analysis is not really to gaze into empty space and come up with the "right" distribution, but rather to achieve a nonarbitrary form of self-consistency. When using any macro-distribution inside deal analysis, this realization implies that the chosen macro-distribution is required to possess a mean of unity since we are assuming, erroneously perhaps, that the micro-distribution is the average case. Because the mean of a standard gamma density function is always γ, the variable used in actual transaction analysis will need to be scaled accordingly to achieve an effective macro-index mean of unity. As we shall see later, this is because the results of the macro-analysis will be superposed on top of the micro-distribution and then inserted inside our Markov chain formalism to generate appropriately scaled credit loss scenarios that will be reflective of the macro-economic disturbances expected to be operative over the life of the pool. Once this is done, credit ratings will be seen as outputs of the analysis, as they should be, instead of the inputs they are today. In fact, the entire raison d'être of our analysis is to accomplish this epistemological reversal in a self-consistent manner.

A Live Example with the Copula Method

As an example of the Clayton copula procedure, exhibit 15.3 shows a VBA code implementation of the macro-economic modulation using the Clayton copula. Macro-index scaling of the mean index to one, as just explained, will take place at the deal level. In addition, figure 15.8 shows the resulting simulated portfolio loss distribution along with a gamma distribution fit to the simulated distribution.

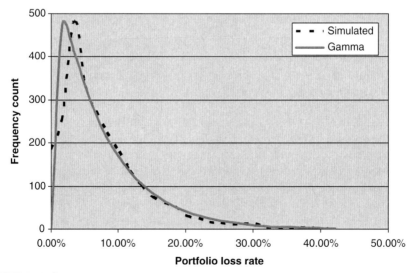

FIGURE 15.8
The macro-economic loss distribution from the Clayton copula.

A few comments are in order with respect to exhibit 15.3. First, as we indicated above, each Monte Carlo scenario is characterized by a single macro-economic index, the variable y in the code. The program generated the 100 uniform random numbers for the 100 loan assets exactly as before and thus they were still independent of each other. Finally, the shape parameter γ used here was 10, a value presumably in line either with the macro-economic data we were given or else selected from a proxy index.

Exhibit 15.3:   Simulation of the Macro-Loss Distribution Using the Clayton Copula Function

Number_of_Scenarios = 2,500

Set the shape parameter

Gamma = 10

For i = 1 To Number_of_Scenarios

Scenario_Loss(i) = 0
y = Application.GammaInv(Rnd, Gamma, 1)

For j = 1 To Number_of_Loans

Compute the correlated index using the Clayton functional form

s = -1 / y * Log(Rnd)
Index = (1 + s) ^ -Gamma
Scenario_Loss(i) = Scenario_Loss(i) - (Index <= Average_Default_Rate) *
Current_Loan_Balance(j)

Next j

Scenario_Loss(i) = Scenario_Loss(i) / Total_Portfolio_Balance

Next i

Looking at figure 15.8, the agreement between the simulated portfolio distribution and the associated best fit to a gamma distribution is not perfect, but it is quite impressive considering the generally poor quality of available data. The simulated distribution cannot be expected to fall right on top of the gamma since, as outlined above, it is somewhat constrained in its appearance by the artificial zero lower bound. In practice, it is not possible to have zero probability mass corresponding to a loss value of zero, which is what the gamma distribution entails.

As expected, within statistical error the mean of the macro-distribution (6.86%) is the same as that of the micro-distribution (6.84%) and predictably, the distribution has spread on both sides of that mean. The positive skew is very obvious and the distribution is highly "peaky." We should mention that the shape parameter of the fitted distribution is 1.07 instead of the ideal value of 1.0 that we indicated was necessary for direct insertion into a Markov transition matrix approach. However, please note that a gamma distribution with a shape parameter of 1.0 is indistinguishable from the one shown in figure 15.8. In addition, at the tail of the distribution, where credit ratings effectively live or die, the two are virtually identical. However, far be it from our intention to stop the purists among you from continuing to use a shape parameter of 1.0 instead of 1.07. In terms of credit rating and pricing, the results will be identical.

At this point, we seem to have squared the circle, having developed a macro-loss distribution out of publicly available data using the issuer's own portfolio data without invoking any magic number or any sort of traditional approach. As far as that is concerned, the above distribution is completely nonarbitrary except that someone might still argue that the selected macro-index, whatever it was, was the "wrong" one. Such arguments are silly and have no place in finance since reasonable men and women can disagree without anyone being definitely right or wrong. Rather, nonarbitrariness is what gives our analysis its fundamental strength. Otherwise, we are back to the drawing board. Replacing one credit religion with another was never our intention. Instead, getting rid of all such religions is our primary goal, one that would let the estimation process return to itself and thereby become self-consistent. Whether we have achieved our objective is for others to judge.

15.5 REVIEW OF TARGET TRANSACTION PARAMETERS

It is now necessary to review the basic parameters of the subprime auto transaction that will occupy us for the remainder of the analysis. The pool cut and other rating variables of interest for this hypothetical transaction are given in tables 15.4 (assets) and 15.5 (liabilities).

In addition, all data elements found in table 15.2 with respect to the 2,000 subprime auto-loans in the target pool were received from the issuer as a flat file. Furthermore, the structured analyst requested and received a basic Markov transition matrix assembled from the combined delinquency history of the obligors in this subprime issuer's managed portfolio. Although building this matrix may entail considerable work, we assume this has been done.

In closing, please note that this transaction is not equipped with a revolving period. A rigorous analysis of revolving structures is much more involved and lies beyond the intended scope of this text. We will have sufficient trouble as it is.

However, revolving structures are far too important to be jettisoned completely and so we devote chapter 23 to a fuller discussion of the analytical challenges that need to be met on the way to an analysis of revolving transactions. Credit card receivables-backed master trust structures and CDOs are just two examples of asset classes that simply could not exist without revolving periods. As we shall see later, it is only after one thoroughly understands amortizing structures from the ground up that similar efforts in revolving deals have any chance of being successful. Although trivial

TABLE 15.4

Asset-side parameters for the target transaction

Issuer name	Yes Financial Corp.
Original pool balance	$37,422,089.37
Closing date	10/01/2010
Revolving period end date	10/01/2010
Pool balance	$37,422,089
WAM	60.34 months
WAC	16.65%
Percent new vehicles	100%
Percent current accounts	100%
Type of vehicle present in the pool	Generic
Eligible investment rate	1%
Recovery delay	3 months
Gross expected loss	17.37%
3-Month averaged 60+ delinquency trigger breach level	15%
Write-off policy	>90 DPD
Clayton copula-based macro-economic modulation	Gamma(1.07,1)

TABLE 15.5

Liability-side parameters for the target transaction

Class A initial principal balance	$29,937,671.49
Class A rating	TBD
Class A interest rate	TBD
Class A average life	TBD
Class B initial principal balance	$7,484,417.87
Class B rating	TBD
Class B interest rate	TBD
Class B average life	TBD
Principal allocation method	Pro Rata
Spread account initial deposit (based on the initial balance)	1.5%
Spread account target (based on the current balance)	3%
Spread account floor (based on the initial balance)	0.5%
PAC IO pass-through rate	1.75%
PAC IO percentage	(see chapter 20)
PAC IO cushion (α)	(see chapter 20)
PAC IO schedule	(see chapter 20)
Residual holder	Sponsor

in theory, revolving periods nevertheless require superlative cash flow modeling skills. Unfortunately, and despite their pre-eminence in the two major asset classes just mentioned, revolving periods are currently all but ignored.

Exercise 15.2

Recall the equation for credit loss from exercise 15.1:

$$L = LEE \ X \ LGD \tag{16}$$

Assuming that some sample portfolio has a constant LEE for all exposures within it, the first two moments of the single-exposure loss density function are the expected (μ) loss and unexpected (σ) loss measures defined by:

$$\mu = E(Loss) = E(LEE \ X \ LGD) = LEE \ E(X \ LGD)$$

$$\sigma = \sqrt{E(Loss^2) - [E(Loss)]^2} = LEE \ \sqrt{E([X \ LGD]^2) - [E(X \ LGD)]^2}$$

Since equation (16) is a bilinear form under the assumption of constant LEE, a Taylor-series expansion carried out to second order will terminate. Thus, the following second-order formulas for expected and unexpected loss should yield the exact answer for all subportfolios:

$$\mu = LEE \ [\overline{X}\,\overline{LGD} + Cov(X, LGD)] \tag{17a}$$

$$\sigma = LEE \ \sqrt{\begin{array}{c} \overline{LGD}^2 \sigma_X^2 + \overline{X}^2 \sigma_{LGD}^2 + 2\left[\overline{X}\,\overline{LGD}\,Cov(X, LGD) + \overline{X} E_{12} + \overline{LGD} E_{21}\right] \\ -Cov(X, LGD)^2 + E_{22} \end{array}} \tag{17b}$$

In equations (17a) and (17b), we have defined the additional moments:

$$E_{ij} = E([X - \overline{X}]^i [LGD - \overline{LGD}]^j)$$

As a reminder, the Taylor-series expansion of a scalar function F about a point x_0 in n-dimensional vector space can be succinctly represented as follows:

$$F(x) = F(x_0) + [\nabla F]_{x_0} \bullet \Delta x + \frac{1}{2}\left[\nabla^2 F\right]_{x_0} \bullet \Delta x^2 + \frac{1}{6}\left[\nabla^3 F\right]_{x_0} \bullet \Delta x^3 + H.O.T. \tag{18}$$

In equation (18), we have defined:

$$\nabla = \sum_{i=1}^{n} \partial / \partial x_i$$

$$\Delta x = \sum_{i=1}^{n} (x_i - x_{i0})$$

$$x_0 = (x_{10}, x_{20}, \ldots, x_{n0})$$

Please derive equations (17a) and (17b) using a Taylor-series carried out to second order.

Exercise 15.3

To verify the mathematical exactness of the last two relationships, please generate a random sample portfolio of 50 independent exposures with constant *LEE* and choose the value $E(X) = \overline{X} = 0.1$. Next, show that equation (2) is indeed exact by computing the expected and unexpected losses in two ways:

1. Using the formulas derived in exercise 15.3
2. Directly from the data you have created

Do the exercise first by using a portfolio where there exists a weak correlation between default events and loss given default (*X* and *LGD*). Select recovery values such that this is the case. Then repeat the exercise with a second random sample of 50 exposures with a correlation of approximately 90% between *X* and *LGD*. You can use any method you wish to cause such correlation to exist.

In both cases, please generate *LGD* values using a uniform distribution with mean 50% and a total dispersion of +/− 5% about the mean. In order to cause a high correlation to exist between *X* and *LGD*, you will most likely have to increase the *LGD* value for default events beyond the confines of the recommended uniform distribution. This can and should be done ad hoc to achieve your 90% correlation objective. In essence, this is what it means to underestimate loan-wise correlation.

Exercise 15.4

Using a Monte Carlo simulation program written in VBA or any other computer language you choose, generate the empirical credit loss distribution of such a sample portfolio and show that its mean μ_p and standard deviation σ_p can be approximated by:

$$\mu_p = \mu$$

$$\sigma_p = \frac{\sigma}{\sqrt{50}}$$

To do this, use binomial default events *X* and uniformly distributed, weakly correlated *LGD* values. Assume the expected loss given by exercise 15.3.

Show further that this distribution is quasi-normal by plotting the theoretical normal distribution given by the central limit theorem along with the empirical distribution you obtain via Monte Carlo simulation on the same graph and showing that they virtually coincide.

As further proof of the similarity of both theoretical and empirical distributions, compute the Kolmogorov–Smirnov D-statistic, defined as the maximum absolute difference between both cumulative distribution functions and show that it is small compared to unity.

16

Markov Chains

"Il est déchaîné"
Astérix le Gaulois

In the space available, we can only engage in a superficial review of our title topic. As a result, this chapter will focus solely on applications of the theory of Markov chains and transition matrices to structured financial analysis rather than on explanations of their origin and underlying intuition. Interested readers can always refer to "*The Analysis of Structured Securities*" (OUP, 2003) for a more in-depth treatment. In addition, most operations research textbooks dedicate entire chapters to the theory and applications of Markov chains.

We feel it would be ill advised to pass over theory completely, otherwise the use of this technique would make no sense at all. We present what we deem sufficient to orient the student and use exercises as the mechanism to correct any obvious weaknesses in this abridged exposition.

16.1 THE IDEA OF A MARKOV CHAIN

The Markov chain is the most important concept in structured finance. It derives its name from the celebrated Russian topologist and algebraist of the same name, a contemporary of Tchebychev. The concept belongs to dealhood in the sense explained in chapter 14, and thus the working out of the essential relationships inherent in Markov transition matrices is but one example of going down the arc.

Our goal is to introduce this concept in relation to the analysis of structured securities and to show how it can be used to model cash flows associated with the credit dynamics of structured pools. Although it will not be necessary for you to become an expert in matrix theory to use Markov chains profitably, understanding the physics will be crucial if you are to make heads or tails out of the results. Even if you end up never writing a single line of code implementing a Markov chain, you still need to have a feel for the cash flow dynamics to which they give rise.

Stochastic Processes

With respect to a system consisting of economic agents, a stochastic process is one that can be described by a random variable x depending on some discrete or continuous parameter t often taken to represent time. In the remainder of this chapter, t will indeed be time and will be integer-valued. A time period or "time step" may be any finite amount, but in general it will represent a single month. Such periods are usually labeled Collection Periods when associated with structured transactions. Practically speaking, the number of time steps will be equal to the number of months or Collection Periods between the Closing Date and the Legal Final Maturity Date of the target transaction. Not knowing the precise Closing Date will not matter since only the difference between these two dates will be used in the analysis.

Stochastic processes in structured finance are characterized by a predefined set of states that the economic agents or obligors are allowed to occupy during a given time step, and thus the indexed variable x will refer to the arbitrary values assigned to such states. It should already be intuitively obvious that the latter will correspond to the delinquency states of the agents in the pool. Because you may define as many states as you like as long as the number remains finite, it is a good idea to use integers to designate them. Later on, they can always be mapped to what they actually mean.

In general, a stochastic process is a sequence of states and their associated properties; these properties define the process in question. However, making suitable assumptions about the process can considerably simplify the ensuing calculations as long as the assumptions have some basis in reality. The Markov property is one such assumption. Basically, it reduces what is nominally a nonlinear process to a linear one. As you can imagine from the previous chapter, this is a big help. This reduction is accomplished by eliminating the memory effect caused by the forward impact of all previous state locations occupied by variable x. Mathematically, the Markov property can be stated as follows:

The Markov Property

For an N-state stochastic process $x(t)$, $t = 0, 1, 2, \ldots, T$, $x(t) \in [1, 2, 3, \ldots, n]$ the Markov property is said to hold if the conditional probability of finding the system in a given state during the next time step depends only on its current location viz.:

$$p(x(t + \Delta t) \mid x(t), x(t - \Delta t), x(t - 2\Delta t), \ldots) = p(x(t + \Delta t) \mid x(t)) \qquad (1)$$

You can surmise that if we had to include prior states in the definition of future conditional probabilities, instead of just the current one, Markov transition matrices would all be linked via the time index and we would not be able to separate each time step from every other one. Thus, the Markov property is a convenient linearization of a general stochastic process and amounts to the physical statement that all you can know with respect to the future of a system is already contained in its current state. In stock market analysis, this belief is referred to as the "efficient market hypothesis."

The notion that memory effects are negligible in economics is plainly wrong. A stock that has been going up for 15 consecutive days does *not* have a 50% probability of going down. Otherwise, technical stock analysis would have stopped long ago. The same is true of the obligors in a static pool, i.e., knowing their delinquency history does enable us to say more than what is implied by the Markov property. However, given the current state of data availability, such detail is difficult if not impossible to either acquire or require. The point is that before you grab a logical formalism like Markov chains, you need to be aware of its limitations and of the fact that you are making an approximation you know to be deficient in some respect a priori. Should data environments improve markedly over the next few years, it would be possible to transition from this linear Markov formalism to a more fully developed stochastic process to get a better feel for the true dynamics of the pool than what is feasible in the linear context. Given the current state of the art with respect to cash flow modeling however, even this admittedly deficient process is a major step forward in analytical sophistication.

16.2 MARKOV PROCESSES IN STRUCTURED FINANCE

Henceforth, we will refer to an n-state stochastic process in which the Markov property holds as a finite-state Markov process. In this exposition, we will be concerned exclusively with finite-state Markov processes. Process states will always refer to the obligors' delinquency states. We will partition the latter into the familiar "buckets" known to most finance professionals.

Thanks to the Markov property, each time step can be conditionally related to each subsequent time step via a square-shaped arrangement of conditional probabilities forming a matrix, one matrix for each time step. The rows and columns of these matrices are the conditional probabilities of entering any state from any other. If you need to, you can always recover the absolute or *unconditional* probabilities of finding the system in any state at time t by summing the conditional probabilities of entering the target state from all other states, including itself, at time step $t - 1$. In other words, in structured finance Markov processes may be conveniently specified by square arrays of conditional time-dependent probabilities. One such array is given as equation (2).

Arrays similar to equation (2) are referred to as "transition" matrices $\mathbf{P(t)}$ for the simple reason that they express the time-dependent probabilities of transitions between states. In each conditional probability, the first index (i) represents the state of the system at time t, while the second (j) represents the state at time $t + 1$. For instance, p_{12} represents the probability of being in State 1 at time t and ending up in State 2 at time $t+1$, and so on.

$$\mathbf{P(t)} = \begin{bmatrix} p_{11} & p_{12} & p_{13} & \cdots & p_{1N} \\ p_{21} & p_{22} & & \cdots\cdots & p_{2N} \\ \cdots\cdots & & & & \\ p_{N1} & p_{N2} & \cdots\cdots & p_{NN} \end{bmatrix} \tag{2}$$

Strictly speaking, a series of consecutive states ruled by a statistical process corresponding to a sequence of transition matrices is a Markov chain.

If the entries of each **P(t)** do not depend on time, the resulting chain will be called *stationary*. Stationary chains are much easier to handle than nonstationary chains and, as we shall see shortly, possess convenient analytical properties.

Although the Markov chains we will be discussing in the rest of the Advanced Part will be nonstationary, an intuitive way of understanding how nonstationary Markov processes behave is to begin by studying stationary chains and to extend that intuition to the nonstationary case. This is because the long-term behavior of a stationary chain where all states communicate is universal, whereas each nonstationary chain has its own idiosyncratic properties. As a result, a nonstationary chain can best be understood from the vantage point of a quasistationary chain as a limiting case of the latter. Learning the behavior of stationary chains is therefore not a waste of time and provides significant insight into the underlying physics.

To set the stage for what we are going to do next, remember that the credit dynamics of structured securities will be derived via the transition dynamics of their static pools. Once the associated matrices are available, they can be used sequentially to obtain the aggregate state of the pool at successive time steps by considering all allowable transitions of the obligors remaining in the pool at any time. We use the word "remaining" since a sizable percentage of the obligors that were initially part of the pool will drop out along the way due to the phenomena of default and prepayment. As a result, it will become necessary to model these two aspects of cash flow dynamics specifically within the Markov-chain formalism. As we shall see shortly, a specific and deterministic cash flow will be associated with obligors undergoing specified delinquency transitions between two given states, including default and prepayment. Much of the work involved in using Markov chains in structured finance will consist in accurately computing such flows via an inversion process enabled by the seller's credit policy. By looping through the live obligors in the pool, we will be able to calculate aggregate pool quantities that will then become target amounts for the liability side of the SPV balance sheet.

In general, delinquency transition matrices are asset class- and issuer-specific and must be empirically derived from portfolio data appropriate to the target issuer. Any issuer with sufficient operating history to enable the synthesis of a delinquency transition matrix is thus a suitable candidate for analysis under a Markov-chain framework. Alternatively, a proxy issuer in the same sector can usually be found. If so, then with little loss of accuracy its base transition matrix can be used instead of the target issuer's. This is because Markov transition matrices tend to be remarkably invariant across issuers in the same market. What cannot be assumed identical, however, is the correspondence between delinquency transitions and cash flows. Minor adjustments, due to idiosyncratic issuer credit policies, will sometimes be needed. Although this will normally involve minor program modifications, the associated cash flow consequences may be sizable in terms of the corresponding changes in credit rating.

The States Found in Structured Finance Markov Processes

Having done so already in our first monograph (*The Analysis of Structured Securities*, OUP, 2003), it would be redundant to dwell at length on the ontology of delinquency states within structured finance Markov processes. Instead, we briefly discuss what matters in applications and try to convey the intuition behind the concepts. First, we review the two broad categories of states found in general Markov processes, and thus in structured finance as well. For ease of understanding, we restrict our attention to stationary chains.

In the remainder of this subsection, we will be referring to the following sample transition matrix:

$$\mathbf{P} = \begin{bmatrix} .2 & .6 & .2 \\ .7 & .1 & .2 \\ 0 & 0 & 1 \end{bmatrix} \tag{3}$$

(a) Recurrent States

Consider the transition matrix shown as equation (3), indicative of some three-state, stationary Markov process. Accordingly, there is a 20% probability that an obligor subject to this statistical process and assumed to be currently in State 1 will remain in that state during the next time step, while the probability that the obligor will move to State 2 is 60%.

On the other hand, if the obligor is now in State 2, there is a 70% probability that he will move back to State 1 and a 10% probability he will remain in State 2. Thus, an obligor in State 1 can leave and re-enter that state according to the transition probabilities given in matrix $\mathbf{P}$. In other words, even when the obligor leaves States 1 or 2, it is possible to come back to that State in subsequent time steps. States that have this property are called *recurrent* because they can thus recur.

In connection with the idea of a recurrent state, if it is possible for an obligor to eventually enter State i from State j and vice versa, States i and j will be said to *communicate*. Please remember that the fact that States i and j communicate does not imply $p_{ij} \neq 0$ and $p_{ji} \neq 0$ simultaneously in $\mathbf{P}$. This is because there is no requirement for the communication between two states to happen in a single step. In other words, as long as there is a path from i to j, which path may take several time steps to play out, the states will communicate. Most structured finance Markov processes will exhibit such patterns.

(b) Absorbing States

Now, consider State 3 in equation (3). Note first that $p_{33} = 1$ and that $p_{3j} = 0, j \neq 3$. Consequently, once the obligor enters State 3 it can never leave; it has been "absorbed" by that state. For this reason, we refer to such states as *absorbing*. In structured finance, we will encounter two absorbing states: prepayment and default.

When an obligor prepays a loan or defaults on it, it is deemed to exit the recurrent part of the process and is no longer regarded as meandering through delinquency space. Therefore, it is considered effectively out of the process. In the case of defaults, the obligor is obviously still "live" in the sense that we need to assess recoveries after foreclosure has taken place (see chapter 17). However, the obligor has essentially left the pool.

16.3 MANIPULATING TRANSITION MATRICES

In this section, the term *system* will refer either individually or collectively to the obligors in a structured pool and we will not distinguish between systems consisting of discrete or continuous obligors. A continuous obligor can clearly not "exist" in the same way a discrete obligor can, but the mechanics of implementation are the same.

Even though we are dealing with a pool of discrete obligors in our automobile transaction, it will be wise to learn how to tackle continuous pools of obligors since credit card master trusts, for example, can be realistically handled only by using Markov chains in a continuum framework.

Recall that a nonstationary Markov process can be specified via a sequence of time-dependent, n-dimensional transition matrices $\mathbf{P(t)}$ each one of whose entries $p_{ij}(t)$ represent the conditional probability with which an obligor in the system, being in State i at time t, will find itself in State j at time $t+1$. Since any obligor must be found at all times in one of its n states, absorbing or not, it follows that the $p_{ij}(t)$ along each row of a Markov transition matrix must sum to unity. This requirement is referred to as the *row sum condition* and turns out to be the main feature of Markov transition matrices:

$$\sum_j p_{ij}(t) = 1, \ \forall i, t \tag{4}$$

Unconditional Probabilities

The main application of the unconditional probability concept is the computation of pool aggregate delinquencies. In other words, as the process unfolds timewise, many obligors drift into given delinquent states from other states in the systems, including remaining in the same state. To compute the total inventory in a target state, we need to sum the contributions to its inventory made by all other states. When weighted by individual account balances, this sum now becomes the delinquent balance in that state within the pool.

To make this clearer, assume the unconditional probability vector in the target pool is defined as $\mathbf{d}(t+1)$, where $\mathbf{d}(t+1)$ is a n-dimensional vector. Its elements $d_i(t+1)$ are the absolute probabilities of finding the system in State i at time $t+1$ regardless of its state at time t (see equation (5)). Of course, the probability vector $\mathbf{d}(t+1)$ is also subject to the row sum condition.

$$\mathbf{d}(t+1) = [d_1(t+1), \ d_2(t+1), \ ....., \ d_n(t+1)] \tag{5}$$

The elements $d_i(t+1)$ can be computed by summing the probabilities of moving to State i from all other states at time t, including State i. For instance, consider some arbitrary four-state Markov process. To find the unconditional probability of finding the system (obligor) in State 1 at time $t+1$, we simply sum all contributions from all other states at time step t, including the probability of remaining in State 1 if that is where the system (obligor) was at time step t, leading to:

$$d_1(t+1) = d_1(t)p_{11}(t) + d_2(t)p_{21}(t) + d_3(t)p_{31}(t) + d_4(t)p_{41}(t) \tag{6}$$

Since vectors are defined as column vectors, we indicate transposed vectors or matrices with a superscript '**T**'. Equation (6) can now be written compactly using matrix notation:

$$\mathbf{d}^{\mathsf{T}}(t+1) = \mathbf{d}^{\mathsf{T}}(t)\mathbf{P}(t) \tag{7}$$

This process can clearly be carried out recursively. For example, starting from time $t = 0$ we have:

$$\mathbf{d}^{\mathsf{T}}(1) = \mathbf{d}^{\mathsf{T}}(0)\mathbf{P}(0)$$
$$\mathbf{d}^{\mathsf{T}}(2) = \mathbf{d}^{\mathsf{T}}(1)\mathbf{P}(1) = \mathbf{d}^{\mathsf{T}}(0)\mathbf{P}(1)\mathbf{P}(0) \tag{8}$$

In general, for n time steps, we will have:

$$\mathbf{d}^{\mathsf{T}}(n) = \mathbf{d}^{\mathsf{T}}(n-1)\mathbf{P}(n-1) = \mathbf{d}^{\mathsf{T}}(0)\mathbf{P}(n-1)\dots\mathbf{P}(2)\mathbf{P}(1)\mathbf{P}(0) \tag{9}$$

Once the initial vector $\mathbf{d}^{\mathsf{T}}(0)$ and the sequence of transition matrices $\mathbf{P(t)}$ are known, equation (9) can be used to derive the evolution of the pool from the Closing Date to the Legal Final Maturity Date and to specify the state occupied by each obligor in the pool. Since the initial inventory vector $[\mathbf{d}^{\mathsf{T}}(0)]$ is usually known from pool data, the derivation of matrices $\mathbf{P(t)}$ is the heart of the analysis of auto-loan-backed structured securities.

Continuous versus *Discrete Chains*

The treatment of discrete chains is similar to that of continuous ones. What we have just gone through applies, strictly speaking, to continuous chains. Therefore, it is useful to make a few comments about discrete implementations, if only to motivate our treatment of the target deal.

The difference between discrete and continuous Markov processes is that individual units or obligors are deemed to exist in the former but not in the latter. Consequently, to implement equation (9) within a discrete framework, we cannot simply multiply matrices by vectors but need to worry about obligor-wise statistics by generating one random number for each obligor in the pool at each time step. If the number of obligors is large enough, the results will be statistically identical to those obtained from a continuous process using the same pool.

In a discrete chain, instead of multiplying a vector of length n by a matrix of shape $n \times n$, thereby obtaining another vector of length n, we need to:

1. Identify the delinquency state of each obligor at each time step t.
2. Generate a single uniform random number α for that obligor

3. Use α to dictate the location of the obligor at time step $t + 1$ via the sequence of conditional probabilities associated with the obligor's delinquency state at time t.

In other words, in the discrete implementation the appropriate rows of Markov transition matrices are transformed into probability distribution functions that statistically determine the delinquency states of the obligors in the pool. This is because, under the discrete regime, we cannot split an account into infinitesimal pieces, the way we implicitly do under a continuous framework, and spread it across all delinquency states in the manner dictated by the current transition matrix.

As a result, cash flows under the discrete framework are associated with individual obligors, whereas under the continuous approximation, they effectively belong to infinitesimal obligors without physical meaning. In a discrete world, an obligor is either delinquent or not.

Last but definitely not least, what does it mean for the number of obligors to be large enough? In general, 1,500 obligors (please don't quote us!) is the magic number at which the pool's statistics start to coalesce. Does this mean that you cannot use Markov chains if the number of obligors in the pool is less than 1,500? No, it does not. However, the variance of the results will increase and with it, the credit enhancement required at given rating levels. This is a good thing since we usually believe that smaller pools are less diversified and riskier. The good news is that this general intuition naturally confirms itself from a strict application of the Markov formalism.

16.4 PROPERTIES OF STATIONARY MARKOV CHAINS

Interesting analytical results can be derived if we assume that the p_{ij} do not depend on time, which is the stationary case. In that case, defining $\mathbf{P}$ as the now unique transition matrix, equation (9) reduces to:

$$\mathbf{d}^{\mathsf{T}}(n) = \mathbf{d}^{\mathsf{T}}(0)\mathbf{P}^n \tag{10}$$

Matrix $\mathbf{P}^n$ is referred to as the n-time step or n-step transition matrix of the process. Physically, p_{ij}^n represent the conditional probability with which the system, being in State i at time 0, will be found in State j at time n.

For the sake of simplicity, let us further assume that our Markov process does not contain absorbing states and that all states communicate. Equation (11) is a typical example of this type of process:

$$\mathbf{P} = \begin{bmatrix} .2 & .6 & .2 \\ .7 & .1 & .2 \\ .5 & .3 & .2 \end{bmatrix} \tag{11}$$

As explained in "The Analysis of Structured Securities" (OUP, 2003), such matrices have characteristic vectors, called eigenvectors, to which are associated characteristic stretching factors called eigenvalues. In the case of matrices like equation (11) and in fact, in that of all transition matrices of this type, the following two facts can be verified concerning its eigenvalues:

1. At least one has unit norm
2. The norm of the others is less than or equal to 1

These two properties are due to the row sum condition, equation (4). It should be mentioned that verifying conditions 1 and 2 is far from trivial, but whether you do or not will have no influence whatever on your career as a structured analyst. Right here and now, just take our word that both of them hold.

Please keep in mind that the fact that *at least* one of the eigenvalues of transition matrices is equal to one does not imply that it has *only* one. What does it mean for a Markov transition matrix to have more than one unit eigenvalue? Briefly, if a transition matrix contains absorbing states, it will have as many unit eigenvalues as there are absorbing states. For instance, the matrix in equation (3) has one unit eigenvalue since the last row indicates that the eigenvalue associated with that state is 1 by definition.

What is the point of bringing up eigenvalues and eigenvectors? The point is that if there is only one eigenvalue with unit norm in the system, iteration in the way of equation (9) will result in the convergence of the unconditional vector $d_i(t+1)$ to the eigenvector associated with this unit eigenvalue. In other words, the eigenvector associated with the unit eigenvalue is a *fixed point* of the iterative process.

To see this mathematically, consider the first few iterates of equation (11) with itself. They are given here with superscripts showing how many times the matrix was iterated with itself:

$$\mathbf{P}^2 = \begin{bmatrix} 0.560 & 0.240 & 0.200 \\ 0.310 & 0.490 & 0.200 \\ 0.410 & 0.390 & 0.200 \end{bmatrix}$$

$$\mathbf{P}^4 = \begin{bmatrix} 0.470 & 0.330 & 0.200 \\ 0.408 & 0.393 & 0.200 \\ 0.433 & 0.368 & 0.200 \end{bmatrix}$$

$$\mathbf{P}^6 = \begin{bmatrix} 0.448 & 0.353 & 0.200 \\ 0.432 & 0.368 & 0.200 \\ 0.438 & 0.362 & 0.200 \end{bmatrix}$$

$$\mathbf{P}^{10} = \begin{bmatrix} 0.440 & 0.359 & 0.200 \\ 0.439 & 0.360 & 0.200 \\ 0.439 & 0.360 & 0.200 \end{bmatrix}$$

As you can see, as $n \to \infty$ the above sequence seems to converge to a limit whereby all the rows of $\mathbf{P}^n$ become virtually identical. Let's call this limiting matrix $\mathbf{P}^\infty$ and label the condition of its attainment *equilibrium*.

According to equation (10), we also have:

$$\mathbf{d}^T(n) = \mathbf{d}^T(0)\mathbf{P}^n \qquad (12)$$

In the limit of $n \to \infty$, we can now write $\mathbf{d}^T(\infty) = \mathbf{d}^T(0)\mathbf{P}^\infty$.

Since the row-elements of limiting matrix $\mathbf{P}^\infty$ are identical, we conclude from the rules of matrix multiplication that, regardless of the initial distribution $\mathbf{d}^T(0)$, $\mathbf{d}^T(\infty)$ will converge to the repeated row of matrix $\mathbf{P}^\infty$. In other words for *any* initial vector $\mathbf{d}(0)$, we will always converge to the unconditional state probability distribution given by the repeated row of $\mathbf{P}^\infty$. You have probably guessed already that this limiting row vector is none other than the eigenvector associated with the unit eigenvalue.

In other words, when a stationary transition matrix of communicating states is iterated a sufficient number of times, it reaches a condition whereby unconditional state probabilities will not change. Further, we shall soon discover that this peculiar equilibrium, far from being static, will in fact be dynamic. Under these conditions, we say we have an *ergodic* set. In fact, this is just an example of the type of process satisfying the so-called ergodic hypothesis discussed earlier (see chapter 14). Somehow, the ergodic hypothesis lies at the heart of structured finance.

If, by some amazing coincidence, we start iterating with the condition $\mathbf{d}(0) = \mathbf{d}(\infty)$ exactly, in some sense we would already be at the limiting equilibrium point and we might expect that the Markov process would have no influence whatsoever on the future of this system. In other words, we might expect that iterating this fortuitous Markov process would simply leave the vector $\mathbf{d}(t+1)$ invariant for all time steps and not merely in the limit $n \to \infty$. In short, we would expect $\mathbf{d}^T(\infty) = \mathbf{d}^T(\infty)\mathbf{P}$ to hold as a special case. And in fact, this is what happens.

Some of you might be wondering where this limiting behavior comes from mathematically. Although we don't time to go into details here, you may recall from "*The Analysis of Structured Securities*" (OUP 2003) how multiplying a matrix by itself amounts to nothing more than letting its eigenvalues "compete" with one another in some sort of Darwinian contest where the fittest, i.e., the largest eigenvalue eventually overwhelms the others in an asymptotic sense. Since matrix (11) possesses only one eigenvalue with unit norm while all others have subunit norms, what happens is that repeated iteration forces the asymptotic extinction of all subunit eigenvectors. As you will know, multiplying a real number smaller than 1 in absolute value by itself results in something smaller than the first number. Thus, the unit eigenvector basically overwhelms the others in the limit, with the result that we end up with the unit-norm eigenvector being the dominant influence on the limiting matrix. Effectively, it is the only one you "see."

If there is more than one unit eigenvalue, for example because of an absorbing state, the same mathematical intuition should tell you that this equilibrium process could not take place. For in that case, two or more unit eigenvalues are competing for ultimate survival, and there is no reason why any particular one should win this battle. Furthermore, since the absorbing state is not letting anyone escape, in the limit the entire probability mass will end up in that state because any other state losing probability to the absorbing state can never recover it from the latter. Through the luck of the draw, eventually everybody will end up being absorbed. In other words, an absorbing state in the fourth row of a four-state stationary chain would produce a limiting unconditional distribution vector given by $\mathbf{d}(\infty) = [0, 0, 0, 1]$ regardless of the initial vector $\mathbf{d}(0)$.

In the case of structured finance Markov processes, this implies that if nothing happens, all obligors in a pool will eventually default or prepay. You will soon realize that this is actually a very good assumption, at least if you regard default as something akin to death. Does not everybody eventually die? In most cases however, something else will happen, and that something we call maturity.

In other words, within static pools default and prepayment states are competing for attention in just the same way, and would eventually absorb all the obligors who did not mature beforehand. As a seasoned structured analyst, it is this differential process of elimination that needs to become second nature to you.

Exercise 16.1

In order to solidify your understanding of the mechanics of implementation with respect to Markov chains in a continuous framework, let us pause to practice a little. The following exercise will require you to write a VBA program. It is designed to give you an intuitive feel for the attainment of equilibrium conditions.

Although this book will only make use of the discrete mode, for obvious reasons entities like credit card master trusts will necessitate the continuous framework. Therefore, a seasoned structured analyst should be proficient in both.

Consider the five-dimensional one-step Markov transition matrix P in table 16.1, one not too distant from what you might encounter in actual structured transactions.

TABLE 16.1
A typical Markov transition matrix

STEP $t-1$ TO t	Average Markov transition matrix $\equiv P$				
	1	2	3	4	5
1	0.98	0.02	0.00	0.00	0.00
2	0.10	0.80	0.10	0.00	0.00
3	0.05	0.10	0.75	0.10	0.00
4	0.01	0.05	0.10	0.64	0.20
5	0.00	0.00	0.05	0.10	0.85

Your task is to use the continuous Markov framework to iterate the matrix until equilibrium is attained using a VBA program specially written for this purpose. At each time step, you are to compute the unconditional obligor distribution for the resulting system. Use the assumption $d_0^T = [1, 0, 0, 0, 0]$ as your initial unconditional distribution and equation (7) to compute subsequent unconditional distributions.

Exercise 16.2

Repeat exercise 16.1, but this time using the discrete framework. This means that you will be starting with a large discrete loan sample (10,000 or more) initially and will reach equilibrium by computing the position of each loan within the state space using the inverse distribution function method (IDFM) reviewed in chapter 18. To generate the necessary uniform random deviates, you may use either the van der Corput method from "Generating Random Numbers from Statistical Distributions" in chapter 18 or the "Rnd" function in Microsoft Excel.

Please note that, although both equilibria are identical, the second, discrete case shows clearly how the macro-equilibrium still implies a rich micro-dynamics of individual loans.

Exercise 16.3

Verify as shown earlier (equation (11) and the following explanatory paragraphs) that the limiting vector obtained in the last two exercises is indeed the unit eigenvector of its associated Markov transition matrix.

16.5 THE PHYSICS OF MARKOV CHAINS

Recall from the last section how the mathematics of Markov chains flowed naturally and directly from the underlying physics. As a result, it is instructive to delve into the latter a little deeper. As we mentioned before, the way to internalize Markov chains is not so much via a string of analytical derivations or esoteric discussions on eigenvectors and their convergence properties, but rather through the physical intuition underlying them. In fact, this is how Markov himself originally conceived of their existence.

The physicist Erwin Schrödinger used to say that you really understand an equation only when you know its solution before solving it. What this means is that you first need an intuitive, nonempirical feel for the subject matter if the logic is to make sense to you. As highlighted back in chapter 14, the mathematics involved in structured finance are trivial once you grasp the truth of the deal. If you do not, merely knowing the mathematics is liable to make you extremely dangerous. Once the physics of Markov chains are properly understood, their mathematical properties become self-evident and can be known a priori. Consequently, we would like to spend some time discussing the road to equilibrium in physical, intuitive terms.

What Is a Markov Chain?

Assume that, instead of a singular system wandering in probability space, our stationary Markov process consists of N individual obligors. Assume further that all of them are initially located in State 1 and that all states communicate. If you want to draw a mental picture of this arrangement, just imagine that these are delinquency states of a group of accounts within a static pool.

Given the foregoing assumptions, the account-wise probability density function is asymptotically equivalent to the population distribution of the obligors in the various states. "Asymptotically" means that if N is large enough, for all practical purposes you cannot distinguish between the two.

Imagine now that there are too many obligors in a given state, where "too many" is to be measured by the difference between the current state population and its equilibrium value. Through the mechanism corresponding to equation (6), such excess capacity in State 1 will cause proportionally more obligors to leave the given state than re-enter it from other communicating states. Conversely, if there were too few agents in the same state, the opposite would apply and proportionally more would enter than leave it.

To see this, simply note that the number of obligors leaving State i for State j at time t is $N\,d_i(t)\,p_{ij}$ and that only the equilibrium distribution $\mathbf{d}(\infty)$ leaves state populations unchanged. As the process marches forward in time, over-populated states will thus be net losers while under-populated states will be net winners. This multi-lateral exchange will continue indefinitely, but there will come a time when an exact dynamic balance will exist between the obligors leaving and entering a state. It is this dynamic balance we call equilibrium. Therefore, although the system's equilibrium macro-structure will remain invariant, its microstructure will be constantly changing. By this, we mean that although the net rate of change of any state population will be zero at equilibrium, individual obligors will be constantly moving in and out of that state.

The Physical Meaning of the Ergodic Hypothesis

Of course, underneath all this, what remains unsaid is that nothing prevents any obligor from entering any state. In other words, all obligors are deemed equivalent from the point of view of their ability to undergo a state transition. If that were not the case, the equilibrium we are talking about would never happen. The assumption that obligors are subject to this absence of differentiation, i.e., that with respect to state transitions all of them are equivalent, is the fundamental meaning of the ergodic hypothesis. In fact, this quite innocuous-looking assumption stands behind all of statistical physics.

What you need to remember is that this is a physical, not a mathematical assumption in the ordinary sense of that word. Although there is no reason why physics of this type should prevail, it *sounds* reasonable. To be sure, we know perfectly well that each obligor represents a living, breathing human being with a name, a job, most likely a family, and specific dreams and aspirations, but we have chosen to ignore all that and regard him or her as just an amorphous blob equipped with a given state transition probability. Beyond that, we pretend to know nothing else about him or her, for if we did, making the ergodic hypothesis would never be justified.

Is any of us really just a number? We have stopped the game of analysis at this level, and beyond that, nothing. On the other hand, even if we have forgotten that we are playing a game, we cannot forget the forgetting. If additional information were to become available on each obligor, we would have no choice but to include that knowledge in the game and our model would thereby improve. It is in this way that each obligor is termed *atomic*. Therefore, the ergodic hypothesis is only a first stage of approximation for a pool of obligors in the face of very little information.

Typical Examples

We can put this physical understanding to the test by predicting what will happen if we relax any of our previous assumptions. For example, what would be the result of letting one of the states be absorbing? According to the definition of a recurrent state provided earlier, that state will no longer communicate with the others as it will be impossible for any obligor to leave once it wandered into it. As a result, we can immediately surmise that this Markov chain can only reach a special type of equilibrium, one in which all obligors eventually end up in the absorbing state.

For example, assume we modify the matrix $\mathbf{P}$ from equation (11) and make State 3 absorbing:

$$\mathbf{P} = \begin{bmatrix} .2 & .6 & .2 \\ .7 & .1 & .2 \\ 0 & 0 & 1 \end{bmatrix} \tag{13}$$

Our physical intuition leads us to expect that the entire probability measure would eventually be allocated to State 3 and that, therefore $\mathbf{d}(\infty) = [0\ 0\ 1]$ must obtain. Does it? Let's see!

Iteration of equation (13) yields:

$$\mathbf{P}^2 = \begin{bmatrix} 0.460 & 0.180 & 0.360 \\ 0.210 & 0.430 & 0.360 \\ 0.000 & 0.000 & 1.000 \end{bmatrix}$$

$$\mathbf{P}^4 = \begin{bmatrix} 0.249 & 0.160 & 0.590 \\ 0.187 & 0.223 & 0.590 \\ 0.000 & 0.000 & 1.000 \end{bmatrix}$$

$$\mathbf{P}^8 = \begin{bmatrix} 0.092 & 0.076 & 0.832 \\ 0.088 & 0.080 & 0.832 \\ 0.000 & 0.000 & 1.000 \end{bmatrix}$$

$$\mathbf{P}^{12} = \begin{bmatrix} 0.037 & 0.032 & 0.931 \\ 0.037 & 0.032 & 0.931 \\ 0.000 & 0.000 & 1.000 \end{bmatrix}$$

And finally:

$$\mathbf{P}^{35} = \begin{bmatrix} 0.000 & 0.000 & 1.000 \\ 0.000 & 0.000 & 1.000 \\ 0.000 & 0.000 & 1.000 \end{bmatrix}$$

Note that it took 35 time steps for equation (13) to reach this pseudo-equilibrium instead of approximately 15 time steps for the almost identical chain in equation (11) without an absorbing state. Note also that [0 0 1] is now the ruling unit-eigenvector of **P**.

As you can see, the rate at which Markov processes reach their equilibrium distribution varies according to the entries of **P**. If the entire population is to end up in the absorbing state, the rate at which obligors communicate with the latter from other states and the initial distribution of state populations are obvious factors in determining the equilibrium timescale.

Now, assume for argument's sake that we have two absorbing states. What happens then? Physically, if not mathematically, the answer is clear. This situation corresponds to a competition between the transitions into one versus the other of the absorbing states, a process made slightly more complicated by the initial distribution. If the rate of entry into the first absorbing state is large compared to that into the second, we should expect that in the limit, most of the probability measure would end up in the former, and vice versa. In that case, there would be two ruling eigenvectors instead of one, and no convergent equilibrium process could take place. To see how this works, say our matrix is now:

$$\mathbf{P} = \begin{bmatrix} 1 & 0 & 0 \\ .7 & .1 & .2 \\ 0 & 0 & 1 \end{bmatrix} \tag{14}$$

Upon iteration of equation (14), we obtain:

$$\mathbf{P}^2 = \begin{bmatrix} 1 & 0 & 0 \\ .77 & .01 & .22 \\ 0 & 0 & 1 \end{bmatrix}$$

$$\mathbf{P}^\infty = \begin{bmatrix} 1 & 0 & 0 \\ .7780 & 0 & .222 \\ 0 & 0 & 1 \end{bmatrix}$$

Here, depending on the initial vector $\mathbf{d}(0)$, we end up with a different $\mathbf{d}(\infty)$ each time contrary to the previous cases where $\mathbf{d}(\infty)$ did not depend on $\mathbf{d}(0)$. This case is important for the following reason:

In addition to the nonstationary nature of their transition matrices, structured finance Markov processes are further complicated by the presence of two absorbing states: prepayment and default. In the limit, the accounts initially in the pool would all either prepay or default in proportions depending on their relative prepayment and default rates. In the case of discrete agents or obligors, this situation will be prevented by causing them to exit the chain upon full repayment of their principal balance, while in the case of continuous Markov processes, the chain would likewise be truncated at the Legal Final Maturity Date, i.e., the final time step. Nevertheless, such complications unleash the full spectrum of Markov chain behavior. Therefore, it will generally not be possible to derive simple analytical formulas for Markov processes in structured finance. If meaningful results are ever to be attained, they will have to be obtained via numerical analysis. However, even assuming the existence of powerful computers, structured credit analysts are unlikely to make significant progress unless they develop an intuitive understanding of the relevant physics.

16.6 CONSERVATION LAWS

Although we did not dwell much on this point, many of the mathematical properties of Markov transition matrices stem from a regularity condition we called the row sum condition. We restate it here merely for convenience:

$$\sum_j p_{ij}(t) = 1, \; \forall i, t \tag{15}$$

Equation (15) expresses the fact that in any Markov process, total probability measure is conserved since we need to account for the obligor's location somewhere among the states defined by the matrix ruling the process. Fields within which conservation laws hold are called *conservative*. Consequently, using Markov processes in structured finance only makes sense when the associated physical field is also conservative.

As explained earlier, the states of a structured finance Markov process are the delinquency states of the obligor. Therefore, to use such processes, we need a conservative field in delinquency space. The only reasonable candidate for this is the number of obligors. By this, we mean that at all times, and contrary to mere cash, the total number of obligors in the system is always conserved. Dollars themselves are not subject to a conservation law in delinquency space due to physical phenomena like interest and fees. For this reason, it is impossible to measure pool cash flows accurately by looking at dollar transitions. For instance, because accrued interest is equivalent to a source of cash, a dollar transition between two states fails to account for it. By contrast, regardless of whether an obligor is current, delinquent, prepaid, or defaulted, the total number of obligors is invariant throughout the life of a structured transaction.

Obviously, a cash flow model can obviously not rely solely on obligor transitions. As a result, dollar balances and cash flows need to be computed from corresponding obligor transitions. The central idea for doing so is the use of an inverted paradigm. Whereas in reality, obligor delinquency states are derived from obligor remittances, simulated structured finance processes need to invert this logic by first determining delinquency states from issuer-specific transition matrices. Associated cash flows can then be computed from issuer-specific transfer functions linking obligor transitions to deterministic cash flows. By deterministic, we mean that a specific cash flow will be associated with each feasible obligor transition within the issuer's Markov process. Rather than a liability of our analytical framework, this feature will turn out to be one of its greatest assets. Cash flow transfer functions can be derived from issuer credit-policy manuals, assuming such exist in the first place. If a target issuer does not have a credit-policy manual, you should seriously reconsider doing the deal.

16.7 COMPUTING MARKOV TRANSITION MATRICES

Before deriving a typical cash flow transfer function, let's review how to get your hands on a basic Markov transition matrix. There are many ways to extract transition matrices from issuer data, and three of them were reviewed in our first monograph (*The Analysis of Structured Securities*, OUP, 2003). Although we skip most complications associated with synthesizing transition matrices and assume that the best situation obtains, in most situations you will be pleasantly surprised to find out that you can use the technique described below.

The first thing you must remember is that the Markov transition matrix you are looking for will be modulated inside your computer program, in the sense that each time step will give rise to a transition matrix valid for one step only. However, if you are dreading some nightmarish scenario whereby each matrix entry is modified at each step, you can relax, for the modulation process is straightforward. What is not as easy is the derivation of an average transition matrix you can then modulate. To do this, you need issuer data.

The basic idea is to select the most recent 12 months of obligor transitions revealed by portfolio data and to compute the average matrix that way. You can do this as follows. In most cases, prospective issuers will have sufficient operating history to derive a valid transition matrix. How much operating history is sufficient? Eighteen months is usually enough but in such minimalist cases, some adjustments will be required to take into account the portfolio's ramp-up phase.

First, ask the issuer for the delinquency status history of its entire portfolio over the last 13 months in the form of a flat file. The names or addresses of the obligors are irrelevant data elements, so there is no need to ask for information that might be regarded as sensitive business knowledge. What you will receive will look like table 16.2 (here the letter **M** means month).

In table 16.2, a status ($\equiv$ S) of 0 represents a current account, 1 means an account delinquent between 5 and 30 days, 2 between 31 and 60 days, 3 between 61 and

TABLE 16.2
Issuer data extract

ID	M1	M2	M3	M4	M5	M6	M7	...	M13
1	0	0	0	P	P	P	P	...	P
2	0	1	0	0	0	1	1	...	2
3	1	1	2	2	1	2	1	...	1
4	0	1	1	2	3	D	D	...	D
...	...	...	...	...	...	...	...	...	...

TABLE 16.3

Sample average Markov transition matrix

i/j	0	1	2	3	D	P
0	P_{00}	P_{01}	0	0	B	SMM
1	P_{10}	P_{11}	P_{12}	0	0	0
2	P_{20}	P_{21}	P_{22}	P_{23}	0	0
3	P_{30}	P_{31}	P_{32}	P_{33}	D	0
D	0	0	0	0	1	0
P	0	0	0	0	0	1

90 days, D a defaulted account (assuming that this particular issuer has a 91-dpd write-off policy) and P a prepaid account.

To begin with, your one-step base Markov transition matrix should be organized as in table 16.3.

The next task is to fill in the entries of the transition matrix in table 16.3. We proceed in a three-step fashion for each entry:

1. Count the number of accounts with S = 0 during **M1**, and add to this the corresponding figure during **M2**. Keep adding until **M12** and call the total α.
2. Out of accounts with S = 0 at **M1**, find the number that still have S = 0 at **M2**. Add the corresponding figure for **M3**. This means, from accounts with S = 0 at **M2**, find the number that still have S = 0 at **M3**. Keep doing this until **M13**. Call the total β.
3. $P_{00} = \alpha/\beta$.

To compute P_{01}, simply repeat steps 2 and 3, but this time counting the accounts with S = 1 at **M2**, etc. Other entries are computed analogously. Normally, numbers less than one basis point are set to zero, at least at this level of approximation.

Table 16.4 shows the result of applying this procedure to 13 months of portfolio data obtained from the issuer in the target transaction. As expected, the majority of the accounts remain current between any two given time steps. By contrast, obligors that reach the 90-day delinquency bucket have a 30% probability of defaulting the following month. The single month mortality SMM is 50 bps and the bankruptcy rate B is 10 bps. The remaining matrix entries are self-explanatory. The results shown in later chapters were computed using the transition matrix in table 16.4

Comments on Transition Matrices

1. Defaults and prepayments are two absorbing states. When an obligor enters either one of them, it effectively exits the pure delinquency process and ceases to generate cash flow per se, except that defaulted accounts give rise to one more cash flow upon collateral liquidation and recovery. However, the source of this cash is unrelated to the terms of the original loan. Please note that since

TABLE 16.4
Transition matrix from portfolio data on the target transaction

i/j	0	1	2	3	D	P
0	98.4%	1.0%	0.0%	0.0%	0.1%	0.5%
1	5.0%	80.0%	15.0%	0.0%	0.0%	0.0%
2	5.0%	10.0%	75.0%	10.0%	0.0%	0.0%
3	0.0%	0.0%	10.0%	60.0%	30.0%	0.0%
D	0.0%	0.0%	0.0%	0.0%	100.0%	0.0%
P	0.0%	0.0%	0.0%	0.0%	0.0%	100.0%

recoveries are an important source of credit enhancement in most automobile transactions, we devote chapter 17 to their detailed modeling.

2. Subscript i refers to the prior month's delinquency state, while subscript j refers to the current month's status. Consequently, P_{ij} is the probability that an account in state i at the prior month will move into state j this month

3. It should be obvious why matrix entries more than one column away to the right of the diagonal must all be zero within the pure delinquency framework. This is basic physics, for how can an account increase its delinquency status by more than one month in a single month? In practice though, you will find pathologies within large organizations, especially in the credit card area, whereby an account will apparently jump from current to three months delinquent within a single month. This nonanalytical behavior usually stems from a dispute with respect to a specific charge that was resolved in favor of the issuer. However, such cases will be relatively few and far between and should be ignored.

4. The letter B in table 16.3 identifies the bankruptcy rate. This is done by counting the accounts that were written off directly from $S = 0$ at prior month. In automobile transactions, this may be relatively rare and, absent any data to back it up, you can usually set that number to zero with little loss of accuracy. On the other hand, bankruptcies are common in the credit card area. In theory, although an obligor may go bankrupt from any delinquency state, under this simplified framework we ignore noncurrent accounts that do so.

5. The expression *SMM* stands for "single month mortality," a term that goes back to mortgage-backed securities (MBS) lore. Although the usual MBS-linked formula is dollar-based, here we define it as the monthly, account-wise prepayment rate. For example, account no. 1 in table 16.2 would contribute one data point (between **M3** and **M4)** to the *SMM* computation. Note that we are implicitly assuming that no obligor can prepay his or her loan from any delinquency state except the current state. Even if this is not quite accurate, it is a fairly benign assumption. The logic is that few people can prepay, i.e., refinance their loan, when they are delinquent on their existing loan because prospective lenders will usually verify credit bureau records before extending

additional credit. Although there is no law against taking risk, for our purposes we assume that all other entries in the prepayment column are zero except, obviously, the unit diagonal element.

6. To be consistent, the entry labeled D in table 16.3 should be labeled P_{34}. We have given it a more descriptive name since it refers to the default roll rate from the 61 to 90 days-past-due delinquency bucket. For obvious reasons, pool cumulative default rates are very sensitive to this value.

7. Although theory is fine, in some cases it will be obvious that later data points are more meaningful and less "noisy" than earlier ones. Suffice it to say that structured analysts need to use their best judgment in deciding which data points are most representative of the situation they are trying to analyze.

8. In constructing your Markov transition matrices, you may have to average ratios of various numbers. Some might therefore argue that geometric averages are more meaningful than arithmetic ones. Since both will lead to approximately the same results, feel free to choose the method you prefer, as long as you stick to it.

Our last remark concerns issuers that cannot, or will not, give you the data you so kindly requested.

1. If they cannot, serious doubts should exist in your mind as to the propriety of securitization for that issuer since the deal itself will invariably call for servicer reports of this type every month after closing. It is unlikely that issuers unable to produce acceptable servicer data during the due diligence period can gear up by the time the deal has to close.

2. If they will not, well, you know how to handle that!

16.8 DERIVATION OF THE FIXED-RATE CASH FLOW TRANSFER FUNCTION

As outlined above, in order to rate the securities, it will be necessary to turn account transitions into cash flows at the obligor level. In "*The Analysis of Structured Securities*" (OUP, 2003), we stated without proof the main type of cash flow transfer functions within structured pools. This section describes in some detail the intuition underlying it.

We restrict our derivation to fixed-rate loans and to a situation whereby the issuer is assumed to collect delinquency fees in the precise amount needed to maintain the yield on the loan at its nominal value. From the majority of obligors, the actual fee is usually worse, so this example is most likely conservative. The derivation of the floating-rate transfer function is left as an exercise. Our notation is shown in table 16.5.

For any fixed-rate loan, we can define the payment due as follows:

$$c_l(t) = \begin{cases} M, \ 0 < t \le T \\ 0, \ t > T \end{cases} \tag{16}$$

TABLE 16.5
Notation for the fixed rate loan cash flow transfer function

ID	SYMBOL	DEFINITION
1	t	Time step (integer)
2	l	Obligor ID (integer)
3	T	Maturity of loan made to obligor l (integer)
4	n	Summation variable (integer)
5	i	Status ID for obligor l at the prior month (integer)
6	j	Status ID for obligor l for the current month (integer)
7	r_l	Periodic loan rate for obligor l (real)
8	$c_l(t)$	Scheduled payment for obligor l at time t (real)
9	$p_l(t)$	Portion of $c_l(t)$ originally allocated to principal at time t
10	$Pmt_{ij}^l(t)$	Total payment made by account l at time t and corresponding to the delinquency transition between state i and state j (real)
11	$Pr_{ij}^l(t)$	Principal payment made by account l at time t corresponding to the delinquency transition between state i and state j (real)

In equation (16), the constant monthly payment M is defined as in chapter 15 (see loan seasoning calculation). To understand the derivation of the cash flow transfer function, one must first become familiar with the mechanics of delinquencies.

For an account to be deemed current requires that each payment be made when due. The amounts due per se do not determine the delinquency status of the account, only those paid in relation to those due. Further, unlike amounts paid, amounts due are always known precisely a priori. Next, we assume obligors make payments corresponding exactly to the associated delinquency transition and that they never make a partial payment. This is clearly wrong. The actual, fine-grained delinquency structure of even a single obligor is a rather complicated affair, much more complicated in fact than we can represent using this simplified view. We also ignore the fact that delinquencies are counted in days, not months. Obviously, we do this to align our assets with our liabilities and we admit that errors are made when doing so. Such minor simplifications amount to damping the noise superposed onto a fundamental structure that is then amenable to analysis.

As far as cash flows are concerned, what matters much more than the microstructure of delinquencies is the issuer's credit policy. If a deal makes sense only when every possible delinquency micro-transition is included in the analysis, it just does not work. Further, when we speak of a "payment," we mean a logical, not a physical payment. Most people write a single check no matter how many logical payments they make. It sometimes happen that obligors take advantage of prepayment possibilities by writing two checks, one for the regular payment and a second check for the principal portion of the next installment, thereby moving through the amortization schedule two lines at a time. Done consistently, this effectively turns a 30-year mortgage into a 15-year mortgage. The trick is that during the early years, principal payments are relatively small, and so this procedure imposes but a small additional burden on the obligor, whereas in later years she will effectively be making two full payments per month.

Now, assume obligor l is one month delinquent and stays one month delinquent for a few months. This really means that the payment *made* each month corresponds to the payment *due* the previous month. In other words, during the second month this obligor makes his or her first payment $c_l(1)$, while during the third month payment $c_l(2)$ is made, and so on. Therefore, in order to maintain the yield on his or her loan at its nominal value r_l, which is what we are assuming, the servicer needs to collect an additional amount $r_l c_l(1)$ from the obligor during the second month because this obligor was effectively made a loan of $c_l(1)$ dollars for one month. The same thing happens during the third month of course, whereby the servicer needs to collect another delinquency fee of $r_l c_l(2)$ to maintain yield on the loan at r_l. The result is that in order to maintain yield, the total payment made during the second month by a one month delinquent account is $c_l(1)(1 + r_l)$ instead of just $c_l(1)$.

Instead of being one month delinquent, assume the obligor is now two months delinquent. The same principle applies here as well, except that in this case we made the obligor a temporary two-month loan instead of a one-month loan as in the first example. To maintain yield, we now need to charge interest on interest for the additional month, and this means that the total payment at month 3, i.e., the time step where the obligor makes his first payment, is now $c_l(1)(1 + r_l)^2$ instead of $c_l(1)(1 + r_l)$. We can clearly keep playing this game for other delinquency states all the way down to default.

Next, let's see what happens when an account becomes less delinquent, or "cures" as people say. For instance, suppose a one month delinquent account suddenly cures. What is the total payment? First, the obligor made a first payment simply to maintain his or her delinquency status where it was, i.e., one month late, but she also made a second payment, i.e., the one actually due this month; for how else can she cure? Thus, this obligor made two payments in order to cure a one-month delinquency. This pattern can also be generalized. To cure an N-month delinquency, you need to make $N + 1$ logically separate payments. In the case of a one-month cure taking place during the second month for example, the total payment made would be:

$$\text{Total payment for a one-period cure at month } 2 = c_l(2) + c_l(1)(1 + r_l) \quad (17)$$

However, an equivalent way of writing equation (17) would be:

$$\text{Total payment at month } 2 : c_l(2)(1 + r_l)^0 + c_l(1)(1 + r_l)^1$$

In other words, with proper notation, the corresponding delinquency state can be made to appear as the exponent of the $(1 + r_l)$ factor in the total payment calculation. If this is a fixed-rate loan, this always works. However, it does not work for loans that have variable compounding factors such as floating-rate loans. For those types of loans, a more complicated transfer function formula needs to be worked out.

Last but not least, all along we have been talking about monthly payments and not merely *principal* payments. In fact, buried inside each payment $c(t)$ is an allocation to interest and principal. We need to take this allocation into account at the time we calculate aggregate amounts due to bondholders.

This fact is normally transparent to the obligor since she makes out one check without breaking it into its interest and principal portions. In other words, the allocation into the two logical components (interest and principal) is logical, not physical. What this means is that in the case of pure cash flow deals, such allocations are arbitrary and may be accomplished in a number of different ways. How to do this is discussed further in chapter 24.

Assembling the foregoing thoughts and features together, we end up with the following yield maintenance, total payment transfer function with respect to fixed-rate loans:

$$\text{Total payment: } Pmt_{ij}^{l}(t) = \sum_{n=0}^{i-j} c_l[t-i+n](1+r_l)^{i-n} \tag{18}$$

As far as the principal portion transfer function is concerned, we obtain:

$$\text{Principal payment: } Pr_{ij}^{l}(t) = \sum_{n=0}^{i-j} p_l[t-i+n] \tag{19}$$

Please note that in all cases where $i < j$ holds, both functions will return a zero result since the summation will be programmatically bypassed.

As always, monies not directly allocated to principal are considered interest. This is the case with delinquency and other fees, which effectively count as interest contributions and are logically part of excess spread. The same is true of recoveries (see chapter 17). Some readers might be puzzled as to why recoveries are considered interest instead of principal since the recovery in question is normally computed based on the principal balance of the loan at the time of default.

However, what really happens is that the entire loan's principal balance at default has already been subtracted from the pool balance and returned to investors as a partial principal payment. Effectively, this de-links recoveries from principal and transforms them into pure interest to the trust. This would not be true if one were to wait before declaring a default until the recovery on that loan were actually received. The difference between the balance at default and the recovered amount would then be considered a *net* default amount. Doing this is inappropriate because it confuses two concepts that ought to be kept separate. In practice, this procedure is usually an attempt by the sponsor to delay default recognition in order to receive incremental excess spread that would be swallowed up were the default recognized immediately. This type of questionable servicing practice is discussed in detail in chapter 24.

As you can see, synthesizing a suitable transfer function took some doing. The good news is that all other transfer functions can be synthesized identically.

Equations (18) and (19) are easily extendable to the more difficult case of floating-rate loans. However, in the remainder of this analysis we focus exclusively on the fixed-rate case.

As an example of the above procedure, table 16.6 presents a typical cash flow history arising from the implementation of equations (18) and (19). In this particular case, the loan defaulted at $t = 26$ and recoveries were received three months later.

TABLE 16.6

Typical account cash flow history

TIME	BALANCE	PRINCIPAL	INTEREST	PAYMENT	DEFAULT	STATUS
0	$21,690	$0	$0	$0	$0	0
1	$21,493	$197	$334	$530	$0	0
2	$21,293	$200	$331	$530	$0	0
3	$21,091	$203	$328	$530	$0	0
4	$20,885	$206	$325	$530	$0	0
5	$20,676	$209	$321	$530	$0	0
6	$20,464	$212	$318	$530	$0	0
7	$20,249	$215	$315	$530	$0	0
8	$20,030	$219	$312	$530	$0	0
9	$19,808	$222	$308	$530	$0	0
10	$19,583	$225	$305	$530	$0	0
11	$19,354	$229	$301	$530	$0	0
12	$19,121	$232	$298	$530	$0	0
13	$18,885	$236	$294	$530	$0	0
14	$18,645	$240	$291	$530	$0	0
15	$18,402	$243	$287	$530	$0	0
16	$18,155	$247	$283	$530	$0	0
17	$17,904	$251	$279	$530	$0	0
18	$17,904	$0	$0	$0	$0	1
19	$17,904	$0	$0	$0	$0	2
20	$17,649	$255	$292	$547	$0	2
21	$17,391	$259	$288	$547	$0	2
22	$17,128	$263	$284	$547	$0	2
23	$16,861	$267	$280	$547	$0	2
24	$16,590	$271	$276	$547	$0	2
25	$16,590	$0	$0	$0	$0	3
26	$0	$0	$0	$0	$16,590	Def
27	$0	$0	$0	$0	$0	Def
28	$0	$0	$0	$0	$0	Def
29	$0	$0	$3,762	$3,762	$0	Def

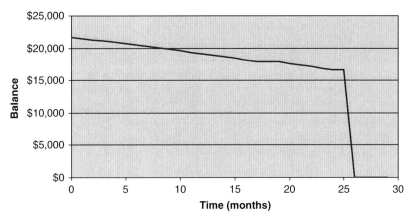

FIGURE 16.1
Principal balance history for a typical loan in the auto pool (default at $t = 26$).

The amount of allocated recoveries is computed according to the loan-wise recovery model described in chapter 17.

Starting in month 18, the account begins its delinquency phase as indicated by a delinquency status of 1 or more from then onward. Thereafter, the account undergoes a rather complicated payment history during which the model allocates delinquency fees according to equation (18).

Please note that recoveries are accounted for as interest collections. This is in keeping with the basic principle that whatever cash received is *not* principal *must* be interest. As discussed above, recoveries cannot be principal since the entire principal balance of the loan has been written off and already included in Principal Due to bondholders at the time of default. In addition, the delinquency fee mechanism implicit in transfer function (18) allocates ca. $17 of delinquency fees while the account remains in delinquency status $S = 2$ (2 months delinquent) but keeps making payments. In actual practice, this amount is most likely conservative.

Figure 16.1 shows the same data graphically. In this case, months when no cash is received show up as flat portions of the curve. Once correctly implemented, the transfer function concept is capable of reproducing practically any conceivable obligor behavior while including delinquency fees at no programming expense, and this is only one of the ways in which the versatility of the Markov chain formalism comes to prominence.

> **Exercise 16.3**
>
> Derive the cash flow transfer function for the case where a loan with maturity T earns a fixed spread r_s over the benchmark Libor index $L(t)$. Assume the same delinquency fee structure as before.

Exercise 16.4

Repeat the above continuous case Markov chain exercise assuming that columns and rows of the Markov matrix given in exercise 16.1 represent the delinquency states of the accounts in the pool. In this case, you are also to compute *principal* and *interest* collections that would accrue to the trust up to maturity assuming you started with 10,000 "continuous" accounts, each with the following identical loan terms:

Initial balance:	$10,000
Coupon:	12% APR
Scheduled maturity:	60 months

In practical applications, these quantities would represent the Average Contract Balance, WAC and WAM (Weighted Average Maturity) of the pool, respectively. Please use equations (18) and (19) to compute total cash flows and principal allocations, from which you can derive interest and principal collections. Please note that this particular formalism denies the accounts the possibility of default or prepayment. These two states will have to wait for a more refined treatment later on.

Exercise 16.5

Repeat exercise 16.4 for the discrete Markov chain formalism using 10,000 discrete loans. Compare the two sets of results and make note of any dissimilarity.

16.9 LOSS CURVE SIMULATION USING BASE MARKOV TRANSITION MATRICES

After these rather lengthy preliminaries, we have finally come to the crux of the matter: how to modulate base Markov transition matrices to reproduce the target issuer's known loss curve. We proceed from the simplest case and then build up to more complicated transactional situations.

You will recall from previous sections that our basic schema hinges on a sequence of T Markov obligor transition matrices $\mathbf{P}(t)$, $t = 1, 2, 3, \ldots T$ in delinquency space and that our task is to write down an expression for each such matrix that anchors the procedure to physical reality. Our first step is to synthesize the cumulative gross loss curve $F(t)$ from issuer data, previous transactions or otherwise. How to do this was demonstrated in chapter 15 using the logistic function as a paradigm of issuer loss curves. For the sake of continuity, we stick to this choice here although you should remember that the precise functional form of the transition matrix modulator is irrelevant to the application of the present method.

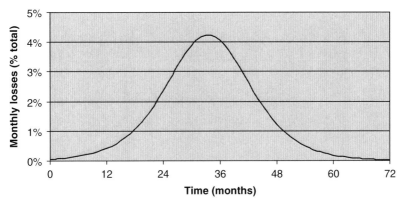

FIGURE 16.2
Marginal gross loss curve.

Specifically, we saw that a generic gross cumulative loss curve can be formally represented by the following function:

$$F(t) = \frac{M_p(n)\,m(L_e)}{1 + b\,e^{-c(t-t_0+t_s)}} \tag{20}$$

For the sake of exposition, we assume that all loans are unseasoned, allowing us to set $t_s = 0$ across the across the pool. With this proviso, we can easily compute the first derivative of a loss curve $F(t)$ that has been synthesized in this manner:

$$f(t) \equiv \frac{\partial F(t)}{\partial t} = \frac{M_p(n)\,m(L_e)\,b\,c\,e^{-c(t-t_0)}}{[1 + b\,e^{-c(t-t_0)}]^2} \tag{21}$$

Equation (21) is the marginal default curve and represents the implied periodic default rate for the obligors in the pool. An example of a marginal default curve given by equation (21) is shown in figure 16.2 for a typical set of parameters in the auto sector.

16.10 THE TWO LEVELS OF CALIBRATION

In order to fairly represent the cash flow dynamics indicative of the target issuer, the basic Markov process derived earlier needs to be modulated in two distinct ways. These two ways are the analogues of the micro- and macrostructure of losses in the pool that we painstakingly derived in chapter 15. Before plunging into the mechanics of Markov chain implementation, we need to become conscious of this *dual* method, which is merely the recognition of the basic physics of the loss process.

To analyze static pools properly, it is a good idea to operate the way economists commonly do, i.e., by partitioning the time-dependent, dynamic aspects of credit losses into two distinct sets of laws or influence factors: the micro- and macro-economic levels. Given that this separation is crucial to the analytical process, we need to treat both levels independently. This is what we did in chapter 15.

Until someone proposes a unified theory of economic behavior that would combine micro- and macro-economics, i.e., a method whereby the behavior of economic ensembles could be derived from that of its agents, it is not unreasonable to view both levels as distinct and separate, no matter how obvious it is that macro-economics should be related to micro-economics through some form of aggregation, convolution, or integration. Since this unification is not exactly imminent, we believe the following method ought to be useful to you in the near future.

In equation (20), we already wrote the loss curve with both levels explicitly shown via its micro- and macro-calibration parameters $m(L_e)$ and $M_p(n)$ respectively. We indicated the curve's micro-dependency through the micro-parameter's dependence on gross expected loss and its macro-dependence via the Monte Carlo scenario index which, you will recall, provides the critical link to the ergodic hypothesis.

Micro-Calibration $[m(L_e)]$

Micro-calibration is implemented by first setting $M_p(n) \equiv 1$. Once the gross expected loss in dollars is available through the technique presented in chapter 15, micro-calibration can begin in earnest.

Via Monte Carlo (MC) simulation, even a single value for m will give rise to an entire distribution of cumulative gross loss rates for the pool no matter how deterministic loss dynamics might appear at first sight. This is because in each MC scenario different obligors will be defaulting merely as a result of the luck of the draw. As a direct consequence of this statistical process, each MC scenario will give rise to a separate and potentially different cumulative gross loss value. Although found on either side of the mean, such loss values will be tightly distributed because the same loss curve will have been used to generate each loss scenario and differences will arise strictly from the micro-randomness inherent in the obligor default selection process. Given a reasonable pool size of 1,500 obligors or more, statistical averaging will cause relatively little variability around the mean value μ of the resulting loss density function.

Each value of m will produce a different μ, enabling us to write $\mu(m)$. As explained before, the expected loss L_e is precisely this mean value. As you can already surmise, the probability that the required L_e will emerge by magic from some arbitrary, initial choice for m is zero, hence the need for calibration at the micro-economic level. The main idea underlying micro-calibration is the specification of the unique value m_0 that will produce the required mean L_e, i.e., $m_0 \equiv \mu^{-1}(L_e)$.

Because parameter m appears linearly in $F(t)$, it will be the case for μ to be a monotonic function of m, making the search for the calibrating micro-parameter m essentially trivial. A simple brute force search can be used to converge onto the desired value m_0.

Macro-Calibration (M)

We have already discussed macro-calibration in chapter 15 when we used the Clayton copula as a means of superposing a macro-influence factor onto issuer portfolio data and its influence on the latter's prospective loss behavior. As we have mentioned many times before, the main reason why credit enhancement exists is not to counter the micro-dynamics of default within structured pools, since diversification alone will largely prevent security-level losses. Rather, it results from the relatively narrow range of loss outcomes achievable under strict micro-economic disturbances. Therefore, credit enhancement levels in structured transactions arises much more due to the influence of macro-economic forces affecting all obligors.

Just as is true of canonical portfolio theory, pool diversification is the mechanism through which unsystematic or micro-risk is eliminated or at least mitigated, leaving the investor with systematic or macro-risk to which all obligors in the pool are exposed in concert. This process is what the copula-based correlation function was attempting to measure. Unlike their equity counterparts, fixed income investors are however not willing to bear this type of risk either and thus demand additional protection via credit enhancement.

How a particular static pool will react to macro-economic factors is largely conjecture since it will depend in large measure on the underwriting standards used to assemble the pool. Clearly, obligors in a prime pool will be less prone to the type of life events that cause delinquency and ultimate default. By contrast, subprime borrowers are generally much more exposed to macro-disturbances, such as lay-offs or temporary unemployment. Therefore, pools of such obligors should exhibit a higher volatility around their mean loss value. The extent of macro-economic impact will also depend on the asset class, for the simple reason that even a subprime borrower will usually pay his electricity bill while defaulting on his auto loan. A mechanism in which asset class and market specificity are to be integrated into a distribution of likely outcomes obviously leaves much room for judgment. Although we did take a stab at it using the Clayton copula in chapter 15, you will recall that, at the time, we strongly indicated that any slavish attachment to this or any other formalism would be dangerous. In other words, the tail should never wag the dog!

Exhibit 16.1:   Macroeconomic Loss Curve Adjustment (from the Clayton Copula)

Adjust the Loss Curve by Overlaying Macro-economic Effects (p is a random number)

```
Sub AdjustDefaultCurve(deal As deal, p As Double)
deal.defC = deal.defMicro * Application.GammaInv(p, deal.defMacroAlpha,
deal.defMacroBeta)
End Sub
```

In general, we find that the process of devising a forecast of likely macro-economic scenarios, i.e., of establishing the probability distribution of parameter M, is relatively painless since published data to do so are plentiful. They can then form a rational basis for a suitable macro-economic parameter probability distribution $f(M)$. Exhibit 16.1 shows a section of VBA code implementing the macro-distribution as a gamma density function with parameters $\alpha = 1.07$ and $\beta = 1.0$ as explained in chapter 15.

By contrast, the decision as to how two given pools would react to the same macro-environment is not nearly as straightforward for the reasons outlined above. The upshot is that some independent source of either opinion or data is usually brought to bear on the case to estimate an "impact" parameter, i.e., some reaction or *transfer* function linking macro-economic outcomes to credit loss levels, but this time based on the specific characteristics of the target market. Although in our target transaction we have subsumed the impact parameter inside M, its implicit existence should never be forgotten.

In computing impact parameters, the analyst is usually better off removing him- or herself from the decision-making process in the name of objectivity. Once the method of credit analysis has been determined as shown herein, it is more defensible and consistent to leave the setting of such crucial inputs to those whose lifetimes have been devoted to the computation of this type of data. Such people are in ample supply and are usually happy to contribute meaningfully to the deal's outcome. In any serious deal analysis, the judge and the jury need to be separated.

16.11 NUMERICAL IMPLEMENTATION OF THE MARKOV CHAIN

Consider the physics of obligor default for a moment. First, note that within the assumed framework all obligors are deemed current at closing. Even in the worst case, they will be at most 30 days delinquent by virtue of the transaction's eligibility covenants.

The vast majority of them will remain current until their loan's stated maturity, at which point the outstanding principal balance will fall to zero. However, a sizable fraction will undergo various *life events*. In fact, the difference between various types of obligors in the credit sense lies in their ability to withstand fundamentally unpredictable events.

Most such events will be minor in the economic sense, like an unexpected medical bill or the death of a parent. Nevertheless, they may create potential shortfalls in the obligor's monthly cash flows that he will be unable to make up from savings alone. These occurrences will show up as long-term delinquencies of all orders, including default. Conversely, a current account which has become 1-month delinquent may also remain in that state until maturity and pay his loan off in $T + 1$ months, where T was its original maturity, and incurring delinquency fees along the way. Such fees provide a priori unexpected cash windfalls to the trust and need to be estimated.

Other life events, such as unemployment, will be major setbacks from which the obligor may be unable to recover, causing the loan to default. As a result, the unfolding temporality of life events in a static pool determines the shape of its loss curve. However, regardless of when they occur, all life events will appear to affect current accounts and may cause a cascading delinquency process leading up to default. Unlike stock prices that can apparently go up and down with 50% probability each way, the probability with which an obligor will make current payments on his auto loan is not 50%. After all, a loan is a legally enforceable claim against him. It is this claim which, in essence, makes up the *real* loan. Once the obligor is delinquent, it has ceased behaving as expected at the outset. It is no longer *lost in a crowd* of similar obligors. Its behavior is more predictable and corresponds quite closely to the dynamics derived from the type of issuer-delinquency data that were reviewed earlier. Thus, the process that causes the initial delinquency is what requires an explanation, i.e., a model, and not what happens once the account becomes delinquent.

Consequently, to simulate this delinquency process, one simply needs to focus on the top leftmost element of the base Markov transition matrix $[p_{00}]$. Recall that this quantity is the probability with which a current obligor at a prior step remains current this month. By modulating p_{00} according to equation (21), we effectively simulate conditions analogous to the physical delinquency process just described.

To do this, first define the modulation function $\Delta p_{00}(t)$ as follows:

$$\Delta p_{00}(t) \equiv f(t), \ t = 1, 2, 3, \ldots, T \tag{22}$$

Next, reduce entry p_{00} by the amount $\Delta p_{00}(t)$ given by equation (22) and increase the entry immediately to its right by the same amount, thus maintaining the row sum condition intact. In other words, assuming p_{00}^0 and p_{01}^0 are the two leftmost entries from the first row of the issuer's base transition matrix, simply set:

$$p_{00}(t) = p_{00}^0 - \Delta p_{00}(t) \tag{23a}$$

$$p_{01}(t) = p_{01}^0 + \Delta p_{00}(t) \tag{23b}$$

All other entries in the transition matrix remain unchanged since they represent life-event dynamics that affect already delinquent accounts. Properly executed, this modulation will give rise to cumulative losses with a profile similar to $F(t)$ because marginal defaults will now be in agreement with its first derivative $f(t)$.

At first sight, readers might be puzzled as to why the bankruptcy rate B and the single-month mortality SMM, two quantities that are also part of the first row, should not be part of the modulation procedure. The reason for this is that these two phenomena are not intimately involved in the fundamental delinquency paradigm. In other words, why would more or fewer obligors prepay their loans simply because a small minority of them have become delinquent? The source of prepayment behavior really lies elsewhere.

Given that only current accounts are allowed to prepay under our paradigm, a higher delinquency propensity simply means that the ratio SMM/p_{00} will be larger than expected. As far as bankruptcies are concerned, the process is nonanalytic in the same way and is independent of what we normally call a "delinquency." In the end however, modifying our framework to modulate SMM and B as well as p_{00} would be essentially trivial. Ultimate results are not significantly affected by extending the modulation to the other two first-row entries, not to mention that a credible rationale for the modulation of bankruptcy and prepayment rates in the context of delinquency transitions is severely lacking. In addition, obligors who become delinquent are no longer eligible for prepayment or bankruptcy and in general, they will not exhibit such behavior.

In practice, it must be borne in mind that a timescale equal to the issuer's default declaration convention, usually 3 or 4 months of delinquency, will offset actual loss recognition. For instance in order to cause peak marginal losses to occur at time step 23 in a case where the issuer recognized defaults at 91 days past due, the value of t_0 inside the Markov chain would be set to approximately 20. In practice, we have found that the formula $t_0 = t_0^* - \sum_{i=0}^{n-3} \frac{1}{p_{ii}}$ works fairly well, where p_{ii} are diagonal entries of the base transition matrix and $n - 3$ is the highest discrete delinquency state in our base transition matrix. Here, t_0^* is the empirically observed mode of the gross marginal loss curve. The summation terminates at $n - 3$ because the last two status codes are default and prepayment and hence do not contribute directly to the delinquency process.

Assume now that we have at our disposal a set of T transition matrices $\mathbf{P}(t)$, where T is slightly higher than the highest maturity of any loan in the pool. Why do we say that T is "slightly" higher than the highest maturity of any loan in the pool? To see why, first remember that owing to delinquencies and to the slow recovery process, cash flows from a loan with any delinquency or, if it should default very late in the game, from its liquidation proceeds, will be collected only after its original maturity. If this troublesome loan happens to be the one with the highest nominal maturity, it is virtually assured that cash flows will be received months after that loan should have theoretically paid off. In practice, this phenomenon is guaranteed to occur at least once inside any random MC simulation. Consequently, the trust will receive its last cash flow at a different time step within each MC scenario, and thus will require the generation of a sufficient number of transition matrices for its computation. It is for this reason that T is not exactly equal, but always higher than the highest loan maturity in the pool.

At the end of each Collection Period during the transaction, the delinquency status of account A_l at time t, defined as $D_l(t)$, can be determined from its delinquency status at time $t - 1$ using the following stepwise procedure:

1. For each A_l, generate $x_l \in [0, 1]$ using a uniform random number generator. You can either use Microsoft's Rnd function, as we did before, or another random selection method of your own choosing. The van der Corput method, although always pristine, is usually overkill at this stage for the simple reason that basic statistical sampling is normally more than adequate to achieve convergence. To get an idea of the statistics involved, note that we need to select one uniformly distributed random number for every obligor on every time step for every MC scenario. Assuming that we have 2,000 obligors in the target pool, that the highest maturity is approximately 72 and that our Monte Carlo simulation involves 5,000 scenarios, we are looking at generating roughly 720 million random numbers for any serious analytical effort. Given this order of magnitude, it is benign to assume that the use of a system-supplied random number generator like the Rnd function is acceptable.

2. Assume that, at time step $t - 1$, account A_l is in delinquency status $j \in [0, n-1]$ and that the jth row of matrix $\mathbf{P}(t)$ is defined as $p_j^t = [p_0^t \ p_1^t \ p_2^t \ \dots \ p_{n-1}^t]$ with the usual row sum condition $\sum_j p_j^t = 1$. Now, defining the row-wise cumulative distribution function $C_j^t = \sum_{l=0}^{j} p_l^t$, $j = 0, 1, \dots, n-1$ with the

artificial boundary condition $C^t_{-1} \equiv 0$, let the new account status j be defined via the condition $D_l(t) \equiv j \mid C^t_{j-1} \leq x_l < C^t_j$. In other words if, for obligor A_l at time t, random number x_l lies between C^t_{-1} and C^t_0 then $D_l(t) \equiv 0$. This means that A_l stays current $(S = 0)$ if it was already current or cures if it was not. Similarly, when x_l lies between C^t_0 and C^t_1 then $D_l(t) \equiv 1$, i.e., the account is deemed to move or stay in Status 1, etc. This process is applied to all the obligors in the pool. For those that have already defaulted or prepaid, the procedure automatically leaves them unaffected since the corresponding state is absorbing.

3. To determine the total payment $Pmt^t_{ij}(t)$ to the trust corresponding to the obligor transition, use the transfer function (equation (18)) appropriate to the target issuer.

Provided each obligor's initial delinquency status is known, this three-step process can be implemented at each time step from the Closing Date to the Legal Final Maturity Date.

Exercise 16.6

This is similar to exercise 16.1 except that now, you are operating within the discrete Markov transition framework instead of the continuous mode of that exercise. The pool has 10,000 discrete obligors and you may use the same transition matrix P to compute monthly obligor transitions. Again, the task is to take the pool to equilibrium and to compute putative cash flows using equation (18) for all obligor-wise transitions. You can assume that all the assets are identical, fixed-rate loans with the following characteristics:

Initial loan balance:	$100,000
Loan rate (APR):	12%
Loan maturity:	72 months

To generate the uniform deviates you will need, please use the van der Corput low-discrepancy sequence[1] method instead of the system-resident generator (Rand). Produce a graph from the sequence of time-dependent unconditional distributions for the 10,000 obligors that clearly shows the attainment of equilibrium. Produce another graph showing the delinquency path taken by obligor no. 2005. What happens when $t > 76$ and why is the number 76 so important here?

Exercise 16.7

Repeat exercise 16.1 but this time compute total cash flows arising from generalized obligor transitions using equation (18) with respect to loans of identical characteristics as those of exercise 16.6. How will you compute cash flows under the continuous regime? Is there a problem here?
Hint: look at equation (6)

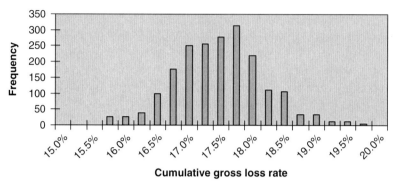

FIGURE 16.3
Calibrated micro-economic loss distribution.

16.12 IMPLEMENTATION OF MICRO-CALIBRATION

Exhibit 16.2 shows a VBA implementation of the micro-calibration procedure discussed above. Figure 16.3 displays the resulting gross credit loss distribution for our static pool of 2,000 obligors, a 25-loan sample of which was given as table 15.2.

▶ **Exhibit 16.2: VBA Code Section Implementing the Microeconomic Loss Calibration**

```
Sub CalibrateMicro()

Dim deal As deal, n As Integer, x as double, s As Double, r As Double
Dim p As Double, q As Double, u As Double, v As Double, i as integer
Dim avgMonthDef() As Double, totDef() As Double, history as Range
```

The basic method is to find the micro-calibration parameter 'r' such that 's', the loss rate associated with r, is within a small tolerance of loss rate 'x'. To find "r," we iteratively use a linear approximation (p and q will bracket r, u and v are the loss rates associated with p and q, respectively)

```
x = Range("ExpectedLoss").Value
n = Range("MicroN").Value
Call ReadDeal(deal)
Set history = Range("MicroHistory")
```

Setup: check the minimum and maximum values for 'r'

```
p = Range("MicroMin").Value
deal.defC = p
u = GetPoolAverageDefaults(deal, n, avgMonthDef, totDef) / deal.poolBal
If u > x Then
MsgBox ("loss(" & p & ") = " & (u * 100) & "%, please choose a lower minimum")
End
```

```
End If

i = 1
history.cells(i, 1) = i
history.cells(i, 2) = deal.defC
history.cells(i, 3) = u
q = Range("MicroMax").Value
deal.defC = q
v = GetPoolAverageDefaults(deal, n, avgMonthDef, totDef) / deal.poolBal
If v < x Then
MsgBox ("loss(" & q & ") = " & (v * 100) & "%, please choose a higher maximum")
End
End If
i = i + 1
history.cells(i, 1) = i
history.cells(i, 2) = deal.defC
history.cells(i, 3) = v
```

Use a linear approximation to find the micro-calibration parameter 'r'

```
Do
r = (x - u) / (v - u) * (q - p) + p
deal.defC = r
s = GetPoolAverageDefaults(deal, n, avgMonthDef, totDef) / deal.poolBal
```

Convergence history

```
i = i + 1
history.cells(i, 1) = i
history.cells(i, 2) = deal.defC
history.cells(i, 3) = s
```

We have come as close as we can (either the tolerance is too low or the number of simulations is too small).

```
If s < u Or s > v Then
Exit Do
End If
If Abs(s - x) < tolerance Then
Exit Do
End If
If s < x Then
p = r
u = s
Else
q = r
v = s
End If
Loop

End Sub
```

For the sake of completeness, we present as table 16.7 the convergence history produced by this code. The micro-calibration is a robust technique that converges under most conceivable scenarios.

While conducting the micro-calibration procedure, it is always a good idea to check whether the simulation produces the desired marginal loss behavior. This is shown as figure 16.4.

Figure 16.4 was created for a single Monte Carlo simulation using equation (20) for $F(t)$ and the following parametric set:

$$c = 0.1, \ m(L_e) = 0.8314, \ b = 0.9, \ M_p(n) = 1, \ t_0 = 20$$

As can be seen, the model does produce the intended nonlinear loss behavior. With a pool of 2,000 obligors, the marginal loss curve is acceptably smooth. When integrated however (see figure 16.5), the result is impressively analytical despite the heavily empirical character of the simulation. At this point, we can conclude with

TABLE 16.7

Micro-calibration convergence history

n	m	$\mu(m)$
1	0.0050	9.70%
2	1.0000	18.69%
3	0.8542	17.57%
4	0.8329	17.40%
5	0.8300	17.36%
6	0.8308	17.36%
7	0.8314	17.37%

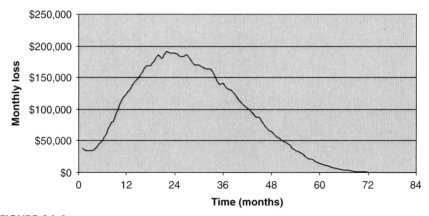

FIGURE 16.4

Marginal loss curve.

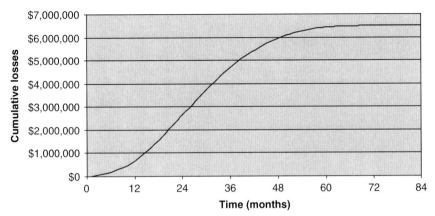

FIGURE 16.5
Cumulative loss curve (integration of the curve in figure 16.4).

relative confidence that our formalism has achieved the stated goal of reproducing the observed aggregate loss behavior of the pool and that statistical behavior can be assumed to rule the dynamics of credit losses, as it should.

16.13 MODIFICATION OF TIME-DEPENDENT TRANSITION MATRICES FOR SEASONING

So far, we have been operating with pools consisting entirely of fresh, unseasoned loans, i.e., whereby the seasoning parameter t_s was effectively zero. Under most field circumstances, this will not be the case and it will be necessary to deal with seasoning. Because seasoning is a loan-wise concept, its handling requires the incorporation of a loan-dependent term inside the Markov chain modulation function, equation (21).

Recall that the modulation function is merely a time-dependent relationship that, so far at least, needs to be computed only once per time step since it can be used indiscriminately for each obligor in the pool. Within a loan-seasoning context this is no longer possible and thus we need to compute a different Markov chain for each obligor in the pool.

This effectively generates the temporality appropriate to each obligor as far as its credit behavior is concerned. In other words a seasoned, but current loan should have a reduced propensity to become delinquent since it would have done so earlier. In other cases delinquency propensity might actually increase since the obligor may now be entering the *modal*, or high-delinquency period of its assumed loss behavior. This can be visualized as the period between the two vertical bars in figure 15.4.

To introduce seasoning, we merely adjust the timescale appropriate to each obligor by increasing the factor above the exponential function by an amount t_s inside modulator equation (21). At each time step, we can do this by defining a unique

Markov transition matrix for each obligor in the pool. Implementation is trivial since it amounts to simply moving the code a few lines down and replacing equation (21) by the following modulator function:

$$f(t) = \frac{M_p(n)\,m(L_e)\,b\,c\,e^{-c(t-t_0+t_s)}}{[1+b\,e^{-c(t-t_0+t_s)}]^2} \tag{24}$$

Exercise 16.8

Starting from the data series in Table 16.8 found below showing U.S. GDP growth for the past 57 years, use the histogram function in Excel (or your own routine if you prefer) to create the probability density function (PDF) of this time series assuming you wanted to use it as the macro-economic index suitable to your transaction. Use at least $m = 50$ points on the I-axis where the PDF will be computed by Excel or by your own routine.

Exercise 16.9

Next, normalize the x-axis values so that the mean of the resulting PDF is unity and then invert the x-axis using a suitable transformation. This is because small GDP growths are what you are looking for in your investigation of stressed credit environments. The maximum value of the initial PDF should now become the origin of the normalized and inverted PDF. You may let the minimum value fall wherever it does naturally.

In general, a well-seasoned pool will exhibit reduced credit losses compared to a similar pools of unseasoned loans for the simple reason that loans that would have been delinquent at the time of securitization have been made ineligible by virtue of deal covenants. Thus, unless seasoning is negligible, we can expect credit risk to be lower within such pools. One of the chief advantages arising directly from the above formalism is that a natural credit loss reduction occurs via the consistent application of the modulator equation (24) because seasoned loans will spend less time inside the high-delinquency region than unseasoned loans. Since default rates will be smaller on average, loss rates will follow suit.

Exercise 16.10

Now that we have a well-formed macro-economic index density function, it is time to synthesize it as a continuous function that includes all of its kinks and curves. Normally, we would first integrate the density function to produce the cumulative distribution function (CDF) and then model the result. However, for this exercise we will stick to the more volatile density function as a starting point in order to illustrate another numerical technique.

In order to follow the PDF precisely, we will use a Fourier half-range expansion. You will recall that Fourier series can be used to model arbitrary periodic functions defined between 0 and 2π. Via a simple affine mapping, the latter range can easily be extended to any real interval. However, if the target function is not periodic, we can still reproduce it precisely if we assume that we are seeing only "half" of its period over the arbitrary interval $[0, L]$ while the other half is simply left alone and is not utilized further. We can thus model the kinks of any function, periodic or not, over any given real interval.

Since Fourier series deal with both sines and cosines as basis functions and we are only looking at half the period, we can use either basis function to implement our half-range expansion. Because the cosine function is even and the sine function is odd, the corresponding half-range expansions are labeled even when cosines are used and odd when sines are used. Herein, we choose an even expansion hence the following treatment. Formally, we proceed as follows:

For a function $f(x)$ sought over the arbitrary domain $[0, L]$, define the Fourier even half-range expansion as:

$$f(x) = a_0 + \sum_{n=1}^{\infty} a_n \cos \frac{n\pi}{L} x, \; 0 \le x \le L \tag{25}$$

From the theory of Fourier series, the various a_n coefficients in equation (25) are computed via:

$$a_0 = \frac{1}{L} \int_0^L f(x)\, dx, \quad a_n = \frac{2}{L} \int_0^L f(x) \cos \frac{n\pi}{L} x\, dx \tag{26}$$

Write a VBA program that implements equation (26).

To integrate a function given solely as a point set, you are required to use the well-known Simpson rule.[2] This is not the only candidate for numerical integration, but it is precise enough for your purposes and can be implemented in less than 10 lines of VBA code.

Exercise 16.11

When you have implemented equation (25) using equation (26), you have a function $f(x)$ that substantially reproduces the wiggles and curves of the given macro-economic index density function.

A critical aspect of this implementation is that, as you will have noted already, the Fourier half-range expansion in exercise 16.10 requires the computation of an infinite array of coefficients a_n, $n \in (0, \infty)$. However, computing machinery always has finite resolution. Therefore, an obvious question relates to the value of n at which one should cease computing the a_n coefficients. Let us define this stopping point as N. How do we know what value N should have?

Using the concept of the Nyquist rate[3] and the wave numbers $\frac{2L}{n}$, demonstrate how the maximum number of Fourier coefficients one may reasonably compute is $N = m$, where parameter m was defined in exercise 16.8.

Exercise 16.12

Via the integration of the density function in equation (25) in exercise 16.10, generate the nonnormalized cumulative distribution function (CDF) defined via equation (27).

$$F'(x) \equiv \int_0^x f(x')\,dx' \tag{27}$$

Starting from equation (25), show that $F'(x)$ is given by:

$$F'(x) = a_0\,x + \sum_{n=1}^N a_n\,\frac{L}{n\pi}\,\sin\frac{n\pi}{L}x \tag{28}$$

Exercise 16.13

Despite our best efforts, the CDF formula in equation (28) will unfortunately not precisely fulfill conditions in equation (29), which is necessary for its use inside IDFM.

$$F'(0) \equiv 0 \tag{29a}$$
$$F'(L) \equiv 1 \tag{29b}$$

Although the boundary condition in equation (29a) is fulfilled because $\sin[0] = 0$, equation (29b) does not follow. As a result, we need to perform an additional normalization to ensure that equation (29b) holds.

To do this, compute $F'(L) = \alpha$ and define the normalized version of the CDF $F(x)$ as:

$$F(x) = \frac{F'(x)}{\alpha} \tag{30}$$

As you did for exercise 16.10, write a VBA program to compute the coefficients $a_n \in [0, m]$ of equation (28) using Simpson's rule.

Exercise 16.14

Implement equation (30) in VBA and verify that boundary conditions (29) are fulfilled.

Exercise 16.15

When the CDF function you generate is not one already programmed in Excel, you will be forced to write your own VBA-based inversion routines to compute the random deviates you need in implementing the IDFM.

A simple and fail-safe way to do this is the *bisection* method. Its basic idea is to split the current root-interval in half and to find out whether the root is located on the left or right side of the interval's mid-point. If it is on the left, simply redefine what was only the left half as the new interval, bisect it and ask the same question again. Keep going this way until the root is located in as small an interval as you need. To see how this works, suppose the entire interval, illustrated earlier in this chapter, is where we start, i.e., $[0, L]$. Then, it is clear that after one bisection, the required answer will be located either inside $[0, L/2, L]$. If we keep doing this, i.e., reducing by 50% each time the size of the x-interval ε where the root is located, after i such iterations we will have bracketed the root within an interval at most equal to $2^{-i}L$.

Show that, under the bisection method, if you wish to bracket the root within an interval $\varepsilon \leq 0.001\,L$, we should use a number of iterates i satisfying $i \geq \frac{3\ln 10}{\ln 2} \approx 10$.

Exercise 16.16

First, select y from some uniform random number generator of your choice. Next, define the required IDFM (see chapter 18) deviate as the value x such that:

$$G(x ; y) \equiv F(x) - y = 0 \tag{31}$$

In other words, the IDFM deviate you need is the root of equation (31), which keeps changing because the uniform deviate y keeps changing.

To find this root, start with the complete interval, here defined by its minimum and maximum values ($a = 0$ and $c = L$), respectively. In other words, the first interval within which the required IDFM deviate is assumed to lie is $x \in [0, L]$.

Please write you VBA code to implement the bisection method described in exercise 16.15 as an IDFM inversion routine and continue iterating until the accuracy bound ε satisfies $\varepsilon \leq 0.0001\,L$. How many bisections do you need?

TABLE 16.8
US GDP growth in constant 2000 dollars

TIME PERIOD	GDP GROWTH (%)	TIME PERIOD	GDP GROWTH (%)
1947q1	—	1976q1	2.2511
1947q2	−0.1146	1976q2	0.7450
1947q3	−0.0446	1976q3	0.4790
1947q4	1.4605	1976q4	0.7162
1948q1	1.5840	1977q1	1.2084
1948q2	1.7635	1977q2	1.9634
1948q3	0.5776	1977q3	1.7903
1948q4	0.2358	1977q4	−0.0104
1949q1	−1.4958	1978q1	0.3219
1949q2	−0.2939	1978q2	3.9414

Continued

TABLE 16.8

(*Cont'd*)

TIME PERIOD	GDP GROWTH (%)	TIME PERIOD	GDP GROWTH (%)
1949q3	1.1238	1978q3	0.9858
1949q4	−1.0202	1978q4	1.3154
1950q1	4.1045	1979q1	0.1947
1950q2	2.9762	1979q2	0.0952
1950q3	3.9203	1979q3	0.7201
1950q4	1.8229	1979q4	0.2948
1951q1	1.2115	1980q1	0.3189
1951q2	1.6994	1980q2	−2.0187
1951q3	1.9967	1980q3	−0.1661
1951q4	0.1700	1980q4	1.8542
1952q1	1.0440	1981q1	2.0261
1952q2	0.0662	1981q2	−0.7800
1952q3	0.6511	1981q3	1.2096
1952q4	3.2848	1981q4	−1.2458
1953q1	1.8837	1982q1	−1.6396
1953q2	0.7588	1982q2	0.5370
1953q3	−0.6053	1982q3	−0.3785
1953q4	−1.5776	1982q4	0.0887
1954q1	−0.4921	1983q1	1.2332
1954q2	0.0930	1983q2	2.2555
1954q3	1.1055	1983q3	1.9749
1954q4	1.9788	1983q4	2.0462
1955q1	2.8798	1984q1	1.9551
1955q2	1.6371	1984q2	1.7211
1955q3	1.3339	1984q3	0.9728
1955q4	0.5328	1984q4	0.8216
1956q1	−0.4676	1985q1	0.9234
1956q2	0.7920	1985q2	0.8545
1956q3	−0.1199	1985q3	1.5630
1956q4	1.6313	1985q4	0.7686
1957q1	0.6035	1986q1	0.9563
1957q2	−0.2478	1986q2	0.3963
1957q3	0.9762	1986q3	0.9580
1957q4	−1.0574	1986q4	0.5038
1958q1	−2.7176	1987q1	0.6579
1958q2	0.5919	1987q2	1.0998
1958q3	2.3090	1987q3	0.9075
1958q4	2.3005	1987q4	1.7464
1959q1	1.9123	1988q1	0.4889
1959q2	2.6286	1988q2	1.2713

TABLE 16.8

(*Cont'd*)

TIME PERIOD	GDP GROWTH (%)	TIME PERIOD	GDP GROWTH (%)
1959q3	−0.0774	1988q3	0.5339
1959q4	0.3545	1988q4	1.3196
1960q1	2.2253	1989q1	1.0148
1960q2	−0.5005	1989q2	0.6562
1960q3	0.1557	1989q3	0.7123
1960q4	−1.2955	1989q4	0.2538
1961q1	0.6058	1990q1	1.1549
1961q2	1.8786	1990q2	0.2559
1961q3	1.6194	1990q3	0.0070
1961q4	2.0433	1990q4	−0.7559
1962q1	1.7972	1991q1	−0.5101
1962q2	1.0937	1991q2	0.6491
1962q3	0.9194	1991q3	0.4826
1962q4	0.2451	1991q4	0.4691
1963q1	1.3102	1992q1	1.0358
1963q2	1.2500	1992q2	0.9643
1963q3	1.8822	1992q3	0.9811
1963q4	0.7788	1992q4	1.1018
1964q1	2.2420	1993q1	0.1208
1964q2	1.1625	1993q2	0.5067
1964q3	1.3636	1993q3	0.5135
1964q4	0.2677	1993q4	1.3455
1965q1	2.4591	1994q1	1.0174
1965q2	1.3513	1994q2	1.3039
1965q3	2.0284	1994q3	0.5604
1965q4	2.4175	1994q4	1.1718
1966q1	2.4455	1995q1	0.2779
1966q2	0.3469	1995q2	0.1793
1966q3	0.6590	1995q3	0.8150
1966q4	0.8044	1995q4	0.7314
1967q1	0.8853	1996q1	0.7051
1967q2	0.0058	1996q2	1.6391
1967q3	0.7938	1996q3	0.8382
1967q4	0.7561	1996q4	1.1693
1968q1	2.0607	1997q1	0.7733
1968q2	1.6960	1997q2	1.5194
1968q3	0.6819	1997q3	1.2451
1968q4	0.4216	1997q4	0.7374
1969q1	1.5764	1998q1	1.1065

Continued

TABLE 16.8

(*Cont'd*)

TIME PERIOD	GDP GROWTH (%)	TIME PERIOD	GDP GROWTH (%)
1969q2	0.2853	1998q2	0.6614
1969q3	0.6195	1998q3	1.1517
1969q4	−0.4730	1998q4	1.5189
1970q1	−0.1673	1999q1	0.8488
1970q2	0.1888	1999q2	0.8277
1970q3	0.8866	1999q3	1.1669
1970q4	−1.0709	1999q4	1.7775
1971q1	2.7741	2000q1	0.2533
1971q2	0.5642	2000q2	1.5708
1971q3	0.7926	2000q3	−0.1147
1971q4	0.2860	2000q4	0.5195
1972q1	1.7770	2001q1	−0.1224
1972q2	2.3614	2001q2	0.3068
1972q3	0.9531	2001q3	−0.3513
1972q4	1.6364	2001q4	0.3941
1973q1	2.5389	2002q1	0.8426
1973q2	1.1567	2002q2	0.5914
1973q3	−0.5327	2002q3	0.6436
1973q4	0.9557	2002q4	0.1838
1974q1	−0.8666	2003q1	0.4785
1974q2	0.2883	2003q2	1.0114
1974q3	−0.9683	2003q3	1.8022
1974q4	−0.3925	2003q4	1.0303
1975q1	−1.1961	2004q1	1.1039
1975q2	0.7315	2004q2	0.8151
1975q3	1.6938	2004q3	0.9857
1975q4	1.3108	2004q4	0.7777

17

Recovery Modeling

Due to the breadth and importance of this topic, we feel it is appropriate to dedicate an entire chapter to the topic of recovery modeling. At the outset, it should be mentioned that the proper modeling of defaulted loan recovery is completely asset-specific and that, given our exclusive focus on automobile-backed securities in this chapter, the following discussion will perforce lack comprehensiveness.

The same, however, cannot be said of the techniques we will use in our modeling exercise. Properly understood, the nonlinear regression analysis underlying our approach can be used to synthesize the recovery curve of any type of ABS collateral. In fact, even taken at face value, the method presented here is valid for all depreciating or appreciating collateral, including rail cars, recreational vehicles, commercial and residential real estate, motorcycles, heavy equipment, and other collateral of similar type. Yes, there are limits to the applicability of this chapter, but they are broader than you might imagine. Further, with minor modifications the following techniques can be used to model any market-based fluctuation superposed onto temporal depreciation.

A second reason for spending this much time on recoveries is that in many important asset classes, such as real estate and automobiles, asset liquidation is the major source of credit enhancement to investors. Yet this topic has so far been a rather neglected aspect of the analysis of structured securities. To assign a single value to recoveries, no matter what that number turns out to be, is to do a great disservice to issuers and investors alike, for it either under- or overestimates the quality of the collateral.

Investors are not looking for conservatism, but for an honest evaluation of credit risk. They can always be conservative on their own via pricing. Similarly, increasing recoveries ad hoc simply to produce the "right" rating outcome, is clearly unacceptable and amounts to the admission that recoveries are really a fudge factor used to achieve a predetermined result. A structured analyst's mission is to produce the fair market value of credit quality, not to engage in ten-minute hack jobs covered up by misleading pronouncements of rigor.

In what follows, we go over much of the same ground covered in "*The Analysis of Structured Securities*" (OUP, 2003), but with an emphasis on implementing the method in practice. As a result, our presentation is curtailed. Interested readers should refer to the above monograph for a fuller treatment.

17.1 DATA SOURCES FOR RECOVERY MODELING

As always, statistical modeling is predicated on the availability of suitable datasets. The good news in this case is that they are generally plentiful and relatively inexpensive. Given America's love affair with the automobile, this should surprise nobody.

The two oldest and most prominent organizations that provide reliable secondary market prices on pre-owned vehicles are the National Automobile Dealers Association (NADA) and Kelley Blue Book. Each of them has over 75 years of operating history, which is essentially as far back as one can go in the automobile business. One should normally compare the prices for the same vehicle found in both publications to estimate the variability of wholesale prices.

The first task is the creation of an average monthly depreciation curve for the models and makes found in the target asset pool. This work can take on nightmarish proportions very quickly since the number of separate curves that need to be synthesized may easily exceed 100. No matter how many interns you have at your disposal, it seems excessive for an output that is bound to show repetition across models of the same make. In addition, strictly speaking the results will not be directly applicable to the target transaction since by definition the vehicles in the pool have not gone through their entire useful life. As a result, we recommend using a single, generic depreciation curve for each make in the pool. In other words, there is no need to specifically model the 1997 Cavalier or the 1999 Taurus when generic Taurus and Cavalier curves will do just as well.

Just to be sure, the analyst should simply compare two different models of the same make to ascertain that depreciation variance across years is no larger than that within a single year. This is the so-called analysis of variance with which any statistician ought to be familiar. You do not have to do this yourself. Most arrangers should already have staff capable of performing this analysis for you. Of course, this should never stop you from trying it alone.

The upshot of this synthetic exercise is an average vehicle monthly depreciation curve like the one shown in table 17.1. It gives the relative depreciation of an arbitrary make over its useful life, starting from an initial wholesale value, which is really the dealer price, to its fully depreciated condition some seven or eight years later.

If a particular vehicle retains significant value over a longer period, for instance a Mercedes Benz, the curve can simply be extended beyond 80 months. Further, note that this curve is monotonic, inflated by definition, and ignores situations whereby market forces might result in a price increase over time. In virtually all cases,

TABLE 17.1

Wholesale depreciation curve for an arbitrary vehicle

MONTH ID	VALUE	MONTH ID	VALUE
0	100.00%	41	15.10%
1	93.92%	42	14.76%
2	88.24%	43	14.44%
3	82.95%	44	14.14%
4	78.02%	45	13.86%
5	73.42%	46	13.60%
6	69.13%	47	13.35%
7	65.14%	48	13.13%
8	61.41%	49	12.91%
9	57.93%	50	12.72%
10	54.69%	51	12.53%
11	51.67%	52	12.36%
12	48.85%	53	12.20%
13	46.23%	54	12.05%
14	43.78%	55	11.92%
15	41.49%	56	11.79%
16	39.37%	57	11.66%
17	37.38%	58	11.55%
18	35.53%	59	11.45%
19	33.80%	60	11.35%
20	32.19%	61	11.26%
21	30.69%	62	11.17%
22	29.29%	63	11.09%
23	27.99%	64	11.02%
24	26.77%	65	10.95%
25	25.64%	66	10.89%
26	24.58%	67	10.83%
27	23.60%	68	10.77%
28	22.68%	69	10.72%
29	21.82%	70	10.67%
30	21.02%	71	10.62%
31	20.28%	72	10.58%
32	19.58%	73	10.54%
33	18.93%	74	10.51%
34	18.33%	75	10.47%
35	17.77%	76	10.44%
36	17.24%	77	10.41%
37	16.75%	78	10.38%
38	16.30%	79	10.36%
39	15.87%	80	10.33%
40	15.47%		

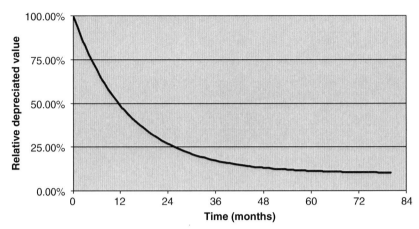

FIGURE 17.1

Vehicle wholesale depreciation curve.

average vehicle prices will decrease with time and the deal will normally see inflated prices. Thus, the last two restrictions are not really limitations of the approach and can safely be made.

Simply looking at table 17.1 will tell you nothing. The only way to make sense of these data is to plot them as we have done in figure 17.1. As you can see, wholesale value falls off dramatically immediately after the vehicle is sold as new (see our discussion of the manufacturing date below). This initial, dramatic drop-off is effectively related to the *vanity* aspect of new automobile purchases. Thereafter, the rate of depreciation decreases precipitously and prices level off asymptotically about seven years after the initial sale.

When trying to discover how to model this curve, you must always keep the foregoing comments on functional behavior in mind. At first blush, a parabola might seem to do the trick, but the curling up of parabolas past their minimum value disqualifies this particular functional form, since there is no guarantee that during deal analysis, the resulting analytical curve would only be used in-sample.

Next, the data themselves can of course be used, but the issue there is one of smoothness. One cannot use a nonmonotonic recovery pattern inside a model since there is no a priori rationale for such behavior. Regardless of the meanderings of the actual empirical curve, the model itself must evidence commonsense, i.e., monotonically decreasing recovery values. Market risk is a factor superposed onto this basic monotonic behavior and does not affect this argument.

Given these remarks, the analyst is left with very little wiggle room in assigning a causal model to the data in table 17.1 once customary curve-fitting efforts such as Lagrange polynomials are excluded as inappropriate. The upshot is that a suitably modulated, negative exponential is usually the preferred embodiment for recovery modeling. The basic form for this model is given by equation (1):

$$R(t) = W_0[a + be^{-ct}] \qquad (1)$$

In the last relationship, vector $R(t)$ stands for the wholesale depreciated value as represented empirically by the appropriate columns in table 17.1, t is time in months, W_0 the initial wholesale value of the new vehicle known from pool data, while a, b, and c are the unknown model parameters to be evaluated from the given data points.

The remainder of this chapter consists of a detailed explanation of how to compute these three parameters within the most basic framework for doing so: the Newton–Raphson method. Before embarking on this trip however, it is a good idea to spend a few minutes discussing whether and why recovery modeling matters.

17.2 WHY DOES RECOVERY MODELING MATTER?

This question is posed primarily because one should always remain open to the possibility that painstakingly modeling recoveries could be *overkill* in asset-backed finance. Why not spend all that precious time working out the *best* structure or the most accurate Markov transition matrix? Would it not be smarter to spend our intellectual capital on obligors that do not default rather than on those that do? After all, if everybody were to default there wouldn't even be a deal.

The simple answer is that transaction modeling does not amount to a trade off between what you can get away with and what you cannot, but more between what makes sense and what does not. Here, what makes sense is that recoveries are obviously dynamic *a priori* instead of static and that we do not have a choice in the matter if this is to be more than a feel-good exercise. The obligors that do default are the life and blood of credit analysis. Saying that detailed recovery modeling is overkill is like saying hurricane insurance in Louisiana is a waste of money because they do not happen very often anyway.

To see why recoveries are dynamic, look at figure 17.2, showing the combination of loan amortization and vehicle depreciation. The loss amount on the vehicle is roughly the difference between the upper and lower curves. We say roughly because auction fees and other minor factors will usually eat into the dollar recoveries seen by the trust. If you compute that difference time-wise and plot it, figure 17.3 will result.

The recovery percentage is simply the complement of losses L divided by the loan's outstanding principal balance P at the time of default, i.e., $1 - L/P$. If you plot that quantity versus time, figure 17.4 is what you obtain.

As you can see, assuming constant recoveries as a percentage of the outstanding principal loan balance, which is what most cash flow models assume, is guaranteed to be wrong all the time, not to mention that it flies in the face of commonsense. Even if we used the actual average recovery given by figure 17.4 as our mean value, it would still be wrong because structured finance is about yield not loss.

Before moving on, note that starting at approximately month 55, recoveries begin to exceed 100%. You will recall the portfolio analysis in chapter 15 where we highlighted this fact in our discussion of functional forms appropriate to loss distributions. Although in practice this should seldom be seen, since an obligor finding

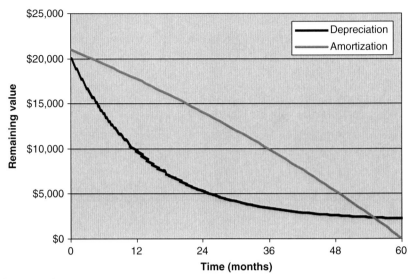

FIGURE 17.2

Loan amortization versus vehicle depreciation.

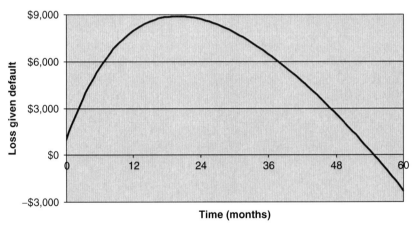

FIGURE 17.3

Vehicle expected loss curve.

herself in this situation could presumably sell her vehicle to a dealer to pay off the remaining balance on her loan, many obligors do not know whether this would in fact happen or do not have the wherewithal to effect this transaction. As a result, and regardless of what consumer protection laws might have to say about it, negative losses do occur. Without accurate recovery modeling of the kind proposed hereunder, this situation can never emerge from the analysis.

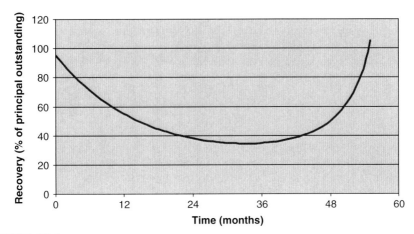

FIGURE 17.4
Vehicle expected recovery curve.

17.3 NONLINEAR REGRESSION MODELING

Coming back to equation (1), our task is now to compute the values of the parameters a, b, and c that really define our simple recovery model.

In its current form, equation (1) is an example of nonlinear regression, so-called not because the functional form is not linear but because the standard regression formalism will result in a set of nonlinear equations to be solved for the values of the three model parameters. In fact, many linear regressions consist of nonlinear functional forms of the raw data. This situation obviously arises from the presence of parameter c in the exponential factor. Note that it would be possible to transform equation (1) to recover linearity, but our aim is to demonstrate the nonlinear regression formalism that would apply in all cases. A linear regression can also be handled as shown here.

The Formalism of Nonlinear Regression

A brief survey of the theory will help us understand what we are doing. Consider a general, possibly nonlinear function $f(t; p)$ of the independent variable t with $t \in [0, T]$ and given at a finite number of $T + 1$ points $f_i(t_i; p)$. Consider also an n-dimensional parametric vector p with $p \equiv [p_1 p_2 \ldots p_n]$. This is what we have in equation (1). The idea is to compute the parameters using the given vector of dependent values $y_i, i \in [0, T]$, which are the available, empirical values obtained in the manner indicated above in "Data Sources for Recovery Modeling". For our purposes, these values will be those shown in table 17.1.

To solve this problem first define the familiar Lagrangian L as follows:

$$L = \sum_{i=0}^{T} (y_i - f_i(t_i; p))^2. \tag{2}$$

The equations for the parameters $p_j, j \in [1, n]$ are obtained by differentiating equation (2) with respect to vector p and setting the result to zero in each case, yielding equations (3) (the factor 2 simply drops out). This is the standard least-squares procedure commonly associated with the regression formalism:

$$\frac{\partial L}{\partial p_j} = \sum_{i=0}^{T} [y_i - f_i(t_i; p)] \frac{\partial f_i(t_i; p)}{\partial p_j} \equiv 0 \qquad (3)$$

In cases where the expression $f(t; p)$ is a linear function of its parameters, this procedure will result in a set of linear equations that can be solved via matrix inversion. By contrast, if $f(t; p)$ should be nonlinear in any of its parameters, at least one equation will present nonlinear features that will preclude matrix inversion and require an iterative solution. This is the present case.

A Sidebar on the Regression Estimator

At this point, it is useful to pause briefly to discuss least-squares regression with respect to its linear optimality vis-à-vis empirical data. Although this was far from evident two hundred years ago, the optimality of regression is something statisticians have now come to accept as Gospel. The simple fact is that most people are quite ready to jump to hasty conclusions in nonlinear regimes just because a formal proof is available in the linear case.

The first hint that least squares *linear* regression could be considered optimal was the heuristic argument provided by Gauss himself at the dawn of the nineteenth century. His starting notion (soon discredited by his contemporaries we might add), was that it was "obvious" that the arithmetic mean y_m was the best estimate of a parameter that could be derived from a set of n independent and equally uncertain observations y_i of this parameter, i.e.,

$$y_m = \frac{1}{n} \sum_{i=1}^{n} y_i.$$

After claiming this was obvious, he simply proceeded to show constructively that the least squares estimate arising from this set was precisely that number. We can see that this is true by defining our Lagrangian via:

$$L = \sum_{i=1}^{n} (y_i - b)^2$$

From this definition, we easily derive the least-squares estimate b using the first order condition $\frac{\partial L}{\partial b} = 0$, leading to:

$$\frac{\partial L}{\partial b} = -2 \sum_{i=1}^{n} (y_i - b) = 0 \rightarrow b = \frac{1}{n} \sum_{i=1}^{n} y_i, QED$$

From this "self-evident" proposition, Gauss concluded that least squares regression was the way to go in all linear cases. As you can see, he had simply assumed his own conclusion. Thus, even someone of Gauss' stature was prone to wishful thinking simply because of his firm intuition that the regression formulation was indeed privileged. However, he later corrected that mistake *via* the brilliant exposition we have come to know as the Gauss–Markov theorem.

Since the above heuristic proof and the Gauss–Markov theorem apply only to linear operators, we cannot make a general statement about the optimality of least squares regression for nonlinear forms. It is, however, a universally accepted notion that regression is the best one can really do with empirical data, i.e., that it is the "truth" in the data. The point here is not to argue with this settled proposition but to remember that this is not as obvious as it might seem.

Other estimators do exist and it is not a forgone conclusion that regression is always optimal in nonlinear cases. The strongest argument in favor of linear regression is not what we just discussed. Rather, it is that owing to the maximization of a quadratic functional in parametric space, it always yields a unique solution. Even though this is something to be prized per se, it is always dangerous to let the tail wag the dog.

17.4 THE NEWTON–RAPHSON IMPLEMENTATION OF THE RECOVERY MODEL

We have now come to the meat of this chapter, the VBA implementation of equation (1) using the Newton–Raphson method.

From equation (1), we can see right away that the three parameters are dependent since by definition, we need to enforce the defining constraint $R(0) = W_0$ as a boundary condition of our solution procedure. In other words, we cannot allow the computation to reach a final solution that violates our fundamental assumption stating that the initial wholesale value of the vehicle is W_0. In turn, this implies:

$$a + b = 1 \tag{4}$$

Instead of simply substituting $b = 1 - a$ into equation (1), a constrained optimization problem will be solved by the introduction of an unknown Lagrange multiplier λ into the original Lagrangian definition, which, in combination with equation (1) and dropping the redundant factor W_0 for the remainder of the exercise yields the final Lagrangian:

$$L = \sum_{i=0}^{T} [y_i - a - b e^{-ct_i}]^2 + \lambda (a + b - 1) \tag{5}$$

Now, instead of three unknown parameters, we have a fourth one (λ) and we have to differentiate equation (5) with respect to λ as well to find its equilibrium value. You might wonder whether we have not made the problem even harder by doing this. Not really, if by *harder* you mean the extra dimension. In theory, a three-dimensional problem is just as difficult as a four-dimensional one. This method also has the huge advantage of being cleaner and much more easily implementable than any other, for obviously you are not learning the Newton–Raphson method to solve such trivial problems, but to be well-equipped later on for some serious modeling effort.

In many cases, there will be no simple relation like equation (4) to play with; the constraint will only be given as an integral, differential, or even integro-differential relation that will preclude simple insertion. Furthermore, there is really no guarantee that substituting $b = 1 - a$ into equation (5) will result in both parameters being positive, as they must be. In the end, you are far better off learning a method that always works rather than using something that might work one day and blow up in your face the next.

Proceeding as dictated by equation (3) within our four-dimensional space, we obtain the set of nonlinear relationships to be solved via Newton–Raphson analysis:

$$\frac{\partial L}{\partial a} = 0 \tag{6}$$

$$\frac{\partial L}{\partial b} = 0 \tag{7}$$

$$\frac{\partial L}{\partial c} = 0 \tag{8}$$

$$\frac{\partial L}{\partial \lambda} = 0 \tag{9}$$

Insertion of the right-hand side of equation (5) into equations (6) through (9) yields the following set of four nonlinear equations $g_i, i \in [1, 4]$, which we henceforth refer to as vector **g**:

$$g_1 \equiv \sum_{i=0}^{T} [y_i - a - be^{-ct_i}] - \frac{\lambda}{2} = 0 \tag{10}$$

$$g_2 \equiv \sum_{i=0}^{T} e^{-ct_i}[y_i - a - be^{-ct_i}] - \frac{\lambda}{2} = 0 \tag{11}$$

$$g_3 \equiv \sum_{i=0}^{T} t_i e^{-ct_i}[y_i - a - be^{-ct_i}] = 0 \tag{12}$$

$$g_4 \equiv a + b - 1 = 0 \tag{13}$$

Exercise 17.1

As a preamble to the vector mode solution, solve for both roots of the analytic function $f(x) = e^x - 5x$ using the scalar version of the Newton–Raphson method. Write a short (three to four lines) VBA program to do this and study the convergence of the method for the initial guess vector $x \in [-10, 10]$ by trying out every integer in the set. Plot the convergence history of each starting value and observe which root is being captured. Think about how you would accelerate the convergence of the scalar method by "jumping" to the root faster if you can figure out how not to jump too far.

The Vector Mode Newton–Raphson Iterative Scheme

First, defining $\mathbf{J}$ as the Jacobian matrix of first derivatives of $\mathbf{g}$ and setting $x_1 = a$; $x_2 = b$; $x_3 = c$; $x_4 = \lambda$ for convenience, we have:

$$\mathbf{J} = \begin{bmatrix} \dfrac{\partial g_1(\mathbf{x})}{\partial x_1} & \dfrac{\partial g_1(\mathbf{x})}{\partial x_2} & \cdots & \dfrac{\partial g_1(\mathbf{x})}{\partial x_n} \\[2ex] \dfrac{\partial g_2(\mathbf{x})}{\partial x_1} & \dfrac{\partial g_2(\mathbf{x})}{\partial x_2} & \cdots & \dfrac{\partial g_2(\mathbf{x})}{\partial x_n} \\[2ex] \cdot & & & \\ \cdot & & & \\ \dfrac{\partial g_n(\mathbf{x})}{\partial x_1} & \dfrac{\partial g_n(\mathbf{x})}{\partial x_2} & \cdots & \dfrac{\partial g_n(\mathbf{x})}{\partial x_n} \end{bmatrix} \tag{14}$$

Now, expand the vector-valued function $\mathbf{g}$ into its first order Taylor-series (i.e., neglect all higher-order terms) about some initial point $\mathbf{x}_0$ in vector space to obtain:

$$\mathbf{g}(\mathbf{x}_0 + \Delta\mathbf{x}) = \mathbf{g}(\mathbf{x}_0) + \mathbf{J}(\mathbf{x}_0)\,\Delta\mathbf{x} + \dots. \tag{15}$$

Because each successive iterate $\mathbf{x_n} + \Delta\mathbf{x_n}$ is meant to drive the function $\mathbf{g}$ toward zero in vector space, it would perhaps be a good idea to calculate the increment $\Delta\mathbf{x}$ so that it could potentially accomplish this in one step by setting:

$$\Delta\mathbf{x} = -\mathbf{J}^{-1}(\mathbf{x}_0)\mathbf{g}(\mathbf{x}_0) \tag{16}$$

Finally, insertion of the definition $\Delta\mathbf{x} = \mathbf{x_n} - \mathbf{x_{n-1}}$ into equation (16) yields the general Newton–Raphson (NR) iterative scheme:

$$\mathbf{x_n} = \mathbf{x_{n-1}} - \mathbf{J}^{-1}(\mathbf{x_{n-1}})\mathbf{g}(\mathbf{x_{n-1}}) \tag{17}$$

Equation (17) is used repeatedly until iterates $\Delta\mathbf{x}$ become too small to matter or the sequence of successive iterates starts to diverge. In general, convergence is reached in less than 10 iterations. Please note that computational and debugging time may be saved by noticing that, with a simple change of variable, the Jacobian matrix can be written as a symmetric matrix. We leave this as an exercise.

The interested reader should consult "*The Analysis of Structured Securities*" (OUP, 2003) for a more detailed treatment of convergence issues. Here and now, note that the NR method is not guaranteed to converge to a root of the vector function $\mathbf{g}$ (local optimum) even when such root is known to exist. As a result, we refer to the NR method as *locally* convergent.

Broyden's method, which is significantly more complicated to implement, does converge for all choices of $\mathbf{x}_0$ and is therefore referred to as *globally* convergent.

TABLE 17.2
Four-dimensional Jacobian determinant for NR solution

J_{ij}	1	2	3	4
1	$-(T+1)$	$-\sum_{i=0}^{T} e^{-ct_i}$	$b\sum_{i=0}^{T} t_i e^{-ct_i}$	$-1/2$
2	$-\sum_{i=0}^{T} e^{-ct_i}$	$-\sum_{i=0}^{T} e^{-2ct_i}$	$\sum_{i=0}^{T} t_i e^{-ct_i}(2be^{-ct_i} - y_i + a)$	$-1/2$
3	$-\sum_{i=0}^{T} t_i e^{-ct_i}$	$-\sum_{i=0}^{T} t_i e^{-2ct_i}$	$\sum_{i=0}^{T} t_i^2 e^{-ct_i}(2be^{-ct_i} - y_i + a)$	0
4	1	1	0	0

However, in all attempts at recovery modeling within structured finance you will be able to take a sufficiently accurate guess at the ultimate root and the simplistic, locally stable NR method will converge. Just be aware that if the method suddenly starts to malfunction, it does not mean that there is necessarily something wrong with your code.

Implementation begins with the theoretical computation of the Jacobian determinant as indicated above. Remember that differentiation in parametric space and summation in time space are independent operations. For ease of exposition, we present the Jacobian definitions in table 17.2 and in the form given implicitly by equation (14).

To see how this works, consider element $J_{11} = -(T+1)$ in table 17.2. How did we get that result? As implied by our definitions, this element is computed via:

$$J_{11} \equiv \frac{\partial g_1}{\partial a} = \sum_{i=0}^{T} \frac{\partial}{\partial a}\{y_i - a - be^{-ct_i}\} - \frac{\partial}{\partial a}\left\{\frac{\lambda}{2}\right\} = \sum_{i=0}^{T}(-1) = -(T+1)$$

The other elements of the first and subsequent rows, are computed analogously. All Jacobian entries must be updated after the computation of each new iterate-vector $\mathbf{X_n}$

Exercise 17.2

Compute the remaining three elements of the first row of the Jacobian determinant to verify the relationships given in table 17.2.

Exercise 17.3

Compute the four elements of the third row of the Jacobian determinant to verify the relationships given by table 17.2.

17.5 NUMERICAL SOLUTION PROCEDURE

In most cases, the required repeated inversion of the Jacobian given in table 17.2 can be done using a system-supplied matrix inversion routine. One such routine already exists in the VBA library. Alternatively, you can use one of the techniques described in reference textbooks like *Numerical Recipes*.[1] In the worst case, four-dimensional matrix inversion can be trivially implemented using Kramer's rule, something most of you will have learned in high school.

As we mentioned before, in the case of a locally stable method such as the NR-iteration scheme, the value of the initial guess vector is critical in determining the iteration's convergence history. This is because for the NR method to be successful, the mapping $x_{n-1} \rightarrow x_n$ must continuously reduce the distance between the solution-vector and the current value of x. We refer to such mappings as "hyperbolic" or "contractive" (see chapter 22 on the importance of contractive mappings). In turn, this means that the initial guess must be close enough to that solution for the mapping to be hyperbolic.

Unfortunately, knowing that one is close enough to *somewhere* implies knowledge of where that is. But if one actually knows the location of the solution to begin with, why bother looking for it? Thus, what remains unexplained and problematic is how to specify in a nontrivial way regions of x space where the method is guaranteed to converge. Such specifications are the subject of convergence analysis, something beyond the scope of this text. The point here, again, is that if the scheme diverges there may be nothing wrong with your code and the problem may simply be one of choosing an appropriate starting guess.

To do this can be nontrivial and is not an exercise in logic. The folowing procedure seems to work all the time:

1. Use a stripped down, linear version of the relevant nonlinear model
2. Solve the (inaccurate) linear case via normal matrix inversion
3. Use the linear solution as the starting guess vector.

The good news is that you will not have to do this. Most vehicle depreciation curves tend to look similar, and we have found that the starting vector $a = 1$, $b = 1$, $c = 0.1$ and $\lambda = 1$ works well in all cases of interest. Please remember that each functional form of a recovery model will require its own NR treatment and that some forms are unduly complicated without adding one iota to basic understanding. Be wary of increasing a model's complexity and believing that you have thereby increased your knowledge of the matter. This is rarely the case. The complexity of any model is a direct function of the intricacy of the available database. Unless you find that the distribution of residuals $(y_i - f_i)$ stemming from equation (1) is strongly nonnormal, we recommend sticking to the simpler functional form.

Exhibit 17.1 is a typical VBA implementation of the above NR iterative scheme based on the use of equation (1) as a depreciation model.

> **Exhibit 17.1: VBA Implementation of the Vector Mode NR Iterative Scheme**

```
Option Base 1
Option Explicit

Sub Newton Raphson ()
Dim T() As Double, Y() As Double, X() As Double, R() As Double
Dim a1 As Double, b1 As Double, c1 As Double, lambda1 As Double
Dim a2 As Double, b2 As Double, c2 As Double, lambda2 As Double
Dim MaxIter As Integer, i As Integer, Epsilon As Double
Dim History As range: Set History = range("History")
```

We iterate until MaxIter is reached or else the difference between two iterations is less than Epsilon

```
MaxIter = 10
Epsilon = 0.00000001
T = ReadArray("T"): Y = ReadArray("Y") :X = ReadArray("X")
a1 = X(1):b1 = X(2) :c1 = X(3) :lambda1 = X(4)

For i = 1 To MaxIter
History.Cells(i, 1) = a1 : History.Cells(i, 2) = b1 : History.Cells(i, 3) = c1:
History.Cells(i, 4) = lambda1
```

*The next iteration: Xn = Xn-1 – J^-1 * F*

```
R = MMult(MInverse(GetJacobian(T, Y, a1, b1, c1, lambda1)), GetF(T, Y, a1, b1, c1,
lambda1))
a2 = a1 - R(1, 1) : b2 = b1 - R(2, 1) : c2 = c1 - R(3, 1) : lambda2 = lambda1 - R(4, 1)
```

We continue until there is no noticeable change

```
   If Sqr((a1 - a2) ^ 2 + (b1 - b2) ^ 2 + (c1 - c2) ^ 2) < Epsilon Then
     Exit For
   End If
   a1 = a2 : b1 = b2 : c1 = c2 : lambda1 = lambda2
Next i
If i > MaxIter Then
   MsgBox ("Unable to converge in " & MaxIter & " iterations")
   Exit Sub
End If
End Sub
```

Compute the Jacobian matrix

```
Function GetJacobian(T() As Double, Y() As Double, a As Double, b As Double, c As
Double, N As Integer, i As Integer, lambda As Double) As Double(),j12 As Double
Dim j13 As Double, j22 As Double, j23 As Double, j32 As Double, j33 As Double

N = UBound(Y, 1)
For i = 1 To N
```

```
j12 = j12 + Exp(-c * T(i))
j13 = j13 + T(i) * Exp(-c * T(i))
j22 = j22 + Exp(-2 * c * T(i))
j23 = j23 + T(i) * Exp(-c * T(i)) * (2 * b * Exp(-c * T(i)) - Y(i) + a)
j32 = j32 + T(i) * Exp(-2 * c * T(i))
j33 = j33 + T(i) ^ 2 * Exp(-c * T(i)) * (2 * b * Exp(-c * T(i)) - Y(i) + a)
Next i

ReDim J(4, 4) As Double
J(1, 1) = -N : J(1, 2) = -j12 : J(1, 3) = b * j13 : J(1, 4) = -0.5
J(2, 1) = J(1, 2) : J(2, 2) = -j22 : J(2, 3) = j23 : J(2, 4) = -0.5
J(3, 1) = -j13 : J(3, 2) = -j32 : J(3, 3) = j33 : J(3, 4) = 0
J(4, 1) = 1 : J(4, 2) = 1 : J(4, 4) = 0 : J(4, 4) = 0
GetJacobian = J
End Function
```

Evaluate the right-hand-side function [F] and return a 4 × 1 matrix

```
Function GetF(T() As Double, Y() As Double, a As Double, b As Double, c As Double,
lambda As Double) As Double()
Dim f11 As Double, f21 As Double, f31 As Double, N As Integer, i As Integer
N - UBound(Y, 1)
For i = 1 To N
f11 = f11 + (Y(i) - a - b * Exp(-c * T(i)))
f21 = f21 + (Y(i) - a - b * Exp(-c * T(i))) * Exp(-c * T(i))
f31 = f31 + (Y(i) - a - b * Exp(-c * T(i))) * Exp(-c * T(i)) * T(i)
Next i
Dim F() As Double : ReDim F(4, 1) As Double
F(1, 1) = f11 - lambda / 2
F(2, 1) = f21 - lambda / 2
F(3, 1) = f31
F(4, 1) = a + b - 1
GetF = F
End Function
```

Compute the inverse of the Jacobian matrix

```
Function MInverse(M() As Double) As Double()
Dim Tmp() As Variant
Tmp = Application.WorksheetFunction.MInverse(M)
MInverse = MDouble(Tmp)
End Function
```

Compute the update by multiplying the inverse Jacobian by the right-hand-side function

```
Function MMult(M1() As Double, M2() As Double) As Double()
Dim Tmp() As Variant
Tmp = Application.WorksheetFunction.MMult(M1, M2)
MMult = MDouble(Tmp)
End Function
```

> **Exercise 17.4**
>
> Using the above code as an example, implement the NR procedure in VBA, debug it and run it to obtain the results shown in table 17.3. Experiment using starting vectors different from those suggested here.

For this selection of the starting vector, the NR procedure is efficient and yields a solution within a few iterations. For instance, table 17.3 gives the Newton–Raphson convergence history for the depreciation data in table 17.1. The agreement between the depreciation data and the model shown in figure 17.5 is impressive and in fact, a little suspicious.

TABLE 17.3
Typical Newton–Raphson convergence history

n	a	b	c
0	1	1	0.1
1	0.147	0.852	0.0909
2	0.096	0.903	0.0599
3	0.091	0.908	0.0661
4	0.095	0.900	0.0696
5	0.099	0.900	0.0699
6	0.100	0.900	0.0700

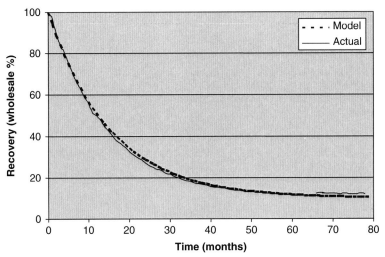

FIGURE 17.5
Actual depreciation data versus the exponential model.

As expected the sum $a + b$ equals unity, showing the correct operation of the Lagrange multiplier λ. In general, we find that functional forms of this type fit the depreciation data extremely well and result in R^2 statistics in the neighborhood of 95% and better. On a Pentium III desktop computer, more than 100 depreciation curves can usually be processed this way in less than a minute. The associated accuracy improvements in recovery estimates are well worth this medium-size effort, not to mention its potential impact on credit enhancement levels.

Exercise 17.5

Instead of functional form (1), use the alternative, quadratic depreciation form:

$$R(t) = W_0 [at^2 + bt + c]$$

For this linear regression, compute the Jacobian and solve the model as if it were a nonlinear regression to verify that, indeed, it converges in one step. Plot the resulting model over time from $t = 0$ to $t = 90$ months. Is there something strange with this model? In other words, would you recommend it to your friends?

Notes on Convergence Acceleration

In practice, the empirical convergence history of any numerical scheme gives us a lot of information on the ways to accelerate that process. For instance, note that model parameter b has already reached its limiting value, at least to three decimal places, by the fourth iterate. This means that Jacobian elements are conspiring to keep b at its limiting value, in effect wiping out numerical error modes via corresponding zero-elements of the current Jacobian. This knowledge can be put to use by advancing the solution vector faster in one or many parametric dimensions compared to others.

In this case, we would most likely be able to accelerate convergence by over-relaxing parameter a or b, or perhaps both, through the introduction of an artificial relaxation term inside the current version of equation (16):

$$\Delta \mathbf{x_n} = -\mathbf{J}^{-1}(\mathbf{x_n})\mathbf{H}(\mathbf{x_n})\mathbf{f}(\mathbf{x_n})$$

In this equation, matrix $\mathbf{H}(\mathbf{x_n})$ would be a diagonal matrix chosen to accelerate convergence in whatever direction was appropriate. You would obviously have to exercise care in choosing the iterate-dependent sequence of diagonal entries of $\mathbf{H}(\mathbf{x_n})$ so as not to overshoot the solution-vector on your way to the ultimate root.

The next level of sophistication would consist in allowing off-diagonal entries of $\mathbf{H}(\mathbf{x_n})$ to be non-zero selectively, again being guided by the convergence analysis. Needless to say, numerical considerations of this sort are beyond the scope of this text. But we should nevertheless mention that although it is the case that convergence analysis is one of the chief weapons in the arsenal of a seasoned numerical analyst, the pitfalls of vector-mode convergence are numerous and can easily turn against their protagonist to quickly become weapons of mass destruction. In other words, unless you really have to, just use the straight NR method.

In closing, we should reiterate that this example requires little numerical sophistication on the part of an analyst. In this case, not much would be gained by spending large chunks of time studying the convergence properties of a particular functional form where convergence is quasi-guaranteed with precious little preliminary work. Were a serious analytical effort ever required, one involving the simultaneous solution of hundreds or even thousands of equations, convergence acceleration would not be a waste of time. In fact, it is only to provide hints as to what to do in such cases that we bring up the topic.

17.6 RECOVERY IMPLEMENTATION IN ACTUAL TRANSACTIONS

In practice, the implementation of the recovery framework developed in this chapter is not as straightforward as would appear from equation (1) alone. The fact is that automobile loans are generally not securitized at the time they are made for the simple reason that it takes any institution, even captive finance arms of large U.S. auto manufacturers, a finite time to assemble the pools necessary to create an efficient transaction in terms of outside-party fees (legal, accounting, etc.), not to mention the ever-rising rating agency fees. As a result, most pools will contain loans with finite seasoning. Since we reviewed seasoning calculations back in chapter 15, readers should consult the relevant section for more details on this issue.

In addition, except for the large U.S. and European auto-makers, most auto-loan pools consist of a mix of new and pre-owned vehicles, which adds yet another twist to the situation since, strictly speaking, equation (1) applies only to vehicles that are securitized immediately following their manufacture. Thus, the VBA code given earlier in this chapter was somewhat contrived in the sense that we assumed that all the vehicles were new. As a result, the time of the deal and the time of the vehicle were identical by definition. In the next few paragraphs, we show how to correct equation (1) for the double impact of a potential delay in securitization from the time the loan is made and of securitizing pre-owned vehicles. For the remainder of this section, we will refer to figure 17.6 showing how time must be partitioned within equation (1).

Securitization Delay

Referring to figure 17.1 for a moment, let's assume that the particular loan under consideration was securitized at time t_0. For purposes of the deal t_0 was by definition equal to zero, but obviously it is not numerically equal to zero and really corresponds to some commonsense time reference, like November 1, 2006. Similarly, the loan was obviously made at a time t_l before it was securitized. Glancing at figure 17.6, assume seasoning t_s satisfies the relationship $t_s = t_0 - t_l$.

The wholesale value W_0 in equation (1) is always given at the time a loan is made, which means that the location $t = 0$ in equation (1) does not correspond to deal time per se, where $t_0 \equiv 0$ holds by definition, but rather to $t = t_l$. In other words, the time of the deal is already ahead by t_s when compared to the time at which wholesale value

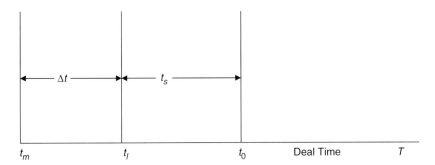

FIGURE 17.6
The recovery time line.

data are available to the analyst. The securitization delay imposes a first modification to equation (1) that compensates for this effect within actual transactions:

$$R(t) = W_0 [a + b e^{-c(t+t_s)}] \tag{18}$$

In the vast majority of cases, seasoning values will be relatively small compared to the maturity of the loans in the pool, and so it would be tempting to ignore the seasoning adjustment in equation (1) altogether. Unfortunately, the problem with doing this is that we are dealing with the wrong end of the curve for this purpose, i.e., the initial portion.

As you can easily see by glancing at figure 17.1, the early portion of the curve is where significant depreciation takes place. It is therefore inappropriate to ignore seasoning in the region where the depreciation gradient takes on its largest values. By contrast, due to the asymptotic nature of depreciation, ignoring the last three to four months around the loan's maturity would cause relatively small errors in the overall scheme of things. Therefore, we recommend that a securitization delay adjustment should always be included, especially in subprime transactions. In any event, the effort in doing so is minimal.

Lending Delay

Unfortunately, adjusting for securitization delays is not sufficient to prepare equation (1) for the realities of deal analysis, because a large percentage of automobiles are sold as pre-owned vehicles. By this, we refer to a lending delay Δt, a much larger quantity than t_s and one we therefore need to include in our recovery calculations.

Specifically, let's assume the target vehicle was manufactured at time t_m, which by definition must take place before the loan was made at time t_l. In other words, the lending delay can be defined as $\Delta t = t_l - t_m$. Again referring to figure 17.6, the boundary condition defining the sale of a pre-owned vehicle is thus:

$$W_0 = W_\infty [a + b e^{-c \Delta t}] \tag{19}$$

Equation (19) expresses the fact that, when the vehicle is known to have a wholesale value W_0 at time t_l, a period Δt from its date of manufacture has already elapsed. Variable W_∞ represents some unknown wholesale value at the time of manufacture. However, please bear in mind that W_∞ does not have to represent any empirically observable value. In effect W_∞ is more akin to a calibration factor than to some physical quantity.

Inversion quickly leads to:

$$W_\infty = \frac{W_0}{[a+be^{-c\,\Delta t}]} \tag{20}$$

Finally, combining equations (18) and (20), we easily derive the general version of equation (1) suitable under all field conditions wherein t is now deal-time proper:

$$R(t) = \frac{W_0\,[a+be^{-c(t+t_s)}]}{[a+be^{-c\,\Delta t}]} \tag{21}$$

What is the Manufacture Date?

Some analysts reading this section are probably wondering how to find out when the vehicle was made. The first point is that the *manufacture* date does not mean this literally, since a vehicle is considered *new* as long as it has not been sold and driven by a consumer. Once it rolls off the assembly line, the first few miles registered by the odometer and logged by safety test-drivers never turn a new vehicle into a used car. Rather, by manufacture date we really mean the first time the car was sold to a bona fide consumer, which may have taken place months after it was physically made. This is the point $t = 0$ in equation (1) and is what t_m truly represents in the context of our calculations.

As far as numbers are concerned, the model year can be lifted from the tenth position of the Vehicle Identification Number (VIN). The VIN is a piece of information each and every lender should have on every automobile in its pools. Second, the paperwork for a pre-owned automobile loan normally contains the exact date of manufacture from which an accurate first-sale date may be inferred if that date is itself not available, which should be rare. In the worst case, the VIN alone can be used to obtain a reasonable estimate of first-sale date. In most cases, analysts should be able to obtain precise sales data on all vehicles sold in the United States.

Please remember that in the case of program-cars, i.e., those sold to car rental agencies that are captives of large U.S. manufacturers, the first-rental date becomes the first-sale date. Such data are even better organized and more readily usable.

18

Covariance Matrices and Laplace Transform Methods

"So much of life, it seems, is determined by pure randomness."
Sydney Poitier

Despite its not being formally involved in the rating exercise we are going through here, we take up once again the subject of covariance matrix simulation. Discussing structured finance while avoiding this topic would be like talking about sailing and ignoring the wind and the ocean.

We strongly encourage readers to read this chapter carefully and to complete the suggested exercises because it is a foregone conclusion that a professional structured analyst will be required to implement the Cholesky decomposition under many circumstances and therefore, that any serious training in structured finance cannot avoid intimate knowledge of this technique. An introductory textbook like this one can obviously not expand endlessly on the topic. Therefore, we restrict ourselves to basic results relevant to structured analysts and to standard implementation mechanics. The Cholesky decomposition is just one version of the broader technique of Lower–Upper (LU) decomposition that can be applied to any matrix. Luckily for us, matrices with special properties, such as symmetry, positive-definiteness and banded structures, present an especially propitious ground for the use of the LU method.

In general, the object of the exercise is the reduction of a full linear, algebraic problem to a sequence of two linked but also linear problems, each of which no longer requires matrix inversion. If the decomposition is less time-consuming than the original, full-blown inversion, it makes sense to do it, and this will happen when matrices possess some of the properties alluded to above. Otherwise, the technique boils down to doing the same work in two steps. In fact, it would be surprising if this were not the case. Otherwise, matrix inversion would have effectively disappeared from the list of basic techniques within numerical analysis. Clearly, low-dimensional (1 to 7) problems are usually not worth the effort of implementing a decomposition since they can be solved quickly anyway. However, when the dimensionality of the problem is in the hundreds or thousands, the operational count can make it worth your while.

In structured finance, LU decomposition is generally not used to solve linear problems, such as least-squares regression, but rather to cause a given covariance structure to exist between hitherto uncorrelated variables. This works because the relation defining covariance is bilinear.

Furthermore, owing to the invariance of correlation matrices under linear transformations, a set of *normally* distributed and suitably correlated deviates with arbitrary means and standard deviations can easily be generated. In many live settings the ability to do this will suffice to solve the problem; for instance in the modeling of a basket of foreign exchange options. However, generating an identical set of correlated deviates with arbitrary distribution functions is much harder and will not be treated or even discussed hereunder. Readers are referred to "*The Analysis of Structured Securities*" (OUP, 2003) for a fuller treatment of this case.

18.1 GENERATING RANDOM NUMBERS FROM STATISTICAL DISTRIBUTIONS

Although this topic was treated in some detail in "*The Analysis of Structured Securities*" (OUP, 2003), it is instructive to review the main technique for generating random numbers. You may recall that selecting random numbers from any distribution boils down to selecting them from a uniform distribution in concert with the inverse distribution function method (IDFM.). The selection of uniform random deviates is what people usually imply when they speak of "random" number selection. The chief figure of merit in this area, other than the obvious requirement of uniformity, is the auto-correlation spectrum of the resulting sequence. In either case we are clearly demanding uniformity, but in the case of the auto-correlation spectrum, we are looking for the presence of identifiable peaks and valleys, indicating that the sequence contains *knowledge*, i.e., that the random character of the sequence is now in question. Although uniform numbers are not a prime target of structured analysis, the proper generation of such deviates cannot simply be assumed away. This operation is of such fundamental importance to structured analysis that we give it priority hereunder.

The Inverse Distribution Function Method

Assuming properly generated uniform deviates are available, the IDFM allows us to satisfy any distributional requirement. In all instances, the goal will be to select a random sample reflecting a given probability density distribution $f(x)$ defined over the interval $[a, b]$.

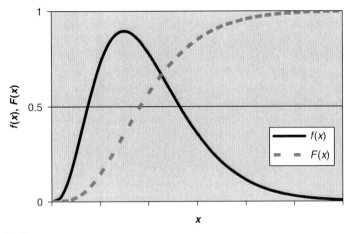

FIGURE 18.1
The inverse distribution function method.

To do this, remember that the associated cumulative distribution function $F(x)$ is defined by:

$$F(x) = \int_a^x f(y)\,dy \tag{1}$$

By definition we have $F(a) = 0$. Now, since $f(x)$ is a probability density function we also have $F(b) = 1$, i.e., the cumulative distribution function spans the entire domain of $f(x)$ over its $[0, 1]$ range. This is shown in Figure 18.1.

Glancing at equation (1), it is clear that the inverse of distribution function $F(x)$ corresponds to $f(x)$. Therefore, by choosing a sample of deviates y from a uniform distribution on the closed interval $[0, 1]$ and setting $F^{-1}(y) = x$, the resulting x will be distributed as $f(x)$. This is the basis of the IDFM.

In implementation, one needs to either obtain a closed-form expression for $F^{-1}(y)$ or else write a small subroutine that locates the proper x given any choice of y.

For example, take the exponential cumulative distribution function defined via:

$$F(x) = 1 - e^{-\alpha x}, \, x \in (0, \infty)$$

It also satisfies the two boundary conditions for a distribution function:

$$F(0) = 0$$
$$F(\infty) = 1$$

In this case, the inverse distribution function is easily derived as:

$$x \equiv F^{-1}(y) = \frac{-\ln(1 - y)}{\alpha}, \, y \in [0, 1]$$

Although in many cases, the analytical derivation of the required inverse function is relatively simple, in many others it is not.

Luckily, the problem of finding distributional inverses has not gone unnoticed at Microsoft. The Excel software is equipped with many resident routines implementing the inverse of most statistical distribution functions of interest. These routines are easy to use and obviate the need to write your own inverse routine. This does not mean that we are encouraging you to rely on Microsoft, quite the contrary. However, it is silly to require students to spend time reinventing the wheel, especially when deal analysis may be unduly slowed down by doing so.

For example, to select a random deviate x from a normal distribution with a mean μ and a standard deviation σ in Excel, one merely needs to enter the formula:

$$x = NormInv(y, \mu, \sigma) \tag{2}$$

The equivalent formula exists for many other statistical distributions, like the gamma distribution employed in chapter 15, or the lognormal distribution that always crops up in connection with stock market analysis.

Note that the numbers forming the sequence y in equation (2) are assumed uniformly distributed. Ensuring this is your job, not Microsoft's.

Methods of Generating Uniform Random Deviates

Armed with our IDFM technique, we have reduced the problem of statistical sampling to that of generating a credible set of uniform deviates y for later insertion into equation (2) or its equivalent with respect to other distribution functions. We review three familiar methods of doing this and explore them via exercises.

(a) The Excel-resident Routine Rand

The first method is the Excel routine Rand, which for some reason is dubbed "Rnd" inside VBA.

Exercise 18.1

Using Excel or any other spreadsheet software, spawn m = 500 uniform deviates using Rand or its equivalent and plot them using a histogram (bar chart) partitioned into N equal sectors from 0 to 1. Do this for the sector-sequence $N \in [1, 5, 10, 25, 50]$ and notice the difference in uniformity when resolution increases. Calculate the uniformity figure of merit κ using the definition:

$$\kappa \equiv \frac{1}{N} \sum_{i=1}^{N} (n_i - {}^m/_N)^2 \tag{3}$$

In equation(3), n_i is the number of random draws in the interval S_i, with $S_i \equiv [(i-1)/N, i/N]$.

Repeat this exercise for m-samples of 1,000 and 5,000 deviates, respectively and compare the three values of κ so obtained. Does uniformity increase as the size of the random sample increases? Can you live with these departures from complete uniformity?

(b) The Antithetic Correction Method

This second method is nothing more than a variation on Rand intended to correct the excessive nonuniformity found in plain-vanilla Rand implementations. It is quasi-trivial in that it boils down to selecting pairs of inversely correlated random numbers together instead of individual values, thereby introducing an "antithetic" bias in successive values. As a result, this works well in instances where the distributional uniformity of the sequence is of paramount importance as compared to its autocorrelative properties.

Exercise 18.2

Using a sequence of 5,000 uniform random deviates x_t, $t \in [1, 5000]$ generated using Rand, plot the sequence's autocorrelation spectrum $\gamma(n)$ for the set $n \in [0, 25]$ with the definition:

$$\gamma(n) = \frac{E[x_t x_{t-n}]}{\sigma_t \sigma_{t-n}}$$

Do you see any unusual peaks? If you do, what are you going to do about them, if anything? Under which circumstances would you not care about autocorrelation? When would you?

Briefly, instead of generating stand-alone values y_i, the pair $(y_i, 1 - y_i)$ is produced at once. Every second call to the random number function would simply reference the antithetic deviate $1 - y_i$. For n such deviates, Rand needs to be invoked only $n/2$ times. Alternatively, one can use y_i on odd calls and $1 - y_i$ on even calls.

The principle underlying the antithetic method can be understood as follows. Suppose there is too much probability sampled around some interval, say $[x_1, x_2]$, the antithetic correction will relocate half of the sample in $[x_1, x_2]$ to the approximate location $1 - \frac{(x_1 + x_2)}{2}$, thereby redistributing the excess probability out where there might be a hole, for how else is there too much probability in $[x_1, x_2]$? In effect, we are using half the sample dictated by Rand and placing the other half symmetrically about the mean value of the original distribution [0.5] instead of relying on system calls to place the other half where it should really lie.

Although introducing inverse correlation should obviously not be done casually, in many cases the occurrence of correlation among deviates will not affect the outcome of the simulation because uniformity is the only feature of interest. For instance, if a distribution of macro-economic influence factors is needed for Monte Carlo analysis, the final output will be the average value over all scenarios. In that situation, we are only interested in having the sample distribution reflect the underlying macro-factor distribution. Therefore, as long as the distribution has been sampled over its entire domain of definition, the results are valid. In practice, one often finds that above a certain random scenario threshold, averages tend to stabilize and become predictably reproducible.

> **Exercise 18.3**

Generate a sequence of 250 random number pairs $(y_i, 1 - y_i)$ using Rand, plot the resulting histogram and compute the value of κ here again. Does this compare favorably with the results of exercise 18.1 for the case of 5,000 deviates? Repeat for 500 and 2,500 deviates and compare the output with the results of exercise 18.1.

> **Exercise 18.4**

Repeat exercise 18.3, but this time calling Rand 500 times and using y_i on odd calls and $1 - y_i$ on even calls. Do these results look like those of the corresponding part of exercise 18.3? Repeat with 1,000 and 5,000 calls to Rand and compare your results with the equivalent output from exercise 18.3.

(c) The Low-Discrepancy Sequence

Although the antithetic corrective scheme is easily implementable and improves our results significantly given the trivial effort involved, it still leaves "holes" in our uniform distribution. By a hole we mean the existence of seemingly empty intervals where no deviates were generated at all. Of course, one might say that we have not sampled *sufficiently* but in fact this is not what happens even if you keep going. If you were still doubtful on this issue, your results from the last few exercises should have convinced you otherwise. What we really need is a method that fills such holes *smoothly* as the number of generated deviates increases. In other words, we are looking for some easy way to partition the numbers we generate across [0, 1] without leaving gaping holes here and there. Can this be done?

The uniformity requirement is especially relevant if one must select relatively few points, say 100. For example, suppose you need a monthly sample of five years, which amounts to only 60 monthly points. The problem with our previous techniques was that the system-supplied random number generator, even when aided by the antithetic correction method, was not uniform and could not really be made so in a simple way. This means that deal outcomes may be unacceptably skewed by a situation whereby small sequences of uniform random numbers could depart significantly from the requirement of uniformity. This happens because high deviates may correspond to high credit losses that are then disproportionately sampled, leading to credit enhancement levels higher than warranted.

Mathematically, the basic requirement is for equal intervals of the deviate range [0, 1] to contain an equal number of draws for all samples. In other words, if we were to separate the whole range [0, 1] into 10 equal intervals, it would be highly desirable to end up with 10% of the sample in each interval no matter where we pick the intervals. This requirement can also be expressed by saying that each interval should contain an equal probability *measure*.

Now, it would be short-sighted to believe that uniformity could be achieved trivially, i.e., by choosing equally spaced points within [0, 1] which, in the 60-point sample above, would amount to defining $y_i = i/60, i = 1, 2, 3, \ldots, 60$. As you can readily visualize, doing so would still leave gaping holes between the regular lattice-points thereby created. Instead, what is needed is a truly random arrangement without holes such that in the limit, the probability measure in each interval dy converges to dy, i.e., a truly uniform distribution. The van der Corput low-discrepancy method is a way of doing this. Although more expensive to implement than the last two, it is well worth the effort.

The basic idea underlying this method is prime number decomposition, a common number-theoretic concept. The uniqueness of such decomposition is the key to the uniformity of the resulting sequence. Specifically, given a prime number p, it is possible to decompose any integer i into a sum of powers of p as follows:

$$i = \sum_{j=0}^{m} c_j p^j \tag{4}$$

The low-discrepancy random numbers are then defined via:

$$x_i = \sum_{j=0}^{m} c_j p^{-(j+1)} \tag{5}$$

It can easily be verified that the deviates x_i satisfy $0 \le x_i \le 1$. First, they are positive by definition, being sums of positive factors. Second, each c_j satisfies $0 \le c_j \le p-1$, which allows us to write:

$$x_i \le (p-1) \sum_{j=1}^{m+1} p^{-j}$$

$$x_i \le (p-1) \left[\frac{1 - \left(1/p\right)^{m+2}}{1 - \frac{1}{p}} - 1 \right] \le 1 - \left(\frac{1}{p}\right)^{m+1} \le 1$$

Therefore, the low-discrepancy sequence satisfies the basic requirements of a probability distribution. That they satisfy uniformity is of course not obvious, but can be tested empirically. In practice, you can adjust the value of m to fit the upper bound of the integer sequence you are using to generate the random deviates.

To find x_i, we have:

$$m = Int\left[\ln(i)/\ln(p)\right] \tag{6}$$

$$c_m = Int(i/p^m) \tag{7}$$

In equations (6) and (7), the expression $Int(x)$ means the integer part of x.

The remaining c_j can be found recursively from:

$$c_j = Int\left(\left[i - \sum_{i=1}^{m-j} c_{j+i} p^{j+i}\right]/p^j\right), \, j = m - 1, m - 2, \ldots, 0 \tag{8}$$

Note in passing that whereas using the Rand function is equivalent to sampling with replacement, the van der Corput sequence amounts to sampling without replacement from a quasi-infinite reservoir. In practice, this issue will not matter because the extent of our knowledge about a credit-risk environment will usually be much scantier than any fine-grained correlation structure introduced by the sampling process. Just be aware that even if both techniques lead to random-looking sequences, they are not random in the same way.

Exercise 18.5

Generate 500 random numbers from the integer sequence $i \in [1, 500]$ using the low-discrepancy sequence method [equations (6) through (8)] and compute the value of κ you obtain with the corresponding κ values from exercises 18.1 and 18.3.

How is uniformity doing now? Repeat the exercise with 1,000 and 5,000 low-discrepancy deviates generated from the corresponding integer sequences. Was it worth the effort?

A Note on the Generation of Lognormal Deviates in Excel

As we mentioned earlier in this section, structured analysts will often be asked to draw random samples from lognormal distributions, with or without Excel. First, recall that a variable x is termed "lognormal" when its natural logarithm $\ln(x)$ is normally distributed. Luckily, you will not have to write your own inversion routine and will be able to use the IDFM method in conjunction with the Excel-resident function LogInv.

As always, using LogInv requires you to specify its two parameters, i.e., the mean and the standard deviation. Unfortunately, they are the ones associated with the corresponding *normal* distribution instead of those that pertain to the *lognormal* distribution you are in fact trying to simulate. Even if you were to write your own sampling routine, you would come across the issue of converting the lognormal parameters into the equivalent normal values. In general, it is much simpler to generate lognormal deviates starting from the associated normal deviates. To do this, proceed as follows.

Assume μ and σ are the mean and standard deviation, respectively, of the lognormal distribution you wish to simulate while m and s are the mean and standard deviation of the associated normal distribution. You can convert the ones to the others as follows:

$$m = \ln \left\{ \frac{\mu}{\sqrt{1 + \left[\frac{\sigma}{\mu}\right]^2}} \right\} \tag{9}$$

$$s = \sqrt{\ln \left[1 + \left(\frac{\sigma}{\mu}\right)^2\right]} \tag{10}$$

Exercise 18.6

Starting from the usual definition of the normal density function:

$$f(x) \equiv \frac{1}{\sqrt{2\pi\sigma^2}} e^{-\frac{1}{2}\left[\frac{x-\mu}{\sigma}\right]^2}$$

Show that, for a lognormal variable x with mean μ and standard deviation σ, the associated normal distribution's equivalent parameters are given by equations (9) and (10), respectively.

To draw a random value x from a lognormal distribution with parameters μ and σ, you would simply use equations (9) and (10) to compute the corresponding normal values and then invoke LogInv using a uniform deviate y as follows:

$$x = LogInv(y, m, s) \tag{11}$$

Exercise 18.7

Draw a sample of 1,000 deviates from a lognormal distribution with $\mu = 1$, $\sigma = 2$, plot a histogram of the values so obtained and verify that it is indeed lognormal.

Repeat the same exercise for a normally distributed sample using the left-hand side of equations (9) and (10) as your parameters and then taking the exponential of each resulting normal deviate. Do both sets of results look similar?

18.2 THE CHOLESKY DECOMPOSITION

In this section, we review the basic principle behind the decomposition and then demonstrate its Visual Basic (VBA)[1] implementation. Implementation into any other computer language is identical.

Suppose you are given a $n X n$ covariance matrix **V** with elements v_{ij} for some hypothetical n dimensional vector whereby a column vector, consisting of an arbitrary group of n components, would correspond to the value of the n variables at time t. Suppose further that you are told to produce another set of m vectors with just such a covariance matrix **V**. In other words, you have to create m separate instances of the n-vector, presumably because you are looking to simulate a process taking place across m time steps. This type of request will crop up repeatedly while doing deals and you must be familiar with a general method of doing this. The easiest way to do so is the Cholesky decomposition.

We have already highlighted the fact that the Cholesky decomposition is just a special case of a more general class of techniques known as LU decomposition. Here, the simplicity of the decomposition is made possible by the fact that the starting matrix **V** satisfies two properties:

1. Nonnegative definiteness
2. Symmetry

You might think such cases are rare, since how many matrices can possibly satisfy two very important properties at the same time? In fact, what is amazing is that both covariance and linear regression matrices do, and that they are by far the most common matrices found in structured financial analysis. As a result, knowledge of the Cholesky decomposition is a must for every structured analyst.

Rationale

As explained above, the use of LU decomposition is possible here only because of the linear definition of covariance. This subsection is only intended to show the rationale underlying the use of the decomposition to correlate a set of vectors subject to a given correlation matrix.

To see this, note that for any vector $\mathbf{x}$ with $E[\mathbf{x}] = \boldsymbol{\mu}$, we can write the covariance matrix as $\mathbf{W} = E[(\mathbf{x} - \boldsymbol{\mu})(\mathbf{x} - \boldsymbol{\mu})^\mathsf{T}]$ where the superscript T indicates the transposition of the associated operand. Please remember that any vector $\mathbf{x}$ is by definition a column-vector, so that the expression $\mathbf{x}\mathbf{x}^\mathsf{T}$ is a matrix while the reverse notation $\mathbf{x}^\mathsf{T}\mathbf{x}$ means a scalar. As always, matrix operations are in general noncommutative.

Given that the covariance matrix satisfies both symmetry and positive-definiteness, we know that it possesses Cholesky decomposition. Therefore, we can write:

$$\mathbf{V} = \mathbf{L}\mathbf{L}^\mathsf{T} \tag{12}$$

The reason why the decomposition takes this simple form is that the given matrix $\mathbf{V}$ is symmetric. Further, since matrix $\mathbf{L}$ with elements l_{ij} is lower-triangular, its transpose $\mathbf{L}^\mathsf{T}$ is upper-triangular.

Now, suppose you have sampled $\mathbf{x}$ as a set of independently drawn *standard normal* deviates in the way indicated in the last section. This means that you have created a vector-mean satisfying $E[\mathbf{x}] = 0$, and that the *covariance* and *correlation* matrices are identical, and both are equal to $\mathbf{I_n}$, the identity matrix of order n. In other words, we now have $E[\mathbf{x}\,\mathbf{x}^\mathsf{T}] = \mathbf{I_n}$.

Remember that in practice, unless you are careful in the sense of the last section the standard normal deviates you have generated will not precisely have the identity matrix as their correlation matrix due to statistical error. This is why it becomes paramount to ensure that you have been diligent in your random number selection.

Now, define a n-dimensional vector $\mathbf{y}$ with elements $y_i, i \in [1, n]$ with:

$$\mathbf{y} = \mathbf{L}\mathbf{x} \tag{13}$$

It is clear from equation (13) that as weighted sums of the constant elements found in matrix $\mathbf{L}$, the components of $\mathbf{y}$ are linear combinations of the variables $\mathbf{x}$. Further, since $\mathbf{x}$ is a set of standard normal deviates with mean zero, the elements of $\mathbf{y}$ will be normal (linearly weighted sums of normal variables are normal), and will have zero mean and variances given by:

$$E[y_i^2] = \sum_{j=1}^{i} l_{ij}^2 = v_{ii}, \; i = 1, 2, 3, \ldots n \tag{14}$$

Now, let's compute the covariance matrix of **y** via direct calculation, remembering that by construction $E[\mathbf{y}] = 0$:

$$E[\mathbf{yy}^{\mathsf{T}}] = E[\mathbf{Lxx}^{\mathsf{T}}\mathbf{L}^{\mathsf{T}}] = \mathbf{L}\,E[\mathbf{xx}^{\mathsf{T}}]\mathbf{L}^{\mathsf{T}} = \mathbf{L}\,\mathbf{I}_n\mathbf{L}^{\mathsf{T}} = \mathbf{LL}^{\mathsf{T}} = \mathbf{V} \qquad (15)$$

Therefore, to the extent of the statistical errors causing $E[\mathbf{x}\,\mathbf{x}^{\mathsf{T}}] \neq \mathbf{I}_n$, the covariance matrix of the vector **y** will be the desired matrix **V**. If the original matrix **V** is itself a correlation matrix, the resulting components of **y** will be standard normal variables since their variances will be equal to the diagonal unit-elements of **V**.

Via Cholesky decomposition, we have thus managed to synthesize a set of standard normal and suitably correlated vectors **y** as weighted sums of normal variables.

The equations of Cholesky decomposition are particularly straightforward and will simply be stated. Students interested in a more detailed treatment should consult *Numerical Recipes*[2] or a similar textbook. The point here is only to learn to use the technique profitably.

To find the elements of **L**, proceed column-wise as follows:

$$l_{ii} = \left[v_{ii} - \sum_{k=1}^{i-1} l_{ik}^2 \right]^{1/2}, i = 1, 2, \dots n \qquad (16)$$

$$l_{ji} = \frac{1}{l_{ii}} \left[v_{ij} - \sum_{k=1}^{i-1} l_{ik} l_{jk} \right], j = i+1, i+2, \dots n \qquad (17)$$

Exercise 18.8

Using the two-step procedure just outlined, generate a set of 360 correlated, seven-dimensional vectors using the correlation matrix in table 18.1:

TABLE 18.1
The correlation matrix to be decomposed

v	1	2	3	4	5	6	7
1	1.00	0.78	0.55	−0.96	0.60	−0.68	0.50
2	0.78	1.00	0.30	−0.75	0.37	−0.94	0.29
3	0.55	0.30	1.00	−0.56	0.99	−0.18	0.96
4	−0.96	−0.75	−0.56	1.00	−0.61	0.66	−0.53
5	0.60	0.37	0.99	−0.61	1.00	−0.25	0.95
6	−0.68	−0.94	−0.18	0.66	−0.25	1.00	−0.17
7	0.50	0.29	0.96	−0.53	0.95	−0.17	1.00

continues to next page

continued from previous page

Once the elements of lower-triangular matrix **L** have been computed using equations (16) and (17), the implementation of the algorithm is simple and proceeds in two steps:

1. Generate a set of m independent column-vectors **x** using a well-designed standard normal deviate generator. This amounts to using a strictly uniform random number generator as shown above.
2. Multiply each one of the m column-vectors in the set **x** by matrix **L** to obtain the set of correlated vectors **y**.

Begin by generating a set of independent normal deviates using the low-discrepancy sequence method from the section "Generating Random Numbers from Statistical Distributions" in the following ways:

1. Using the same prime number p to generate the entire seven-set of 360 vectors
2. Using a different prime base p for each dimension to do the same thing

When you are finished, compute the correlation matrix of the resulting **y** vectors and compare it to the original matrix **V**. To have an idea of the performance of the Cholesky method under cases 1 and 2 above, compute the root mean square (RMS) difference between the entries of the empirically obtained correlation matrix, i.e., the elements of the correlation matrix for the vectors **y**, and those of matrix **V** in both cases. What do you notice about the performance of the method in each case? If there is a big difference in accuracy, why do you think there is?

Next, repeat the vector-correlation exercise with the winner between cases 1 and 2 24 more times, and calculating the RMS difference in each instance.

Answer the following questions:

1. Are the 25 RMS norms clustered around some mean value or are they all over the place?
2. In each instance, what is the largest deviation (maximum norm) from the required correlation matrix from among all matrix entries?
3. Is it much larger than the RMS value?
4. If so, do you think the maximum norm is a better measure of Cholesky decomposition performance than the RMS norm?
5. Whether you said yes or no to question 4, please explain why.

VBA Code Implementation

Coding the Cholesky decomposition is straightforward. Furthermore, since the problem is symmetric it can also be implemented in the reverse order from what was given via equations (16) and (17). For instance, exhibit 18.1 is a VBA implementation of Cholesky decomposition taken from a CDO analysis code that first computes the transpose of matrix **L**. Note that, even if this is redundant, the code checks directly that the decomposition was correctly done. This is good programming practice as bugs can inadvertently creep into codes that used to work.

> **Exhibit 18.1:   VBA Implementation of the Cholesky Decomposition**

```
'
Initialize Cholesky matrix
'
For i = 1 To N
For j = 1 To N
V(i, j) = 0
Next j: Next i
'
Acquire the given correlation matrix
'
For i = 1 To N
For j = 1 To N
Sigma(i, j) = Range("Correlation_Matrix").Cells(i, j).Value

Next j: Next i
'
Cholesky decomposition
'
VT(1, 1) = Sqr(Sigma(1, 1))

For j = 2 To N

For i = 1 To j - 1
Scratch = 0
For k = 1 To i - 1
Scratch = Scratch + VT(k, i) * VT(k, j)
Next k
VT(i, j) = (1 / VT(i, i)) * (Sigma(i, j) - Scratch)
Next i
Scratch = 0
For k = 1 To j - 1
Scratch = Scratch + VT(k, j) ^ 2
Next k
VT(j, j) = Sqr(Sigma(j, j) - Scratch)

Next j
'
Transpose VT for correlated deviate generation
'
For i = 1 To N
For j = 1 To N
V(i, j) = VT(j, i)
Next j: Next i
'
Check the result
'
```

continues to next page

```
continued from previous page
Error = 0
For i = 1 To N
For j = 1 To N
Scratch = 0
For k = 1 To N
Scratch = Scratch + V(i, k) * VT(k, j)
Next k
Error = Error + Abs (Scratch - Sigma(i, j)) ^ 2
Next j: Next i
If [Error/N^2] > Allowable Error Then Stop Else "Cholesky OK"
```

The Further Use of the Cholesky Decomposition

(a) Use of the Invariance Property

Note that since correlation matrices are invariant under linear transformations of their constituents, the Cholesky decomposition can be used to generate normal vectors with arbitrary means and standard deviations. In other words, once the set of normal vectors $\mathbf{y}$ is available, a normal vector z with mean μ and standard deviation σ may be simulated via the following affine transformation:

$$z = \mu + \sigma y \qquad (18)$$

Doing this will not change the correlation between the affected component of $\mathbf{y}$ and the other components. Obviously, the covariance itself will change by a factor σ.

Exercise 18.9

From its basic definition, show that a correlation matrix is invariant under the linear transformation (18).

If distributional normality of the resulting vectors is required, our modeling effort can be halted at this point. For instance, in the modeling of stock prices or currency options, we can simply interpose arbitrary linear transformations to further specify the mean and the standard deviation of the normal vectors. This can be done by setting $z = \sigma y + \mu$, whereby parameters μ and σ are the mean and standard deviation, respectively, of the desired normal distributions.

(b) Default Correlation Process

On many occasions, for instance in modeling a CDO, it will be necessary to simulate a correlation process taking place in default space whereby you will be asked to investigate the creditworthiness of a transaction consisting of a pool of highly rated corporate bonds known to be subject to a given correlation structure. Whether this epistemological claim is believable is a question we can luckily avoid debating.

Note further that this is different from what we did in chapter 15 when we used the Clayton copula to simulate a macro-economic correlation process. For in that case, each loan was in fact independent of every other loan in the pool even while correlated to a single macro-economic variable. This allowed us to simplify the problem compared to the present case, i.e., where every bond is now assumed to default characteristically in relation to other bonds in a manner specified by matrix **V**.

If this should be the task, you would first have to represent the default process as shown above, but in addition, you would need to default each bond in accordance with its corporate rating on a stand-alone basis, the latter assumed known a priori,. To do this, proceed as follows.

Assume you are given a set of bond ratings R_i, $i \in [1, n]$ to which corresponds a set of cumulative default rates $D_i(R_i)$ over a time span equal to the length of the target transaction.

Once you have obtained the variables **y** as explained earlier, simply declare bond i defaulted if either of the following conditions holds:

1. $y_i \leq F^{-1}(D_i)$
2. $y_i \geq 1 - F^{-1}(D_i)$

The symbol $F^{-1}(\bullet)$ stands for the inverse standard normal distribution function. In practice, one would alternate between 1 and 2 in successive Monte Carlo scenarios. This gives the same results as the Gaussian copula.

The idea behind this method is easy to visualize. Since the standard normal deviates **y** generated via the decomposition are expected to have probability mass D_i in the intervals $(-\infty, F^{-1}(D_i)]$ and $[1 - F^{-1}(D_i), \infty)$, selection rules 1 and 2 should force a default with the required cumulative probability. In addition, the rule "once a default always a default" applies here as well.

If one is analyzing a five-year transaction using monthly draws from statistical distributions, conditions 1 and 2 must be modified to reflect the draw frequency. In that case, since the default could occur at any time from closing to maturity, we would use $D_i/60$ instead of D_i as a default threshold since the total default probability of an exclusive OR under an independence assumption is additive.

This basic default model can also be made slightly more sophisticated by using the survival concept, whereby the nondefault of a bond at any time changes the marginal default probability function, which is then called the survival or "hazard" function. Effectively, this is the *thinning of the herd* idea that makes it more difficult to cause the default of bonds that have survived for a long time. You should note that there is an empirical basis for using this concept. The bond default studies performed by rating agencies show that in some rating categories, especially below investment grade, companies that survive beyond a few years tend to survive much longer. This shows up as a decreasing marginal default probability past the threshold value, usually in the neighborhood of five to seven years. It is usually straightforward to modify this procedure to simulate the marginal default curve representative of each rating category, as long as you are not making assumptions without at least some empirical basis.

The realization that marginal default probabilities are subject to a characteristic pattern has provided much grist for the mill of enterprising analysts. The fact is that such patterns are at best secondary driving factors in the analysis. However, this does not mean that they can be totally ignored, for the truth is quite the opposite. Structured finance is about loss not default, and hence the temporal default distribution does matter for a given cumulative default rate. What we mean is that no one should spend an inordinate amount of time trying to derive the *optimal* hazard function when the same time could be spent much more productively on enhanced liability features and better asset cash flow modeling. To be sure, if time were not the most precious commodity in finance things might look quite different.

18.3 THE GENERAL USE OF LU DECOMPOSITION

We should note at the outset that the most interesting aspect of LU decomposition is its paradigmatic character with respect to the solution of difficult mathematical problems, i.e., their reduction to simpler problems. This principle is of such fundamental importance that it was commonly used centuries ago as a measure of promise in mathematical studies.

In the previous section, we focused on the use of the LU matrix decomposition technique, in the special case where the matrix was symmetric and positive definite, as a means to correlate independent vectors according to a given correlation structure.

However, LU decomposition finds its main utility in the solution of linear systems of algebraic equations characterized by matrices with convenient properties. The Cholesky decomposition is just one example of how a matrix with two special properties can give rise to a decomposition with an especially simple form. Clearly, it would not make sense to use decompositions in reducing matrices to LU form if the CPU time involved in doing so were in fact greater than what could be achieved using either Gaussian elimination or Gauss–Seidel iteration. In the case of the Cholesky decomposition, there is a clear benefit in taking advantage of the properties possessed by correlation matrices, properties that are handed to us on a platter.

Now, suppose you are asked to solve numerically some arbitrary equation containing a second derivative term like $\partial^2 f / \partial x^2$, or two or three such terms in multidimensional problems. Assume further that you have chosen to use a finite difference scheme to do this. Somewhere in the process, you will clearly have to discretize the second derivative terms and will most likely come up with discrete expressions such as:

$$\frac{f(x + \Delta x) - 2f(x) + f(x - \Delta x)}{\Delta x^2} \tag{19}$$

If you factor out the denominator and think of applying this form across the x domain, you will end up with a matrix, the rows of which will consist of instances of equation (19) for each x_i along the axis, and likewise for the other dimensional axes, if any. Thus, each matrix row to be solved will have $- 2$ on the diagonal, 1 on either side and 0 everywhere else. For obvious reasons, this is called a *tridiagonal* matrix, and is yet another property that can be put to good use via LU decomposition. In such cases, the solution will be much simpler than for fully fledged matrices, i.e., those with nonzero elements everywhere. As you can readily imagine, the solution of differential equations naturally produces many such banded structures that can all be handled in the same way.

The Solution Algorithm for LU-Decomposed Linear Systems

The objective is the solution of general systems of the form:

$$\mathbf{M}\mathbf{x} = \mathbf{y} \tag{20}$$

After executing the LU decomposition, either as shown above or in some other way, the square matrix $\mathbf{M}$ of rank n can now be expressed as the product of two matrices, one of which [$\mathbf{L}$] is lower triangular while the other [$\mathbf{U}$] is upper triangular.

You will recall that in the special case treated in the previous section, it turned out that $\mathbf{U} = \mathbf{L}^{\mathsf{T}}$. However, in general $\mathbf{L}$ and $\mathbf{U}$ have the following forms:

$$\mathbf{L} = \begin{bmatrix} l_{11} & 0 & 0 & 0 \dots \\ l_{21} & l_{22} & 0 & 0 \dots \\ l_{31} & l_{32} & l_{33} & 0 \dots \\ & \cdot & & \\ & \cdot & & \\ l_{n1} & l_{n2} & l_{n3} & \dots l_{nn} \end{bmatrix} \qquad \mathbf{U} = \begin{bmatrix} u_{11} & u_{12} & u_{13} & \dots \\ 0 & u_{22} & u_{23} & u_{24} \dots \\ 0 & 0 & u_{33} & u_{34} \cdot \\ & \cdot & & \\ 0 & 0 & 0 & \dots u_{nn} \end{bmatrix} \tag{21}$$

As a result, system (20) can now be written:

$$\mathbf{L}\mathbf{U}\mathbf{x} = \mathbf{y} \tag{22}$$

Have we achieved anything simpler by doing this? Yes, we have. To see this, note that we can now partition the system into two separate linear equation systems as follows:

$$\mathbf{U}\mathbf{x} = \mathbf{z} \tag{23}$$

$$\mathbf{L}\mathbf{z} = \mathbf{y} \tag{24}$$

So far, we seem to be going backwards, i.e., from one system we end up with two. However, note that the two solutions of systems (23) and (24) can be done almost trivially in succession due to the respective forms of $\mathbf{L}$ and $\mathbf{U}$.

As a first step, a lower-triangular system can be solved sequentially by starting with the first equation on top, which of course is already solved, and sweeping downward in a recursive manner, i.e., solving each z_i using the calculations from the previous step. This works as follows for the first two unknowns:

$$l_{11} z_1 = y_1 \ \rightarrow \ z_1 = \frac{y_1}{l_{11}}$$

Then,

$$l_{21} z_1 + l_{22} z_2 = y_2 \ \rightarrow \ z_2 = \frac{y_2 - l_{21} z_1}{l_{22}}$$

As you can see, any time some z_i is required on the right, it has already been computed on the left somewhere. You will remember that this is what happened when implementing the above Cholesky decomposition. In fact, this *sweeping* tactic is of general applicability to LU methods.

The upward sweep occurs when we solve equation (23) for the required solution vector **x** viz.:

$$u_{nn} x_n = z_n \;\rightarrow\; x_n = \frac{z_n}{u_{nn}}$$

$$u_{(n-1)(n-1)}\, x_{n-1} + u_{(n-1)n}\, x_n = z_{n-1} \;\rightarrow\; x_{n-1} = \frac{z_{n-1} - u_{(n-1)n}\, x_n}{u_{(n-1)(n-1)}}$$

Just like what happened with the downward sweep, whenever x_i is needed on the right it has already been computed from a prior calculation. You can see how simple this solution procedure becomes once the LU decomposition is available. That, of course, is the entire issue.

The lesson to be drawn from this section is that before plunging into a full-blown Gaussian elimination with pivoting, one should look at the structure of the monster we have created, for that monster can sometimes be tamed easily.

Exercise 18.10

For the correlation matrix given in exercise 18.8, i.e., assuming it now represents some linear system, and the right-hand side vector **y** defined by $y_i = 2^i$, $i \in [1, n]$, solve for **x** using a generalization of the algorithm presented in here, either using a VBA program or any other non-Excel related method of your own choosing. ◁

18.4 LAPLACE TRANSFORM METHODS IN STRUCTURED FINANCE

This chapter has dealt in very broad outline with what is, in fact, a vast amount of analytical material across many fields. In finance, transformations are not considered intrinsic to the subject matter, and hence the above topics would probably be categorized as lying squarely in the *"geek"* corner. Yet, if the truth were told, any structured transaction involves the transformation of assets into liabilities. In chapter 16 we used the term *transfer function* to describe the way cash was generated given any delinquency state transition. In fact, such functions are nothing but special cases of a more general transform framework that applies to structured finance a priori.

What we want to show now, more in an effort to point the way towards a more mature treatment of financial structures than because we intend to dwell on it, is that the fundamental financial structure is itself a transform. In fact, it is the most illustrious of them all: *the Laplace transform.*

Formally, the Laplace transform $F(s)$ of a function $f(t)$, where t normally stands for time, is defined via:

$$L(f(t); s) \equiv F(s) = \int_0^\infty e^{-st} f(t) \, dt \qquad (25)$$

The Laplace transform, named after the legendary eighteenth-century French mathematician and physicist Pierre Simon Marquis de Laplace, finds its main applications in the solution of linear ordinary and partial differential equations,[3] as well as in many other fields. The Clayton copula used in chapter 15 was nothing but a thinly disguised Laplace transform.

Why are we saying that the Laplace transform is the fundamental structure in finance? After all, by-and-large financial analysts do not spend their time solving ordinary differential equations and in fact, the use of the copula formalism is completely peripheral to the essence of the deal. There are ways to skin this cat that do not involve copulas at all.

To see why this is so, consider the standard computation of the expected yield r of an investment I_0 expected to produce N future cash flows c_i over its lifetime:

$$I_0 = \sum_{i=1}^N \frac{c_i}{(1+r)^i} \qquad (26)$$

As everybody will know, the yield of the investment is the *root* of the last equation, i.e., the value of r that produces the equality of the left- and right-hand sides of equation (26).

Now, using a continuous cash flow density function $f(t)$ instead of the discrete flows c_i, we can set $c_i = f(t_i)\Delta t$ and pass to the limit $\Delta t \to dt$, thereby transforming the summation sign to the right of equation (26) into an integral sign, while the factor $(1+r)^{-i}$ is just the first term of e^{-rt}.[4] Putting all this together, we realize that equation (26) is simply the discrete version of the continuous time yield relationship:

$$I_0 = \int_0^T e^{-rt} f(t) \, dt \qquad (27)$$

However, by arbitrarily setting $f(t) \equiv 0$, $t \in [T, \infty)$, which we can do without loss of generality, we see immediately that equation (27) fulfills the basic definition of the Laplace transform, and that, glancing back at equation (25), we can redefine generalized yield via:

$$r \equiv F^{-1}(I_0) \qquad (28)$$

Please note that the inverse, or "pre-image," on the right-hand side of equation (28) is not the same as the inverse Laplace transform $L^{-1}(F(s)) = f(t)$. For instance, the inverse transform of $\frac{1}{s^2}$ is t and not simply s^2.

Under this framework, yield is now conceived as one of the real or imaginary roots of an algebraic equation describing the current meaning of future time, i.e., what the deal always "is." When we characterized finance as the *algebra of original time* in chapter 14, this is what we meant. The yield of an investment thus conceived is the *truth* of finance. In other words, in reality finance is an imaginary game played in a Riemann-space on differentiable manifolds. Are you having fun yet?

Among other things, the Laplace transform formalism enables the extension of yield to cases that are far from obvious and where previously, one would have to solve equation (26) iteratively, discovering precious little about the structure of original time in the process.

Effectively, we have transformed what, up to now, has been a nonlinear, discrete and iterative computational scheme into an algebraic root-locus problem. Remember also that via the procedure of analytical continuation,[5] any discrete set of cash flows can be turned into a continuous function representative of the same set. Even better, the resulting function is not required to be differentiable everywhere but only integrable. Therefore, the functional universe that can be inserted into equation (27) has now been expanded.

Examples of Laplace-Transform Yield Solutions

Let's go through a couple of examples to firm this up. Say you are dealing with a perpetual bond, something sovereigns and municipalities used to be quite fond of issuing.[6].

Because of the absence of any principal maturity date, a perpetual bond is characterized by a constant cash flow density function. Thus, we have:

$$f(t) = k$$

Equation (28) then leads to:

$$I_0 = \int_0^\infty k e^{-st} \, dt = \frac{k}{s} \Rightarrow r = \frac{k}{I_0} \tag{29}$$

To solve equation (29), you could either write down directly the Laplace transform of some constant a as $\frac{a}{s}$, or simply look it up in a handbook. Most functions known to man have already been Laplace-transformed or else reduced to others that have been.

▶ **Exercise 18.11**

Verify via direct integration of equation (25) that the Laplace transform of a is $\frac{a}{s}$. ◀

This first calculation tells us that the yield on a perpetual bond is simply the periodic payment divided by the original investment, which is just a restatement of the meaning of interest rate. In other words, this was a reality check, no more.

> **Exercise 18.12**

Assume that an investment has the following cash flow density profile for positive times:

$$f(t) \equiv \begin{cases} k, t \leq T \\ 0, t > T \end{cases} \tag{30}$$

By insertion of equation (30) into equation (27), show that the yield of this investment is the root of the algebraic relation:

$$1 - \frac{I_0 r}{k} = e^{-rT} \tag{31}$$

Next, via a Taylor expansion of the right-hand side of equation (31) carried out to second order, show that an approximate solution for the yield r is given by:

$$r \cong 2\left[\frac{1}{T} - \frac{I_0}{kT^2}\right] \tag{32}$$

Now, using equation (32), compute the yield of a $10,000 investment expected to throw off $2,500 of free cash flow for the next five years, and compare that result to the exact analytical solution which, according to Microsoft, is 7.94% APR. How far off were you?

Please note that even the approximate solution (32) has the correct leading behavior for the case where the investment throws off $2,000 of free cash flow for the next five years. The exact solution is obviously a 0% yield and equation (32) leads to:

$$r = 2\left[\frac{1}{5} - \frac{10^4}{2^3 5^2}\right] = 2\left[\frac{1}{5} - \frac{1}{5}\right] = 0$$

Next, take the Taylor-series of e^{-rT} to third order, and show that the solution for r is the quadratic-root formula:

$$r \cong \frac{3}{2T} - \sqrt{\frac{9}{4T^2} - \frac{6}{T^3}(T - I_0/k)} \tag{33}$$

How did we know to select the negative root from the two available quadratic roots?

Now, compare the result of using equation (33) with the same investment parameters as before, i.e., those with the exact solution 7.94% APR. How far off are you this time? Is it getting better or worse? Either way, can you explain why? ◄

For another example, let's assume you are trying to find the yield on some weird investment displaying a strange periodicity, perhaps like a resort, but with built-in obsolescence due to aging and shifting consumer preferences.

In other words, we will presume that the cash flow density function for this company can be defined as follows:

$$f(t) \equiv K e^{-at} \cos(\omega t) \tag{34}$$

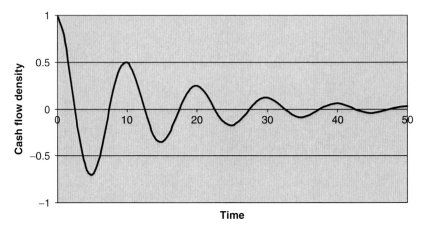

FIGURE 18.2
A decaying periodic cash flow density function.

This type of cash flow density function is shown in figure 18.2. In this case, equation (28) gives:

$$I_0 = K \int_0^\infty e^{-st} e^{-at} \cos(\omega t) \, dt \qquad (35)$$

To find the yield of this investment, we need to find the Laplace transform of a decaying cosine wave like equation (34). Fortunately, we can rely on the fact that that if we find the Laplace transform $F(s)$ of some function $f(t)$, the transform of the same function multiplied by the factor e^{-at} is just $F(s+a)$. This is the *shifting* theorem and is one of the main properties of Laplace transforms.

> **Exercise 18.13**
>
> Derive the shifting theorem as it applies to Laplace transforms.

The same handbook that gave you the Laplace transform of a constant value will also give you that of the cosine function:

$$L\left(\cos[\omega t]\right) = \frac{s}{s^2 + \omega^2} \qquad (36)$$

Insertion of equation (36) into equation (35) in conjunction with the shifting theorem determines the yield of this investment as one of the roots of the following algebraic equation:

$$I_0 = K \frac{r+a}{(r+a)^2 + \omega^2} \qquad (37)$$

A few lines of algebra easily lead to the required yield r :

$$r = \frac{K - \sqrt{K^2 - 4I_0^2\omega^2}}{2I_0} - a \tag{38}$$

Unlike the example of the perpetual bond, result (38) for yield is not exactly self-evident given the initial cash flow density function (34), not to mention the significant insight produced by an analytical formula like equation (38).

Exercise 18.14

Derive equation (38) starting from equation (37). ◀

But wait, someone is already objecting, you are assuming negative cash flows in some "down" years, and that cannot be true can it? Of course, negative cash flows are quite conceivable to anyone even remotely acquainted with finance, but let's play along for argument's sake. To prevent negative cash flows, let's modify equation (34) as follows:

$$f(t) \equiv Ke^{-at}[\cos(\omega t) + 1] \tag{39}$$

Now, after insertion of equation (39) into equation (28), in place of equation (37) we obtain:

$$I_0 = K\left\{\frac{r+a}{(r+a)^2 + \omega^2} + \frac{1}{r+a}\right\} \tag{40}$$

To solve equation (40), first make the obvious substitution:

$$y = r + a \tag{41}$$

Next, rearrange equation (40) to get:

$$y^3 - \frac{2K}{I_0}y^2 + \omega^2 y - \frac{K}{I_0}\omega^2 = 0 \tag{42}$$

Next, you need to solve the cubic equation (42) and then use equation (41) in reverse. Luckily, cubic algebraic equations have been solved in general. What normally happens is that one of the roots is real and positive while the other two are usually not appropriate, being either complex conjugates or more negative than -1.

Sticking to reality for the moment, the cubic solution is straightforward and can be looked up in a handbook. First define the subsidiary quantities:

$$Q = \frac{\omega^2}{3} - \frac{4K^2}{9I_0^2}, \quad R = \frac{16K^3}{I_0^3} + \frac{9K\omega^2}{I_0}, \quad D = Q^3 + R^2$$

$$S = \sqrt[3]{R + \sqrt{D}}, \quad T = \sqrt[3]{R + \sqrt{D}}$$

Combining the real root of equation (42) with equation (41) leads to the solution r:

$$r = S + T + \frac{2K}{3I_0} - a \tag{43}$$

Perhaps you too are thinking what we are thinking, i.e., that this is a lot of work for something that could be done so easily in Excel. What matters however, is the insight into the structure of original time (yield) that can be obtained from this method, not that the same answer can be obtained via a brute force method, which it obviously can.

In general, the cash flow densities appropriate to real transactions will be piecewise continuous and consist of a series of analytic functions $g_i(t)$, each of which will be deemed valid over a time interval $[t_i, t_{i+1}]$ and where interval boundaries t_i will be arbitrary. Using a sequence of impulse functions $u_i(t)$ like the one shown in figure 18.3, we will then be able to construct arbitrary, piecewise-continuous cash flow density functions as sums of boundary-matched analytic functions as follows:

$$f(t) \equiv \sum_{i=1}^{N} [u_i(t) - u_{i+1}] g_i(t) \tag{44}$$

Impulse functions like the one in figure 18.3, equal to unity on the interval $t \in [A, B]$ and zero elsewhere, are important because they enable you to manufacture just about any functional shape.

Finding the Laplace transform of equation (44) is actually straightforward if one takes advantage of another basic theorem, the time-shifting theorem. Without going into detail, let's simply state that the transform $F(s)$ of a form like equation (44) will

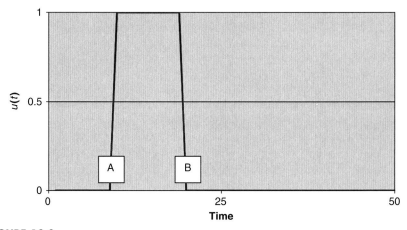

FIGURE 18.3
Impulse function.

always work out to be:

$$F(s) = \sum_{i=1}^{N} [e^{-t_i s} - e^{-t_{i+1} s}] L(g_i(t)) \tag{45}$$

In addition, the Laplace transforms $L(g_i(t))$ of the analytic functions inside equation (45) will be relatively straightforward since these functions will normally end up as time-dependent quadratic polynomials of the form:

$$g_i(t) = a_i t^2 + b_i t + c_i \tag{46}$$

This will happen, for example, as a result of spline-function approximations to the cash flow environment under consideration. Whence, each transform will take the form:

$$L(g_i(t)) = \frac{2a_i}{s^3} + \frac{b_i}{s^2} + \frac{c_i}{s} \tag{47}$$

Exercise 18.15

Show that the transform of t^2 is given by $2/s^3$ and that in general the transform of t^n where n is an integer is equal to $n!/s^{n+1}$.

Insertion of the appropriate versions of equation (47) into equation (45) will lead to the algebraic equation to be inverted. Like terms will be collected and the algebraic inversion will proceed without a hitch. In a nutshell, the imagination of the structured analyst is the only obstacle to the versatility of this method.

Speaking of imagination, note that the other two roots of equation (42) may have, in principle at least, imaginary components. Since equation (43) is but one of the three potential roots of equation (42), you might perhaps reflect on these other *imaginary* roots. At least, the Laplace transform formalism has the advantage of making explicit the full structure of yield with its inherent root-multiplicity. You have probably heard before that the standard yield [equation (26)] is known in some cases to have multiple solutions that depend on the number of times cash flows c_i change sign. Here, such multiplicity comes about quite naturally from the very structure of time itself.

What about the two imaginary roots? Although they are not physical in the ordinary sense of that word, is it possible that they have meaning, i.e., that they represent a form of reality hitherto either hidden or merely imagined? In other words, are complex roots completely useless in finance? If not, it is reasonable to ask what type of *reality* might be lurking behind an imaginary root. In the next section, we discuss this issue with respect to an important special case.

18.5 THE SINGULARITY OF THE YIELD KERNEL

Our investigation into yield and its properties has taken an unexpected turn, one that compels us to consider the daunting possibility that yield as currently conceived, as a purely real quantity, might in fact not tell the whole story. Could a more fundamental and synthetic form of knowledge not be extracted from this intuition? Maybe, but where exactly should we look for such insight?

First, we say the roots are *imaginary* simply because they are not *real*. Yet you already know that two imaginary numbers can easily combine via $i^2 \equiv -1$ to produce a real number, so they could be *potentially* real could they not? In this manner, the imaginary might reveal itself as nothing but an original, nascent form of reality. Does this make sense? Yes, it does.

Pure Liquidity Propositions

To see how to approach yield primordially, consider the following sheer *liquidity proposition*. You are presented with a four-year, $100 investment expected to produce the cash flow sequence C_j shown as equation (48) (each paid out at the end of year j):

$$C_1 = 25 \quad C_2 = 25 \quad C_3 = 25 \quad C_4 = 25 \tag{48}$$

To know what this *means*, a savvy investor would first compute the yield r of this proposal in the following, time-honored way:

$$100 = \frac{25}{(1+r)^1} + \frac{25}{(1+r)^2} + \frac{25}{(1+r)^3} + \frac{25}{(1+r)^4} \tag{49}$$

In general, solving for r requires an iterative solution, but in this case mere inspection reveals that $r = 0$ satisfies equation (49) identically. Consequently, the yield of this investment is zero. Not great, but it's a deal!

Next, say someone else proposes another four-year investment evidencing a different cash flow pattern:

$$C_1 = 0 \quad C_2 = 0 \quad C_3 = 0 \quad C_4 = 100 \tag{50}$$

Solving for r in the same manner, we have:

$$100 = \frac{0}{(1+r)^1} + \frac{0}{(1+r)^2} + \frac{0}{(1+r)^3} + \frac{100}{(1+r)^4} \tag{51}$$

The yield of this second investment drops out as easily as the first and is also zero, and this despite the fact that nobody in his right mind would ever claim that these two investments are *the same*. Yet, they are signaled as identical by the yield function.

An objection that this could always be resolved by including subsidiary returns arising from the reinvestment of intermediate flows from the first proposal would be naïve, for in that case we would be analyzing more than one proposal, and anything goes, as they say. Therefore, we have to deal with this problem on its own, and not via some facile argument obviously aimed at circumventing it or else wishing it away.

In addition, the problem remains whole if we extend the formalism to a continuous cash flow framework whereby a normalized liquidity proposition can be redefined as follows:[7]

$$\int_0^\infty f(t)\,dt = 1 \tag{52}$$

To see this clearly, consider only one such liquidity proposition, for instance the standard gamma distribution used to define the Clayton copula in chapter 16.

$$f(t;\gamma) \equiv \frac{t^{\gamma-1}e^{-t}}{\Gamma(\gamma)}, \gamma > 0 \tag{53}$$

Since by definition, all density functions integrate to unity, the yield of this liquidity proposition with initial investment I_0 can be represented via equation (54):

$$I_0 \int_0^\infty e^{-rt} f(t;\gamma)\,dt = I_0, \ \forall \gamma > 0 \tag{54}$$

Applying our previous results for yield in terms of Laplace transform pre-images, we can immediately write down:

$$r \equiv F^{-1}(I_0;\gamma), \ F(r;\gamma) \equiv L[f(t;\gamma)]$$

Using definition (53) and equation (54) together, we obtain:

$$I_0 = \frac{I_0}{\Gamma(\gamma)} \int_0^\infty t^{\gamma-1} e^{-(1+r)t}\,dt \tag{55}$$

Next, recall what happened when we derived the Clayton copula via the Laplace transform of density function (53), to produce:

$$1 = (1+r)^{-\gamma}, \ \forall \gamma > 0 \tag{56}$$

This indicates that $r = 0$ is the only possible real solution for *all* values of γ, the shape parameter. Thus, here again we are faced with a situation whereby yield is apparently not an adequate measure of investment potential, and this always happens because yield is vanishingly small, effectively zero.

In fact, we can extend definition (52) to all such propositions, whether they are liquidity plays or not:

$$\int_0^\infty f(t)\,dt = \begin{cases} <1 \to r<0 \\ 1 \to r=0 \\ >1 \to r>0 \end{cases} \tag{57}$$

The Kernel of the Yield Function

It appears that sets of cash flows producing zero-yield possess a privileged status in finance, because they can all be rearranged without affecting the result, i.e., investors ought to be indifferent to receiving any one of them. This includes such absurd transactions as no cash at all, since the maturity date can be pushed out as far as necessary without affecting the result.

In fact, this is nothing new. Over the last century, mathematicians have wrestled with this curious state of affairs on many occasions, and their research eventually led to a deep investigation of its root causes. To begin with, the common mathematical name for the set of domain points that map to zero-range is the *nucleus* of the function. However, for historical reasons we use the word *Kernel* instead, a word of German origin more-or-less meaning nucleus.

Next, the fact that so many combinations of the same cash flows lead to zero-yield is evidence for what we call *singularity*. The use of the word *singular* should not surprise you, since it can easily be seen via definition (57) that the problem occurs when cash flows integrate to 1, the normal mathematical representation of the singular. As Conan Doyle put it so well in *The Boscombe Valley Mystery*, "singularity is almost invariably a clue." In this case, we note with amazement that the Kernel of the yield-function is highly singular, and thus provides a clue to an uncanny, largely unthought aspect thereof. Most likely, some of you are already saying "please tell me why I should care about this nonsense?" Yes, maybe we are insane, or perhaps insanity is just the ground of sanity.

In passing, this goes all the way back to a time in our history where the very idea of zero was conceived (in India). As you now know, the idea of the zero, of nothing, boils down to circularity, which is just another word for nonlinearity. This is because cyclic behavior is the only possible way something infinite can remain essentially bounded, as Poincaré knew down to its very foundations. Thus, it came to be that *zero*, the *nothing*, acquired a circle as its representation. At the same time, this state of affairs is precisely why the yield function must be singular at zero, for what else does the word *singularity* imply but the ability to give rise to the *one*, the singular, the *unit*. In more mathematical terms, contour integrals around a closed loop (circulation) can have multiple and equally acceptable real solutions, the range of which is tied to the imaginary. Thus, what we so fondly dub *reality* is always subject to a basic indeterminacy arising from nonlinearity. This is the essential import of Heidegger's celebrated aphorism "whatever happens to us, even though it is not defined for all times, happens at the right time." As everybody knows, there is more than one right love for any person.

Unfortunately, this is no mere academic obfuscation, for the singularity of the yield Kernel seems to be literally persecuting us, given the obvious conclusion that the various liquidity propositions indexed by γ can certainly not be deemed identical from an investment standpoint. Could it be that we are being persecuted for our beliefs? In other words, yield as currently conceived fails to inform us as to the radical difference existing between a series of apparently equally good, or equally bad, investments when measured via the standard yield definition. Apparently, the yield we talk about all day long is woefully incomplete. Can we help that? Yes, we can.

18.6 MEASURE AND MEANING

In the first instance, when we normally talk about yield, we always expect it to be greater than zero, for why else would anyone invest money, if not to receive more than their money back? Nevertheless, zero is certainly an allowable value for yield and we cannot simply bury our heads in the sand saying "this will never happen" or some similar adolescent rubbish.

A yield of zero means that, in some sense, *nothing* happened, and yet *something* happened. We really did invest $100 and the deal really did give it back to us. However, in the financial sense that something is *really* nothing since it has zero-yield. Consequently, $r = 0$ appears to be something that is really nothing. Is this a contradiction? No, it is not. How is this so?

It is not a contradiction if you define what is real, what is something, simply as what is meaningful, and thus what is nothing as what is meaningless. It is not so much that $r = 0$ is *nothing* in the linear sense of that word, but merely that it *means* nothing. In mathematics, the word for meaning is *measure*. Thus, we can define nothing simply as something with zero measure. In other words, what is meaningless is also worthless.

Because of this, we can take hold of the fact that the Kernel of any function is just its domain of meaninglessness. What lies outside the Kernel is thus *real* in the usual way, and we then say either that it *means* something or that it has *measure*. In a nutshell, measure theory is the theory of meaning.

This should be obvious to you if you have stayed with us from the very beginning. As was pointed out in chapter 14, reality is about meaning and nothing else. What is real is only what is measurable. What you do not *measure*, what does not *count*, is what is *imaginary*. It is called *imaginary* only because, although it is still part of our world in some sense, it lives in our *imagination*. However, that does not mean it is not *there*, quite the contrary. When we defined the Dao of Dealing back in chapter 14, we remarked that deals must be extracted out of the "nothing," and that the latter was just a shorthand way of representing Moment A at the top of the arc. Far from being *nothing*, what comes out of our own selves is the very stuff of reality. Thus, the imaginary essence of yield comes through loud and clear via the singularity of its Kernel.

The real, and hence the measurable, is what must first be extracted out of nothing as something self-identical. We are talking about a negation, a restriction of the freedom operating at the level of the World. As a direct consequence of this, the realm of the imaginary is simultaneously that of the nonlinearity out of which *logic* can emerge. It is the *negative* that allows the *positive* to reveal itself for itself out of itself.

The imaginary, the simple, is merely the ground of the real. As we saw earlier, it shows itself as the essential core out of which the real acquires meaning. Since it is both negative and nonlinear, we have no choice as to how to define the imaginary. Whereas the real, the positive, needs to be defined so that $1 + 0 \equiv 1$ obtains, imaginary numbers demand a different *basis*, one we label i for obvious reasons. From the foregoing discussion, it is clear that i must be defined via $i \times i \equiv -1$, i.e., as the confluence of nonlinearity and negativity.

Even better, the concept of imaginary numbers does not only enlighten us about the essence of yield but finds applications in accounting as well. Here, imaginary processes are what we might call *inter-company* transfers when speaking of a consolidated annual report. We do not *see* transfers taking place between the various business units of the group because we only measure the *real* cash, i.e., the external, audited report of consolidated cash flows that, for us, represents the *company*. However, those inter-company transfers are real, for after all, they *really* took place and perhaps resulted in cash showing up at the level of a subsidiary. In fact, this is how they became real in the original sense of the word. When executed inside the group, such transfers are regarded as imaginary, but once they show up outside, i.e., as part of what we measure, they become real. By ignoring what goes on inside the various business units of a company, we are admittedly ignoring its internal structure. The good news is that our Laplace transform formalism is not ignoring them, so that when internal transfers combine to become *real*, something hitherto imaginary has now become measurable. If you grasp this thoroughly, now or ever, you also know how to eliminate Ponzi schemes altogether.

18.7 THE EXTENSION OF YIELD TO THE COMPLEX PLANE

A New Definition for Yield

At this point, a resolution is clearly in our sights. The yield Kernel is singular because we have failed to account for the full structure of yield that emerges when yield becomes either meaningless, or else fails to have measure. The concomitant incompleteness of yield stems from the failure to capture the full nonlinear reality underlying it. Thus, to restore yield to its original form, we need to correct this oversight and let it be what it has been all along, i.e., a complete number that includes an imaginary component.

As was already made abundantly clear in our introductory chapter on the Dao of Dealing, the incompleteness of yield finds its origin in that of logic. What logic lacks is a spark of intuition, and that is what imagination is all about. Consequently, to recover the full import of yield, we need to rewrite it as follows:

$$r = r_n + i r_c, \quad i^2 \equiv -1 \tag{58}$$

In equation (58), we have defined r_n as the *real* (credit) component of yield and r_c as its *imaginary* (liquidity) component. Thus, in singular cases r_c is itself an imaginary number enabling the disappearance of the yield measure associated with such situations. In other words, one does not normally measure liquidity yield, but only credit yield, the most readily accessible yield notion that has been handed down to us as *yield* tout court.

The following example ought to convince you that definition (58) allows us to explore the singular range of the yield Kernel albeit at the expense of slightly more cumbersome calculations. Obviously, under normal, nonsingular circumstances yield can be handled as it has always been.

An Example of Singular Yield

As a preamble, consider the standard gamma density function described above in "The Singularity of the Yield Kernel", and select just one of its infinitely many incarnations, say $\gamma = 2$. Assume further that this represents as accurately as possible the cash flow density function applicable to some transaction. Being a probability density function, it integrates to unity and as such, satisfies the requirement imposed on all liquidity propositions.

$$I_0 = I_0 \int_0^\infty \frac{t e^{-t}}{\Gamma(2)} e^{-rt} \, dt, \ \Gamma(n) \equiv (n-1)! \tag{59}$$

Next, introduce definition (58) using the known result $r_n = 0$ arising from equation (56), and rearrange,[8] leading to:

$$1 = \int_0^\infty t \, e^{-(1+ir)t} \, dt \tag{60}$$

Using De Moivre's theorem $[e^{i\theta} = \cos(\theta) + i \sin(\theta)]$, we then have:

$$1 = \int_0^\infty t e^{-t} \cos(rt) dt - i \int_0^\infty t e^{-t} \sin(rt) \, dt \tag{61}$$

You should already be objecting, but bear with us for a moment and define:

$$A = \int_0^\infty t e^{-t} \cos(rt) dt \tag{62a}$$

$$B = \int_0^\infty t e^{-t} \sin(rt) \, dt \tag{62b}$$

To tackle factor (62a), the obvious trick is integration by parts.

$$u = dt, \ du = dt$$

$$dv = e^{-t} \cos(rt) \, dt, v = e^{-t} \left[\frac{r\sin(rt) - \cos(rt)}{(1+r^2)} \right]$$

The mechanics of integration by parts easily lead to:

$$A = t e^{-t} \left[\frac{r\sin(rt) - \cos(rt)}{(1+r^2)} \right] \Bigg|_0^\infty - \int_0^\infty e^{-t} \left[\frac{r\sin(rt) - \cos(rt)}{(1+r^2)} \right] dt$$

This simplifies to:

$$A = \frac{-1}{(1+r^2)} \int_0^\infty [r\sin(rt) - \cos(rt)]\, e^{-t}\, dt \tag{63}$$

Straightforward integration of equation (63) then yields:

$$A = \frac{r}{(1+r^2)^2} \left[e^{-t}(\sin(rt) + r\cos(rt)) \right]\Big|_0^\infty + \frac{1}{(1+r^2)^2} \left[e^{-t}(r\sin(rt) - \cos(rt)) \right]\Big|_0^\infty$$

Simplifying, we obtain:

$$A = \frac{-r^2}{(1+r^2)^2} + \frac{1}{(1+r^2)^2} = \frac{1-r^2}{(1+r^2)^2} \tag{64}$$

Because it is completely analogous to factor A, we omit most of the algebra for factor B. The following then emerges:

$$B = \frac{2r}{(1+r^2)^2} \tag{65}$$

Next, combining equations (61), (62), (64), and (65), we get:

$$1 = A - iB = \frac{1-r^2}{(1+r^2)^2} - i\,\frac{2r}{(1+r^2)^2} \tag{66}$$

Rearranging equation (66), we have:

$$(1+r^2)^2 = 1 - 2ir - r^2 \tag{67}$$

To solve, postulate the obvious solution $r = iy, y \in \Re$, and substitute into equation (67):

$$(1-y^2)^2 = (1+y)^2 \tag{68}$$

The solution $y = -1$ drops out immediately. However, notice from equation (68) that r_c has a multiplicity of 2, and so we conclude that in this case singular yield is an imaginary quantity given by the square roots of $r_c = -i$ in the complex plane, i.e., $[3\pi/4, 7\pi/4]$. As advertised, yield redefined via equation (58) is sufficiently complete to partition liquidity propositions via an imaginary number that effectively restores it to nonsingular status and lets it produce unity on the left-hand side of equation (60).

Last but not least, one has the sneaking suspicion that, had we selected $\gamma = 3$ in equation (59), the upshot would have been identical save for the root-multiplicity of $r_c = -i$ in the complex plane. In that case (see the next exercise), the cube roots of $-i$ would have been our solution, i.e., $[3\pi/6, 7\pi/6, 11\pi/6]$.

We can now *imagine* liquidity-yield as a *vector* going around a quantized circle indexed by the roots of $-i$. Complex-root multiplicity thus provides a simple differentiation between the one-parameter set of liquidity propositions represented by equation (53). The extension of this formalism to the general case of noninteger γ is straightforward, beyond the intended scope and will not be discussed further.

Exercise 18.16

Show that the imaginary yield for the standard gamma density function with $\gamma = 3$ consists of the cube roots of $r_c = -i$.

Our brief excursion into the complex plane and its import to structured finance has taken us on financial byways that opened up veiled possibilities within a world begging to be discovered. If the truth be told however, we have barely scratched the surface of what awaits us out there.

A more sophisticated analysis than that currently in vogue could easily bring to light the manifold possibilities of finance. We called the Laplace transform the *fundamental* structure of finance precisely because it clearly shows what was hitherto hidden, i.e., the full algebraic structure of yield and the way something that does not *exist* can suddenly become *real* via convolutions in complex space. If you ever want to grasp the inner structure and meaning of finance, this is where you must begin.

18.8 THE BOX–MULLER ALGORITHM

We conclude this chapter with another analytical transformation useful in solving the basic problems of structured finance. Recall how we employed the concept of Jacobian determinants in chapter 17 while implementing the multi-dimensional Newton–Raphson iterative method. The Box–Muller (B–M) algorithm is yet another important application of Jacobian determinants aimed at the generation of Gaussian deviates. If you are ever called upon to write your own Gaussian-deviate routine, as in exercise 18.18 for instance, you will find the following technique quite helpful and easy to use.

The theory behind the B–M method is straightforward and amounts to applying the chain rule of differentiation for functions of many variables. The rule says that the total derivative of a real and differentiable function of several variables $g(x_1, x_2, x_3, ..., x_n)$ can be written as follows:

$$dg = \sum_{i=1}^{n} \frac{\partial g}{\partial x_i} dx_i \tag{69}$$

Equation (69) implies that if you have two such functions of the same variables, say g_1 and g_2, a two-dimensional area element $dx_1\, dx_2$ in the original space will be related to a corresponding area in g space $dg_1\, dg_2$ via the following relationship:

$$dx_1\, dx_2 = |\det[J]|\, dg_1\, dg_2 \tag{70}$$

You can verify equation (70) yourself by writing both versions of equation (69) underneath each other and solving for the left-hand side of equation (70) as a linear system in terms of dx_1 and dx_2. Here again, the symbol J stands for the Jacobian matrix of the transformation equations, the same equations we derived in chapter 17:

$$J \equiv \begin{Bmatrix} \dfrac{\partial x_1}{\partial g_1} & \dfrac{\partial x_1}{\partial g_2} \\[2ex] \dfrac{\partial x_2}{\partial g_1} & \dfrac{\partial x_2}{\partial g_2} \end{Bmatrix} \tag{71}$$

Relationship (70) also applies to functions of those same variables, i.e., x and g, and enables you to switch from one space to the other.

For instance, if you are given a joint probability density function $f(x_1, x_2)$, equation (70) allows us to write the following relationship between the density functions in the original space x and the transformed space g :

$$f(g_1, g_2)\, dg_1\, dg_2 = f(x_1, x_2)\, |\det[J]|\, dg_1\, dg_2 \tag{72}$$

Note that the functional values on either side of equation (72) will not be the same since the two sets of variables are related via arbitrary coordinate transformations. Now, consider the following special case of transformations between coordinate systems x and g :

$$\begin{aligned} x_1 &= e^{-\{g_1^2 + g_2^2\}/2} \\ x_2 &= \tfrac{1}{2\pi} \arctan[\tfrac{g_1}{g_2}] \end{aligned} \tag{73}$$

Admittedly, one cannot simply *guess* these particular transformations without prior experience in this sort of thing. To be sure, this was no mere guess on their part.

When you compute the determinant of the two-dimensional Jacobian matrix along the lines of equation (71), the following result obtains:

$$\det[J] = - \left[\frac{1}{\sqrt{2\pi}} e^{-\frac{g_1^2}{2}} \right] \left[\frac{1}{\sqrt{2\pi}} e^{-\frac{g_2^2}{2}} \right] \tag{74}$$

Exercise 18.16

Starting from equations (73), derive equation (74) by applying equation (71).

Amazingly, the right-hand side of equation (74) is the product of two independent standard Gaussian density functions, those of g_1 and g_2, respectively.

Effectively, this means that the transformed variables will be standard normal variables if the original variables x_1 and x_2 were uniformly distributed. However, this merely implies that one started from a uniform, Cartesian x space. The B–M algorithm is given by equations (73). It is equivalent to an exponential mapping of the unit square onto the plane.

Inversion of equations (73) quickly leads to our transformation equations:

$$g_1 = \sqrt{-2\ln x_1} \cos[2\pi x_2] \tag{75a}$$

$$g_2 = \sqrt{-2\ln x_1} \sin[2\pi x_2] \tag{75b}$$

Exercise 18.17

Starting from equation (73), derive equations (75).

Exercise 18.18

1. Using Excel's Rand uniform deviate routine in combination with the antithetic correction method from the section "Generating Random Numbers from Statistical Distributions" above, generate 2,500 pairs of uniform random deviates x_1 and x_2.
2. Use equations (75) to derive standard normal deviates from the uniform deviate pairs.
3. Plot a histogram of both the original uniform deviates and of the resulting normal deviates. How normal are g_1 and g_2? How would you measure their departure from normality? Are your results good enough for deal simulation purposes?

Note: The monograph *Numerical Recipes*[2] uses polar coordinates to eliminate the use of the sine and cosine functions within equations (75). Interested readers should peruse the appropriate pages of this authoritative textbook to find out how to do this.

18.9 CONCLUDING REMARKS

In this chapter, we reviewed some of the more mundane and technical aspects of structured finance, issues largely peripheral to our main deal focus. However, we feel such techniques should always reside in the quiver of any self-respecting structured analyst. We introduced Laplace transforms not so much to open Pandora's Box, but to plant the seeds of a more general (i.e., more abstract) approach to financial analysis. It should come to you as no surprise to discover that the Laplace transform is the cornerstone of cybernetics, the essence of finance.

Strictly speaking, the Cholesky and Box–Muller transformations have nothing to do with structured finance, and yet they have everything to do with it. A seasoned analyst ought to write and debug his algebraic and random number generation routines well ahead of their use in actual transactions. In fact, such routines ought to be developed as deal-independent blocks ready to be popped into any transaction at a moment's notice. A serious structured analyst cannot afford to waste time, especially when a transaction is on the table and the clock is ticking, because a Cholesky decomposition routine needs to be written from scratch.

Excellence in structured finance does not consist in writing routines more sophisticated than those of other people, but in ensuring that pseudo-randomness means exactly that. Over-sampling one end or the other of some loss distribution will cost the deal far more than a failure to use the sexiest random number generation scheme available. Regardless of how much number-crunching there might be in a transaction, finance is not an exercise in numerical analysis. Believe it or not, it is an exercise in financial analysis. One day, losing sight of this fact may cost you dearly.

APPENDIX: PRINCIPAL-ONLY CREDIT RATINGS

Of late, some of the major U.S. rating agencies have found it in their heart to assign *principal-only* credit ratings to structured securities issued in connection with selected transactions. Although we certainly applaud any extension of credit analysis that attempts to rise above the current horizon, we wonder whether investors have stopped to think about the propriety of doing this. In the context they are used, there is no doubt as to the rationale behind this type of credit rating, but the issue is whether this informs investors considering a purchase. Although the dubiousness of principal-only credit ratings should be transparent enough to anyone encountering them in practice, does a more formal argument exist that could enable us to concretize and solidify our opposition to this practice? The answer to this question is an overwhelming *yes*, and this becomes obvious when one realizes that a principal-only promise is nothing but a liquidity proposition, the singularity of which was reviewed above.

The painfully clear and obvious objection to ratings subscripted with the letter "p" is that they defeat the basic intent of a credit rating. They are unacceptable simply because liquidity propositions lead to zero-yield and, as a result, are meaningless. Because coupon payments are not intended to be part of the rating exercise, the "promise" can always be fulfilled by buying a principal guarantee, a zero-coupon or surety bond maturing on the trust's legal final maturity date. As mentioned above, the latter can be extended almost at will as long as it does not exceed a life in being plus 21 years,[9] i.e., approximately 100 years. This is not exactly what we mean by a credit rating.

Whatever trade those buying into such ratings are plying, investment is not one of them. We conclude that, regardless of the prevailing politics, principal-only credit ratings are singular and thus improper.

19

Cash Flow Model: Building Blocks

"Ideas are the building blocks of ideas"
Jason Zebehazy

This chapter is intended as a reinforcement of some of the asset-side cash flow modeling techniques that were demonstrated in chapters 15–18. At this point, the analyst should be ready to assemble the building blocks he has coded up to let the deal finally come together as a whole, as a logical construct. As a result, there is likely to be nothing new in what follows. In fact, we hope that there is indeed nothing new, since the reader should be fully prepared to go through the process that makes up the synthetic half of the arc in figure 14.1. This phase consists of two separate sections, each addressing one side of the SPC balance sheet. While this chapter focuses on the left side, the next tackles the liabilities. As already indicated, the latter are much more straightforward to model than the assets.

19.1 DELINQUENCY STRUCTURE IMPLEMENTATION

You will recall how, in chapter 15, we showed at least in principle how to implement our Markov transition matrix formalism using the IDFM coupled with random number generation. Exhibit 19.1 shows a straightforward VBA implementation of this process using the system-resident random number generator (Rnd).

▷ Exhibit 19.1: Implementation of Markov Transition Matrix

Get Markov Transition at Time = t; 'I' is the current state. Return the following state.

Function GetMarkovTransition(deal As deal, t As Integer, i As Integer) As Integer
Dim r As Double, v As Double, j As Integer, tij As Double, m12 As Double

```
With deal

If using prepayment model, set element (1, 5) to SMM and keep elements (1,1) and
(1,5) so they add up to the same value.

If .enablePrepayModel Then
.mmat(1, 1) = .mmat(1, 1) + .mmat(1, 5) - .prepaySmm(t)
.mmat(1, 5) = .prepaySmm(t)
End If
m12 = .mmat(1, 2)
.mmat(1, 2) = m12 + (.defA * .defB * .defC * Exp(-.defA * (t - .defT0)) / (1 + .defB *
Exp(-.defA * (t - .defT0))) ^ 2)
.mmat(1, 1) = .mmat(1, 1) - .mmat(1, 2) + m12
r = Rnd()
v = 0
For j = 1 To 6
tij = .mmat(i, j)
If (r <= v + tij) Then
Exit For
End If
v = v + tij
Next j
GetMarkovTransition = j
.mmat(1, 1) = .mmat(1, 1) + .mmat(1, 2) - m12
.mmat(1, 2) = m12


End With
End Function
```

Note that this code section fulfills two goals of the Markov process:

1. It implements the delinquency structure expected to be applicable to this pool
   and given implicitly by the issuer's portfolio data. We reviewed this subject in
   chapter 15.
2. It ensures that the loss curve expected to prevail after considering the issuer's
   static pool data is properly reflected in the delinquency patterns likely to be
   observed within the simulated process.

The first goal is reached by strict adherence to the issuer's portfolio delinquency
structure as submitted to the analyst while the second is achieved by using as a
delinquency modulator $\Delta p_{00}(t)$ the first derivative $f(t)$ of the issuer's loss curve $F(t)$
inside the first row of a time-dependent sequence of Markov transition matrices.
In effect, this procedure ensures that marginal losses will develop in accordance
with the dictates of $F(t)$, and thus result in the same default pattern as the loss curve
corresponding to this type of asset pool. The target issuer's loss curve behavior can be
known either from proxy situations or from previous transactions by the same issuer.

> **Exercise 19.1**
>
> Implement the above formalism in Visual Basic (VBA) inside your own ABS deal
> analysis code, and verify that the resulting loss pattern reproduces the input loss
> curve $F(t)$.

19.2 ABSORBING STATES: DEFAULT AND PREPAYMENT

In our treatment of delinquencies, we remarked that since Markov processes in
structured finance are not stationary, they can never reach the equilibrium state
demonstrated in chapter 16. Mainly, this is due to the presence of absorbing states, i.e.,
states with 1.0 on the diagonal of the corresponding row of their Markov transition
matrix. At the time, we mentioned that there were two such states (i.e., default and
prepayment), and that they were extremely important in terms of cash flow dynamics.
In this section, we take up the analysis of these two states in some detail and give an
example of their implementation in VBA.

Default

There is nothing mysterious about default, the heart and soul of credit risk analysis.
Rather, the question is how to treat defaulted loans properly via the normal cascading
process equivalent to a sequence of Markov transitions. This is because defaulted
loans are subject to recovery upon foreclosure. Our purpose here is to indicate how
to implement recoveries easily in code.

We pick up the loan once its delinquency status is set equal to D via the transition
process, i.e., as it effectively exits the issuer's analytical delinquency structure. The
simplest way to proceed is to "mark time" during a known time interval (months)
during which the foreclosure process is expected to take place. We define this time
interval as t_r. Once t_r collection periods have elapsed, simply invoke the recovery
function in accordance with the Newton–Raphson method of chapter 17, and deposit
the proceeds into the trust as a recovery. Since each loan is treated independently
within the Monte Carlo simulation, the timing of recoveries is handled automatically.
This basic principle is shown schematically in figure 19.1, where a loan is assumed
to have defaulted at time t_d with a principal balance $P(t_d)$ whereupon a recovery in
the amount $R(t_d + t_r)$ takes place t_r months later.

This method, in addition to being straightforwardly implemented (see below) also
gives full credit to issuers that manage their recoveries to lower the interval t_r. In
the case of automobiles, the normal recovery delay t_r is relatively small compared
to what we see in the mortgage arena. In general, recovery delays of three months or
less are common in automobile ABS.

Again, please note that defaulted loans are automatically excluded from further
Markov transitions since the corresponding state-wise diagonal entry in all transition
matrices is 1. The time sequence of defaulted loans is crucial since it needs

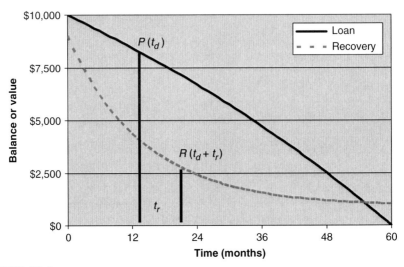

FIGURE 19.1
Loan amortization and vehicle depreciation.

to correspond as closely as possible to the given loss curve $F(t)$. Therefore, analysts should verify whether this is indeed the case before moving on with their modeling effort. Recall that the function $F(t)$ is the *gross* loss curve easily obtained by cumulating the principal balance of defaulted loans as they occur through time. In other words, assuming $P(t_d^i)$ is the principal balance of loan i at default, an estimate $\widetilde{F}(t)$ for $F(t)$ can be defined via:

$$\widetilde{F}(t) \equiv \sum_{i=1}^{t} P(t_d^i) | \forall t_d^i \leq t \tag{1}$$

Once the curve given by equation (20) in chapter 16 is constructed, the analyst can adjust the parameters of the Markov modulator, i.e., equation (25) in that chapter, so that $\widetilde{F}(t)$ will be as close as possible to $F(t)$.

For an arbitrary loan, the default and recovery events taking place at times t_d and $t_d + t_r$, respectively, are handled via the following two lines of code:

1. $TD(t_d) = TD(t_d) + P(t_d)$ (2a)

2. $TR(t_d + t_r) = TR(t_d + t_r) + R(t_d + t_r)$ (2b)

In equations (2a) and (2b), we have defined $TD(t)$ and $TR(t)$ as Aggregate Defaults and Aggregate Recoveries at time t, respectively. Therefore, the system keeps track of defaults and recoveries in real time and gives explicit recognition to the realistic dynamics of the default process. In addition, the easiest way to insert the mechanics of default into the flow chart is to use two distinct paths, the first one for loan-assets still part of the analytical delinquency structure and the other one defaulted or prepaid loans (see below).

Assuming that, within a Markov transition process consisting of n distinct status codes, the first $n - 2$ of which are normal delinquency states and the last two absorbing states, and assuming default is given status code $n - 1$, this method could be coded up schematically as shown in exhibit 19.2 (bold letters are VBA reserved words):

Exhibit 19.2:   Implementation of Defaulted Loans

Time Loop (takes care of each time step)

Asset Loop (runs through each asset one by one)

Markov Transition Process Simulation

Select Case Status ID

Case 1 to $n - 2$

(This is the normal delinquency process discussed in detail in the section "Delinquency Structure Implementation")

Case $n - 1$

$t_r = t_r + 1$

If $t_r = 0$ **then** $R(t) = F_R(t, W_0, a, b, c, t_s)$

End Select

In exhibit 19.2, the function $F_R(t, W_0, a, b, c, t_s)$ is the recovery function created from the Newton–Raphson-based depreciation model derived in chapter 17. On entry into each Monte Carlo (MC) scenario, loan-wise parameter t_r is given a *negative* value equal to the length of the recovery process. For instance if we know that three months will elapse on average before the sale of the vehicle at auction and the subsequent remittance of proceeds to the trust, the value of t_r on entry would be $t_r^0 \equiv -3$. This would capture recoveries on defaulted loans at the right time and prevent double counting. In addition, setting the delinquency status of a defaulted loan to a value above n post-recovery would completely remove it from consideration altogether and would save precious CPU cycles.

It cannot be sufficiently stressed how important it is to capture the appropriate default dynamics in a credit risk analysis code. The ability to simulate complex credit behaviors is by far the greatest contribution that Markov transition matrices can make to structured finance.

Prepayment

In some asset classes, such as mortgages, the issue of prepayments is of the essence, and thus we devote an entire section (Implementation of Prepayment Models inside Markov Transition Matrices) later in the chapter to the topic of prepayment modeling and the implementation of prepayment models inside a Markov model. In addition, due to the importance of this issue to mortgage-backed security analysis, all of chapter 10 was devoted to prepayment modeling. With respect to the target transaction, although prepayments are a much less critical piece of the credit analysis, by no means are we implying that prepayments can just be ignored. At this point however, we simply want to indicate how to account properly for the principal balance of loans that prepay throughout the simulation.

Since prepayment is just another absorbing state within Markov transition matrices in structured finance, our treatment will perforce parallel that of default and appear somewhat redundant. The major difference is that, unlike defaults, prepayments are not subject to trailing cash flows i.e., recovery. Here, once the loan pays its balance in full at some time t, it effectively exits the deal and its delinquency structure.

Clearly, the cash flow arising from a prepayment is the sum of the interest and principal allocations from the combined payment made by the obligor. In this case, this amount is usually assumed to be the periodic interest plus the principal balance remaining. With reference to our earlier formulations, whereby an obligor with periodic interest rate r, maturity T, periodic payment M and principal balance $B(t-1)$ at time $t-1$ prepays her loan entirely[1] at time t, we would compute a total payment partitioned into interest $I(t)$ and principal $P(t)$ allocations defined via:

$$I(t) = rB(t-1) \tag{3}$$

$$P(t) = \frac{M}{r}\left\{(1+r)^{t-1-T} - (1+r)^{t-T}\right\} + \frac{M}{r}\left\{1 - (1+r)^{t-T}\right\} \tag{4}$$

The interest component is shown as being paid in arrears as always, while the principal component has been dissected into its two logical portions. In other words, logically speaking the total principal amount consists of an expected principal payment portion, shown as the first term on the right-hand side of equation (4), and a "prepayment" shown as the second term. This was done to highlight the separate existence of these two components in prepayment modeling. In general, prepayments are defined as principal payments in excess of expected principal payments.

In terms of principal due to bondholders, this distinction is obviously immaterial. However, if one is forecasting prepayments using some analytical model, properly accounting for expected and unexpected payments becomes very relevant. Recall also that in the mortgage world a default is classified as a "prepayment" since MBS prepayments are defined as any reduction of pool principal balance beyond the expected reduction from scheduled loan amortization.

Prepayments are handled like defaults, i.e. via a separate branch of the Markov transition flowchart. Assuming that a loan prepays at time t and defining the prepayment status number as n, we can simply add the following short section to exhibit 19.2 to handle prepayments:

Exhibit 19.3:   Implementation of Prepaying Loans

Select Case Status ID

[Same as before]

Case $n - 1$

[Code for defaulted loans shown above]

Case n

$$TI(t) = TI(t) + r B(t - 1)$$

$$TR(t) = TR(t) + \frac{M}{r} \left\{ (1 + r)^{t-1-T} - (1 + r)^{t-T} \right\}$$

$$TP(t) = TP(t) + \frac{M}{r} \left\{ 1 - (1 + r)^{t-T} \right\}$$

End Select

In exhibit 19.3, we have defined Aggregate Interest Collections at time t as $TI(t)$, Aggregate Regular Principal Collections as $TR(t)$ and Aggregate Prepayments as $TP(t)$. As explained earlier, we have shown explicitly the partitioning of the assumed total principal payment made into its regular and prepayment portions.

The difficult aspect of prepayment modeling is clearly not such trivial code but the determination of actual prepayment values. Before we take this up separately in a subsequent section, the next section discusses the way our cash flow transfer function would be altered for different delinquency fee regimes, as this will significantly affect the cash flows assumed to accrue to the trust.

Exercise 19.2

Derive the amortization analytics of a piecewise level pay loan with principal balance $p(t)$ and level payment m_i over the restricted time interval t_i within the total interval $t \in [0, T]$. In this case, the intervals are defined as follows:

$$t_1 \equiv t \in [0, T_1]$$

$$t_2 \equiv t \in [T_1, T_2]$$

$$t_3 \equiv t \in [T_2, T]$$

continues to next page

---

continued from previous page
In other words, during interval t_1 the obligor pays the periodic amount m_1 and so on. Please compute the entire amortization schedule and graph the resulting formulas over $[0, T]$.

19.3 OTHER DELINQUENCY FEE REGIMES

In chapter 16, we derived the cash flow transfer function appropriate to a situation whereby delinquency fees were assumed to always precisely equal the amount necessary to bring a curing, or a partially curing account to a yield-neutral status, i.e., to the state whereby yield to the trust would not be impaired given its cure level. After much discussion, the upshot was equation (18) in chapter 16, reproduced here for convenience:

$$Pmt_{ij}^l(t) = \sum_{n=0}^{i-j} c_l[t-i+n](1+r_l)^{i-n}$$

Yield maintenance is provided by factor $(1+r_l)^{i-n}$, which is then multiplied by the monthly scheduled loan payment $c_l[t-i+n]$. Thus, this is where we need to look for any discrepancy in the delinquency regime applicable to our target issuer. We review some of the more common delinquency fee variations.

(a) No delinquency fee

Although this is probably a limiting case, it is quite possible that in some circumstances, issuers might not assess delinquency fees. In view of our previous comments, the cash flow transfer function would then look like equation (5):

$$Pmt_{ij}^l(t) = \sum_{n=0}^{i-j} c_l[t-i+n] \tag{5}$$

(b) Flat delinquency fee

Our second case deals with the most common situation, whereby an account is assessed a flat additional fee for any monthly collection period during which the account is delinquent. Let us assume this fee is d dollars per month, regardless of the level of delinquency applicable to the account.

$$Pmt_{ij}^l(t) = \sum_{n=0}^{i-j} c_l[t-i+n] + \sum_{n=1}^{i} \frac{d}{i} \tag{6}$$

In other words, we are simply allocating delinquency fees in an amount aggregating to d after all delinquent payments are counted. This way of expressing the situation may seem odd, and there are other ways of formulating this delinquency regime, but this method comes in handy when looking at alternative delinquency fee regimes whereby delinquency fees are graduated depending on the level of the delinquency.

(c) Graduated delinquency fee

Another possible scheme is a situation whereby the obligor is assessed a total fee proportional to the number of months by which the payment made is delinquent. In other words, we need to multiply the last summand in equation (6) by the index n, yielding:

$$Pmt_{ij}^l(t) = \sum_{n=0}^{i-j} c_l[t-i+n] + \sum_{n=1}^{i} \frac{nd}{i} \qquad (7)$$

(d) Delinquency fee allocation to interest collections

In general, the vast majority of obligors in certain sectors will not be able to make payments that include a specific amount allocated to their delinquency status in addition to the payment they "believe" they owe. This is because most people simply can not compute what delinquency fees actually mean. Taking account of this fact considerably complicates matters with respect to cash flows. For instance, suppose we assumed obligors are simply making scheduled total payments c_l without regard for delinquency fees. What would happen is that, upon receipt of the payment, the issuer would recharacterize some of the cash as interest instead of principal for this is what delinquency fees truly represent. This would proportionally lower the principal allocated as amortization and thus raise the loan's principal balance to a level higher than what would be calculated from the same payment absent the fee. Specifically, assume a delinquent obligor makes his payments according to delinquency fee regime (a) above, and thus makes a total payment given by equation (5).

Now, instead of actually receiving the delinquent fee amount d, we would simply subtract it from what would otherwise be allocated to principal amortization. Therefore, the allocated monthly principal amortization $Pr_{ij}^l(t)$ would be computed as:

$$Pr_{ij}^l(t) = \sum_{n=0}^{i-j} p_l[t-i+n] - d \qquad (8)$$

As a result, the periodic interest allocation for this obligor would be computed as:

$$I_{ij}^l(t) = \sum_{n=0}^{i-j} c_l[t-i+n] - Pr_{ij}^l(t) \qquad (9)$$

As can readily be seen, the sum of interest and principal allocations still equals the total payment made by the obligor.

The complication comes from the fact that the aggregate amounts d from all collection periods would have to be computed so as to represent a trailing stream of payments that would be tacked onto the original maturity structure of the loan. This would require additional lines of VBA, but would not add an undue CPU burden to code performance. Alternative fee regimes can be implemented in a similar fashion.

(e) Pro rata delinquency fee

Our last delinquency fee method ties such fees to the scheduled obligor payment but foregoes the compounding appropriate to the basic method. In essence, we are simply adding a factor of d percent to each payment $c_l[t-i+n]$ made by the obligor, resulting in the following imputed cash flow transfer function:

$$Pmt_{ij}^l(t) = \sum_{n=0}^{i-j} c_l[t-i+n](1+id) \tag{10}$$

In this case, although principal allocations would remain the same as for the case of zero delinquency fees, the factor $\sum_{n=0}^{i-j} id\, c_l[t-i+n]$ would be counted as additional interest collections accruing to the trust.

Exercise 19.3

Implement a cash flow transfer function for a floating-rate loan based on one-month LIBOR as the floating index. What is the main difference between fixed and floating-rate loans when it comes to cash flow transfer functions?

The Varieties of Delinquency Experience

It will surprise no one to discover that issuers are rather creative in their use of interest allocation with respect to payments made by their obligors. Borrowers that start on the slippery delinquency slope often find that the amount they actually owe to get out from underneath a mounting pile of additional fees is sometimes much higher than they could have ever imagined. One can obviously not scan through the universe of possible real-life permutations. Some percentage of noise is thus acceptable as part of delinquency fee analysis. Although one can often *intend* much more than what can be conceptualized, such noise will in general never make the difference between a deal that works and one that does not. If it does, it is a foregone conclusion that the transaction has much bigger problems.

Delinquency modeling is a prime instance where the fundamentally atomic nature of our conceptual analysis comes to the fore. Good judgment as to how far to push the recognition of delinquency fees and their associated mechanics is critical to the structured analyst and the well-worn phrase "the devil is in the details" is especially applicable to this context. At some point, it becomes counter-productive and unnecessarily time-consuming to work out the precise modalities of interest and principal allocations that follow logically from a particular credit policy. At best, this can only evidence a few additional basis points. On the other hand, the complete neglect of this crucial aspect of cash flow modeling is also inappropriate since delinquency fees are a source of cash that cannot be summarily dismissed. The extent and depth to which one needs to resort to properly reflect the delinquency-based earning potential of the trust is a matter in which credit analysts ought to prove their mettle.

19.4 IMPLEMENTATION OF PREPAYMENT MODELS INSIDE MARKOV TRANSITION MATRICES

This section discusses how prepayment models can be inserted inside time-dependent Markov transition matrices as a precursor to deal analysis. What will emerge from this discussion is the ease with which this can be done, adding further support to the notion that this formalism, unlike any other, is especially appropriate to the task of prepayment modeling.

As was pointed out in chapter 10, prepayment models are delicate animals to tame because they are created from painstaking data analysis over long periods, and yet can only deliver on their promise in the form of a two-fold conditionality. By the latter expression, we mean that on the one hand, such models can only predict prepayments subject to external and a priori unknown quantities like interest rates, and on the other hand, prepayment rates are always communicated as conditional rates, which means that accounts that have already prepaid are obviously not eligible for current prepayments.

Thus, the Conditional Prepayment Rate (CPR) put out by all prepayment models is primarily conditional on the account being part of the trust, and most likely still current, at the time the prepayment rate is calculated. If absolute rates were used, it would be theoretically possible for more than 100% of the pool to prepay.

The task of creating a prepayment model is arduous, something to which readers of chapter 10 can probably testify. Unlike the recovery models of chapter 17, prepayment models usually cannot be derived in a few days simply to suit the requirements of deal analysis. If any prepayment model is expected to be used, it must usually be made available before a deal needs to be analyzed.

In general, prepayment models are asset-class specific because the variables that turn out to be major performance drivers will normally vary across asset classes. Most well-known prepayment models are driven by interest rates, something clearly designed for real estate assets. In some asset classes, such as autos, prepayment rates are however largely insensitive to the vagaries of the yield curve, which is not to say that prepayment rates are negligible, for this could not be further from the truth. Interested readers are referred to chapter 10 for further details on how to build a prepayment model for mortgage collateral.

In what follows, we assume a simplistic form of prepayment model, one that nevertheless affords certain well-known characteristics like burn-out. We then show via code samples and an accompanying discussion how this particular model was used to generate cash flows to the trust.

Markov Transition Matrices and Prepayment Modeling

The easiest way to insert a prepayment model into our Markov chain formalism is to use the element of the first-row labeled *SMM*. Since the Markov transition matrix is itself a conditional probability of moving between two states given an account currently found in one of them, the Markov chain formalism automatically takes care of the first "conditional" aspect of prepayment analysis, i.e., that the target obligor's current loan balance is the relevant parameter for prepayment purposes.

In addition, in the following we assume it is impossible for a delinquent obligor to prepay his loan. Strictly speaking, this is incorrect. However, as a rule this assumption is remarkably accurate given that prepayments mainly stem from early amortization, i.e., from the refinancing of an existing mortgage or from the purchase of a new vehicle. Although delinquent-account prepayments are not impossible, in most cases it will be difficult for an obligor to refinance his mortgage, or else to buy a new vehicle, if a delinquency on the same type of collateral shows up in his credit bureau report. Therefore, restricting prepayments to current accounts is probably the simplest, and the best, first-order approximation that can be made. If we were later asked to allow prepayments on delinquent loans, the necessary matrix modifications would be relatively minor.

When the single month mortality is assumed constant, as with our basic approach to prepayments from chapter 16, prepayment modeling effectively reduces to a constant conditional rate, say α_0. In fact, this might be an acceptable model given the amount of a priori information available. Despite many claims to the contrary, prepayment rates are remarkably stable within many transactions.

However, for any time-dependent specification of the $SMM(t)$ entry inside our time-dependent Markov transition matrix, subsidiary models addressing prepayment drivers will need to be available. For instance, a prepayment model meant to apply to mortgage assets will need to be driven by an estimate of the key interest rate since it is the major prepayment driver. In general, interest-rate models are labeled *short-rate* models because they address mainly the near end of the yield curve, leaving to arbitrage-free arguments the task of computing the remaining points. Although many such models exist, we briefly mention one of the most popular short-rate models, the Cox–Ingersoll–Ross (CIR) algorithm, which is little more than a variation on the well-known Vasicek model.

The next subsection is not meant as advertising for the CIR model. Any other model is acceptable and we encourage credit analysts to use the model they know best. All short-rate models can be made to produce comparable outputs and the difference in their respective predictive accuracy is negligible.

The CIR Short-Rate Model

Within the CIR[2] model, the short-rate increment dr is estimated using:

$$dr = \mu (r_0 - r) dt + \sigma \sqrt{r} \, dz \tag{11}$$

It should first be mentioned that the main innovation in both the CIR and the Vasicek model is the introduction of a *steady-state* short rate r_0 rather than through terms like $\mu \, dt$ and $\sigma \, dz$ that were present in previous modeling efforts. As can readily be seen, for all values of r such that $r > r_0$, the increment dr would on average satisfy $dr < 0$ and hence the rate r would tend to be brought back closer to r_0, and vice versa in the opposite case. Therefore, the value r_0 acts as an "attractor" in yield space.

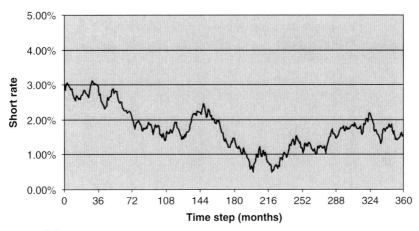

FIGURE 19.2
Typical short-rate sequence from the CIR model.

Thus, a dynamic sequence of short rates r regards the line $r = r_0$ as a limit-cycle of the system. The ratio σ/μ then determines the volatility of rates on either side of this limit-cycle.

We can therefore expect that, most of the time, the model will cause interest rates to oscillate around the value $r = r_0$ while still allowing rate excursions dictated by the value of σ. The $\sqrt{r}$ term was added to recognize the fact that absolute rate volatility tends to increase when rates are relatively high and vice versa. The Vasicek model simply omits this term but preserves the basic limit-cycle intuition.

The essence of the CIR model is its *mean reversion* feature captured by the value r_0 and requires that a reasonable estimate for that quantity exist already. Figure 19.2 shows a typical short-rate sequence arising from the CIR model, whereby the limit cycle was set at $r_0 = 0.02$ and where the initial rate was $r(0) = 0.03$. For this run, we used short-rate volatility $\sigma = 0.10\%$ and a drift (μ) of 25 bps.

As long as rates remain within the realm of the possible, any short-rate model may be used.

The Basic Prepayment Model

Our basic prepayment model consists of Brownian motion coupled with an inverse rate driver and a burn-out factor. According to this model, single-month mortality can be represented as follows:

$$SMM(t) = e^{-at} \left[\alpha_0 + \beta_0 \left(\frac{K}{r(t)} - 1 \right) \right] + \sigma_p\, dz \qquad (12)$$

In equation (12), we have defined the relevant parameters as follows:

t = time (months)
$r(t)$ = CIR short-rate model output (equipped with a floor and a cap)

K $= r(t_0)$ [calibration variable]

$r(t_0) =$ short rate on the closing date of the target transaction

α_0 $=$ base prepayment rate

β_0 $=$ interest-rate effect multiplier

a $=$ burn-out factor

dz $=$ Wiener process

σ_p $=$ prepayment rate volatility

Variable K is a calibration variable introduced in order to force the initial prepayment rates to be approximately the base rate. We do this because we expect that in the initial stages of the transaction, obligors will lack the incentive to refinance their mortgage or indebtedness because interest rates will tend to hover around the value at which the loan was issued, which is likely to be in the neighborhood or $r(t_0)$ in most cases. In other words, when current rates are near their closing value, obligors will commonly not have a financial incentive to repay their loan, nor can they usually afford to do so immediately post-closing. We recognize this situation by setting $K = r(t_0)$, leading to the condition $K/r(t) - 1 \approx 0$ in the first two years or so after closing.

Exercise 19.4

Implement the CIR model on a spreadsheet and plot a graph similar to figure 19.2. Next, run various values of the limit cycle variable r_0 and volatility σ over a wide range and look at the output in the form of graphs like figure 19.2. Satisfy yourself that you understand the rate excursions that can be expected from various combinations of parameters.

The burn-out factor a is included to reflect the fact that no matter how high the economic incentive to prepay, obligors who have not yet prepaid in spite of large incentives are presumably immune to economic pressure and will not prepay at speeds that would otherwise be dictated by a standalone model. The burn-out rate is an attempt to reflect the increased resistance to prepayment from such *die-hard* obligors.

The implementation of this prepayment model merely amounts to the insertion of equation (12) into the time-dependent sequence of Markov transition matrices. Because we are attributing prepayments exclusively to current accounts, doing this involves a two-step procedure that leaves intact the initial calibration of the loss process reviewed in chapter 16 and simply modulates the conditional prepayment rate $SMM(t)$ to the extent it is different from its formerly constant value α_0, the base prepayment rate.

Therefore, we proceed as follows:

1. Loss Curve Modulation

This is a repetition of the procedure undertaken in chapter 16. Here, we set the entry $p_{00}(t)$ on the first row of our transition matrix to the value given by equation (23a) in chapter 16, where we have relabeled the probability with which an account will remain current $p_{00}^L(t)$ merely to indicate that the operation is dealing with losses only:

$$p_{00}^L(t) = p_{00}^0 - \Delta p_{00}(t) \tag{13}$$

Note that loss curve modulation and calibration should be done prior to, and independently of any prepayment model implementation. The use of a prepayment model will obviously disturb the micro-loss dynamics during calibration, and so it is critical to execute the loss calibration exercise while maintaining the single-month mortality level at the constant value α_0. Because the prepayment rate represents a second-order credit driver, doing this is both acceptable and reasonable.

2. Prepayment Model Modulation

Next, the prepayment model is applied on top of the modulation represented by equation (13) to yield the final value $p_{00}^P(t)$ for the probability with which a loan will remain current within this collection period, and where the capital superscript 'P' indicates that prepayment rates are now dynamically conceived.

First, equation (12) is used to compute the variance to the base prepayment rate α_0:

$$\Delta P(t) = SMM(t) - \alpha_0 \tag{14}$$

Next, the left-most Markov chain entry is further modulated to account for variable prepayment rates while preserving the time-dependent row sum condition, which can be written $\sum_{j=0}^{n} p_{0j}(t) = 1$.

$$p_{00}^P(t) = p_{00}^L(t) - \Delta P(t) \tag{15}$$

Exercise 19.5

Implement the prepayment model (12) on a spreadsheet and plot a graph similar to figure 19.3. Next, run various values of burn-out rate a, prepayment volatility σ and multiplier β_0 and look at the output in the form of graphs like figure 19.3. Satisfy yourself that you understand the prepayment rate excursions that can be expected from various combinations of the parameters within model (12).

Exhibit 19.4: Prepayment Model Implementation inside a Markov Process

Calculate SMM and short-rate values according to the CIR model (equation 11).

Sub CalcPrepaySmm(deal As deal)

continues to next page

```
continued from previous page
Dim t As Integer, r As Double, dr As Double, dz As Double
ReDim deal.prepaySmm(0 To deal.maxTerm) As Double
ReDim deal.cirRates(0 To deal.maxTerm) As Double
With deal
.cirRates(0) = .prepayK
For t = 1 To .maxTerm
dz = Application.Normsinv(Rnd())
r = .cirRates(t - 1)
r = r + .cirMeanDrift * (.cirLimitCycle - r) * .cirDt + .cirVol * r ^ 0.5 * dz
r = Application.Max(.cirMin, r)
r = Application.Min(.cirMax, r)
.cirRates(t) = r
.prepaySmm(t) = Exp(-.prepayA * t) * (.prepayAlpha + .prepayBeta *
(.prepayK / r - 1)) + .prepayVol * dz
.prepaySmm(t) = Application.Max(.prepayMin, .prepaySmm(t))
.prepaySmm(t) = Application.Min(.prepayMax, .prepaySmm(t))
Next t
End With

End Sub
```

Figure 19.3 shows a typical sequence of prepayment rates produced by model (12) for reasonable values of its parameters. Given a judicious choice of model parameters, $SMM(t)$ values are reasonably distributed over the feasible historical range within a 20-year maturity transaction.

In actual implementations, it is customary to impose a hard cap and a hard floor on the allowable values of $SMM(t)$ to avoid either negative prepayment rates or rates

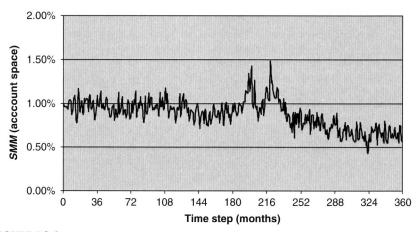

FIGURE 19.3
Typical SMM sequence from prepayment model 19.12.

that have never been seen historically. Exhibit 19.4 shows a VBA implementation of algorithm (12) within our target transaction code.

19.5 PREPAYMENT MODELS WITHIN MARKOV CHAINS

Clearly, we have barely scratched the surface of prepayment modeling and its implications for structured finance, not to mention that the approach we have outlined here is far from pristine. We now wish to discuss some of the more obvious weaknesses of our algorithm in order to bring to light the many pitfalls that lurk on the threshold of hasty conclusions.

At the outset, it can be seen that the main advantage of Markov chains lies in their being essentially *ready-made* both for prepayment modeling and its cash flow consequences. The programming effort involved in implementing a prepayment model inside transition matrices is benign and speaks volumes as to the appropriateness of this technique to structured analysis in general.

Disruption of the Initial Micro-Loss Calibration

For starters, the introduction of the basic prepayment model has obviously modified the initial expected loss micro-calibration described in chapter 16, and one might be tempted to redo the loss calibration, but this time including the additional variability arising from the dynamics of prepayments. Doing this would be a mistake since, owing precisely to prepayment stochasticity we would never be able to calibrate the expected loss properly.

This is because there is no feasible solution for the micro-loss parameter $m(L_e)$ if additional cash flow variance is introduced in the form of a prepayment model. As you will know, a single defining equation with more than one unknown coefficient produces an under-determined system. In other words, it is strongly advisable to use the constant prepayment rate α_0 that best fits the target pool or issuer and to leave the micro-level loss calibration unscathed, letting the deal itself find its new micro-loss distribution, i.e., the one produced by the incorporation of our prepayment model equation (12). If α_0 has been properly selected to begin with, the micro-loss distribution output by a prepayment model like equation (12) will be close enough to what would result from a constant CPR.

Correlations at the Obligor Level

A potentially important, yet neglected aspect of the above cash flow formalism is the possibility that an observable correlation structure might exist between loans that become delinquent and those that prepay. At the outset, it is clear that loans that default cannot prepay and thus, that as soon as a loan is seen to enter the pool's delinquency structure by exiting the current status, it would no longer be available to prepay unless it returned to currency via enhanced payment activity. By definition, our Markov transition formalism allows loans that were once delinquent to prepay just the same. This means that the delinquency process is modeled without a memory effect. You will recall from "The Idea of a Markov Chain" in chapter 16 that the central tenet of Markov-chain analysis is the absence of memory. Thus in our delinquency world, a current loan is subject to the same prepayment probability regardless of its previous delinquency history. Without this condition, Markov himself would have been unable to linearize the ensuing process and we would be forced to deny the validity of the efficient market hypothesis. Whether this view accurately reflects empirical prepayment dynamics is still an open question.

Yet another potentially neglected correlative factor is the notion that increased prepayment rates would somehow reduce the propensity of a given loan to become delinquent via some sort of *conservation* argument whereby the sum of prepayment and delinquency propensities would be kept nearly constant over time. Although it may be interesting and fruitful to speculate idly on such matters, there is precious little reliable evidence for this type of pool behavior. In any case, the statistical nature of the beast renders this point rather moot. The assumption of independence between prepayment and default behavior, which is effectively the strong assumption that all relevant statistical moments vanish simultaneously, is a good approximation at the basic level. This type of correlation would come about much more from macro-economic factors than because obligors are somehow "correlated" with each other. It is a fairly well-accepted notion that obligors are indeed independent in the real sense of the word. In the event interest rates were to drop suddenly, thereby causing relatively higher prepayment rates, obligors would most likely react precisely in the manner we have already conceived because the drivers of default and prepayments are fundamentally different. We conclude that, at first blush at least, the independence between delinquency and prepayment propensities is a defensible assumption.

Short-Rate Model Performance

Probably the most neglected factor in all this is the performance of the short-rate algorithm (CIR) lying at the heart of prepayment dynamics. Historically, short-rate models have been little more than pithy ways of organizing one's thoughts rather than "predictions" of anything that was truly believed to be highly probable. The statistical R^2 measure appropriate to most short rate-models hovers in the single-digit range, hardly a shining example of predictive accuracy.

Yet it would be wrong and unfair to indict such a dismal performance and attribute it to a lack of analytical expertise on the part of modelers. As everybody knows, prediction of interest rates really amounts to prediction of future events, which is a nonstarter anyway. The best we can really do is to create a mental image of how the world looks to us currently and to stop attempting to gauge interest-rate prediction the way we do with weather prediction. Until something like a *front*, a concept familiar to all weather forecasters, is invented in this context, interest-rate prediction will remain what it is today, i.e., an expensive hobby. As a practical matter, most people have stopped trying to predict rates altogether and simply seek to hedge it out. The upshot is that what really matters is not how high or low rates are computed to be, but rather the *view* they afford on the current situation. In other words, short-rate models are not to be referred to as good or bad, but rather as helpful or useless.

The Relevance of Prepayment Modeling

It is always tempting and in some corners, impressive, to demonstrate one's familiarity with the latest and greatest prepayment model. Wall Street definitely has no dearth of analysts looking to serve up the latest concoction of edible research, one that usually includes the most avant-garde concepts known to man.

Readers likely to fall for the lure of the esoteric should think twice before launching on a sophisticated modeling exercise that may, in fact, turn out to be much ado about nothing. In many cases, inherent transaction value-drivers will lie totally outside prepayment analysis and precious time will be wasted trying to reproduce models and algorithms that fail to hit the nail on the head. We are obviously not talking about mortgage-backed securities, where prepayment modeling is the crux of the analysis, but of more exotic asset classes such as structured settlements (see chapter 24) and automobile-loan-backed securities in which investments are unlikely to be misguided merely because someone has failed to predict prepayments accurately.

Our central message is this: unlike prepayments, time is *always* of the essence. Every analytical minute should be allocated to the area where it will have the greatest impact in terms of relevance to the deal's credit loss drivers. In most non-MBS transactions it is still acceptable to optimize structures with effectively no prepayment model save a constant single-month mortality rate. This does not mean that prepayments have somehow been *neglected* and that the results may be thrown away as irrelevant. On the contrary, results become much more meaningful when the effective loss drivers have been accurately modeled. Rather than spending countless hours churning air in the hope of displaying one's analytical virtuosity, one ought to refrain from rushing in and instead, engage in a meaningful reflection on the truth of the relevant asset class. Sometimes, the low-tech solution is the smarter way to go.

APPENDIX: *In Memoriam*

Martin Heidegger (1889–1976)

Introduction

Martin Heidegger, now regarded by most as the greatest philosopher of the twentieth century, was born in the Swabian (Baden, Germany) town of Messkirch in 1889. He had begun novitiate studies leading to ordination as a Jesuit priest but had to abandon them on the advice of his superiors because of asthma and heart problems. It was then that he turned his amazing powers of synthesis to the study of philosophy and mathematics. Shortly thereafter, he came under the influence of Franz Brentano and Edmund Husserl, two leading German philosophers associated with the Phenomenological school. Most likely as a result of such encounters, the young Heidegger decided to focus the remainder of his life's work on the "Question of Being" as prefigured in Aristotle's famous remark "τι το ον" ("What is a being?").

During his long and tumultuous life, Martin Heidegger wrote only one book, and this merely in order to become eligible for an academic position in Germany. Entitled *Being and Time*, it is considered a sublime masterpiece. Published in 1927, it was to be followed by a second volume which, regrettably, never saw the light of day.

Instead, Heidegger produced lecture notes now being published as books by Vittorio Klostermann GmbH (Frankfurt am Main). The entire corpus of Heidegger's works, known as the "Gesamtausgabe," is to contain 102 volumes and is scheduled to be fully available in German by the year 2025 or thereabouts. It is in such other treatises that the second part of *Being and Time* will be transmitted to the public.

Heidegger is famous, or perhaps infamous, for his misunderstood declaration that the goal of his life's project was to accomplish the destruction of traditional metaphysics. However, this destruction must be grasped in the positive rather than the negative sense that is nowadays so common. The word ought to be conceived as a *de-struktion*, i.e., a deconstruction. In passing, the latter expression became the name for an entire philosophical school, one most strongly associated with the recently deceased Frenchman Jacques Derrida.

Heidegger's Place in the Western Tradition

Positioning Heidegger within our tradition is not easy. Methodologically, Heidegger descends directly from Socrates in being a consummate teacher and in never bothering to write books, as too many so-called philosophers are wont to do. To him, understanding the world on its own terms from *die Sache selbst* (the thing itself) is what philosophy is really all about. Once you lose your connection to the world, what you are doing is not philosophy but religion. Reading or writing books is only a path to doing so but, per se, can never amount to anything.

Revered by his students as a God, Heidegger still expressed himself in the language of the common man without pedantry or conceit. He never talked down to people and never pretended that what he was saying was "too complicated" for them. On the contrary, he stressed time and again that the soul of philosophy lay in its simplicity. What he really meant was not so much simplicity in the usual manner of speaking, but more the elementariness we attempt to demonstrate in chapter 22 via the two fair coin problems. Nieztsche used to say that a philosopher was much more afraid of being understood than misunderstood. That was never an issue with Heidegger. As always with him, the negative and the positive were inextricably intertwined and complementary rather than viewed as opposites, which is how we have come to conceive them generally in the West.

The Western tradition had started a long time before Socrates, with the speculations on Being and Becoming of Parmenides (Eleatic School) and Heraclitus (Milesian School), respectively. The mere existence of two apparently irreconcilable but plausible points of view was in itself evidence of a major philosophical problem, one that became known as the problem of existence or "Being." What does it mean to be? This problem is still with us today and is just as real and seemingly as unsolvable as ever. Pretending there is no problem, à la early Ludwig Wittgenstein for instance, or that if you just said the *right* words, all would be well, does not amount to a solution. In fact, it is a tribute to his towering intellect that Wittgenstein was willing to abandon his early manifesto[3] to embrace metaphysics, much to the dismay of his erstwhile mentor Bertrand Russell.

During the turmoil of the Peloponnesian War and its aftermath, where two incompatible organizational frameworks (Sparta [communism] and Athens [capitalism]) were being tested on the battlefield, there was a lull in philosophical output. Soon afterwards, freedom of speech was restored, and men like Socrates and the Sophists went on exercising that freedom in different ways. Socrates, benefiting from a modest war pension, was able to charge nothing for his advice whereas the average Sophist was a hired gun, the forerunner of the modern-day management consultant. Socrates, like his Eastern counterpart Confucius, never wrote books, preferring simply to teach people everywhere and anywhere, but usually on the street. His students propagated whatever is known of his teachings, assuming they had the time to write it down. Thus, by definition we really do not know exactly what Socrates said. The same is true of Confucius.

Socrates' legacy was left in the hands of his loyal student Plato who emphasized theory or *ideas*, and the latter's protégé Aristotle who, for his part, emphasized practice and physical investigation, i.e., what the average person would call the *real* world. These two points of view, once more seemingly irreconcilable, gave rise to empiricism and idealism, respectively, the two brands of philosophy known to most people. The first type is associated with the United Kingdom and the second with France and Germany.

It should be noted that much of that early Greek speculation was passed down to us via translations by Arabic philosophers, such as Avicenna, and Sufis, like Rumi, without whom we might never have known the sources of our own tradition.

Heidegger's Contribution to the West

The fact that it was to take centuries for someone to bring to light and harmonize the existence of two dissimilar philosophical schools is nothing but the symptom of something more original, i.e., of the *a priori* lying at the heart of the possibility of our knowledge of the world. The de-construction, grounding and bringing to light of such possibility is Heidegger's fundamental and massive contribution to the West.

When we say *original*, we do not mean it in the sense of time, but rather in the sense of what must come first, at the source—what specifically grounds the possibility of knowledge. Not surprisingly, in practice this is usually the last thing we learn, having dabbled for decades with the mistaken notion that what "is" today, what we plainly see beforehand, is somehow privileged and unquestionable. Holding out in the questionable, which for us is the *question of the deal*, is the process by which we can synthesize deals *ex nihilo* from our negative determinations unto their positive elaboration from the ground up. Only then can finance understand itself out of itself; only then does it have any chance at all to rank amongst the sciences instead of being relegated to the bottom of the pile as something dirty and debased or even worse, as Applied Economics.

Heidegger and Structured Finance

Heidegger speaks to us today as currently as he did 50 years ago. Of course, as a philosopher he never talked about finance as such. If the truth were told, he would probably be shocked to find that his ideas are being adapted to something as perverse and commonplace as Wall Street finance. On the other hand, by showing the way forward to an elusive synthesis of being and becoming for the first time in modern

458 • ELEMENTS OF STRUCTURED FINANCE

history, Heidegger gave us the hope that structured finance, this most metaphysical of endeavors, can one day stand on solid ground. Perhaps then, it can become accessible to those who want to learn it, not as religion, but as science.

If structured finance is ever to emerge from the depths of its own ignorance, come of age, assert itself, and become a respectable profession like all others, it will be solely on the basis of a fundamental self-understanding, i.e., of something that lies outside finance. Before there can be a deal, there must be *deal-hood*. Understanding deals and doing deals is not feasible unless, and until, one understands the meaning of the deal as the essence of deal-hood. When this is finally accomplished, all deals will merge into that essence and appear as the one, essential deal.

Thanks to Martin Heidegger, this hitherto unattainable dream is now realistically within reach.

20

Cash Flow Model: Advanced Liabilities

Mephistopheles:

"Mein guter Herr, Ihr seht die Sachen,
Wie man die Sachen eben sieht;
Wir müssen das gescheiter machen,
Eh uns des Lebens Freude flieht."

J. W. von Goethe, Faust (First Part)

Compared to asset-side modeling, liability modeling will seem like a bit of an anti-climax. Although a single chapter will be sufficient to cover this topic, we saw that the effort necessary to produce a fair representation of asset pools took us on wild roller-coaster ride of analytical by-roads and detours. This is not an exception or a peculiarity of subprime automobile ABS transactions. Rather, it is a feature of structured finance in general, at least at this stage of maturity.

Unfortunately, it is a regrettable feature of the U.S. capital markets that the bulk of ABS transactions across the entire spectrum of asset classes are neither optimized, nor is any such optimization ever really attempted. In the final analysis, the sponsor or seller is usually happy to escape with his life intact, to have gone one more time around the Wall Street wheel of fortune, and to be able to go on fighting another day, or perhaps "die another day" would be more accurate. Through no nefarious conspiracy, sellers and investors are both ill-served by the current structured finance environment, one that brings together the worst of both worlds, i.e., where neither sponsors nor investors can fully benefit from, respectively, the true credit quality of their assets or securities. To do otherwise would require a level of conceptualization that simply does not exist at present and that, furthermore, is unlikely to emerge for some time.

If the truth be told, structured finance has only begun to realize its own possibilities. If it is there at all, comprehensive deal analysis is largely in its infancy and will not grow up until, and unless, the silly and inaccurate notions that now prevail (many of which were shamelessly borrowed from corporate finance) are jettisoned altogether and replaced by those native to the relevant field. Structured finance must first be allowed to come out of itself, for itself, before serious liability structuring can come of age in a meaningful way.

The upshot of all this is that our seemingly ambitious title is really nothing but a faint hope. Liability "modeling" now amounts to following simple rules of logic usually already written down in the prospectus, otherwise known as the *waterfall*. Although creativity at this level is nonexistent, there is still much to learn when it comes to the implementation of these rules. Therefore, what follows is, unfortunately, restrictive and largely incomplete.

We now present a detailed description of the target transaction's liability structure and a rough guide toward programming it in VBA. Interestingly, many of the structural features commonly encountered while wandering through asset-backed securities are in fact included in the target deal. Although by no means exhausting the realm of structural variation, the concepts covered over the next few pages will account for a surprisingly large percentage of outstanding ABS transactions.

20.1 AGGREGATE QUANTITIES

Before embarking on a treatment of liabilities, we need to spend a few moments discussing the preliminary quantities that need to be made available to the right-hand side of the Special Purpose Vehicle (SPV) balance sheet, most of which have coincidentally been reviewed in earlier chapters. Although the following remarks are meant to apply solely to the target asset class, the overlap with other classes is extensive.

As an adjunct to the Markov-chain-based modeling of the pool, the time-dependent quantities shown in table 20.1 need to be computed before waterfall distributions can be made.

Available Funds and Current Collections

One of the crucial distinctions in liability implementation is the difference between *Available Funds* and *Current Collections*. As we shall soon see, this distinction will become paramount when dealing with the mechanics of Reserve Accounts within the waterfall.

As its name implies, the expression "Available Funds" refer to the totality of funds available for distribution to bondholders and shareholders on any Distribution Date, not to what was collected during the immediately preceding Collection Period. Thus, at its most basic level, Available Funds is the sum of Current Collections plus any form of credit enhancement, surety bond proceeds, or cash collateral deemed to be included in the trust estate.

In the target transaction, the existence of a reserve account forces us to write $F_0(t)$ as follows:

$$F_0(t) = C_C(t) + R_b(t) \tag{1}$$

TABLE 20.1
Aggregate quantities for liability modeling

ITEM	DEFINITION
$A(t-1)$	Current Class A Principal Balance
$B(t-1)$	Current Class B Principal Balance
$V(t)$	Current Pool Balance
$V(t-1)$	Previous Pool Balance
$D(t)$	Current Aggregate Defaulted Receivables
$PP(t)$	Current Aggregate Prepayments
$P_R(t)$	Current Aggregate Regular Principal Collections
$P_D(t)$	Current Principal Due $[P_D(t) = D(t) + PP(t) + P_R(t)]$
$C(t)$	Current Cumulative Principal Due $[C(t) = C(t-1) + P_D(t)]$
$R_b(t)$	Current Reserve Account Balance
$P(t)$	Current Aggregate Principal Collections $[P(t) = P_R(t) + PP(t)]$
$I(t)$	Current Aggregate Interest Collections
$R_c(t)$	Current Aggregate Recoveries
$C_C(t)$	Current Collections $[C_C(t) = P(t) + I(t) + R_c(t)]$
$F_0(t)$	Available Funds

In other cases, the availability of a line of credit or some other asset, such as security deposits from defaulted lessees in aircraft lease transactions, may be included in Available Funds. Failure to abide by equation (1) will usually result in mistaken risk analyses. Exhibit 20.1 shows how the distinction between these two concepts is made explicit in the target transaction's VBA code.

Exhibit 20.1:   Distinction between Available Funds and Current Collections

```
cf(CF_AVAIL_FUNDS_1, t) = cf(CF_POOL_CASHFLOW, t) [Current Collections] +
cf(CF_RESERVE_BEGIN_BALANCE, t)
```

20.2 WATERFALL-LEVEL DESCRIPTIONS

What follows is a short description of the major items found in the vast majority of structured finance transaction waterfalls. Instead of being exhaustive, our goal is to set the stage for assembling the deal and let it come together as a deal that reveals its own value without any presupposition.

Servicing Fees

The way servicing fees $[S(t)]$ are calculated may vary with the transaction. Servicing fees are paid monthly in an amount equal to one-twelfth the annual servicing fee rate calculated from some measure of managed assets known as the *basis*. We normally use the previous month's ending pool balance as the basis since in amortizing pools the latter will be a conservative estimate in terms of investor protection. This means that monthly servicing fees are computed using:

$$S(t) = \frac{s_f}{12}V(t-1) + S_S(t-1)\left(1 + \frac{s_r}{12}\right) \qquad (2)$$

In equation (2), as we saw in earlier chapters, the quantity s_f is the normal servicing fee while the much higher shortfall rate s_r would only apply had shortfalls occurred during prior collection periods. The subscript S refers to shortfalls in all cases.

Other servicing compensation schemes are possible. For example, the servicer could receive an amount corresponding to the mean of the previous and current pool balances:

$$S(t) = \frac{s_f}{24}\{V(t-1)+V(t)\} + S_S(t-1)\left(1 + \frac{s_r}{12}\right) \qquad (3)$$

Yet a third scheme could consist of assessing servicing fees based on the average daily pool balance. This would amount to using a basis $V_b(t)$ equal to:

$$V_b(t) = \frac{1}{\Delta t}\int_{t-1}^{t} V(t)dt, \ \Delta t \equiv 1 \qquad (4)$$

The quantity $V_b(t)$ would then be substituted into equation (2).

Note that in pure cash flow deals (see "Structured Settlements" in chapter 24) it may make more sense to compute servicing fees on the basis of collections rather than managed assets. In such cases, the rate s_f would represent a larger portion of collections and we would compute the servicing fee via:

$$S(t) = s_f C_C(t) + S_S(t-1)\left(1 + \frac{s_r}{12}\right) \qquad (5)$$

This latter scheme is usually counterintuitive in terms of credit quality because we have the unintended consequence that no servicing fee is due without collections. Theoretically speaking, there can therefore be no servicing fee shortfalls at any time during the deal, something quite possible in other cases.

Trustee and Other Senior Fees

The question as to where other senior fees ought to be placed within the waterfall has many answers. Normally, such fees will be much smaller than servicing fees and it will not really matter where exactly they are paid out. Sometimes, specific third parties feel better seeing themselves higher in the waterfall than the servicer, although in practice the point is largely moot. Please note that, either implicitly or explicitly, taxes and regulatory assessments are always paid at the highest level.

Surety bond fees are an interesting case and deserve a few words. When present, they are usually immediately below trustee fees, although transactions where the surety provider's fee is actually placed below principal and interest allocations to the wrapped classes do exist. Obviously, this makes some sense since the surety provider is eventually called upon to pay any interest and principal shortfalls to investors in the insured classes. If insufficient cash to pay interest and principal on such classes is on hand, the insurer will have to pay up anyway. If this is true, the potential premium paid by the trust is clearly irrelevant. But the truth is that there may be situations where the wrap provider will prefer to receive its premium from current funds and delay principal reimbursements, thus creating principal shortfalls, until the funds are actually "due" to investors, i.e., on the transaction's Legal Final Maturity Date.

In these cases, the placement of surety bond fees after interest and principal allocations is awkward and makes little sense. The existence of principal shortfalls, albeit harbingers of impending doom, are not necessarily events of default causing immediate acceleration of the bonds. The surety provider thus maintains more flexibility with respect to exposure management if it elevates its surety premium above its potential obligations. In the worst case, it's a wash.

Exhibit 20.2 shows an actual implementation of servicing and other senior fees, all subsumed under the heading *servicing fees*, in an actual transaction.

Exhibit 20.2:   VBA Code Implementation of Senior Fees

Servicing Fees

```
cf(CF_FEE_DUE, t) = deal.feeRate / 12 * cf(CF_POOL_BALANCE, t - 1) +
cf(CF_FEE_SHORTFALL, t - 1) * (1 + deal.feeShortfallRate / 12)
cf(CF_FEE_PAID, t) = Application.Min(cf(CF_AVAIL_FUNDS_1, t), cf(CF_FEE_DUE, t))
cf(CF_FEE_SHORTFALL, t) = cf(CF_FEE_DUE, t) - cf(CF_FEE_PAID, t)
cf(CF_AVAIL_FUNDS_2, t) = cf(CF_AVAIL_FUNDS_1, t) - cf(CF_FEE_PAID, t)
```

Interest Due

For some reason, this item seems to cause implementation dilemmas. Interest Due consists of current interest and past-due interest accruing at some past-due rate, which rate may in turn be linked to triggering mechanisms. This is why we write past-due interest using a rate different from current interest. Please note that in the vast majority of transactions, interest will be paid on schedule and thus the issue of penalty interest rates is largely moot. However, this is not the case in the *modeling* of transactions, since a Monte Carlo scenario under consideration may cause severe cash flow shortages which, in turn, lead to interest shortfalls. The notion that interest shortfalls will never occur, and hence can be neglected, is one of the biggest mistakes in liability modeling. As a rule, we can write Interest Due to Class A bondholders on any Calculation Date as follows:

$$I(t) = \frac{r_A}{12}A(t-1) + I_{AS}(t-1)\left(1 + \frac{r_{AS}}{12}\right) \tag{6}$$

An analogous equation obviously applies to Class B bondholders. The quantity r_A is the annualized Class A interest rate while r_{AS} is the shortfall rate which in general, as we already pointed out, may be different from r_A.

Through the second term on the right-hand side of equation (6), we are assuming that interest on interest is payable. If that were not the case, we could simply set $r_{AS} = 0$. Finally, the quantity $I_{AS}(t-1)$ represents the cumulative interest shortfall from previous periods. Exhibit 20.3 shows a VBA implementation of this waterfall level for the target transaction.

Exhibit 20.3: VBA Implementation of Class A Interest Due

Class A Interest Allocation

```
cf(CF_A_INTEREST_DUE, t) = deal.aRate / 12 * cf(CF_A_BALANCE, t - 1) +
cf(CF_A_INTEREST_SHORTFALL, t - 1) * (1 + deal.aRate / 12)
cf(CF_A_INTEREST_PAID, t) = Application.Min(cf(CF_AVAIL_FUNDS_2, t),
cf(CF_A_INTEREST_DUE, t))
cf(CF_A_INTEREST_SHORTFALL, t) = cf(CF_A_INTEREST_DUE, t) -
cf(CF_A_INTEREST_PAID, t)
cf(CF_AVAIL_FUNDS_3, t) = cf(CF_AVAIL_FUNDS_2, t) - cf(CF_A_INTEREST_PAID, t)
```

Current Principal Due

This quantity is by far the most important concept in a waterfall since it enforces the maintenance of full collateralization. As you will recall, this condition must be fulfilled at all times to keep the transaction working as intended. Cash flow leaks usually show up as failures to account for this rule properly. Regardless of the structure, the amount of "Current Principal Due" must be entirely allocated to the tranches of our transaction. The difference between pro rata and sequential, structures shows up at this level by modifying the way principal is allocated. What is important to remember is that an allocation is not a payment, the latter depending solely on the amount of Available Funds remaining at the appropriate level in the waterfall. Without accounting for the pool's total principal amortization at each time step, the repayment mechanism would fail to maintain the par collateralization requirement at the heart of structured analysis.

For instance, exhibit 20.4 is a VBA code section showing the difference between pro rata and sequential principal allocations inside the waterfall. Note especially how Cumulative Principal Due is used to allocate Principal Due in a sequential structure.

Exhibit 20.4: Principal Due Allocations in Pro Rata and Sequential Structures

Class A Principal Allocation

Pro Rata Structure

```
cf(CF_A_PRINCIPAL_DUE, t) = Application.Min(cf(CF_A_BALANCE, t - 1), deal.alpha *
cf(CF_PRINCIPAL_DUE, t) + cf(CF_A_PRINCIPAL_SHORTFALL, t - 1))
```

Sequential Structure

cf(CF_A_PRINCIPAL_DUE, t) = Application.Min(cf(CF_A_BALANCE, t - 1),
cf(CF_PRINCIPAL_DUE, t) + cf(CF_A_PRINCIPAL_SHORTFALL, t - 1))

---

cf(CF_A_PRINCIPAL_PAID, t) = Application.Min(cf(CF_AVAIL_FUNDS_4, t),
cf(CF_A_PRINCIPAL_DUE, t))
cf(CF_A_PRINCIPAL_SHORTFALL, t) = cf(CF_A_PRINCIPAL_DUE, t) -
cf(CF_A_PRINCIPAL_PAID, t)
cf(CF_AVAIL_FUNDS_5, t) = cf(CF_AVAIL_FUNDS_4, t) - cf(CF_A_PRINCIPAL_PAID, t)
cf(CF_A_BALANCE, t) = cf(CF_A_BALANCE, t - 1) - cf(CF_A_PRINCIPAL_PAID, t)

Class B Principal Allocation

Pro Rata Structure

cf(CF_B_PRINCIPAL_DUE, t) = Application.Min(cf(CF_B_BALANCE, t - 1),
(1 - deal.alpha) * cf(CF_PRINCIPAL_DUE, t) + cf(CF_B_PRINCIPAL_SHORTFALL, t - 1))

Sequential Structure

cf(CF_A_PRINCIPAL_DUE, t) = Application.Min(cf(CF_A_BALANCE, t - 1),
Application.Max(0,cf(CF_CUM_PRINCIPAL_DUE, t) -
Application.Max(cf(CF_A_BALANCE, 0), cf(CF_CUM_PRINCIPAL_DUE, t-1))) +
cf(CF_A_PRINCIPAL_SHORTFALL, t - 1))

---

cf(CF_B_PRINCIPAL_PAID, t) = Application.Min(cf(CF_AVAIL_FUNDS_5, t),
cf(CF_B_PRINCIPAL_DUE, t))
cf(CF_B_PRINCIPAL_SHORTFALL, t) = cf(CF_B_PRINCIPAL_DUE, t) -
cf(CF_B_PRINCIPAL_PAID, t)
cf(CF_AVAIL_FUNDS_6, t) = cf(CF_AVAIL_FUNDS_5, t) - cf(CF_B_PRINCIPAL_PAID, t)
cf(CF_B_BALANCE, t) = cf(CF_B_BALANCE, t - 1) - cf(CF_B_PRINCIPAL_PAID, t)

20.3 RESERVE ACCOUNT MECHANICS

The implementation of a reserve account is rather straightforward once the concept is properly understood. Please note that the mechanics of liquidity facilities and reserve accounts are formally identical save for their position in the waterfall. As its name implies, a liquidity facility is not intended to provide credit enhancement to any class of notes or certificates. It is for this reason that reimbursements on draws are effected above principal distributions on both classes.

Conversely, reimbursements on draws from reserve accounts take place below principal repayments, and this is how one can tell that the facility is credit enhancement and not liquidity. The fact that a certain piece of collateral is available in the form of cash in no way qualifies it as "liquidity" for purposes of the deal.

For example, reimbursement mechanics (see below) on previous draws from a dedicated Class A liquidity facility would be inserted below the Class A interest level but above Class B interest. Likewise, reimbursement mechanics on a dedicated Class A reserve account (*credit enhancement*) would be inserted below Class A principal but above Class B principal. What follows is thus a generic implementation sequence that can be applied to any combination of such facilities. General reserve accounts are available to fund both interest and principal distributions as the case may be.

Please note that if multiple reserve accounts and/or liquidity facilities are included in a deal, the following lines of code simply need to be repeated as many times as necessary while ensuring that funds residing in any particular facility are available solely for distribution to the appropriate party.

Implementation of a General Reserve Account
Applicable to Both Classes

You will recall that Available Funds were originally defined as the sum of Current Collections and Reserve Account Beginning Balance. In this context, note that the Reserve Account is deemed to be earning the relatively low Eligible Investment Rate, which means that, defining $R_e(t-1)$ as the cash balance in the Reserve Account at the end of the prior Distribution Date and r_e as the Eligible Investment Rate, we can write:

$$R_b(t) = R_c(t-1)\left(1 + \frac{r_e}{12}\right) \tag{7}$$

As observed above, the tricky part of Reserve Account implementation lies in the proper placement of draw reimbursements depending on whether we are dealing with a Liquidity Facility or a Reserve Account and how to handle Available Funds when this occurs. The main concept to keep in mind is that reserve account draws are automatically handled via the application of equation (1). However, reimbursements of such draws need careful handling. In addition, it follows logically that draws and reimbursements cannot take place simultaneously, i.e., during the same Collection Period.

To begin reimbursements, we must first remove the balance in the Reserve Account from Available Funds and use the remaining amount, if any, to refund draws made on previous Distribution Dates. Once this is done, it is a trivial matter to extract from remaining funds the amount necessary to top-up the Reserve Account to its target percentage (based on the current pool balance $V(t)$) and allow excess funds to escape the transaction to SPV shareholders.

Table 20.2 introduces some familiar notation for any given time step t:

TABLE 20.2

Notation for reserve account mechanics

ITEM	DEFINITION
$V(t)$	Current Pool Balance
$F_R(t)$	Available Funds remaining after Class B Principal
R_P	Reserve Account Target Percentage
$R_r(t)$	Reserve Account Target Amount
$R_d(t)$	Reserve Account Current Draw Amount
$R_a(t)$	Reserve Account Current Contribution Amount
$F_{XS}(t)$	Excess Spread flowing back to SPV shareholders

Give the above notation, the code sequence implementing a Reserve Account can be written as follows, where χ is a dummy variable:

$$R_d(t) = Max\,[0,\, R_b(t) - F_R(t)] \tag{8}$$

$$\chi = Max\,[0,\, F_R(t) - R_b(t)] \tag{9}$$

$$R_r(t) = R_P V(t) \tag{10}$$

$$R_a(t) = Min,\,[\chi,\, R_r(t) - R_b(t) + R_d(t)] \tag{11}$$

$$R_e(t) = R_b(t) - R_d(t) + R_a(t) \tag{12}$$

$$F_{XS}(t) = \chi - R_a(t) \tag{13}$$

Exhibit 20.5:   VBA Implementation of a General Reserve Account

Reserve Account Mechanics

```
cf(CF_RESERVE_DRAW, t) = Application.Max(0, cf(CF_RESERVE_BEGIN_BALANCE, t) -
cf(CF_AVAIL_FUNDS_6, t))
cf(CF_AVAIL_FUNDS_7, t) = Application.Max(0, cf(CF_AVAIL_FUNDS_6, t) -
cf(CF_RESERVE_BEGIN_BALANCE, t))
cf(CF_RESERVE_TARGET, t) = Application.Max(deal.reserveTarget *
cf(CF_POOL_BALANCE, t), deal.reserveFloor * deal.poolBal)
cf(CF_RESERVE_CONTRIBUTIONS, t) = Application.Min(cf(CF_AVAIL_FUNDS_7, t),
cf(CF_RESERVE_TARGET, t) - cf(CF_RESERVE_BEGIN_BALANCE, t) +
cf(CF_RESERVE_DRAW, t))
cf(CF_RESERVE_END_BALANCE, t) = cf(CF_RESERVE_BEGIN_BALANCE, t) -
cf(CF_RESERVE_DRAW, t) + cf(CF_RESERVE_CONTRIBUTIONS, t)
cf(CF_AVAIL_FUNDS_8, t) = cf(CF_AVAIL_FUNDS_7, t) -
cf(CF_RESERVE_CONTRIBUTIONS, t)
```

> **Exercise 20.1**
>
> Implement a surety bond and a reserve account inside the Excel cash flow model you
> built in earlier chapters.
>   How would you implement a surety bond inside our target transaction in Visual
> Basic? Remember that the *wrap* provider must pay the structured note promise, i.e.,
> timely interest and ultimate principal. How does that affect principal allocations and the
> mechanics of the waterfall? How is investor yield affected by the presence of a surety
> bond? Is a wrap a good idea in general? How about in this case?

Equation (11) includes the quantity $R_d(t)$ to handle rare cases where simultaneous
draws have taken place in amounts still too small to reduce the reserve account
balance below its target amount at the same time step. Exhibit 20.5 shows the VBA
implementation of a reserve account within a transaction similar to ours.

20.4 BASIC PRINCIPAL ALLOCATION REGIMES

Introduction

In previous chapters, we reviewed and demonstrated the two most common principal
allocation methods, i.e., sequential and pro rata. Our main objective at the time was to
highlight the difference between an allocation and a payment. This was done via the
distinction between pro rata principal allocation and pari passu payment. Too many
times, the availability of cash hides the fact that principal allocated pro rata is not
paid pari passu, i.e., at the same level, for doing so would significantly undermine the
subordination concept at the heart of the waterfall. It is not our intention to discuss
ad nauseam the universe of possible variations in principal allocation regimes, but
simply to lay out broad lines of thinking in that area. Therefore, this section is nothing
more than a brief primer on allocation schemes and their implications.

Multiple Classes

Thus far in this text, we have restricted our discussions to two-tranche transactions.
This was not done because two is the most common number, but simply because two-
tranche transactions are relatively simple and a good way to bring out the fundamental
concepts underlying the analysis of structured securities without getting bogged down
in algebraic details. However, the most important reason was left unsaid, which is
that the demarcation between two and three is fundamental, not accidental.

   In essence, with two tranches we can simply use the advance rate α for the first
tranche and its complement $1 - \alpha$ for the other tranche, thereby turning two into
one. But as soon as we have three tranches this is no longer possible and we have no
choice but to deal with the *group* or *ensemble* concept without being able to reduce
it to a unitary notion. If you believe this is trivial nonsense, think again, for the same
principle also holds at much higher levels of abstraction.

   For example, consider the solution procedure with respect to the incompressible,
steady-state flow of a fluid within some arbitrary domain. From the relevant equations

of motion, the Navier–Stokes equations, we know that such flows satisfy the so-called continuity equation. Defining U as the velocity vector, the latter equation can be written as the vanishing of its divergence:

$$\nabla \bullet U = 0 \qquad (14)$$

Now, it is well known that solving equation (14) can be done automatically by defining a special function Ψ, usually called the *stream-function* for reasons that are not important right now, and defining U as the curl of Ψ:

$$U = \nabla X \Psi \qquad (15)$$

Since the divergence of the curl of anything is zero identically, the continuity equation is satisfied by definition and we have solved our problem. What is the point of this?

The point is that suppose we are operating in two dimensions instead of the nominal three, i.e., we have defined $\partial/\partial z \equiv 0$, and assume further that $U = \{u, v\}$ where the letter-symbols inside the curly brackets are the components of U in the x and y direction, respectively. In that case, equation (15) reduces to:

$$\nabla X \Psi \equiv \begin{vmatrix} i & j & k \\ \dfrac{\partial}{\partial x} & \dfrac{\partial}{\partial y} & 0 \\ \psi_x & \psi_y & \psi_z \end{vmatrix} \qquad (16)$$

From equation (16), we can easily derive the definitions of u and v as:

$$u = \frac{\partial \psi_z}{\partial y}, \qquad v = -\frac{\partial \psi_z}{\partial x} \qquad (17)$$

Notice that both components of the velocity vector depend only on the z-component of the stream-function. Thus, although the stream-function is formally a three-dimensional vector, in two dimensions it can be reduced to a scalar without any loss of generality. We can use the resulting scalar field to solve our problem. In this way, we have effectively transformed a problem that had two unknowns, namely the velocity components u and v, into a new problem with a single unknown ψ_z, the scalar stream-function.

However, if you try this trick in three dimensions, i.e., with velocity components u, v, and w, you will discover that equation (15) will compel you to deal with the corresponding three components of the stream function, ψ_x, ψ_y, and ψ_z. In the three-dimensional case, you have merely exchanged the original three velocity components for the three stream-function components and have gotten effectively nowhere. In other words, here too a three-dimensional problem seems to defeat all attempts at a reduction.

The good news is that this seemingly strange border between two and three is unique, i.e., it is no more difficult to implement a deal with four or more classes than it is to implement one with three. As a result, in what follows we restrict our discussion to three-tranche transactions simply because more complicated ones do not require additional analytical understanding.

Pro Rata Principal Allocation of the Three-Tranche Deal

In a pro rata principal allocation of a three-tranche transaction the solution is clear and can be solved as a simple extension of the two-tranche case, i.e., whereby we simply define appropriate pro rata factors and allocate based on them while maintaining a running count of shortfalls. Thus, using the notation of table 20.1 and defining $P_A(t)$, $P_B(t)$, and $P_Z(t)$ as current principal allocated[1] to the deal's three classes respectively, we can define the pro rata factors:

$$\alpha = \frac{A(0)}{V(0)} \quad \beta = \frac{B(0)}{V(0)} \quad \delta = \frac{Z(0)}{V(0)} \tag{18}$$

The three-class principal due allocation equations may be defined respectively via:

$$P_A(t) = \alpha P_D(t) + P_{AS}(t-1) \tag{19a}$$

$$P_B(t) = \beta P_D(t) + P_{BS}(t-1) \tag{19b}$$

$$P_Z(t) = \delta P_D(t) + P_{ZS}(t-1) \tag{19c}$$

In equations (19a), (19b), and (19c), we have defined the class-wise subscript S as the respective cumulative shortfall from prior periods.

Sequential Deals

As most readers will have surmised from our previous formulas with respect to a two-tranche sequential deal, this allocation regime is recalcitrant to efficient generalization. Recall from previous chapters that for Class A, the formula for monthly principal due under a sequential scheme was given by:

$$P_A(t) = Min[A(t-1), P_D(t) + P_{AS}(t-1)] \tag{20}$$

Inside equation (20), we simply set the class-wise principal due to the entire principal due $P_D(t)$ and make sure that no leakage occurs via a minimization procedure ensuring that principal is either paid on schedule or simply ends up in the cumulative shortfall variable. In other words, once an amount $A(0)$ has been allocated, the value of the cumulative shortfall variable is by definition equal to the outstanding balance of the Class A bond, for otherwise no shortfall would exist and the bond would have paid down completely. As can easily be verified, this method works for the first class of any deal regardless of how many tranches it has.

Next, consider the slightly modified principal allocation formula for the Class B of a two-tranche transaction:

$$P_B(t) = Min[B(t-1), Max[0, C(t) - Max[k(2), C(t-1)]] + P_{BS}(t-1)] \tag{21}$$

You will recall that parameter $k(2)$ in equation (21) was set equal to $A(0)$ in senior-subordinated transactions. In that case, we could get away with a simple formula like (21) because the deal only had two tranches. As soon as cumulative principal due satisfied the condition $C(t) = V(0)$, an amount of Class B principal exactly equal to $B(0)$ would have been properly allocated while, by definition, no additional principal due would ever be allocated owing to the basic condition $V(T) = 0$. The above definition for $k(2)$ further ensures that before $C(t) \geq A(0)$ held, no principal amount would ever be allocated to Class B, which is exactly what a sequential allocation is intended to accomplish. Thus, formula (21) provides a clue to the handling of the *last* credit tranche in generalized sequential schemes.

In other words, in the three-tranche case, this principle no longer applies to Class B but it is still valid for the Class Z with a slight modification that takes into account the additional tranche. The formula for the last tranche is formally identical to that of the two-tranche case and reduces to:

$$P_Z(t) = Min\,[Z(t-1),\, Max\,[0,\, C(t) - Max[k(3),\, C(t-1)]] + P_{ZS}(t-1)] \quad (22)$$

In equation (22), we have defined parameter $k(3)$ as follows:

$$k(3) = A(0) + B(0)$$

As you will have already guessed, the apparent problem lies with the middle class, i.e., Class B. Here, it is no longer permissible to use either equation (21) or (22) to allocate principal and a logical extension has to be introduced, one that allows us to target a specific range of principal amortization rather than either the beginning or the end.

To do this, we can take our cue from equation (21) and seek to organize the allocation of principal so as to ensure that, on the one hand, no principal can be allocated to Class B unless cumulative principal due crosses the $k(2)$ threshold, while on the other hand, principal allocations must cease entirely as soon as cumulative principal due crosses the $k(3)$ threshold. This is accomplished *via* the following modification of equation (21):

$$P_B(t) = Min\,[B(t-1),\, Max\,[0,\, Min\,[k(3),\, C(t)]$$
$$- Max[k(2),\, C(t-1)]] + P_{BS}(t-1)] \quad (23)$$

Unless Cumulative Principal Due $C(t)$ crosses the $k(2)$ barrier, no principal can ever be allocated to Class B. The first time $C(t)$ traverses level $k(3)$, the term $Min\,[k(3),\, C(t)]$ becomes effective and causes the principal amount allocated to Class B to equal the exact difference between $k(3)$ and $C(t-1)$, as it should.

For all later time steps, the term $Min\,[k(3),\, C(t)]$ prevents additional principal due amounts from being allocated to Class B as dictated by the mechanics of sequential allocation. At that moment, cumulative principal shortfalls to Class B will equal the outstanding Class B balance and both will step down dollar-for-dollar using available funds, if any.

Exercise 20.2

Devise a general formula for the sequential allocation of principal due in a multi-tranche deal regardless of the number of tranches n. Express your answer using the same nomenclature as that used to derive equations (22) and (23) ◀

We have thus reached our objective with a minor, easily generalizable modification. In fact, equations (20), (22), and (23) are sufficiently close to enable the generalization of the sequential principal allocation scheme to a single formula. The problem with this type of formalism is that it is error prone. One can become dizzy just staring at equation (23) with all its parentheses, minimizations, and the like.

You might therefore ask: is there a way to allocate principal sequentially that is perhaps a little *cleaner*? Devising such a method will entail going back to the drawing board and asking about the *essence* of the sequential allocation phenomenon. A place to start would seem to be the above formula for pro rata allocation of principal. It looked pretty clean compared to equation (23). Would you like to give it a shot?

Exercise 20.3

Devise an alternative sequential principal allocation formalism that does not take its lead from equation (22) but is rather inspired by the formulas for pro rata allocations. What must you do to achieve this?

20.5 TARGETED AMORTIZATION CLASSES

Introduction

The Targeted Amortization Class (TAC) concept came of age in the world of Mortgage-Backed Securities (MBS) at roughly the same time as the more sophisticated Planned Amortization Class (PAC) (see "Planned Amortization Classes" below) made its appearance. Due to its relative simplicity we treat the TAC first.

The basic philosophy at the heart of the TAC is to allocate principal in a manner that is neither pro rata nor sequential, but somewhere in between. In a two-tranche transaction for instance, let's assume the structuror wished to allocate principal to Class A in an amount less than what it would receive in a purely sequential scheme, whereby it would have simply been allocated all principal due, including defaults, until its balance had been reduced to zero. Normally, the only other option would be the pro rata regime whereby strictly speaking, only its proportional share of the initial investment would be allocated to Class A.

Why someone would want to do this in the MBS world is rather obvious: prepayment protection. Of course, doing this in non-credit-risk environments makes much more sense since principal reimbursements are virtually guaranteed via credit insurance policies provided by US Government agencies like Fannie Mae and Freddie Mac. In a credit-risk world however, the motivation for a TAC is less transparent and is usually aimed at reducing the long-term credit exposure of the class that benefits from the additional allocations, while at the same time maintaining significant protection to the senior class. In other words, as long as Class A is paying down and maintains its prescribed level of over-collateralization, what is wrong with giving Class B some principal since the deal is working out anyway? What Class A investors might think of this *philosophy* is debatable.

Mechanics of Implementation

Let's say we wanted to achieve an intermediate Class A principal allocation schedule that is more restrictive than strictly sequential yet more permissive than strictly pro rata. We can do this by computing the Class A amortization schedule under both regimes and steering a middle course, thereby computing a targeted amount of Class A principal amortization, or "TAC schedule" at each time step. This technique is displayed in figure 20.1 for an arbitrary 10-year transaction and a given pool amortization profile.

The top curve is the pro rata Class A schedule and the bottom curve is its sequential-based amortization profile. The middle curve (i.e., the TAC schedule) was computed as one half of the sum of the upper and lower curves. In other words, if $S_P(t)$ is the pro rata schedule and $S_S(t)$ the sequential schedule, the TAC schedule $S_{TAC}(t)$ in figure 20.1 was derived using the admittedly simplistic rule:

$$S_{TAC}(t) = \frac{S_P(t) + S_S(t)}{2}$$

Of course, any conceivable schedule may be derived using formulas limited in scope only by the imagination of the analyst, but provided the full amortization of the pool be allocated in aggregate to both classes. The restriction to some intermediate value between purely sequential or pro rata is obviously not an actual limitation. It was used merely as a didactic aid to introduce the TAC.

In this context, it would be quite straightforward to devise a TAC schedule causing an effective *lock-out* period to exist for the Class B, after which it would begin receiving a greater share of principal than it would have achieved under a purely

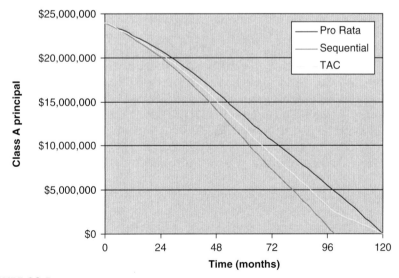

FIGURE 20.1
A Simple TAC Schedule.

sequential regime. In a world where significant credit risk might be entailed, as opposed to the more comfortable credit environment generally prevailing within MBS, this particular use of the TAC concept may in fact make perfect sense.

Formulaically, things are even simpler once it is understood that the TAC schedule becomes the target that Class A needs to meet, after which remaining current principal due may be allocated to Class B to keep up with the pool's total amortization profile.

To illustrate, we define the following two subsidiary quantities:

$$\Delta V(t) = V(t-1) - V(t) \tag{24}$$

$$\Delta S_{TAC}(t) = S_{TAC}(t-1) - S_{TAC}(t) \tag{25}$$

Now, using equations (24) and (25), we can easily write down the Class A and Class B principal allocation formulas:

$$P_A(t) = \Delta S_{TAC}(t) + P_{AS}(t-1) \tag{26}$$

$$P_B(t) = \Delta V(t) - \Delta S_{TAC}(t) + P_{BS}(t-1) \tag{27}$$

Note that the above formulation is only physically valid as long as the following condition holds for all time steps $t \in [0, T]$:

$$\Delta V(t) \geq \Delta S_{TAC}(t) \tag{28}$$

This is a mathematical reflection of the fact that, in order to still allow excess spread to escape from the deal once equations (26) and (27) are both satisfied, the sum of Class A and Class B amortizations must still equal the pool's total amortization from a combination of regular payments and prepayments. Glancing at equation (27), it can be seen that any violation of condition (28) would show up as a negative principal due amount on Class B, a situation that cannot be countenanced. To prevent this from happening, any structuror would have to ensure that (28) always held, which would amount to selecting the schedule $S_{TAC}(t)$ appropriately. This could be done in practice by picking the targeted amortization schedule more restrictively than the smallest payment speed ever seen on similar collateral over a given time interval or else by linking the TAC schedule to the actual pool's amortization history. But in any event, there appears to be no logical impediment to this type of implementation.

The real problem is not the maintenance of equation (28). Rather, it is that excess spread should still be able to escape as before within the purely pro rata or sequential schemes. If that condition is relaxed however, the use of the TAC concept is trivial. As a result, in some structures an alternative TAC formulation is used whereby the allocation is effectively *turbo*, which means that no excess spread is allowed to escape until both classes are paid off. To accomplish this, the allocation formulas are modified in the following manner.

Class A Principal Due is given via:

$$P_A(t) = Min[A(t-1), A(t-1) - S_{TAC}(t)] \tag{29}$$

Class B Principal Due is simply set equal to whatever available funds $F(t)$ are available at that point in the waterfall, i.e.,

$$P_B(t) = Min[B(t-1), F(t)] \qquad (30)$$

Assuming the TAC schedule is devised properly, this mechanism guarantees that excess spread can never escape until both classes are paid off. As a result, the concept of principal shortfall is not applicable to this case since it is automatically included in the definition of $P_A(t)$ via the TAC targeting process. This process further guarantees that, should Class A fail to keep up with its TAC schedule, the difference would show up during the next period via a reduction in the TAC scheduled balance. Thus, Class A is still regarded as senior to Class B and no cash flow leak can occur.

In summary, the TAC concept is a convenient way to allow variable principal allocations to more junior classes while still affording relatively senior classes the protection to which they feel entitled. In benign credit risk environments, such as agency MBS, their use is straightforward.

As explained earlier, one must tread more carefully within risky ABS asset classes where allocated principal may not be available when due. Although investment bankers can always use their creativity to devise TAC schedules meeting specific goals within given transactions, the extent to which credit-risk-prone ABS asset classes may be equipped with TAC tranches will vary. On the other hand, once investors have become comfortable with either an asset class or a sponsor, the TAC feature affords a simple and transparent mechanism whereby the average life of the Class B may be shortened to reduce the all-in cost of funds to the sponsor or seller. In general, this is always a worthwhile endeavor.

20.6 PLANNED AMORTIZATION CLASSES

Introduction

A more interesting allocation concept closely related to the TAC is the Planned Amortization Class (PAC). As the name implies, it is similar to the TAC except that the problem encountered when dealing with equation (27) is automatically avoided. In fact, the PAC was probably conceived ahead of the TAC, despite its higher level of abstraction, for the simple reason that it does not present the practical implementation difficulty we experienced with the TAC.

Although a detailed explanation of PAC mechanics was given in chapter 11, we have no choice but to repeat ourselves somewhat here, at least in broad outline, if only as a refresher and primer to implementation. Students seeking additional information should, however, consult the above chapter. This section covers both the PAC bond and the PAC IO, a now common ABS feature that amounts to piggy-backing on the straight PAC bond.

The Philosophy of the PAC

Essentially, PACs were conceived to give prepayment protection to certain classes of investors who would suffer either yield erosion or a relatively less favorable set of reinvestment opportunities should prepayment speeds severely exceed historical norms. This situation may arise in many different ways, but the most interesting is probably that facing the purchaser of an Interest Only Class (IO) in a pool of mortgages. Since the buyer's cash flows stem exclusively from interest payments, it is conceivable that, should the entire pool prepay on day one, interest cash flows would be effectively zero. In that case, the return on the IO would be –100%, i.e., the buyer would lose his entire investment.

Please note that the risk taken by buyers of a straight PAC bond is sometimes mislabeled *prepayment* risk when in fact it is simply *reinvestment* risk. In the context of credit risk, we reserve the term prepayment risk for a situation whereby the inability to predict prepayment speeds within the current deal would cause a loss of principal instead of a less-attractive reinvestment universe on subsequent transactions. As every body knows, loss of principal is the quintessence of credit risk. Even given such an extreme prepayment scenario, the buyer of a PAC bond would simply receive his principal earlier than anticipated, and would have suffered no principal loss. Hence, straight PAC bonds do not experience credit loss solely due to excessive prepayments. The fact that such extreme prepayment speeds would normally take place within a decreasing-rate environment only means that a bond investor would be facing a reduced opportunity set on the next deal, not this one. Although this may upset the investor's asset-liability management forecast, it does not amount to credit loss. By contrast, the buyer of a principal-only (PO) security would welcome this situation, as she would experience an above-average return relative to the pricing scenario.

Even if reinvestment risk is not specifically discussed hereunder, we do recognize that it is a risk, and that it should not be marginalized. Although it does not equate to credit risk per se, the PAC concept is designed to address it. On the other hand, a PAC IO buyer *does* bear credit risk even when extreme prepayments speeds *do not* result from either defaults or credit events. This mode of credit risk can occur regardless of the fact that the IO might have been rated *Aaa* by a major rating agency.

Despite the fact that such cases are rather academic, the point is that an investor potentially exposed to this type of return volatility will usually demand some modicum of downside protection. Someone might retort that the IO downside risk is compensated by the *opportunity* of perhaps an equally probable and lower than expected prepayment speed, in which case the IO buyer would receive the windfall gain instead of the PO buyer. Unfortunately, given the predictive power of most prepayment models, which are essentially interest-rate forecasting models[2] if hedging is ignored for the moment, this argument is unlikely to be well received by investors considering a purchase.

As explained above, although IO buyers are fully aware that their investment entails prepayment risk, they have gotten comfortable over the years with a certain universe of prepayment speeds, which universe was clearly derived from actual prepayment history with similar collateral. Regardless of the fact that the price of the IO was negotiated freely between the buyer and the seller given their relative views on prepayments, these views were heavily influenced by historical patterns in concert with current thinking on interest-rate fluctuations over the life of the pool.

If interest-rate volatility should be such as to take the pool outside the prepayment universe initially contemplated, the PAC IO buyer would have no recourse. In other words, risk aversion usually creates an asymmetry behind the risk perceptions of an otherwise risk-neutral pricing scenario. As a result, even assuming equal low and high prepayment speed probability mass on either side of the pricing curve, IO investors nevertheless require additional security against excessive prepayment speeds. This additional security is what the PAC was designed to achieve.

Please keep in mind that the PAC mechanism is not supposed to remove *all* downside risk from the IO, just that portion of risk that could arise from prepayment speeds in excess of most conceivable historical norms. In the end, nothing can save a PAC IO buyer from the cash flow consequences of a doomsday prepayment scenario.

The Mechanics of the PAC

The basic technique at the heart of the PAC is the partitioning of the pool's outstanding principal balance $V(t)$ into two components, the PAC portion $P(t)$ and the Companion Class $H(t)$. At all times the following condition holds:

$$V(t) = P(t) + H(t) \qquad (31)$$

Assuming sufficient cash is always available for distribution, the IO buyer would receive the following periodic allocation $F(t)$, paid in arrears:

$$F(t) = rP(t-1), \ 0 < r \leq R \qquad (32)$$

In equation (32), the parameter r is the IO periodic pass-through rate. R, the upper bound, is much smaller than the pool's weighted average coupon or WAC.

The following step is the crucial one. Based on prepayment speeds considered high given historical norms, a PAC schedule $S_{PAC}(t)$ is established at closing. The latter schedule may be derived in a number of different and equally valid ways, but for our purpose we can assume it represents some fixed percentage α of the pool's outstanding principal balance $V_h(t)$ under an extreme prepayment scenario by historical standards. In other words, here $S_{PAC}(t)$ is computed based on the highest historical prepayment speed seen with similar collateral over a comparable period. Thus, the amount of cushion available to either straight PAC or PAC IO buyers may be conveniently defined as $1 - \alpha$.

Once the ratio $\alpha = \frac{S_{PAC}(t)}{V_h(t)}$ is agreed upon, the IO price is negotiated between buyer and seller based solely on cash flows allocated to the $P(t)$ using a suitable pricing yield, defined as y. The balance $P(t)$ required as input to equation (32) is then computed for each time step according to the following scheme. First the companion bond's balance $H(t)$ is calculated from:

$$H(t) = Max\,[0, (1-\alpha)V(t) - Max[0, S_{PAC}(t) - \alpha V(t)]] \qquad (33)$$

Then, the PAC balance $P(t)$ is computed from equation (31).

Keeping in mind that PAC IO cash flows are based on $P(t)$ only, this technique offers IO investors the following three prepayment regimes:

1. For prepayment speeds between zero and speeds such that $V(t) \geq \frac{S_{PAC}(t)}{\alpha}$ holds, we have the identity $P(t) = \alpha V(t)$. In such cases, the IO holder is taking prepayment risk within the universe originally contemplated.

2. For prepayment speeds such that $V(t) \leq \frac{S_{PAC}(t)}{\alpha}$ and $H(t) > 0$, we have $P(t) = S_{PAC}(t)$. This is the chief PAC prepayment protection feature. In essence, over a range of prepayment speeds in excess of historical norms, the IO buyer is assured of a known principal balance schedule for the purposes of IO cash flow allocation. Obviously, this range depends entirely on the value of α. This particular prepayment region has historically been labeled the *PAC structuring band*, or the *PAC range*.

3. For prepayment speeds such that $V(t) \leq \frac{S_{PAC}(t)}{\alpha}$ and $H(t) = 0$, we have $P(t) = V(t)$. In other words, in this case IO investors suffer a dollar-for-dollar reduction in the basis of their cash flow allocation formula. This would be considered extreme by any measure although this does not mean that it has never happened. Speeds in that range did indeed occur in the aftermath of 9/11.

Exercise 20.4

Verify that under the prepayment speed ranges 1, 2, and 3 defined above, the stated PAC bond balance indeed results from using equation (33).

As a practical example of PAC IO mechanics, exhibit 20.6 shows the VBA code section implementing this feature for the target deal. As you can see, the mathematical formalism either of the straight PAC or the PAC IO is relatively simple compared to the design of its PAC schedule. The latter is wrapped up in the physics of the deal, something that can only emerge as an integral part of the valuation process

---

Exercise 20.5

Using the asset side of the cash flow model you have built in earlier chapters, implement a PAC IO using the following basic data:

$$r = 3\%$$

$$\alpha = 0.8$$

$$y = 12\%$$

To properly implement the PAC IO, proceed as follows:

1. Arbitrarily choose some reasonable prepayment speed as your pricing speed and use parameter δ to index prepayment speeds. Define the pricing speed as $\delta = \delta_{Pr}$. This can easily be done by first focusing on the familiar prepayment model parameter N_P (from before) and normalizing it to create a prepayment

index that equals zero when $N_P = 0$ and unity when prepayment speeds are at their maximum allowable value. A simple scaling function will accomplish this trick.

2. Increase the prepayment speed to some significantly higher value $\delta_{PAC} > \delta_{Pr}$ and use that speed to define the schedule $S_{PAC}(t)$ as shown earlier.

3. Compute the cash flows accruing to the PAC IO buyer at speed $\delta = \delta_{Pr}$ using equation (32) and discount them at the rate y to compute the PAC IO price P_{IO}.

You are now ready to witness first hand the workings of the PAC's prepayment protection feature. To do this, run the cash flow model you have already built and compute the yield to the PAC IO buyer using the Excel IRR function and the initial investment P_{IO} over a range of prepayment speeds indexed by the parameter δ. In doing this, please ensure that the minimum value of δ_{min} satisfies $\delta_{min} < \delta_{Pr}$ while the maximum δ_{max} satisfies $\delta_{max} > \delta_{PAC}$ to guarantee that the full unfolding of the PAC protection region becomes explicit. You should discover that over a region dictated by the cushion α, the PAC IO yield will remain constant. In other words, build a table showing the yield on your IO for a given prepayment speed and note the range of prepayment speeds δ over which the IO yield is both invariant and equal to the expected value.

Next, to confirm that the PAC range is indeed ruled by the value of α, redo the exercise but this time using $\alpha = 0.9$, everything else remaining constant. Add a new column to the table you have already created showing the resulting IO yield for the same range of prepayment speeds and compare the results to the case $\alpha = 0.8$. ◁

Exhibit 20.6: PAC IO Implementation Mechanics

Companion and PAC Notional Balance Calculations, equations (33) and (31)

cf(CF_C, t) = Application.Max(0, (1 - deal.pacAlpha) * cf(CF_POOL_BALANCE, t) -
Application.Max(0, deal.pacS(t) - deal.pacAlpha * cf(CF_POOL_BALANCE, t)))
cf(CF_P, t) = cf(CF_POOL_BALANCE, t) - cf(CF_C, t)

Class A and PAC IO Interest Amounts Paid Pari Passu

cf(CF_A_INTEREST_DUE, t) = deal.aRate / 12 * cf(CF_A_BALANCE, t - 1) +
cf(CF_A_INTEREST_SHORTFALL, t - 1) * (1 + deal.aRate / 12)
cf(CF_IO_DUE, t) = deal.ioRate / 12 * cf(CF_P, t - 1) + cf(CF_IO_SHORTFALL, t - 1) *
(1 + deal.ioRate / 12)
cf(CF_IO_PAID, t) = Application.Min(cf(CF_AVAIL_FUNDS_2, t) * cf(CF_IO_DUE, t) /
(CF_IO_DUE + cf(CF_A_INTEREST_DUE, t)), cf(CF_IO_DUE, t))
cf(CF_IO_SHORTFALL, t) = cf(CF_IO_DUE, t) - cf(CF_IO_PAID, t)
cf(CF_A_INTEREST_PAID, t) = Application.Min(cf(CF_AVAIL_FUNDS_2, t) -
cf(CF_IO_PAID, t), cf(CF_A_INTEREST_DUE, t))
cf(CF_A_INTEREST_SHORTFALL, t) = cf(CF_A_INTEREST_DUE, t) -
cf(CF_A_INTEREST_PAID, t)
cf(CF_AVAIL_FUNDS_3, t) = cf(CF_AVAIL_FUNDS_2, t) - cf(CF_IO_PAID, t) -
cf(CF_A_INTEREST_PAID, t) ◁

TABLE 20.3

PAC IO yields under various SMM speeds and cushions $1 - \alpha$

PAC IO YIELDS (%) FOR THE TARGET TRANSACTION USING EQUATIONS (31) AND (33)			
IO PRICE	$1,181,163	$1,118,997	$1,056,830	$994,664
$SMM/1 - \alpha$	5%	10%	15%	20%
0.5%	16.80	16.80	16.80	16.80
1%	12.00	12.00	12.00	12.00
2%	2.77	2.77	2.77	2.77
5%	−21.86	−18.66	−15.52	−12.54
10%	−62.99	−59.83	−56.48	−52.97

Table 20.3 is what happens within our target transaction when this is done for the cushion values $1 - \alpha$ shown at the top of the table and the constant SMM values shown at the left. The pricing yield was set to 12%, the pricing speed $SMM = 1\%$ while the stressed pool amortization schedule $V_h(t)$, and hence the PAC schedule, was computed in each case using $SMM = 2\%$. Since an isomorphic mapping function can be derived that turns SMM values into CPR speeds, there is no advantage in defining PAC IO performance in terms of CPR speeds. Our prepayment formalism is designed around the SMM index because that is the parameter referenced by the Markov transition matrix.

As can be seen, for the range of average prepayment speeds within the expected universe, i.e., $SMM \in [0\%, 2\%]$, the benefits of the PAC IO are nonexistent, since yield is identical under all values of the cushion $1 - \alpha$. Thereafter as expected, yield goes up with the value of the cushion.

It should be mentioned that the range $SMM \in [2\%, 5\%]$ is actually much more significant than the numbers shown in table 20.3 would tend to indicate. To do a conscientious job, an analyst ought to explore the so-called *PAC range* further in an attempt to compute the conditional probability distribution of prepayments within it. Only then can the true value of the cushion to the investor be gauged accurately. Clearly, this is beyond the scope of this chapter.

Table 20.3 is given for illustration only, since SMM values are changing constantly in accordance with our prepayment model, i.e., equation (12). Therefore, in practice the advantage of a PAC IO may not be as clear as may appear at first sight. This is something that has been known for quite a long time.

Exercise 20.6

Using either the code presented earlier, or preferably your own VBA or C++ program written for the target transaction, implement the PAC IO as shown hereunder using the SMM method and further refine the analysis by exploring the PAC range in detail. Next, compute the conditional, weighted average yield to the PAC IO holder using various functional forms for the conditional probability distribution function to the right

of the stressed *SMM*, which is 10% in table 20.3. As a first experiment, try the uniform, exponential and beta distributions and observe their differential impact on yield at various cushion levels $1 - \alpha$.

20.7 CONCLUDING REMARKS

We have broached the topic of structuring more for the sake of completeness with respect to the target deal than out of any real desire to tackle the subject comprehensively. In addition, it would be rather odd to ignore altogether the *structure* inside structured finance. As indicated in the introductory remarks to chapter 14, we need to realize that we have fallen short of the mark, and for very good reasons. In fact, almost every page of this chapter is filled with nice-looking but misleading equations and concepts that lend an air of respectability to something that is anything but respectable.

At first sight, one could not be blamed for naively believing that the myriad structural possibilities currently found in actual transactions results from the brilliance and creativity of the investment banking profession. Unfortunately, this could not be further from the truth. Anyone even remotely acquainted with the practice of structured finance knows first hand the shoddy nature of the average structuring process, one whereby reserve accounts are traded like old toasters while triggers are designed in approximately five minutes by well-meaning lawyers and bankers with little fundamental understanding of the basic dynamics of triggering. The result is a hodge-podge of conflicting, and sometimes even contradictory, requirements that end up looking like what everybody else calls a *deal*, but we would call a *mess*.

The reason why most structured transactions perform has nothing whatsoever to do with structuring excellence, but is simply the result of the fact that the vast majority of assets perform, and in that case structuring is moot. The rating process is usually haphazard and ungrounded, effectively amounting to an exercise in black magic in which answers (i.e., ratings) are derived from an iterative process during which sheer physical exhaustion is the only telltale sign of convergence. Analysts structuring deals work such long hours because they are forced to plod through the same steps 50 times over, preparing uncountable versions of presumably the same deal in search of never-to-be-found excellence. Regrettably, to do this in no way amounts to a process, let alone to a science. At best, it is a waste of time.

When a carpenter behaves this way on the job, he is usually fired within a week, but when an investment banker does it, he is usually promoted.

In the current world of structured finance deals are like sausages, i.e., those who like them should never watch them being made!

21

Triggers

Triggers are an important aspect of structured financial analysis because they represent a relatively cheap form of credit enhancement. Whether they are as cheap as people think is another matter. In most cases, triggers are reluctantly inserted inside transaction documents, more as an afterthought than consciously, and usually amount to the same reduction in optical credit enhancement (ca. 50 bps) regardless of the situation. The truth is that in many cases, they are in fact worthless.

In "*The Analysis of Structured Securities*" (OUP, 2003), we spent quite a bit of time discussing trigger theory and the process of trigger optimization. Although some repetition is unavoidable, it is not our intention to go over well-trodden ground one more time but merely to get down to the business of triggers and show how an analyst can implement a simple trigger. In addition, we will spend some time on peripheral issues pertaining to triggers and their use inside structured transactions.

Before embarking on a journey through trigger-land, it is a good idea to reintroduce the topic to help bring this important feature into focus in the context of structured analysis.

21.1 WHAT IS A TRIGGER?

As their name indicates, triggers are automatic provisions within Pooling & Servicing Agreements that cause hitherto dormant actions to be taken upon the occurrence of certain asset- or liability-based events. Triggers can be partitioned by reference to the steps that must be taken when the trigger is breached or "hit." We discuss the most common types in the following passages.

Cash Flow Triggers

From an analytical standpoint, the most interesting triggers are those whereby a breach causes the trapping of cash that would otherwise escape back to the residual holder, or its allocation to someone else. This diversionary process is clearly aimed at strengthening the transaction by providing a relatively inexpensive form of on-demand credit enhancement, albeit at the price of operational constraints.

In the analysis of cash flow triggers, it is both possible and desirable to weigh benefits against costs to arrive at an unambiguous definition of the optimal breach level. We discuss how to do this below in "Trigger Valuation and Optimization."

Deal-Type Triggers

An alternative form of cash flow reallocation is the *deal-type* trigger, an expression we have coined for lack of a better term. By this, we mean for instance that a formerly *pro rata* principal allocation regime could become sequential following a trigger breach event, or vice versa.

In this category also lies the so-called "lock-out" trigger feature, one mostly found in mortgage-backed structures whereby no principal is paid to junior tranches while senior tranches are being refunded. The junior tranches are then said to be "locked out." Under one implementation, this may happen during a given time period, e.g., the first two years after closing. Alternatively, the junior class can start amortizing after an agreed-upon percentage of the senior class has paid down. Instead of trapping cash inside the transaction as with the first type of trigger, here risk is managed while simultaneously reducing the all-in cost of funds to the sponsor by paying down relatively high coupon classes, once it becomes clear that the deal is performing, ahead of what would happen under a purely sequential regime. Senior investors usually deem too risky the idea of paying down lower classes right after closing.

Strictly speaking, implementing this type of trigger is not difficult. Waterfall formulas need to change but the asset-side analysis remains untouched. Basic questions here would revolve around when to initiate the switch to the new allocation scheme or by how much the senior class should amortize before allowing the junior class to start paying down. With respect to deal-type triggers, it is often the case that triggers statistically unlikely to be breached are rarely tested in situ and that, as a result, operational problems are never discovered. The potential economic advantage of the trigger is therefore nullified.

> **Exercise 21.1**
>
> How would you implement a deal-type trigger in your own code? Write a hypothetical section of Visual Basic (VBA) code that would switch the waterfall from pro rata to sequential upon breach, insert it and cause the breach to occur so you can watch the trigger in action.

Wind-Down Triggers

In contrast to the above, some triggers act more as failsafe devices than cash reallocation schemes. For instance, if the servicer is placed into bankruptcy by a court of competent jurisdiction, legal documents may force the transaction to unwind ahead of schedule. In other cases, the securities backed by the pool may become due and payable upon the occurrence of certain events. In yet others, a revolving period may end immediately, thus causing the deal to amortize early. This is just another form of wind-down.

The macro-events that are the subject matter of these triggers are usually disruptions in the deal's operational environment on a scale that was never contemplated at the outset. Such events are thought to fundamentally change the nature of the transaction and force it to be wound down in as orderly a manner as possible.

Although wind-down triggers are interesting in practical terms, they are stochastic in nature and hence, in contrast to cash flow triggers, not amenable to statistical analysis. Owing to their strictly binary character, wind-down triggers are trivially implementable within the waterfall and rarely require optimization. In addition, the definition of the relevant trigger events is unambiguous and leaves no room for analytical creativity. In many instances, they will fall within the category of "force majeure," i.e., situations about which very little can be done. For this and other reasons, we will focus the following discussion exclusively on cash flow triggers, an area where structuring expertise can be reasonably expected to matter.

Exercise 21.2

Think of an alternative trigger type in some asset class of your own choosing, a type not represented here, and discuss the reason why it would be used in this case. What are the particular characteristics of the asset class that would make it attractive to both issuers and investors? Does this exist anywhere in the capital markets? Has it ever existed? What general method would you use to design alternative triggers if that were your job?

Taxonomy of Triggers

The field of triggers is vast. They can be used to cause a variety of behaviors and to introduce ad hoc operational constraints. In this text, we restrict our discussion to the binary trigger both because it is relevant to the target transaction and because it is by far the most common type. Nevertheless, the reader should be conscious of the fact that binary triggers are only the tip of the iceberg when it comes to trigger analysis. As explained in our previous monograph, *"The Analysis of Structured Securities"* (OUP, 2003), one can easily design *differential* triggers, whereby a breach would have greater or lesser impact depending on the speed of deterioration of some appropriate index. One can also conceive of *integral* triggers, where the impact of a breach would be based on the cumulative effect of deterioration in the same index.

Why one would use such complicated triggers in the first place was discussed at length in the above monograph, and that discussion will not be repeated here. As of this writing, most triggers found in live transactions are binary. As always, the market has a long way to go to before taking advantage of what is possible, and nothing will change that until investor education catches up.

21.2 INTRODUCTION TO BINARY CASH FLOW TRIGGERS

In this section, we review the basic dynamics of binary cash flow triggers, i.e., those that are either fully on or fully off. Despite their crudeness, these triggers are by far the most common.[1] In most cases, either cash reallocation or a similar result is effected via an index defined with respect to a variety of transaction variables, the most common of which are delinquencies, defaults, and principal balances. The main difference between binary triggers lies in the index with which they are associated.

Although such cash reallocations are usually permanent, they can also be temporary. When they are permanent, we will refer to the trigger as *noncurable*. When temporary or even reversible, we will refer to it as *curable*. Note also that, although trigger indices are computable on any Calculation Date, the basis for such computation may include data from more than one Collection Period. For instance, the average of the asset pool's 60+ delinquencies over the last three Calculation Dates is a standard example of a trigger index. Such quarterly-averaged delinquency indices are common and are generally designed to avoid accidental triggering due to seasonality and other transitional, noncredit-related factors (see chapter 23). In its basic operation, a trigger is referred to as *breached* if the associated index exceeds a suitably chosen threshold on any periodic Calculation Date. In most cases in the U.S., the trigger is tested every month.

Related Considerations

(a) Cash Flow Trapping Mechanics

One should always distinguish between the index upon which the trigger is based, something that can vary considerably, and the impact of the breach which tends to be singular. In general, a breach causes cash that would normally escape the transaction to be instead captured inside a separate account. That cash is then available on future Distribution Dates to fulfill debt obligations should current collections fall short of the mark. As explained earlier, triggers mainly serve as additional, dynamic forms of credit enhancement.

Note that in a pure cash flow environment whereby liabilities amortize using all available cash after servicing fees and coupon payments, the inclusion of a cash flow trigger is clearly irrelevant. In other words, in such transactions the trigger is implicitly breached at all times. Another important aspect of triggers is that even though cash is theoretically available from excess spread, one has to test whether the breach level is low enough for excess spread to remain after the demands of the waterfall above the affected level have been met. It is quite common for structures to have perfectly fine-looking triggers that are in fact ineffective due to the inappropriate positioning of the threshold level. To properly and consistently position trigger breach levels is not as trivial as it may seem.

(b) Alternative Impact of Trigger Breach (Turbo)

Some of you are probably wondering why, instead of trapping cash inside the structure to be available on future Distribution Dates, it is not returned to investors as additional principal distributions. If the deal is not doing well, why not bite the bullet now and amortize further? Such triggers do exist and they are dubbed *turbo* triggers. When they are breached, the deal simply uses the excess cash to build over-collateralization (OC) instead of accumulating it inside a spread account. Even better, since the spread-account earnings rate is invariably lower than the average coupon on the liabilities, doing this actually reduces the load on the structure by eliminating the associated negative carry. The downside for the issuer is obviously that the cash is gone, i.e., it cannot be retrieved later should the deal recover, assuming for the sake of argument that the contents of the spread account could be released.

The turbo aspect of a trigger in no way affects the allocation of monthly principal due. The liabilities simply amortize that much faster. This does however mean that the parity condition no longer strictly holds and that the OC percentage slowly approaches infinity. Last but certainly not least, turbo triggers clearly do not make sense in the case of pure cash flow deals. As we indicated in item (a) above, the use of any cash flow reallocation trigger is predicated on the presence of excess spread that would otherwise escape to the residual holder.

(c) Binary Triggers and Moral Hazard

In all cases, the choice of the index is a crucial component of its effectiveness. For instance, a coincident default trigger may be completely ineffective against a slowly deteriorating pool, allowing too much excess spread to escape before the trigger level, set for example at two times expected losses on a run-rate basis, is finally reached. Rather than a coincident default index, the way around this problem would be to use a suitably chosen cumulative default index as a signal of impending doom. Therefore, in general, trigger indices and breach levels ought to be designed with specific asset behaviors in mind. Consequently, knowledge of the asset class is critical to the art of constructing realistic triggers.

By far the most inconvenient aspect of binary triggers is their "all-or-none" feature. More often than not, this introduces moral hazard that would not exist but for the trigger. We are referring to situations whereby the issuer can manipulate delinquency or default data, as the case may be, in precisely the amount necessary to avoid a breach simply because the consequences of such breach are simply too horrendous to be contemplated. As a result, the transaction and the trigger do not work as intended, and everyone loses. In other words, triggers are much easier to include than to respect. From the standpoint of the sponsor, what we have casually labeled "excess spread" is nothing short of its profit margin. Convincing an executive or businessperson to forego that cash *just in case* usually takes some persuasion.

This moral hazard is unavoidable and highlights the need for proper analysis of sponsor operations to ensure that no "black hole" exists in which nonperforming assets might be parked to avoid a breach. In the prototypical case, a default-trigger breach could be avoided via payment holidays or some other form of account-level debt restructuring. The affected accounts, usually highly delinquent, would then be prevented from rolling into default, forestalling the inevitable. The obvious fix is to supplement the default-based trigger with a delinquency-based trigger capturing the resulting increase in delinquencies, provided of course no fraud takes place. Properly defining the right incentive structure requires detailed knowledge of the issuer's credit policy, something over which we already locked horns when discussing cash flow transfer functions in chapter 16. Therefore, trigger design is yet another reason why the detailed knowledge of sponsor operations is so important.

(d) Triggers as Free Lunches

When structuring a two-tranche transaction for instance, it is commonly observed that the presence of a trigger will raise both credit ratings simultaneously. However, as we have mentioned several times before, given an asset pool with fixed cash flow potential and a given basic structure, it is theoretically impossible to improve simultaneously both tranche credit ratings if one excludes hypothetical arbitrage opportunities stemming from market inefficiencies. How can this *impossible* thing happen?

The answer is that the trigger traps cash that was not being counted as credit enhancement to pay interest and principal on the liabilities before the introduction of the trigger. In other words, while the pool's cash flow potential has not changed at all, the amount of *available* cash has indeed increased. Remember that credit analysis lives and dies at the tail of loss distributions, where commonsense and intuition usually fail us. Without a proper cash flow analysis, it is impossible to tell by how much credit ratings would improve via trigger inclusion.

In cases like deal-type triggers, their impact might be to decrease the senior rating for the benefit of the junior class, or vice versa. Why would we be interested in doing this? There are many answers to this question. First, the senior rating might be overkill and Class A investors would be just as interested in a slightly lower rating at the identical or nearly identical spread. In such instances, yielding some credit quality to the junior class would be a neat way to optimize the structure at very little cost. Alternatively, it is quite possible for the senior class to be rated at the top end of its rating band, thus allowing it a bit of downward maneuvering room at the same letter-grade rating. Clearly, this type of credit arbitrage would disappear instantly should credit ratings move to a numerical scale instead of sticking to the alphanumeric nomenclature currently in vogue.

As neat as this may appear, there is trouble in paradise. This is because, as mentioned before, regardless of its index and declaration mechanics, the benefits of a trigger are realized immediately via either reduced interest costs or increased advance rates. Even better, the presence of the trigger will not matter at all and will normally count as little more than a dead letter should the feared stressed cash flow scenario never materialize. In that sense, the trigger may appear costless. However, the costs of the trigger are only palpable when the transaction and sponsor are experiencing difficulties, i.e., when they can least afford to give up cash. Therefore, issuers and investment bankers playing fast and loose with trigger levels may live to regret it.

21.3 TRIGGER DEFINITION AND INDEX SELECTION

Since we will be dealing exclusively with binary triggers in the remainder of this chapter, let us formally specify the set of assumptions underlying them.

Binary Trigger Definition

In keeping with the nomenclature we are using in this transaction, the trigger environment can be characterized as follows:

1. The transaction has maturity T, resulting in a time domain $t \in [0, T]$.
2. A suitable trigger index $I(t)$ and associated breach level $I_s(t)$ have been defined (see below).
3. The transaction documents (P&S Agreement) include the concept of a spread account with an outstanding principal balance of $R(t)$ at time t.
4. The impact of the trigger is to reallocate to the spread account any cash left over after distributions needed to maintain the pool's parity condition.
5. Define $P(x(t))$ as the proportion of the available excess spread to be so reallocated. By definition, we have $P(x(t)) \in [0, 1]$.
6. The trigger variable $x(t)$ is a known function of the trigger index $I(t)$ and other deal parameters.
7. Although $R(t)$ is usually capped at a given percentage of the outstanding aggregate bond or pool balance, we assume no such cap exists. Amounts remaining in the spread account at time T are simply returned to the residual certificate-holder.

As a result of these basic definitions, we can define the following trigger mechanics:

$$P(x(t)) = H[g(x(t))] \tag{1}$$

In equation (1), we have defined the Heaviside step function $H[\bullet]$, the curing functional $g(x(t))$ and the trigger variable $x(t)$ via:

$$H[y] = \begin{cases} 0, & y < 0 \\ 1, & y \geq 0 \end{cases} \tag{2}$$

$$x(t) = I(t) - I_s(t) \tag{3}$$

$$g(x(t)) = \begin{cases} x(t), & \text{curable} \\ \int_0^t H[x(t)] \, dt, & \text{noncurable} \end{cases} \tag{4}$$

As you can see, breaching this trigger results in the reallocation of 100% of available excess spread to the spread account indefinitely and with no allowance for subsequent withdrawals. This is an extreme example of a binary trigger's most troublesome feature.

One could also conceive of binary triggers that:

• On any Calculation Date, allocate excess spread to the spread account up to a given maximum percentage of the total amount available, thereby according the residual holder a grace period in curing the breach and somewhat reducing concomitant moral hazard (this is already more sophisticated than what is currently being done); or

• Increase the spread account balance up to a target percentage of the pool's ending balance instead of indefinitely (see below); or

• Allow trapped funds to be released from the spread account should the index again fall below the breach level $I_s(t)$ (see exercise 21.5).

Index and Breach Level Definitions

In the above definitions, we left out the definitions of the trigger index $I(t)$ and its breach level $I_s(t)$ on purpose. This is where the rubber meets the road in trigger design. Although the number of possibilities is quasi-infinite, the following are some of the most common varieties:

(a) 60+ Delinquencies

In this example, the index $I(t)$ is equal to either the coincident or the quarterly rolling average 60+ pool dollar delinquencies $d_{60+}(t)$. The latter are defined as the aggregate principal balance of all accounts with delinquencies greater than 60 days past due on any Determination Date.

If the definition calls for coincident delinquencies, we have the following relation for $t \in [1, T]$:

$$I(t) = d_{60+}(t) \tag{5}$$

If quarterly averaged 60+ delinquencies are used, we need to use:

$$I(t) = \frac{d_{60+}(t-2) + d_{60+}(t-1) + d_{60+}(t)}{3}, \; d(-1) \equiv d(0) \equiv 0 \tag{6a}$$

Here, the breach level would be some constant value k_d to be determined later after negotiation between buyer and seller:

$$I_s(t) = k_d \tag{6b}$$

As explained above, the reason why one would define a trigger index on a rolling, quarterly-average basis is that this definition normally prevents an accidental breach arising from noncredit-related causes, for instance normal seasonality in the pool's delinquency structure. Unfortunately, this definition also introduces its own idiosyncratic behavior. Specifically, the issue is that breach will be deemed to occur only when the average of the arguments in the numerator of equation (6a) exceeds $I_s(t)$. Depending on the speed of delinquency deterioration, there may in fact be no spread left to sweep into the spread account when the trigger is actually breached. This is generally not a problem if the issuer adheres to its credit policy manual precisely, but how often is that the case? In any event, simply recognizing this effect is already winning half the battle.

(b) Coincident Defaults

Defining defaulted receivables during any collection period t as $l(t)$, we have:

$$I(t) = l(t) \tag{7a}$$

The breach level k_l is similarly defined:

$$I_s(t) = k_l \tag{7b}$$

(c) Cumulative Defaults

Coincident default is not common in ABS transactions since it is a poor leading indicator of trouble. A far more compelling index is cumulative defaults as a percentage of the pool's initial principal balance. In that case, we would define the index via:

$$I(t) = \int_0^t l(\tau)\,d\tau \tag{8a}$$

Please note that in practice, the integral in equation (8a) would be represented either as a straight sum or an integration formula like Simpson's rule. Here, the breach level can obviously not be defined as a simple constant as in our first two examples and must instead follow a pre-established schedule of cumulative pool default levels. The latter schedule can be devised in many ways and in all cases be represented as some continuous function of time $F_c(t)$:

$$I_s(t) = F_c(t), \ t \in [0, T] \tag{8b}$$

(d) Coincident Prepayments

In certain asset classes and special situations, it is possible for triggers to be based on the level of coincident prepayments at time t. In such cases, the structure might switch from *pro rata* to sequential to extend the average life of the junior class or for some other purpose. Obviously, this type of trigger makes sense mainly in asset classes, like mortgage-backed securities (MBS), where prepayment speeds are a pricing concern.

Defining coincident prepayments as $P_p(t)$ we can write the trigger index as:

$$I(t) = P_p(t) \tag{9a}$$

The breach level here is just a predetermined constant k_p:

$$I_s(t) = k_p \tag{9b}$$

(e) Cumulative Prepayments

In the case of cumulative prepayments $C_p(t)$ we proceed in a manner similar to cumulative defaults:

$$I(t) = \int_0^t P_p(\tau)d\tau \tag{10a}$$

$$I_s(t) = F_p(t), \ t \in [0, T] \tag{10b}$$

In some situations, holders of PAC IO instruments might be interested in downside protection following doomsday scenarios in which the Companion Class[2] associated with such IO securities would have been exhausted. Under this structure, amounts deposited into the spread account pursuant to a breach could be re-allocated to IO holders as yield enhancement to compensate them for the sudden demise of their interest-rate play via the original PAC IO. In such cases, the breach function $F_p(t)$ defined by equation (10b) would be designed to keep track of the pool's amortization history and would enter the fray only when the Companion Class had been effectively exhausted at each corresponding time step. This way, PAC IO holders would not be entitled to yield enhancement except under extreme prepayment speeds.

Alternative Forms of Triggering

Obviously, the creativity of investment bankers is the only real obstacle to the creation of triggers of all kinds. Advanced students are encouraged to consult actual deal prospectuses to find out what is currently being done in the capital markets with respect to triggering. The foregoing was merely intended as a brief overview of what we believe to be a promising area for capital structure optimization in years to come.

21.4 TRIGGER VALUATION AND OPTIMIZATION

Our intention hereunder is not so much to repeat what was laid out in "*The Analysis of Structured Securities*" (OUP, 2003) but simply to orient the student while giving him reason enough to keep digging into this topic. In addition, the intimate relationship between valuation and optimization will be explored fully in the next chapter. Although they are clearly not the same thing, valuation and optimization with respect to trigger design are certainly close cousins.

Before one can manage or "optimize" a risky portfolio, one must first measure risk within it. To state, for instance, that Value at Risk (VAR) is being used as a measure of risk in no way amounts to a risk management system. Risk management cannot take place unless and until that risk has been measured. For us, this means that triggers can only be *optimized* once they are *valued*. But what does this mean exactly?

In the next section section, we review briefly the idea underlying trigger valuation and then move onto actual implementation inside a deal code.

21.5 THE VALUE OF A TRIGGER

It is sensible to first take a step back and ask what is to be accomplished through valuation. On the one hand, this requires knowledge of the impact of the trigger on the issuer, and on the other hand, of what is prevented by the breach.

Given the foregoing, it should not be difficult to convince ourselves that there is really no magic involved in trigger valuation. Triggers are things that ostensibly give you something tangible and immediate, albeit at the cost of some other things that might cost you in the future if the deal turns out to be headed south. Valuation amounts to computing the immediate benefits of such *good* things and weighing them against the *average* cost of the *bad* things should they in fact materialize. Of course, if the deal performs well and such bad things never come to pass, the trigger gave you something for nothing, a free lunch so to speak. The valuation process cannot engage in this form of idle speculation. What the future holds nobody really knows and thus, trigger valuation can clearly never be predicated on a pretense. Regrettably, this happens all too often.

For starters, the trade-offs involved are intuitive. Because valuation requires the sampling of loss distributions far into their tail to justify the assignment of high credit ratings, relatively high breach levels have essentially no practical impact on issuers, since they neither view such levels as realistic nor seriously contemplate their occurrence. However, because extreme loss events contribute disproportionately to the creditworthiness of structured securities, and of all securities for that matter, high breach levels confer relatively small, but still tangible funding benefits on issuers at essentially no perceived cost to them. Conversely, at relatively low breach levels triggers become effective, and hence cumbersome, operational and working capital constraints on sponsors. Not surprisingly, issuer resistance to breach thresholds is inversely related to their location. On the other hand, the ratings-derived borrowing cost advantage that low breach levels confer is much more significant, and usually much more in line with the issuer's original expectations.

Given these unavoidable philosophical considerations, our marching orders are clear. First, we need to formally define the benefits and the costs of a trigger for a given tranche of debt, from which the *Value* of the trigger can be computed. The extension to multiple tranches is obvious and will not be explicitly considered. In addition, given the basic method presented here, extensions to more complicated structures can easily be implemented.

The Benefits of a Trigger

The aggregate benefit of a trigger $T_B(I_s)$ is the cost of funds advantage it gives an issuer. The latter is clearly dependent on the trigger breach level I_s, here assumed to be some unknown constant. To compute these benefits, we will need the parameters in table 21.1.

Please note that the *weighted* average life of a tranche is not the same as its average life within a particular Monte Carlo scenario. The former is defined as the arithmetic mean of individual average lives over the entire simulation.

TABLE 21.1

Parametric trigger definition (benefits)

PARAMETER	DEFINITION
B_0	Tranche initial principal balance ($)
L_{avg}	Weighted average life of the tranche (years)
r_n	Credit spread without the trigger (%)
r_t	Credit spread with the trigger (%)
$\Delta r = r_n - r_t$	Credit spread benefit (%)

It is now relatively straightforward to define formally the benefits of our binary trigger at any given breach level I_s :

$$T_B(I_s) = \Delta r \, B_0 \, L_{avg} \tag{11}$$

The benefits of a trigger can only be computed from two separate numerical simulations, one with and one without the trigger. Since there is no guarantee that both simulations will yield the same weighted average life, if the respective weighted average lives in the two cases are noticeably different, their mean value should be used. In general, we find that weighted average lives are so close as to be indistinguishable.

The Costs of a Trigger

As a result of the basic trade-offs associated with triggers, the aggregate cost of a trigger $T_C(I_s)$ can be defined as the difference between earnings on funds invested in the spread account versus what would have been earned had the same funds been invested in normal operations, which latter number is more or less equal to the issuer's return on equity. In doing this, we are assuming that the spread account would be empty but for the presence of the trigger. An obvious modification can be made if this is not the case.

Note that funds withdrawn from the spread account to pay for liability coupon or principal due are implicitly counted under benefits and should not be double-counted. Hence, the measure of the trigger's real cost is the spread account balance multiplied by the difference between the two yield environments. Table 21.2 defines the parameters involved in the cost estimate.

From the foregoing, the aggregate cost of this binary trigger for any given breach level I_s can be expressed formally as follows:

$$T_C(I_s) = \frac{\Delta i}{N} \sum_{j=1}^{N} \int_0^{T_j} R_j(t) \, dt \tag{12}$$

In general, each Monte Carlo (MC) scenario will give rise to a different transaction maturity since defaulted accounts may experience recoveries beyond the last maturity

TABLE 21.2
Parametric trigger definitions (costs)

PARAMETER	DEFINITION
N	Number of Monte Carlo scenarios
$R_j(t)$	Spread account balance at time t in scenario j ($)
T_j	Computed maturity of the transaction in scenario j (years)
ROE	Issuer estimated return on equity (%)
r_s	Spread account earnings rate (%)
$\Delta i = ROE - r_s$	Differential yield cost (%)

date of any loan in the pool. However, since most simulated maturities will lie within a tight neighborhood of the transaction's nominal maturity T, these effects will be second order at best. Finally, the spread account earnings rate can usually be set equal to the Eligible Investment Rate.

The *Value* of a Trigger

As explained above, the *Value* $V_T(I_s)$ of a binary trigger at any given breach level is equal to benefits less costs, whether that difference is positive or negative:

$$V_T(I_s) = T_B(I_s) - T_C(I_s) \qquad (13)$$

Once the trigger has been so valued, the optimization of the breach level becomes a fairly routine and transparent operation.

The Basis of Trigger Optimization

If relatively high breach levels confer modest benefits on the issuer, and relatively low levels are simply too onerous in operational terms, then it follows that some intermediate level must exist at which an optimal balance between costs and benefits can be struck. The search for this ideal level is the crux of trigger optimization.

Trigger optimization is normally accomplished via a sequence of MC simulations no different from those leading to valuation (see chapter 22). In addition to requiring a significant amount of CPU time, the trigger space itself can be tricky and nonlinear, and might leave no choice but to sample a large number of breach levels in search of the optimum without any expeditious way of narrowing the search a priori. In spite of these factors, the resulting savings are usually well worth the effort given the relatively low cost of triggers to sponsors compared with other forms of credit enhancement.

The optimal breach level I_{opt} is the one leading to the highest *Value* across the entire I_s range:

$$I_{opt} \equiv \max_{I_s} V_T(I_s) \qquad (14)$$

Obviously, I_{opt} might be different for different trigger types within the same structure. Following the above procedure, it is possible to find the optimal breach level for any

TABLE 21.3

Delinquency status definitions

STATUS CODE	DEFINITION
0	0 to 4 days past due
1	5 to 29 days past due
2	30 to 59 days past due
3	60 to 89 days past due
D	90 days or more past due

trigger within a transaction. If the breach I_s level is not a constant, but is instead an entire schedule of values (see "Trigger Definition and Index Selection"), the optimization process is exactly analogous as long as the said schedule is invariant across MC scenarios.

21.6 TRIGGER IMPLEMENTATION

In this section, we focus on what needs reinforcement, i.e., on the details of trigger implementation. As soon as implementation becomes second nature to a structured analyst, optimization really boils down to basic number crunching.

Assuming we have decided to include a binary, quarterly-rolling-average delinquency trigger inside our target transaction, how do we do this? First, we need to compute aggregate delinquencies within the pool so we can judge whether the trigger has been breached. This is easy with the help of our Markov transition matrix formalism from chapter 16.

Delinquency Calculations

To compute 60+ day delinquencies, proceed as follows. Recall the definition of 60+ delinquencies $d_{60+}(t)$ as the aggregate principal balance of all accounts greater than 60 days past due. This includes all accounts in delinquency States 3 and higher according to the delinquency nomenclature defined in table 21.3.

Therefore, we can compute $d_{60+}(t)$ by cycling through the pool while aggregating the principal balance of all accounts satisfying $j \geq 3$. Exhibit 21.1 is a section of VBA code that computes all pool delinquencies.

> **Exhibit 21.1: Computation of Trust Delinquency Vector**

If state(j) = 0 Then

cf(CF_POOL_CURRENT, j) = cf(CF_POOL_CURRENT, j) + bal(j) / CF_POOL_BALANCE

Elself state(j) = 1 Then

```
cf(CF_POOL_30DAY_DELINQ, j) = cf(CF_POOL_30DAY_DELINQ, j) + bal(j) /
CF_POOL_BALANCE

Elself state(j) = 2 Then

cf(CF_POOL_60DAY_DELINQ, j) = cf(CF_POOL_60DAY_DELINQ, j) + bal(j) /
CF_POOL_BALANCE

Elself state(j) = 3 Then

cf(CF_POOL_90DAY_DELINQ, j) = cf(CF_POOL_90DAY_DELINQ, j) + bal(j) /
CF_POOL_BALANCE

End If
```

Trigger Implementation

Once $60+$ day delinquencies have been calculated, the index $I(t)$ itself is easily calculated in real time using equation (6a). Thereafter, a conditional statement is inserted in the code to indicate a breach.

Now assume that some Boolean trigger-breach indicator B has been initialized to FALSE at the beginning of every Monte Carlo scenario within the simulation. If the binary trigger being implemented is *curable*, the conditional statement that includes B contains an *else* clause resetting the breach indicator to FALSE at every time step should the breach condition no longer be TRUE. For a *noncurable* trigger, simply omit the *else* clause.

To illustrate, consider the following schemata for some constant breach level $I_s(t) = k_d$ for Monte Carlo scenario j:

(a) Curable Trigger Implementation

$$\forall j, \, t = 0 \Rightarrow B \equiv FALSE$$

Now for $t \in [1, T_j]$, we have:

$$\text{IF } I(t) \geq k_d \text{ THEN } B = TRUE \text{ ELSE } B = FALSE$$

(b) NonCurable Trigger Implementation

$$\forall j, \, t = 0 \Rightarrow B \equiv FALSE$$

Now for $t \in [1, T_j]$, we have:

$$\text{IF } I(t) \geq k_d \text{ THEN } B = TRUE$$

Exhibit 21.2 is a VBA code section implementing a noncurable trigger inside the target automobile transaction.

Exhibit 21.2: Noncurable Binary Trigger Implementation

```
deal.enableTrigger = TRUE
trigger_breach_level = 0.15 (15% trigger breach level as described in chapter 15)

For j = 0 To maxM
sum = sum + cf(CF_POOL_90DAY_DELINQ, j)
If j - i = 3 Then
sum = sum - cf(CF_POOL_90DAY_DELINQ, i)
i = i + 1
End If
cf(CF_POOL_MOVING_AVG_DELINQ, j) = sum / (j - i + 1)
```

Trigger index is quarterly moving average 60+ delinquency rate

```
cf(CF_TRIGGER_INDEX, j) = cf(CF_POOL_MOVING_AVG_DELINQ, j) /
CF_POOL_BALANCE
```

The trigger is breached when the Boolean variable 'CF_TRIGGER' is set to 1

```
If cf(CF_TRIGGER_INDEX, j) > trigger_breach_level Then cf(CF_TRIGGER, j) = 1

Next j
```

Figure 21.1, taken from a stressed Monte Carlo loss scenario experienced with the target pool, shows how a breach would have been declared at $t = 17$. The breach

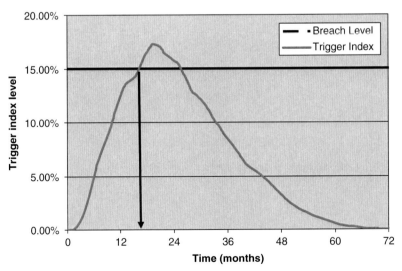

FIGURE 21.1

Noncurable trigger example. Breach at $t = 17$ months.

level was set at 15%, an arbitrarily chosen level. In the case of interest, the impact of this noncurable trigger would remain in effect for the duration of the transaction regardless of subsequent collateral performance. Furthermore, since the effect of the breach is the accumulation of excess cash inside the spread account, a breach would cause all excess spread to remain trapped inside the deal. By contrast, a curable trigger would have been reset at approximately $t = 28$, i.e., when $d_{60+}(t)$ fell below 15%, thus causing excess spread to be released back to the sponsor on a current basis as before. The status of funds residing in the spread account is another matter. Several alternatives are of course possible, from outright instantaneous release to remaining trapped inside the reserve account for *rainy days*. Further discussion on this topic would however be speculative.

Exercise 21.3

Implement this delinquency trigger inside your transaction code using a switch enabling both curable and noncurable triggers. Ensure Boolean indicator B is properly treated.

Impact on Residual Holder and Spread Account Mechanics

If the trigger is deemed breached, the impact on the transaction is felt immediately at the bottom of the waterfall where excess spread would normally escape back to the sponsor. Instead of being returned to the residual holder, excess spread is now trapped inside the deal until the balance in the spread account reaches some prearranged percentage R_p of the remaining pool balance.

Exhibit 21.3 shows the VBA code section effecting the reallocation of cash from the residual holder to a spread/reserve account created expressly for this purpose. In many cases, this being an exception to this rule, the spread account may not be intended to keep building forever, and excess cash allocations may terminate once the spread account balance reaches the predetermined pool fraction R_p on any Calculation Date. In this case, the reserve keeps on building effectively forever.

Exhibit 21.3: Trigger-Related Spread Account and Residual Mechanics

Upon a breach, the reserve target amount is set equal to the pool balance

```
If deal.enableTrigger And cf(CF_TRIGGER, t) = 1 Then
cf(CF_RESERVE_TARGET, t) = Application.Max(cf(CF_POOL_BALANCE, t),
deal.reserveFloor * deal.poolBal)
Else
cf(CF_RESERVE_TARGET, t) = Application.Max(deal.reserveTarget *
cf(CF_POOL_BALANCE, t), deal.reserveFloor * deal.poolBal)
End If
```

As already indicated, the impact of a cash flow binary trigger on residual value is severe and abrupt. As a result, sponsors are often tempted to forestall a breach, hoping to keep more of their spread when, at least in their own mind, there is "nothing wrong." There is, of course, no way to predict when or even whether this moral hazard will be present, and this is where the monitoring of transactions in the secondary market becomes critical.

The average issuer will usually not start out on the wrong path, since in most cases deals will require significant time to reveal themselves as either performing or not. Until then, we can reasonably expect that the rules of the game will be followed. Because the vast majority of transactions perform, this type of risk is relatively small in absolute terms. But if the transaction starts to perform poorly, one should not be surprised to discover that corners were cut along the way in an effort to prevent a breach that could further exacerbate an already dire situation. Readers might be wondering if it is possible to know from performance data alone whether an issuer is playing number games with his portfolio. The answer is an overwhelming *yes*, but only once the analyst has conceptualized the transaction in depth. It can never be done using the standard, shoddy Wall Street shuffle technique.

Exercise 21.4

1. Write a section of VBA code implementing a cumulative gross default trigger using equation (8).
2. Construct a trigger-breach schedule $I_s(t) = F_c(t)$ using equation (27) (loss curve) from chapter 16 by stressing it across the board by 20%.
3. Insert this brief code section into your deal analysis and cause an intentional breach on the first MC scenario by increasing the time-dependent delinquency propensity $p_{01}(t)$ inside your Markov transition process until this occurs.
4. Verify that the accumulation of cash inside the spread account reaches the suitably chosen level R_p before credit losses begin to nullify asset performance. What if it doesn't? What would you do to correct the situation?

Exercise 21.5

Write a code section implementing a delinquency trigger that also allows funds to leave the spread account if, and when, the trigger index falls below the breach level i.e., a curable trigger.

In this case, the functional $P(x(t))$ can be negative as well as positive. To find out how much cash to let go from the spread account, simply compute the excess spread, which is positive by definition, and flush out the same amount from the spread account. This method has the advantage of matching cash releases from the spread account to equivalent benefits actually conferred on the trust by the sponsor's improving operational performance.

APPENDIX: *In Memoriam*

Thomas Simpson (1710–1761)

The allusion to Simpson's rule in the main body of this chapter was but a clumsy excuse to highlight and honor the life of this pioneer in mathematical education, a man who made significant contributions to the furtherance of knowledge with respect to data analysis as a lone voice in the wilderness.

Trained as a weaver, Simpson was deeply involved in the real world and attempted to solve real-world problems at a time when theology, agriculture, and warfare were the three main polite occupations. He was an early proponent of the now accepted view (effectively post-Gaussian) that the arithmetic mean of a set of observations is a better measure of the underlying phenomenon than any one of them. In 1754, he was appointed editor of the *Ladies Diary* where he attempted to promote the mathematical education of the "common woman," a part of society that was hitherto restricted to the kitchen and the bedroom. By the way, he did not invent the rule that bears his name although he used it profusely. An itinerant teacher who could be found in coffee shops and pubs across London, Thomas was known to end every lecture with a pint of beer and gin. Although many of his contemporaries looked down on him for "degrading science," they still elected him to the Royal Society. From the age of 27 until he died, he taught mathematics.

Strangely enough for an Englishman, Simpson was very much in the French tradition. As is well known, the British school is generally hostile to analytical methods, preferring empirical observation as a guide to theory. Logical positivism is just one example of this odd approach. For most of his life, Simpson tried to counter that mindset by promoting the seemingly strange idea that theory ought to be the guide to observation. This heretical reversal of the accepted framework did not endear him to his colleagues and, unfortunately, he remained relatively obscure. Today, this view is the unquestioned paradigm of science, one brilliantly codified by Sir Karl R. Popper in contradistinction to the Wittgenstein–Russell positivist school. Thomas Simpson was clearly a man ahead of his times, but it should never be forgotten that people like him are the very reason why such *times* ever see the light of day.

22

The Valuation of Structured Securities

"Μελέτα τό πάν"
Periander

Will we be wrong in assuming that many of you have skipped the previous 500-odd pages entirely to focus your attention on this, a chapter with such a promising title? Perhaps some profound piece of wisdom is lying here, and this is why the discriminating analyst really ought to forego all that preliminary, useless philosophy to concentrate on what really matters: valuation. Since we have been talking about the target deal for at least eight chapters, isn't it about time we got somewhere fast? If not now, then when?

Unfortunately, if you did end up here rightaway, you will be sorely disappointed. Not that reading what follows is a waste of time, quite the opposite. In fact, over the next few sections you will be presented with a self-consistent method of valuing, and hence pricing, structured securities that will heed the call to dealing through the explicit recognition of the nonlinear nature of the beast. Regrettably, even if you know precisely what to do, still your victory will remain depressingly Pyrrhic for there is no shortcut to essential dealing. The truth is that the *answer* or the *right number* is to be found neither here nor via the magic of some multifarious algorithm or model. Numbers are not right and wrong, but merely high and low. As you should have realized by now, the answer is really the question, the question of the deal.

The truth of dealing does not lie in vacuous pronouncements like "the Class B bears an interest rate of X and a credit rating of Y". On the contrary, that truth literally irrupts on the scene while traveling the lonely, winding and treacherous road to *Value*. For those of you who have patiently taken each careful step along the byways of finance, it will turn out that you have simultaneously laid the groundwork for valuation, work without which a *price* is just an opinion, something everyone and their mother already have.

Valuation is quite a let down compared to what we have gone through thus far. As we shall soon discover, it does not involve any sort of esoteric mathematics. Instead, it merely drops out of the analysis as its natural outgrowth, almost by surprise. Can something so momentous be so simple? What must be understood is that the issue is exactly the other way around. What looks *simple* only seems so because it is fundamentally difficult. Simplicity, mathematically understood, always and only means rigor; it is the way truth reveals itself. Valuation is not easy, it is simple.

For example, here is an easy problem. You are shown a fair coin and asked to calculate the probability that on the next toss, heads will turn up. The answer can be computed in the following, logically formal way using P_1 and P_2 as the probabilities of heads and tails turning up, respectively.

A fair coin is defined as having equal probability on either side, so we have our first equation:

$$P_1 = P_2 \tag{1}$$

Next, the total probability space must be contained in each toss. Thus, our second equation follows:

$$P_1 + P_2 = 1 \tag{2}$$

Combining equations (1) and (2), and solving for P_1 we find:

$$2P_1 = 1 \Rightarrow P_1 = \frac{1}{2} \tag{3}$$

That was a lot of work for something so obvious! Yes, it was. Now, let's look at a *simple* problem, which is this: how many tosses will be required on average before heads turns up? At first sight, this second problem looks as easy as the first one, but upon further reflection, it belongs to a separate category of problems, of which this is but a basic example. Actually, people who breeze right through the first problem are usually stumped by this one.

The answer is clear and has to be two, for otherwise something would be amiss. In arriving at that answer, we nevertheless had to pause ever so slightly to think about why it had to be two. However, that was the easy part of this most elementary problem. The simple part is to prove formally that it is indeed two. Just saying it is obvious will not cut it here. How do we proceed? The *simple* way is to calculate the answer, say n, directly in a manner that goes something like this.

Assume there are two possibilities with this fair coin, i.e., heads and tails.[1] If tails shows up, we toss it again and maybe heads will turn up. Each toss is of course independent of the previous one. If, on the other hand, heads turns up the first time, we are through. By doing this, we have effectively partitioned the space of tosses into two distinct and equally likely events, one where the answer is 1, and another one where it is $n + 1$. It follows that, on average, the combined result from these two sets must yield the answer we seek, and we can therefore write directly, i.e., intuitively:

$$n \equiv \frac{1 + (n + 1)}{2} \tag{4}$$

Solving for *n*, we easily find $n = 2$, and we are done.

What is *hard* in arriving at the solution is to pose equation (4) for the first time. But why is it hard? If you think about it, you will recognize that it is because *n* appears on both sides of the definition sign [≡]. In the second case, the answer does not trivially follow from the logical rules of probability applied to the problem statement. The fact that equation (4) can be readily inverted to yield *n* explicitly does not take anything away from the elementariness of the situation, for in many cases this will not be possible.

In other words, the difficulty in solving the second problem is that to do so, *insight* was required whereas none was needed for the first one. Insight is what is properly *mathematical* in the solution; it is what is learnable or teachable in the true sense of these words. We will come back to insight later in this chapter when discussing *Value*, but for now, note how insight cannot come from logic alone. Rather, it is something hovering beyond the obvious, something that can only be known in advance without being derived from the thing itself. What is remarkable is that insight can be learned at all.

Valuation is about insight not logic, for logically speaking, any number will do. It is in this way that valuation is *simple*. Do you still believe it is that easy?

22.1 WHAT DOES IT MEAN TO PRICE A DEAL?

In chapter 14, we introduced the question of nonlinearity by showing how the deal would come together inside a feedback loop in yield space and whereby, for lack of a better word, yield was redefined as original time, i.e., as the transcendental horizon for the understanding of dealing. Before discussing this process in familiar terms, we need to pay careful attention to *what* is really measured when a deal is valued, as opposed to *how* it is actually measured.

To answer the question "What does it mean to price a deal?" by saying that it is the process of assigning interest rates or prices to its various securities is meaningless, for it amounts to defining poverty as the lack of money, or corporate bankruptcy as a filing under Chapter 11 of the U.S. Code. Such answers are but restatements of the original question. Of course, a poor man is one that has no money, but the real question obviously was: Why doesn't he have any? By the same token, a bankrupt corporation is *not* one that has filed under Chapter 11, for the truth is exactly the opposite, i.e., a company files under Chapter 11 *because* it is already bankrupt. This *already* business is the soul of structured security valuation.

The purpose of inverting the common understanding of bankruptcy is that it clearly shows that the truth of bankruptcy comes first, before the filing, and likewise, that of poverty comes before the lack of money. Facts and data are not the same. Data only become "facts" when viewed in the light of an underlying theory, when projected against the backdrop of some manmade conceptual framework. There is no such thing as a "pure" fact. If you ever hear someone say "it is a fact that …" you should smile, because the definition of a fact is precisely what *is* for someone, and only that. That sentence has the same epistemological status as "the Pope is Catholic." He sure is!

The commonplace notion, no doubt inherited from the Chicago School of Economics, that a market can arise spontaneously, i.e., before *Value*, is nonsense. It is *Value* rather, what we normally call *fair value* that comes first, a priori, and then allows the market and hence the price, to come into being. Any other way to look at it leads either nowhere or to the "two fools make a market" type of thinking. Where was the option *market* before Sprenkle and Black? *Value* comes first, the market second.

The Intrinsic NonLinearity of Value

The basic problem of finance, and thus what is truly difficult to achieve, is not the establishment of the so-called secondary market, for the latter is nothing but a linear construct derived from *Value*, i.e., from the primary market. Rather, the real issue is the specific way in which the valuation process is to be carried out from the ground up in a self-consistent manner. Thereafter, price simply coalesces around *Value* in an obvious manner to enable trading.[2] When that happens, the number so derived is henceforth regarded as the security's *equilibrium* price or its *fair market value*. In fact, this is precisely and exclusively how a market can develop for it.

Having insight means to know that it is valuation that allows interest rates to exist in the first place, instead of following the linear crowd in believing that the existence of the yield curve is what allows pricing to be carried out. Understanding *Value* means understanding it as an inversion of commonsense, for it is on that basis, and that basis alone, that commonsense can even begin to exist. Strangely, here again we have stumbled upon both sides of the equation at the same time.

Valuing a deal does not amount to an exercise in logic, whereby an answer can be found as it was in our first problem. In other words, security valuation does not consist in finding a *solution* in the way the equation $x + 3 = 7$ can be *solved* by saying $x = 4$. Not surprisingly, financial analysts trying to value deals while still operating within the realm of linearity, of logic, commonly talk about such nonentities as the "right number," "market momentum," or "current conditions," as if they were discussing an absolute that could be defined without reference to something already existing. Such arguments are merely escape mechanisms from the inescapable conclusion that logic is not something that merely hangs out there, free-standing, complete, and sufficient unto itself; in short, they are but means of breaking the essential nonlinearity, the symmetry somewhere, in order to achieve closure, linearity, and nonarbitrariness. The truth is that logic must be grounded in something that stands above and beyond it, something that itself can obviously not be logical. That something is what we called *ground* in chapter 14. A deal can be valued only when it provides its own ground, i.e., ground needs no ground because it "is" for its own sake, in itself. So the next time the man or woman of your dreams corners you during one of those New-York-style cocktail parties by asking "pray tell, what is the essence of dealing?" you can answer clearly and truthfully: it is the ground of the inner possibility of *Value*.

To *Value* a deal means to give it ground, and nothing else. That is why we first had to go through the last 500 pages. Only then, could the deal emerge out of itself and yield its *Value*, its true price. This will now be accomplished by linking interest rates to themselves within a cybernetic feedback loop, allowing them to come to their final, *unique* resting place on their own. When it exists, this fixed point will be termed the *Value* of the deal. Valuation is how the deal comes together *as* a deal, as a manifold unity. What gives *Value* credibility and elevates it above the rank of mere opinion is not that it is cheap or rich, high or low, or originates from a pre-established, purported fount of human wisdom, but rather that it is grounded, i.e., *unique*.

We can express this way of thinking by saying that in valuing a deal we are not so much looking for a solution, as for a *re-solution*. Here the prefix *re* is used to convey the notion of linking input and output in yield space. By contrast, to *solve* the deal would amount to a claim of perfect knowledge of the future, something that would completely annihilate the market in one fell swoop if it ever happened anyway. In fact, it is crystal-clear that the market's very possibility is grounded in its own freedom, i.e., in a lack of absolute certainty about future events. To resolve the deal is not the best thing one can do, it is the only thing. Contrary to public opinion, valuation is not something that can be taken for granted. It is anything but a routine procedure that gets boring after a while. Valuation takes a lifetime to master and can only begin seriously once we stop taking ourselves so seriously.

From the foregoing, you can perhaps catch a glimpse of what a misconception it is to look for a solution by reference to something no more grounded than the sheer opinion of some analyst. Pricing by asking yourself what you would *really* say if you were someone else is the height of silliness, and yet it is still by far the most common approach to pricing deals. To ask a rating agency the same question is not a solution, it is a mistake, because it leads to the naïve belief that something magical has happened when you receive the *right* answer, the one you so desperately need. The accepted notion that you can change that answer almost at will is all you need to know that it never was an *answer* in the first place.

22.2 NONLINEARITY REVISITED

At this point, it is worthwhile to recapitulate some of the basic tenets of structured security valuation before moving on to a live example. In truth, we started talking about the end game of structured analysis as far back as chapter 14, but did not elaborate on how this would actually take place. Many questions were left unanswered on purpose as we ploughed our way through the assets and the liabilities. Luckily, valuation is the easy part of transaction analysis compared to what was involved in giving the assets their due.

Brief Review of the Structured Valuation Problem

You will recall from chapter 14 that the crux of structured security analysis is the resolution of the proverbial "chicken and the egg" problem whereby the rates, or ratings, from which prices will be determined are dependent on the average reduction of yield a security-holder would experience over a range of realizations explored via Monte Carlo (MC) simulation. This technique, coupled with the invocation of the ergodic hypothesis, enabled us to relate the results of MC simulation to the specific transaction under review. Otherwise there would be no empirically valid way to equate the performance of the ensemble to that of the target.

The fundamental dilemma lay in the fact that, in order to compute the average reduction of yield from the nominal coupon promise, one had to know that promise in the first place, the latter being in turn dependent on credit ratings, and thus on the average reduction of yield. In other words, knowledge of the rating requires knowledge of the rate, but knowledge of the rate requires knowledge of the rating. The circle around which we are obviously moving was then referred to as the *nonlinearity* of structured finance. It will not do to merely redefine credit ratings as something that can be known a priori since the same problem will simply reappear from another angle. It is an *essential* nonlinearity because it cannot be removed via some mapping or transformation. To resolve this essential problem is our task.

Nonlinearity is not something mysterious or fanciful. Napoleon Bonaparte, easily the greatest tactician of his generation, was known to use the expression "the logic of the situation" when referring to his uncanny, intuitive knowledge of the enemy's battlefield reactions. What he meant was that it is not possible to know your own actions beforehand since the enemy's moves are obvious inputs to yours. Napoleonic fame ought to be sufficient to convince you that, far from being easy, essential nonlinearity is difficult to grasp because it seems not to exist at all.

Nonlinear Solution Procedure

The resolution of the structured valuation problem is unique. The identical problem has been faced and dealt with many times before in a variety of contexts and the key has always been cybernetics. For the sake of argument, we reiterate the basic nonlinear convergence algorithm described somewhat cryptically in chapter 14:

1. Estimate some initial and provisional yield vector, one rate for each credit tranche in the deal. This can be done, for example, by using the back of the envelope method reviewed earlier.
2. Perform a first MC simulation using this provisional yield vector and derive tranche credit ratings as average yield reductions from the nominal promise.
3. Use an empirically derived yield curve, or a model thereof, to compute output interest rates from both the average reduction of yield and the weighted average life of each security.
4. Using a relaxation method, transform the output rates into a new input-rate vector and substitute the latter into the MC engine.
5. Compute the absolute value difference between the input and output rates and express it as a percentage of the input rates. Define the convergence parameter δ as this percentage weighted by initial tranche balances.
6. Repeat the sequence 1 through 5 until δ falls below a specified error bound, usually in the neighborhood of 0.5%.

The final yield vector can now be defined as the *Value* of the deal. Further, because *Value* is fair, the offered price of each security should be par.

The *Value* of a deal is none other than the limit point of an iterative procedure operating in a multidimensional and nonlinear space, which dimensionality is perforce equal to the number of credit tranches in the deal. In the case of the target transaction, we are operating in two-dimensional Cartesian space because the yield on any fixed income security can be regarded as a real number $r \in [-1, 1]$.[3]

As you can imagine, the potential for numerical instability increases in lock-step with the dimensionality of the space, something over which we have relatively little control. This does not bode well for those analyzing transactions with 10 or more credit tranches. The upshot is that the skills of a structured analyst must be commensurate with the dimensionality of his or her deals, something bound to cause problems when intricate structures are analyzed, as they will be. In anticipation of this problem, the rest of this chapter is devoted to a familiar conceptual framework aimed at recognizing and diagnosing trouble when it occurs, and knowing what to do about it.

22.3 VALUATION AS THE FIXED POINT OF A NONLINEAR MAP

Before tackling the valuation process mathematically, we need to conceptualize it more precisely. Glancing at the steps laid out in the previous section, we can formally schematize the valuation sequence as the process shown in Figure 22.1 whereby we have purposely left out all variables save those related to tranche yields.

As such, the vector-valued mapping function $g(r)$ in figure 22.1 stands for the complete deal cycle consisting of an entire MC simulation. Each simulation represents thousands of deal realizations involving perhaps 300 time steps each, not to mention the thousands of obligors processed during each MC scenario. Depending on the computing power at the analyst's disposal, a single valuation exercise may require hours of CPU time.

The modeling of the yield curve is involved in this process, and so is the calculation of credit spreads. For future reference, we have shown the rate-relaxation algorithm separately from the rest of the valuation process. However, this step can usually be subsumed under the mapping function $g(r)$ without loss of generality.

Our iterative valuation scheme can be represented as follows:

$$r^{n+1} = g(r^n) \tag{5}$$

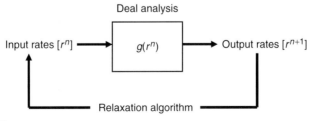

FIGURE 22.1
The valuation schema in structured finance.

It is now a trivial matter to define theoretically the *Value* of the deal *V* as the fixed point r^∞ of the map $g(r)$:

$$V \equiv r^\infty = g(r^\infty) \tag{6}$$

In other words, the *Value* of the deal is the set of rates that simply reproduce themselves upon iteration. The *practical*, as opposed to *theoretical* definition of *Value* will have to wait a while longer (see "The Value of the Deal" below), but the concept will remain the same. In other words, since we are dealing with an asymptotic process, it is to be understood that the word *reproduce* is intended to leave room for a small error margin. Even theoretically, a fixed point is never actually reached.

The practical problem now becomes the determination of conditions under which the sequence of rate vectors r^n will converge to some fixed limit. We take up this topic in the next sections.

22.4 CONTRACTION MAPPINGS AND DEAL VALUATION

Most of you probably remember the opening line of Tolstoy's great novel *Anna Karenina*: Все счастливые семьи похожи друг на друга, каждая несчастливая семья несчастлива по-своему. (All happy families are happy in the same way, but every unhappy family has its own way of being unhappy.) Had he been a mathematician, the illustrious Russian novelist would have said that all linear functions are linear in the same way, whereas every nonlinear function has its own way of being nonlinear. What this means is that the behavior of nonlinear iteration is idiosyncratic. Whereas linearity is a formal concept that can be treated monolithically, nonlinearity can mostly be discussed as a black box, using statements like "this is due to nonlinear effects" or "this happened because of nonlinear instability." In essence, numerical analysts use nonlincarity the way physicians use stress, i.e., as a catch phrase to say more than they know while giving their ignorance the veneer of knowledge.

The upshot is that we must tread carefully when making general statements regarding nonlinear iteration. Whereas well-posed linear systems, with very few exceptions, can always be solved, nonlinear maps present special problems that seem to disguise themselves every now and then. Because of their rarity, formal proofs in nonlinear mathematics are always welcome. One such result is Banach's celebrated contraction mapping theorem.

Stefan Banach was an early twentieth-century Polish mathematician who, despite his untimely demise, made significant contributions to functional analysis.[4] The following fixed-point theorem is only one of his many accomplishments. Before we begin, remember that a theorem is supposed to be an unmediated traversing to a parcel of truth, a spark of godliness. The truth of a theorem is what you cannot plainly see, what lies underneath the logic. In other words, a theorem is like a window: although you can see the truth through it, it still separates you from it. This being said, as much as possible we try to avoid discussing and proving theorems for the simple reason that knowing and rattling off theoretical proofs will never make you into a great credit analyst. However, this one is unavoidable because it strikes at the heart of the matter.

The Banach Contraction Mapping Theorem

Let X be a complete[5] metric space equipped with metric d and let the map $g(x)$ be given by $g(x): X \rightarrow X$, mapping every element of X onto another element of X. The elements of X are conceived as vectors, i.e., groups of numbers with as many dimensions as we like.

In addition, this type of mapping is said to be a *contraction* mapping when any two elements of the domain are mapped to a pair of images that are closer to each other than the original pair, i.e., when the following condition holds for any choice of elements x and y in X for some q, $0 \leq q < 1$:

$$d(g(x), g(y)) \leq q\,d(x, y) \qquad (7)$$

Just to refresh your memory, in one dimension the metric or *norm* is usually the distance between two elements and is simply the absolute value of their algebraic difference, i.e., $|x - y|$. In multiple dimensions, we need to consider each dimension in turn and use some other form for the norm. In two dimensions, where each element would be represented by $x \equiv [x_1, x_2]$, we could define the metric as the distance between the two elements x and y using the Euclidean norm:

$$d(x, y) = \sqrt{(x_1 - y_1)^2 + (x_2 - y_2)^2} \qquad (8)$$

This metric can be generalized to more than two dimensions in an obvious way. In fact, this type of space is a basic example of a more general type of space called, believe or not, a Banach space. In structured finance, we will generally need as many dimensions as there are credit tranches in the deal, which is unlikely to be greater than 10 in the worst case. Historically, mortgage-backed securities transactions apparently containing dozens of tranches usually had no more than three or four credit tranches.

We are now ready to state without proof Banach's contraction mapping theorem:

Theorem 1 (Banach):

For constant q, $0 \leq q < 1$, every contraction mapping in X with metric d has a unique fixed point.

The proof is not difficult[6] and interested readers should consult appendix B at the end of this chapter for a full treatment. Briefly, it begins by first showing that the series of iterates under $g(r)$ will form a Cauchy sequence, i.e., that they get closer to each other under the given map. Next, we need to show that all such sequences will converge to some fixed limit. This is not difficult because the definition of a complete metric space is one in which all Cauchy sequences converge. The remainder of the proof consists in demonstrating that this fixed limit-point is unique, which is done by first assuming that it is not and then obtaining a contradiction.[7]

Proving this theorem is not important. What matters, rather, is to know what it means to us budding structured analysts, which is that if we can show that the deal's map $g(r)$, referred to above in "Nonlinearity Revisited", is contracting over some domain, a fixed point will exist and, even better, that it will be unique. In other words, Theorem 1 guarantees that under relatively generous preconditions and assumptions, we will be able to uniquely value structured securities. Therefore, Banach's contraction mapping theorem is the fundamental valuation theorem in structured finance.

Applications of Banach's Contraction Mapping Theorem

How do we know in advance that some mapping will be contractive? The basic answer is that we do not. What the theorem tells us, in fact, is that if the deal's mapping function is *not* contractive, the deal may not be *valuable* at all, i.e., the deal may not "work" and, in general, it will not.

At least under this conceptual framework, it is therefore possible for deals not to work, to be *non-deals*. This is a major step forward for at this very moment, Wall Street believes that by definition, all the deals it wants to underwrite actually work. The task of structured analysis is to create the environment within which a deal can be valued and reach its fixed point by itself, not to value it by *fiat* or simply tout it to unsuspecting investors as a *great* deal. In other words, you do not have to value deals, for deals can value themselves.

The application of Banach's fixed-point mapping theorem is not difficult, since in the case of an ill-posed transaction the algorithm will eventually start to diverge, causing the processing to abort and wasting very little time. What we really need to know is how to tell right away that a deal will eventually diverge, so we can stop the valuation sequence immediately and start over with a different, hopefully better, structure. We need a criterion by which to judge the deal's contractive property. Thus, our problem is the determination of the conditions under which a deal's mapping function will be contractive. We will go over the algebra in one dimension to let the concept speak for itself, but in the end true learning only happens by doing deals, not by proving theorems about doing deals.

Some of you will recall that, in "*The Analysis of Structured Securities*" (OUP, 2003), we developed a convergence criterion with respect to the basic nonlinear optimization technique, the Newton–Raphson [NR] method. Back then, we showed how, in one dimension at least, a sufficient condition for the NR iteration to converge was for the slope $g'(x)$ of the associated mapping function $g(x)$ to be less than unity in absolute value everywhere within the domain of interest, including the starting guess, hence the criticality of that location.

In other words, the one-dimensional NR iteration *will* converge if the slope of $g(x)$ satisfies $|g'(x)| < 1$ everywhere. This sufficiency condition is strangely reminiscent of the assumption $q < 1$ involved in Banach's theorem. Could there be a connection? Do you really think we would bring this up if there were not?

In our first demonstration, after assuming that the mapping function $g(x)$ was continuous, we used the Mean Value Theorem to show that for any two iterates, x^i and x^{i+1}, in the sequence leading to the root of the NR mapping algorithm, we could always find a location ξ^i somewhere between x^i and x^{i+1} for which the following condition held:

$$g'(\xi^i) = \frac{g(x^{i+1}) - g(x^i)}{x^{i+1} - x^i} \tag{9}$$

The next step was to show that if the absolute value of the mapping function's slope at the location ξ^i was always less than unity, from the initial guess $[x^0]$ down to the location of the root $[x^\infty]$, the iteration would always converge. In other words, the process would always converge if the following held along the way:

$$\left| g'(\xi^i) \right| < 1, \, \xi^i \in [x^0, x^\infty] \tag{10}$$

This happens because equation (10) guarantees that the following condition holds:

$$\lim_{n \to \infty} \left| x^{n+1} - x^n \right| \to 0 \tag{11}$$

The absolute value is just a red herring here. Why? Because, according to Banach, the distance between two iterates is what we are really looking for, and in one dimension distance is nothing but the absolute value of the difference between two iterates.

Now, look at equation (9) and note that a sufficient condition for the convergence of the scheme is really:

$$\frac{\left| g(x^{i+1}) - g(x^i) \right|}{\left| x^{i+1} - x^i \right|} < 1 \Rightarrow \left| g(x^{i+1}) - g(x^i) \right| < 1 \bullet \left| x^{i+1} - x^i \right| \tag{12}$$

Now if we replace the 1 on the right-hand side of equation (10) by q with the standard proviso that $q < 1$, we have simply reproduced the condition guaranteeing that Banach's contraction mapping theorem will hold, and wouldn't you know: equation (11) is precisely the definition[8] of a Cauchy sequence. What a coincidence! In the scalar case, the two concepts are one and the same but in practice, it is much easier to check whether equation (10) holds somewhere in X than whether equation (7) holds everywhere in X.

In passing, although we have shown the correspondence between Banach's fixed-point theorem and our original NR convergence analysis, some readers might still be wondering whether this also applies to deals with multiple tranches. Indeed, it would be strange if we concluded that only single-tranche transactions could be properly valued. Rest assured that the same principle applies to the vector case, although the demonstration is more involved.[9]

We now have the outline of a workable strategy for deal valuation. Before trying this out however, let's become a little more comfortable with how the slope of the mapping function controls the convergence process.

Nonlinear Convergence in Banach Space

Let's go back to our friend, the function $f(x) = e^x - 5x$ and examine the convergence history of the NR iterative method applied to it. We will need the following quantities:

$$f(x) = e^x - 5x \tag{13}$$

$$f'(x) = e^x - 5 \tag{14}$$

$$g(x) = x - \frac{f(x)}{f'(x)} \tag{15}$$

$$f''(x) = e^x \tag{16}$$

$$g'(x) = \frac{f(x)f''(x)}{f'^2(x)} = \frac{e^x(e^x - 5x)}{(e^x - 5)^2} \tag{17}$$

This function has two roots, one around 2.54 and the other one at ca. 0.26. Let's see how equation (17) behaves over a segment bracketing both roots. Figure 22.2 shows the behavior of $g'(x)$ in the interval $x \in [0, 5]$. The location of each root is shown in the figure via the label R_i.

To begin with, note that $|g'(x)|$ is always less than unity in the neighborhood of both roots, so we can be assured that the algorithm will converge as long as the initial guess is chosen close enough to either one. Now, contrary to what Banach seems to have implied, the fixed point to which a Cauchy sequence will convergence is not unique, since there are two of them even in the case of a pretty dull looking one-dimensional function. God knows what could happen in more than one dimension!

What we discovered in "*The Analysis of Structured Securities*" (OUP, 2003) is that, under the above restrictive condition, the NR algorithm in fact converges everywhere, but that the root to which it does converge depends on the starting guess. Is this in conflict with Banach's theorem?

No, because the theorem only says that if the mapping is contractive everywhere in X, the solution is unique. Sure enough, if we restrict ourselves to regions of figure 22.2 where $|g'(x)| < 1$ holds everywhere we also find that, just as Banach claimed, the solution is unique.

Exercise 22.1

For the function given as equation (13), use the Newton–Raphson iterative scheme and monitor its convergence to one of the two roots (0.26 and 2.54) over the range $x \in [0, 5]$. Redo this exercise for the series of functions given by the form $f(x) = e^x - \alpha x$, and explore the integer domain $\alpha \in [1, 9]$ in terms of convergence behavior. Is there any difference between the convergence properties of the function when α varies across its domain of definition? What about making α itself a function of x? ◀

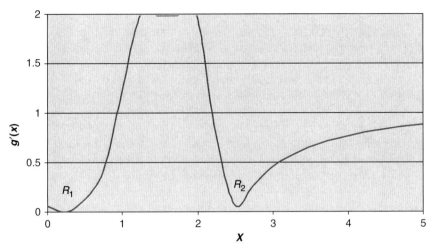

FIGURE 22.2
Slope of the Newton–Raphson iterative map.

In more than two dimensions, things actually get better and worse at the same time. They get better in the sense that the number of distinct roots in the domain of interest actually decreases, and we usually find that when the algorithm reaches a limit point at all, it converges to the same limit point each time.

Exercise 22.2

Redo exercise 22.1 using $f(x) = e^x - \alpha(x)x$ and the following definition:

$$\alpha(x) = ax^2 + bx + c \qquad (18)$$

To explore the disturbance effect of using equation (18) on the convergence of the NR iterative method, use the following range for its three parameters:

$$a \in [-1, 1] \quad b \in [-5, 5] \quad c \in [-10, 10]$$

They get worse in the sense that the mapping's region of convergence, which for obvious reasons we also call its *basin of attraction*, is much less forgiving with respect to the starting guess. In such cases, we find that if the corresponding criterion is not met around the starting guess, the iteration quickly diverges. This is good and bad. It is good because the solution is unique in the global sense, but bad because it tells us that unless we begin close enough to the deal's sole limit point, the iterative scheme will most likely diverge even though the transaction can definitely be valued.

22.5 THE VALUATION SPACE IN STRUCTURED FINANCE

What does Banach's theorem amount to in terms of the deal's valuation space? First, what we know is that as soon as we have more than one tranche, the valuation exercise gets easier and harder at the same time. On the one hand, practically speaking the solution becomes *unique*, but determining an appropriate starting guess requires some thinking. Otherwise, the iteration may diverge and the deal may have no *Value*. Can we create some practical rule around this idea?

In essence, we are asking whether we can extend the concept of mapping functions to handle cases that do not converge. For any given structure, there must be some finite initial set around the solution vector within which the process will converge and another set, hopefully distinct from the first one, where it will diverge. If this is true, these two regions must be separated by some border where the deal will neither converge nor diverge. Yes, but what does this mean exactly?

To see how to handle this situation generically, we need to introduce concepts that apply to all mappings, whether they are contractive or not. By this we mean the geometry of the mapping. In broad terms, you can think of the deal's root locus as behaving like that of a quadratic function, such as the one defined via equation (19) and depicted in figure 22.3.

$$ax^2 + bx + c = 0 \qquad (19)$$

As is well known, roots of quadratic forms such as equation (19) are determined by their determinant D given by:

$$D = b^2 - 4ac \qquad (20)$$

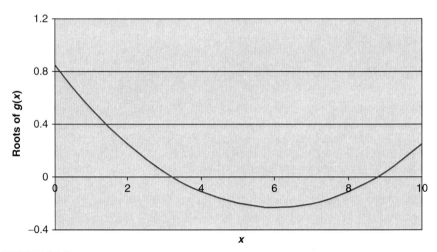

FIGURE 22.3
The concept of the hyperbolic map.

Depending on the value of D, there will be two real roots $[D > 0]$, a single real root $[D = 0]$, or two imaginary roots $[D < 0]$. In what follows, situations whereby $D > 0$ will be referred to as *hyperbolic*, i.e., where the roots are *real* and therefore *exist.* Those whereby $D = 0$ will be called *parabolic,* and those whereby $D < 0$ will be referred to as *elliptic.*

In the case of figure 22.3, the three parameters on the right of equation (19) were:

$$a = 0.03 \quad b = -0.36 \quad c = 0.85$$

The determinant is thus: $D = (0.36)^2 - 4(0.03)(0.85) = 0.0276 > 0$

As a result, the equation has two real roots. If $D = 0$ had prevailed, the graph would have barely touched the y-axis and if $D < 0$ had been the case, the curve would have been completely above the y-axis. In that case, both roots of equation (19) would have been imaginary.

What must be understood is that this is also how the deal's valuation process presents itself with respect to mapping functions $g(x)$, i.e., the process of finding the roots of equation (19) is akin to that of finding the roots of $g(x)$.

By strict analogy with the above scheme, we will refer to mapping functions using the same nomenclature. When the roots are real, we will be referring to a hyperbolic iteration whereby the determinant of $g(x)$ will be greater than zero. In terms of Banach's theorem, this will be the situation $q < 1$. In other words, a hyperbolic deal is one where a solution exists. Please remember that *Value* in structured finance implies existence as well as uniqueness. We will sometimes label such deals *well-posed* since their mapping function will always lead to *Value.* A well-posed deal does not mean a risk-less deal. On the contrary, such deals can be extremely risky.

When the roots are the same, we have the parabolic situation and $D = 0$ holds, which corresponds to $q \approx 1$. In that case, a real solution barely exists. We will refer to this situation as *meta-stable* for reasons to be explained shortly. Last but not least, when $D < 0$ the roots are imaginary and the deal will diverge. While we would describe this situation as *elliptic*, to Banach this would merely indicate $q > 1$ on average across its domain of definition. In these cases, we will simply say the deal does not work, or is *ill-posed.* In other words, it is a non-deal.

In the foregoing, we have conceptualized an environment within which a given deal's valuation space can be regarded as simply connected, in that it can be divided into two distinct regions:

1. A hyperbolic region where it is well-posed (deals)
2. An elliptic region where it is ill-posed (non-deals)

If this is so, then at the border between the first and the second region the deal must be parabolic, right? Yes, it is. What does this mean? Simply put, it means that you do not want to operate near that region when valuing the deal because you may not actually know that you are in fact inside it. This is because the most noteworthy feature of the parabolic border is that it is *fuzzy.* By contrast, under the ideal, Platonic case corresponding to equation (19), it would be sharp. Why is there a difference?

In a nutshell, the reason is that we are dealing with a statistical ensemble, whereby a single Monte Carlo iteration may tip the balance either way and actually make the difference between a convergent and a divergent iteration, i.e., between a hyperbolic and an elliptic transaction. In other words, although theoretically the convergence probability measure contained in the parabolic region vanishes as the number of Monte Carlo scenarios increases toward infinity, in practice this will not be feasible.

As a result, the topology of structured financial analysis contains a fuzzy region wherein the deal will be neither strictly hyperbolic nor elliptic. Instead of a line, the parabolic region will reveal itself as a strip, whereby deals lying thereon will move in and out of convergence due to the irreducible randomness and the vagaries of Monte Carlo analysis (see "Meta-Stability in Structured Finance" below). In other words, valuations launched inside the parabolic strip may very well converge in one MC simulation and diverge in the next one. Therefore, this is a region generally to be avoided, one where the deal may behave erratically and yet it is by far the most tempting area of deal space.

Some of you will have most likely raised an objection and now be saying: Can't we just increase the number of MC scenarios at will, effectively up to infinity? We can, but we may not. In fact, the notion that doing this is feasible while adhering to statistical theory is mistaken.

The Two Vector Spaces Inherent in Structured Finance

So far, we have been referring to deal valuation space, or deal space for short. In fact, deal space really consists of two distinct subspaces: yield space and parametric space. In effect, this means that we need to conceive of two distinct and independent forms of convergence. To understand deal valuation in structured finance, the separate and independent existence of these two subspaces needs to be borne in mind. For future reference, they are defined in boxes 22.1 and 22.2.

Box 22.1: Yield Space

As its name indicates, yield space refers to the space of liability interest rates. It makes up the schema that enables us to talk about the *uniqueness* of structured valuation. This space is a natural outgrowth, generalization, and consequence of Banach's fixed-point theorem.

Box 22.2: Parametric Space

This more abstract space involves basic deal parameters, things like issuance levels, reserve accounts, and delinquency triggers. It is within this space that the notion of "optimality" within structured analysis can be defined. As a result, it is just as important as yield space. More importantly, it is *freedom* space.

These two concepts address completely different aspects of the valuation puzzle and require separate discussions. The good news is that their topological properties are closely related, and thus understanding achieved in one space can be carried over to the other.

22.6 META-STABILITY IN STRUCTURED FINANCE

Before continuing our convergence analysis in deal space, it is a good idea to spend a few moments highlighting and describing the notion of meta-stability, which holds inside the parabolic strip.

Meta-stability is a concept borrowed from the field of dynamics and is of significant import to structured analysis. When we think of stability *tout court*, we usually refer to a system that has basic integrity, i.e., one that will not spin out of control at the slightest disturbance. Physical systems that display such stability are obviously desirable, while those that may become unstable under relatively mild disturbances are generally avoided, and are in fact described as unstable. Mathematically, the latter situation is reflected in the fact that the system is stable "in theory" but not in practice. This happens because the stability condition is satisfied locally, but not globally. What does this mean?

Let's take a financial example to clarify what this is all about. Think of the concept of *convexity* as a market risk measure. Conceptually speaking, the duration[10] D of a bond can be taken as the first derivative of its value with respect to yield (i.e., $D = \partial V / \partial r$), while its convexity C is the second derivative of its value with respect to yield (i.e., $C = \partial^2 V / \partial r^2$).

As you will know, it is quite possible for a bond or a portfolio of such bonds to have zero duration while simultaneously displaying significant convexity, which means that the bond is on the edge of some mathematical cliff. If rates were to shift even mildly, upward or downward, the value of the bond might collapse precipitously in an environment that appeared rather benign. When we refer to a situation as locally stable, but globally unstable, this is what we mean. Alternatively, we might simply say that the bond is "meta-stable." In other words, meta-stability refers to instability to relatively small disturbances. In the present case, disturbances with respect to the convergence behavior of the system are produced by the randomness inherent in the Monte Carlo techniques at the heart of the valuation process. As a final example, consider figure 22.4a, representing a truly stable environment, while figure 22.4b tries to convey the physical and intuitive notion underlying meta-stability.

Figure 22.4b shows a case where instability would result from any disturbance, regardless of whether it is to the right or left. Cases that are more complicated also exist, i.e., ones that exhibit instability along one direction and stability along another. Such locations are called *saddle points*. For instance, imagine how one statistical disturbance could push the deal inside the hyperbolic region while the next could take it into the elliptic domain. Saddle points also exist in structured finance, but they lie beyond the intended scope of this text. At this juncture, just be aware that nonlinear space is intricate.

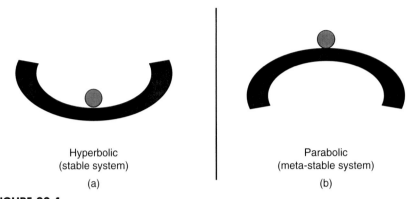

Hyperbolic
(stable system)

(a)

Parabolic
(meta-stable system)

(b)

FIGURE 22.4
The distinct but related notions of stability and meta-stability.

Now you can see why the parabolic strip is the most tempting region of deal space. For instance, consider a deal with a delinquency trigger. At constant trigger level, total issuance barely inside the parabolic strip will clearly be maximal, and thus most attractive to the issuer. The parabolic region's meta-stability property is how the deal tells us that we are pushing the design envelope to its breaking point. In baseball terms, this is the deal's *warning track*.[11] Not surprisingly, issuers able to execute transactions on the far side of the strip often refer to them as *home runs*.

As expected, a deal's stability region is finite since no matter how much we would like to issue, and neglecting legal constraints for the moment, transactions will eventually run up against unavoidable cash flow and statistical constraints. In other words, the most beautiful pool in the world can only give what it's got!

22.7 YIELD SPACE CONVERGENCE: BANACH LAND

You will recall that, under Banach's leadership, we were able to define the deal's existence region as that area wherein an iterated sequence of tranche rates became a Cauchy sequence. What are we to make of this? Is this something we can use in actual transactions? Yes, it is. In fact, for the first time in finance we are in a position to define in nonambiguous terms what it means to be a deal at all.

To understand the behavior that naturally arises from our basic topological conceptualization, consider figure 22.5, showing an idealized schematic of what yield space could look like for a typical two-tranche transaction. In this case, we have defined the rate-vector as r_1 for Class A and r_2 for Class B. The dark spot in the middle of the lightly shaded portion is the solution rate-vector r^∞. The width of the parabolic strip has been exaggerated for didactic purposes; practically speaking, the parabolic region would be much thinner.

As already explained, the three convergence regions are nonoverlapping. Given any starting rate-vector in the hyperbolic region, iteration of the deal's mapping function $g(r)$ converges to the unique fixed point shown in figure 22.5. Note that

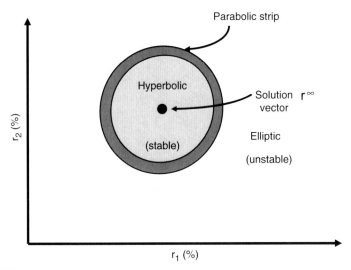

FIGURE 22.5
Convergence in yield space: Banach Land.

the hyperbolic region does not extend to the level of vanishing interest rate since initial estimates are constrained from below by the yield curve (see "A Live Example of Deal Convergence in Yield Space" below). In other words, we normally have no choice but to initiate the nonlinear iterative loop at some level above zero, thus preventing the convergence region from touching the axes. This means that under our iterative scheme the trivial solution $r_1 = r_2 = 0$ is ruled out a priori.

As outlined earlier, although in theory the width of the parabolic strip can be made smaller by increasing the number of Monte Carlo scenarios, that number is fundamentally constrained by the basic uncertainty inherent in issuer data and by the limited resolution compatible with the capital markets' measure of value, whichever is smallest. In other words, one cannot ask the simulation to be more precise than the resolution found either in the original data or in our own limits of measurability. As a result, even on a theoretical basis, the width of the parabolic strip will always remain finite. In practice, the maximum number of scenarios N_M can be set equal to the minimum value, such that an additional scenario would change the overall deal average reduction of yield by at most one hundredth of a basis point:

$$N_M = \min_{N} \{|\Delta IRR(N+1) - \Delta IRR(N)| \leq 0.01 bps\} \qquad (21)$$

Some will argue with this arbitrary definition and there is certainly room for debate here. But arguing this point is counterproductive and anyone should feel free to set any limit they please, as long as no attempt is made to simply raise the value of N so as to crunch one's way out of trouble. In all cases, N_M will remain finite and, in fact, will be surprisingly small.

At the outset of the analysis, the deal's hyperbolic region would need to be mapped out via trial and error, preferably before the deal goes to market. Thereafter, prior experience would normally provide guidance as to the location of an appropriate starting rate-vector r^0 that would more or less guarantee a relatively speedy convergence to the fixed point. Similar transactions will clearly lead to similar convergence behaviors.

Note also that the size of a deal is irrelevant to its convergence properties, although in absolute terms a deal with a more intricate structure or many more obligors will obviously require more CPU time to converge than a relatively less demanding one.

22.8 THE VALUE OF THE DEAL

We are finally in a position to define formally the *Value* of a deal V in non-ambiguous and practical terms as the unique solution-vector r^∞ located in the hyperbolic region:

$$r^\infty \equiv r \mid \left\| \frac{g(r)-r}{r} \right\| \leq \varepsilon \tag{22}$$

$$V \equiv r^\infty \tag{23}$$

In equation (22), the error bound ε should be set somewhere around 0.5%. Again, randomness will usually prevent ε from being set too close to zero.

As dictated by Banach's theorem, equation (22) is a practical definition of when to quit when attempting to reach the fixed point. As already pointed out, statistical error and other constraints will always prevent us from getting infinitely close to the asymptotic limit implied by equation (22) and we will have to remain content with the stop law measured by ε. However, the deal's basic *Value* range thereby implied is not something "wrong" with this method, for it merely represents the explicit recognition that knowledge has limits. On the other hand, what *is* wrong is the pretense to perfection so commonly seen in finance.

Value and Positive Freedom

Recall how, in chapter 14, we claimed without proof that once the deal reached Moment C (Life), it would have given itself to itself and that for the first time, it would exist as a positively free object. Therefore, a legitimate question would appear to be whether in defining *Value* as we have done here, we have achieved our stated objective in any meaningful sense, and if so, how we can prove it.

To see that we have indeed reached our goal, assume equation (6) holds identically. As we have just indicated, this never happens numerically since all we can do is *tend* to *Value* asymptotically without ever, actually reaching it. For the sake of argument though, assume this is possible. As a result, we would then be able to write the following vector equation:

$$\vec{g}(r) = \vec{r}$$

Now, apply the divergence operator, which is the freedom operator, to the n-dimensional vector on either side of this fixed-point relationship, to obtain readily:

$$\vec{\nabla} \bullet \vec{g}(r) = \vec{\nabla} \bullet \vec{r} = n$$

Amazingly, we are done! Mathematically speaking, this is how the deal tells us it has finally reached its maximum point of positive freedom. It is but the logical reflection of the fact that the deal has emerged out of itself and is now able to move freely within its original n-dimensional yield space.

By contrast, an incompressible fluid conceived as a continuum is required to have no freedom at all since together, continuity and incompressibility mean that disturbances in any direction will displace a fluid element in such a way as to leave invariant the space it occupied before the disturbance took place. If v is the fluid velocity vector, the incompressibility of the continuum can be expressed via the so-called *continuity* equation:

$$\nabla \bullet v \equiv 0$$

In essence, all fluid elements are intimately tied together and thus unable to move independently. Such freedom restrictions enable the explicit calculation of fluid trajectories and demonstrate how freedom and determinism are intimately related. The same logic holds true in yield space.

Once literally extracted from its own negativity into a positive object, the deal is now conceived as a fully articulated organism behaving with as much or as little freedom as is compatible with its basic construct. Although we call this condition "free," it is clearly not identical with the negative freedom of Χαως (chaos), of the nothing, for the deal is now bound up with itself in a world restricted by the rules of its evolution in yield space, and yet it is free to reveal itself as a deal for the first time. The loop has been closed and *logic* can now take over in the secondary market.

Value and Calibration

Although this may sound really simple, on closer examination it is only deceptively so. For starters, it took us about 500 pages to get here. How easy can that be? In truth, such simplicity both hides and yet reveals how difficult it is to achieve the simple.

It should always be remembered that, strictly speaking, the *Value* of the deal does not refer to a specific numerical figure but to a process, namely the process of valuation. Deal valuation is merely the re-enactment of this process, not the computation of some particular number. In practice, one obviously needs to do just that, but as far as pricing goes, a wide array of choices will work just as well in allowing markets to clear.

To assign a numerical figure to *Value* is to *linearize* the deal. However, because the latter concept is so ambiguous, we instead use the word *calibration*. Basically, calibration refers to the determination of the basis on which a price will be computed. Assuming the deal will be sold at that price, the latter becomes its *fair* value. The word *fair* means that price and *Value* are the same number, and nothing else. When this is done and widely agreed upon, we refer to the associated figure as the *fair market value*.

Likewise, any freshman chemistry student knows that a thermometer needs to be calibrated before being used. Most people do not know this because the thermometers they buy from hardware stores are already calibrated. Just as is true of financial calibration, what matters to physical calibration is that the standard be widely accepted. In the end, it does not matter whether water freezes at 0 or 32 degrees, for what really matters is that we are all using water. The world of chemistry looks the same either way, and so does the world of finance. What must be seen clearly is that the crucial ingredient in the valuation recipe is the degree of acceptability of the benchmark used, not what the price turns out to be. In other words, although structured securities will have many *prices*, they can only have one *Value*. The specific scale of prices in use is irrelevant to the correct operation of the capital markets just as that of temperature is to the correct operation of chemistry.

Value and Essential Freedom

If you reflect on this for a moment, you will realize that the condition of basic indeterminacy we have just outlined is precisely what is necessary for the world, as we know it, to keep going. If this were not the case, we as economic agents would be subject to full determinism and would literally cease to *care*. In turn, this physical indeterminacy is but a reflection of the basic freedom that must exist within economic analysis, hence the arc of freedom from chapter 14. It is in this way that the limits of our knowledge reappear in the rearview mirror, at the very moment we thought it was safe to go back to the trading floor.

Although the inner possibility of finance is not predicated on reaching some necessary numerical conclusion as to what *Value* needs to be, how does one compute some particular figure for it? As we shall readily see, one does so via nothing but an act of will. It is quite remarkable that the possibility of *Value*, this most mathematical of constructs, is in fact predicated on the a priori potential for something not derived from any one party attempting to reach it. Thus, *Value* implies in advance the possibility of some act of faith, of sheer will.[12] How can this be? Is there not something *absolute* we can rely on to value securities?

For now, the answer is no, but what matters is that it does not matter. Even though calibrating a deal can lead to various dollar prices, this affects neither the validity of our credit knowledge nor the uniqueness of *Value*. Uniqueness of price can only arise based on the uniqueness of *Value*. It can never come from the secondary market because that market is itself predicated on the prior existence of *Value*. The fact that the latter can lead to various numbers, whereby each is considered an acceptable *Value*, does not imply that *Value* is non-unique since the truth of *Value* does not rely on its numerical representation. Similarly, when a man is on his third wife and counting, he cannot tell himself that the first two were somehow *mistakes*, for this is not how life works.

Value and Agreement

Let us look at this strange *agreement* a little more closely. In saying that equation (23) defines the *Value* of a deal, what have we really said? In essence, we are asking the more basic question: what is *valuable* in *Value*? A while ago, we answered this question in an apparently trite manner by saying that *Value* was credible because it was *unique*, i.e., that uniqueness is what is valuable in *Value* and thus that uniqueness 'is' *Value*. Although this makes perfect sense, it says nothing at all, for how is *Value* supposed to become unique in the first place?

The answer to this puzzle is obvious and for now, equally trivial. It is that uniqueness comes about through the *agreement* of the parties standing in the light of *Value*. Objects over which widespread agreement exists are truly valuable in the sense we mean. The real question is clearly how this agreement is to be achieved within a lifetime. Here, *Value* does not simply mean something like "This is €3 per kilogram and that is €4 per kilogram, hence that is more *valuable* than this." All such talk is silly nonsense for it is confusing more *valuable* with more *expensive*. Of course, there lies the crux of the problem.

The entire basis of security valuation is precisely the fact that price is *linear*, whereas *Value* is *nonlinear*. Between the two lies an unfathomable gap, an abyss that cannot be traversed simply by doing a little more of the same. *Value* can never be attained from the standpoint of linearity. Reading one or, for that matter, 1,000 annual reports or prospectuses will never tell you whether a stock or a bond is valuable or not. Analysts with 10 years of experience are no more likely to determine *Value* than those with 10 days of experience. Valuation is not a statistical exercise whereby if you close a sufficient number of deals, eventually you will get the hang of it. This cannot and will not happen, because valuation is something stochastic, not statistical. In finance, there are no points for second place.

Discounting five years of free cash flow and calling that the *Value* of a stock or security is not only amateurish, it belies a complete misunderstanding of the inner sufficiency and necessity of *Value*. "Value-investing," if this label can be used at all, only means the recognition that price and *Value* are mutually alien concepts. After all, is not *every* investor interested in *Value*? What if some fund manager told you "Oh no, I'm not a value-investor. What I buy is truly worthless!"

The point is precisely to find situations where the price is lower than the *Value*. Usually, this means waiting patiently until, via the normal insanity of the markets, the price drops significantly below an already and independently determined *Value* for some security, and then buy into it. Of course, to the vulgar understanding it is obvious that one makes money when one *sells*. In fact, the situation is exactly the other way around. It is upon *purchase* and not sale that money is in fact made. Realizing a gain and recovering *Value* are two different things. The notion that *Value* can be derived from price is nonsense because it would amount to squaring the circle, something that has eluded mankind since time immemorial. The problem is not that quadrature has yet to be discovered. The problem, rather, is the naïve belief in the outer possibility of *Value*.

The wild gyrations of the capital markets can never tell you about *Value*, only about price, and a true value-investor is just someone who knows perfectly well that *Value* is not something he can change. It is, as we have repeated so many times now, unique. Therefore, the only consistently successful investment avenue is to buy when the price falls below the *Value*, and wait till the former floats back up to the latter (as it always does). Although the idea that doing this is making money could not

526 • ELEMENTS OF STRUCTURED FINANCE

be further from the truth, most analysts believe it is the purview of demigods. As simple as this concept is to grasp, its consistent application is usually considered an unbelievable prowess and a sign of utter transcendence. In fact, when an investor keeps to this elementary formula for a few years, he is usually declared *legendary*, no doubt to his greatest surprise.

Well then, how are agreement and *Value* related? What do we call a thing over which quasi-universal agreement exists? The answer is: a *commodity*. But, what is *commode* in a commodity? The word *commode* comes from a Latin expression meaning useful; thus being a commodity means being useful. Somehow, there seems to be a connection between usefulness and *Value*. Yes, but where is it? More specifically, how come we find that useful things are more valuable than other things?

For example, gold is valuable and yet for almost all intents and purposes it is truly useless. The answer is that gold itself is not what is valuable. Rather, it is the use we can extract from gold by exchanging it for something truly useful. A thing that derives its *Value* purely via exchange is called *money*. So it is clear that money itself, i.e., money qua cash, is not what is valuable but that, here again, *Value* rests fundamentally on the usefulness of the exchange. To *define* money as "a store of value," the way economists are unfortunately wont to do, is to understand nothing about money. If the best a chemist could do were to define a fuel as "a store of energy," then it is chemistry and not economics we would be calling the dismal science.

In the usefulness of a thing lies its *Value*, that is all. We can already hear you say: "What's the point?" The point is that usefulness does not exist as a property independent of our own selves. People are the source of *Value*, not the other way around. Commodities do not exist a priori, they are manmade. What about soy beans, crude oil, and pork bellies? Don't they *exist* beforehand? Sure, they do, but what *exists* in that way is not a commodity, it is nothing. Agreement can never and will never exist about some random pork belly lying out there in Chicago. The *commode* in the commodity, i.e., its *Value,* is only what is manmade in it, what came out of our own heads. What we are trying to intimate to you, not so subtly perhaps, is the realization that that which comes out of our selves is the simple.

The commodity *gold* is not some piece of gold around your finger. Rather, it is a relational construct consisting of metal with specific mathematical properties like Carat weight, purity, and so on. Agreement, which is the ultimate source of *Value*, arises solely based on that construction. The truth of the agreement comes about only because it is predicated on something manmade. This will not make sense until you realize that whatever we find valuable in something is always manmade, otherwise it is worthless, i.e., nothing. What we are, in fact, in agreement about is not the gold or the pork belly, but our own thinking; not something *out there*, something unknown, but something *in here*.

A commodity is nothing but a mathematical construct and we can agree on it only because we *know* it in advance. Thus, mathematical reduction is the fundamental presupposition of the inner possibility of knowledge. When you know something, *what* you know is something mathematical. Perhaps now you can understand why reducing an object to mathematics allows us to agree, for to agree only means to be sure. You're sure because you're already sure.

Value agreement on commodities is more universal simply because numbers are the most accessible formation of the mathematical. However, they can no more exhaust the mathematical than King Lear can exhaust family values. The *Value* of a deal can be unique only when derived from a mathematical analysis and cannot come from the deal itself, for it is only based on valuation that a deal can first emerge. *Value* comes first, the deal second.

The more something can be mathematically de-constructed via the reductive process outlined previously, and then re-constructed, the more agreement will exist on its *Value*. What must be understood is that *Value* derives exclusively from that process, that everything else is in fact nothing. A building per se is *not* valuable; people living in it, now that's *Value*!

Now, do you not see how *Value* and usefulness are really the same?

Value and Liquidity

After all this, if you still believe that deals have *Value* you understand nothing about finance and you should go back to chapter 1. Rather, it is *Value* that "has" deals because the latter can only come into existence based on the valuation process. *Value* does not somehow attach to a deal already existing and just waiting for a kind and clever soul to assign it a *number*. Rather, it is through valuation that deals first reveal themselves as such. This is why it is impossible for a deal to have two *Values*, for that would be like a country having two *Presidents.* If this is true, then the country simply has *no* President. The deal and its *Value* are the same notion. The *Value* of the deal is the reason for its existence; it is the *ground* of the deal. In other words, deals have one *Value* and one *Value* alone because this is how they become deals in the first place. Their value "is" what they are. What they are "is" their *Value*. The concepts *Deal* and *Value* are therefore inseparable, i.e., nonlinear. Such essential relatedness is the very magic that allows deals to be uniquely valued.

When disagreement arises on deal valuation, it simply means that those who disagree are looking at *different* deals. Disagreement can only come about from the voluntary incompleteness of our own logical construction, from wanton, unnecessary, and always convenient assumptions. The deal is simply what it is. It always remains equal to itself. To say that the *Value* of a deal is *uncertain* is a barefaced lie, for it hides the plain truth that *we* are the ones who are uncertain, who have no ground. Valuation is not difficult because it is complex, but on the contrary, because it is so simple.

Doing a deal only means reducing its world to a set of deterministic, mathematical substructures that let it emerge by itself. The difference is that now, the formations of the mathematical we must employ go far beyond the sheer numerology that circumscribes the concept of a commodity. Once this is accomplished, we have *created* the deal, our own deal. We can value deals, i.e., we can *know* deals, simply because they are the products of our own minds. Otherwise, valuation means nothing.

Agreement on commodities can be so widespread only because the level of mathematical knowledge they require is so basic as to be intuitive to almost everyone.

Such quasi-universal agreement is the essence of what we call *liquidity*. Hence relatively speaking, commodities are highly liquid assets. In fact, the most liquid of all assets is the one that has no other function than to be the measure of itself, the commodity that is most exclusively mathematical. What is that? Cash of course!

To increase liquidity simply means to increase agreement, which in turn amounts to achieving uniqueness of *Value*. To do this is our task here, the task of dealing. It will not do to blame deals for being *too complex* to model, as if they were somehow thrown onto the markets from on high *via* a process over which we had no control. Deals are not too complex, for they are just what they are. It is we, who are too simplistic, too ignorant. As that deservedly famous English playwright would surely have said, "the fault, dear trader, lies not in our deals but in our selves."

The upshot of this convoluted discussion is that uniqueness defines *Value* merely because it is the precondition for the possibility of the deal. This is what we mean when we say that the essence of dealing is the ground of the inner possibility of *Value*. When you can feel this down to the very depth of your own-most soul, only then have you paid the price of admission to the inner sanctum of finance.

22.9 PARAMETRIC SPACE CONVERGENCE: OPTIMALITY

With the expression "parametric space," we wish to define the multidimensional manifold formed by the deal's basic parameters. Although unlimited theoretically, there will seldom be more than 10 arbitrary parameters in any realistic transaction. What follows is a short account of convergence properties inside parametric space.

The Topology of Parametric Space

As shown in the last section, convergence to a fixed point in yield space is the process whereby self-consistency in structured analysis is achieved. It is fairly intuitive to see that a fixed point can only be "fixed" for given structures, i.e., that only as long as basic deal parameters like tranche sizing, trigger levels, and others remain unchanged can we truthfully claim that a fixed point will exist and that it will be unique. Some of you may already be wondering what happens to the fixed point, specifically to its uniqueness property, if structural parameters are modified.

It stands to reason that the deal will not work at arbitrary issuance levels, regardless of what lawyers, investment bankers, and accountants might say about it. Otherwise, what would stop you from raising issuance indefinitely, perhaps under the spell of some romantic story? As a result, we will find that deals will not possess *Value* outside a finite region of parametric space and in a way highly reminiscent of yield space. Inside this stable region, the deal will converge to a different fixed point, in theory at least, with respect to each parametric combination. Outside the stable region, it will diverge. Furthermore, as you have already guessed, an intermediate region will also exist where the situation will be "iffy," i.e., where the deal may or may not converge depending on the scenario-count and other factors. The intuition garnered from yield space can therefore be carried over unaltered to parametric space where we observe the same three convergence regions.

By analogy with yield space, we designate convergence regions in parametric space using the labels hyperbolic, elliptic, and parabolic, respectively. Again, please do not confuse *yield* space (figure 22.5), where the dimensions are the various tranche interest rates in the deal, with *parametric* space (figure 22.6) for the same deal, where they are the axes along which we measure its parameters. You should think of a deal's parameters as the values *a*, *b*, and *c* on the right-hand side of equation (19). While the deal's topological behavior is formally identical in both cases, the spaces themselves are not.

To better visualize this new space, consider figure 22.6, which is nothing but the analogue of figure 22.5 in parametric space. It shows what happens topologically inside a deal where we have conceptually reduced the number of degrees of freedom to two, here arbitrarily chosen as *Total Net Issuance*[13] and *Delinquency Trigger Level* as a percentage of the currently outstanding pool balance.

Just like figure 22.5, note how the hyperbolic region in figure 22.6 is finite. For ease of presentation, we have shown only the relevant portion of the deal's stability region. For instance, in the case of the Total Net Issuance dimension it is clear that we can issue an aggregate amount of securities equal to zero out of any pool and that this "solution" is feasible and stable in the trivial sense. Here, we are mainly interested in what happens at the high end of the issuance range.

As advertised, a parabolic strip can be found around the hyperbolic stability region. As expected, the range of allowable trigger levels compatible with a feasible solution decreases as issuance increases.

The second noteworthy behavioral pattern is the generally negatively sloped orientation of the stable region. This is merely a reflection of the fact that as total issuance increases, the range of delinquency trigger levels leading to convergence

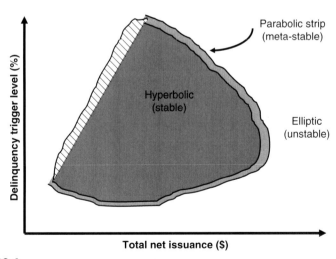

FIGURE 22.6
The parametric space and deal pricing.

must perforce decrease since more spread must be captured inside the structure to justify the same rating or to simply allow the deal to converge at all.

Toward a Definition of the "Optimal" Deal

Now consider figure 22.7, showing the situation as it is likely to present itself to an analyst after mapping out the hyperbolic manifold. As you can imagine, in practice the parametric space will be multidimensional and nowhere near as intuitive or smooth as what shows up in figure 22.7. In this case, the situation is clear. Looking at the top branch of the stability region for the moment we see that as trigger levels increase, Total Net Issuance T compatible with a convergent solution decreases. This is simply a reflection of the fact that less spread can be accumulated inside the structure under stress cases. In fact, it would be amazing if this were not the case for how else could deals put an end to themselves except via instability. In other words given a delinquency trigger level, something usually decided a priori by the issuer from unrelated considerations, we are in a position to recommend to the client a one-parameter family of solutions to the liquidity problem, i.e., those extending from zero to the *Issuance Limit* line shown in figure 22.7. This family represents the deal's corresponding issuance window and can be defined as the range $T \in [0, T_M]$ whereby T_M is the maximum feasible issuance. As shown in figure 22.7, given trigger level L_0 this seller could only issue an amount T_m, where $T_m < T_M$.

The thought that one would automatically select the far end of the hyperbolic region as the best proposal to the client is *nonsense* since this solution might unduly constrain the issuer operationally and lead to counter-productive behavior, one that would in fact undermine the very performance we seek to ascertain. Too much of a good thing may well turn out to be a bad thing.

In other words, the parabolic strip's entire inner border should be considered the locus of optimality for this transaction, and not simply the point T_M. The issuer and

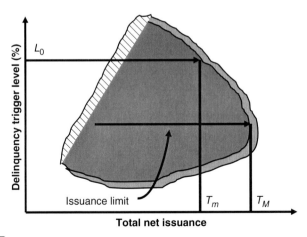

FIGURE 22.7

Deal optimality and structured analysis.

the investors can be left to decide where along that border the deal should go to market. Now at least, the full range of possibilities can be presented to the client in an unequivocal manner and the parties can come together with something to discuss. In the end, all deals are optimal in some sense.

For instance, if ad hoc restrictions on credit ratings are present, we might be forced to choose a lesser issuance level than we might have otherwise contemplated. For any given deal, there exists an infinite array of structuring possibilities, each offering its own brand of optimality. The only constant in all of this is that the one-size-fits-all framework in structured finance is a nonstarter.

The Credit Spectrum Inherent in Parametric Space

Some readers might be wondering what happens inside the hyperbolic region. If all the associated structures are convergent, does this mean that they converge to the same point? Clearly not, for how can we speak of an issuance *range* if nothing changes? What does change is the location of the fixed point in yield space, i.e., the credit ratings associated with the various tranches of the deal.

Going from zero to the maximum issuance T_M, we are in fact traveling the entire credit spectrum. At relatively small issuances, the deal will converge to a sequence of structures in which both classes will be rated "Aaa." At or near T_M however, the A Class might be rated Ba1 while the B Class would barely make it to Caa3. The fact that the deal converges in no way obligates it to converge to an acceptable investment opportunity. Although all converged transactions are equally good from the numerical standpoint, whether they *work* from other points of view is another matter.

As we have said so many times before, it is a common investor misconception that a good deal in terms of investment potential is a risk-less deal. In fact, a good deal is just a deal priced below its *Value* and vice versa for a bad deal. Thus, to know whether a deal is good or bad merely requires knowledge of its *Value*, because the market price itself is obviously known. For an investor, buying a deal below its *Value* is what is *good*. Doing this obviously requires *Value* to be known in the first place for only then can the price be given its true meaning. This is what investing is really about.

Therefore, across the issuance window, $T \in [0, T_M]$ the deal's tranches will be spanning the whole spectrum of creditworthiness, at least one point of which potentially satisfies both issuer and investor. Obviously, the same game can be played vertically for a given issuance size with respect to the delinquency trigger level. Since the concept is entirely analogous, we skip the discussion altogether.

22.10 A LIVE EXAMPLE OF CONVERGENCE IN YIELD SPACE

As highlighted in chapter 14, some readers may rightly be wondering whether this method works at all. It seems so complicated and uncanny that perhaps it is nothing but smoke and mirrors designed to fool unsuspecting investors If you are asking yourself such questions, you are already on your way to an answer. Believe it or not, this is the simple in a deal. The simple is what lasts when a deal meanders through time, i.e., through original time. It is the only way a deal can come to itself from out of itself and reveal its essence, its *Value*.

However, the proof is in the pudding. In the space allotted to us (no pun intended), we do not have the luxury of fully exploring parametric space, but let's peek into Banach Land a little bit.

As an example of convergence in an actual transaction, table 22.1 and figure 22.8 show the target deal's convergence history in yield space for the parametric set given in table 22.2. *Alpha* in table 22.1 is the convergence criterion, here set to 10 bps. The initial rate-vector was set to 7.0% for the Class A and 10.0% for the Class B using the back of the envelope (BOTE) approach reviewed in earlier chapters.

TABLE 22.1

Target deal convergence history in yield space

RUN ID	A DIRR (BPS)	B DIRR (BPS)	A RATE (%)	B RATE (%)	ALPHA
0	–	–	7.00	10.00	1.0
1	0.97	129.98	5.12	8.86	0.2375
2	0.39	62.06	5.36	7.78	0.0623
3	0.33	66.32	5.30	7.63	0.0137
4	0.28	62.45	5.29	7.54	0.0028
5	0.32	66.47	5.31	7.58	0.0028
6	0.26	58.38	5.28	7.47	0.0061
7	0.26	58.97	5.29	7.46	0.0010

Class A *WAL*: 27.5 months   Class B *WAL*: 28.0 months

Class A Rating: *Aa*1   Class B Rating: *Ba*1

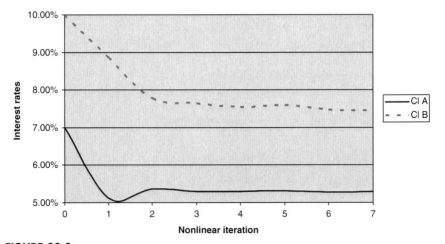

FIGURE 22.8

Non–linear convergence history in yield space.

TABLE 22.2

Parametric set for the target deal

PARAMETER ID	VALUE
Asset Class	Autos
Principal Allocation Scheme	Pro Rata
A Class Initial Balance	$29,937,671.49
B Class Initial Balance	$7,484,417.87
Delinquency Trigger Type	Binary
Delinquency Trigger Index	Quart. 60+ DPD
Delinquency Trigger Level	10%
Reserve Account Target Level (% Current Balance)	3.0%
Pool Balance	$37,422,089.37
Estimated Recoveries	See chapter 17
Percent Current Loans at Closing	100%
Gross Expected Loss	17.37%
Macroeconomic Simulation Method	Clayton Copula
Estimated Recovery Delay	3 months
WAC	16.65%
WAM	60.34 months

Finally, as an example of coding the nonlinear valuation loop, we present as exhibit 22.1 the VBA implementation that led to table 22.1, but without relaxation mechanics (see "Successive Relaxation in Yield Space" below). As you can see, the code is trivial compared to what we have already gone through to get here.

With a 10 bps threshold value for alpha, the rates converge self-consistently to within 1 bps, which is far more accurate than any current or past method of analysis. The equilibrium interest rates are given in the last row (Run ID: 7) of table 22.1 and the corresponding letter-grade ratings, shown in the last row, drop out as a byproduct. This is the end of the road for this deal.

Exhibit 22.1: Nonlinear Convergence in Yield Space

Run the nonlinear loop

```
Sub AnalyzeDeal()
Dim deal As deal, n As Integer, alpha As Double, r As Range
Call ReadDeal(deal)
deal.enablePrepayModel = True
randVdc_seq = 1
Dim aInitBal As Double, bInitBal As Double
```

continues to next page

```
continued from previous page
alnitBal = deal.alpha * deal.poolBal
blnitBal = (1 - deal.alpha) * deal.poolBal
Set r = Range("NonLinearConv")
r.ClearContents
Range("Ratings").ClearContents
Dim i As Integer

For i = 1 To max_non_linear_iterations
Dim ayr As Double, byr As Double, ata As Double, bta As Double, ar As Double, br As
Double
Call RunDealSim(deal, n, ayr, byr, ata, bta)
ar = YieldCurvePlusSpread(deal, ata, ayr)
br = YieldCurvePlusSpread(deal, bta, byr)
alpha = (alnitBal * Abs((ar - deal.aRate) / deal.aRate) + blnitBal * Abs((br - deal.bRate)
/ deal.bRate)) / deal.poolBal
r.Cells(i, 1) = ayr
r.Cells(i, 2) = byr
r.Cells(i, 3) = ar
r.Cells(i, 4) = br
r.Cells(i, 5) = alpha

Once we have reached the convergence threshold, exit the loop

If alpha < threshold Then Exit For
End If
deal.aRate = ar
deal.bRate = br
Next i

Obtain corresponding Moody's letter grade credit ratings

Range("Ratings").Cells(1) = GetRating(ayr)
Range("Ratings").Cells(2) = GetRating(byr)
End Sub
```

22.11 SUCCESSIVE RELAXATION IN YIELD SPACE

Within the nonlinear context, a critical component of the analytics of structured finance is the introduction of relaxation methods as convergence-control mechanisms. Although the transaction as structured may in fact lie inside the hyperbolic region, some of the transitional stages leading to a converged result may cause the iteration to diverge for purely numerical reasons. It is to avoid an erratic convergence history, which may in certain cases lead to numerical divergence, that we introduce the use of relaxation methods.

You will recall that, as shown in figure 22.1, following every iteration in yield space, each of which consisting of an entire MC simulation, we are able to compute new tranche rates for each class of note in the deal. The latter rates are then fed back into the structure to become the input rates for the next nonlinear iteration. The relaxation concept refers to the mechanism through which tranche rates are updated between two linear simulations. When precisely the full update is allowed to take place, the process is said to be *fully* relaxed. When less than the full update is permitted, we talk about *under-relaxation* and conversely, when more than the full update is enforced, we speak of *over-relaxation*.

What immediately comes to mind is why we would even consider under- or over-relaxing any tranche in the first place? After all, isn't this system supposed to work by itself? The truth is that the transaction's drivers will subject different tranches to different effective yield scales. In practical terms, exhibit 22.1 cannot represent a general solution to the relaxation problem because, while Class A may be relatively stable, more junior classes will clearly display higher volatility, both numerically and practically speaking. In fact, their empirical volatility arises from their numerical volatility, not the other way around. In other words, senior classes are *less* nonlinear than junior classes. As we move down the capital structure, each tranche will thus be associated with a corresponding yield-range that will make it increasingly susceptible to secular instabilities due to the requirement of increased resolution brought about by such scales. If we did nothing, the deal could diverge merely for lack of control at the junior level when in fact a stable solution does exist.

The upshot is that we should allow tranche-wise convergence within yield space in accordance with a scaling factor appropriate to each class, and this means that senior classes can be over-relaxed while junior classes commonly need to be under-relaxed. Obviously, this does not amount to a theory of relaxation, only to a rule of thumb.

To implement relaxation, proceed as follows. First, assume that in the target deal we have performed Monte Carlo simulation n using yield-vector r^n and that we are now ready to compute the next iterate-vector r^{n+1} using a yield update rule formulated as follows:

$$r_i^{n+1} = r_i^n + \lambda_i \, \Delta r_i^n \tag{24}$$

In equation (24), parameter λ_i is a tranche-wise relaxation coefficient of order one. As indicated here, this parameter rules the relaxation process via the tranche increment Δr_i^n computed from the yield curve function Y_c as follows:

$$\Delta r_i^n = Y_c(\overline{t_i^n}, \Delta IRR_i^n) - r_i^n \tag{25}$$

This yield curve model (see "Yield Curve Modeling" below) takes as inputs, with respect to tranche i, the weighted average life $\overline{t_i^n}$ and the average yield reduction ΔIRR_i^n, both of which are tranche-wise outputs of any given MC simulation.

This means that if $\lambda_i = 1$ the new rates are simply set equal to the output of the yield curve model (i.e., the abscissa of the Y_c function) resulting from the last MC simulation.

It would be nice if credit spreads and yield reductions were in fact numerically identical, but the market does not work like that. The average yield reduction should be conceived as a measure of risk commanding a given credit spread, a risk premium, rather than as the spread itself. Otherwise, all Aaa structured bonds would sell at the Treasury rate, which hardly seems reasonable since most ABS issuers do not have nuclear weapons at their disposal to enforce their claims.

We can now formally define the familiar notions of successive over- and under-relaxation, *SOR* and *SUR*, respectively, as follows:

$$SOR \equiv \lambda_i \in (1, \infty) \tag{26}$$

$$SUR \equiv \lambda_i \in (0, 1) \tag{27}$$

This implies that whenever $\lambda > 1$, tranche rates will be updated by a greater amount, either positive or negative, than that warranted by the yield curve transformation. When $\lambda < 1$ holds, the opposite will be the case. Over-relaxation drives the system to its fixed-point solution faster than it would reach it on its own, and vice versa for under-relaxation. Under-relaxation has the advantage of damping yield oscillations that otherwise could cause provisional solutions to spin out of control when a bona fide fixed-point solution does exist.

Since we would like to reach the solution rate-vector as fast as possible, over-relaxation is usually the way to go as long as it does not destabilize the deal. As explained above, senior tranches more stable than junior tranches and better able to withstand over-relaxation. As a rule, initially you will want to drive the provisional solution vector to its fixed point using over-relaxation on senior tranches and under-relaxation on junior tranches. However, as the solution progresses, it is propitious to modulate tranche-wise relaxation factors in a cascading manner, thereby allowing increased relaxation on junior tranches in concert with the convergence properties of senior tranches. In other words, once senior tranches have settled down sufficiently, one can increase junior relaxation factors to try and accelerate convergence as much as possible.

Investigating this process obviously makes more sense when the number of tranches is in the high single digits rather than the low single digits. In deals with five credit tranches or more, CPU-time savings from a properly designed tranche-wise relaxation plan may be significant. Taking our lead from numerical analysis in general, the appropriate metric for relaxation-factor modulation is the slope of the yield curve update Δr_i^n as a function of n, the iterate counter. This means that the value of each tranche-wise relaxation parameter λ_i should be specified as a negatively sloped, monotonic function of Δr_i^n as shown in figure 22.9.

As you can see, if the pure yield-curve update for a given class is relatively large, the tranche should be under-relaxed, and conversely if the update is relatively small. The entire MC simulation can thus remain on autopilot along the path to convergence. Under this system, all tranches will successively over-relax themselves as they approach their final yield space location. Otherwise, numerical experiments need to be performed beforehand by simply letting the system crunch numbers. In the case of our two-tranche target transaction, relaxation analysis is clearly not needed. In general, we find that with respect to transactions containing two or three credit tranches, the effort expended in determining the optimal relaxation pattern is

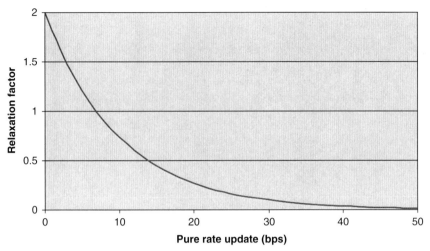

FIGURE 22.9
Suggested form for the λ_i modulating function.

simply not worth the computational savings since the deal will usually converge in less than 10 nonlinear iterations. For the target transaction, relaxation factors of order one were used.

Exhibit 22.2:   The Successive Over-Relaxation Algorithm inside the Nonlinear Loop

```
------ (same nonlinear code as before) ---------
br = YieldCurvePlusSpread(deal, bta, byr)
ar = deal.aRate + deal.aRelax * (ar - deal.aRate) (Class A relaxation)
br = deal.bRate + deal.bRelax * (br - deal.bRate) (Class B relaxation)
alpha = (aInitBal * Abs((ar - deal.aRate) / deal.aRate) + bInitBal * Abs((br - deal.bRate)
/ deal.bRate)) / deal.poolBal
------ (same nonlinear code as before) ---------
```

Exercise 22.3

In order to become familiar with the notion of relaxation in structured finance and in numerical analysis in general, it is appropriate to experiment with the technique in a completely different setting, albeit one that clearly brings out the issues. Rather than belaboring some unknown structured deal and compounding the mystery, let's stick to something everyone should understand intuitively: heat. In what follows, we explore the technique of relaxation using the steady-state heat equation.

continues to next page

continued from previous page
Problem Statement

Say you are designing a Roman-style house where heating is provided through the floor. The room you are presently designing is shaped as a thin rectangle with sides A and L, and with the property $A \gg L$. This is shown in figure 22.10.

You have decided to provide heat using electrical wires located in the floor itself. However, in order to economize, you want to manage the density of the wires by placing more of them toward the center of the room, where people are going to live, and fewer toward the walls where the furniture will be placed. This type of arrangement is shown in a cross-view through the floor in figure 22.11.

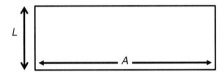

FIGURE 22.10
Economic heating inside a Roman-style house.

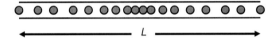

FIGURE 22.11
Electrical wire probability density function.

The problem is to calculate the temperature distribution that will result from this variable density arrangement and hence to optimize the placement of the wires. In order to do this, you will need to solve the steady-state heat equation with heat sources or sinks.

Skipping the standard heat balance derivation from your first-year college physics course, we arrive at normalized equation (28) for the temperature in the slab. Normalization simply means that some of the physical constants have been absorbed inside others so you do not see them explicitly.

$$\nabla^2 T = q(\mathbf{x}) \tag{28}$$

On the right-hand side of equation (28), we have formally defined the quantity $q(\mathbf{x})$ as the variable heat flux issuing from the electrical wiring in the floor. Note that the flux is variable because it varies across the floor, not across time. This is still a steady-state problem.

Now, by assumption we have $A \gg L$. This allows us to stick to a one-dimensional version of the heat equation, thereby considerably simplifying our problem. Please note that the same would obtain, if instead of a semi-infinite floor, we assumed the floor to be infinitesimally thin. This is another example where *zero* and *infinity* are the same.

As a result of this simplifying assumption, we can rewrite equation (28) as follows:

$$\frac{d^2 T}{dx^2} = q(x) \tag{29}$$

Now, assume that the symmetry of the situation coupled with the variable density of the wires across the floor allow us to specify the flux $q(x)$ as a parabolic function similar to equation (18). Therefore, we can state:

$$q(x) \equiv Lx - x^2 + b \tag{30}$$

You may assume $b = 1$ because the actual value of this parameter has nothing to do with the intent of the problem. As you can see, the maximum flux occurs at the location:

$$\frac{\partial q(x)}{\partial x} = 0 \Rightarrow x = \frac{L}{2}$$

For the purpose of this exercise, you will be asked to solve the following Dirichlet problem:

$$T(0) = 0 \tag{31a}$$

$$T(L) = 0 \tag{31b}$$

Now, using a Cartesian grid for the independent variable x with $x_i \equiv \frac{i}{n}L$, $i \in [0, n]$, you can express equation (29) using the standard second-order discretization formula on this grid in the form of equation (32):

$$\frac{T_{i-1} - 2T_i + T_{i+1}}{\Delta x^2} = q(x_i) \tag{32}$$

You have elected to use successive over-relaxation to solve equation (32) by using the basic technique of red–black ordering. Essentially, this means that you regard odd-numbered points as *black* and even-numbered points as *red*. Doing this to equation (32) is equivalent to labeling T_i as black during one pass while T_{i+1} and T_{i-1} will both be red during the same pass, and vice versa during the next.

Now, solve equation (32) by successively updating the black and red grids. While you are solving the black points, the red points are assumed known, and vice versa. Doing this allows you to place the off-color points on the right-hand side of the update equation, obviating the use of the tridiagonal solver that would normally be required to obtain a one-step solution to equation (32). Effectively, this amounts to solving odd-numbered points in one pass and even-numbered points in the next.

On each separate grid, we can state the basic update rule via:

$$T_i^{n+1} = \frac{1}{2}\left[q(x_i)\Delta x^2 + \left(T_{i-1}^n + T_{i+1}^n\right)\right] \equiv F(T_i^n) \tag{33}$$

In order to start, you need to assume some initial distribution for the temperature, which will most likely be wrong. Say you are starting with the following unreasonable start-up temperature distribution:

$$T^0(x) \equiv 0, \forall x \in [0, L] \tag{34}$$

However, instead of letting the solution converge *naturally* to its final position using update rule (33), you have decided to go faster and use successive over-relaxation, or SOR. To do this, you first define the update factor:

$$\Delta_i^n = F(T_i^n) - T_i^n \tag{35}$$

continues to next page

continued from previous page

Then, you create the over-relaxed temperature update rule:

$$T_i^{n+1} = T_i^n + \alpha \, \Delta_i^n, \ \alpha \in [0, \infty) \tag{36}$$

With respect to our target transaction, update rules (35) and (36) are formally identical to equations (25) and (24), respectively. Parameter α is clearly the relaxation factor and is restricted to the domain indicated on the right-hand side of equation (36).

Assignment

Your task is to solve equation (32) using the rule (36) but with 20 different values of α in the range $\alpha \in [0, 10]$. How fast does the iteration converge with this selection of over-relaxation parameter?

As a first check, use a sequence of discretization grids where the number of points n is in the set $n \in [10, 50, 100, 250, 500, 1000]$. Does the normalized solution converge faster with more points, slower? In other words, where do things stand with respect to convergence as a function of n?

Next, change the value of b in equation (30) and do this again. Does the value of b make a difference? Now, change the left, right, and both boundary conditions in equation (31) and redo the same exercise. Use the range $T(0), T(L) \in [-10, 10]$. Does a change in boundary condition make a difference to the rate of convergence to the final solution?

Next, instead of the initial temperature distribution (34), use the one-parameter family of distributions defined via equation (37):

$$T^0(x) \equiv c \frac{e^{-(x-\frac{L}{2})}}{\left[1 + e^{-(x-\frac{L}{2})}\right]^2}, \ c \in [-3, 3] \tag{37}$$

For each experiment, plot the rate of convergence as a function of α. You can define the convergence rate any way you like, but if you do not have a favorite norm already, just use the well-known Sobolev norm:

$$\Sigma(n) = \frac{1}{L} \int_0^L [\Delta T^n]^2 dx \tag{38}$$

In equation (38), we have defined $\Delta T^n = T^n - T^{n-1}$.

After thoroughly going through this exercise, you should have a good idea of how to make judicious use of relaxation methods in structured finance.

Note: We should mention that in numerical analysis, spontaneous and unreflected impulses to be creative should be resisted as much as possible, for such unclean thoughts are usually punished severely and immediately. ◀

Many pitfalls lie in wait for you on the path to success, and we recommend that while doing a live deal is not the right time to attempt something new. Rather, you should perform the experiment quietly, i.e., without the added pressure of dealmaking on your shoulders. For a method to go smoothly in practice, you should have had so much practice with it that even thinking about it makes you sick.

As a simple example of relaxation in situ, we present as exhibit 22.2 a VBA implementation of equations (24). The relatively equal size of Classes A and B makes much of this section's arguments moot. Even though the two tranches might seem widely different to the casual observer, they are in fact of the same order of magnitude, which is what we really mean by *equal size.*

22.12 ILL-POSEDNESS IN STRUCTURED FINANCE

Over the last few sections, we have outlined how deal space could be conceived as two separate vector subspaces: yield space and parametric space. In each one, we then defined nonoverlapping regions where the deal would either converge (hyperbolic) or diverge (elliptic), as well as a third, parabolic region consisting of a thin strip at the border between the first two regions where the ultimate outcome depended on certain global system parameters like the number of Monte Carlo scenarios.

Although the divergence of the iterative process was labeled *ill-posedness* in both cases, the latter term refers to something markedly different in each one. In this section, we want to stress the conceptual difference between ill-posedness in each vector space as guidance to analysts struggling with live implementations.

Yield Space Ill-Posedness

As you will recall, yield space is the place where the deal comes together as long as the initial yield vector is selected inside the hyperbolic region, turning the iteration into a Cauchy sequence. The deal can then be valued as the vector r^∞ lying at the fixed point of the iterative map $g(r)$. Outside this region, the deal diverges and cannot be valued. This is the behavior we label ill-posedness in yield space. In other words, as long as starting rate-vectors are properly selected, the value V of the deal is unique, i.e., the deal *exists*.

The selection of suitable initial guesses is not difficult once prior transactions of the same type are factored into the analysis. You will soon discover that yield space is in fact quite robust and will usually display reproducible behavior under similar circumstances. Here, ill-posedness is simply caused by a misunderstanding of the deal's basic possibilities on the part of the structured analyst and not due to some fundamental problem. In a nutshell, the issue is simply that the analyst is unable to locate the hyperbolic region despite his or her best efforts.

This situation can be remedied relatively quickly, either by using a back-of-the-envelope (BOTE) credit analysis, letting it dictate the starting yield-vector, or *via* proxy values on similar transactions. In both cases, the deal will normally begin to converge rightaway. For example, if the WAC of the pool is 12%, the deal can obviously not converge with an initial Class B rate of 35%. Hopefully, it is not too hard to see why this initial guess lies inside the elliptic region.

In all cases, physical or legal constraints will exist prior to the valuation exercise that will guide the analyst as to the rough location of the hyperbolic region. As a result, once you have valued a few transactions, recognizing the hyperbolic region will usually not pose a problem because the basic existence of the deal will already be assured. Banach's theorem tells us that once a deal can be shown to exist its

Value is unique. The strange beauty of structured analysis lies in the fact that this is so.

Parametric Space Ill-Posedness

As a result of the foregoing, it is easy to surmise that the authentic struggle, characteristic of ill-posedness, is found not in yield space, but rather in parametric space for there, special situations can arise whereby deals may not exist at all. In the absence of existence, the uniqueness issue is moot.

Recall from "The Value of the Deal" how the deal's Value spanned the entire credit spectrum as you traversed the hyperbolic region in parametric space. Although the fixed point was still unique given each parametric combination, its location had to change to reflect the credit consequences of variable issuance levels and other deal parameters. In fact, this movement through the credit scale was the mechanism that allowed the deal to *speak* to us and to reveal itself as more or less risky. Here, ill-posedness is far more serious since there may be no solution in yield space despite the analyst's utter familiarity with this collateral. In other words, the deal may not *work*.

The problem is not that this happens, for we should all be thankful that it does. Rather, it is that an inexperienced structured analyst may mistake this second type of ill-posedness for the first one, thereby engaging in a futile experiment, diligently looking, wide-eyed and bushy-tailed, for something that can never be found. It is problematic especially because, as you will remember, from the client's standpoint optimal transactions are bound to lie inside the parabolic strip, i.e., exactly where the analyst is likely to encounter the case of vanishing regional stability. This is an area where deal space intricacy comes to the fore quite forcedly and compels structured analysts to tread carefully lest they spin their wheels forever, effectively turning deal valuation into meaningless number crunching.

The solution to this conundrum is to begin the valuation exercise in a region of parametric space where the second type of ill-posedness is unlikely to occur and to let the deal stabilize inside its preliminary feasible universe. Starting from this feasible domain, the parametric envelope can then be pushed out one dimension at a time on the way to optimality. As this is done, the sensitivity of the deal's valuation vector can be monitored, thus allowing the detection of incipient instability. In most cases, various physical, investor, accounting and legal constraints will preclude the valuation search from exploring more than one or two parametric dimensions and the process will soon terminate around the credit point considered optimal given the regions of parametric space that must remain unexplored owing to such constraints. A secondary advantage of doing this is that the valuation exercise can usually be terminated at any time and the current structure declared locally optimal.

Please note that this does not amount to an exhaustive search for the global optimum, something lying clearly beyond the scope of this text.

22.13 YIELD CURVE MODELING

We close this topic with a short discussion of yield curve modeling, a necessary corollary to the mechanics of valuation. At the outset, remember that a yield curve *model* is not a *conditio sine qua non* of the analysis since the yield curve itself is observable. A simple polynomial form fitted to the daily values found in widely circulated financial publications will usually suffice.

However, the valuation problem is sufficiently nonlinear on its own without adding the additional noise arising from the vagaries of the marketplace, i.e., those causing discontinuous yield curves to emerge. As a result, it is usually a good idea to introduce a yield curve model that is both smooth and well-behaved rather than to ape empirical yield curves precisely, those that will all be wrong tomorrow anyway.

To do this, we first need to recall that total yield can be conceived as the sum of contributions from three distinct sources:

1. The equilibrium price of risk-free exchanges, i.e., whereby time vanishes
2. The credit risk premium, i.e., whereby nonlinear time is the essence
3. The liquidity premium, i.e., whereby linear time is the essence

Of these, only the first two can usually be referred to as analytic since the liquidity spread is obtained via difference, i.e., as the difference between the observed rate and the sum of the average credit spread and the risk-free rate. For instance, if the market rate on a tranche is 6.5%, the risk-free rate 4.2%, and the average credit spread 200 bps, it follows that the liquidity premium must have been $6.5 - [4.2 + 2] = 30$ bps. In other words, the liquidity spread is nothing more than a fudge factor often used as a prop to communicate to wondrous analysts how markets actually cleared.

Some might wish to explain liquidity spreads away by saying that primary market bonds expected to undergo few secondary market trades will command higher liquidity premiums than more *liquid* bonds. This is liquidity as fear of being stuck. But how do we then explain such fear, if not by the presence of a liquidity premium? This type of circular thinking obviously leads nowhere and the only reasonable approach is to subsume liquidity spreads under credit spreads, i.e., to assume that average liquidity spreads will vanish. Therefore, in what follows we ignore the deal's liquidity aspects since the basic promise of financial analysis is the elimination of all distinctions save that of economic loss. In other words, theoretically speaking liquidity spreads ought to converge to zero as well. Those of you who bother to reflect on our discussion of chapter 18 concerning liquidity propositions will understand immediately why this must be the case.

The Basic Yield Curve Model

Following the above considerations, we can formally state our yield curve model's basic schema:

$$\text{Yield curve} = \text{Treasury yield} + \text{credit spread}$$

This relation can be formalized using the continuous functions we used in chapter 21 of "*The Analysis of Structured Securities*" (OUP, 2003) where we dealt with the CDO of ABS. You will recall that we had introduced the following simple diffusion model:

$$Y_c(\bar{t}, \Delta IRR) = f(\bar{t}) + \alpha \sqrt{\bar{t}} \, \Delta IRR \tag{39}$$

In equation (39), the first term on the right is the risk-free rate and the second term is a diffusive credit spread with the familiar square root behavior. As the risk-free rate functional form $f(t)$, we had selected our old friend the logistic curve, but this time equipped with carefully chosen parameters:

$$f(\bar{t}) = \frac{r_\infty}{1 + \beta e^{-\delta \bar{t}}} \tag{40}$$

In equations (39) and (40) the input and output variables were defined as shown in table 22.3.

For example, using common structured rating definitions in terms of average reductions of yield, figure 22.12 shows total yield Y_c as a function of broad rating category using the following parametric set:

$$\alpha = 0.02 \quad r_\infty = 0.08 \quad \beta = 0.9 \quad \delta = 0.21$$

Exhibit 22.3 shows the VBA implementation of the same algorithm. As shown above, the yield curve comes into play inside the nonlinear portion of deal analysis.

Exhibit 22.3: Yield Curve Model Implementation

```
Sub ReadYieldCurveModel(deal As deal)
Dim r As Range
Set r = Range("YieldCurveModel")
deal.ycRInf = r.Cells(1)
deal.ycAlpha = r.Cells(2)
deal.ycBeta = r.Cells(3)
deal.ycDelta = r.Cells(4)
End Sub

Function YieldCurvePlusSpread(deal As deal, ta As Double, yr As Double) As Double

YieldCurvePlusSpread = ((deal.ycRInf * 100) / (1 + deal.ycBeta * Exp(-deal.ycDelta *
(ta / 12))) + deal.ycAlpha * Sqr((ta / 12) * yr / 100)) / 100

End Function
```

The advantage of using the above rate model, or any model for that matter, is that results will always make intuitive sense, i.e., the output from an analytical model will never contain the quirks that empirical yield curves commonly display. In other words, a yield curve model normally guarantees *smoothness* of the solution. Any remaining deal discontinuities will normally arise because of structural features kicking in under

TABLE 22.3
Variable definitions for the basic yield curve model

VARIABLE	DEFINITION
Y_c	Total rate as the sum of the risk-free rate and the credit spread (%)
$\bar{t}$	The weighted average life of a tranche (years)
ΔIRR	The average reduction of yield on a tranche expressed as a percentage
α	Calibration multiplier
r_∞	Limiting value of the risk-free rate as $\bar{t} \to \infty$
β	Logistic curve (equation 40) shifting parameter
δ	Logistic curve (equation 40) spreading parameter $(\text{year})^{-1}$

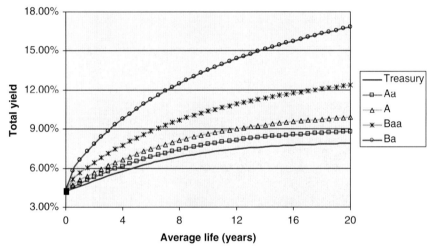

FIGURE 22.12
The basic yield curve model.

specified conditions, and never because the yield curve is somehow discontinuous at $\bar{t} = 2$ years for instance. We strongly encourage the use of a model fitted to actual market data rather than the direct use of the same data.

Exercise 22.4

Implement the yield curve model given by equations (39) and (40) and watch the behavior of credit spreads as average life is increased as compared to the average reduction of yield. Compute the first derivative of yield with respect to both weighted average life $\partial Y_c / \partial \bar{t}$ and average yield reduction $\partial Y_c / \partial \Delta IRR$ and plot them (*on separate graphs*) as a function of average life and average yield reduction, respectively.

22.14 VALUE AND THE BIRTH OF MARKETS

One of the most quotable lyrics from the legendary rock-and-roll song "Stairway to Heaven" is the phrase "and you know sometimes words have two meanings." At this point, it should not surprise you to hear that money is just one of those words. What should remain questionable is why words are said to have two meanings instead of three or four. What is all the excitement about two anyway?

In the case of money, the two meanings are obviously money *qua* <u>cash</u> and money *qua* <u>Value</u>. If the situation amounted to the fact that there are two meanings like there are two banks to the Hudson River, it would be easy. However, the central issue is that one meaning comes before the other and in essence, makes the other one possible. For us, this means that *Value* precedes price and enables it. Although over the short term price can sometimes project the illusion that it will prevail, in the end *Value* always wins the day. A situation whereby the two are *out of whack*, as finance people like to put it, is commonly described as a *liquidity crisis* or conversely, a *bubble*, and this mostly in retrospect after the latter has burst, leaving moans and groans in its wake, not to mention childish confessions of ignorance. It is not a coincidence that "two fools make a market" means precisely the opposite.[14]

Value as a Precondition to Markets

What does the foregoing preamble have to do with the birth of a market? To begin with, despite the best efforts of everyone concerned to the contrary, it appears that brokers and intermediaries can never quite be eliminated from most active markets. Yet, such elimination is the one thing buyers and sellers are intent on achieving. Brokers are universally resented, especially by other brokers, and are at best regarded as a necessary evil to be jettisoned at the first opportunity.

If you think about it, the sole promise of the Internet during its so-called bubble was precisely that of eliminating brokers, and of going *directly* to a consumer deemed to be just waiting there, ready to be taken. The logic of the Internet was apparently flawless, at least to those hapless investors who forked out megabucks in search of capitalism's Holy Grail. Unfortunately, the Internet provides everything but the only thing it has to provide: *Value*. Without *Value*, a market can never begin, let alone thrive.

What is the problem with this logic? The problem is always the same it seems, and boils down to the fact that logic is predicated on something that itself cannot be logical. In other words, logic is incomplete. Parenthetically, logic knows itself formally to be insufficient at least since the 1931 publication of Kurt Gödel's incompleteness theorem. What is amazing is not the existence, necessity and unavoidability of this theorem, for it only expresses logic's underlying self-referential groundlessness, but rather that it took someone of Gödel's caliber to demonstrate a fact every schoolgirl knows.

Value and Agreement Revisited

But if *Value* cannot come from logic, whence does it come? Obviously from outside logic, but where is that? Although this chapter apparently gave a full answer to this question, we left something out. What we omitted was a discussion of the basis of our fundamental assumption with respect to the copula function for instance. How do we determine the range of loss rates compatible with the asset class or the deal? There seems to be no answer to this question, for any particular choice of γ will do, right? Actually, that isn't right.

If you recall our discussion about Agreement versus *Value* from "The Value of the Deal", you will remember that the truth of *Value* lies in agreement and nothing else. In order to understand *Value* from the ground up, we have no choice but to abstract one more level and see how it comes into being out of nothing.

In other words, the answer to the apparent indeterminacy of *Value* is the existence of an external reference, of what we call an *honest broker*, for it is plain as day that agreement between buyers and sellers can never come from something internal to either one of them. Absent such external reference, *Value* can never be computed because agreement can never be reached. Putting 10 people in a room with something to sell, and 10 more in the same room with loads of cash looking to buy the same thing will never give rise to a market unless *Value* already exists.

Long before the so-called Black–Scholes formula was created, buyers and sellers of options were desperately seeking to make deals en masse, but to no avail. Why? You might say because the bid–ask spread was too wide, but that only means that *Value* did not exist. Once *Value* was created, the market arose spontaneously and liquidity turned up as if by magic. One would think that, given an example of this magnitude, the average investor would first ask how *Value* ought to be determined before handing over his cash. *Value* cannot come from price since price is itself predicated on *Value*. In other words in the absence of *Value* the secondary market is inherently unstable and will eventually collapse.

The critical point is that due to the fundamental symmetry of the linear problem, buyers and sellers need a third party to whom they can relate. Thus, brokers arise completely spontaneously in *Value* creation as a natural consequence and necessary precondition of market agreement. It really does not matter which datum, legal, or natural person acts as the external reference as long as it does not reside in either the buyer or the seller. Further, it is solely on this basis that cash can eventually move. Cash moves for V*alue*, not the other way around because *Value* is *in itself* while cash is only *for itself*, i.e., it requires a benchmark to have meaning.

As with all such arguments, this one must be understood metaphysically, not physically. Whether, as the case may be, the buyer or the seller is *physically* computing *Value* is irrelevant as long as a recognizable external reference exists that would enable the other party to go through the same calculation. The essence of broking, the *real* broker, is not the party that computes, but the reference itself. Thus, getting rid of *physical* brokers is easily done once both buyers and sellers can agree on a suitable external reference. The pervasive existence of physical brokers is a living testament to how difficult it is to find such a reference. To answer that *data* are the solution is to miss the point entirely, for data per se are always meaningless. Only information means something.

Valuation is simply the process of transforming data into information. Therefore, structured securities are more *valuable* than corporate securities, as opposed to more *expensive*, because comparatively speaking they are issued within a data-rich, and hence potentially information-rich, environment. As we discussed earlier when talking about commodities, the entire rationale of the advanced approach to valuation is the mathematical reduction of the valuation basis to an extent sufficient to enable unaided human intuition to agree. When this happens, *Value* becomes unique and liquidity arises spontaneously.

22.15 RATING AGENCIES AND STRUCTURED ANALYSIS

In structured finance, the quintessential broker is the rating agency that provides an unbiased estimate of *Value*, or at least one would like to think so. From this vantage point, it is easy to understand why so-called *split* ratings are so undesirable. Since the defining characteristic of *Value* is its uniqueness, split ratings deny *Value* its essence. On the other hand, every now and then one hears repeated calls for the removal of rating agencies from the operations of credit markets, usually after mega-scandals like Enron and the subprime mortgage crisis have surfaced, as they always do. At first blush, it is tempting to answer this call with a resounding yes! Unfortunately, those asking for such removals commonly fail to apprehend what would happen if rating agencies were suddenly to disappear.[15]

No doubt, investment bankers would reply that *Value* is *pretty well understood* and that value-agreement would readily ensue. What would in fact happen is exactly the opposite. The first time a deal truly needed to be valued, as opposed to this year's 25th FNMA deal, a major disagreement would occur and an external broker would immediately have to step in to arbitrage the difference. Getting rid of rating agencies is no more difficult than getting rid of physical brokers, but those wishing for this dream to come true must first provide a blueprint of what will replace them. In this context, securities regulators should be leery of half-baked proposals that purport to bring about valuation nirvana and that would effectively undo in one day what took decades to assemble. Rather than the enemy they are thought to represent, rating agencies are the glue that holds bond markets together. This is not to say that reform at those august bodies is not sorely needed, quite the contrary. However, the way out of either rating agency hegemony or of any *yield-depressing* broking situation is not to substitute one rating agency or broker for another cheaper one, but rather to conceptualize *Value* from the ground up in a way that achieves self-consistency. As you have probably noticed, this topic has occupied us from the very first page of this textbook.

One thing is clear at the outset: as it now stands, finance is in a state of transition characterized by massive confusion in the investing public. The centuries-old framework of the linear firm is increasingly being replaced by the more nimble and abstract special purpose entity paradigm whereby the typical corporation is reduced to the status of mere servicer. In its soul-searching transition for meaning, finance is re-inventing itself practically against its own will. Unfortunately, transitions are like revolutions: they are normally characterized by chaos hiding under various pseudonyms like CDO-squared, PIK bonds and the like; and chaos is precisely where we find ourselves at this very moment. How is this so?

The Self-Contradiction Embedded in the Current Rating Agency Paradigm

To convince yourself that this is indeed the case, consider the inevitable conclusion that structured securities must be valued, which obviously means rated, in the way we have outlined above, i.e., through nonlinear iteration, and that this is never done by any of the U.S. rating agencies. In fact, it is highly doubtful they are even aware there is a problem at all, at least not until now.

As already stated, the central focus of nonlinearity is self-reflexivity, which only means the condition whereby inputs are linked to outputs a priori, forcing us into an iterative solution procedure. In terms of credit ratings, this leads to the inescapable result that the currently implemented reduction of yield methodology at the heart of the rating agency analytical framework contains the fatal flaw of self-contradiction.

No way. Yes, way.

Recall that the essential problem embedded in the current rating agency paradigm is that it assumes known the very thing it seeks to compute. Just think about it. Why do we need credit ratings? Obviously to compute the promised yield and price the bond; everybody knows that. If you assume you already know the yield-promise in order to calculate a reduction of yield, you have assumed the problem away. In that case, the bond's credit rating is clearly superfluous since you only wanted to know it to find its yield. If one cannot assume the yield to be known a priori, one clearly cannot rate the bond. Therefore, logically speaking credit rating in structured finance is *impossible*. Obviously, there must be a flaw in this argument somewhere.

As was demonstrated above, structured ratings and yields are nonlinearly coupled and cannot be de-linked just because one is only capable of solving linear problems. By wrongly assuming the yield to be known a priori, rating agencies have ipso facto assumed deals to have already been valued while at the same time seemingly engaging in a bona fide valuation process. In other words, up to now rating agencies have *simultaneously* taken deals to be and not to be. The rule that tries to enforce the condition that one cannot take something to be and not to be at the same time is called the Principle of Non-Contradiction. As stated by Aristotle, it serves to ensure that one does not speak from both sides of one's mouth, although it is still true that speaking without contradiction in no way guarantees that one is saying something meaningful. What is amazing is that this most venerable principle of logic and hence, of linearity, is itself grounded in nonlinearity.

Unfortunately, there is a heavy price to pay for violating the Principle of Non-Contradiction in finance, and that is total confusion and ridiculously large arbitrage opportunities. What is even more amazing is that such opportunities are actually created every day by the self-contradictory paradigm of structured credit analysis currently in use. Mind you, confusion is not that bad since it always benefits one set of individuals, namely those who actually understand the situation.

Does this mean that virtually all structured credit ratings ever produced are wrong? No, it does not since ratings can never be *wrong* in the ordinary, linear sense of that word. However, it does mean that all of them are potentially inconsistent and hence wrong in a relative way. But wait a minute! There are thousands of deals out there doing just fine. How can all those ratings be incorrect? This cannot be? You might as well ask why airplanes don't crash all the time since it is a plain fact that 99% of all pilots know essentially nothing about aerodynamics. The reason deals do not *crash* has nothing to do with credit ratings, but is merely a reflection of the fact that most Americans pay their bills, something over which rating agencies have no control. Ratings or not, most transactions would perform.

The real issue is not the threat of wholesale dislocation in the capital markets, but of the gross economic inefficiencies that attend self-contradiction. In the end, inefficiency helps no one, let alone those who think they are benefiting by taking advantage of the countless others who naïvely believe in the current paradigm. Financial rationality implies nothing more than the self-consistent measurement of risk. By itself and over time, such self-consistency would actually bring about the congruence of empirically observed credit risk and whatever rating scale happened to have been chosen, and would single-handedly give structured credit analysis something it can never have as things now stand: credibility. To be or not to be, that is indeed the question!

22.16 THE VALUATION OF REVOLVING PORTFOLIOS: FRACTAL MEASURES

Although this section probably lies beyond the intended scope of this text, we include it merely to prod students and analysts into a broader engagement with structured security valuation, potentially achieving a level of analytical dexterity that could enable them to conduct heterogeneous-portfolio liability analysis, a topic that has of late received much more attention than it really deserves.

Here and now, we do not have time to go into this subject in detail. This is regrettable because traded portfolios are entitled to a better deal. Our comments are offered more as an impetus to further research and as a cautionary tale than as a blueprint for hedge-fund valuation, for that would require a complete review of the empirical basis underlying them (see section 24.6 below for a more detailed treatment).

Strictly speaking, the valuation method described earlier in this chapter is valid only for a transaction backed by a static pool whereby fixed-point convergence according to equation (22) is achievable. Many existing structures do not fit this paradigm and, therefore, a question should have arisen as to how transactions equipped with revolving asset bases ought to be valued. From the preceding analysis, it should be obvious that those in which no yield space fixed-point solution exists do not have a *Value* in the sense of the word we mean. However, by no means does this automatically imply that we have no choice but to remain silent about the situation and the associated securities. Instead, it means that the concept of *Value* must be raised to yet another level of abstraction.

Hausdorff Dimensions

In order to conceptualize revolving structures and their *Value* properly, it is appropriate to introduce the notion of Hausdorff-dimensionality, named after Felix Hausdorff,[16] a leading twentieth-century German mathematician who, like Banach, made significant contributions to functional analysis in addition to authoring *Grundzüge der Mengenlehre*,[17] *the* seminal text on set theory. Rather than simply state the definition of the Hausdorff dimension, which accomplishes precious little, let's spend some time understanding it from the ground up.

The first thing to notice is that Hausdorff dimensions and measures are derived by reference to the notion of *analytic continuation*, a simple and hence powerful idea. Before launching into the subject matter in earnest, it is perhaps worth our while lingering over its foundation for a minute.

(a) Analytic Continuation

Analytic continuation is formally defined as the extension of the range of a function beyond its domain of definition. By far the best-known example is the gamma function we encountered in chapter 15 when discussing the Clayton copula. For real-valued arguments γ, the gamma function $\Gamma(\gamma)$ is defined as follows:

$$\Gamma(\gamma) \equiv \int_0^\infty t^{\gamma-1} e^{-t} dt, \ \gamma > 0 \tag{41}$$

As first sight, this definition looks like it means nothing else than the fact that it is just that, i.e., a definition to be taken at face value and then used. But the truth of the gamma function lies in seeing how it is the analytical continuation of some other function which is not defined for all values of its argument γ. To see what happens and why the above definition makes eminent sense, set $\gamma = 5$ for example and insert it inside equation (41) to obtain:

$$\Gamma(5) \equiv \int_0^\infty t^4 e^{-t} dt$$

To solve this, use integration by parts and set:

$$u = t^4 \rightarrow du = 4t^3 \, dt$$

$$dv = e^{-t} \, dt \rightarrow v = -e^{-t}$$

The usual operations of integration by parts then yield:

$$\Gamma(5) = -t^4 e^{-t} \Big|_0^\infty + 4 \int_0^\infty t^3 e^{-t} \, dt \tag{42}$$

Now, since the exponential function rises faster than any finite power of t, equation (42) quickly leads to:

$$\Gamma(5) = 4 \int_0^\infty t^3 e^{-t} \, dt$$

In passing, this is how the Clayton copula [equation (14) in chapter 15] was derived from the definition of the gamma density function [equation (3) in chapter 15]. There was never an explicit need to compute the Laplace transform of $f(y)$ in equation (13) because a simple substitution inside the defining equation led directly to the result $g(s) = (1+s)^{-\gamma}$ in two steps. To see this, first substitute the definition of the gamma density function into equation (10) in chapter 15 to obtain:

$$g(s) = \int_0^\infty e^{-sy}\, dF(y) = \frac{1}{\Gamma(\gamma)} \int_0^\infty e^{-sy} e^{-y} y^{\gamma-1}\, dy = \frac{1}{\Gamma(\gamma)} \int_0^\infty e^{-(s+1)y} y^{\gamma-1}\, dy$$

Next, introduce the transformation $y' = (s+1)y$, yielding:

$$g(s) = \frac{1}{\Gamma(\gamma)(1+s)^\gamma} \int_0^\infty e^{-y'} (y')^{\gamma-1}\, dy' = \frac{\Gamma(\gamma)}{\Gamma(\gamma)(1+s)^\gamma} = (1+s)^{-\gamma}$$

The next step is to do the same thing again but this time starting with $u = t^3$, leading to:

$$\Gamma(5) = 4 \bullet 3 \int_0^\infty t^2 e^{-t}\, dt$$

As you will have already surmised, in the end the result will turn out to be:

$$\Gamma(5) = 4 \bullet 3 \bullet 2 \bullet 1 = 4!$$

Now you see why the above definition was chosen, for the gamma function $\Gamma(n)$ in the case of integer arguments n will always yield the result $\Gamma(n) = (n-1)!$ Obviously, we don't need a complicated expression like equation (41) to compute the factorial function, except that equation (41) is defined for all real values of its argument γ, not just the integers. This means that it allows us to extend the factorial concept to the real space, i.e., the gamma function is the *continuation* of the factorial notion to real-valued arguments. In terms that are perhaps more intuitive, it effectively represents the *geometrization* of factorials, their extension into a realm fundamentally different from their arithmetic origin.

(b) The Hausdorff Dimension

Let's see how to apply analytic continuation to the notion of a dimension. To begin with, when one imagines a line, one normally thinks of one dimension; a plane, two dimensions, and so forth. In short, you need a single coordinate to define a line, two coordinates to define a plane, etc. As a result, the integer n is the proper *topological* dimension of an n-dimensional manifold. At first blush, there seems to be no middle ground here. In other words, how could a manifold have anything other than an integer as a measure of its dimensionality? However, the same could have been said of factorials before the invention of the gamma function. The answer is that it is possible, but that understanding what happens requires a little intuition.

The Hausdorff dimension represents the extension, or continuation, of the concept of a dimension to any number not necessarily an integer. To grasp the notion fully, you need to ask what it would be like for a manifold to be more than a line but still less than a plane. Does it make sense? It does in the same way that $\Gamma(4.7) = 3.7!$ makes sense.

To get a more intuitive feel for the idea of Hausdorff-dimensionality, consider figure 22.13, showing two concentric circles of finite radius r_1 and r_2, respectively inside an arbitrary set F within a two-dimensional topological manifold. For illustration purposes, we have specifically marked with dots a few elements in F.

Since the underlying manifold is topological, it has the cardinality of the two-dimensional continuum, which means that any couple (x_1, x_2), whereby x_1 and x_2 are real numbers, is allowable as a location on this manifold. Consequently, one would expect that, were F to have the same cardinality as the manifold underlying it, elements belonging to F would be able to occupy any position on it. In practice, this means that since the two circles in figure 22.13 cover respective areas πr_i^2, $i \in [1, 2]$, the number of elements of F contained in each circle should scale as r^2. Suppose n_1 is the number of elements of F contained in the circle with radius r_1 and n_2 the corresponding number for the circle with radius r_2, we would expect to find:

$$\frac{n_1}{n_2} = \frac{r_1^2}{r_2^2} = \left(\frac{r_1}{r_2}\right)^2 \tag{43}$$

In essence, we are saying that if the elements of F are generated under complete *freedom*, equation (43) would have to hold because this is as good as it gets. Under this construction, the dimensionality of any set meant to represent some physical or strictly mathematical process cannot be higher than that of the underlying topological continuum, in this case 2.

Now just imagine that somehow, the process leading to the creation of elements in F is operating under a set of constraints and that, because of the latter, certain

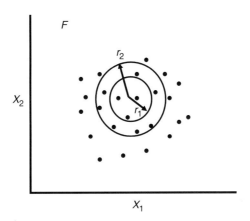

FIGURE 22.13
The Hausdorff dimension.

bona fide locations within the topological manifold are in fact forbidden to F. What would happen then? Clearly, rather than scaling as the square of the radius according to equation (43), the elements of F would behave according to some other scaling law $(r_1/r_2)^d, d < 2$. This is because, as we just saw, 2 is the upper bound for d in the case of a two-dimensional topological manifold. The difference is that now, d is no longer restricted to integers as was the case for the topological dimension.

In the same way the gamma function extended the factorial concept, Hausdorff was able to specify a formal way to calculate d so it would capture the fine-grained process generating elements in F, thereby providing an intuitively appealing analytical continuation to the commonsense notion of a dimension. The types of constraints we are talking about and how they arise physically are not important issues at this point. What *is* important is to realize that this state of affairs stems from something fundamental and transcendental at the heart of the elemental process underlying F.

If you recall the low-discrepancy sequence method reviewed in chapter 18, you can easily convince yourself that Hausdorff's concept becomes extremely useful there. In that case, since we were only using integers to derive random numbers lying between 0 and 1, it followed that many locations inside the interval [0, 1] were forbidden to the process generating such numbers. For instance, take any two consecutive numbers in the low-discrepancy sequence, say 55 and 56. From the low-discrepancy generating function, you can easily see that a real number lying between those two integers will never have a chance to produce a random deviate belonging to F, where F is here taken to mean the set of low-discrepancy values corresponding to the integers $i \in [1, 2, \ldots k]$. Thus, the set of low-discrepancy random deviates is unable to achieve the cardinality of the one-dimensional continuum. Therefore, its Hausdorff dimension is smaller than its topological dimension. This is what we mean when we say that Hausdorff-dimensionality is transcendental. By construction, the low-discrepancy generation process belongs originally to a genus different from that of the continuum. Those familiar with the idea behind Cantor's set have probably noticed the obvious similarity.

Exercise 22.5

Find the Hausdorff dimension of the van der Corput process from chapter 18. In what range do you expect it to lie? Should it be smaller or greater than that of Cantor's set, first found by Hausdorff to be $d = \ln(2)/\ln(3) \approx 0.63$?

Still missing from the above dimensionality treatment is the limiting process Hausdorff applied to the definition of his generalized concept of dimension. In effect, rather than using finite circles, he defined dimension by letting the circle shrink down to a limiting radius of zero, i.e., the value d was thought to be the one corresponding to $r \to 0$, the transcendental limit. The reason for this is that we are looking for the *essence*, the origin of the process leading to elements of F. If we used finite (large) circles to compute d, we could only derive an approximate measure for the *local* process where the elements of F are created. Of course, practically speaking this can never be done save in a few simple cases, and so the way to compute d is to use an asymptotic numerical method that lets us extrapolate this limit as we approach it from above. This is also how physicists compute absolute zero experimentally. By definition, *absolute* zero is a temperature than cannot be reached physically; it is a *concept*, not a *percept*. The same principle holds true in the notion of Hausdorff-dimensionality.

For instance, consider the standard definition of the functional derivative $df(x)/dx$ given by equation (44):

$$\frac{df(x)}{dx} \equiv \lim_{h \to 0} \frac{f(x+h) - f(x)}{h} \tag{44}$$

Clearly, the limit involved in this definition is superfluous in situations where $f(x)$ is linear, i.e., where $f(x) = ax + b$, for in that case any value of h will lead to the correct first derivative, namely a. However, in cases where $f(x)$ is *nonlinear*, local definition (44) readily imposes itself.

Finally, what happens if we apply Hausdorff's idea to a process always yielding the same location, which is the situation we described above in "The Value of the Deal?" In other words, what would be such a set's corresponding Hausdorff dimension? Applying our intuitive definition, it is clear that no matter how small a circle we chose, the number of points contained in it would remain the same, in this case one. The rate of change would therefore be zero and consequently, the Hausdorff dimension of processes associated with fixed-point solutions is zero. Since the topological dimension of a transaction is equal to the number of credit[18] tranches it has, we conclude that the Hausdorff dimension of a deal with n credit tranches is a real number $d \in [0, n]$.

Can we say more? Yes, but before that let's ponder Hausdorff's penetrating analysis a little more.

Reflections on the Intuition Underlying the Hausdorff Dimension

In the end, the logical definition of the Hausdorff dimension is not of primary significance, which is why we did not even bother to write it down. Instead, what really matters is the ability to take up Hausdorff's seminal intuition and make it our own. As we tried to suggest earlier, the soul of a thinking that creates an idea or concept does not lie in its explicit, logical statement because mathematics addresses a level of truth that cannot be said, but only experienced, only felt.

As you will know, every mathematical proposition can be reduced to the tautological statement $A = A$, which is nothing but the bare statement of apparently meaningless self-identity. Thus, what mathematics is *really* trying to say it cannot tell you through *logic* for logical statements are always tautological and hence, meaningless. What is difficult to grasp is that the truth of a logical statement is not itself contained in it, that it is hidden in a fundamental way and cannot be expressed in words or symbols, but only intimated. Consequently, what you need to hold onto are not the equations or the proofs, but that which lies a priori beneath the latter, what is already *thrown under*, i.e., the subject.[19] The proper sense of the mathematical is this *already* business concealed inside logic.

There is clearly a problem here, which is this: How can we learn anything if we need to have learned it already?

The literal translation of the word *theorem* is *a thing of God*. In other words, theorems are trying to tell us about God. Wait a minute, you say, this is finance! How the Devil did God get in here? The answer is that God did not *get in here* as you put it; she was there from the very beginning. The answer is that the truth of a theorem is not explicit, but implicit. It is such truth that we call an *intuition*.

Since the thing to be grasped cannot be learned via mere erudition and so-called theorems, how then is knowledge at all possible? The unique resolution of this dilemma, which is simultaneously the heart of intrinsic nonlinearity and the essence of valuation, is that we knew it all along. What is astounding is that knowledge is latent inside each of us and may not be given or imparted the way we usually think it can. When you learn something, *what* you learn is something you already knew, something that in a sense you brought with you into the classroom. The truth of the mathematical is this *about* things we already know.[20] Properly conceived, knowledge is nothing save a simple *remembrance* of what we, really, already know. Otherwise, it is impossible.

Every other type of knowledge is predicated on such intuitions. As a direct consequence of this, we can see that mathematics is but an attempt to transmit simple intuition. Numbers and arithmetic are only particular formations of the mathematical, not the other way around. We can know things only because knowledge is something that comes from within, something that we somehow carry along with us whenever we learn. Now, the source of our ability to learn can obviously not itself be something we have learned. This ability is the essence of the mathematical. A great mathematician is not a clerk able to recite 20 pages of algebra in 10 minutes. Rather, he is just someone who can clearly see what was there all along. Hausdorff was such a thinker, and we honor a thinker only when we ourselves think.

If you have stayed the course, you have most likely realized that because knowledge originates from your own mind, there is no way *nature* can tell you anything that amounts to a fact, let alone to knowledge. Facts only become so in light of a fundamental a priori preconceptualization we call a theory. Otherwise, all we have are mere data elements without meaning. Knowledge is about conveying meaning and besides that nothing. A sheer prospectus has no meaning whatsoever, and this is why finance cannot work empirically.

Whatever happened to Charles Darwin, he did not develop his great intuition concerning evolution while observing species living on the Galapagos Islands, for it is crystal-clear that nothing theoretical could ever come out of such a procedure. What he did, in fact, was go there with a pre-established notion of evolution he was merely seeking to confirm. Absent such preconceptualization, Darwin could have traveled his entire life without ever encountering evolution in the flesh. Seriously, have you ever seen a species *evolve* no matter how long you stared at it? The source of Darwin's inspiration is not hard to guess since, at the time, Hegel's dialectics was all the rage in Europe and is also known to have greatly influenced another famous Londoner: Karl Marx.

Nevertheless, it would be wrong to read a radical embracing of idealism into a rejection of the official version of the scientific method. If placing the emphasis on the object (empiricism) is wrong, why would it be right to place it on the subject (idealism)? The answer is that both points of view are misguided because they miss the central problematic. What requires an explanation, instead of being regarded as self-evident, is precisely the origin of the relationship between the subject and the object. The answer is that it is our singular and a priori ability to relate to things that enables knowledge to arise in the first place, and thus to create the subject–object dichotomy out of nothing. Fundamentally, to know only means to relate, i.e., to apply one's intuition.

Hold on. Is it not generally believed that intuition cannot be learned, that you either have it or you don't? Although this is completely bogus, what is true is that learning is not *easy*. Instead, it is *simple* and as such demands constant dwelling on things. One cannot learn intuition in a few minutes the way we can with the proof of Banach's fixed-point theorem. If that were possible, then you could literally become Banach in a few minutes. In fact, even if you did learn each and every one of his proofs, you would never even come close to his amazing powers of intuition. This is why we insist on lingering over deals and doing deals, on engagement with deals, for only then can one have at least the faint hope of developing the intuition necessary to deal more simply than ever before. Finding yourself in deals requires first and foremost losing yourself in them.

The Value of Revolving Portfolios

Over the last few pages, we have engaged in a huge sidebar, talking about seemingly off-base things like analytic continuation, Hausdorff dimensions, and the essence of intuition. Are we wasting your time or does this have something to do with revolving portfolios? See for yourself.

As you are about to discover, the Hausdorff dimension is the key concept underlying the valuation of revolving portfolios. By extension, it is of paradigm importance in valuing both traded tranches like those found in a market-value CDO and the vast majority of hedge fund liabilities.

(a) The Valuation Framework

As we did when introducing Hausdorff dimensions, our approach to revolving portfolio valuation will be strictly conceptual. Any more than that, and we would quickly become embroiled in esoteric algebra, losing the point along the way.

To contextualize the discussion, we first postulate a situation whereby a fund manager may choose any combination of assets from among three basis portfolios within each of which assets are assumed independent of each other. It should be emphasized that the intended form of independence is the *vertical* type discussed in chapter 15, not *horizontal* independence. By this we mean that amount, default, and loss given default with respect to each exposure can still be correlated in any manner whatever without affecting the validity of our conclusions. In addition, the case of inter-asset correlation can easily be recovered by assuming that each exposure represents its own portfolio.

Consider figure 22.14, showing the three distinct fixed points that resulted from our valuation procedure applied to the same liability structure paired with the three basis portfolios (P_1, P_2 and P_3).[21] Furthermore, unless otherwise specified, when we use the word *correlation* we always mean it vis-à-vis credit risk, i.e., default or loss correlation.

(b) The Independent Case

To begin with, assume that not only are the assets within a single portfolio independent, but macro-economic independence obtains across all portfolios as well. In other words, the macro-economic forces driving the performance of each basis portfolio are different and assumed independent of each other.

Before venturing further, remember that independence is a very strong statement compared to that of vanishing linear correlation. With respect to two arbitrary variables x and y, not only does independence imply the vanishing of the bilinear, central moment $E[(x - \bar{x})(y - \bar{y})]$, which is how we normally describe the absence of correlation, but that of all higher moments $E\left[(x - \bar{x})^i (y - \bar{y})^j\right] \forall i, j \in [1, \infty)$ as well.

Independence implies the absence of correlation of any order, not just first order. As was shown in Appendix XI of "*The Analysis of Structured Securities*" (OUP, 2003), it is quite possible for linear correlation to be zero but, at the same time, for higher-order correlation to exist, thereby indicating that the two variables are far from independent.

It is too often assumed in practice that lack of linear correlation is equivalent to independence. In fact, the exactly opposite situation may very well be the case.

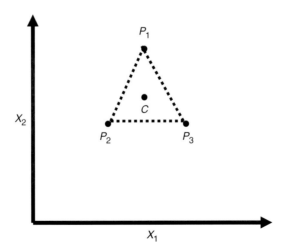

FIGURE 22.14
The valuation framework for revolving portfolios.

The notion of independence is equivalent to the self-identity concept discussed earlier. Self-identity is the reason why we can factually state that two independent variables x and y must satisfy:[22]

$$E[xy] = E[x]\,E[y] \tag{45}$$

Exercise 22.6

Using a Taylor-series expansion, computed in terms of its respective moments of all orders in terms of x and y, show that $E[x\,y]$ must satisfy equation (45) identically when all moments vanish simultaneously. Which equation does $E[x\,y]$ satisfy if all moments except those up to second order vanish identically? Could you then generalize the notion of independence from its current *stochastic* meaning to a more *statistical* one?

Exercise 22.7

Using the results and intuition gained from the previous exercise, could you devise a method to ferret out instances whereby variables, while appearing independent are in fact dependent to some degree, from cases where they are truly independent?

Independence is usually a convenient assumption made to simplify derivations, but it is rarely justified fundamentally since that would imply some sort of constructive proof that statistical moments of all order vanish identically, something quite difficult to do.

With the *Values* P_1, P_2, and P_3 in hand, assume now that our portfolio manager starts to combine the respective assets of P_1 and P_2 via trading. Due to the independence assumption within and without our basis portfolios, you can already guess what will happen: the resulting *Value* will fall somewhere on the dashed line linking P_1 and P_2 in figure 22.14. This is not to say that the combination [0.5 P_1, 0.5 P_2] would give rise to a *Value* exactly half-way between the two ends of the relevant line segment, for *Value* itself already contains its own brand of nonlinearity. But owing to strict independence, the *Value* axis will perforce be acting along the line joining the anchor-points P_1 and P_2. This is because an independent system behaves homogeneously, i.e., it cannot support nonlinearity.

From our earlier comments on the meaning of fractal measures, it should now be clear that the dimensionality of this set will be equivalent to that of a line ($= 1$). In other words, we expect the Hausdorff dimension of a two-dimensional deal constructed out of an arbitrary combination of two independent portfolios to increase by one, i.e., from zero-dimensional in the case of a single portfolio to one-dimensional in the case of two portfolios whereby the parameterization could be the percentage of either basis portfolio in the combined portfolio. Therefore, although the *Value* of the deal is no longer restricted to a unique fixed point, *Value* can still be quantified meaningfully by specifying both end-points of the relevant line segment and the associated Hausdorff dimension. Although this is really overkill in this simple example, we shall soon come to realize that the concept turns out to be invaluable in the quantification and qualification of *Value* within more intricate asset environments.

If we now combined all three portfolios and calculated the *Value* of each combination, it should be clear from the preceding homogeneity argument that all such *Value*s must fall inside the triangular shape defined by the dashed lines in figure 22.14. Further, since by definition all locations inside the said triangle are accessible simply by varying the respective proportion of each basis portfolio contained in the target pool, no single individual manifold location would be *forbidden* as a possible *Value*. Given the foregoing discussion, we conclude that the Hausdorff dimension of a traded universe of at least three distinct, independent portfolios is equal to two, the relevant topological dimension.

If a potential investor were to insist on a single *Value* for this type of deal, he could probably be talked into using the centroid of the triangle, shown as point C in figure 22.14, as a *proxy* for *Value*. Nevertheless, this simplification would only make sense as long as he remained conscious of the fact that a single point would in no way convey the truth of *Value* within a traded environment. The obvious advantage of using one *Value* is that it makes pricing easier, albeit at the expense of clarity. What *is* clear however is that investors in traded portfolios ought to demand and receive the triangular or polygonal version of *Value,* for only then can informed judgments be made.

(c) Generalized *Value* within Correlated, Revolving Portfolios

Now, let's make the valuation game a little more interesting by introducing inter-portfolio correlation into the mix. Instead of independence across basis portfolios, let's assume that some form of macro-economic correlation exists even though within a single portfolio we are still assuming asset independence. If we found any identifiable correlation among basis portfolio assets, they would be segregated and constitute yet another basis portfolio. Thus, intra-portfolio independence is not a *sine qua non* of this approach, but merely expresses the provisional and conditional state of our knowledge.

Remembering that the basic intuition underlying the concept of dimensionality turned out to be the freedom to occupy any topological location, what will happen in this situation is easily guessed, for the essential import of correlation is to impose a priori constraints on the ability of *Value* to occupy certain positions in the valuation space. Effectively, these are the forbidden locations we alluded to when introducing the notion of Hausdorff-dimensionality. They arise naturally because of implied ties between the assets in one portfolio with those in another, which, of course, is what correlation is all about. If you recall our macro-economic correlation treatment from chapter 15, where we observed how the Clayton copula widened the originally Gaussian loss distribution due to inter-asset correlation, the current situation will appear straightforward. Here, the linking of assets from various groups prevents certain locations from being visited by the Value-creation process F. Topologically, this situation amounts to a falsification of the ergodic hypothesis normally operative within the structured security valuation paradigm. As a result, the *Value* space will

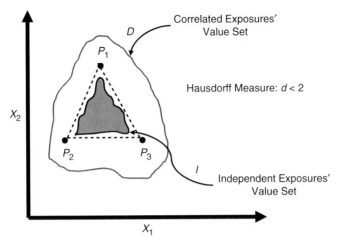

FIGURE 22.15
Generalized value concept within traded portfolios.

fail to evidence a Hausdorff dimension equal to its topological dimension. This is shown in figure 22.15. Obviously, the precise value of the applicable Hausdorff dimension will be related to the correlation structure that happens to exist among the basis portfolios.

What is important to remember is that traded portfolios can be characterized via their Hausdorff dimension. What this means in practice is that such environments will exhibit significant *Value jumpiness* once the most current estimate of trust assets is taken into account within a revolving pool. For those of you familiar with the analytical meaning of this term, this is the type of behavior commonly referred to as *chaotic*. In other words, such transactions will display unusually erratic behavior whereby large changes in *Value* will result from seemingly small changes in portfolio composition. This is to be sharply contrasted with the independent case whereby small differences in asset composition could only generate small changes in *Value*. In other words, independent portfolios behave *smoothly* rather than *chaotically*.

Therefore, the first lesson to be drawn from our cursory treatment of correlation is something that should be obvious to anyone who has observed correlation trading in action, which is that apparently innocuous modifications of the eligibility criteria across transaction structures can lead to much larger changes in outcome. The difference is that, under the above framework, such chaotic behavior can be characterized and priced *a priori* rather than a posteriori. Finally yet importantly, given that correlation is so notoriously difficult to nail down, the foregoing analysis should be viewed more as a way to think about correlation than as some sort of magical pricing engine.

An important consequence of the type of nonlinearity introduced through inter-portfolio correlation is what we call the *spillover* effect in *Value* space. This phenomenon refers to the fact that *Value* will no longer be restricted to the inside of the triangular region in figure 22.14, which was the case under independence. This time, it will spill over the edges of the triangle and access neighborhoods outside the triangle. The extent of this spillover can be measured by using the *moment* method, whereby the moment of each potential *Value* about the centroid can be computed, summed, and used as a measure of uncertainty about the centroid and thus, of credit risk in the deal.

If you think about it for a minute, this secondary effect is intimately tied to the reduction in Hausdorff dimensionality, for where have those forbidden locations gone if not outside the triangle itself? The upshot is that instead of being constrained to the roughly triangular shaded region in figure 22.15 (the arrow labeled I), *Value* can now globally occupy a larger region of yield space (the arrow labeled D). Obviously, the concomitantly increased risk, as measured by the now potentially wider uncertainty in *Value*, is but the corollary of the reduction in Hausdorff dimension from its topological limit. As we highlighted earlier, the power of this approach lies in its ability to exhibit the full range of *Value* possibilities within a given structure, thereby better informing investors as to the formal risk properties of the securities they might consider buying.

Last but not least, negative correlation among a given subset of basis portfolios, combined with positive correlation among another, can certainly lead to less risky environments and to *Value* maps whereby Hausdorff measures of almost any value could be manufactured *ex nihilo* using the appropriate mix. However, it would be speculative at best to belabor this possibility when the average Wall Street fund manager would be hard pressed to qualify his real-time exposures in any meaningful way.

As mentioned at the beginning of this section, most of the concepts developed herein are meant to prod students into a deeper engagement with the field of structured valuation than we can afford at this time. One thing is however clear: Research in this area has barely begun.

APPENDIX A: *In Memoriam*

Stefan Banach (1892–1945)

Those accustomed to thinking of mathematicians as dull and "un-cool" will perhaps wish to revisit that assumption upon hearing the story of Stefan Banach, one of the twentieth-century's leading mathematicians.

Stefan Banach was the illegitimate son of Stefan Greczek, a local tax official who was not married to Banach's biological mother, the latter vanishing from the scene shortly after the boy's baptism at the age of four days. On his birth certificate, the mother was listed as one Katarzyna Banach, who is believed to have been either his real mother's servant or someone who took care of him as an infant. Later on, every time Stefan Jr. tried to find out the truth about his natural mother, his father simply told him he had been sworn to secrecy. Thus, with Banach the search for his inner self took on a very personal dimension.

Young Stefan was first brought up by his grandmother in the small village of Ostrowsko, about 50 km south of Krakow. After she took ill, however, he was taken to Franciszka Plowa, a woman who lived in Krakow with her daughter Maria and the latter's guardian, Juliusz Mien, a Polish intellectual who taught Stefan to speak French, to have respect for education, but more importantly, who recognized the boy's mathematical talent immediately.

In high school, Banach and his best friend Witold Wikosz did well in mathematics and physics, but not so well in other topics. Things got worse as they approached graduation, with the result that Banach failed to obtain a pass *with distinction*, an honor granted to about 25% of the class. In other words, in high school, Banach was considered mediocre at best. Upon graduation, Banach and Wikosz both wanted to study mathematics but were somehow convinced that there was nothing left to prove. Banach decided to study engineering (a wise choice says SR!) while Wikosz chose Oriental languages (a wise choice says AR!)

Banach attended the Technical University at Lvov (Lemberg in German) from 1910 until 1914 and in fact took longer than usual to earn his degree, most likely because he was receiving no financial support from a father who was very happy to get rid of that financial burden. Thus, while in Lvov he had to support himself by tutoring. Because he was ineligible for combat due to poor vision, Banach spent the World War I years in Krakow working as a construction worker, attending lectures on mathematics at the famous Jagiellonian University, and earning extra cash by teaching in local schools.

The event that changed Banach's life forever was a 1916 chance encounter with Hugo Steinhaus, a leading Polish mathematician who was about to start teaching at Lvov. Steinhaus told Banach about a problem he had been struggling with, but to no avail. Banach found a solution in a few days. As a result, both of them co-wrote a paper published belatedly in 1918 in the *Bulletin of the Krakow Academy.* More significantly though, it was through Steinhaus that Banach was to meet his future wife, Lucja Braus, whom he married in 1920 at the mountain retreat of Zakopane.

Banach started his academic career in Lvov as an assistant to Lomnicki and later submitted a doctoral dissertation entitled *On Operations with Abstract Sets and their Applications to Integral Equations*, a work now believed to mark the birth of functional analysis. Although this path to a doctorate was irregular, Banach having no mathematics qualifications, an exception was made in his case and he obtained the Ph.D. degree. Then in 1922, he presented his *Habilitationsschrift* on measure theory. This is the post-doctoral thesis that allows someone to teach at a University under the German system. Banach was now a professor of mathematics at the Jan Kazimierz University in Lvov.

In the inter-war years, Banach and Steinhaus remained close collaborators. In 1931, they started editing a new series of mathematical monographs from Lvov, while colleagues based in Warsaw were also contributing material. The first of these tomes, written in Polish by Banach himself in 1931, quickly became a classic after its publication in French around 1932 under the title *Théorie des Opérations Linéaires*. The Warsaw editors of the series were Knaster, Kuratowski, Mazurkewicz, and Sierpinski. Of these, Kuratowski in particular was to have a lasting influence on Banach and the two wrote several joint papers during the late 1920s and early 1930s.

For an academic, Banach worked rather unconventionally. He spent countless hours at the "Scottish Café" in Lvov, a hang-out for mathematicians where people like Steinhaus, Banach, and Stanislas Ulam would congregate to talk and breathe mathematics. The latter recalls Banach during those feverish times:

> "It was difficult to out-last or out-drink Banach during these sessions. We discussed problems proposed right there, often with no solution evident even after several hours of thinking. The next day Banach was likely to appear with several small sheets of paper containing outlines of proofs he had completed."

On a separate occasion, this is how Andrzej Turowicz, another professor of mathematics at Lvov, reminisced about Banach the bon vivant:

> "Banach would spend most of his days in cafés, not only in the company of others but also by himself. He liked the noise and the music. They did not prevent him from concentrating and thinking. There were cases when, after the cafés closed for the night, he would walk over to the railway station where the cafeteria was open around the clock. There, over a glass of beer, he would think about his problems."

In 1939, Banach was appointed President of the Polish Mathematical Society. Luckily, when World War II started Banach's life remained unaffected, mainly because he had been on prior good terms with Russian mathematicians, particularly Sobolev and Aleksandrov, and had visited Moscow several times. They protected him and he was able to both retain his University appointment and continue his research activities. The German occupation of Lvov in 1941 changed all that. He was arrested on suspicion of forgery although later released and went on to survive a tragic period when many Polish academics were murdered, for instance his advisor Lomnicki. He spent the remaining war-years working as a janitor in a German institute on infectious diseases, and died of lung cancer late in 1945 just as he was about to assume the Chair of Mathematics at the Jagiellonian University in Krakow. He never met his mother.

Immediately after the war, Sobolev met Banach outside Moscow, when it was obvious that the illustrious Pole had but a few months to live. The legendary Russian analyst, who gave the eulogy at a memorial conference in Banach's honor, had this to say about that fateful encounter:

> "Despite heavy traces of the war years under German occupation, and despite the grave illness that was undercutting his strength, Banach's eyes were still lively. He remained the same sociable, cheerful, and extraordinarily well-meaning and charming Stefan Banach whom I had seen in Lvov before the war. That is how he remains in my memory: with a great sense of humor, an energetic human being, a beautiful soul, and a great talent."

Banach's accomplishments are too numerous to recount in detail. As mentioned above, he is credited with the foundation of functional analysis and, of course, with the axiomatic definition of a so-called Banach space (a word however coined by Fréchet), which, as we saw, is so central to structured financial analysis. He made major contributions to the theory of topological vector spaces, measure theory, integration, and orthogonal series. He also proved a number of fundamental theorems, notably the Hahn–Banach theorem, the Banach–Steinhaus theorem, the Banach fixed-point theorem (see Appendix B), the Banach–Alaoglu theorem and the well-known Banach–Tarski decomposition theorem.

Stefan Banach was a brilliant mind and a great man who laid the theoretical foundations of structured finance.

APPENDIX B: Annotated Proof of Banach's Fixed-Point Theorem

Due to its criticality, it is generally not possible to learn structured security valuation without discussing, if not proving, Banach's celebrated fixed-point theorem. In the end however, doing deals is what structured finance is all about, not proving theorems. Thus, although you may find the following proof "neat" and intriguing, please remember that it has nothing whatsoever to do with deals or with what you are supposed to learn by reading this book. No one who tells you differently understands finance.

We plow through the proof of this landmark theorem merely to provide a deeper and more rigorous mathematical foundation to structured finance than it currently has. In finance, analytical results are so rare that we should celebrate any time we come across something that holds water, and we do.

The canonical statement of Banach's fixed-point theorem runs as follows:

Premise: Let (X, d) be a nonempty, complete metric space and let T be a contraction mapping on (X, d) with constant q. Choose an arbitrary $x_0 \in X$ and define the sequence $(x_n)_{n=0}^{\infty}$ by $x_n = T^n x_0$. Further, let $a \equiv d(Tx_0, x_0)$.

Conclusion: Then, it follows that T has a unique fixed point in X.

Before laying out the formal proof, a few comments are in order. First, it is clear that most finance students will need some basic terminological background before being able to understand this proof. If you start cold with no prior knowledge of analysis, reading this is a total waste of your time. So let's go through a few concepts that will clarify the theorem's perhaps foreboding statement.

Metric Space

A metric space is a vector space equipped with a metric. For instance, two-dimensional Euclidean space is such an animal, but the Pressure–Volume–Temperature space of thermodynamics is not. Obviously, when you define a metric space, it is a good idea to define the metric as well. In a two-dimensional, Euclidean space for example, the metric d with respect to the two points P_1 and P_2 with coordinates (x_i, y_i), $i \in [1, 2]$ would be defined as follows:

$$d \equiv \sqrt{(x_1 - x_2)^2 + (y_1 - y_2)^2}$$

As you have probably noticed already, the above metric looks suspiciously like the distance measure in planar geometry, and this is in fact why we use the letter d to label it. In the vast majority of cases, the metric d applied to two points will be the Euclidean distance between them.

Complete Metric Space

A complete metric space is one in which all Cauchy sequences converge to a limit. You can already see how critical this assumption will turn out to be to prove Banach's theorem.

Now, what is a Cauchy sequence? A Cauchy sequence is one whereby successive elements a_n, $n \in [0, \infty)$ taken as a pair become increasingly close to each other. With respect to the above metric space with metric d, a Cauchy sequence can be defined formally as follows:

$$\lim_{\min (m,n) \to \infty} d(a_m, a_n) \to 0$$

As you can see, this definition is more general than what we have just said, but the intent is identical. Most of the time in mathematics, too much generality hinders rather than helps.

Contraction Mapping

A contraction mapping, also called a *hyperbolic* mapping, is characterized by the fact that the mapping of any two points in X will result in a reduction, or *contraction*, of the distance between their images compared to that between the original points. If x and y are chosen arbitrarily in X, then for T to be a contraction mapping in X the following condition must hold for some scalar q with $0 \leq q < 1$:

$$d(Tx, Ty) \leq q\, d(x, y) \text{ (cf. inequality (7) in this chapter)}$$

Note that, according to the condition, the scalar q needs to be the largest value over X that can be found since the requirement is for the ratio of the distances between the mapped and unmapped points to always be less than q. Also, note that q cannot be *equal* to unity, as this would simply move some of the points around the space without changing the distance between them. In effect, if this held everywhere in X we would have a simple rotation followed by a potential shifting of the origin.

Last but not least, the parameter a is merely the distance between the first two iterates in the sequence, i.e., $a \equiv d(x_1, x_0)$.

Proof of Banach's Fixed-Point Theorem

First, we need to show by mathematical induction that for any $n \geq 0$, we have:

$$d(T^n x_0, x_0) \leq \frac{1-q^n}{1-q} a \qquad \text{(B.1)}$$

For $n = 0$, the result is obvious. For $n \geq 1$, suppose $d(T^{n-1} x_0, x_0) \leq \frac{1-q^{n-1}}{1-q} a$ holds, and it does so trivially for $n = 1$. Then, we have from the assumption of the contraction mapping:

$$d(T^n x_0, x_0) \leq d(T^n x_0, T^{n-1} x_0) + d(T^{n-1} x_0, x_0)$$

$$\leq q^{n-1} d(Tx_0, x_0) + \frac{1 - q^{n-1}}{1 - q} a$$

$$= \frac{q^{n-1} - q^n}{1 - q} a + \frac{1 - q^{n-1}}{1 - q} a$$

$$= \frac{1 - q^n}{1 - q} a$$

Hence, we have proved inequality (B.1) by using the triangle inequality (the sum of the length of two sides is always greater than the length of the third) and repeated application of the contractive property $d(Tx, Ty) \leq q d(x, y)$ that holds for T. By induction, the property holds for $n \geq 0$.

The next part of the proof consists in showing that the elements $T^n x_0$, $n \in [1, \infty)$ of the sequence starting at x_0 form a Cauchy sequence, which means that successive elements get increasingly close to each other. Once this is done, we can conclude that the sequence has a limit, since the metric space is assumed complete. As you will have already guessed, this limit will turn out to be a fixed point of operator T.

Given an $\varepsilon > 0$, we can find an integer N such that $\frac{q^n}{1-q} a < \varepsilon, \forall n \geq N$ because the ratio $\frac{q^n}{1-q} a \to 0$ as $n \to \infty$. Now, for any pair m, n (and where we assume without loss of generality that $m \geq n$), we have:

$$d(x_m, x_n) = d(T^m x_0, T^n x_0)$$

$$\leq q^n d(T^{m-n} x_0, x_0)$$

$$\leq q^n \frac{1 - q^{m-n}}{1 - q} a$$

$$\leq \frac{q^n}{1 - q} a < \varepsilon$$

Thus, the sequence is a Cauchy sequence, and by our theorem's assumptions, it possesses a limit point, say x^*. Next, we need to show that x^* is a fixed point of the operator T. We will do this by the negative method, also called reductio ad absurdum that consists in demonstrating that the converse of what is to be proved leads to a contradiction, hence what is to be proved must be true. You will probably know that this method has been the subject of much debate over the years, whereby mathematicians of the so-called Intuitionist School have insisted that this technique is not really a proof, and that only the *positive* method will do. The latter technique forces you to construct the thing you need to prove from the ground up instead of simply saying the opposite is false. We shall leave such transcendental debates to better people.

Suppose that x^* is not a fixed point of the operator T, then by definition we have $\delta \equiv d(Tx^*, x^*) > 0$. Because x_n converges to x^*, there is an integer N such that $d(x_n, x^*) < \delta/2$, $\forall n \geq N$. Playing the same game as before (triangle inequality), we find:

$$d(Tx^*, x^*) \leq d(Tx^*, x_{N+1}) + d(x^*, x_{N+1})$$

$$\leq q\, d(x_N, x^*) + d(x^*, x_{N+1})$$

$$< \delta/2 + \delta/2 = \delta$$

Therefore, the condition $d(Tx^*, x^*) = 0$ must hold and x^* is a fixed point of the operator T inside metric space X.

The last part of the proof is to show that the fixed point x^* is unique. To do this, we again have recourse to the negative method. To wit, suppose there exists another fixed point x' of T in X and that $x' \neq x^*$. This means $d(x', x^*) > 0$, but then:

$$d(x', x^*) = d(Tx', Tx^*) \leq q\, d(x', x^*) < d(x', x^*)$$

This is clearly a contradiction, and we have shown that if two fixed points exist, they must in fact be the same point.

Relationship to Linear Iterative Sequences

You may recall our earlier discussions on the action of linear operators as they related to eigenvalues. At the time, we mentioned that the latter could be conceived as shrinking or stretching factors that modify input vectors upon the operation of a matrix. We would like to bring to your attention the analogy between the linear, matrix operators we discussed previously and the hyperbolic, nonlinear operators at the heart of Banach's proof.

In effect, the parameter q is the equivalent of the stretching or shrinking factor, and thus can be regarded as the "eigenvalue" of operator T. Since q is always less than one, the iteration of T leads to an "equilibrium" solution here as well. As before, the equilibrium solution is reached asymptotically in the limit $n \to \infty$.

Note also that the properties of the fixed point are transcendental, which means that as long as we are not exactly at the fixed point x^*, the operator keeps the process moving ever so slightly. It is only at the precise equilibrium location that the operator simply reproduces its input. Thus, in practice the fixed point is an ideal limit that is never truly reached. As we approach equilibrium, spurious elements (cf. Markov chain eigenvalues less than unity in absolute value) tend to vanish and the dominant behavior is recognized as that corresponding to the leading eigenvalue.

We can also imagine a situation whereby $q > 1$ holds and a fixed point can still exist. Unfortunately, unless you start your iterative sequence precisely there by sheer luck, the system will never approach its fixed point on its own and will generally diverge. We point this out to highlight the close relationship between eigenvalue analysis and the discovery of fixed points within nonlinear systems.

23

Revolving Periods

"Eppur, si muove"
Galileo Galilei

This chapter will give an overview of the implementation and of the special difficulties associated with transactions that include revolving periods. This feature is usually the key structural protection in most Collateralized Debt Obligations (CDO) transactions and all credit card master trusts (CCMTs) operated within the United States, Europe, and elsewhere.

Given such wide usage, the dollar amounts involved and the criticality of the concept to structured analysis, it is perhaps surprising that we would only present a mere introduction coupled with a Victorian cautionary tale. The reason is that a full-blown discussion of the ramifications of revolving periods with respect to credit ratings, monitoring and pricing is way beyond the scope of this textbook, and would assume a level of understanding that cannot be presupposed from a majority of the intended readership. The fact of the matter is that, in terms of programming sophistication and complexity, there is as much difference between a static pool analysis and a revolving period as there is between a row boat and an aircraft carrier. One way or another, revolving periods bring into view the full spectrum of analytical skills that can comfortably reside within a single analyst's toolbox.

Second, and more importantly, it is only after one has thoroughly mastered the analysis of static pools that the investigation of revolving periods makes any sense at all. As we have pointed out many times before, the current approach to revolving periods at rating agencies and investment banks is to ignore them completely, which testifies to the level of difficulty involved. In fact, from direct experience it has become clear that analysts challenging our assessment of the difficulties of revolving period implementation have never personally implemented one, for only *in theory* are they simple.

Some readers may also argue that this entire line of argumentation is fallacious. After all, deals with revolving periods are done all the time, so what is the problem? The problem is that such deals are in fact not *done* at all; they are underwritten. If an arranger has the implicit confidence of investors who do not, and in most cases do not care to, understand the risk they are taking, nobody can stand in the way of a CDO with an amazingly complex structure. What is amazing, rather, is that such arrangers believe themselves incredibly sophisticated, as opposed to incredibly naïve, to have pulled this off.

It should never be forgotten that, as things now stand, the credit rating of *all* securities inside revolving structures does not depend formally on the length of the revolving period as it obviously should. The simple reason for this state of affairs is that the revolving period is ignored. Apparently, primary market investors are quite comfortable with the claim that five-year revolvers bear no more credit risk than three-year revolvers, which is patently false.

23.1 THE CONCEPT OF A REVOLVING PERIOD

At the outset, we should point out that the concept of a *revolving* period is closely related to that of a *ramp-up* period, the latter term referring to a time span during which new assets are purchased with a view to including them in the trust estate. However, in the remainder of this chapter we voluntarily restrict ourselves to revolving periods since ramp-up periods represent yet another level of sophistication lying squarely beyond our intended scope. Once revolving periods have been mastered, the student can usually graduate effortlessly to their generalization, which is how the ramp-up period ought to be conceptualized. In other words, a revolving period is but a special case of the more general idea of a ramp-up period. The difference between the two is that during a ramp-up period, liability balances increase in lockstep with the purchase of additional assets while during a revolving period they remain constant. In other words, within revolving structures assets are bought merely to the extent necessary to keep up with pool amortization in whatever form. In a plain-vanilla, static-pool transaction, a suitable package of loans has already been originated and assembled, usually on the sponsor's balance sheet. Therefore, ramp-up periods are by definition absent from the vast majority of Asset-Backed Security (ABS) transactions. Only when the purchase of assets post-closing becomes necessary to create a securitized pool may we properly speak of a *ramp-up* period.

Last but not least, transactions with ramp-up periods are clearly riskier than those without, since, by definition, the former cannot disclose the actual composition of their pool. Instead, the analyst is simply presented with a set of eligibility criteria that are to be followed as best they can. The moral hazard involved in such schemes is obvious and generally causes pools arising from deals with such features to depart significantly from what would have been postulated solely on the basis of eligibility criteria.

The Basic Mechanics of Revolving Periods

In its basic make-up, the revolving period is trivial, and yet such simplicity conceals an amazing array of complications. Rather than being returned to investors as they come in piecemeal, principal payments due are instead re-invested into newly minted or purchased receivables that meet the eligibility criteria found in deal documents. The reason why eligibility criteria must be met is that otherwise, the pool might start deteriorating right after closing and give rise to an effective credit profile completely outside the intent of the transaction. Although respecting a transaction's eligibility criteria represents but one of the new difficulties involved in modeling revolving deals, it is by no means the most challenging one.

Given such a simple state of affairs, why then are these animals so difficult to tame? There are many reasons for this, not the least of which is that the concept of time now takes on meanings alien to static pool analysis. Whereas static pool transactions can be conceptualized using a single interpretation of time, within revolving structures we are faced with having to partition time into three distinct concepts, i.e., the time of the deal, of the assets, and of the liabilities. In what follows, we address these difficulties one by one. But first, let's review the rationale for revolving periods.

As a rule, the goal of a revolving period is the transformation of a short-dated asset structure into a long-dated liability structure. For instance, credit-card receivables do not have an amortization schedule like those associated with mortgage loans. Consequently, on any given payment date the entire outstanding principal balance of the pool could be available for distribution, thereby effectively terminating the deal. If nothing were done to counter this situation, investors would constantly be at risk of receiving principal early or late depending on the vagaries of the marketplace. As you should know by now, and regardless of what people might tell you, the capital markets loathe volatility.

Likewise, say you have a CDO with corporate exposures consisting exclusively of short-term loans with maturities of one year or less, while the associated ABS bonds are designed as five-year hard bullets. If the loans in the pool are originated precisely on the closing date, which is unrealistic anyway, the deal would wind down one year thereafter when everybody paid back what they owed, and you can probably imagine many more circumstances under which a similar situation might arise. One way or another, each example of this type requires a mechanism aimed at keeping the deal alive via the purchase of new loans. Such purchases amount to the recycling back into the deal cash that would normally return to investors. This is what is meant by the term *revolving*. Thus in a revolving structure the assets, not the liabilities, revolve.

Logically speaking, the loan purchase process must take place continuously, i.e., during each collection period, if the deal is to run smoothly. However, the way it actually operates in this respect can vary. For example, in order to insure that no cash leaks out of the transaction, the trustee usually deposits the proceeds of asset repayments into the collection account, thereby suffering a mild negative carry, and then waits until the next Distribution Date to distribute Available Funds according to the Pooling and Servicing Agreement (PSA). Otherwise, one could be prematurely reinvesting cash that should instead be allocated to other parties. However, recent indentures have allowed managers to reinvest idle cash immediately upon receipt during the revolving period. How this works out in practice is anything but clean.

Analysts ought to be on the look-out for such minute transaction details. A CDO may be disadvantaged by a restrictive procedure as asset managers will often insist on maximal flexibility with respect to asset purchase. Whether they get it or not is another issue. The rationale is that good managers need flexibility if they are to take advantage of market opportunities, especially in the case of a market value CDO, something better characterized as a hedge fund.

Despite these minutiae, the basic concept operative during each cash cycle is identical, whether or not the transaction is revolving. Fundamentally, the goal is to keep the trust in a zero-equity position via the principal-based parity of assets and liabilities. In a static pool transaction, you will recall that this was accomplished by returning just enough principal to investors to enable that equality to be maintained at all times. If insufficient Available Funds remained after interest and other distributions had been made, the trust became insolvent. It was not bankrupt because bankruptcy-remoteness was the very raison d'être of the transaction.

Defining $P_d(t)$ as the principal due to investors at time step t, $D(t)$ as the receivables that were tagged as defaulted during the most recent collection period, $P_p(t)$ as prepayments from whatever source, and $P_r(t)$ as regular principal collections, the amount of principal that had to be returned to investors at time t was given in earlier chapters via the following basic relationship:

$$P_d(t) = P_r(t) + P_p(t) + D(t) \qquad (1)$$

Equation (1) is valid under all circumstances, including revolving periods, except that here the amount $P_d(t)$ is not given back to investors but is instead deemed available for new asset purchases. Excess cash can be returned to the sponsor or SPC equity-holder as a dividend. As long as actual cash remaining at the level of principal within the periodic waterfall exceeds or at least equals the amount given by the right-hand side of equation (1), the transaction is presumed to be operating as intended, since total funds collected are more than sufficient to pay all servicing and other fees, interest due, and defaults. Defaults have obviously not been received as cash and are simply *due* to investors in order to maintain the trust in a fully collateralized position.

At this point, one can imagine various creative and not so creative schemes to try and force the satisfaction of equation (1) despite the absence of any cash. For instance, the asset manager could wait to declare a default until the recoveries on such default have been received as cash. This would create a black hole in terms of yield because loans labeled as performing would in fact not be generating any cash. It would also improperly allow funds to escape from the transaction at the bottom of the waterfall. The proper way to deal with this issue in cases where the deal is too coarse to handle the default would be to use a liquidity account specifically created for this purpose that would be replenished from recovery proceeds ahead of principal distributions on the notes. This way, cash would never escape in contravention of the deal's intent. Inside a market value CDO for instance, the purchase of cheap assets in the open market can cause the same situation to occur. In that case, such assets are booked at par when, in fact, they are generating much higher yield, all of which ends up at the bottom of the waterfall during the revolving period, thus escaping the deal into sponsor pockets.

Although there are other ways to play this game, in the majority of cases there will be more than enough cash to satisfy the left-hand side of equation (1) via the purchase of new loans in the required amount. The source of additional loans during the revolving period will vary depending on the asset class and may eventually make a big difference to the outcome. In this context, we briefly review a couple of major asset classes.

Sources of Receivables during the Revolving Period

Credit Card Master Trusts

In the case of credit card master trusts, the obvious source of assets is the balance sheet of the sponsor. Most large commercial banks are in the business of apparently issuing credit cards to anybody who wants one.[1] The receivables generated by purchases on these cards are in the billions weekly and are usually financed off-balance-sheet.

To do this with sufficient flexibility, most card issuers have created massive trust structures within which several *series* of notes are issued. Each series may be created with its own set of features and modalities, thus enabling the bank to take advantage of changing market conditions to lower its all-in cost of funds. In order to ensure that mechanical or nonanalytical glitches, such as dilution, do not inadvertently cause the trust to become insolvent, the bank is not allowed to securitize the entire principal balance of the receivables in its master trust but requires a certain cushion as security against such risks. The fixed percentage amount of this cushion is usually set by rating agencies and varies by institution depending on the quality of the receivable base and the bank's operating history. This amount has drifted downward in recent years as investors and rating agencies have become more comfortable with the asset class. As of this writing, it is commonly in the neighborhood of 4%.

What is important to understand is that this portion of the master trust's principal balance is not considered credit enhancement to the issued notes but ranks pari passu with the latter. In effect, it represents a co-investment by the sponsor in its own receivables and is still effectively on its balance sheet. In the next section, we come back to the intricacies of credit card master trusts in the context of early amortization.

Collateralized Debt Obligations (CDOs)

This popular funding mechanism sources its receivables mostly in the open market. In transactions based on corporate assets, high-yield and other types of loans are bought and sold with relative liquidity, thus creating a propitious playground for enterprising asset managers.

In the early CDO market, transactions were intended to pay down their liabilities based exclusively on cash flows generated by the assets according to their terms, i.e., merely with the passage of time. Therefore, minimal trading was supposed to take place, at least if one excludes from the definition of *trading* ineligible assets that had to be re-purchased from the trust. The revolving nature of these pools was caused solely by the natural amortization of the usually high-quality loans in the pool. In such cases, normal bank operations were normally sufficient to supply the required assets.

Over the past 10 years, the advent of the market-value CDO concept changed all that. In these transactions, assets are bought and sold at will by managers not engaged in the banking business, thus drastically changing the transaction's credit profile versus that of the initial pool. The main difficulty faced by the manager of a market-value CDO is to locate assets that fit the constraints imposed a priori by the Pooling and Servicing Agreement. Fortunately, the panoply of eligibility criteria commonly encountered in market-value CDO transactions is largely ineffective.

In this respect, it should be noted that the market-value CDO is an *innovation* lying squarely outside the scope of structure finance as originally conceived. In other words, the use of market value as a metric is highly dubious and leads to self-fulfilling prophecies with respect to such value. Remember that the idea of market value as a viable basis for a leveraged investment portfolio was developed into an art form during those heady days when hedge funds were buying CMOs, i.e., whereby asset managers would purchase a diversified portfolio of essentially Aaa-rated securities with positive and negative duration, thus potentially achieving neutral portfolio-wide duration. While doing this, managers commonly earned slightly more than the portfolio's financing costs. That small difference was then magnified by the significant leverage in the capital structure, giving rise to the abnormal equity returns earned by hedge funds, returns that eventually led to their overrated status within the investment community.

In fact, the inverse correlation structure inherent in pool assets is the only feature that made this technique viable. In the original hedge fund concept, trading was used exclusively to re-balance the portfolio in order to maintain approximately zero duration, which in practice usually meant that duration remained within a band of +/- 3%. The hedge fund concept was based on market value because the funding for such schemes came in the form of short-term credit lines from prime brokerage firms entering into matching repurchase agreements collateralized by the very same securities. The brokerage firm simply could not afford to be short liquidity and thus had to be able to liquidate the portfolio into the marketplace within days.

However, although the task of computing the market value of an Aaa-rated instrument is usually not a major challenge, that of doing the same thing for a Ba1-rated telecommunications corporate loan is a different matter. As a result, the market-value CDO lacks the solid theoretical foundation that made CMO-based hedge funds into the gold mine they once were. As Eve told Adam when they first met "don't confuse paradise with fantasy land!"

23.2 EARLY AMORTIZATION

By now, it should be clear to the reader why, as long as sufficient cash is on hand to satisfy the demands of equation (1), the transaction is deemed performing and is left to its own devices. Although a revolving structure is indeed expected to experience defaults over its lifetime, such defaults are expected to be sufficiently small to be reimbursable from excess spread alone. The problem begins when this is no longer the case.

In that situation, something has to be done to protect investors who are clearly exposed. The solution comes in the form of the early amortization trigger, henceforth the main protection mechanism operating within revolving structures. Market value structures, which will not be pursued further, are also equipped with early amortization triggers but for the reasons indicated above, they work according to a different principle.

By way of rationale, recall from the previous section how, within a normally functioning revolving transaction, the assets of the trust should generate periodic yield in amount more than sufficient to pay for servicing and other fees, and for coupon on the liabilities backed by such assets. Even after compensating investors and the seller for receivables that have defaulted during the most recent collection period, excess collections should remain, the so-called *excess spread*. If this excess were to fall to zero however, for instance through a rise in defaults, a decrease in the effective yield of the trust, or some combination thereof, investors would run the risk of principal loss. This situation cannot be allowed to continue since the deal was originally construed so that this would not happen. At that moment, no further spread is available and investor protection can only come from whatever form of credit enhancement is available to them. It is at this time that the process of investor reimbursement is triggered ahead of schedule and allowed to use that enhancement. This is the idea of early amortization within revolving structures. The word *early* refers to the fact that amortization happens ahead of schedule.

As a direct consequence of this mechanism, it follows that, at all times leading up to the potential declaration of any early amortization event, credit enhancement in the form of a reserve account, a surety bond or any other, cannot be used to effect distributions pursuant to the waterfall. The reason is that doing this would postpone the effective declaration of the early amortization event in an obviously deteriorating credit environment.

The Early Amortization Trigger

The early amortization trigger is the single most important feature within a revolving structure. As indicated, it allows the transaction to start amortizing early should collateral performance deteriorate outside the bounds originally contemplated. The foregoing discussion should provide ample rationale to motivate the definition of zero excess spread as the level at which the transaction will be triggered into early amortization within most revolving structures, i.e., exactly at the point where excess spread vanishes. It should however be noted that some foreign jurisdictions use a higher percentage. For example, Japanese credit card master trusts commonly set early amortization levels at 2% APR. This provides additional credit protection since investors are already on their way out before excess spread falls to zero.

This simple amortization trigger definition may be fine in theory, but practically speaking trusts do not behave as analytically as one would hope. In order to prevent the early amortization feature from being triggered accidentally or for nonanalytical reasons, for instance due to seasonality or other predictable causes, the actual trigger index is not the *periodic* excess spread percentage but its *quarterly-averaged* value. In other words although coincident excess spread could very well be negative during any given collection period, the trust should recover over the following period or two if the collateral starts performing as expected, which effectively forestalls early amortization. If it does not, the deal enters early amortization. Unfortunately, this procedure significantly complicates the numerical implementation of revolving periods.

The Excess Spread Index

Table 23.1 lays out the parameters needed to compute the quarterly-average excess spread index.

Assuming monthly collections, a simple cash balance around the trust leads to the following definitions and boundary conditions for early amortization declarations:

$$A_t = 12 \frac{I_t - S_t - C_t - D_t}{P_{t-1}}, \quad t \in [1, T], \quad A_0 \equiv 1, A_{-1} \equiv 1$$

$$X_t = \frac{A_{t-2} + A_{t-1} + A_t}{3}, \quad t \in [1, T]$$

A cash flow situation whereby $X_t \leq 0$ normally causes the trust to start amortizing. As explained above, $X_t \leq 0.02$ is used to trigger early amortization within Japanese credit card master trusts.

Once a transaction enters its amortization period, new loans are no longer being purchased and principal collections, including of course prepayments and defaults, are due to investors whether received or not. Although the mechanics are virtually identical, it is still customary to differentiate early amortization from that occurring

TABLE 23.1

Nomenclature for the computation of the excess spread index

PARAMETER	DEFINITION
T	The Legal Final Maturity Date of the transaction
t	An arbitrary Collection Period, indexed with an integer, $t \in [1, T]$
I_t	Interest Collections at time t (including recoveries on defaulted receivables, earnings on the PFA (see below) and potentially on any reserve or spread account.)
S_t	Servicing and other fees due at time t
C_t	Coupon due on all outstanding classes of debt at time t
D_t	Defaulted receivables at time t
P_t	Pool balance at time t
A_t	Current excess spread at time t
X_t	Early amortization index at time t

according to the terms originally contemplated. Not surprisingly, the mere fact of experiencing early amortization, even though it should have no bearing on a potential loss to them, is viewed by most investors as a dramatic event. Somehow, they equate such declaration with impending doom. If the rules of the game have been followed precisely, there is no a priori reason why that should be.

Exhibits 23.1 and 23.2 show our own VBA implementation of an early amortization trigger inside a cash flow CDO.

Exhibit 23.1:   Computation of the Coincident Excess Spread Amount

First, the coincident excess spread index needs to be calculated:

Excess Spread = Early Am Available Funds – Swap Payment Due – Aggregate Write Down – Servicing Fee Due – Trustee Fee Due – Aggregate Note Coupon
'
Compute annualized excess spread level as a percentage of the total invested amount
'
Early Amortization Trigger = 12 * Excess Spread / (Previous Pool Balance + Principal Collections Account Balance)

Now, compute the quarterly-averaged excess spread index, remembering that the early months must be handled via the aforementioned boundary conditions and that all subsequent early amortization indices need to be computed based on this rolling value of excess spread.

Exhibit 23.2:   Computation of the Quarterly Average Early Amortization Index

Select Case Time Step

Case 1

Early_Amortization_Trigger_M1 = Early Amortization Trigger
'
Neutralize the first month (will not trigger)
'
Early Amortization Trigger = 1

Case 2

Early_Amortization_Trigger_M2 = Early Amortization Trigger
'
Neutralize the second month (will not trigger)
'
Early Amortization Trigger = 1

continues to next page

---

continued from previous page
Case 3

Early_Amortization_Trigger_M3 = Early Amortization Trigger

Early Amortization Trigger = (Early_Amortization_Trigger_M1 + _
Early_Amortization_Trigger_M2 + Early_Amortization_Trigger_M3) / 3

Case Else

Early_Amortization_Trigger_M1 = Early_Amortization_Trigger_M2
Early_Amortization_Trigger_M2 = Early_Amortization_Trigger_M3
Early_Amortization_Trigger_M3 = Early Amortization Trigger

Early Amortization Trigger = (Early_Amortization_Trigger_M1 + _
Early_Amortization_Trigger_M2 + Early_Amortization_Trigger_M3) / 3

End Select

It is rare, although not impossible, for an early amortization event to be defined in terms of delinquencies instead of excess spread. In such cases, the index would be trivially implemented by quarterly-averaging the percentages of suitably defined delinquencies in the pool, most likely 60+ days past due. This feature will not be demonstrated as it follows an identical format to the one given above and is currently not a major feature of ABS transactions.

23.3 THE BASIC MECHANICS OF ASSET PURCHASE

As mentioned before, the main difficulty presented by the revolving feature is the fact that, in any serious numerical implementation, new loans must be synthesized in real time, placed within the pool, and then allowed to interact with the granular assets already there. The programming skills involved in doing so are nontrivial. What we present here is merely an outline of what actual implementation entails.

The Time Line

Figure 23.1 presents an idealized time line for an arbitrary revolving transaction. Please note that the above fourfold sequence repeats itself every Collection Period. We will use the definitions from table 23.2.

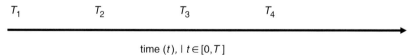

$$T_1 \qquad T_2 \qquad T_3 \qquad T_4$$

$$\text{time } (t), \mid t \in [0, T]$$

FIGURE 23.1
The time line.

TABLE 23.2

Timing definitions for revolving asset purchase

PARAMETER	DEFINITION
T_1	Arbitrary Record Date for the transaction
T_2	Time when new purchases begin during this Collection Period
T_3	The following Record Date
T_4	Distribution Date corresponding to Collection Period $t \in [T_1, T_3]$

We pick up the transaction at time T_1 and assume that all current collections are now sitting in the Collection Account, waiting for the next Distribution Date. In essence, the interval $t \in [T_1, T_3]$ is the time between two record dates during which obligors will make their monthly payments, default, or prepay their loan according to the transaction's synthetic Markov transition matrix. This process takes place during any period, whether it is classified as amortizing or revolving. This interval is also the basis on which principal and interest collections from all obligors are computed, and when defaulted and prepaid loans are handled normally.

By contrast, the interval $t \in [T_2, T_3]$ embedded within this periodic Markov process is the span during which revolving period purchases are made. Although this can physically represent any finite interval, numerical implementation will set it equal to zero since, as far as the model is concerned, revolving purchases are deemed instantaneous. Assets are purchased using either an external line of credit or cash balances evidenced in the Principal Funding Account (PFA, see "Special Accounts within Revolving Structure Implementations" below). To achieve any sort of success in the modeling of revolving periods, the mechanics of asset purchase need to be modeled precisely and explicitly, since PFA mechanics will closely interact with them.

Note also that, although in most cases the assets that have just been purchased will usually not default or prepay right away, a serious numerical implementation cannot differentiate between such new assets and those which have been outstanding for some time, since even new assets were most likely originated prior to their purchase date. As a result, all assets are subjected to the full Markov chain dynamics from the moment they are placed in the trust.

Finally, the interval $t \in [T_3, T_4]$ represents the time from the second Record Date to the corresponding Distribution Date. In practice, this is approximately two weeks, during which time the Trustee gathers and computes appropriate transfers to investors and third parties in concert with the Servicer. Again, numerical implementations usually collapse this interval to zero.

The Two Extremes of Loan Purchase Modeling

In modeling asset purchase, although many different methods can be used, they invariably fall on an axis whose endpoints roughly corresponding to random and historical simulation, respectively. Instead of using these common definitions, let's introduce the more expressive labels of *Chinese* and *French* methods.

Effectively, the French method corresponds to historical simulation. This is because of its vector-based, all-or-none selection bias with limited substitution (a truly French technique would not allow any variation). The Chinese system implies a more flexible and intricate approach whereby loans are synthesized in real time by considering the pool's horizontal correlation structure. To understand what we are trying to achieve we devote a few paragraphs to each one.

The French Asset Selection Method

The basic idea underlying the French method is the *prix fixe* restaurant menu. As may you know, this does not mean that the price is fixed but rather, that the menu is fixed. In structured finance, this amounts to re-selecting individual assets found in the original pool while allowing the principal balance to change according to the corresponding pool distribution. This avoids the major problem involved in synthesizing assets (addressed by the next method), i.e., the faithful representation of the pool's asset-wise correlation structure.

This issue arises because assets cannot be created in a vacuum. For instance, in transactions sponsored by issuers actually pricing for risk, assuming there are still any, a loan's FICO score and its interest rate will be correlated in some way because this is how rates are set in the first place. This implicit correlation structure needs to be heeded if the pool is to make any sense at all. In fact, this is nothing but one of the many examples of implicit correlation. We call it *horizontal* by analogy with chapter 15, where we assumed that *vertical* correlation addressed the possibility that individual assets were dependent, something ruled out a priori except for the potential link between independence and a common macro-economic index modeled explicitly via some copula function. Although neglecting vertical correlation beyond copula-function-based linkages is justifiable, the proper modeling of horizontal correlation structures is a *conditio sine qua non* of any serious revolving analysis.

It is simply not permissible to pick asset parameters at random, put them together and pretend that this is an eligible asset. Errors of this type are widely committed when, for example, it is assumed that subsequent lessees in a revolving aircraft lease transaction have the same, low credit rating, for the simple reason that such airline-lessees do not exist. As a result, pools created during the revolving period have no connection to the real world and completely exaggerate the risk involved in aircraft ABS transactions.

The French method obviates this problem by ensuring that the horizontal asset correlation structure is implicitly followed via the selection of feasible assets simply because they were originally in the pool. Another advantage of this method is that it reduces asset synthesis to a table look-up function, thereby considerably accelerating Monte Carlo analysis. As an example of the straightforwardness of this method, exhibit 23.3 presents a VBA code implementation of the French selection method for a CDO of ABS. In the code, "Save Asset ID" is the label for the granular asset that was in the original pool.

> **Exhibit 23.3: VBA Implementation of the French Asset Selection Method**

Case "French"
'

Pick the entire vector from a single line, the same as the target asset class
'

.Interest Type = Tranches (Save Asset ID).Interest Type
.Tranche Swap Flag = Tranches (Save Asset ID).Tranche Swap Flag
.Tranche Rate = Tranches (Save Asset ID).Tranche Rate
'

Adjust the WAC selection to account for LIBOR variation on floating-rate loans
'

Select Case .Interest Type
Case "Fixed"

.WAC = Tranches (Save Asset ID).WAC

Case "Floating"
Fac(1) = LIBOR(Tranches(Save Asset ID).Purchase Month, 1) + Tranches(Save Asset ID).Tranche Rate
Fac(2) = Tranches(Save Asset ID).WAC - Fac(1)
.WAC = Fac(2) + LIBOR(.Purchase Month, 1) + .Tranche Rate

End Select

.WAM = Min (Tranches (Save Asset ID).WAM, Legal Final Maturity Date - .Purchase Month - 1)
.Number of Loans = Tranches (Save Asset ID).Number of Loans
.Seasoning = Tranches (Save Asset ID).Seasoning
.Asymptote = Tranches (Save Asset ID).Asymptote
.Multiplier = Tranches (Save Asset ID).Multiplier
.Time Constant = Tranches (Save Asset ID).Time Constant
.Time Offset = Tranches (Save Asset ID).Time Offset

End Select

The Chinese Asset Selection Method

In contrast to the relatively straightforward French selection method, the Chinese scheme is based on the columnar system in use at most Chinese restaurants. This scheme is based on the selection of one parameter at a time from the pool's original parametric density function. As mentioned previously, the main programming difficulty encountered in the implementation of the Chinese method rests in following the dictates of the horizontal, asset-wise correlation structure that inheres in the original pool. As a result, specific loan parameters must be selected in concert with others inside a coherent scheme implicitly respecting this structure. For example, in a corporate CDO, the loan rate or spread and its credit rating can obviously not be separately chosen since the two are inextricably linked via the yield curve.

Therefore, once the credit rating is selected, the rate needs to be determined in a manner consistent with it. How to do this quickly and logically is the crux of the Chinese method.

Clearly, in practice certain parameters need to be considered primordial and subjected to a basic random selection algorithm, after which the parameters deemed associated or correlated to such primordial variables are co-determined in a consistent manner. To the extent possible, these determinations are effected within a correlation structure simulated via Cholesky decomposition (chapter 18), thereby slightly lengthening the extent of the programming task but fully accounting for the pool's internal structure. There are, however, less onerous methods of doing this that do not impose the burden of Cholesky decomposition. Given that we already introduced the latter technique in chapter 18, we would like to now focus on simplified methods, leaving readers the task of giving free rein to their creativity in using the Cholesky decomposition to solve the same problem.

As an example of a simple method, exhibit 23.4 is a VBA code section showing the implementation of the Chinese method for the same CDO of ABS transaction used to illustrate the prior method. This implementation uses simple uniform distributions to select the primordial and correlated parameters while ensuring that correlated parameters fall in line with the original pool's distributional features.

Exhibit 23.4:   VBA Implementation of the Chinese Asset Selection Method

```
Case "Chinese"

Fac(2) = 0

For Counter = 1 To Number of Tranches - 1
Fac(2) = Fac(2) - (Tranches(Counter).Interest Type = "Floating") * _
Tranches (Counter).Current Tranche Balance
Next Counter

Fac(2) = Fac(2) / Pool Balance

Fac(1) = Random Number Generator (I)
'
Handle floating or fixed-rate tranches
'
Select Case Fac(1)
Case Is <= Fac(2)
.Interest Type = "Floating"
Case Else
.Interest Type = "Fixed"
End Select
'
Pick the tranche rate at random from the target universe
'
Fac(3) = 0.5: Fac(4) = 0
```

```
Fac(5) = 0.2: Fac(6) = 0
Fac(2) = 0: Fac(7) = 0

For Counter = 1 To Number of Tranches - 1
Select Case Tranches (Counter).Interest Type

Case "Fixed"

Select Case Tranches (Counter).Tranche Rating
Case Target Rating
'
Find the minimum and maximum rates of all classes with this rating in the current pool
'
Fac(3) = Min(Fac(3), Tranches(Counter).Tranche Rate)
Fac(4) = Max(Fac(4), Tranches(Counter).Tranche Rate)
End Select

Case "Floating"

Fac(7) = Fac(7) + 1
Fac(2) = Fac(2) - 1 * (Tranches(Counter).Tranche Swap Flag = True)
Select Case Tranches (Counter).Tranche Moodys Rating
Case Target Rating
'
Find the minimum and maximum rates of all classes with this rating in the current pool
'
Fac(5) = Min(Fac(5), Tranches(Counter).Tranche Rate)
Fac(6) = Max(Fac(6), Tranches(Counter).Tranche Rate)
End Select
End Select
Next Counter
'
Pick a random number between the min and the max for the tranche rate
'
Select Case .Interest Type
Case "Fixed"

.Tranche Rate = Fac(3) + Random Number Generator(l) * (Fac(4) - Fac(3))

Case "Floating"

.Tranche Rate = Fac(5) + Random Number Generator(l) * (Fac(6) - Fac(5))
'
Determine from the target universe whether a swap exists at the tranche level
'
Fac(1) = Fac(2) / (Fac(7) + Random Residual)
Scratch = Random Number Generator (l)

Select Case Scratch
```

continues to next page

continued from previous page
Case Is < Fac(1)
.Tranche Swap Flag = True
.Tranche Swap Rate = LIBOR (.Purchase Month, 1)
Case Else
.Tranche Swap Flag = False
.Tranche Swap Rate = 0
End Select

End Select
'
Continue with the remaining parameters
The WAC is chosen by reference to the tranche rate to model the behavior of the target
universe.
'
This next group of parameters must be chosen together to fit the loss model
'
i = 1 + Int(Random Number Generator (l) * (Number of Tranches - 1))
'
Cap maturities at the legal final date
'
.WAM = Min(Tranches(i).WAM, Legal Final Maturity Date - .Purchase Month - 1)
.Number of Loans = Tranches (i).Number of Loans
.Seasoning = Tranches (i).Seasoning
.Asymptote = Tranches (i).Initial Asymptote
.Multiplier = Tranches(i).Multiplier
.Time Constant = Tranches(i).Time Constant
.Time Offset = Tranches(i).Time Offset
'
WAC selection is tricky because [WAC – Tranche Rate] depends on the WAM
'
Fac(3) = 0.2: Fac(4) = 0
Fac(5) = 0.2: Fac(6) = 0

For Counter = 1 To Number of Tranches - 1
Select Case Tranches (Counter).Interest Type

Case "Fixed"
Scratch = Abs((.WAM - Tranches(Counter).WAM) / .WAM)
Select Case Scratch
Case Is <= WAM Cut Off Limit
Fac(3) = Min(Fac(3), Tranches(Counter).WAC - Tranches(Counter).Tranche Rate)
Fac(4) = Max(Fac(4), Tranches(Counter).WAC - Tranches(Counter).Tranche Rate)
End Select

Case "Floating"
'
In the floating-rate case, pick the maximum and minimum of the difference between the
WAC and the total rate of all floating-rate tranches that pass the WAM cut-off.
'

```
Scratch = Abs((.WAM - Tranches(Counter).WAM) / .WAM)
Select Case Scratch
Case Is <= WAM Cut Off Limit
Fac(5) = Min(Fac(5), Tranches(Counter).WAC - _
(Tranches(Counter).Tranche Rate + LIBOR(Tranches(Counter).Purchase Month, 1)))
Fac(6) = Max(Fac(6), Tranches(Counter).WAC - _
(Tranches(Counter).Tranche Rate + LIBOR(Tranches(Counter).Purchase Month, 1)))

End Select
End Select

Next Counter
'
Pick a random number between the min and the max for the WAC selection
'
Select Case .Interest Type
Case "Fixed"
.WAC = .Tranche Rate + Fac(3) + Random Number Generator(I) * (Max_WAC
-Min_WAC)
Case "Floating"
.WAC = .Tranche Rate + LIBOR(.Purchase Month, 1) + Fac(5) + _
Random Number Generator (I) * (Max_Spread - Min_ Spread)
End Select

Calibrate (Number of Tranches)

In the case of the Chinese selection method, an ABS tranche has now been synthesized
and needs to be re-calibrated according to the selected parameters.
```

Some Final Remarks on the Chinese Selection Method

The first thing to notice with respect to the Chinese method is how much more involved it is to implement programmatically than the French method. These complications mostly stem from the correlation structure we discussed earlier and the concomitant need to restrict our freedom in selecting related asset parameters. The implementation highlighted in exhibit 23.4 is by no means a sophisticated one. We would expect serious structured analysts to do much more than this illustration to implement live revolving transactions.

However, the good news here is that a Cholesky-based approach would in fact be easier than the above code would suggest and would more clearly demonstrate the way in which correlations can be automatically incorporated into transaction analysis. This is yet another example where a numerical method never intended to handle revolving periods finds an ideal application in the trenches of structured finance.

Last, but not least, the calibration required to effect the Chinese method, and shown at the end of exhibit 23.4, refers to the first stage of the CDO of ABS analysis discussed in "*The Analysis of Structured Securities*" (OUP, 2003), whereby the average reduction of yield of this synthetic tranche must be made consistent with its credit rating. You will recall that such consistency was a precondition of the analysis of the CDO of ABS transaction, whether or not it had a revolving period. In the case of the French method, calibration was made redundant by the fact that all synthetic tranches had already been calibrated at the outset. Conversely, in the Chinese method the tranche is essentially brand new and, to be credible, requires an initial calibration.

As you can imagine, doing this in real time considerably lengthens the Monte Carlo simulation. As a result, and despite the added realism inherent in the method, we recommend it only to those with sufficient computing resources at their disposal.

23.4 MODIFICATION OF MARKOV TRANSITION MATRICES DUE TO REVOLVING PERIODS

From the standpoint of simulation, allowing revolving period purchases to take place imposes an additional burden on the analyst that requires an explicit modification of the time-dependent synthesis of Markov transition matrices. Specifically, modulator-equation (30) in chapter 16 must be modified to take into account revolving period assets meeting eligibility covenants at the time of purchase (see "Implementing Eligibility Criteria within Revolving Structures" below). This is because these assets cannot be handled using the same time-dependent pattern used to model the assets in the original pool.

Further, since the asset purchase process operative within revolving structures takes place from the Closing Date to the scheduled end of the revolving period, or earlier should the transaction enter early amortization, a general analytical code needs a way to continuously modify transition matrices without regard for the particular terms of the target transaction.

Recall that equations (28) and (30) in chapter 16 implicitly assumed that $t = 0$ for the deal and the assets were the same notion. In other words, $t = 2$ was the second time step for the deal and for the loans too, and this meant that all loans were effectively originated on the closing date. Although this was admittedly an approximation, better or worse depending on the issuer and the asset class, the magnitude of such errors inside static pool transactions was relatively small and, in the case of seasoned loans, could easily be handled via the seasoning-based transition-matrix modification reviewed in chapter 16. Once this was done, the respective time scales of the transaction and its assets were ipso facto restored to their original equality.

Within revolving structures however, this approximation can no longer be countenanced since newly purchased assets inside cash flow CDOs will most likely be newly originated, and will require their own time scale. The latter needs initialization at the moment an asset is purchased. Of course, the purchase of seasoned loans during the revolving period is by no means excluded from this formalism. For now, we leave such complications aside.

The foregoing considerations should provide ample motivation for the conclusion that a loan-wise modification of Markov transition matrices is best effected via the inclusion of a revolving period time parameter t_p equal to the time at which the loan is purchased within the revolving period. Since revolving period assets are effectively delayed purchases, this parameter will perforce appear negatively above the exponential found in modulator-equation (30) in chapter 16.

As a result, the standard revolving period modulator can be defined as follows:

$$f(t) = \frac{M_p(n)\,m(L_e)\,b\,c\,e^{-c(t-t_0+t_s-t_p)}}{[1+b\,e^{-c(t-t_0+t_s-t_p)}]^2} \qquad (2)$$

Since the implementation of this modification is innocuous, it will not be demonstrated here. If need be, you can simply refer to equation (31) in chapter (16) and implement the change implied by equation (2) when appropriate.

Lastly, note that the presence of a revolving period per se introduces an explicit loan-wise factor inside a Markov transition matrix, in addition to its already existing time-wise features. As a result, a revolving period implementation which uses an ad hoc scheme will always fail to reflect the dynamics of asset purchase properly.

23.5 ELIGIBILITY COVENANTS IN REVOLVING STRUCTURES

We have now come to the second major challenge of revolving period implementation: the appropriate selection of new assets based on pool eligibility criteria, something of even greater critical import to the credit rating of the deal than asset-wise correlation. You will recall how, within most revolving transactions, whether of the cash flow or market-value type, rating agencies and investment bankers usually develop a series of eligibility criteria or *covenants* aimed at ensuring that the pool's composition does not drift too far away from the intended portfolio composition as a result of adverse revolving period purchases. To be sure, this risk looms much larger with respect to market-value structures, where unlimited trading is allowed, than within cash flow deals where trading is largely incidental and where normal issuer originations are the main source of new assets, i.e., where market speculation induced by asset managers is not a major factor.

In this work, we leave strictly alone any discussion or opinion as to whether such eligibility criteria, which can run into the dozens, in fact accomplish their stated goal. What is certain, however, is that nobody has ever bothered to check whether they do.

Implementing Eligibility Covenants

The general idea underlying the implementation of eligibility covenants within revolving structures is the creation of a Boolean loop inside which assets are generated in real time while eligibility covenants are enforced. Should the resulting, provisional pool breach any covenant, the code simply rejects the would-be asset and starts all over again with a new prospective loan, each time verifying that all covenants are indeed satisfied. The obvious Catch 22 aspect of this type of implementation is that, depending on the allowable universe of new assets, the loop might never terminate. This simply means that loans with the required characteristics simply do not exist with sufficiently high probability. In other words, the deal as currently structured does not work. It is a forgone conclusion that many CDOs of this type have in fact been issued.

The obvious solution is to relax some or all of the eligibility criteria to allow the covenant loop to terminate. In terms of CPU time, it is easy to guess that the higher the number of covenants that need to be enforced simultaneously, the longer the code will run inside a single Monte Carlo scenario. Luckily, the liberality of the covenants found in many transactions is usually sufficient to allow the simulation to march forward at high speed.

Someone might reasonably argue that a transaction can always be properly structured and that statistical artifacts are solely to blame for the supposedly mistaken notion that the deal does not work. Unfortunately, the combinatorial possibilities inside revolving-period statistics are such that even on the first time step of the first Monte Carlo scenario, i.e., when the initial pool is still intact, badly designed eligibility covenants will invariably cause the deal to crash, whereas in properly designed transactions, asset selection will proceed smoothly. Of course, those arguing as above are commonly and falsely assuming that such structures were designed in the first place, instead of being thrown together hodgepodge, Wall Street style, in the forlorn hope that something would eventually stick, as it apparently did. As a live example of the covenant loop, exhibit 23.5 shows how two such covenants (asset class and subinvestment grade credit rating) can be implemented in real time inside transaction code.

Exhibit 23.5: Implementing Eligibility Covenants within a CDO of ABS

Select new tranche parameters using the Chinese or French method while respecting the two assumed covenants:
1) The aggregate principal balance of all sub-investment grade tranches must be kept below the target percentage.
2) The maximum dollar concentration by asset class must be kept below the target percentage.
'

Additional covenants may be inserted; this is the minimum set.
'

Covenant Breach = True
Do Until Or (Covenant Breach = False, Trial ID > Maximum Selection Trials)
'

' Principal balance
'

Do

Target Balance = Max (0, Norm Inv (Random Number Generator (I), Portfolio Mean Balance, New Tranche Standard Deviation))

Loop Until Or (I > 2 * Maximum Selection Trials, And (Target Balance > Minimum Par Amount, Target Balance < Available Principal))
'

If the algorithm has gone through more than a set number of trials, just pick a uniform deviate for the target balance.
'

If I > 2 * Maximum Selection Trials Then

```
Target Balance = Minimum Par Amount + Random Number Generator (I) * _
(Available Principal – Minimum Par Amount)
End If
'
Credit rating
'
i = 1 + Int(Random Number Generator (I) * Number of Tranches)
Target Rating = Tranches(i).Tranche Rating
'
Asset class
'
i = 1 + Int(Random Number Generator (I) * Number of Tranches)
Save Asset ID = i
Target Asset Class = Tranches(i).Tranche Asset Class
'
This is the temporary repository of the asset class index for the new tranche
'
j = Int(VLookup (Target Asset Class, Asset Class Array, 2, False))
'
First covenant
'
Scratch = 0
For Counter = 1 To Number of Tranches
With Tranches(Counter)

Select Case .Tranche Rating
Case "Ba1", "Ba2", "Ba3"
Scratch = Scratch + .Current Tranche Balance
End Select
End With
Next Counter
'
If the target tranche is in the range, include it too
'
Select Case Target Rating
Case "Ba1", "Ba2", "Ba3"
Scratch = Scratch + Target Balance

End Select
'
Calculate the aggregate balance of Ba1, Ba2, Ba3 Tranches (including the target
tranche)
'
Fac(1) = Pool Balance + Target Balance
Fac(2) = Scratch / Fac(1)
If Fac(2) > Non Investment Grade Covenant Then First Covenant = True Else First
Covenant = False
```

continues to next page

```
continued from previous page
'
Second covenant
'
Scratch = 0
For i = 1 To Macro Indices
Fac(i) = 0
For Counter = 1 To Number of Tranches
With Tranches(Counter)
Fac(i) = Fac(i) - (.Tranche Index = i) * .Current Tranche Balance
End With
Next Counter
Fac(i) = Fac(i) - (j = i) * Target Balance

Next i
'
Calculate the maximum aggregate balance by asset class
'
Scratch = Fac(1)
For i = 2 To Macro Indices
Scratch = Max(Fac(i), Scratch)
Next i

Scratch = Scratch / (Pool Balance + Target Balance)
If Scratch > Asset Class Limit Covenant Then Second Covenant = True
Else Second Covenant = False
'
If more covenants are imposed, add them here.
'
If And (Not First Covenant, Not Second Covenant) Then Covenant Breach = False
'
Update the Trial ID to prevent an infinite loop.
'
Trial ID = Trial ID + 1

Loop
'
If we have not succeeded before the allowable number of attempts, stop and
investigate. Most likely, the covenants are too tight and need to be changed.
'
If (Trial ID > Maximum Selection Trials) Then Stop
'
If OK, spawn the exposure and fill in the remaining parameters
'
Number of Tranches = Number of Tranches + 1

Re Dim Preserve Tranches (Number of Tranches)
```

23.6 REVOLVING PERIODS AND FLOATING-RATE ASSETS

After all this trouble, the addition of floating-rate assets inside a structured transaction should not represent a large amount of work on the part of the analyst, especially in view of our discussion of short-rate models in chapter 19.

At the time, you will recall that we reviewed the implementation of the Cox–Ingersoll–Ross (CIR) short-rate model as a precursor to prepayment modeling. We inserted the CIR output rate inside the time-dependent sequence of Markov transition matrices, which led to the implementation of a basic prepayment model used to investigate the performance of the deal over a range of prepayment speeds. In a similar way, the CIR model can be put to use in modeling floating-rate assets. Interested readers should refer to chapter 19 for more information on the CIR algorithm.

It will sometimes happen, for instance in mortgage markets, that issuers contribute floating-rate assets with constant or variable spreads during revolving periods. The first task is to assign the proper spread to the assets in real time. The deal then simply unfolds by letting the CIR model compute interest payments owed by the new assets.

Although exhibit 23.4 provides an indication as to how floating-rate assets are to be treated, the situation is complicated by the fact that their cash flow transfer function is more difficult to derive than that of fixed-rate assets. In most cases, LIBOR spreads on consumer assets will be high and sticky while in others, issuers will be pricing for risk and spreads will depend on risk measures like FICO scores. If this is the case, there will be a requirement to model credit scores. The technique used above for the other loan parameters can be used here as well.

For corporate loans however, one can reasonably expect that bond spreads will depend on the maturity of the loan and the credit rating of the borrower, i.e., on the yield curve. To do this, the yield curve model presented in chapter 22 can be used profitably, and spreads can simply be read of the yield curve by subtracting the output of the model from the risk-free rate at that maturity. The vast majority of corporate exposures have bullet maturities, thus obviating the need to compute the average life before using the yield curve model.

A simpler method to compute spreads is to use the original pool and select a spread from the spread distribution of all like-maturity assets with a credit rating comparable to that of the target asset. Granted, this assumes that credit ratings tell the whole story, and they commonly do not. However, it does have the advantage of linking the chosen spread to a more relevant, local measure, i.e., the original pool, than to a global index like the yield curve. This is really a matter of choice and preference than of accuracy. The use of a yield curve model is cleaner and allows the explicit use of maturities in the computation of spreads, although spread differences over a typical target-maturity range within a given issuer will usually be overwhelmed by other sources of error.

The point is that floating-rate assets do not present a serious obstacle to the implementation of a revolving period once short-rate and yield curve models, which abound in the literature, are available to the analyst. There is no point re-inventing the wheel by creating a different short-rate model for the purpose of revolving-period analysis, not to mention the obvious inconsistency in doing this.

> **Exercise 23.1**
>
> Derive the floating-rate asset cash flow transfer function. Remember that rates on past due payments are variable, i.e., equation (25) in chapter 16 can no longer be used.

23.7 SPECIAL ACCOUNTS IN REVOLVING STRUCTURES

In closing this chapter, we would like to dig a little deeper into the programmatic details of implementing revolving structures as well as discuss some of the major implementation pitfalls.

So far, we have chiefly expounded on the strictly theoretical aspects of loan creation, asset-wise correlation structure, covenant handling, and internal asset modeling. It is remarkable that, within revolving structures, all these features are present simultaneously and interact in real time. The upshot is that the cash balancing problem at the heart of all structured transactions now takes on nightmarish proportions on that basis alone. Yet, the very practical problem of dealing with reality is still hiding underneath this structural challenge. A Monte Carlo simulation needs to take into account the way actual transactions work, and cannot make simplifying, completely unrealistic assumptions in the name of tractability.

Chief among the brand new, strictly practical problems created by revolving periods are two phenomena that never needed to enter the analysis of static pool deals:

1. What to do with idle cash balances allocated to principal purchases during the revolving period.
2. How to deal with the cash flow implications associated with the declaration mechanics of early amortization events based on quarterly moving averages.

Although these two phenomena arise merely as unwanted mechanical consequences of revolving structures, it is virtually certain that structured analysts who do not take the time to address them in their own implementations end up with codes that leak cash, and hence produce misleading results and security values. Serious analysis eventually has to come to grips with the unintended consequences that plague the numerical implementation of revolving structures. In what follows, we review the basic problematic and indicate briefly how to achieve resolution in one case.

The Principal Funding Account (PFA)

As we have already mentioned, the main headache underlying the implementation of a revolving period is that a loan generation routine needs to be included. Leaving aside for the moment considerations pertaining to the difficulties of an implementation attentive to transaction requirements in terms of covenants and correlation structure, it stands to reason that the actual process of buying loans must be situated within a realistic framework. What we mean is that loans of exactly the right size, maturity, etc., will not materialize by magic before the asset manager to help him or her get rid of cash sitting in the Collection Account. In practice, asset managers will have to scour the capital markets in search of fixed income excellence.

During the acquisition process, it is a foregone conclusion that, both on practical and theoretical grounds, a certain amount of cash will remain idle until the appropriate investment presents itself. This cash, in an amount precisely equal to the difference between the aggregate liability balance and the aggregate principal balance of earning assets in the trust, must somehow be accounted for and invested until opportunity knocks. Therefore, to hold idle balances dedicated to asset purchases between two collection periods, structured analysts need to create a special cash account, dubbed the Principal Funding Account (PFA), whose contents are to be duly invested in Eligible Investments pending further asset purchases.

On a periodic basis, the balance in the PFA would always equal the difference between Total Principal Due during the revolving period and assets purchased pursuant to it. Each month, the remaining PFA balance from the previous period would be added to Total Principal Due from current collections and would be made available to the asset manager for additional purchases, or else to satisfy other revolving period constraints.

In this context, it would be wrong to presume that the PFA could simply be zeroed out each month by assuming that, by sheer coincidence, a *clean-up* asset with a principal balance exactly equal to the remaining PFA balance could be found. First, this type of artificial, market-clearing purchase, which could potentially amount to buying a $50 loan, simply does not make sense because these loans are obviously too small to be realistically considered by the manager. To model this kind of artificiality is silly and should never be done. It is a simple fact that idle balances exist and have to be treated as such, i.e., as an integral part of the analytical exercise at the outset. Furthermore, transactions are normally equipped with minimum purchase requirements which prevent any asset with an initial principal balance smaller than such minimum from entering the pool. Thus, for reasons having nothing to do with the putative ability of asset managers to find the right asset at the right time, the explicit modeling of the PFA is necessary.

The PFA is an interest-bearing account earning the Eligible Investment Rate. These earnings represent cash that needs to be counted as part of any amortization trigger calculation. In addition, PFA earnings need to be removed from the account itself and added periodically to Available Funds so as never to allow the trust's aggregate asset balance to exceed its aggregate liability balance. This would happen if the balance in the PFA were grossed up by the earnings thereon and allowed to be regarded as funds available for asset purchase. In addition, PFA excess earnings should be permitted to escape the deal since they represent yield of the same type as that arising from the other assets in the pool.

A fundamental PFA boundary condition, which also provides a check to its correct implementation, is that at all times during the revolving period the sum of pool and PFA balances should equal aggregate liability balances, the latter remaining unchanged from the Closing Date. Finally, at the end of the revolving period the contents of the PFA are to be added to Total Principal Due and returned to investors either immediately after the declaration of an Early Amortization Event or otherwise. It will generally be true that the average PFA balance during the revolving period will depend on the smallest loan that may be either purchased or originated by the trust.

A Live Example of PFA Mechanics

In actual transactions, the correct implementation of the PFA presupposes a formal handling of the revolving period that keeps track of Total Principal Due in the way it was done within static pool transactions. In terms of interaction, the PFA is not directly related to the early amortization mechanics and can be treated separately. Remember that if an amount less than Total Principal Due is available for deposit into the PFA on any Distribution Date, the transaction is on its way to early amortization even though the early amortization trigger has yet to be declared. Formally speaking, the PFA balance could be reinvested in new assets despite any shortfall, reflective of the fact that the trust has just become insolvent. To correct this situation, the PSA (treated in this section) needs to be introduced. Exhibit 23.6 shows sections of the VBA code implementation of a PFA inside a CDO.

Exhibit 23.6: Simplified VBA Code Section Implementing the PFA

Available Funds = Available Funds – Reserve Account Balance

Buy new securities with principal collections and make up defaults when feasible

Available Principal = Principal Funding Account Balance + Min (Principal Owed, Available Funds)
Available Funds = Available Funds – Min (Principal Owed, Available Funds)

Acquire new assets using the PFA balance

Do While Available Principal > (1 + Error Margin) * Minimum Par Amount
Spawn New Exposure
Loop

Restore the PFA to its remaining balance using unused principal funds

Principal Funding Account Balance = Available Principal

Notes on PFA Implementation

We should mention that the above code section was somewhat sanitized in order to bring out more clearly the crux of implementation mechanics. Actual CDO codes will contain fail-safe features that have nothing to do with deal mechanics.

The first thing to notice is that the contents of the reserve account, if one exists, are first removed from Available Funds since this account cannot be used to purchase new assets during the revolving period. The variable "Principal Owed" is more or less what we called "Total Principal Due" above. The devil is obviously in the meaning of "more or less." Within a properly functioning transaction, this variable would merely consist of the total pool amortization for the current Collection Period. As you can see, Principal Owed is simply added to the PFA balance left over from the prior period before entering the asset purchase routine (labeled "Spawn New Exposure"). Exactly how assets are bought was discussed earlier in this chapter. An amount equal to Principal Owed is then removed from Available Funds and what remains falls to the bottom of the waterfall, returning to the sponsor in the form of excess spread.

The code allows for an "Error Margin," which can later be set to zero, in order to avoid an infinite loop inside the asset generation routine due to statistical artifacts. Under this implementation, the transaction is not allowed to buy an asset with a principal balance less than a given minimum. This minimum can be reduced at will, thus automatically resulting in increased pool granularity and diversification as smaller assets can now enter the trust. In this way, the analyst maintains complete flexibility over pool composition during the revolving period.

The PFA balance at the end of the asset purchase phase is equal to the amount remaining in Available Principal, which balance is then deemed to earn the Eligible Investment Rate during the next Collection Period. This cycle is repeated until the deal starts to amortize according to its original terms or else upon the declaration of an Early Amortization Event. In fact, the above code section forms the bulk of the revolving period treatment within the main waterfall.

The Principal Shortfall Account (PSA)

Although the Principal Shortfall Account (PSA) is our last revolving period topic, it is by no means the end of the road for those actually implementing revolving periods. The simultaneous interaction of all these features is much more problematic that anyone could first surmise. The PSA is an important feature meant to avoid cash flow leaks. In what follows, we review the origin of the PSA and demonstrate its implementation within a live setting.

Fundamentally, the introduction of a PSA is made necessary by the declaration mechanics of early amortization events. Recall that in actual transactions, the quarterly moving average excess spread, rather than its coincident value, is used as the trigger index pursuant to early amortization. This was done to counter seasonality and other factors and to ensure that transactions do not flippantly enter early amortization when, in fact, they are performing in line with original expectations. It follows directly from this feature that coincident excess spread may in fact be negative while the transaction is still revolving, because its quarterly moving average value is still positive. The frequency with which this will happen depends in large measure on the speed of deterioration in asset performance, something that cannot be predicted. The entire raison d'être of the early amortization trigger is precisely the ability to avoid having to make this prediction.

As a result of this loophole, the aggregate trust balance, including both high-yield assets and the PFA balance, will be allowed to drop below its aggregate liability balance and the trust, albeit now insolvent, will still be permitted to revolve for a month or even two. Therefore, unless one somehow keeps track of such differential negativity, which in essence would correspond to the amount by which the PFA balance would otherwise fall below zero, the deal-code will start to leak cash. The PSA was conceived to prevent just that.

In a nutshell, the PSA simply accumulates shortfalls between Total Principal Due and Available Funds during the revolving period until the transaction starts to amortize. Obviously, once the deal triggers out of its revolving period, the amount contained in the PSA must be added to what is already owed to bondholders since it represents the extent of total trust insolvency. In other words, the PSA does not represent cash but the absence of cash, and thus is not an interest-bearing account. Although its balance is considered positive, the latter stands for cash deficiencies arising out of an operational and necessary quirk in the mechanics of revolving structures.

On any Payment Date during the proper operation of the transaction, Available Funds should be more than sufficient to make up for defaulted receivables, the only portion of Total Principal Due that has not been received. In this case, the balance in the PSA would be zero at all times. On the other hand, if Available Collections were insufficient to cover Aggregate Defaults after paying for servicing fees and interest on the liabilities, the difference would show up as a positive balance in the PSA. If the trust should not recover, the entire PSA balance would be added to Total Principal Due on the first month of the Amortization Period and could be paid to investors using available credit enhancement.

It is somewhat tricky to manage the PSA should the trust recover. In the unlikely event that asset performance should indeed go back to normal in subsequent Collection Periods, the quarterly averaged excess spread index would never fall below zero and remaining Available Funds would then be used to make up previous shortfalls as evidenced by the PSA. Thus at each time step, in addition to the amounts mentioned above, Total Principal Due includes the principal balance in the PSA.

The import of the PSA with respect to credit ratings should be clear. Unless PSA mechanics are properly implemented, the trigger-based trust insolvency mechanics described above will prevent the cash flow engine from accounting for all liability balances and thus, will fail to refund a portion of such balances to investors even if sufficient funds are made available for this purpose. These principal shortfalls will then cause an artificial reduction of yield to appear on some or all of the structured bonds in the deal and will negatively affect their credit rating. To supposedly fix this by dictating that the entire principal balance of the bond is due at all times, or even simply on the Legal Final Maturity Date is clearly a nonstarter since the timing of principal reimbursements is critical to the accurate reflection of the principal allocation scheme (pro rata, sequential, etc.). Structured analysts do not have a choice as to how the deal operates. An ad hoc fix or a patch will not do either.

Unfortunately, the necessity of a PSA only starts to dawn on an analyst once revolving period mechanics are fully implemented, which of course may never happen. It is thus a theorem that CDOs and credit card master trusts that have been rated using the techniques presented here but without a PSA are over-enhanced.

We close this topic with a short VBA section highlighting the way a PSA is implemented within a live deal. Exhibit 23.7 is taken from the deal code used in exhibit 23.6. It shows how the PSA is fitted into the cash flow mechanics of the revolving period.

Exhibit 23.7 consists of two parts:

1. Computing Principal Owed to the PFA during the revolving period.
2. Flushing the PSA into Principal Owed upon amortization, early or not.

Exhibit 23.7: Simplified VB Code Section Implementing a PSA

Part 1

Principal Owed = Total Principal Collections + Aggregate Shortfall + Principal Shortfall Account Balance

Note: "Aggregate Shortfall" represents ABS tranche-assets that have suffered a write-down, but that have not defaulted yet. This is because ABS collateral does not "default" until the Legal Final Maturity Date at which time all remaining unpaid principal becomes due.

Part 2
'
```
' -----------------------------------------------------------------
'            AMORTIZATION PERIOD TREATMENT
' -----------------------------------------------------------------
'
```
As soon as amortization begins, flush the principal funding account balance into Available Funds to redeem principal as soon as possible and avoid negative arbitrage on cash.
'
Available Funds = Available Funds + Principal Funding Account Balance

Principal Owed = Principal Owed + Principal Funding Account Balance + Principal Shortfall Account Balance

Principal Funding Account Balance = 0
Principal Shortfall Account Balance = 0

23.8 CREDIT ENHANCEMENT IN REVOLVING STRUCTURES

Although we have made scattered remarks throughout this chapter on the use of credit enhancement within revolving structures, it is worthwhile spending a few moments on a matter of considerable importance with respect to implementation mechanics.

You will recall how, save for excess spread, other sources of external credit enhancement available to the trust may not be used during the revolving period. For instance, although a reserve or spread account may fund from excess spread during the revolving period, it may not be drawn while the deal is still revolving. This is why, for instance, we had to remove the Reserve Account Balance from Available Funds in our handling of the PFA (see exhibit 23.6 above). Otherwise, Early Amortization might be forestalled when, in fact, unaided collateral performance has deteriorated to the point at which current excess spread alone is insufficient to make up for current defaults.

Speaking of excess spread, it is completely appropriate to make an exception to this rule with respect to earnings on either reserve or spread accounts. Since such amounts are technically not credit enhancement, although in many transactions they act as such, spread account earnings may be counted as part of Available Funds to forestall early amortization. However, such amounts are unlikely to be a material factor in delaying impending doom. In addition, if a surety bond is available, it may similarly not be drawn before the Amortization Period begins, early or not.

Last but not least, amounts due to, or owed by swap counterparties under a swap agreement, although they have been considered by some as credit enhancement, are in fact market-risk mitigation techniques since they are always found above the principal level in the waterfall. Thus, technically speaking they may never be viewed as credit enhancement. No one claiming the opposite understands structured finance. Of course, the default of the swap counterparty itself is a different matter. In this respect, a transaction that can achieve investment-grade status only when the swap counterparty is assumed default-free has serious problems.

23.9 CONCLUDING REMARKS

We have now come to the end of our cursory look at revolving periods. To be sure, their implementation contains many remaining byways, unexpected difficulties, and treacherous dead-ends we have either not bothered to mention or else merely glossed over. In the final analysis, the only way to know anything about a revolving period is to dig right in and write your own routine. When it finally does work, you will know more about cash flow modeling that you can possibly imagine. People who have done this already do not need to be reminded of how difficult, tedious and unforgiving this process can be.

In terms of CPU requirements, a revolving period increases fixed-point convergence time considerably, but taking this time is the only acceptable way to do justice to the deal's intricate mechanics. If you care to embark seriously on this meandering path, you will soon discover that the accurate modeling of revolving periods will consume many of your best years and undoubtedly raise your market value far above that of your peers. Besides, you might even enjoy it.

24

Special Topics

"Ah! Yes, the truth, that ingenious concoction of desirability of appearance."
Anatole France (on the Dreyfus Affair)

Throughout the first nine chapters of the Advanced Part, we have focused our efforts on a single asset class, in fact on a single deal, and we did so mainly to impress upon the reader the care and attention that all structured analysts need to lavish on a transaction, no matter how mundane or trivial it might appear at the outset.

It is a huge and politically convenient misconception to believe that work done in one asset class is only valid there. Unfortunately, the truth is that there is only one way to do deals, a way we sought to bring out as best we could in chapter 14. Obviously, this cannot and does not mean that all automobile-loan-backed securitizations, let alone all structured transactions, look alike. Instead, the essential lesson we wish to teach is that knowledge of a single transaction, when sufficiently deep and thorough, provides a general method valid under all circumstances and asset classes. When people say "all is one and one is all," this is what they mean. Nothing of what you have learned up to now will ever have to be unlearned, re-learned, or forgotten, in order to move on in the wide world of structured finance. Of course, things will get a little more complicated. Perhaps not mathematically, for that is really up to you, but merely because your codes will get bigger. Maybe bigger is better, but bigger is definitely not harder.

What dawned upon us over the last few chapters is that even a routine and commonplace transaction has the potential to take us on a tour of various concepts and paradigms, the successful implementation of which requires mastery of some of the more recondite practical aspects of statistical analysis. Perhaps some of you are now wondering whether any transaction can be done at all if this is how things truly stand in structured finance. In fact, it is just the other way around. If you came along without pretense or self-conceit, and especially without taking yourself too seriously, you have accomplished far more than you probably wish to contemplate at this point. Take a good look in the rear-view mirror, and see for yourself how small Wall Street really seems now. Yet, if the truth be told, we have barely scratched the surface of structured finance as a whole.

In this ultimate chapter of the Advanced Part, we will meander through finance and its dynamics as a preamble and, hopefully, an impetus to further engagement with the field. The asset classes and topics discussed here in were not chosen with some sneaky or macabre agenda in mind, but because they too represent paradigms for some specific concept bound to crop up if you persevere in doing deals, as we hope all of you will. In the main, they are intended to reinforce the idea that, when viewed properly, structured finance forms a unity. This is an idea severely in need of a reminder.

24.1 TAX LIENS

Our first topic is delinquent tax lien securitizations, an asset class that was once *promising* but that, since then, has not quite lived up to those early dreams. We have selected tax liens for this cursory treatment for two main reasons and a minor one. First, they are a paradigm example of an asset class with risks of an entirely different sort than those encountered in mainstream asset classes like autos and credit cards. Second, they require more expertise and dexterity on the part of the average analyst than the ones just mentioned. The minor reason is that, along with tobacco settlements and a few others, these transactions display the peculiar feature of self-annihilation. By this, we mean that if all goes well, the market will self-destruct. This strange characteristic is perhaps related to the lack of enthusiasm it has met in some circles. We will have more to say on this topic later.

The Political Environment Surrounding Tax-Lien Securitizations

By way of background, we should first mention that a few cities in the United States, New York (NYC) and Philadelphia among them, have instituted delinquent tax-lien securitization programs. Mainly due to the political will underlying it, the NYC program has been quite successful. By contrast, similar programs in other U.S. cities have not been nearly as successful for the same reason in reverse. Investors in the latter transactions probably wondered how deals with such similar profiles could turn out so differently.

The stated goal of a tax-lien securitization program is the collection of unpaid real estate taxes owed on mainly vacant or partially occupied, commercial, and high-density residential buildings in some target market. As can be surmised, landlords who do not receive income from a property lose their incentive to pay their real estate taxes rather quickly, wishfully thinking that the city will not mind too much making them what amounts to a short-term loan until the building's financial situation improves, if and when it does. Not surprisingly, many of the affected properties are located in marginal neighborhoods and the landlords in question are effectively slumlords.

However, it would be wrong to assume that slumlords are as poor as their tenants, quite the contrary.

In general, the business model used by slumlords is such that tax delinquencies can drag on almost forever unless action is taken at the highest administrative levels. The vast majority of these people have more than enough cash to pay their taxes, but standard avoidance tactics are in fact cheaper. However, once the top political echelons have decided that they would really like to collect delinquent taxes, a special servicer is hired to carry out the legal process of collection, and landlords face the prospect of potentially forfeiting the building altogether once penalties and legal fees are factored into the mix.

Due to the nature of the beast, the dollar amount of delinquent taxes is, in most cases, much smaller than the appraised value of the building. The extent to which this is true is measured via the LTV concept, which here translates to "Lien to Value" as opposed to the more common "Loan to Value" concept used in real estate transactions. The intuitive meaning is the same in that, from the servicer's standpoint, a low LTV ratio indicates easy pickings, and conversely for high LTV ratios. The LTV ratio distribution is therefore a consistent metric that can be put to work in estimating aggregate cash flows accruing to the trust in any particular tax-lien securitization. In other words, if the LTV is 20% the property owner will usually pay promptly since the building is worth five times the delinquent taxes.[1] However, when the LTV rises to 50% for instance, the landlord is usually slow in reflecting on his past sins and might require some encouragement before forking over half the building's market value simply to satisfy a tax lien. In such cases, legal proceedings may need to be instituted to help him make up his mind.

Because of this phenomenon, the percentage of total collections the servicer may keep as a collection fee is normally computed using an acceleration scale, whereby each new dollar is deemed more difficult to collect than the previous one, resulting in an increasing servicing fee as collections increase. This built-in positive correlation between collections and servicing fees is unusual in securitization-prone asset classes and demands careful modeling and attention if the deal's credit risk is to be properly assessed. As usual in such situations, the transaction's cash flow profile is far from intuitive and the creditworthiness of the associated securities cannot be casually eyeballed in a manner reminiscent of how most analysts, under normal circumstances, tend to deal with real estate transactions.

A Cautionary Tale in Structured Finance

At this point, we may elaborate a little more on the pitfalls of this asset class with respect to its politics, something that regrettably lurks in the background of any asset class.

The difference between a successful deal and a disaster is not the quality of the documentation or law firm, or that of the investment bank for that matter. All these aspects are secondary in most cases anyway. Rather, it is the seriousness and professionalism with which the entire exercise is undertaken in the first place. This is, in fact, what we are trying to determine when looking at the players involved. The types of risk that can be handled mathematically, and that are discussed in this book, operate within the realm of statistics. They are not of the binary, stochastic sort of risk one comes across within law. When invoking Markov chains and random number generators, we are implicitly assuming that deals are already equipped with true sale and non-consolidation opinions. However, if the basic tenets of the field are violated, it is useless to speak of *structured finance* in any meaningful way. In some cases, and this is one of them, taking something for granted is not a good idea.

The problem with binary events of this kind is that they represent the worst possible environment for, and hence impediment to, serious analysis. The reason is obvious. If the answer is yes the deal will do fine but will collapse in the opposite case. The capital markets commonly expect the insurance industry to reduce this unacceptable variance by absorbing it completely. However, even a naïve reading of history ought to convince you that placing the sins of the world onto your shoulders can lead to major catastrophes. Before embarking, happy-go-lucky, on some beautiful statistical exercise, a mature analyst should tread with extreme caution and circumspection, and would do well to investigate whether the deal adheres strictly to its *sine qua non* stochastic laws. Otherwise, all that beauty might end up being only skin-deep.

In fixed income finance, which people believe to be *money good* in most cases of interest, the reason why investors end up losing 80% or 90% of their investment is not that the standard deviation or the kurtosis of some statistical distribution was somehow misjudged, or that the trust experienced a six-delta event or an Act of God. Rather, it is always because the most sacred principles of structured finance[2] were ignored or else that some even more fundamental premise, like respect for contracts, was questionable. Only when this is not the case can we even begin to start debating the merits and demerits of statistics. If anything can be learned from this asset class, it is that not all that shines is gold. Contrary to popular belief, God does not send people to Hell, they volunteer.

A Primer on Asset-Side Modeling for Tax-Lien Securitizations

The basic physics described above ought to motivate the acceptance of the rationale for the fact that the normal cash flow environment seen within tax-lien securitizations takes the form of a bi-modal distribution like the one shown in figure 24.1. Time, measured in months, is displayed on the abscissa. Arbitrary dollar units are shown on the ordinate.

The first modal period results from payments made by low-LTV and easy-going proprietors responding positively to a friendly but firm letter advising them that their real estate taxes are delinquent and that the servicer is serious. This step is usually perfunctory since the landlords have known for some time that the grim reaper is coming. Because the vast majority of property owners view themselves as simply benefiting from a no-interest loan from their local official, they usually pay up after some quick negotiation aimed at lowering their total bill, avoiding interest, penalties, and so on.

The second hump is the result of a legal process aimed at convincing recalcitrant property owners who insist on going through it, hoping to delay the inevitable.

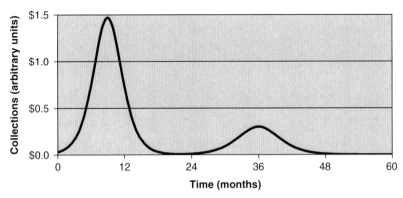

FIGURE 24.1
Typical cash flow pattern in a tax-lien securitization.

Judging from the approximately one-year delay between the end of the first wave and the beginning of the second, they are in fact quite successful at doing this. This is where political will comes into play. In successful jurisdictions, i.e., where the politics are aligned as they should be, the trust is usually able to collect a sizable amount in or out of court.

The last noteworthy feature of this distribution is that it is largely independent of the total amount collected by the servicer. In other words, no matter how much cumulative cash is collected during the life of the deal, the distribution will generally exhibit the two modes shown earlier. Thus, this feature provides the key to the modeling exercise.

Model Conception

Glancing at figure 24.1, the chief task of the analyst is to develop a continuously differentiable analytical expression for this implied functional form, one that will be modulated via suitable boundary conditions. Here and now, we cannot explain how this should be done from the ground up, but the upshot will seem strangely familiar. We leave it up to you to decide why the resulting function needs to be continuously differentiable.

An analytical cash flow expression $G(t)$ of almost any shape and possessing the above distributional properties can be derived via sums of analytic functions. It will not take long before you realize that our old friend the logistic curve can once again come to the rescue.

Specifically, we will build our cash flow curve using continuous and smooth analytic functions $f(t)$ of the form:

$$f(t) \equiv \frac{\partial F(t)}{\partial t} \tag{1}$$

$$F(t) = \frac{a}{1 + e^{-s(t - t_0)}} \tag{2}$$

Figure 24.1 tells you that it will be necessary to superpose two distinct incarnations of equation (1), defined as $f_1(t)$ and $f_2(t)$, respectively, to generate the required behavior. Hence, we can write immediately:

$$G(t) = f_1(t) + f_2(t) \tag{3}$$

Exercise 24.1

How do we know that equation (3) can do the job of reproducing figure 24.1? Is this the only way?

Now, the challenge is to come up with some way to determine the numerical value of the six unknown parameters of your model, i.e., the value of a, s, and t_0 for each incarnation of equation (2). In theory, reasonable assumptions leading to the exact numerical specification of both versions of equation (2) would be developed in concert with the special servicer and the sponsor of the transaction, for instance the New York City Tax Department. In practice though, and as is common in most asset classes in structured finance, the underwriters together with appropriate analysts from the investment side would derive those assumptions.

In this hypothetical case, let's suppose that you are an investment analyst assigned to this tax-lien transaction and that you have, after endless deliberation and negotiation, derived the following six defining conditions in collaboration with your opposite number at the investment bank. In items 1 through 6 below the expected amount of total collections has been defined as N_0.

1. The first mode is located at $t = 9$ months.
2. Ninety percent of all cash collected during the first modal period is received between $t = 3$ and $t = 15$ months. Define $b_1 = 6$ and $m_1 = 0.9$.
3. The second mode is located at $t = 36$ months.
4. Eighty percent of all cash collected during the second modal period is received between $t = 24$ and $t = 48$ months. Define $b_2 = 12$ and $m_2 = 0.8$.
5. Sixty percent of aggregate cash flows to the trust are collected during the first two years after closing. Defining $c_1 = 0.6$ and $t_1 = 24$, this means $\int_0^{t_1} G(t)\, dt = c_1 N_0$.
6. Eighty-eight and one half percent of aggregate cash flows to the trust are collected during the first three and a half years after closing. Defining $c_2 = 0.885$ and $t_2 = 42$, this means $\int_0^{t_2} G(t)\, dt = c_2 N_0$.

In passing, the above definitions or boundary conditions could have been formulated in a more complicated way, one that would have forced you to solve a two-dimensional nonlinear problem. In that case, it would have been necessary to write your own Newton–Raphson routine to achieve closure (see chapter 17).

Exercise 24.2

Create a short table allocating conditions 1 through 6 in the above list to each of the six required parameters in equation (2), and reflect in writing on why these conditions would be arrived at instead of others in the same vein.

Exercise 24.3

Some of these definitions require the solution of a two-dimensional, linear system of equations. This can be done using Cramer's rule, obviating the need to write a matrix inversion routine. Implement Cramer's rule inside an Excel spreadsheet or in VBA code. Which parameters are we talking about here?

As you can see, in structured finance the same basic schemata keep coming up again and again no matter what the asset class or the situation. Thus, learning how to deal with them generically is time well spent that can easily improve your productivity by an order of magnitude.

Exercise 24.4

By assuming that the first modal period's collections can be attributed exclusively to $f_1(t)$ and that the second modal period's collections can be attributed exclusively to $f_2(t)$, show analytically that the spreading parameter s inside equation (2) is found from the relationship:

$$s = \frac{1}{b} H^{-1}\left(\frac{1}{m}\right)$$

and that the function $H(x)$ is given by:

$$H(x) = \coth(x) + \csc h(x) \tag{4}$$

Note: the two expressions on the right-hand side of equation (4) refer to the hyperbolic co-tangent and co-secant, respectively.

As a result, you can compute the two spreading parameters as inputs to model equation (2) from:

$$s_1 = \frac{1}{b_1} H^{-1}\left(\frac{1}{m_1}\right)$$

$$s_2 = \frac{1}{b_2} H^{-1}\left(\frac{1}{m_2}\right).$$

In practice, you will find that the two assumptions at the origin of equation (4) are quite accurate in the sense that the contribution of $f_1(t)$ to the second modal period's aggregate collections is negligible, and the same can usually be said of $f_2(t)$ with respect to the first modal period.

Exercise 24.5

Analytically invert the function $H(x)$ (equation 4) to derive the Yampol[3] formula:

$$s = \frac{1}{b} \ln\left[\frac{1+m}{1-m}\right]$$

Total Collections

Although you have done well by creating a time-dependent distribution of cash flows for the transaction, not a word has been spoken about the total amount of cash that will be flowing through the Special Purpose Vehicle (SPV). As you might imagine, the statistics of that quantity will ultimately drive the value or rating of the structured securities you will issue. No matter how carefully you have allocated the cash that does come in via equation (2), nothing will save the investors if total cash is wanting.

You should also realize that our previous modeling implies that the behavior of the cash flow density function is invariant. Remembering the comments we made in chapter 14, the number of degrees of freedom remaining in our conceptualization is thus effectively zero. If we did not allow total collections to be the dimension via which uncertainty, i.e., variance, crept back in, it is clear that this deal would either be *Aaa* or would never see the light of day. In essence, when freedom disappears we have effectively reached the infinite. This is what *Aaa* really means.

The determination of the statistical distribution for total collections is nontrivial and imposes an additional burden on the analyst. To begin with, one would have to determine the expected value of total collections N_0 in consultation with the jurisdiction's tax department. To be sure, the deal's LTV distribution alluded to earlier would be the workhorse index for that exercise. Thereafter, from the same LTV distribution you would have to investigate LTV variability and estimate the range of possibilities given the tax department's prior collection experience with the same type of delinquent taxpayers. This is not as difficult as it may seem. Finally, boundary conditions would enter the fray. On the one hand, you would never collect more than the total nominal amount of outstanding liens plus penalties. On the other hand, total collections clearly have to be greater than zero. This is quite different from the case of automobile loans whereby recoveries can exceed the outstanding loan balance without violating any physical constraint.

When you are done, these restrictions would by themselves pretty well dictate the shape of the distribution. From what we have just said, it should not be difficult to convince yourself that among others, a beta distribution fulfills the above requirements without any drawbacks. As a reminder, the standard beta probability density function $f_d(x)$, given as equation (5), can be understood as a generalization of the binomial distribution on the real unit-interval. As before $\Gamma(x)$ is the standard gamma function.

$$f_d(x) = \frac{\Gamma(\alpha+\beta)}{\Gamma(\alpha)\,\Gamma(\beta)}\,(1-x)^{\beta-1}\,(x)^{\alpha-1} \tag{5}$$

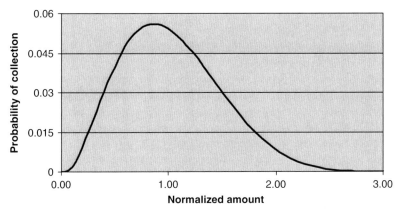

FIGURE 24.2
Beta distribution for total collections in a tax-lien securitization.

After reasoning this way, you would have arrived, quite naturally it seems, at a distribution like that in figure 24.2 for total collections to the trust.

To use the beta distribution in this case you first need to calibrate the abscissa to generate total cash flows N with a mean equal to the agreed upon expected value N_0, i.e., you need to enforce $E[N] = N_0$. This can be done quite easily by writing the following expression for each N_i:

$$N_i = CDF^{-1}(y_i; \alpha, \beta) N_0 \frac{\alpha + \beta}{\alpha} \qquad (6)$$

In equation (6) above, we have defined $CDF^{-1}(y_i; \alpha, \beta)$ as the inverse cumulative distribution function for the chosen beta distribution with parameters α and β, N_i as the value of total tax-liens collections to the trust in one Monte Carlo scenario, and y_i as a uniform random deviate for that scenario.

Exercise 24.6

Using a standard beta distribution like the one in equation (6) with parameters $\alpha = 3$ and $\beta = 7$, write a short Visual Basic (VBA) program that enables you to generate a series of total cash flows N for input to equation (2).

Use the inverse distribution function method (equation 6) to select the required uniform random deviates from the above beta distribution. To select the deviates y_i, use the van der Corput low-discrepancy sequence method with $p = 3$. This method was described in detail in chapter 18.

Note: Although you are welcome to use the Excel-resident subroutine "Beta Inv" to simplify your effort in this exercise, remember that if Excel or any other package were to be unavailable, you would have to write the inverse distribution routine from scratch. Many examples of how to do this are provided in *Numerical Recipes*[4], a monograph we recommend to anyone seriously interested in pure numerical analysis.

Implementation Issues

Calculation of the Legal Final Maturity Date

In implementing equation (2) using equation (6), you will need to calculate the transaction's Legal Final Maturity date so that exactly 100% of aggregate cash flows have been received by that time. The five-year value shown in figure 24.1 in no way implies that by that time precisely N_0 dollars have been collected, and yet this is what you imply using equation (6). In other words, once you have computed the values of the six unknown parameters in equation (2) you still have to enforce physically the termination of the asset cash flow stream at $t = t_{max}$ using the natural boundary condition $G(t_{max}) = N_0$. Because of the invariance condition enforced throughout, this will work out to be the same value for each Monte Carlo scenario. Otherwise, the claim that N_0 represents aggregate cash flows would be wrong.

The Legal Final Maturity Date, which is normally some reasonable time after the Expected Final Maturity Date, will instead be defined as t_{max}. The Expected Final Maturity Date is usually defined as the time at which the liabilities have been paid off under the *expected* cash flow process, hence the expression *expected* final. Its calculation is one of the liability-side modeling requirements.

Cap/Stress Parameter

If it becomes necessary, you also need to ensure that your implementation code is equipped with a parameter capping collections at some fixed number since, as we mentioned above, the trust will never be able to collect more than the total amount of tax liens owed by delinquent taxpayers. Clearly, most conceivable scenarios would involve situations where total collections would be far less than this theoretical maximum, but your program should never be allowed to compute physically impossible events. In addition, this maximum is a convenient way to stress the environment for testing purposes prior to rolling out the model to an actual transaction.

Miscellaneous Issues

As you can see, even a plain-vanilla tax-lien securitization involves nontrivial cash flow modeling at the asset level, saying nothing of liability modeling that also presents its own challenges. This is because this asset class is unique in the way servicing fees are computed. Overall, tax-lien securitizations present unusual modeling challenges, both from the asset and the liability standpoints, in addition to letting the creativity of the analyst shine brightly.

First, the servicer behaves in a much more aggressive manner than would a normal servicer, because it is motivated by the acceleration scale that allows it to keep an increasing share of each incremental dollar collected. The positive correlation between collections and servicing fees is a special feature of tax-lien transactions that needs to be modeled correctly. Thus, investors in a tax-lien deal do not benefit to the same extent that they would when servicing fees are calculated as a fixed percentage of monthly collections.

The problem is that the servicer may seek to *optimize* the transaction from its own standpoint by relaxing its collection efforts when the dynamics of the servicing scale become unfavorable. The elaboration of this schedule is therefore paramount to the smooth operation of a tax-lien securitization.

In addition, the pure cash flow environment associated with this asset class restricts the range of alternatives available to the structuring team. A sequential principal allocation structure is almost *de rigueur* unless some reasonable TAC structure can be worked out across the investor group. Next, triggers are more difficult to specify since no outstanding principal balance exists on the asset side. Finally yet importantly, do not forget that no obligor has yet agreed to any specific amount at the outset. This is in sharp contrast to most asset classes whereby a promise to pay exists a priori.

But perhaps the most depressing aspect of tax-lien transactions is their potential evanescence. As mentioned before, if all goes well U.S. cities will eventually run out of assets to securitize. This is not exactly a recipe for a major asset class. However depressing, the situation is not as dire as what will most likely happen to tobacco-settlement transactions, for in that case an investor carefully reading a prospectus would be surprised to find that a portion of deal proceeds must be allocated to an advocacy fund warning consumers about the nefarious side-effects of smoking. Given that smokers are precisely the people paying the interest and the principal on the bonds, we arrive at the interesting conclusion that tobacco settlement is an asset class whereby proceeds are actively used to force the bonds into default. Freud would have a field day with this.

24.2 LEGAL SETTLEMENTS

Legal settlements make up another pure cash flow asset class. At the risk of repeating ourselves, we bring them up because their *purity* is of different sort than that of tax liens. In essence, legal settlements represent an intermediary stage between the completely free cash flow environment of the prior section and those of mainstream asset classes like automobiles and mortgages.

In the case of tax liens, not a single dollar was promised to the trust by any obligor as of the closing date. In fact, the truth was exactly the opposite, i.e., fiendish proprietors had already shown themselves willing to break their original promise to the municipality. In that instance, servicing and political will were definitely the keys to the yield kingdom.

With legal settlements though, we have a different story. Instead of starting at the beginning, i.e., via the cajoling of obligors into coughing up some cash and ending up making credible threats of legal action if payment is not forthcoming, we pick up the money trail somewhere down the road, after the noble fight between man and the system has taken place. In legal settlement securitizations, either the court has already ordered third parties to pay up, and that decision is usually meaningful and easily enforceable, or they have an outstanding commitment to pay such amounts on a regular basis. Even better, parties that become obligors under the settlement agreement are commonly much more creditworthy on an individual basis than the average landlord-obligor. In other words, the transaction benefits from a pre-established set of cash flow obligations that are much more difficult to avoid than the original ones and that usually originate from highly creditworthy sources.

If you think about it for a minute, this makes perfect sense. Suppose someone told you about a proposed structured transaction consisting exclusively of loans made to consumers who just declared bankruptcy. At first sight, this might look like a terrible deal because such people are already known to have defaulted on their pre-existing obligations. On the other hand, the deal could be regarded as much better than average since the relevant obligors no longer have the option, at least for another 7 years, to declare bankruptcy to avoid paying the new loans. Further, their personal balance sheet is likely to be much cleaner than that of the average consumer precisely because of the bankruptcy proceedings. Therefore, the situation may not be so bad after all.

This pre-established set of legal obligations is what we meant by an *intermediate* stage of cash flow purity. Although one cannot identify a priori the allocated principal and interest components of the future payments' stream, as one easily could with a mortgage, the temporal sequence of dollar obligations and their amounts are known exactly on the closing date. If this is true, it is a simple matter to use discounting to manufacture synthetic principal and interest payments and to do the same with respect to defaults and prepayments. Thus, although you are not given a schedule of principal and interest allocations, the job simply falls to you, the structured analyst. In some sense, it even makes things easier because an expanded realm of possibilities now exists compared to that of more mainstream asset classes. In what follows, we will come back to this aspect of legal settlement securitizations.

Review of Legal Settlement Transactions

If one excludes parceling out the market in political terms, the field of legal settlements is usually partitioned into three distinct categories.

Structured Settlements

This name refers to the securitization of cash flows owed on a monthly or periodic basis by insurance companies arising from successful lawsuits by plaintiffs that became incapacitated or injured. Such tax-free payments will usually be made over years, sometimes decades, and are meant to compensate injured parties for the associated lost income opportunity. The settlement is supposed to make the claimant *whole* and hence, is tax-free. As you can readily surmise, such determinations are largely arbitrary decisions.

In the vast majority of cases, the private finance companies that sponsor these transactions will offer the injured claimants immediate cash in exchange for the right to receive the stream of monthly payments. Brokers are usually involved and they are paid hefty fees. Discount rates vary but are usually in the 20–30% range. The sponsor then turns around and securitizes the same payment stream at an average of ca. 7–10%, collecting the arbitrage difference at closing or according to some other pre-arranged formula. Servicing is minimal since the insurance companies involved have already agreed to pay and the sponsor simply asks the original claimant to assign his or her payment stream to a lock-box account for the benefit of the trust, usually via a letter to this effect addressed to the obligor (insurer) under the settlement agreement.

In principle, this payment redirection order is uneventful, except that some claimants, once they have the cash in hand, take it upon themselves, usually via another letter, to redirect the payment to the original address, thus depriving the trust of the corresponding periodic income. The sponsor clearly has an airtight case and usually prevails at law or in equity. However, the payments that were sent to the wrong location, although recoverable as damages, are normally lost to the trust owing to the poor credit of the original claimant. Even though these circumstances are rare, they do occur and can drag on, especially given that the injured party has commonly spent most of the up-front cash, not to mention that he or she *looks* injured and helpless in the courtroom compared to the monsters from Wall Street. Such reassignment potential is in fact the largest risk factor in a structured settlement securitization and, at this point, has generally been addressed.

A secondary risk factor is the possibility that a sale of the payment stream from the insurer might be avoidable altogether. This is possible because the insurer can claim that such purchases are illegal under the original settlement due to special tax provisions. Remember that claimants take their settlement tax-free, because it is regarded simply as compensation for what they have lost, i.e., it is not income per se.

The market power of the insurance industry was brought to bear on this question since, from a strictly economic standpoint, it is difficult to see how paying money to Party A might be more expensive than paying the same amount to Party B. The legal issues are non-negligible because courts must eventually decide if the original settlement agreement is a bona fide contract between two parties, or simply a right to receive cash that can be treated as freely disposable property. This argument is as old as securitization itself and has usually been decided in favor of property over against contract law. The real issue is that insurers simply do not like the notion that they can be arbitraged in this bold manner.

It is probably fair to state that any remaining legal uncertainty surrounding the area of structured settlements could put a damper on the bulk securitization of such agreements.

Life Settlements

Regrettably, this asset subclass has sometimes been associated with shady operators and unscrupulous principals. Essentially, it consists of the securitization of proceeds from life insurance policies issued by highly creditworthy companies, albeit with certain exclusions. In the mean time, the trust must have sufficient cash to pay the monthly premia or else forfeit the right to receive the proceeds in the event the policy matures. Maturity is what insurers call the death of the insured.

The difficult, ethical aspect of this asset class is related to the underwriting performed by the sponsors. This boils down to the selection of individuals with impaired health whose remaining life expectancy can be estimated with relatively high accuracy. In other words, the life of the target insured is already in jeopardy due to some chronic condition such as HIV, cancer, or another chronic and usually fatal illness. The sale proceeds of the insurance policy are usually earmarked for healthcare costs. In addition, the beneficiary under the policy, normally the spouse or life-partner of the insured, must be convinced to assign his or her rights upon maturity to a third party. The moral dilemma involved in doing this is obvious.

It should be noted that transactions holding pools of viatical settlements to AIDS victims were once caught unaware by a sudden increase in the life expectancy of the average insured, which in turn was due to the availability of drug-cocktails able to prolong life much beyond the original estimate. When yield to the trust arises solely from someone's death, it should surprise no one that the insured persons generally have little incentive to help things along. From the strictly economic standpoint however, the deal can make sense if the underwriting is done properly. Whereas viatical settlements are based on abnormal conditions, most life settlements address older insured about whom much more is known with respect to remaining lifespan. Further, there exists an obvious negative correlation between age and expected remaining life. Eventually, everybody dies. Thus, as long as the yield lost to cover current premia and coupon on the issued securities is less than the return from maturing policies, the trust should come out ahead.

At one point, life settlements constituted a hopeful avenue for another large asset class of repeat issuers since a large percentage of adult citizens have life insurance and there is no lack of chronic illness in the United States. For whatever reason such early hopes have so far been dashed, possibly because of the ethical dilemmas involved, or perhaps because a significant benchmark transaction, one that would attract a critical mass of investors, has yet to appear.

Gambling Receivables

We include this would-be asset class not so much because it is a factor in today's ABS marketplace, but more to highlight the breadth of investment possibilities offered by the investment banking community. Among other things, these transactions are made possible by the fact that people winning a lottery must agree to receive periodic payments over many years instead of an immediate lump sum, although many State lotteries will also discount the stream into a lump sum at the winner's option. Clearly, these payments are not tax-free and tax consequences greatly affect the economic calculus within these transactions.

Save for potentially deal-killing tax issues, the economics facing credit analysts are identical to those encountered in the first two cases. The best we can say at this juncture is that some transactions have seen the light of day, but that fundamental impediments, not the least of which is taxation, have prevented this asset subclass from achieving any credibility. Liquidity clearly suffers due to the relatively few deals that have thus far been closed. Additionally, the market consists mainly of relatively small operators within a cottage industry. In a nutshell, no single overriding factor is pushing the market in any direction. Until and unless a paradigm transaction emerges, this asset class is likely to remain largely an interesting curiosity.

The Liability Constraints of Settlement Transactions

At the beginning of this section, it was pointed out that the absence of an a priori principal and interest allocation schedule opens up a field of possibilities with respect to liability structuring. In this case, it can be seen that no single cash receivable or principal balance can be said to be defaulted since the trust will simply collect what it collects.

This is not that different from what obtains in other asset classes. In a mortgage loan for instance, consumers make monolithic payments and the lender, not the consumer, partitions the full amount it receives into its principal and interest components. The method of doing so is far from unique. As an example, recall the notorious "Rule of 78" still allowed in some States. The latter algorithm is a reallocation of interest and principal amounts which effectively frontloads interest payments in excess of what would happen under an actuarial amortization schedule, without increasing the total amount paid by the obligor over the loan's expected maturity. The only way to recover principal is to discount the monthly payments stepwise at the loan rate, and call the result the *principal* balance. In a similar fashion, the settlement-assets in the trust are nothing but pure streams of cash to which no particular amortization schedule has been attached. One is thus at liberty to do so in any way needed to achieve a stated objective.

Pure Discounting

For instance, if one discounts the cash flow payments $y_i, i \in [1, T]$ from one obligor at discount rate r, the resulting value P, obtained via $P = \sum_{i=1}^{T} \frac{y_i}{(1+r)^i}$, can simply be defined as the principal balance contributed to the deal by that obligor. Assuming par issuance, the aggregate amount of such balances would then constitute the total liability balance of ABS debt issued at closing.

Many other combinations are possible, for instance the use of different discount rates for obligors of different credit quality, or some other dynamic scheme. In the end, you can devise a system that allows you to allocate portion p_i or every cash payment f_i to principal and the difference to interest, where we can define $p_i = \frac{f_i}{(1+r)^i}$. In this way, each cash flow could be designed to retire a specific principal amount and the difference used to pay liability coupon. Any remaining amount would constitute excess spread. Otherwise, all cash collected needs to be allocated to amortization, and sponsors must wait practically until the end of the transaction to extract cash from the bottom of the waterfall, even though the transaction might be performing ahead of expectations. Using the method described here, excess spread can be manufactured almost at will by raising the discount rate.

Under this scheme, defaults would show up as missed payments as explained earlier and would be computed as the present value (as of the closing date) of such payments. Prepayments, if any, would be computed similarly. In other words, if three separate payments f_t^1, f_t^2, f_t^3 were wrongfully diverted by various claimants at time step t, we would simply declare defaults d_t in the amount:

$$d_t = \sum_{i=1}^{3} \frac{f_t^i}{(1+r)^t}$$

This amount then becomes part of "Total Principal Due" and would have to be promptly returned to ABS bond investors at time t. Prepayments can be treated similarly.

The advantage of this structure is that sponsors would be motivated to remain actively engaged with the deal until maturity, since they would be collecting excess cash on each Payment Date. The way most deals currently work, sponsors have a direct incentive to securitize the maximum amount because the up-front gain on sale is likely to be their only cash flow for a long time. Thus, a small structural change could go a long way toward removing some of the moral hazard that now exists in this asset class.

TAC Structure

Alternatively, the deal can be structured as a single-class TAC, whereby an arbitrary TAC schedule $TAC(t), t \in [1, T]$ (see chapter 20 for further details) would be established by the sponsor. Any amortization beyond that schedule on any collection period would be allocated to equity or simply flow back to the residual holder. Missed payments would result in the trust falling behind and cause a larger Total Principal Due at the next time step. This is because principal due under a TAC bond is the difference between the current outstanding principal balance and the current TAC schedule $TAC(t)$, which difference is thus reduced to zero if precisely that difference is paid out to investors. If nothing is paid, Total Principal Due is the difference between the previously outstanding balance, which has not changed, and $TAC(t+1)$. By definition, $TAC(t+1) < TAC(t)$ thus forcing the trust to catch up, using potentially all the cash it has collected, as well as stopping cash flow leaks to sponsors.

Turbo-Triggered Liability Amortization

In yet a third structural alternative, one could impose a priori requirements on structured liability amortization via a schedule of time steps t_i and corresponding liability balances B_i. This sequence could be created so that cash could still escape even if the trust met the schedule. Failure to meet any benchmark B_t at time t would immediately cause the invocation of the turbo trigger, trapping cash inside the deal and amortizing the bonds as fast as possible.

As described in "*The Analysis of Structured Securities*" (OUP, 2003), one could also contemplate an infinite array of hybrid structures whereby, for example, proportional triggers could be used intelligently to raise the benchmark amortization schedule and let cash escape in the hope of encouraging the sponsor or servicer to get back on track, without immediately removing all incentive to do so by cutting off its cash supply entirely.

General Remarks

Unfortunately, so far legal settlements have yet to acquire the status to which they could be entitled if handled professionally. Although the reasons elicited earlier in this chapter with respect to ethics and moral hazard are perhaps to blame for this situation, the simple fact is that given the favorable hedging and counter-cyclical cash flow characteristics inherent in these structures, the tremendous potential for U.S. issuance has not materialized to any significant extent. Whether this can ever happen is a question that awaits a better answer than the one provided by today's capital market players.

24.3 WRITE-DOWN MECHANISMS

One of these days, while taking a random walk down Wall Street, you are bound to encounter the structural feature known as a "write-down," and perhaps wonder why it is used at all given that insolvency is not a deal-killer in structured finance the way it usually is in corporate finance. On the contrary, bankruptcy-remoteness is one of the central tenets of structured finance. Because the write-down mechanism is important when used, we believe it merits a detailed discussion. The next few pages present a review of two write-down modifications, highlighting their implementation and rationale, or lack thereof, inside structured transactions. While the first is symptomatic of certain MBS and CDO transactions, the second ought to be a mandatory yet often forgotten feature of the CDO of ABS.

The Interest Subordination Write-Down Feature

This write-down mechanism applies to transactions with subordination whereby the waterfall is of the type shown piecewise in table 24.1 for a two-tranche structure.

This waterfall layout is common in structured finance, and applies to both sequential and pro rata structures. As you will recall, it is not possible to tell from table 24.1 alone which principal allocation scheme is being used.

The Mechanics of the Write-Down Process

Within a two-tranche transaction, the main write-down feature refers to a process whereby a decrease in the aggregate, performing pool balance $P(t)$ below the sum of Class A and Class B balances [$A(t)$ and $B(t)$, respectively] would cause the write-down

TABLE 24.1
Partial asset-backed transaction waterfall

LEVEL ID	DISTRIBUTION
1	Class A interest
2	Class B interest
3	Class A principal
4	Class B principal

of the Class B by the difference. For obvious reasons, the senior class is usually not written down.

In other words, defining $w_d(t)$ as the Write-Down Amount, we would have:

$$w_d(t) = Max\{0, [A(t) + B(t)] - P(t)\}$$

$$B(t) = B(t) - w_d(t)$$

In essence, after the application of the above write-down mechanism, the remaining Class B balance plus the currently outstanding Class A balance would precisely equal the pool balance $P(t)$. In subsequent collections periods, the written-down Class B balance then becomes the basis for interest due to Class B holders at Level 2 in table 24.1, thereby effectively subordinating Class B Interest to senior principal payments.

Therefore, this write-down mechanism is nothing but an interest subordination feature benefiting senior investors at the expense of junior investors, the latter's acceptance of which is rather odd, since subordinated investors normally invest out of yield hunger. To be sure, should the trust undergo a miraculous recovery in future periods, an event with small probability when write-downs do take place, Class B investors are entitled to "write-ups" in an aggregate amount equal to all previously written-down amounts. Unfortunately, such amounts commonly do not bear interest at the nominal security rate, and the Class B all-in yield obviously suffers. But since the original promise to Class B investors contains the write-down feature, the effective reduction in current yield is not considered a default under the indenture.

For illustration purposes, we present in exhibit 24.1 a portion of a typical VB code analyzing a two-tranche home equity transaction with this type of write-down feature.

Exhibit 24.1: Section of VB Code Implementing a Write-Down/Write-Up Feature

```
'
Write down amounts to Class B
'
Total_Write_Down_Amount = Max(0, Total_Certificate_Balance - Pool_Balance -
Cum_Defaults)

With Certificates (B)

.Write_Down_Amount = Min(.Balance, Total_Write_Down_Amount)
.Cum_Write_Down_Amount = .Cum_Write_Down_Amount + .Write_Down_Amount
.Balance = .Balance - .Write_Down_Amount

End With

'
Write-up amounts to Class B
```

```
With Certificates (B)

.Principal_Due = .Cum_Write_Down_Amount
.Principal_Paid = Min(Available_Funds, .Principal_Due)
.Payments(Time) = .Payments(Time) + .Principal_Paid
.Cum_Write_Down_Amount = .Cum_Write_Down_Amount - .Principal_Paid
Available_Funds = Available_Funds - .Principal_Paid

End With
```

The Trouble with Write-Downs

It would be silly to find fault with structures that, for better or for worse, do exist. Monday morning quarterbacking is not the point. Instead, what we want to discuss are the rating implications of this feature in terms of yield reduction. The common objection that this line of argument is moot or specious since, it is objected, write-downs of this type are virtually unthinkable, misses the point completely because we are talking about risk, not fact. In fact, this mechanism has already been used in actual transactions and their offspring to raise the credit rating of securities sponsored by an issuer in trouble. That issuer later went bankrupt and investors lost a significant portion of their principal.

You will recall that a structured credit rating can be regarded as the average reduction of yield from the original bond promise that investors in a given class would experience should they hold a well-diversified portfolio of similar securities, whether or not the investors in question indeed held such a portfolio. In defining credit ratings this way, we made an implicit but important assumption, which was that the promise to investors was in fact known a priori. This assumption is the reason why equity securities cannot be assigned a credit rating, i.e., they do not carry any promise. Thus, although stocks cannot be rated like bonds, they can be assessed via the relationship between the average return and the standard deviation of that return in the context of a distribution of returns over some time horizon. As long as investors are conscious of the difference, all is well.

However, in the case of the write-down feature just described, the natural assumption is to equate the promise to the nominal coupon usually written on the first page of the prospectus or offering memorandum. The reason why this would seem natural is that in the vast majority of structured transactions this is indeed the case. Investors in the B-piece are more comfortable with their subordinated position because they are confident that their interest distributions will remains current. This is something made more likely by the fact that Class B interest is positioned above Class A principal in table 24.1. However, the truth is that under a write-down structure this assumption is erroneous, for in that case their promise is not the same as in the vast majority of bond structures. It is smaller.

The problem is not the use of write-downs per se, for why should we restrict freedom in this way? The problem, rather, is that the rating exercise must clearly be adjusted to reflect the reduced investor promise. If the transaction promises less, the probability of fulfilling that lower promise is obviously greater, and hence the Class B credit rating moves up even though on the surface things look structurally identical. Even better, the Class A rating also increases for the same reason. In other words, introducing a write-down mechanism in this manner has managed to work magic, i.e., to simultaneously raise the credit rating of both classes at the same time while the expected cash flow performance of the asset pool and the rest of the structure remain identical to what they were before the change.

As you will probably remember from earlier chapters, it is a mathematical theorem that, save for market inefficiencies, structured finance is a zero-sum credit game. By this we mean that the credit rating of two structured securities backed by a given pool of assets cannot both increase or decrease at the same time. This is because all tranches share the same pot. Whatever additional cash is given to someone must implicitly be taken away from someone else. As a result, if the numerical credit rating of Class A goes up, that of Class B must go down. Note that on a letter-grade credit basis, this is not always true because the rating scale is piecewise continuous instead of merely continuous. Because of this artifact, the credit rating of one class can easily decrease numerically but insufficiently to cause a letter-grade rating change, while simultaneously allowing the rating of the Class B to go up in an amount that *does* enable it to enter another rating notch. In this situation, the letter-grade rating of the senior class will remain unchanged while that of the lower class will rise, seemingly in violation of our zero-sum game principle. In fact, playing this game is precisely how structures are *optimized* in the first place. If the rating scale were continuous, as it should be, this type of *magic* would cease.

Что делать со списаниями? (What is to be done with write-downs?)

In summary, via a subtle modification of the original promise to one class of investors, the use of the write-down feature has managed to invalidate the theorem that both credit ratings cannot move in the same direction at the same time, a modification that, we might add, usually goes unnoticed. If we are going to rate securities based on the promise to investors, how can we avoid using that very promise in the definition of the reduction of yield?

Actually, there are a couple of workable solutions. The first one is to forego the write-down feature altogether, thereby restoring the associated structured ratings to their original meanings. If, as is usually claimed, the probability of an *actual* write-down is remote, this should not be objectionable to the issuer. The second solution is simply to ignore the write-down mechanism for valuation and rating purposes, i.e., to assume that coupon is due on the entire principal balance of the bond regardless. This would cause any write-downs, even those later written-up (due to the absence of interest paid on written-down amounts) to reduce the all-in yield on the bond and add to the reduction of yield, thus resulting in a lower rating.

Under the current framework, the seller really gets something for nothing, i.e., a higher rating for Class B and potentially for Class A too, which of course was the intention all along. If the investors are in agreement with this situation, and we doubt they would be if this were explained properly, they could simply be told that the *Baa2*

Class B rating they are shown is, in reality, some other, unknown rating. In all cases, they would ask for a recomputation of the rating on the original basis. Who knows, maybe the write-down feature does not move the Class B rating that far down?[5]

Final Remarks on the Interest Subordination Write-Down Feature

The foregoing discussion has taken us into some of the more recondite aspects of structured finance, those secretive nooks and crannies that should make the life of a structured analyst more interesting. As we saw, the world of structured finance is not quite as transparent as it might appear at first blush. Here too, *follow the money* is excellent advice.

Even though we have barely scratched the surface of structural possibilities, already we have been placed on guard against the *magic* of fixed-income analysis. It can perhaps be seen as disingenuous on our part to ascribe nefarious motives to investment bankers trying to make an honest living. After all, everything was done above board, and no one is hiding anything from investors. Unfortunately, the sad fact is that investors have few friends and that reading a prospectus looking for a needle in a hay stack is no more exciting than watching grass grow. Our recommendation is to ignore all such structural creativity and to communicate credit ratings on the same basis in all transactions. The last thing we need in structured finance is a floating promise. A floating return is sufficient.

The Write-Down Account in the CDO of ABS Structure

The second write-down feature we wish to discuss really consists not of a mechanism in the above sense, but of a special cash investment account we will henceforth label the "Write-Down Account," or WDA for short. As already indicated in our introductory remarks, this should be a mandatory structural feature of the CDO of ABS, if the latter is to make any sense at all. The fact that the WDA is mostly absent from actual transactions is not an argument against it, but for it.

Review of the CDO of ABS in Contradistinction to the Corporate CDO

Much attention has of late been paid to the CDO market, something that will surely change once the capital implications of the Basel II accord are fully integrated into the operational procedures of commercial banks. There are many incidental reasons to execute a CDO, outside of credit and regulatory arbitrage. In fact, countless hedge funds used to call themselves CDOs in order to attract capital. What will occupy us in this subsection is not the difference in terms of strategy or capital structure. Instead, we will restrict our attention to the asset side of the SPV balance sheet and to transactions based on cash flows, as opposed to market values, as the source of repayment. A market-value CDO is nothing but a thinly disguised hedge fund.

A corporate CDO consists of bank loans or corporate bonds of variable credit quality, while a CDO of ABS, as its name implies, is put together from ABS bonds bought in the secondary market. The fact that ratings assigned by the major U.S. rating agencies bear the same letter designation does not imply that they mean the same thing in practice. Corporate ratings are based on the default or bankruptcy paradigm while ABS ratings are based on loss. Even if rating agencies insist that both mean the same, they do not. To change that would require a completely new approach to bond default studies, something that has been neither attempted nor achieved.

This is not the end of the world. The fact that corporate and structured ratings mean different things does not matter because the two scales are monotonic. In other words, what matters is that, given that in corporate land "*Aaa*" is more secure than "*Aa*1," the same should be true in structured finance, and it is. It is silly to insist on something patently false, i.e., that both ratings mean the same, for it does not matter one whit whether they do. Life will go on quite nicely even if they do not. Whether they should is another matter. In any event, the asset side of a corporate CDO is always analyzed in terms of default events to which recoveries are later attached, for obviously finance is still about cash. Therefore, in practice the rating agencies' claim is ignored.

The Write-Down Account [WDA] in the CDO of ABS

Now, assume you have purchased a pool of N structured securities in the secondary market, each an *asset-tranche*, and that each of them has been issued out of a different Special Purpose Vehicle (SPV). Assume further that you have deposited these asset-tranches into yet another SPV created specifically for that purpose. On the right side of the new SPV balance sheet, you will be creating a fresh set of linked structured bonds (the CDO securities proper) that will then be sold to CDO investors.

Now recall that structured securities are issued by vehicles that are bankruptcy-remote, in the sense that insolvency does not cause a default as it normally would in corporate finance. Note also that bankruptcy is a default concept, not a loss concept. Because of this, there is no reason why, in the underlying SPV of any asset-tranche, the transaction would be aborted simply because the SPV that issued the tranche has become insolvent.

To see the reason for the WDA, imagine that some underlying asset-SPV (labeled i hereunder) is now insolvent because of bad credit performance, in the sense that the current underlying pool balance $P_i(t)$ is now smaller than its current aggregate liability balance $D_i(t)$. Assume further that the deal in question consists of two tranches and that you have purchased the subordinated class, for else your arbitrage-based yield is likely to be too small.

By definition, the following holds at all time on the right-hand side of the SPV, where $A_i(t)$ and $B_i(t)$ are the class-wise liability balances:

$$D_i(t) = A_i(t) + B_i(t)$$

The insolvency implies that, should the underlying assets be liquidated immediately, the Class B would suffer a theoretical loss $L_i(t)$ equal to:

$$L_i(t) = Min\{B_i(t), D_i(t) - P_i(t)\}$$

(In the following discussion, we ignore the possibility that the pool balance is also smaller than $A_i(t)$.)

In corporate finance, this would not normally happen since only interest would be due until the maturity of any tranche. In that sense, the underlying company could be considered "performing" until it eventually defaulted. In structured finance however, this cannot be countenanced since defaults occur stepwise over time.

The WDA is simply the account that contains the sum $W_i(t) = \sum_{i=1}^{N} L_i(t)$ across all asset-tranches in the CDO of ABS.

If one were to wait for an underlying default to be *declared* within the asset-tranche SPV, there would be nothing left to recover since all cash flows would have ceased. Even worse, asset-tranche balances inside the CDO of ABS would be reckoned as performing while this took place, since that would be only way to represent the situation. After all, the asset-tranche SPV does owe the entire Class B balance to CDO investors no matter what is going on inside its trust. Since the amounts $L_i(t)$ would not be recorded anywhere, the excess spread from all other asset-tranches would simply escape back to the sponsor in a deteriorating situation in which the CDO of ABS would be insolvent by the aggregate amount $W_i(t)$. If this were allowed to continue unabated, the cumulative effect of this phenomenon would spell doom for the CDO of ABS since credit enhancement in the form of spread would not be available to make up for securities that would eventually experience severe write-downs. In other words, a CDO of ABS without a WDA is exposed to risks that are theoretically not present in a corporate CDO and that stem from a misunderstanding of the nature of structured securities.

On the other hand, if excess spread in the amount $W_i(t)$ is trapped on the fly, subject of course, to being released if any of the underlying SPV recovers in subsequent periods, this situation cannot arise. This is because, at the time the ABS asset-tranche default is declared, the aggregate balance of the insolvent portion of all asset-tranches would have been trapped inside the deal and could be used to absorb fully the write-down of asset-tranches. Further, the trapping of cash in this manner would provide a real-time signal to the asset-tranche manager as to the curing prospects of such insolvencies. Note that the WDA mechanism must also allow cash to escape in synchronization with asset-tranche behavior, otherwise there would be no incentive on the part of asset managers to cure any write-down.

What should be done with funds trapped in the WDA is debatable. One thing is clear however: the asset manager cannot be allowed to re-invest them into new ABS asset-tranches and run the risk of compounding the problem, for write-downs should never have happened in the first place. These funds should either be left uninvested, i.e., as cash, or else placed into eligible investment accounts pending a review of the asset manager's suitability for the job. Following the latter, the deal can either enter an alternative *turbo* mode whereby the contents of the WDA are returned to investors immediately as partial prepayments, or the asset manager may be replaced and the deal can go on as described above. Investors should always pause and review asset managers who have purchased ABS securities that undergo partial write-downs. Of course, the review may result in a clean bill of health, for by definition someone has to hold the securities that do default, i.e., risk management does not mean risk elimination. However, a disproportionate share of such purchases in one transaction should be cause for investor concern.

The cash flow mechanics of a WDA are nontrivial and require nonnegligible technical expertise. To help the reader visualize this, exhibits 24.2–24.5 present, with minimal commentary, relevant VBA sections showing some of the steps necessary to implement a WDA inside the analysis code for a CDO of ABS.

First, exhibit 24.2 shows how tranche-wise insolvency write-downs are computed via the calculations of asset-level shortfalls inside a slimmed-down version of each underlying SPV.

▷ Exhibit 24.2: Computation of Tranche-Wise Shortfalls

```
Defaulted_Balances = Defaulted_Loans * .Current_Loan_Balance

.Remaining_Loans = .Remaining_Loans - Defaulted_Loans

.Principal_Paid = -.Remaining_Loans * PPmt(.WAC / 12, Temps - .Purchase_Month,
.WAM, .Initial_Tranche_Balance / .Number_of_Loans)

.Current_Loan_Balance = .Current_Loan_Balance + Application.PPmt(.WAC / 12,
Temps - .Purchase_Month, .WAM, .Initial_Tranche_Balance / .Number_of_Loans)

.Interest_Paid = -.Remaining_Loans * IPmt(.WAC / 12, Temps - .Purchase_Month,
.WAM, .Initial_Tranche_Balance / .Number_of_Loans)

Tranche_Available_Funds = .Principal_Paid + .Interest_Paid + Tranche_Swap_
Payment
'
Asset-tranche waterfall (fixed- and floating-rate tranches are allowed)
'
Scratch = .Tranche_Rate - (.Interest_Type = "Floating") * LIBOR(Temps - 1, 1)
Tranche_Interest_Due = Scratch / 12 * .Current_Tranche_Balance + _
.Tranche_Interest_Shortfall * (1 + Scratch / 12)
Tranche_Principal_Due = Min(Defaulted_Balances + .Principal_Paid + _
.Tranche_Principal_Shortfall, .Current_Tranche_Balance)

Tranche_Interest_Paid = Min(Tranche_Available_Funds, Tranche_Interest_Due)

.Tranche_Interest_Shortfall = Tranche_Interest_Due - Tranche_Interest_Paid

.Cum_Interest_Paid = .Cum_Interest_Paid + Tranche_Interest_Paid

Tranche_Available_Funds = Tranche_Available_Funds - Tranche_Interest_Paid
Tranche_Principal_Paid = Min(Tranche_Available_Funds, Tranche_Principal_Due)

.Tranche_Principal_Shortfall = Tranche_Principal_Due - Tranche_Principal_Paid  ◁
```

On exit from this section, we potentially have a shortfall vis-a-vis each asset-tranche and need to keep track of them globally. This is shown in exhibit 24.3.

Exhibit 24.3   Aggregate Write-Down Computation for the CDO of ABS

Write-down tranches in real time
Aggregate_Write_Down = Aggregate_Write_Down + Max(0, Defaulted_Balances + .Principal_Paid - Tranche_Principal_Paid)

Write-up tranches in real time

Aggregate_Write_Up = Aggregate_Write_Up + Max(0, Tranche_Principal_Paid - (Defaulted_Balances + .Principal_Paid))

At this point, aggregate write-downs need to be adjusted using write-ups. In essence, we are writing down net amounts only, and keeping track of the latter via the Aggregate Write-Down variable. In addition, since the WDA is a cash account, it earns interest at the eligible investment rate. Aggregate Write-Downs are preserved between time steps but Aggregate Write-Ups are not. When write-downs are negative, the code automatically releases cash into Available Funds and sets Aggregate Write-Down to zero (not shown here). Effectively, this is how the write-up feature is implemented. The net write-downs are first computed in Exhibit 24.4.

Exhibit 24.4:   Use Net Write-Downs (and Set Write-Ups to Zero between Time Steps)

Aggregate_Write_Down = Aggregate_Write_Down - Aggregate_Write_Up

(Increase Available Funds through earnings from principal collections and the WDA)

Available_Funds = Available_Funds + Eligible_Investment_Rate / 12 * _ (Write_Down_Account_Balance + Principal_Collections_Account_Balance)

At the principal distribution level in the waterfall of the CDO of ABS, the WDA balance needs to be incremented by the Aggregate Write-Down Amount computed above using remaining Available Funds allowed to be used for this purpose, which means excluding Principal Collections and the funds in the Reserve Account, both of which cannot be used for this purpose. Remember that the Reserve Account is part of Available Funds at all times. In addition, we must use funds in the WDA when each underlying SPV matures and the asset-tranche in the CDO of ABS experiences a shortfall that must be absorbed as explained above. Remember that under the CDO of ABS framework, a default can normally be realized only upon the maturity of each underlying ABS asset.

Finally, the update to the WDA is implemented as long as asset-tranches are still outstanding, after which the WDA becomes redundant and can be flushed out to Available Funds. This process is shown in exhibit 24.5.

Exhibit 24.5: Maintenance of the WDA in Real Time

Select Case Pool Balance

Case Pool Balance is > 0 (i.e. during the transaction)

Fac = Min(Max(0, Available_Funds - Total_Principal_Collections - _
Reserve_Account_Balance), Aggregate_Write_Down)
Write_Down_Account_Balance = Write_Down_Account_Balance + Fac
Available_Funds = Available_Funds - Fac
Aggregate_Write_Down = Aggregate_Write_Down - Fac

Use up as much of the write-down account as needed to cover Aggregate Shortfalls as they occur.

Fac = Min(Aggregate_Shortfall, Write_Down_Account_Balance)
Available_Funds = Available_Funds + Fac
Write_Down_Account_Balance = Write_Down_Account_Balance - Fac

Case Pool Balance is = 0

When the write-down account is no longer relevant, flush it out to available funds.

Available_Funds = Available_Funds + Write_Down_Account_Balance
Write_Down_Account_Balance = 0
Aggregate_Write_Down = 0

End Select

As you can see, the implementation of the WDA feature, even under the simplified treatment shown here, is a nontrivial programming task. If the mechanics of a revolving period are also involved, and this happens frequently, just keeping track of cash, shortfalls, write-downs, write-ups, and Available Funds becomes quasi-nightmarish. Unfortunately, this trial by fire is what each structuror of a CDO of ABS has to undergo, for it is a *conditio sine qua non* of the asset class.

Final Remarks on Write-Down Accounts

The real implementation challenge of a WDA begins when the myriad of possible cash flow combinations arising from the various structural and asset-tranche features of an actual CDO of ABS start to interact in real time and anything goes. In this connection, one cannot undertake the task of faithful deal representation in a vacuum, but only after growing into it from the ground up. The first few chapters of the Advanced Part were an attempt to do just that and to prepare the student to tackle the type of situation bound to arise within live deals.

The VBA code presented in this section makes up but a few dozen lines chosen from among the more than 3,000 found in a typical CDO cash flow analysis. In this type of intricate situation, the most trivial programming error can be magnified beyond any reasonable proportion and force you into a formal mode of thought whereby trial and error simply won't cut it. Unless the code is logically correct, it will not work. The probability that something will go wrong in any serious cash flow analysis is 100%. Only by being rock solid on the basics can an analyst ever hope to achieve any sort of closure.

24.4 THE VALUATION OF FLOATING-RATE SECURITIES

Throughout this work, we have voluntarily restricted ourselves to the credit analysis of fixed-rate ABS tranches. We have done this primarily for didactic and expository reasons, but also because this is how one should be introduced to structured finance. The fixed-rate bond comes first, not only historically, but thematically as well. This is also the way the meaning of credit ratings, i.e., the reduction of yield, ought to be understood and grasped. However, the plain fact is that the capital markets have been dealing with floating-rate securities for decades. In particular, European investors seem to have a fondness for them. Therefore, the chances are that you will one day be asked to either assign a credit rating or else evaluate the safety of floating-rate tranches issued out of a SPV. The next few paragraphs explain how to do this consistently.

Cursory Review of Current Approaches

The standard approach to rating floating-rate liabilities, assuming this is even recognized as an issue in the first place, is to turn them artificially into fixed-rate tranches. How can this be done?

In many cases, this is trivially accomplished when the tranche benefits from a swap or a cap, hence the swap or cap rate could be regarded as the *implied* fixed rate on the bond. Doing this in the case of a cap is clearly inappropriate since the cap rate represents a nonanalytical rate which is supposed to be, in some sense, a ceiling for the deal. Thus, assuming the coupon to be the cap rate is ipso facto assuming that the bond carries a much higher interest rate than it, in fact, does. Since a structured rating is related to the reduction of yield from the nominal bond promise, making an a priori false assumption vis-à-vis the security's coupon sets the bar unnecessarily high and causes the associated securities to be underrated. Penalizing floating-rate deals compared to fixed-rate transactions is highly amateurish because, depending on the prevailing rate conjecture, the floating-rate coupon might actually be lower. Ignoring prepayment issues for the moment, why else would one issue floating-rate bonds?

In the case of a transaction with a fixed-to-floating swap, the swap rate plus the credit spread could, at first blush, be viewed as the net rate on the bond, but only synthetically. Making that assumption is also shallow since in truth, swap payments are formally separate from coupon payments. Assuming that rate to be the effective, fixed coupon ignores an event of default on the part of the swap counter-party, which probability is definitely finite, not to mention the possibility that the trust will be *out of the money* when the swap provider defaults. This would bring up a brand new set of potential cash outcomes. Last but not least, it assumes no mismatch in the deal's basis, hence no basis risk related to the swap, which is false in many cases of interest. In a nutshell, serious analysis requires the formal separation of all payments inside a floating-rate transaction.

We should also mention that selecting an analyst's best guess for the worst or the average coupon, no matter how brilliant this analyst might be, is a nonstarter if the rating is to be statistically based, which it always pretends to be. The upshot of all this is that one has no choice but to grab the bull by the tail and face the situation.

The Analysis of Floating-Rate Structured Liabilities

The attempt to turn floating-rate tranches into fixed-rate ones is obviously motivated by the desire to reduce the problem to one that has already been solved. This is a noble instinct, albeit a misguided one in this case.

However, a solution can be found via a trick here as well, which is to step back one more level and to ask what credit ratings really mean as opposed to what they say. If you think about it, the average yield reduction is computed based on the promise to investors and in the case of floating-rate securities, the dilemma is that no one is quite sure what the *promise* really means.

However, there is no logical ambiguity whatsoever about that promise when it comes to the actual transaction. The mistake is to conceptualize such promises in physical, rather than metaphysical terms. On the one hand, floating-rate bonds promise their coupon, i.e., something unknown a priori. On the other hand, they also promise something unambiguous and known at closing i.e., a constant spread over the index (normally LIBOR). The problem is that spreads are relative, not absolute, so that only in real time does the rate become a specific and calculable value. In other words, inside actual transactions there is no problem since rates always become known when they are needed. This is the clue to the solution.

Floating-Rate Tranche Rating Algorithm

The calculations proceed as follows for a floating-rate structured security promising a constant periodic credit spread Δr_c over the index.

The first task is to compute the absolute interest promise using your favorite short-rate model. Nonlinear codes for floating-rate transactions are always equipped with one such model, for instance the Cox–Ingersoll–Ross (see chapter 19) or the Black–Derman–Toy short-rate model.[6] As you will know, such models produce the origin $r_0(t)$ of the yield curve, leaving us the task of deriving rates corresponding to other maturities via arbitrage-free arguments. The particular short-rate model used is irrelevant as long as it is used consistently. Again, some *absolute* truth is not what we are attempting to ferret out with a short-rate model. The model you should use is the one you know best.

Now, say you have derived the index rate $r_1(t)$ from $r_0(t)$. Once the required absolute periodic interest rate $r_1(t) + \Delta r_c$ has been calculated in real time, the corresponding *coupon promise* $I(t)$ at time t may be computed based on the outstanding principal balance $B(t - 1)$ of the security at the prior time step:

$$I(t) = B(t-1)[r_1(t-1) + \Delta r_c]$$

This first expression gives us the current interest amount due. On the principal side, since the actual promise of a structured security is timely interest but only ultimate principal, the *principal* promise is simply the principal amount *paid* $P(t)$ until the transaction's Legal Final Maturity Date, at which time the bond's remaining principal balance, if any, becomes its ultimate principal promise.

These two separate streams of promised cash flows, i.e., $I(t)$ and $P(t)$, are then substituted inside the internal rate of return (IRR) formula to compute the promised yield $r_p(i)$ for scenario i. This is the rate to be used within this scenario to compute the security's reduction of yield, if any. The quantity $\Delta IRR(i)$ is simply the difference between the synthetically calculated promise $r_p(i)$ and the actual yield $r_a(i)$, i.e., we have $\Delta IRR(i) = r_p(i) - r_a(i)$. Just as before, these differences are then summed over all scenarios and averaged to obtain the second input to the yield curve necessary to value the bond.

In summary, the main distinction between the rating procedure for fixed- versus floating-rate securities is that for fixed-rate bonds we compute the average yield over all Monte Carlo scenarios and then subtract that value from the fixed-coupon promise. By contrast, for floating-rate bonds we compute one such yield difference for each scenario and average those differences. It is interesting to note how the fixed- and floating-rate credit rating procedures turned out to be essentially inverses of each other.

Implementation Mechanics

In order to concretize our floating-rate valuation procedure, exhibit 24.6 is presented. It is taken from an actual transaction with floating-rate tranches and shows the initialization of promised payments. Failure to do this is a common error.

Exhibit 24.6:   Initialization of Promised Payments at the Inception of Monte Carlo Scenarios

For Monte Carlo = 1 To Monte Carlo Scenarios

Reset tranche data

.Current_Tranche_Balance = .Initial_Tranche_Balance
.Current_Loan_Balance = .Initial_Tranche_Balance / .Number_of_Loans
.Remaining_Loans = .Number_of_Loans
.Cum_Principal_Paid = 0
.Cum_Interest_Paid = 0
.Tranche_Interest_Shortfall = 0
.Tranche_Principal_Shortfall = 0

For Time_Step = 1 To .WAM
.Payments(Time_Step) = Empty

continues to next page

---

continued from previous page
.Promised_Payments(Time_Step) = Empty
Next Time_Step

The next step is to generate LIBOR paths for floating-rate calculations. Here, the model is plain-vanilla Brownian motion, i.e., no specific short-rate model is used. This is shown in exhibit 24.7.

Exhibit 24.7: Generation of LIBOR Paths for Floating-Rate Valuation

If .Interest Type = "Floating" Then Generate LIBOR Paths

One Month LIBOR

For i = 1 To WAM
Scratch = Norm Inv (Random Number Generator(I), LIBOR Drift, LIBOR Volatility)
LIBOR(i, 1) = Max(0, Min(LIBOR Cap, LIBOR(i - 1, 1) + Scratch * LIBOR(i - 1, 1)))
Next i

As explained above, we accumulate the promised stream of dollar payments to the floating-rate ABS and insert them into a dummy vector in anticipation of the *IRR* calculation. This is shown in exhibit 24.8.

Exhibit 24.8: Calculation of Interest and Principal Promises to the ABS Tranche

Scratch = .Tranche_Rate - (.Interest_Type = "Floating") * LIBOR(Time_Step - 1, 1)
Tranche_Interest_Due = Scratch / 12 * .Current_Tranche_Balance +
.Tranche_Interest_Shortfall * (1 + Scratch / 12)
Promised_Payments(Time_Step) = .Promised_Payments(Time_Step) + Scratch / 12 *
.Current_Tranche_Balance
Tranche_Principal_Due = Min(Defaulted_Balances + .Principal_Paid + _
.Tranche_Principal_Shortfall, .Current_Tranche_Balance)
Tranche_Interest_Paid = Min(Tranche_Available_Funds, Tranche_Interest_Due)
.Tranche_Interest_Shortfall = Tranche_Interest_Due - Tranche_Interest_Paid
.Cum_Interest_Paid = .Cum_Interest_Paid + Tranche_Interest_Paid
Tranche_Available_Funds = Tranche_Available_Funds - Tranche_Interest_Paid
Tranche_Principal_Paid = Min(Tranche_Available_Funds, Tranche_Principal_Due)
.Promised_Payments(Time_Step) = .Promised_Payments(Time_Step) +_
Tranche_Principal_Paid

Finally, the reduction of yield on the tranche is computed. exhibit 24.9 shows the yield-reduction calculation for both fixed- and floating-rate tranches as well as the final computation of the average reduction of yield on the tranche.

Exhibit 24.9:   Reduction of Yield Calculations

Select Case .Interest Type

Case "Floating"

.Promised Payments (Time Step - 1) = .Promised Payments (Time Step - 1) + .Current Tranche Balance
.Yield Promise = 12 * IRR (.Promised Payments, (.Tranche Rate + .Tranche Swap Rate) / 12)
.Yield Reduction = Max (0, 10000 * (.Yield Promise – Max (-1, 12 * IRR (.Payments, .Yield Promise / 12))))

Case "Fixed"

.Yield Reduction = Max (0, 10000 * (.Tranche Rate – Max (-1, 12 * IRR (.Payments, .Tranche Rate / 12))))

End Select

.Average Yield Reduction = .Average Yield Reduction + .Yield Reduction

Next Monte Carlo

.Average Yield Reduction = .Average Yield Reduction / Monte Carlo Scenarios

---

Exercise 24.7

Using the spreadsheet model given in earlier chapters, introduce a cap inside a version of the deal where the Class B rate is now floating with a spread of 250 bps over one-month LIBOR and perform the following three tasks:

  a) Assuming the cap provider never defaults, rate the security using the assumption that the effective Class B rate is the cap rate.
  b) Using the same asset-side model as in item a), rate the Class B using the promised coupon implied by the Brownian motion-based, one-month LIBOR model shown above.
  c) Observe the difference between the ratings assigned to the same class under both modes, and comment on it. What does that difference, if any, imply in terms of investor risk?

As always, the last step in this floating-rate tranche-valuation exercise is the nonlinear update. Nonlinear implementation is straightforward and boils down to computing the credit spread that corresponds to the total yield obtained via the yield curve, as was done previously to value fixed-rate securities.

To see how this works, assume you have conducted the floating-rate analysis as we have outlined so far in this section. Now, you are asked to update the credit spread of each floating-rate bond in the transaction on your way to a converged structure.

Clearly, upon accessing the yield curve using the calculated weighted average life and average reduction of yield, the result will be the total coupon promise as before. According to our yield curve concept from chapter 22 however, this value can be decomposed into a risk-free component and a credit spread. In essence, the liquidity premium is the *residual* vector ε from a bona fide regression analysis of market yields, and thus the relationship $E[\varepsilon] = 0$ must hold by construction. When this is done, the yield *curve* has been effectively deconstructed into its risk-free and credit spread components.

The required provisional credit spread Δr_c^n needed for the next nonlinear iterate drops out as the difference between the current total yield r_T at the security's weighted average life t_A^a and average reduction of yield ΔIRR, and the risk-free rate r_f for the same set of yield curve input values. This is depicted in figure 24.3 for a structured bond evidencing an approximate five-year average life.

The provisional promise on the bond would equal the sum of the floating-rate index for any time interval and the provisional credit spread for nonlinear iterate n as follows:

$$r^n(t) = r_1(t) + \Delta r_c^n$$

The rate-relaxation process discussed earlier is still valid in the case of floating-rate securities and must be used to compute the next value of Δr_c^n on exit from the yield curve. Once convergence is achieved, the resulting spread is the fair value Δr_c^∞.

Final Remarks on Floating-Rate Liability Ratings

As it turned out, the rating of floating-rate securities involved essentially the same procedure as that used with respect to fixed-rate tranches, but carried out in the reverse order. In the end, only a few additional lines of codes were necessary for

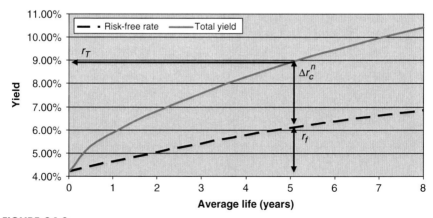

FIGURE 24.3
The nonlinear convergence process for floating-rate securities.

the rating to be interpreted in the same manner without any approximation or ad hoc assumption. This procedure has the advantage of giving credit to situations whereby the current rate is below the cap rate, above the floor rate and does not assume the continued existence of some artificial and synthetic swap counter-party, letting the deal unfold by itself. Therefore, this nonlinear technique is bound to produce higher ratings than those produced via current methods. More importantly, it will give rise to consistent and reproducible outcomes, since it explicitly includes forecasted rate environments via a short-rate model, no matter how simplistic it might be.

▶ Exercise 24.8

Statement

You will recall how, as part of the exercises in chapter 16, we showed how to construct the value at risk (VAR) of a portfolio of bank loans using a model derived from a second-order Taylor-series expansion of the basic credit loss equation and making use of the central limit theorem when the loans are independent. Alternatively, the portfolio's VAR can be obtained via a variety of commercially available models. In all cases however, the upshot will be a portfolio-wise dynamic measure that will meander in time according to the vagaries of the target portfolio's aggregate credit risk.

Remember that although the computation of VAR or of some other index is necessary to *measure* credit risk, per se that step is only a precondition to *managing* it. By itself, measurement is by no means sufficient. This lengthy exercise is intended to familiarize you with the spectral approach to credit risk management with a view toward optimally allocating bank-wide capital. In addition, it will further solidify your knowledge of the breadth of applications accessible via the techniques you have learned thus far.

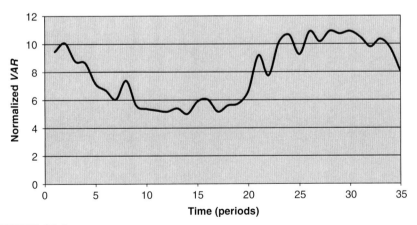

FIGURE 24.4
The temporal variation of VAR in a typical bank portfolio.

In general, a rational framework for capital allocation would partition the bank's required capital into long-term and short-term components. In this exercise, we develop

continues to next page

continued from previous page

a practical method to do this. Ideally, the bank would only require long-term capital, a much cheaper form than short-term capital, usually available only in the form of standby letters of credit with commitment and other unavoidable fees. Unfortunately, the stochastic nature of risk will impose constraints on our ability to constrain VAR-related variance, and hence in required economic capital, under the basic requirement that the bank's default rate, and hence its credit rating, must remain constant. You will remember that, because credit risk cannot be eliminated, only shifted, the constancy of default risk as measured by the chosen model is the long-term goal and fundamental desideratum of all risk management efforts.

Thus, in practice a bank will be faced with having to procure both long- and short-term capital to meet its economic or regulatory capital needs. In general, we can imagine a situation like that depicted in figure 24.4 where the abscissa is time in arbitrary units and the ordinate is the value of VAR at that time, normalized as a percentage of the target portfolio's aggregate nominal exposure. In most cases, financial regulators will impose capital requirements equal to a multiple of VAR. This multiple will hopefully be as low as possible, but in most cases it will be equal to, or higher than unity. It is understood that any approach to capital optimization should be indifferent to the particular value of this multiple.

To investigate the optimal allocation of capital given the above VAR stochasticity, assume first that the VAR time series, rather than displaying the random gyrations of figure 24.4, behaves periodically according to the functional form displayed as figure 24.5:

$$VAR \equiv V(t) = v_0 + v_a \cos\left(\frac{2\pi t}{T}\right) \tag{7}$$

In addition, assume further that capital can be procured either as long-term capital at a fixed cost p_l or as short-term capital at a fixed cost p_s. The problem is to find the optimal value of long-term capital C_0^{opt} the bank should hold under this VAR scenario, and assuming total required capital is equal to VAR; in other words a multiple of one is assumed. For any other multiple, the optimal value of long-term capital would simply be that much larger.

Note that the assumption of a fixed short-term capital cost over the period T is not as stupid as it may seem. For instance, a bank may have entered into an agreement with a particular source to provide it with a standby line of credit at a fixed cost over the period T in exchange for exclusivity or some other benefit. Therefore, assuming a fixed cost of short-term capital in no way implies that the cost of short-term capital in the market in fact remains fixed.

Given that total required capital is the sum of long-term capital plus whatever short-term capital is needed to meet the VAR target, and defining the current value of long-term capital as C_0, we can write down the instantaneous capital needed by the bank to meet its regulatory requirements:

$$\text{Required capital: } C_0 + Max\,[0,\, VAR - C_0] \tag{8}$$

In other words, during times where the condition $VAR - C_0 \leq 0$ holds, and shown in figure 24.5 as the interval $t \in [t_0, t_1]$, the bank will be holding too much capital. As odd as it may seem, this situation may turn out to be optimal because in general the cost of short-term capital is significantly higher than that of long-term capital.

Therefore the period between t_0 and t_1 will be compensated by the reduced total cost of capital during the rest of the cycle.

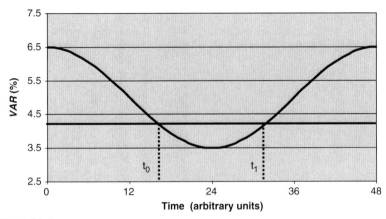

FIGURE 24.5
The assumed co-sinusoidal variation in the portfolio.

In view of definition (8), we can write down the total cost of capital C_T over the period T as:

$$C_T = \int_0^T \left[p_l C_0 + p_s \left[V(t) - C_0 \right] H\left(V(t) - C_0 \right) \right] dt \qquad (9)$$

In equation (9), we have defined the Heaviside step function in the usual way:

$$H(x) \equiv \begin{cases} 0, x \le 0 \\ 1, x > 0 \end{cases}$$

Tasks
Via a standard parametric optimization procedure and making use of Leibniz's differentiation rule for definite integrals, show that the value of C_0 that minimizes C_T is given by equation (10).

$$C_0^{opt} = v_0 + v_a \cos \left(\frac{p_l}{p_s} \pi \right) \qquad (10)$$

Next, suggest what you would do with any excess capital available under this scheme. How would you further optimize the bank's capital situation given such excess?

Exercise 24.9

Clearly, it would be utopic to hope that *VAR* time series would reveal themselves as perfect cosine waves. Rather, we can expect that as a rule, we will be dealing with

continues to next page

continued from previous page

arbitrary, nonperiodic functions of time $f(t)$. However, any function of time defined over the interval $t \in [0, T]$ can always be expanded as a half-range Fourier series for a hypothetically periodic function with period $2T$. In effect, we are assuming that we can only *see* half the cycle over the period of interest, i.e., T. If we make the further and mild assumption that the function is even, it can be expanded as a sum of cosine terms:

$$f(t) = v_0 + \sum_{n=1}^{\infty} v_a^n \cos \left(\frac{n\pi t}{T} \right) \tag{11}$$

The usual manipulations lead to the definition of the coefficients for the half-range expansion as:

$$v_0 = \frac{1}{T} \int_0^T f(t) \, dt \tag{12a}$$

$$v_a^n = \frac{2}{T} \int_0^T f(t) \cos \left(\frac{n\pi t}{T} \right) dt \tag{12b}$$

Task

By introducing definition (11) for *VAR* into the above optimal capital formalism, show that optimal long-term capital under arbitrary *VAR* specifications can be defined as:

$$C_0^{opt} \equiv v_0 + \sum_{n=1}^{\infty} v_a^n \cos \left[\frac{p_l \, n\pi}{2p_s} \right] \tag{13}$$

Exercise 24.10

Admittedly, the assumption that the variation of *VAR* in $t \in [T, 2T]$ is symmetric about the interval $t \in [0, T]$ is rather unrealistic. In practice, we cannot really expect this to be the case and must find some way of estimating the sensitivity of optimal capital to various inaccuracies in our, most likely, mistaken assumption about the shape of *VAR* stochasticity. In other words, it would be advantageous to know the range of errors we might be making when using the half-range Fourier series formalism used in exercise 24.9 to define optimal long-term capital. Remember that we are only observing half the data and merely assuming that the second half is the mirror image of the first one.

To evaluate the magnitude of this type of error, it is propitious to investigate the behavior of optimal capital under some assumed variability of the above Fourier amplitudes. This is because it is fairly safe to assume that under normal circumstances, the *VAR* time series from for $t \in [T, 2T]$ will still be characterized by similar variability but with perhaps some errors in the value of the assumed amplitudes. As a result, you might need to study the vulnerability and sensitivity of C_o^{opt} to such amplitude variance.

Tasks

Using the *VAR* time series data given as Table 24.2 in Appendix A, first introduce the following time-dependent amplitude functions $w_n(t)$:

$$w_n(t) = w_n(t-1) + \frac{\sigma}{\sqrt{n}} z(t) \tag{14}$$

In equation (14), we have defined $w_n(0) = v_a^n$, $z(t) = N(0, 1)$, where $N(0, 1)$ is a standard normal deviate.

The volatility index σ is a measure of how amplitudes might be changing from their base value over time and, practically speaking, could be estimated by looking at previous *VAR* time series samples within the same half-range Fourier formalism. Each of these samples will generate a different set of amplitudes v_a^n that we can use to define the range of likely σ values. However, for the purposes of the exercise, simply choose σ via:

$$\sigma \equiv \alpha \, v_a^1, \ \alpha \in [0.05, 0.5]$$

Instead of equation (11), use the more general formula:

$$f(t) = v_0 + \sum_{n=1}^{\infty} w_n(t) \cos\left(\frac{n\pi t}{T}\right) \tag{15}$$

As a first step to the investigation of the variation in optimal long-term capital, please conduct Monte Carlo experiments by generating a sequence of 2,000 *VAR* time series using equation (15) and the value of σ corresponding to $\alpha = 0.05$. To find the normal deviates you need to implement equation (14), please use the Box–Muller transformation reviewed in chapter 18 in concert with the Excel-resident Rand function or some alternative uniform random number generator.

In order to calculate the amplitudes v_0 and v_a^n, fit a cubic spline function through the given data points and use Simpson's rule[7] to compute the integrals required by equations (12a) and (12b) using at least five times more data points than the number (36) you are given in Appendix A . The cubic spline equations are available in "*The Analysis of Structured Securities*" (OUP, 2003).

Exercise 24.11

As the next step in your study of optimal long-term capital sensitivity, please conduct the same type of random simulations as those you did in exercise 24.10, but this time with various values of σ chosen from among the set defined in that exercise.

Exercise 24.12

Redo exercise 24.11, but this time compute the total cost of capital under various trial values of long-term capital C_0. Choose C_0^{opt} as the value that results in the minimum average total cost of capital across a given set of Monte Carlo runs.

Exercise 24.13

Determine how close to the right hand side of the equation (13) the limiting value of optimal long-term capital converges under this Monte Carlo method. To do this, plot the sequence of optimal long-term capital $C_0^{opt}(\sigma)$ obtained in exercise 24.12 as a function of σ and compute the asymptote:

$$C_0^\infty \equiv \lim_{\sigma \to 0} C_0^{opt}(\sigma)$$

You may easily compute this asymptote as the constant term of the least-squares linear regression line corresponding to $C_0^{opt}(\sigma)$. The value of C_0^∞ should be comparable to the right side of equation (13). To find the required regression coefficient, please use the Cholesky decomposition (see chapter 18) applied to the regression matrix.

   You will recall that the regression matrix satisfies two conditions guaranteeing that its Cholesky decomposition exists. What are these conditions?

24.5 AVERAGE LIFE, DURATION, AND ALL THAT!

Despite the fact that the concepts of *duration* and *average life* could not be more different from each other than they already are, there appears to exist widespread confusion in the mind of many practitioners as to their possible kinship, a confusion that sometimes takes the form of outright identification. For some, duration even seems to stand for another way of expressing the idea of average life. The following section is intended to dispel as much of that confusion as possible, hopefully without introducing more.

   To begin with, one could not be faulted for believing that the two concepts are in fact one and the same. After all, the word "duration" certainly connotes a time determination, and so does "life." What else but time could be hiding under the pseudonym of "duration"? On the other hand, mathematically speaking the situation could not be clearer. Duration is an attempt to measure the sensitivity of bond prices to instantaneous changes in interest rates, while average life speaks of the *average* maturity of a stream of principal payments extending over possibly many years. Thus in the concept of duration, linear time per se is absent, whereas it is of the essence when computing average life since it represents the sole integration variable. In other words, duration is a *local* and transcendental concept while average life is a *global* and linear concept.

   In addition, and more importantly, duration involves total cash flow received by bondholders whereas average life solely addresses flows allocated to principal. Yet, there remains a lingering feeling in many quarters as to their putative kinship. Why is that? Contrary to all mathematical notions, not to mention commonsense, why do so many people still harbor the secret intuition that they are somehow connected? The answer is quite simple: they are.

The Connection between Average Life and Duration in the Standard Case

Ostensibly, the story of duration begins in 1938, the year in which Frederick Macaulay introduced the first attempt to characterize the volatility of bond prices with respect to interest rates. By using the word *duration* to refer to his concept, he could perhaps be regarded as the best man to blame for the confusion that now exists. Yet, to pass judgment so hastily on one of the few people who ever tried to bring clarity to Wall Street would be to commit a grave error. His original formulation eventually acquired the label *Macaulay* duration and still constitutes the basic intuition underlying duration in the capital markets.

In the standard case of a plain-vanilla corporate bond, i.e., one not subject to the sort of call risk that affects mortgage-backed securities for instance, it ran as follows:

$$D_M \equiv \frac{\displaystyle\sum_{i=1}^{T} \frac{t_i C_i}{(1+r)^{t_i}}}{\displaystyle\sum_{i=1}^{T} \frac{C_i}{(1+r)^{t_i}}} \tag{16}$$

In this relationship, we have defined the following quantities:

D_M ≡ Macaulay duration
T ≡ stated maturity of the bond
i ≡ integer time index with $i \in [1, T]$ (i.e., $t_1 = 1$, etc.)
C_i ≡ total cash flow received during period t_i
r ≡ periodic discount rate of interest

Although Macaulay probably did not have calculus in mind when he devised equation (16), analytically minded readers will immediately recognize the denominator as corresponding to the definition of the value V_0 of a bond as of $t = 0$ and expected to receive T cash flows at future times $t_i, i \in [1, T]$, while the numerator looks suspiciously like the first derivative of the denominator with respect to yield r. Yet, Macaulay did not propose equation (16) by backing out of a rigorous mathematical derivation. Instead, he was operating on pure instinct.

As you can see, save for the missing minus sign in the numerator and a factor $(1 + r)$ in the denominator, the definition of D_M given by equation (16) is simply a modified version of the more modern formulation of duration which, not surprisingly perhaps, came to be known as *modified duration*, or duration *tout court*:

$$D(r) \equiv -\frac{1}{V_0} \frac{\partial V_0(r)}{\partial r} \tag{17}$$

Here, $V(r)$ is the fair market value of the bond at some time, and without loss of generality, we have defined $V_0(r)$ as its fair market value at $t = 0$. In any event, the current time can always be normalized to zero. In essence, practitioners simply filled in the elements of the definition of first derivative that were missing from Macaulay's original insight.

Most of you will already know that there are many practical reasons why the price of a bond might fall or rise with interest rates in ways that would falsify the result obtained using equation (17), which factors go beyond the simple logic of equation (16). We reiterate that the former equation merely addresses the standard case where risk-free cash flows are received, and where investors simply look to the opportunity cost of alternative, current investments to value an existing plain-vanilla bond. In our treatment, we thus fully abstract from these various, real-life effects and consider the impact of interest-rate fluctuations on a pure cash flow stream in a totally fluid environment. Far from being unimportant, this case is actually the way most financial analysts are first introduced to duration within an academic setting.

By contrast, the canonical definition of average life t^a, reproduced here for the sake of argument, runs as follows:

$$t^a \equiv \frac{1}{P_0} \int_0^T t\, dp(t) \tag{18}$$

In equation (18), we have defined the following additional quantities:

$p(t) =$ outstanding principal balance of the bond at time t
$dp(t) =$ amortization schedule from $t - dt$ to t

As always, we postulate the following two boundary conditions:

$$p(0) \equiv P_0 \tag{19a}$$

$$p(T) = 0 \tag{19b}$$

In the absence of any information to the contrary, it is customary to renormalize instantaneously and assume a *fair* market, which implies that price and value are numerically equal,[8] leading to:

$$P_0 = V_0 \tag{20}$$

Now, recall our fundamental cash flow balance equation for the plain-vanilla renormalized bond, from which we can also derive the principal balance schedule $p(t)$:

$$f(t)\, dt = r\, p(t)\, dt - dp(t) \tag{21}$$

In equation (21), $f(t)$ represents the total cash flow density function experienced by bondholders, which is then partitioned into principal and interest allocations.

The next step is to transform the basic definition for the value of a plain-vanilla bond, usually conceived as a discrete sum of payments made over the T periods, into an integral from zero to maturity:

$$V_0 = \int_0^T f(t) e^{-rt}\, dt \tag{22}$$

Passing to the limit will enable us to manipulate the above relations more easily. In doing so, $f(t)\, dt$ takes the place of the discrete payments C_i shown in equation (16) while the factor $(1 + r)$ in the denominator is simply the first two terms of the Taylor-series expansion of e^{-r}. Applying definition (17) to equation (22) leads to:

$$D(r) = -\frac{1}{V_0} \frac{\partial}{\partial r} \left[\int_0^T f(t)\, e^{-rt}\, dt \right] = \frac{1}{V_0} \int_0^T t f(t)\, e^{-rt}\, dt \tag{23}$$

In deriving the last identity, we can take the differential operator inside the integral sign without recourse to Leibniz's rule because r and t are independent variables.

Now, substitute equation (21) inside equation (23) to obtain:

$$D(r) = \frac{1}{V_0} \int_0^T t e^{-rt} [r p(t)\, dt - dp(t)] = \int_0^T r t p(t) e^{-rt}\, dt - \int_0^T t e^{-rt} dp(t) \tag{24}$$

Next, use integration by parts on the second term to the right of equation (24). As usual, we have:

$$u = t e^{-rt}, \ du = (e^{-rt} - r t e^{-rt})\, dt \tag{25a}$$

$$dv = dp(t), \ v = p(t) \tag{25b}$$

The mechanics of integration by parts quickly yield:

$$D(r) = \frac{1}{V_0} \left[-t e^{-rt} p(t) \Big|_0^T + \int_0^T p(t)\, (1 - rt)\, e^{-rt}\, dt + \int_0^T r t p(t) e^{-rt}\, dt \right] \tag{26}$$

Applying boundary conditions (19) and effecting the obvious cancellation inside equation (26), we finally obtain:

$$D(r) = \frac{1}{V_0} \int_0^T p(t) e^{-rt}\, dt \tag{27}$$

Now, making use of our fair value condition (20) we can write:

$$D(r) = \frac{1}{P_0} \int_0^T p(t)\, e^{-rt}\, dt \qquad (28)$$

Glancing at the definition of the average life given above, we note that in all[9] continuous principal balance cases, it can be rewritten under a Riemann framework instead of the Lebesgue formulation given by equation (18):

$$t^a = \frac{1}{P_0} \int_0^T p(t)\, dt \qquad (29)$$

Equations (28) and (29) should provide ample motivation for the generalization of the average life definition as the transcendental limit of duration for vanishing yield:

$$t^a \equiv \lim_{r \to 0} D(r) \qquad (30)$$

As can readily be seen, there does indeed exist an intimate relationship between these two seemingly disparate concepts. This relationship, which remains for the most part hidden in the background of our calculations, is precisely what gives rise both to the prevailing confusion about duration and average life and to the intuition that they are "the same." In fact, the transcendence of average life vis-à-vis duration is why Macaulay himself was led to his brilliant intuition. What he saw so clearly, in sharp contrast to the vast majority of financial men of our generation, is that duration does indeed have something to do with time. It has to do with *nonlinear* instead of *linear* time, the latter being, of course, what average life is all about.

Exercise 24.14

Use equations (28) and (30) to compute explicitly the duration and average life of a bond with initial principal balance P_0 and amortizing in a straight line pattern across the interval $t \in [0, T]$. Note that, in this simple case, the use of equation (30) to compute t^a is clearly superfluous since triangulation quickly leads to the well-known result:

$$t^a = \frac{T}{2} \qquad (31)$$

The goal here is to verify that equation (30) reproduces the known result given by equation (31).

Hint: The amortization schedule of a straight-line bond satisfying boundary conditions (19) is given by:

$$p(t) = P_0 \left(1 - \frac{t}{T}\right) \qquad (32)$$

Exercise 24.15

Show that the duration of a continuous time bond can be redefined as the renormalized Laplace transform of its principal balance schedule:

$$D(r) \equiv \frac{1}{P_0} L(p(t)) \tag{33}$$

Exercise 24.16

Extend the above Laplace transform formalism to convexity by defining $C(r)$ as follows:

$$C(r) \equiv \frac{\partial D(r)}{\partial r} = D'(r) = \frac{\partial}{\partial r}\left[\frac{1}{P_0} L(p(t))\right]$$

Next, using the basic properties of Laplace transforms, derive the generalized definition for the convexity $C(r)$ of any bond.

Exercise 24.17

Derive formulas for the duration and average life of a security with the following principal balance schedule:

$$p(t) = P_0\, e^{-\alpha t}\, [1 + \sin(\omega t)]\,, \; p(\infty) \to 0 \tag{34}$$

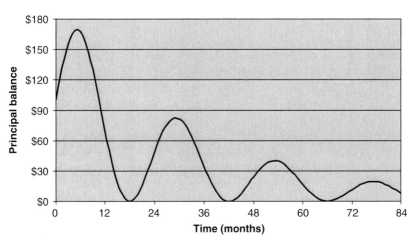

FIGURE 24.6

Amortization schedule of an exponentially decaying sinusoidal bond.

Figure 24.6 shows a typical pattern produced by equation (34). This type of profile could arise, for instance, in the case of a graduated-payment student loan in which the

continues to next page

continued from previous page
initial total payment made would be insufficient to pay even the interest on the loan
when due, thus causing negative amortization to take place, but soon followed by
higher payments that would let principal amortize, and so on.

The striking similarity to the renormalization group in particle physics can be seen
in the analogy between the generalized definition of duration via equation (33) and
the Callan & Symansik version of the Gell–Man equation from quantum field theory.
In that case, the coupling parameter g in a particle-system is known to be related to
the energy level μ through the following equation:

$$\frac{\partial \ln g}{\partial \ln \mu} = \psi(g) = \frac{\beta(g)}{g}$$

In this case, if we formally define the soul-energy as $\mu = e^{-r}$ and the coupling
parameter as the value V_0 at any point in time, thus linking the *present* to the *future*,
the left side of the last equation immediately drops out as:

$$\frac{\partial \ln g}{\partial \ln \mu} = -\frac{1}{V_0}\frac{\partial V_0}{\partial r} = \frac{\beta(V_0)}{V_0}$$

Then, it becomes obvious that, since we have postulated all along the relation $P_0 = V_0$,
the function $\beta(V_0)$ is the Laplace transform of the principal schedule $p(t)$. In other
words, by setting $\beta(V_0(t)) \equiv L(p(t))$, we have derived the renormalized value V_0.

Exercise 24.18

Extend the above definition of duration to discrete bonds, i.e., those with principal
balance $p(n)$ at time n making periodic principal and interest payments. By using a
finite sum containing the factor $z \equiv (1 + r)$ in the denominator, show that duration can
be redefined and generalized via:

$$D_d(r) \equiv \frac{1}{P_0} \sum_{n=0}^{\infty} p(n)\, z^{-n} \tag{35}$$

What is the standard mathematical name given to the summation in equation (35)?

Exercise 24.19

By strict analogy with the continuous case, show that the convexity of a discrete bond
can be defined as:

$$C_d(r) \equiv \frac{1}{P_0} Z\big[n\, p(n)\big] \tag{36}$$

Exercise 24.20

Show that the duration of a standard, amortizing, and continuous bond with the familiar principal balance schedule given by:

$$p(t) = \begin{cases} \frac{M}{r_0}\left[1 - e^{r_0(t-T)}\right], & 0 \le t \le T \\ 0, & t > T \end{cases}$$

can be given by the following relationship:

$$D(r) = \frac{1}{1 - e^{-r_0 T}} \left\{ \frac{1 - e^{-rT}}{r} + \frac{e^{-r_0 T} - e^{-rT}}{(r_0 - r)} \right\} \qquad (37)$$

Exercise 24.21

Construct a first-order Taylor-series approximation for the interest-rate-bound variation in the price of the bond in exercise 24.20.

Exercise 24.22

Using the result of exercise 24.21 and the concept of duration, express the sensitivity of the bond's price to interest rates. You may assume that the current level of interest rates is r_c,

Exercise 24.23

Assuming $r_c = 0.1$, $T = 5$ years, and $r_0 = 0.12$, find the value of duration using equation (37).

Exercise 24.24

Assuming the bond now sells for 105.5 and that the conditions of exercise 24.23 apply, what would be your estimate for the value of this bond if interest rates jumped up by 200 bps?

Exercise 24.25

Construct a second-order Taylor-series approximation for the interest-rate-bound variation in the value of the bond in exercise 24.20.

> **Exercise 24.26**
>
> Assuming the relationship $C(r_c)/D(r_c) = -\frac{1}{r_c}$ holds when rates are 10%, what would be your new estimate for the market value of this bond if interest rates were to jump by 200 bps?

> **Exercise 24.27**
>
> Compute the duration of the bond in exercise 24.20 for $r_c = 0.14$.

In closing, we might add that since the Laplace transform operator is linear, aggregate portfolio duration can be easily obtained by summing the individual durations of exposures found on the balance sheet of any institution. Given this, it is a routine matter to recalibrate the said institution's portfolio *via* deconvolution of aggregate duration into the re-calibrating principal profile. The latter then becomes the target, calibrating exposure to be either purchased or sold short. This is what we emonstrate in the next section.

As long as you remember that the calculations on duration and convexity described in this section can only be deemed to hold for an instant of linear time with zero measure, you will not commit significant errors. What "an instant of linear time with zero measure" actually means in practice is different in different markets, and is obviously related to the liquidity properties prevailing in the target market. This should not surprise those who have read chapter 22. Since the secondary market is a linear market, i.e., inherently unstable, one needs to be careful when casually engaging in recalibration operations in highly illiquid environments.

> **Exercise 24.28**
>
> Using the Fourier–Mellin integral, show that the cash flow density-function $f(t)$ of a bond with initial principal balance V_0 and exhibiting amortization profile $p(t)$ satisfying the duration relation $D(r) = (1/V_0) L(p(t))$ can be recovered explicitly from complex-space integration around the set of algebraic singularities s_n, $n \in [1, N]$ of its yield-space duration function as follows:
>
> $$f(t) = -\frac{V_0}{2\pi i} \int_{\gamma-i\infty}^{\gamma+i\infty} \left[\int_{-\infty}^{r} D(s)\, ds \right] e^{rt} dr, \gamma > Re[s_n] \; \forall n$$

24.6 HEDGE FUND IMMUNIZATION

As was true of our treatment of Hausdorff measures and dimensions in chapter 22, this section is probably beyond the scope of an introductory text like this one.

However, we feel that the topic of hedge funds has received too little attention thus far, especially considering the aggregate amount of capital invested in them across the planet. As we mentioned while discussing revolving portfolios, we believe that the entire rationale for hedge fund valuation is woefully inadequate and, to be credible, would require a complete revamping. Unfortunately, we have neither the space nor the necessary background to do this here.

Nevertheless, assuming hedge funds rested on more solid theoretical foundations than they actually do, practitioners have a right to wonder how they could make immediate use of the generalized formulation of duration and convexity as Laplace transforms acquired in the last section. In this spirit, we review in some detail the important area of portfolio immunization.

The Concept behind Hedge Funds

Specifically, hedge funds were originally conceived as portfolios of assets with positive and negative duration. In the once thriving world of collateralized mortgage obligations, this could be accomplished relatively easily by purchasing a pool of interest-only and principal-only securities pegged off the same index, usually LIBOR. The weighted-average duration of this portfolio was controlled, normally via trading, to ensure that it remained within given, fixed bounds. These *logical* bounds were however conceived as having zero measure. In other words, it was deemed impossible to achieve greater precision around zero duration in the actual world of mortgage-backed securities, as opposed to the make-believe world of *theory*. The standard bound was ca. ±3%, meaning that if the portfolio exhibited duration with an absolute value smaller than this, no corrective action needed to take place.

One question might arise at the outset, which is this: why do we need to maintain duration-neutrality in the first place? After all, garden-variety portfolio managers are not similarly obsessed with duration. What makes hedge funds so special that their managers need to lose sleep over an elusive target like duration? The answer is that investment banks invented hedge funds when they did not have direct access to the Federal Reserve window. Therefore, they had to borrow the majority of the invested funds from someone else who, in turn, needed to enter into repurchase agreements with the investment banks to borrow from the Fed. The associated, so-called *repo* lines were short-term instruments that could mature any given day. As a result, the investment banks were forced to provide internal liquidity via the secondary market liquidation of the same securities, which in most cases were highly rated mortgage-backed securities. If the market value of the collateral were to drop precipitously, even without any corresponding credit concern, the fund's equity might be wiped out when, in fact, there was nothing wrong. Thus, the liquidity requirements imposed on hedge funds arose completely spontaneously and did not originate from the economic or mathematical basis underlying such funds. By contrast, most hedge funds today are neither hedged nor funds.

A true hedge fund, by its very nature, is a balancing act, or more precisely, a *rebalancing* act. Indeed, periods during which the market value of all hedge fund collateral collapsed discontinuously were rare, but they did occur. Each of them was mistakenly dubbed a *liquidity* crisis when, in fact, it was a *valuation* crisis.

A real liquidity crisis is impossible unless national currency, i.e., the Federal Reserve, has mysteriously vanished. In all such cases, what had vanished was the previously smooth and continuous bond pricing environment that had prevailed. Of course, the same phenomenon can happen today. Obviously, knowing that a hedge fund needs to remain essentially duration-neutral throughout its existence is one thing. Knowing how to achieve it is quite another.

Duration Immunization

The rebalancing of a portfolio usually means the trading of one set of exposures for another one with anti-correlated duration. For example, if the current portfolio displays too much positive duration, the manager could sell selected exposures contributing disproportionately to such positivity and swap them for another group with smaller duration, thus reducing the average portfolio duration below 3%. Mathematically speaking, this can be also conceived as adding negative duration to the current portfolio. Alternatively, if too little duration is obtained, the opposite trade would be executed, effectively keeping average portfolio duration within the target range. Such actions came to be known as rebalancing or *immunizing* the portfolio against interest-rate movements.

In the remainder of this section, we show how to compute the cash flow stream that effectively immunizes a hedged portfolio and restores it, theoretically speaking, to zero duration at any point in linear time. We do this using the Laplace transform formalism derived in the last section.

The mathematical situation is as follows. We are presented with a portfolio of n exposures, indexed with i, each with its own absolute duration $d_i(r)$, $i \in [1, n]$. Since duration is a linear operator, the portfolio's total absolute duration $D_p(r)$ is simply the sum of all n individual contributions to absolute duration:

$$D_p(r) = \sum_{i=1}^{n} d_i(r)$$

As a reminder, the absolute duration of a single exposure can be defined as the Laplace transform of the associated renormalized amortization schedule with time reset to zero prior to each rebalancing exercise:

$$d_i(r) = L(p_i(t))$$

As was explained above, the immunizing exposure's associated duration $D_I(r)$ needs to be such as to cause the new portfolio to have zero duration, and this for a instant of linear time[10] with zero measure. Therefore, our portfolio-wide immunization condition is as follows:

$$D_p(r) + D_I(r) = 0 \tag{38}$$

The immunizing exposure's principal balance schedule can now be recovered easily from the inverse Laplace transform of the current portfolio's duration before the change:

$$P_I(t) = -L^{-1}(D_p(r)) \tag{39}$$

Duration and Convexity Immunization

If a position with the precise profile, and hence functional form, corresponding to equation (39) can be found, then we have ipso facto immunized our hedged portfolio with respect to convexity and other moments as well, since obviously:

$$C_p(r) \equiv \frac{\partial D_p(r)}{\partial r} = -\frac{\partial D_I(r)}{\partial r} \tag{40}$$

However, it is unlikely that, by sheer coincidence, such an exposure can be found just lying about and ready to be plucked. More often than not, we will need to be satisfied with less than perfect immunity. In most cases, the functional form we would be in a position to access would fall short of the mark at some level, and we would only be able to duration-immunize the current portfolio at the prevailing rate conjecture. For the sake of argument, assume we are faced with a situation like the one shown in figure 24.7.

Here, the added duration $D_I(r)$ is indeed immunizing at the prevailing rate of about 5.5% since the slopes of the portfolio's value $V_p(r)$ and of the hypothetical, immunizing exposure $V_I(r)$ are inverses of each other. Thus, our portfolio is indeed duration-immunized at 5.5%. However, it is apparent from figure 24.7 that the convexities of the current portfolio and of the proposed immunizing exposure have the same sign, and thus that $D_I(r)$ will not convexity-immunize this portfolio at the

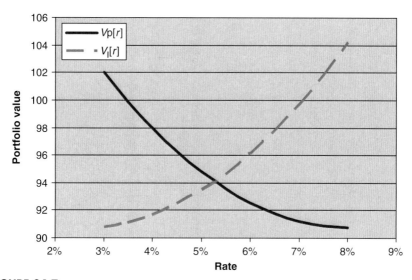

FIGURE 24.7
Portfolio immunization exercise.

current interest rate. In this example, we would have $C_p(r) + C_I(r) > 0$ and would have failed our convexity objective, or so it seems.

Therefore, in some sense the last exercise was trivial. We were simply asking what principal balance schedule, positive (long) or negative (short), was required to ensure provisionally that the combined portfolio would be brought to zero duration, at least for a while. The other moments were left uninterrogated. In some circles, this might be viewed as a cavalier attitude.

As we all know, our provisional victory may in fact be short-lived because, although zero duration has indeed been achieved, a portfolio with zero duration at some moment in yield space may in practice be standing on the edge of a rate cliff.

This is the situation shown in figure 24.8. In that case, although we do indeed have zero duration at the prevailing rate of 5.5%, the actual situation is anything but stable. What we want is a situation similar to figure 24.9, whereby the portfolio does not face significant price decreases, or increases, when rates undergo relatively benign movements. Do not forget that many hedge funds are thinly capitalized to begin with.

In the second situation, our portfolio could be described as having greater *integrity*. In fact, this is the very situation we are trying to achieve when attempting to keep average portfolio duration to within known targets. Can this be done? As stated above, it cannot be done through duration alone. Here convexity, the second derivative of value with respect to rate, needs to enter the picture as well. This second problem is more difficult because of the direct relationship between duration and convexity shown via equation (40).

Thus, any attempt to reduce convexity independently of duration is bound to fail a priori, since it is not possible to do this without simultaneously changing duration. The two measures are linked and, therefore, a global solution requires both zero-conditions to be met as part of a locally and quadratically immunized condition. In other words,

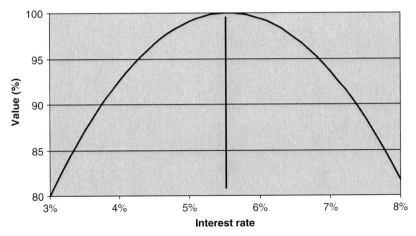

FIGURE 24.8
High-convexity portfolio.

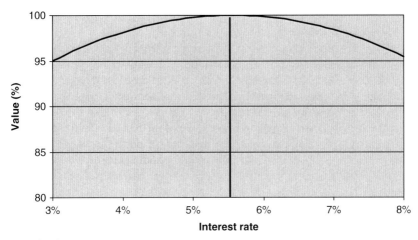

FIGURE 24.9
Low convexity portfolio.

we need to somehow add duration and convexity to an existing, hedged portfolio in an amount just sufficient to reduce both measures to zero together and, at least, locally if a global solution is not available. Our first equation is identical to equation (38):

$$D_p(r) + D_I(r) = 0 \tag{38}$$

Our second equation expresses the required convexity immunization condition for the portfolio as a whole at the current rate r:

$$C_p(r) + C_I(r) = 0 \tag{41}$$

The likelihood that equations (38) and (41) can be satisfied simultaneously is remote. Instead, equation (42) will hold at the prevailing interest rate r for some number β not equal to zero:

$$C_p(r) + C_I(r) = \beta \tag{42}$$

At this point, there seems to be no other way but to keep chasing our tail ad infinitum. In other words, we could always add or subtract convexity in an effort to drive the absolute value $|\beta|$ towards zero, but that would invariably upset the duration requirement represented by equation (38). We could try and nullify the difference by adding or subtracting duration, and keep doing this in ever smaller increments within some, hopefully, converging sequence.

However, note that there was never a real need to enforce equation (38) in the first place. As stated earlier, we only had to maintain the post-addition $D_p(r)$ within the target $\pm\alpha$, and we were given α at the outset. Therefore, we can *give up* duration in exchange for a tighter, i.e., lower, absolute convexity bound.

Specifically, simply postulate equation (38a) as a replacement for equation (38):

$$D_p(r) + D_I(r) = \delta \tag{38a}$$

The way to proceed is to start moving duration away from zero as long as it remains within the range $\pm\alpha$. This may be done formally through an optimization method. For example, one might first introduce an arbitrary parameter λ inside the duration correction $D_I(r; \lambda)$, define the Lagrangian[11] $L(\lambda) = \beta^2 + \delta^2 + \chi\,(\delta - \alpha)$ as an explicit function of λ and then solve a constrained, one-dimensional optimization problem by differentiating the Lagrangian with respect to λ, thus finding the value of λ that minimizes the Lagrangian while keeping $\delta \leq \alpha$. Granted, this method assumes that a point of duration is *worth* the same as a point of convexity, and this cannot be countenanced even as a theoretical matter.

There are many other approaches, from simply monitoring convexity without worrying too much about it, all the way to maintaining convexity as close to zero as possible while simultaneously meeting the duration target $\pm\alpha$. The practical, as opposed to theoretical, possibilities are however much more restricted than this analysis might let one presuppose. Needless to say, hedge fund investors need more circumspection and knowledge in this area than they usually care to have.

APPENDIX A

TABLE 24.2
VAR time series

TIME	VAR
0	10.850
1	9.455
2	10.067
3	8.774
4	8.635
5	7.143
6	6.689
7	6.047
8	7.382
9	5.594
10	5.360
11	5.254
12	5.156
13	5.395
14	5.002
15	5.897
16	6.017
17	5.156
18	5.606
19	5.738
20	6.612
21	9.180
22	7.737
23	10.097
24	10.653
25	9.247
26	10.894
27	10.172
28	10.910
29	10.721
30	10.904
31	10.461
32	9.785
33	10.338
34	9.674
35	8.013
36	8.893

APPENDIX B

Simpson's rule is a numerical integration method based on the analytical integration of Lagrange polynomials. The higher the order of the polynomial, the more sophisticated the formula. This one is based on quadratic polynomials.

In economics, discretization arguments are usually moot since one can normally use as many points as one likes and remain well within the accuracy of the given data.

If the goal is to find the integral I of a function $f(x)$ given at the $2n + 1$ points $f_i \equiv f(x_i), i \in [0, 2n]$ over the real interval $[a, b]$, Simpson's rule for the integral is given by:

$$I \equiv \int_a^b f(x)\,dx = \frac{h}{3}\left(f_0 + 4f_1 + 2f_2 + 4f_3 + \ldots\ldots + 2f_{2n-2} + 4f_{2n-1} + f_{2n}\right)$$

In this formula, we have defined $h = \frac{b-a}{2n}$

Epilogue

The Task of Dealing

It is probably fair to say that some of you may be entertaining serious doubts as to the practicality of the approach we have carefully laid out in the Advanced Part, as well as to its usefulness in the practice of structured analysis. If you do, you are not alone. In fact, most investment bankers secretly harbor similar fears.

It would indeed be remarkable if the *Dao of Dealing* made perfect sense to you. This is because the usual upshot of one's initial encounter with deal-hood is total confusion. In other words, if on a first reading you believe this is plain as day, you really do not understand, if only because what makes perfect sense is that talk about making sense cannot itself make any sense. The French say l'appétit vient en mangeant, and so it is with finance. Unbelievably perhaps, one can only learn how to do deals by doing deals and not by talking or reading books about deals, including this one, and certainly not by attending expensive seminars, lectures, and conferences on the topic. Doing deals is difficult not because it is complex but because it is so simple and requires of you the clear realization of what was staring you in the face all along and yet remained *passed-over*. Nonevasion is critical, for that is the only secure path to a real understanding of the deal.

Structured securities cannot be extirpated from assets and sold like weasels jumping out of boxes. A structured bond is simply a piece of a deal and must be regarded as such if its creditworthiness is to make sense. Deals live and die as deals, and this means that once you understand deal-hood you can never buy or sell bonds, only deals.

Given the current state of American finance, learning the Dao is obviously not a necessary precondition to gainful employment. On the contrary, the time and effort involved in doing so will certainly take you away from the ubiquitous politics of the office. Thousands of transactions have been and are now being done without it, and apparently, no one is any worse off on that account. Even better, the consensus among self-appointed financial luminaries seems to be that this stuff is total overkill and that "all is well" in structured finance, at least until now.

The realization that there is only one way to do deals no more implies that all deals must look alike than the fact that there is only one way to build bridges implies that all bridges must look alike. In fact, it means just the opposite. The ignoble and, alas, commonplace underwriter practice of plagiarizing deals from competitors, other issuers, and asset classes ought to be sufficient proof that deals are never conceptualized from the ground up. Instead of admitting our own ignorance via such copycat demeanor, what we must do is recognize that each asset class or issuer has its own truth, one that forces us to look upon each transaction with fresh eyes if the client is to be served as opposed to betrayed. In this way, every deal is the first and only deal. Aping other people's structures makes as much sense as borrowing Michael Jordan's sneakers in the hope of playing great basketball.

As far as you are concerned, avoiding the painstaking work of essential dealing may lead to immense wealth, a cabinet post, giving the prizes at your old prep school, a fashion model as a spouse, and a beach house in Southampton. Conversely and needless to say, equally likely, it may end in tears, disgrace, prosecution, and Club Fed. It really doesn't matter, for in both cases finance would have remained a mystery to you, and in the final analysis you would know as much about deals as an usher at Yankee Stadium *knows* about baseball.

Only when it finally becomes control theory can structured analysis ever hope to rise above the angst of adolescence and achieve the stature to which it is surely entitled. As pure metaphysics, it deserves the most delicate of treatments and the most refined of worlds. Restoring finance to its own-most inner possibility is the task of dealing. It is your task.

Bon Voyage and May the Deal Be With You!

notes

6 ANALYSIS OF ASSET-SIDE CASH FLOWS

1. Bartlett, William W., "*The Valuation of Mortgage-Backed Securities*," New York: Irwin, 1994, pp. 201–207.
2. This expression reads "for all t from 0 to termination."
3. The first time derivative of the *CDF*, the *PDF*, is defined as $f(t)$ and is given by:

$$f(t) \equiv \frac{\partial F(t)}{\partial t} = \frac{abce^{-c(t-t_0)}}{[1+be^{-c(t-t_0)}]^2} \tag{1a}$$

It will not be used in the cash flow model, and is given for reference only.

7 ANALYSIS OF LIABILITY-SIDE CASH FLOWS

1. The main exception is found within prepayment-defensive structures like Planned Amortization Classes (PACs) and Targeted Amortization Classes (TACs), which have notional amortization schedules. However, these are not enforceable: to deviate from the notional schedule is not a default. During the height of CDO madness, some junior tranches were underwritten with "ultimate interest, ultimate principal" repayment features.
2. Guidelines for modeling other types of credit enhancement are provided in later chapters, where the associated analytical concept is introduced. For example, the end of this chapter presents the algebra of reserve accounts. Chapter 8 presents the early amortization trigger used in static-mode modeling of collateral whose risk profile has been treated conventionally by scenario-driven analysis. A simple treatment for analyzing the impact of credit enhancement from third parties is discussed at the end of chapter 9. That is because exogenous *CE* works by transforming the collateral risk into a correlated structure of asset and counterparty risk, altering the risk distribution. Chapter 11 profiles the PAC, a common CMO feature that mechanically skews the allocation of cash to protect investors against the effects of early principal repayment. Chapter 20 offers guidance on advanced liability structuring in a cash flow model, while chapter 21 provides a practical, indepth treatment of triggers.
3. A Yield Supplement Account (YSA) is a liquidity reserve for deals going to market under water (with negative *XS*), where in the expected case *XS* turns positive after the close and the transaction becomes feasible on its own. Deals with a YSA surfaced in the early 2000s, when

manufacturers provided soft credit and subvented loans (offering borrowers an initial grace period on interest) to stimulate sales. The mechanics of a YSA are not included in this chapter (nor are step-down mechanics) because the interruption of the downward flow of cash introduces complexity in the form of a trigger.

8 STATIC ANALYSIS OF REVOLVING STRUCTURES

1. Short-term investors, who park their funds for additional yield, are said to be less sensitive to prepayment than long-term investors, many of whom may be carefully managing their asset/liability gap.

2. From a risk disclosure standpoint, the static PVA model permits maximal transparency on assets and liabilities, so that participants earn their right to a cheaper cost of funds. From a cynical vantage point, the purpose of revolving phase structures seems to be to allow banks to amortize their set-up costs over many transactions, by contrast with PVAs that encourage bank clients to generate more fees.

3. An exception is amortizing CDOs, which have represented a small percentage of the total CDO market.

4. For a fuller treatment on their valuation methods, see "*The Analysis of Structured Securities*," (OUP, 2003), or consult the piecemeal methods and criteria publications by Moody's, S&P, and Fitch on these sectors.

5. The financial objective of a securitization of properties whose value is too uncertain to allow them to be laced on the balance sheet is problematic. However, this transaction could make sense as an investment in tax-loss carry forwards with a call option on their future value.

6. Note that, given expected credit performance, amortization occurs naturally at the end of every transaction. We use the term "early" merely to distinguish amortization caused by a worsening credit environment from that normal case.

7. The worst environment on record is probably the State of Texas in the early 1980s. In that case, as a result of trouble in the oil industry, *peak* loss rates in the neighborhood of 12% were experienced for a short while. However, such extreme loss rates were never sustained and, furthermore, that situation was symptomatic of aberrant local conditions not seen before or since.

8. It is important to note that, although the credit derivative industry goes to great lengths to stay away from the insurance analogy, it is obvious that credit default swaps are a form of credit insurance. The word "swap" is used merely to place the transaction outside the purview of insurance, and hence of insurance regulation. If this were an acknowledged insurance contract, which by its economic substance it is, we would be talking about an *insurer* and an *insured*, but in this artificial world the insurer has now become the *protection seller* while the insured is labeled the *protection buyer*. The crux of the analysis now consists of establishing the premium to be paid by the protection buyer in exchange for the desired credit protection.

9 MONTE CARLO SIMULATION

1. As you will remember, this was a loss *curve*, not a loss *distribution*.

10 INTRODUCTION TO PREPAYMENT MODELING

1. See section 6.4 for an introduction to the logistic curve, colloquially known as the '*S*-curve'.

2. Note that there are such things as "callable" bonds and that prepayment analysis does apply to them as well.

3. As we shall see, the quantities $C_i(r)$ in equation (4) are the outputs from conditional prepayment models.

11 PACs

1. Given interest rates, conditional prepayment models are remarkably accurate. However, absolute prepayment speeds are mainly related to interest rates, i.e., to fundamentally unpredictable quantities.

12 INTERMEDIATE CASH FLOW MODELING

1. Guidance on the use of these parameters is also provided in *"The Analysis of Structured Securities"* (OUP, 2003).
2. Capital structure is also referred to as *liability structure, hierarchy of claims* and *the waterfall.*

14 THE DAO OF DEALING

1. Physics, chemistry and so on.
2. G.W.F. Hegel, "Phenomenologie des Geistes", pp. 157 ff.
3. As most of you probably know, reading an offering circular is enough to make you sick to your stomach, and that's just the beginning.
4. At least, this is the stated goal of the "free" markets. What happens in practice is another matter.
5. The title of this work was qualified in order to avoid confusion with Aristotle's Eudemian Ethics, another ethical treatise believed to have been written earlier. The qualifying word stems from the fact that it was edited and published posthumously by Aristotle's loyal son Nicomachus.
6. Modern physicists would say that the entropy of the system must always increase.
7. The usual dictionary definition of the word "eschatological" refers to death and related matters. This is a special meaning of this term that fails to capture its essence.
8. For a prime example, see Hull, J. *Options, Futures and Other Derivative Securities*, 1989, Prentice Hall International, pp. 64ff.
9. This principle is usually referred to as "the preponderance of the evidence". Thus, civil actions are more like physics than ethics.
10. Every married man knows this extremely well.
11. These were general traverse, special traverse, demurrer, and confession & avoidance.

15 DATA ANALYSIS

1. Although this is not an endorsement of the Fair, Isaac Companies, their products have become the de facto standard in consumer lending.
2. The geometric mean, which is less stable than the arithmetic mean, can also be used.
3. "Taken to the Limit: Simple and Not so Simple Loan Loss Distributions," Philipp J. Schönbucher, Department of Statistics, Bonn University; August 2002 Version. Two of us (SR & AR) would like to thank our co-author Nenad Ilincic for providing us with a copy of the above paper.
4. Please refer to the Section "Rating Agencies and Structured Analysis" (in chapter 22) for a full derivation of equation (15).

16 MARKOV CHAINS

1. This method is fully described in chapter 18.
2. Those readers not familiar with Simpson's rule should consult the appendix to Chapter 24 where it is defined in detail.
3. Those readers not familiar with it should spend some time researching it and the legendary sampling theorem.

17 RECOVERY MODELING

1. "*Numerical Recipes*," William H. Press, Saul A. Teukolsky, William T. Vetterling, Brian P. Flannery, Cambridge University Press, 2nd Edn, 1992.

18 COVARIANCE MATRICES AND LAPLACE TRANSFORM METHODS

1. Please note that the VBA language is quirky in that it uses True $= -1$ instead of 1, but with False $= 0$ as always.
2. "*Numerical Recipes*," William H. Press, Saul A. Teukolsky, William T. Vetterling, Brian P. Flannery, Cambridge University Press, 2nd Edn, 1992.
3. Please note that the extension of Laplace transforms to partial differential equations and equation systems is mainly due to the work of Gustav Dötsch (1892–1977).
4. The latter equality was highlighted in "*The Analysis of Structured Securities*" (OUP, 2003) when deriving the average life formula.
5. Please see chapter 22 for a more detailed treatment of this technique in connection with Hausdorff dimensions.
6. Believe it or not, financial history tells us of early European investors receiving their principal back with "tears in their eyes" because of the unexpected refunding of such fixed income instruments.
7. In passing, this looks suspiciously like the definition of some probability density functions.
8. For readability's sake, we have dropped subscript "*c*" from r_c.
9. This is the canonical definition of the maximum life of a trust.

19 CASH FLOW MODEL: BUILDING BLOCKS

1. Under this formulation, we do not allow partial prepayments.
2. This model is just a modified form of the van der Pol equation, whose work predates the financial modeling literature by many decades.
3. His illustrious "Tractatus Logico-Mathematicus."

20 CASH FLOW MODEL: ADVANCED LIABILITIES

1. The last class is dubbed "Class Z" merely to signify its status as the ultimate class. This class is not related to the Z-bond of MBS lore.
2. See chapter 10, which treats prepayment modeling in more detail.

21 TRIGGERS

1. In control theory, this form of control is referred to as the "bang-bang" principle.
2. The concept of a Companion Class was reviewed in chapter 20.

22 THE VALUATION OF STRUCTURED SECURITIES

1. Don't laugh, for this is not true in practice.
2. If the price is less than the *Value*, buy. If the price is more than the *Value*, sell.
3. For convenience, we assume that the maximum nominal interest rate is 100% although this is by no means a constraint.

4. See Appendix A for a fuller account of his life.

5. See Appendix B for the definition of metrical completeness.

6. Please do not conclude that because the proof is easy to follow it was as easy to conceive, for this could not be further from the truth. As you have probably guessed already, proving this theorem was far from easy; it was "elementary."

7. This technique is called "reductio ad absurdum."

8. In fact, the canonical definition of a Cauchy sequence is $\lim_{\min(m,n) \to \infty} d(a_m, a_n) \to 0$, but the intent is to guarantee that successive elements get increasingly close to reach other. The canonical definition is obviously more general and can address pathological cases that are beyond the scope of this text.

9. Interested readers should consult "*The Analysis of Structured Securities*" (OUP, 2003) where we analyze vector-valued fixed-point iteration in more detail.

10. We do not wish to cloud the issues with qualifying terms such as "modified" or "Macaulay."

11. We apologize to all non-American readers for the obsessive sport metaphors. On the other hand, this is an excellent opportunity to become familiar with America's national pastime.

12. In Latin, the phrase "I believe" translates to "credo" from which we have the word "credit." In other words, credit analysis is a religious process, something anyone involved in it knows only too well.

13. This can be defined as the aggregate principal balance of bonds issued less any initial deposit into a spread or reserve account.

14. In this section and elsewhere in this chapter, the word *market* refers exclusively to the secondary market in the sense of Wall Street. As should be clear by now, the entire contents of this book are devoted to the establishment of the primary market based on which the secondary market can come into existence. As we have defined them herein, the secondary market is linear-logical while the primary market is nonlinear-transcendental.

15. In passing, this is nothing new since the vast majority of teenaged children regularly complain that their parents don't understand them and that life would be much better without daddy. That usually lasts till they need some hard cash to go out partying. At that moment, the virtues of parenthood are extolled and praised to no end.

16. It should be mentioned that Hausdorff, his wife Charlotte née Goldschmidt, and her sister Edith all committed suicide on January 25, 1942, the night before being sent on the first leg of a trip to Oswieciem (Auschwitz) in Poland. As the son of wealthy merchants, he had many opportunities to escape, but instead chose to remain true to his craft until the very end. Hausdorff was much more than a mathematician.

17. First published in 1914; the title can be roughly translated as "Foundations of Set Theory."

18. Liquidity tranches should be rolled up as a single credit tranche, which is how the former are constructed in the first place.

19. The word *subject* comes from the Latin words for under (sub) and to throw (jacere). Properly conceived, the subject is what already lies beneath a logical statement.

20. For a detailed treatment of this topic, readers should consult Heidegger's penetrating analysis from the lecture course "Die Frage nach dem Ding," Max Niemeyer Verlag, Tübingen 1962, pp. 59–86.

21. In what follows, we use the label P_i to designate the *Value* of portfolio i as well as to refer to the underlying portfolio itself.

22. This can easily be shown by expanding the left-hand side about zero in terms of its moments, multiplying the resulting Taylor-series, and then setting the said moments to zero (see exercise 22.6).

23 REVOLVING PERIODS

1. It is well known that many household pets have received credit card offers from U.S. commercial banks. Whether they accepted them, or not, is not as well known.

24 SPECIAL TOPICS

1. Whereas civil servants working in the tax department of the average U.S. urban agglomeration usually lack the proper incentive to collect, i.e., a piece of the action, this is not the case for the special servicer hired by the transaction's sponsor.

2. These are: true sale and nonconsolidation.

3. This formula is named after Michael Yampol, a former student at Baruch College.

4. "*Numerical Recipes*," William H. Press, Saul A. Teukolsky, William T. Vetterling, Brian P. Flannery, Cambridge University Press, 2nd Edn, 1992.

5. Two of us (SR and AR) would like to acknowledge the help of our former student Oksana Londorenko in devising this subsection's title.

6. The fact that we mention these models by name should not be construed as an endorsement of either one.

7. See Appendix B.

8. In passing, this is the financial equivalent of the renormalization group (RG) in particle physics. In this case, the interest rate r acts as a measure of energy. Within Greek metaphysics, the concepts of interest rate and energy are tightly linked since they effectively refer to the same underlying reality. In other words to produce something, to have "yield," one needs to expend energy in the linear sense. The essential notion hiding behind the Greek word for energy (εv-$\varepsilon \rho \gamma \varepsilon \iota \alpha$) is $\varepsilon \rho \gamma o v$, literally a work. Thus, energy is the "being-produced" of something. Financially speaking, yield is what is produced out of nothing since principal is always excluded, having *already* been produced. Without production, positive or negative, it is a trivial proposition that yield is identically zero. Remember that there exists a rate of interest on everything (spoons, computers, coffee, etc.) As far as we can tell, of all modern economists only J.M. Keynes actually understood why the rate of interest on cash holds such a unique and privileged position.

9. Lebesgue and Riemann integrals have different values only in very special cases that lie squarely outside the scope of this investigation.

10. The length of this time interval can be small or large depending on trading volume and other parameters, but it can be known when required.

11. The parameter χ is the familiar Lagrange multiplier.

Index